LADIES' HOME JOURNAL ADVENTURES IN COOKING

LADIES' HOME JOURNAL

ADVENTURES IN COOKING

By the Editors of Ladies' Home Journal

Drawings by Preston Fetty

BONANZA BOOKS · NEW YORK

INTRODUCTION

We at the *Ladies' Home Journal* feel this is a new kind of cookbook—and a very necessary one. It truly is all things to all cooks—the new bride who is wondering how to plan a meal and cook a hamburger or the experienced cook who would like to experiment with classic dishes of the world's exotic cuisines.

It is many cookbooks under one cover . . . and a lifetime cooking course as well. Each recipe explains not just *what* to do but *why*, as well as how to use the same techniques in other dishes. Make the Creamed Chicken in Patty Shells in Chapter One, for instance, and, as the note explains, you have mastered a simple white sauce. Other ways of making white sauce are discussed too. And you not only have a delicious dish, you are a wiser cook than when you began.

To get full value from this book we suggest browsing through it on occasion instead of just pulling it off the shelf to find a certain recipe. There's a world of helps that most cookbooks never mention. For instance, almost every chapter includes a host of menus built around the dishes in that chapter, with the dishes for which specific preparation instructions are included in the book set off in THIS STYLE—a wonderful boost for days when you just can't dream up something different to entice family or guests.

How to describe all the wonders of *Adventures in Cooking?* The best way is to give a peep into each chapter.

Chapter One, The Art of Good Cooking is an excellent introduction—a treasure trove of good advice on how to plan meals nutritionally, how to shop ahead, how long various foods keep, how to halve a recipe or substitute ingredients, how to watch calories . . . even how to pack a lunchbox. Be sure to notice the menus—for year-round, hot weather and two solid weeks of family meals.

Chapter Two, Hearty Main Dishes, includes all the meat, fish, fowl and casserole entrees you'll ever need, plus tips on how to plan a meal for appetite appeal, how to carve, buy and cook meat, which herbs, seasonings and garnishes are soulmates with which main dishes. There's even a section of main dishes and menus *just for two.*

Fruits and Vegetables are the subject of *Chapter Three,* but you'll also find advice on herbs, dessert sauces, pickling, home freezing, home canning and lots of menus. *Chapter Four, Creative Baking,* will turn any bride into a prize-winning baker. Festive breads from around the world, cake decorating, pastries plain and fancy, even what to do if you don't have the right cake pan—it's all here.

Chapter Five, An Introduction to Gourmet Cookery is a special bonus—a complete cook's tour of the world's cuisines. What could be timelier in these days when everyone is travelling abroad? Don't worry if you don't know a Bordeaux from a Brie. After reading the sections on great wines and cheeses of the world and how to serve them, you'll never be guilty of a *faux pas.* The special equipment used for gourmet cookery is explained. There's a complete guide to seasoning with herbs, spices and seeds. Best of all are the recipes and explanations of French gourmet cooking, exotic dishes from Spain, lively Italian cuisine, famous dishes from Central Europe, translations from the Scandinavian, dishes from the land of pilaff and kebab, curries out of India, foods from the Far Pacific, Oriental meals, Mexico's spicy theme, Canadian traditions, regional cooking of the United States, and, of course international gourmet menus.

We're especially proud of the last two chapters, geared for today's young, adventurous, active housewives. *Chapter Six* is called *Parties Large and Small.* It's not just party recipes, but hints on everything from the guest list to decorations. There are menus and preparation plans for dozens of parties: informal or formal, buffet, barbecue, teas, cocktail parties, dessert-and-coffee parties, teen-age parties, holiday entertaining . . . and lots more.

Chapter Seven, The Bridal Corner, is just for the bride. At the *Journal* the new bride is a Very Important Person, so we've included this section to take her through the first days of entertaining, meals for unexpected guests, and all the special parties that cluster around a wedding, from announcement parties to showers to the Golden Anniversary.

Don't overlook the *Appendix* at the back—the guide to planning a perfect kitchen and a glossary of cooking terms.

All this in addition to countless recipes, 32 beautiful color pages and hundreds of black-and-white illustrations!

Now you know why we call this the cookbook that has everything for everyone. Browse in it, try the recipes—you'll find it a lifetime adventure in good cooking and good eating.

The Editors of the Ladies' Home Journal

CONTENTS

CHAPTER SEVEN

The Bridal Corner 331

Appendix 345

Index 357

LADIES' HOME JOURNAL ADVENTURES IN COOKING

1
~
The Art of Good Cooking

THE DAILY FOOD GUIDE

These foods are healthful and should be eaten every day.

The Basic Foods. Every successful pattern of 3 meals a day for family nutrition and health begins with an understanding of 4 essential food groups.

If your household's 3 daily meals include foods recommended in the Daily Food Guide, you can be sure that your family is receiving all the nutrients necessary for a complete and well-balanced diet and that your meals are nutritionally sound.

Milk. Milk is our best source of calcium, which is necessary for strong bones and teeth. It also supplies proteins for body building and repair. The daily milk quota may be fulfilled in many ways—as a beverage, in soups, sauces, puddings, custard and ice cream, or on cereals and puddings.

> Children, 3 cups*
> Adolescents, 4 cups
> Adults, 2 cups
> Expectant or nursing mothers, 4 cups
> *1 cup = 8 fluid ounces

Meat and Fish

2 servings meat, poultry, fish, eggs or cheese. Dried beans or peas, nuts or peanut butter in place of meat occasionally.

Meat

This group supplies proteins, B vitamins and iron. Two servings are recommended daily; adolescents and expectant or nursing mothers need more. One serving should provide as much protein as that in 2 ounces cooked lean meat without bone. An equal amount of protein is obtained from 2 eggs, 2 ounces (2 slices) cheese, 1/4 cup cottage cheese, 1/4 cup peanut butter or 1 cup cooked dried beans or peas. Don't forget salads and casseroles here, as well as many variations in broiled, braised and roasted meats. Such variety meats as liver, heart, kidney and sweetbreads are especially high in B vitamins and iron and should be served occasionally.

Vegetables and Fruits. Vegetables and fruits provide considerable vitamins and minerals. Include 4 or more servings every day.

For vitamin A: 1 serving dark green or deep yellow vegetable at least every other day.

Citrus fruits, cantaloupe, strawberries, tomatoes, broccoli, green peppers, and cabbage are important sources of vitamin C. Include 1 serving every day.

Plan on servings of other vegetables and fruits, including potatoes, every day. They can be served with dinner or at other times in soups, salads, stews and casseroles. Fruits and juices can be served at any desired time: at breakfast, as dessert for lunch or dinner or as tomato-juice cocktail at the start of a meal. Fruits in the menu may be in cocktails, salads and so forth.

Breads and Cereals. 4 or more servings whole grain or enriched breads and cereals.

Cereals provide protein, iron, B vitamins and energy. The quality of vegetable protein is improved by serving it with animal protein as in milk. This group includes whole grain or enriched breads, cooked and ready-to-eat cereals, crackers, grits, spaghetti and macaroni, noodles, rice, quick breads and other baked goods made with wholegrain or enriched flour.

In addition to being served plain, toasted and in sandwiches, bread may be introduced in stuffings, meat loaves, toppings for casseroles, puddings, and fine crumbs for frying or baking.

Cereals may be in hot cooked or ready-to-eat form for breakfast or the major ingredient in griddle cakes, waffles, hot breads and muffins.

Additional Foods

Fats and sugars, plus more servings from each of the first 4 food groups to meet energy needs and round out meals.
400 international units vitamin D added to daily diet for children and expectant mothers.

PLANNING AHEAD

It's easy to plan meals for your family a week in advance by making a chart—with days across the top as in a calendar. You can list 3 menus under each day. You may wish to start with Sunday's meals, but, if you do your marketing on Thursday or Friday, it may be better to start with the day following the shopping routine. You can avoid monotony in your meal pattern by serving different foods on the same days of the week. Plan your meals so that the family does not know in advance it will be "Sunday—roast beef, Monday—stew."

Plan your menus so that leftovers may be prepared and served in attractive ways when they reappear at the table—preferably 1 or 2 days later, rather than at the very next meal.

When you have planned your menus for the week, check each day, keeping an eye on "The Daily Food Guide." Have you included foods from each group? You may need to make some changes in your original plan to be sure that you are following the guide. If your budget must be kept to a minimum, savings can be made by selecting the least expensive foods in each category.

Stocking Your Kitchen. Certain products that you buy for meal preparation must be used quickly; to overstock is thus to run the risk of

waste. Buy fresh foods only for your foreseeable needs. Many other supplies, however, keep well for weeks, months—even years, in the case of canned goods—and there is no risk of overstocking if you have plenty of kitchen space.

Your Shopping Plan: Prepare in Advance.

Make out your list before you leave home. Check the forthcoming week's menu needs, supplies on hand, the state of your budget and your family's preferences ahead of time.

An Organized Expedition. If you have the time, it is to your advantage to shop in person rather than by telephone. Telephone ordering and delivery service usually cost more, and you cannot select foods personally and choose the best buys. You can save time by shopping at an hour when the stores are least busy.

If you shop in a supermarket it would be useful to organize your list according to groups of foods: all the refrigerated foods like milk, cream, cheese, butter and margarine together; meats, poultry and fish together, frozen foods together, and so on down the list. After you have come to know your supermarket, try to keep these groups in the order in which foods are displayed in the store, which will save tiresome backtracking, so that 1 trip through each aisle will be sufficient.

If you have outlined your menu plan, ensuring that it is nutritionally right by checking it with "The Daily Food Guide," you can readily make a list for your marketing. A planned shopping list prevents your overlooking needed supplies and eliminates unnecessary items. A good shopping plan includes special and seasonal buys as announced in newspaper advertisements or on radio and television. Besides your list of needs for each meal, be sure to include staples. It is a good idea to keep a checklist handy in the kitchen and to jot down items as they are used up. Remember to check your refrigerator supplies too, so that items can be added to your list as necessary.

Storage Up to 1 Year

Canned fruits, vegetables, juices, meats, fish, milk
Freeze-dried foods
Packaged desserts, gelatin
Macaroni, spaghetti, noodles
Rice, tapioca, barley
Dried peas, beans
Sugars, syrups
Flour, cornstarch
Hard cheeses

Storage Up to 6 Months

Frozen fruits, vegetables, juices, roasts, poultry (at 0° F.)
Shortening, salad oil (in refrigerator)

Packaged cereals
Crackers
Nuts (in refrigerator or freezer)
Dried fruits (in covered container)
Spices, condiments
Baking powder, soda

Storage Up to 1 Month

Ice cream
Cookies
Potatoes, onions, carrots

Storage Up to 1 Week

Fresh milk, cream
Soft cheeses
Butter, margarine
Eggs
Breads, cakes
Roasts, cold cuts

Use as Soon as Possible

Ground meat, fresh poultry, fish, chops, variety meats
Fresh fruits, vegetables

Whether you wish to shop only once a week or at more frequent intervals is a point to be taken into account when planning your list. Your food budget and your family's preferences will also affect your shopping. Remember also that it is unwise to buy more food than you can store properly. Try not to overstock perishables. Cross items off your list as they go into your basket, in order to avoid overlooking any item.

How Much to Buy

Your shopping list of course should indicate the required amounts of each item, according to the number and ages of family members. Following is a guide to show you how much raw or packaged foodstuff in various categories is generally found adequate for 1 serving per person. Allow 1/3 less per serving for young children or elderly people. For special recipes be guided by amounts called for.

Amount to Buy Per Serving

Steaks, 3/4 pound
Meat with fat and bone, 1/2 pound
Lean meat with some bone, 1/3 pound
Broiling or frying chicken, 1/2–3/4 pound
Roasting chicken and turkey, 1/2–1 pound
Geese and ducks, 1 pound
Whole fish, 1/2 pound
Fish fillets, 1/3 pound
Shrimp, 1/3–1/2 pound (6–8)
Whole lobster, 1–1 1/4 pounds
Oysters (shucked), 1/3 pint
Cooked and canned meat and fish, 2–3 ounces

Shopping for Value

If you plan your shopping, you can save money and time and make your meals more interesting and better balanced. Haphazard shopping is expensive so check the food supplies you have on hand, and then plan your shopping list to cover next week's meals, taking advantage of the specials.

Compare prices at your local stores, and shop where you get the best value for your money. Try not to buy unnecessary items. For family meals "convenience foods" can save your time but often cost more. Notable exceptions recommended by the United States Department of Agriculture are frozen orange juice, frozen lima beans and peas, packaged and canned spaghetti, canned cherries, canned chicken chow mein and devil's food cake mix.

Read labels on containers, and compare costs per edible portion before you buy. This comparison should be made both between brands and between package sizes of the same brand. Sometimes large sizes are less economical than are medium sizes. Premiums you do not need can upset your food budget.

Ways to Save

Choose the grade or quality of canned goods that best suits your purpose. Fancy whole tomatoes are not necessary for a mixed dish, and fruits packed in light syrup have the same vitamins and minerals—and fewer calories—than do those packed in heavy syrup, which cost more.

Skim milk or skim-milk powder is as rich in minerals as is whole milk and much less expensive for both cooking and drinking. Whole milk is cheaper in 1/2 gallons and costs even less if bought at the store rather than delivered to your door. Ice cream costs less when you buy it in large quantities if you have freezer storage facilities, and if you know it will be eaten before it develops an off-flavor associated with prolonged storage. The best money values in cheese are Cheddar and cottage varieties, and process cheeses are a great convenience.

How Much Waste?

Compare prices of fresh, frozen and canned vegetables; buy the best value available. Potatoes are an inexpensive mainstay; good menu planning makes use of them often, along with a dark-green or deep-yellow vegetable at least every other day. Use the coarse outer leaves of green vegetables to flavor salads. Some fresh vegetables, like peas in the pod, have a good deal of waste, but there is no waste when you buy the canned or frozen packs. Use liquids from canned or cooked vegetables for soup, sauces, gravy. The good cook will find interesting uses for many of these by-products. Juice from canned beets, for example, can be used in making Harvard sauce, or soup.

Buying Fruits

Economical frozen or canned fruit juices are a year-round source of vitamin C. When you buy fresh oranges or grapefruit for eating, shop for the thin-skinned heavy ones, which give you more for your money. Of course, some varieties naturally have thicker skins than do others. Other kinds of fruit should be eaten regularly— buy them when they are in season. Fresh apples and bananas are inexpensive during most of the year. Supplement them with frozen, canned and dried fruits.

Study Egg Sizes

Buy small, medium or large eggs according to their ounce-for-ounce cost. Although all eggs are sold by the dozen, you can get more actual money's worth from eggs if you follow this guide: Take the medium size when they cost less than 7/8 what large eggs cost; take the small size when they cost less than 3/4 what the medium size costs. Grade A eggs are good for frying and poaching, but grade B eggs are less expensive and are fine for scrambling and as an ingredient in baked goods and the like.

Meats, Fish and Poultry

Buy only required amounts of meats, fish or poultry. Estimate amounts of edible meat in various cuts to make sure you are getting the best value. For economy, buy meats that are lower in price and those featured as weekend specials. Steaks, chops and oven roasts add up to an expensive meal pattern. Meats for stewing and braising cost less, yet they are just as nutritious as the expensive cuts, and with proper cooking they lack nothing in appetite appeal. Large chickens and turkeys are more economical than are small ones, and what is left from 1 meal can be used up later.

Inexpensive chicken wings and backs from cut-up poultry displays make flavorful casseroles and soups. Fish is as nourishing as is red meat and has the additional value of vitamin A. Dark-fleshed fish also gives vitamin D. You may serve fish at least once a week for both economy and menu variety.

Meatless Main-Dish Foods

Eggs and cheese are inexpensive sources of high-quality protein, and dried beans and peas, nuts and peanut butter can be used occasionally

for economical protein. Home-style baked beans and split-pea soup are steady favorites. Peanuts and peanut butter offer both food and money value and are almost essential in a household with children.

Breads and Cereals

Serve products of the grain family at every meal. There is a wide variety of breads, crackers and baked goods to choose from. Cereals you cook are less expensive than the ready-to-eat kind. Use noodles, macaroni, rice, rolled oats to stretch leftover meats in interesting dishes. Breads, too, have versatility in stuffings and toppings.

Save on Beverages

If you wish, have coffee beans ground at the store, or use instant coffee. Both types are less expensive than is the ground coffee in the can, and there is no waste with the instant type. For family use loose tea is less expensive than are tea bags and instant tea. When shopping assess the advantages of large sizes versus those of small sizes for your particular household.

Fats and Flavorings

Fats provide calories and some vitamin A. Butter and margarine are comparable in food value; both have vitamin A, but margarine is less expensive. Shortening, oils, lard and salt pork help to make meals enjoyable. Save meat drippings for cooking.

Condiments, flavorings, herbs and spices add appetite appeal. It is best to buy spices in small quantities because they lose strength after they are opened.

What To Look For. Your family enjoys better meals, and your food dollar goes further when you do your shopping with a keen eye for food-grading marks that guide you to quality with economy.

There are many considerations in selecting the food for your family's meals, and of course you want to be assured that your selections are right —that you have chosen wholesome foods of good quality and have obtained good value for your money. With some foods there are very definite points to look for when you shop.

Buying Meat

The first thing to look for in meat is the Federal inspection stamp. It is a round purple stamp that assures you that the meat is "U.S. Inspected and Passed." This phrase means that the meat has been inspected by the Government and that the animal from which it came was healthy and slaughtered under sanitary conditions. The meat is wholesome and safe for your family. Government inspection is compulsory only for meats entering interstate or foreign trade, but it is safer to choose a dealer who carries only inspected meats. The Federal inspection stamp is not to be confused with the grade marking on meats. The grade mark indicates the quality of the meat. It is shield-shaped and is repeated in a ribbon the full length of the carcass. As some meat cuts lack an outside layer of fat, this mark may be trimmed off. Certain meat packers put their own brands on better beef, veal, lamb and cured meats. Fresh pork is usually not branded or graded because there is less variation in quality thanks to greater uniformity in the age of animals when slaughtered. The grades used for beef are, in order of quality, USDA prime (seldom found on the retail market), USDA choice, USDA good, USDA standard, USDA commercial and USDA utility.

As grading is not compulsory and as trimming may remove the colored ribbon stamp on branded beef, you should learn to recognize good meat when you see it. Here are the signs for beef:

Lean—uniform, bright-red color; firm and smooth but moist; high proportion of meat to bone; good marbling, which means that small flecks of fat are well distributed throughout the lean.
Fat—moderately thick outer covering of firm, creamy-white, flaky fat.
Bone—cut surfaces of bones that are porous and reddish-pink.

Good young pork should be grayish-pink in color; pork from older animals is a delicate rose color.

Good lamb is pinkish-red; mutton, coming from an older animal, is a deeper red.

Good veal is pale pink, almost gray, in color. Veal is never marbled with fat because the animal is very young when slaughtered.

Always choose the right cut for the right dish. The quick-cooking cuts—steaks and chops—are most expensive, but they are no more nutritious than are the less expensive cuts. The latter take a little more time and skill to prepare. They are excellent for casseroles, stews, pot roasts and braised dishes.

Poultry

Look for the government grade mark on fowl, chickens, turkeys, geese and ducks. This mark is either printed on the bag or appears on a tag attached to the breast of the bird.

Grade A—well-fattened and well-fleshed birds, normally shaped.
Grade B—Not so well fattened or well fleshed as Grade A; slightly crooked bones that do not affect the meat arrangement permitted; slight tears and pinfeathers that do not detract from the appearance of the bird also allowed.
Grade C—fairly well-fleshed, but not well-fattened birds; may have tears, pinfeathers, and discolorations that do not seriously detract from their appearance.

You should also buy the poultry that is best suited for your purposes. Capons are large, desexed male birds, raised for their tender flesh and flavor. A capon has a high proportion of white meat and is splendid for roasting. Broiler-fryers or roasters may be prepared with a dry-heat method. A bird of broiling size may also be fried or roasted. A bird with a wide body, a broad full-fleshed breast, and thick, short legs, rather than a long, thin, poorly fleshed bird is your best buy, because the latter offers more bone and less meat. Stewing fowl should be stewed or braised.

Today most poultry is sold "ready to cook." It has had the head, feet and feathers removed; the giblets and neck have been removed and wrapped separately. The bird has been thoroughly cleaned and is all ready to cook.

Chickens and turkeys are available whole or cut up, as well as in selected parts.

Fresh Fish and Seafood

There are many varieties and forms of fish from which to make your selection. Be sure to buy fish that is really fresh. Fresh fish has little or no odor: Do not buy fish if it has a strong odor. In a whole fresh fish, the flesh should be firm and elastic and should show no signs of separation from the bone. The eyes should be clear and bright and the gills red. Fish steaks are slices cut crosswise. Fish fillets are boneless, lengthwise slices. If you buy oysters or clams in shells, see that the shells are tightly closed. Fresh crabs and lobsters should be alive and moving.

Fruits and Vegetables

Fresh vegetables and fruits are graded for the wholesale trade, but the grade is not necessarily

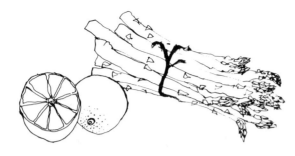

be springy to the touch. Do not choose those with very coarse skins or soft decayed areas. Limes should be green; yellow ones do not have such pungent flavor.

Bananas are ripe when they are all yellow or mottled with brown spots. Green-tipped bananas ripen at home in a few days. Pineapples should be heavy and fragrant, without soft areas at the bases. They are perfectly ripe when the flesh yields *slightly* to pressure. The freshest grapes are those that are still well attached to the stem. Ripe cantaloupes, honeydew melons and muskmelons have characteristic aromas. Watermelon is best when it is firm, with a fresh, good color and slightly yellow or whitish skin on the lower side. Berries of all kinds should be solid, clean and bright in color. Strawberries should have hulls still attached and be bright, solid red. When the caps cling tightly to the berries, the berries are underripe. Avoid buying overripe berries, which are dull in color and soft. Rhubarb should not have a musty odor.

Canned Fruits and Vegetables

Read the labels on cans to learn the weight and contents and to compare prices. A dented can is not a sign of spoilage unless the dent has caused a leak. A bulging can could denote spoilage.

Once opened, canned fruits and juices should be covered and stored in the refrigerator. They may safely be left in their original containers, but high-acid juices, like those of tomatoes, pineapples and so forth keep their flavor better and develop no metallic taste if they are poured into clean glass jars or plastic containers before refrigerator storage.

Frozen Fruits and Vegetables

The weight and contents of frozen fruits and vegetables must be shown on the main part of the label.

Butter

Butter is sold salted or sweet. Both kinds are made from cream, but sweet butter has no salt added. The grade mark must be shown on the main panel of the carton or wrapper in which the butter is sold. Your retailer carries these grades of butter, in order of quality: U.S. Grade AA, U.S. Grade A, U.S. Grade B, U.S. Grade C.

Eggs

Eggs are sold by grade and size. Grade AA and grade A eggs are clean, with unbroken shells, and are practically perfect in shape. The whites

indicated in the retail market. The grades used are U.S. Fancy, U.S. No. 1, U.S. No. 2, U.S. Commercial, U.S. Combination and Unclassified. For some products, there are more grades than for others. As the grades are often not available to you, select fresh produce by the following standards.

Vegetables should appear garden fresh, with no soft, discolored spots or blemishes; leafy vegetables should not look wilted, and the outer leaves should not be discolored. Vegetables are best when they are not too mature. Undersized vegetables may lack flavor, and oversized ones may be tough and fibrous. Green and wax beans should be fresh and should snap crisply. Potatoes and onions should be firm. Also note the care that your dealer gives to fresh vegetables. They are best kept covered with chipped ice or kept moist with frequent ice-water sprays. They should be protected from dust and flies and should not be handled unnecessarily.

In choosing fresh fruit, judge color and firmness, degree of ripeness and absence of decay. The larger fruit may not have so much flavor and juice as the smaller fruit. The use for which it is intended will also affect your choice. Oranges to be used for juice need not be large; on the other hand, if they are to be served whole or in salads, large ones are a better choice. Bargains in overripe fruit are not always economical, as they may be partly decayed.

Oranges, tangerines, grapefruit, lemons and limes should be well shaped. The heavier ones are your best choice, as they have less pulp and more juice. A thin, fine-grained skin is also an indication of juicy citrus fruit. Florida oranges usually have more juice. California oranges are better for sections or for peeling and eating. Navel oranges have a sweeter flavor and are seedless. Oranges need not be bright in color to be good (indeed, juice oranges are frequently color-sprayed for eye appeal). Grapefruit should are thick and firm, and the yolks are well centered. These eggs are especially suitable for cooking in the shells, for poaching and for frying. Grade B and grade C eggs have reasonably clean and unbroken shells, which may show definite ridges or some roughness. Their whites are less firm and the yolks less well centered than those of grade A eggs. These eggs may be used for scrambling, baking and other cooking purposes. Eggs are also sold with definite size markings: Extra Large, Large, Medium and Small. When selecting eggs, it is advisable to look at the bottom of the carton for stain or soil, which usually denotes that there may be some breakage in the eggs in that carton. Do not choose them, as cracked or broken eggs will not keep fresh as long as those with unbroken shells. These eggs are also difficult to remove, as they may stick to the carton and be a complete loss to you, a waste of money.

Bread and Bakery Products

The best method for storing bread is in your home freezer: Keep fresh bread in its original wrapper, and immediately place in the freezer. The next-best method for home storage is to keep bread in its original wrapper in a ventilated container at room temperature. The least desirable method of storing bread is to keep it in the refrigerator. Refrigerator storage hastens rather than retards staling. Bread properly wrapped and stored in the refrigerator, however, is less subject to mold than is bread kept at room temperature. Refrigerator storage is only recommended when freezing facilities are not available and your bread use is so limited that mold growth becomes a problem.

All cakes should be covered to keep them fresh. Most plain cakes keep well in a ventilated cake tin or breadbox for several days. Unfrosted or butter-frosted cakes may be wrapped in moisture-vapor proof paper and frozen. If icing is soft, it is a good idea to freeze cake for a few minutes; then as soon as top is firm, wrap cake for freezer storage. Large cakes should be cut before wrapping and freezing, to reduce thawing time.

Cakes or puff pastries containing whipped cream and cream fillings should be refrigerated until served; plan to use them quickly. Fruit cakes should be left in their original wrappings until served.

Crisp cookies should be stored in a container with a loose-fitting cover that permits some circulation of air. Soft, chewy cookies should be stored in an airtight container. Filled cookies should be stored in a cool place and used within a reasonable time.

Cream or fruit pies should be refrigerated until used. But, even when refrigerated, cream pies should not be kept more than 1 day before using.

Staples

Packaged foods, canned foods, dried foods and freeze-dried foods can be stored on kitchen shelves or in any cool, dry place. Flour and cereal products should be stored in tightly covered containers in a dry place; treat granulated sugar in the same way. Brown sugar should be stored in a tightly covered container in a cool place.

Herbs and spices will keep their full flavors longer if they are tightly covered and stored in a cool dry place.

Coffee

Ground coffee should be stored in a tightly covered container in as cool a place as possible. If you have space in your refrigerator, it is the best storage place, and there will be less loss of flavor and aroma.

Shortening and Oils

Shortening and salad oils keep best when tightly covered in a cool place. Some oils may cloud and solidify in the refrigerator, but such changes are not harmful. If returned to room temperature, they will become clear and liquid again. It is helpful to keep some shortening at room temperature for ease in creaming when making cakes and cookies. For making pastry, however, shortening should be used straight from the refrigerator, otherwise the flour soaks up the shortening and the pastry becomes heavy.

Salad Dressing

Commercially-made salad dressing does not need refrigeration to keep it fresh, but it is an advantage to chill it before using it in salads. Once it has been opened, it should be refrigerated.

Dried Fruits

Keep dried fruits in tightly closed containers. They may be stored at room temperature, except in warm humid weather, when they should be refrigerated.

Nonfat Dry Milk

Dry milk should be stored in a tightly closed container and will keep for several months on the kitchen shelf. When it has been reconstituted, it should be stored in the same way as is fresh fluid milk—covered and in the refrigerator.

Evaporated and Condensed Milk

These items may be stored at room temperature on the cupboard shelf until opened. Then cover and refrigerate.

Measures for Success. *Read the recipe carefully! Assemble all the ingredients; measure the quantities accurately.*

When following a tested recipe, it is important to measure the ingredients as accurately as they were measured when the recipe was developed and tested. Otherwise the recipe may be thrown out of balance, and may yield disappointing results. In all reliable test kitchens, the same methods are used, and certain basic rules are maintained. So if you follow the following suggestions you are assured of success.

Always use standard measuring cups and spoons.

Use 8-ounce glass measuring cups for liquids. The glass permits you to see the level of the liquid being measured. The cup for liquids should have additional space above the 1-cup line, so that a full cup can be accurately measured without spilling. Stand cup on level surface, and fill to amount indicated. Check the measurement at eye level.

When measuring thick liquids like honey and syrup, do not let them overflow the measuring cup or spoon. Be careful to scrape out the cup or spoon thoroughly. A light greasing of the cup or spoon helps in measuring sticky ingredients.

To measure dry ingredients, use standard individual cups (as in a nested set), in 1/4-, 1/2-, 1/3- and 1-cup sizes. Lightly spoon dry ingredients into appropriate cup, heap up and level off with edge of spatula by cutting across the top. Use measuring spoons in this way, too, for dry ingredients. Flour need not be sifted before measuring unless recipe specifies. Sifting flour onto a sheet of waxed paper instead of into a bowl cuts down on dishwashing. Brown sugar is always packed firmly into measuring cup.

Shortening, lard and butter can be measured accurately by using the same fractional measuring cups used for dry ingredients. Fats are more easily measured if they are soft and measured at room temperature.

If the recipe calls for "2 tablespoons melted shortening," the shortening should be melted first and then measured. On the other hand, if the recipe calls for "2 tablespoons shortening, melted," the shortening should be measured first, and then melted.

How To Use Half a Recipe. *Do you want to make only 1/2 the amount? Some recipes may be successfully "halved."*

Measuring-spoon sets do not include 1/2-tablespoon measures. When you want to measure 1/2 tablespoon of a dry ingredient or fat, fill 1 tablespoon, level off with a flat knife or spatula and cut in half from tip to handle. Flick off 1/2 the ingredients in the spoon, and you will have accurately measured 1/2 tablespoon. Or you can measure out 1 1/2 teaspoons, which equals 1/2 tablespoon. For measuring 1/2 tablespoon of liquid, use 1 teaspoon and 1/2 teaspoon.

When a recipe calls for 1/3 cup of an ingredient and you wish to use 1/2 this amount, remember that 1/3 cup is 5 1/3 tablespoons or 5 tablespoons plus 1 teaspoon. Half this amount can be easily and accurately measured by using 2 1/2 tablespoons plus 1/2 teaspoon or 2 tablespoons and 2 teaspoons.

If you are using a cake mix and a whole cake is more than you require at one time, remember that a mix that yields a cake to fill an 8-inch square pan will make 2 thinner 8-inch layers. Cut one layer in half horizontally, spread filling over one half, place other half on top and frost. This method will give you 1/2 a fresh layer cake for immediate use. The other layer can be tightly wrapped and frozen for future serving. Or, instead of two 8-inch layers, you might prefer to make 1 layer and bake the remaining batter as cupcakes. Some of the commercial cake mixes are packaged in 2 parts, so that you can use 1/2 the quantity and save the other.

In dividing a recipe, the time for cooking may need adjustment—although not necessarily by an exact 1/2 of the normal period. For instance, a casserole that requires 45 minutes' baking time will cook nicely in 30–35 minutes when you are preparing 1/2 the recipe.

In making 1/2 the regular recipe for meat loaf or salmon loaf, you might like to vary the usual plan by baking the mixture in individual custard cups or muffin pans. In this case, you will find that cooking can be completed in a little less than 1/2 the usual time. A family-sized meat loaf to serve 6 people will bake in a loaf pan at 350°F. 1 1/4 hours. By dividing all ingredients in half and baking mixture in 1/2 dozen custard cups, the oven time can be cut to 30 minutes at 350°F. When you double a recipe, it is important to remember that, beside doubling ingredients, you must allow longer cooking time, depending on the depth of pan.

MEASURES
(All measurements are level)

1 cup (8 fluid ounces) = 16 tablespoons
3/4 cup (6 fluid ounces) = 12 tablespoons
2/3 cup (5 1/3 fluid ounces) = 10 tablespoons plus 2 teaspoons

1/2 cup (4 fluid ounces) = 8 tablespoons
1/3 cup (2 2/3 fluid ounces) = 5 tablespoons plus 1 teaspoon
1/4 cup (2 fluid ounces) = 4 tablespoons
1/8 cup (1 fluid ounce) = 2 tablespoons
1 tablespoon (1/2 fluid ounce) = 3 teaspoons

TABLE OF EQUIVALENTS

1 gallon (144 fluid ounces) = 4 quarts
1 quart (32 fluid ounces) = 4 cups
1 pint (16 fluid ounces) = 2 cups

If you have to convert weights to measures in a recipe, this table will help you.

FOOD	WEIGHT OF 1 CUP	MEASURE IN OUNCES
Butter	8 oz.	1 oz. = 2 tbsps.
Cocoa	4 1/2 oz.	1 oz. = 3 1/2 tbsps.
Cornstarch		1 oz. = 3 1/2 tbsps.
Gelatin		1 oz. = 3 tbsps.
Flour (all-purpose, sifted)	4 1/2 oz.	8 oz. = 1 7/8 cups
Macaroni	4 oz.	8 oz. = 2 cups
Rice	6 1/2 oz.	8 oz. = 1 1/6 cups
Rolled oats	2 3/4 oz.	8 oz. = 3 cups
Sugar (brown, packed)	7 oz.	8 oz. = 1 1/8 cups
Sugar (granulated)	7 oz.	8 oz. = 1 1/8 cups
Sugar (confectioners', sifted)	4 1/2 oz.	8 oz. = 2 cups
Shortening	7 oz.	8 oz. = 1 1/8 cups

If a recipe calls for an ingredient like 4 1/2 cups cooked macaroni, you have to know the amount of raw macaroni to be cooked. Here is a guide.

ESTIMATING RAW INGREDIENTS

Macaroni	1 cup uncooked = 2 1/4 cups cooked
Rice	1 cup uncooked = 3 cups cooked
	1 cup precooked = 2 cups cooked
Confectioners' sugar	1 pound = 3–4 cups sifted
Brown sugar	1 pound = 2 1/4 cups packed
Granulated sugar	1 pound = 2 1/4 cups
Heavy cream	1 cup = 2 cups, whipped
Cheese	1 pound = 4 cups grated
Egg whites	1 cup = 8 egg whites

Occasionally, you may find that you do not have the exact ingredient called for in the recipe. The following list will help in easy adjustment of recipes with replacements.

SUBSTITUTION CHART

1 ounce chocolate	= 3 tablespoons cocoa plus 1 tablespoon fat

1 tablespoon flour (for thickening)	= 1/2 tablespoon cornstarch or 1 egg or 2 teaspoons quick-cooking tapioca
1 egg (in custards)	= 2 egg yolks
1 egg (in batter)	= 1/2 teaspoon baking powder
1 cup whole milk	= 1/2 cup evaporated milk plus 1/2 cup water or 1 cup reconstituted nonfat dry milk plus 2 1/2 teaspoons fat
1 cup sour milk	= 1 tablespoon vinegar with sweet milk to make total of 1 cup (let stand 5 minutes to sour) or 1 cup buttermilk
1 cup instant flour	= 1 cup sifted all-purpose flour
1 cup cake flour	= 7/8 cup all-purpose flour plus 2 tablespoons cornstarch
1 cup butter or margarine	= 1 cup shortening or oil plus 1/2 teaspoon salt
1 cup light cream	= 3 tablespoons butter, plus 7/8 cup milk
1 cup granulated sugar	= 1 cup brown sugar, packed, or 1 cup honey or corn syrup* (reduce other liquids in recipe by 1/4 cup)
1 teaspoon baking powder	= 1/4 teaspoon baking soda plus 5/8 teaspoon cream of tartar

*Never replace more than 1/2 the prescribed sugar with syrup.

BEST COOKING METHODS

Knowing the best ways of cooking means good eating and good economy. Here are some tips on preparing and cooking various kinds of food.

Meat. Washing meat destroys some of its soluble nutrients and diminishes its flavor. Wipe it on all sides with clean, damp cloth or damp paper towel.

During cooking, do not pierce meat with fork, thus allowing juices to escape; to lift or turn meat, use kitchen tongs or spatula.

For less shrinkage, roast meat in slow-to-moderate oven, and do not overcook. A meat thermometer is the best way to determine when roast is done.

Do not discard fat or meat juices from pan. Use in gravies, sauces, stews or casseroles.

The roast should stand in a warm place for a short time before carving, to let meat absorb juices and make carving easier and more economical.

When you cook meat bones for soup or stock, start cooking in cold water. This method ensures extraction of more food value and flavor from the bones into the liquid; the bones are to be discarded.

Poultry. Follow the same hints when you cook poultry. Most poultry on the market today has been thoroughly cleaned but, for safety's sake, still must be washed. Wash bird in water, and dry it well inside and out with paper towels.

Fish and Seafood. Unlike meat, fin fish, which has very little connective tissue, should be cooked quickly at high temperatures, to retain its flavor and keep it moist and juicy. The thickness of fish determines cooking time. In general, fin fish needs only 10 minutes' cooking time for each inch of thickness. Whereas fin fish may fall apart if overcooked, shellfish will become tough, so particular care not to overcook is required with lobster, crab, shrimp, oysters and clams.

Milk. When heating milk, use low heat, or cook it in top of double boiler. When scalding milk, do not discard the skin that forms on top; it contains milk solids and valuable nutrients.

Vegetables. In preparing any vegetable—fresh, canned, or frozen—be careful not to overcook.

Overcooking destroys color, flavor and palatability and results in greater loss of nutrients. Vegetables that are reheated also lose many of their nutrients. Cook only enough vegetables for 1 meal at a time, and serve as soon as cooking is done. And remember that, for variety of flavor and texture, raw vegetables should be served often.

Some minerals and vitamins in vegetables may be destroyed by dissolving them in water or by exposing them to heat and air during cooking. Mineral content will also be lost if too thick a layer of skin is removed, as most iron in root vegetables is right under the skin.

So remember:

1. Bake vegetables in their skins whenever possible, in order to retain nutrients. Pressure-cooking is next best. Waterless cooking, in special heavy pots for the purpose, is very satisfactory and steaming is another good method.

2. In peeling, remove as thin a layer of skin as possible. Scraping is better than peeling. Cooking in the skin, after thorough scrubbing, retains even more food values.
3. Do not soak vegetables in water before cooking. If you find it necessary to prepare vegetables in advance, put them in a covered container or storage bag in the refrigerator until time to cook them.
4. Do not cut vegetables into small pieces for cooking. There will be less nutrient loss if they are left in larger pieces. Mashing after cooking causes still more nutrient loss.

5. Cook mild-flavored vegetables in as little water as possible, and cover tightly. Cook leafy greens in water that clings to leaves after washing and in tightly covered saucepan; they require only a few minutes' boiling. More water is necessary when cooking strong-flavored vegetables like cabbage, but never drown them—use only enough water to cover, and cook quickly. *Never add baking soda*—it destroys some vitamins.

6. To shorten cooking time, which means less loss of vitamins and minerals, bring water to boiling point *before* vegetables are added.
7. Do not pour away liquid in which mild-flavored vegetables have been cooked. Use it for gravies, sauces and stews. However, do not use liquid from green vegetables.
8. Serve vegetables as soon as they are cooked; much of their value is lost if they are kept waiting, and flavor is lost too.

Canned Vegetables. When heating canned vegetables, do not discard liquid in can. Drain it, boil until reduced by 1/2, add vegetable and heat through as quickly as possible. Save vegetable juice for use in gravies or soups.

Frozen Vegetables. All frozen vegetables (except corn on the cob) should be cooked without thawing. Use only a small amount of boiling water, and cover tightly. Cook only for time given in package directions. Do not overcook. These vegetables need much less time than do fresh vegetables. Serve at once.

MENUS AND RECIPES

Beginning a special portfolio of well-balanced family meals with recipes planned for consecutive days over 2 weeks, menus for year-round use and for hot weather, including uses for leftovers.

Good meals don't simply "happen." They are the result of planning. The care you take in shopping, storing, refrigerating and all other preliminary activities helps you to give your family satisfactory year-round menus.

Plan your timing well in advance: Chill dessert; wash salad stuffs, and keep in plastic bags; open new bottles; make dressing; measure flour for thickening; separate eggs for last minute use if necessary. Start longest-cooking item (roast, stew or the like) a little ahead of required cooking time. Get out all tools necessary; beater, shredder and so forth to save endless opening of drawers and cupboards. Set table. Start vegetables cooking at desired time. Warm plates and platters. Measure coffee, and water into pot. Organize dessert service on side table or in kitchen. Complete table with bread, water and so forth. Start coffee, and serve first course.

In this section of consecutive days' menus with recipes, note how planning from many angles is demonstrated. Although breakfast may be a standard meal, its components of vitamins, proteins and other food elements have a bearing on the evening dinner plan.

Contrast in food colors, textures and flavors is considered in every menu. Planned leftovers become tempting in fresh guises. Planning covers cooking methods too; while the oven is hot it can be utilized for more than 1 dish. Seasonal variety in menus is always worth forethought,

and the hot-weather menus make full use of summer's bounty.

Recipes are given for items printed IN THIS STYLE. THIS STYLE is used too when the recipe will be found by reference to other chapters of the book.

Year-round Menus

Sunday

BREAKFAST	LUNCHEON	DINNER
Citrus-fruit cup	PUREE MONGOLE	Oyster stew
EGGS IN CREAM	WITH	ROAST CAPON with
WITH BACON	CROUTONS	SAVORY BREAD
CURLS	Grilled-cheese	STUFFING
Pecan rolls	sandwiches	BAKED COTTAGE
Coffee Milk	Pears	POTATOES
	Tea Milk	BAKED CRUMBED
		TOMATOES
		Tossed green salad
		Peach pie
		Coffee Tea Milk

Eggs in Cream with Bacon Curls

    6 eggs
    1 tablespoon butter or margarine
    1/2 cup heavy cream
    Salt and pepper to taste
    1 recipe FRIED BACON CURLS

Butter shallow baking dish generously. Break eggs into dish, dot with butter, pour cream over eggs and bake at 350°F. until eggs are barely set, about 15 minutes. Garnish with crisply fried bacon curls. Serves 6.

Fried Bacon Curls

    12 bacon slices

Place bacon in cold skillet. Cook slowly over low heat, turning occasionally, until evenly crisp but not brittle. Pour off excess fat. Remove from pan, and curl with fork. Drain on paper towels. Serves 6.

Puree Mongole with Croutons

    1 (10 1/2-ounce) can condensed tomato soup
    1 (10 1/2-ounce) can condensed green-pea soup
    2 cups milk or 1 cup milk and 1 cup cream
    Croutons

Combine and stir two cans soup. Add milk, stirring to smooth out any lumps. Heat thoroughly. Serve soup sprinkled with croutons. Serves 4–5.

Roast Capon

    1 5-pound drawn capon, completely thawed
    1 teaspoon salt
    1 recipe SAVORY BREAD STUFFING
    1/4 cup soft butter or margarine
    1/2 cup melted fat
    Salt to taste

Remove any pinfeathers from bird. Wash bird under cold water tap, inside as thoroughly as outside, and make sure all traces of red, spongy lungs near ribs are removed. Pat as dry as possible, using clean cloth or paper towels. Sprinkle inside with a little salt.

Stuff with dressing, placing a little against upper breast meat under neck skin and filling body cavity from rear vent. Do not pack dressing, as it swells during cooking. Using small poultry skewers, pin vent closed, and hold together with twine laced round, or sew up with heavy thread and darning needle. Truss bird for roasting by tucking wing tips under back and pressing legs close to body. Loop middle of yard-long piece of twine over tail; bring ends up tightly to loop legs and hold them securely against the body; then carry each length along side to wing and up over wing joint; tie together over neck skin at back. This method avoids marks across breast.

Rub softened butter or margarine over entire bird. Place breast up on rack in open roasting pan. Use no water in pan; do not cover and do not sear. Place in oven pre-heated to 325°F. Dip small square of clean, dry cheesecloth in melted fat and place over bird for self-basting.

Cook at low-to-medium temperature, allowing 35 minutes to the pound—or about 3–3 1/2 hours for 5-pound capon. Salt bird midway in the cooking.

Remove basting cloth about 45 minutes before end of cooking time, for nice browning of skin. When bird is done, allow it to stand in warm place for 5 minutes before serving. This period allows for absorption of juices and easier carving. Serves 4–6.

Note: Allow ample time for frozen bird to thaw completely before beginning preparation.

Savory Bread Stuffing

    1/3 cup butter or margarine
    1/4 cup chopped onion
    1/4 cup chopped celery
    5 cups soft bread crumbs
    2 teaspoons poultry seasoning
    1 teaspoon salt
    Pinch of pepper

Melt butter or margarine, add onion and celery and cook gently over low heat until vegetables are tender but not brown. Mix in crumbs and seasonings. Cool completely before inserting in bird. Do not pack stuffing in tightly, because bread must have room to swell during cooking. Also it will cook more thoroughly—and not be too damp—if it is loosely packed. Makes enough stuffing for 5-pound bird.

Note: Discard brown crusts of bread before preparing crumbs.

Baked Cottage Potatoes

    6 medium potatoes
    6 tablespoons skim milk
    6 tablespoons onion-flavored cottage cheese
    Salt and pepper to taste

Scrub potatoes. Prick skin all over with fork. Bake in oven last 1 1/2 hours with capon. Just before serving, slash top of each, and split open, remove potato pulp. Mix skim milk and cottage cheese. Season with salt and pepper to taste. Divide mixture evenly into empty potato shells. Return to oven for 10 minutes to reheat. For a crisper skin, brush each potato with fat before putting it in oven. Serves 6.

Note: Usually, potatoes are baked about 1 hour at 450°F. As oven is set for 325°F. for capon, allow longer, slower cooking time.

Baked Crumbed Tomatoes

    6 medium tomatoes
    Salt to taste
    1/4 teaspoon ground cloves
    4 salt-flavored crackers, crushed
    2 tablespoons melted butter or margarine
    1/4 teaspoon savory
    1/4 teaspoon oregano
    Dash of Worcestershire sauce
    1/2 cup water

Wash tomatoes, and cut out stem ends. Place in baking dish, cavity side up, and sprinkle with salt and cloves. Combine salt-flavored crackers with butter or margarine, savory, oregano and Worcestershire sauce. Spoon some of this mixture into each cavity. Pour water around tomatoes, and bake at 350°F. about 30 minutes. Serves 6.

Monday

BREAKFAST	LUNCHEON	DINNER
Orange sections	CHEESE PUFF	SWISS STEAK
Cornflakes	Celery hearts	Mashed potatoes
CINNAMON	Fresh apple	Green beans with
TOAST	Cookies	pimento
Coffee Milk	Tea Milk	Chocolate pudding
		Coffee Tea Milk

Cinnamon Toast

    6 slices white, whole wheat or raisin toast
    2 tablespoons butter or margarine
    3 tablespoons granulated sugar
    1 teaspoon cinnamon

Butter toast lightly. Trim crusts if desired. Blend sugar and cinnamon; sprinkle over toast.

Place on rack in shallow baking pan. Toast in moderate oven (350°F.) or under broiler until sugar melts. Cut in triangles or strips. Serves 6.

Cheese Puff

        8 slices day-old bread
    1/2 lb. Cheddar cheese, sliced thin
        3 eggs
        2 cups milk
        1 teaspoon finely chopped onion
        1 teaspoon prepared mustard
        1 scant teaspoon salt
    Pepper to taste

Remove crusts from bread. Arrange 4 slices in greased shallow baking dish. Add cheese slices; cover with remaining bread. Beat eggs; add milk, onion and seasonings. Pour into dish, and refrigerate about 1/2 hour. Bake at 325°F. about 45 minutes or until puffed and golden brown on top. Serve immediately. Serves 4.

Swiss Steak

    1 1/2 lbs. round or rump beef, 1 1/2 inches thick
        2 tablespoons flour
        1 teaspoon salt
    1/8 teaspoon pepper
        2 tablespoons salad oil or melted fat
        1 (1-pound) can tomatoes
        3 large onions, peeled and thinly sliced
        1 stalk celery, diced
        1 clove garlic, crushed
        1 tablespoon thick meat sauce

Trim excess fat from meat. Combine flour, salt and pepper. Lay beef on chopping board, sprinkle with 1/2 flour mixture; with rim of saucer pound flour into meat. Turn meat over, and pound remaining flour into other side. Cut into serving pieces if desired. Heat salad oil in heavy skillet or Dutch oven. Brown meat well on 1 side over medium heat. Turn and brown other side. Add remaining ingredients. Stir well, cover and simmer 1 3/4–2 hours or until meat is tender. Skim off fat if necessary. Serves 4–5.

Tuesday

BREAKFAST	LUNCHEON	DINNER
Prunes with	Consommé	ROAST PORK LOIN
cream	CABBAGE SALAD	BAKED SWEET
SOFT-COOKED	WITH FRUIT	POTATOES
EGGS	AND CREAM-	Broccoli with lemon
Toasted English	CHEESE BALLS	butter
muffins	Melba toast	BAKED APPLES
Coffee Milk	Tea Milk	Coffee Tea Milk

Soft-cooked Eggs

        6 eggs
        Cold or lukewarm water

Cover tops of eggs with water by at least 1/4 inch. Cover pan. Heat rapidly until water boils; turn off heat, and, if necessary, set pan aside to prevent further boiling. Let stand, covered, for following time periods:

For very soft-cooked eggs, about 2 minutes
For medium soft-cooked eggs, 3–3 1/2 minutes
For firmer soft-cooked eggs, about 4 minutes

Serves 6.
Note: If eggs are extra large or very cold, you may have to increase cooking time 2–4 minutes. If 4 or more eggs are being cooked, lower heat to keep water hot but not simmering, and cook 4–6 minutes.

Cabbage Salad with Fruit and Cream-cheese Balls

        10 dates, pitted
    1/4 cup seedless raisins
        3 cups shredded raw cabbage
        1 teaspoon cream
    1/2 cup mayonnaise
        6 large lettuce leaves
    6–12 small cream cheese balls

Cut dates into small pieces. Add dates and raisins to cabbage. Add cream to mayonnaise and use to moisten cabbage thoroughly. Serve in lettuce cups, and garnish each with 1 or 2 little balls of cream cheese. Serves 6.

VARIATIONS:

● Add 1 cup diced, cored, unpared red apples; increase amount of dressing if necessary.
● Sprinkle coarsely chopped nuts over each salad mound after arranging.

- Omit cream-cheese balls and crumble blue cheese over each salad.
- Use peanut-butter balls rolled in coarsely chopped peanuts in place of cheese.

Roast Pork Loin

1 (5 1/2–6 pound) pork loin roast
Salt and pepper to taste

Take pork loin from refrigerator at least 1/2 hour before placing in oven. Wipe with damp cloth or damp paper towels. Place on rack in uncovered roasting pan, fat side up, and roast at 350°F., allowing 35 minutes per pound. If meat thermometer is used, it will register 185°F. when meat is done. Season about 40 minutes before cooking is completed. Do not baste or turn roast during cooking. Serves 6.

Note: The first rule for pork is that it must be thoroughly cooked. Underdone pork should never be eaten.

Baked Sweet Potatoes

6 medium sweet potatoes
2 tablespoons salad oil
2 tablespoons butter or margarine

Scrub potatoes well, and dry with paper towels. Rub each with a little salad oil, and arrange on small baking sheet or oven rack. Cooking time will be approximately 1 hour at 350°F., so put potatoes in 1 hour before pork roast is done. Test potatoes with fork for tenderness. When baked soft, remove from oven, and prick with fork to let steam out. Cut 1 1/2-inch cross in top of each potato. While holding with clean towel, press each potato from bottom until it partially bursts through cross. Top with butter or margarine. Serves 6.

Note: Select firm smooth-skinned sweet potatoes of bright appearance.

Baked Apples

6 firm medium-sized baking apples
3/4 cup granulated sugar
1 cup water

Wash apples; then with knife or corer remove cores and seeds as neatly as possible. To help prevent skin from bursting during cooking, pare each apple about 1/3 the way down from stem end. Arrange in shallow baking pan, allowing apples to touch one another. Make syrup by

boiling sugar and water 10 minutes. Some red parings may be added to syrup for extra color. Remove parings before pouring syrup over apples. Put apples into a moderate oven 350°F. Baste with syrup from time to time. Apples are done when they can be pierced easily with fork. Serve apples warm or chilled, with plain or whipped cream. Serves 6.

Note: For an extra touch, try sprinkling 1 teaspoon sugar on each cooked apple and broiling under low heat a few minutes.

VARIATIONS:

To vary baked apples by filling centers, leave base intact when removing cores. Set in baking dish, fill each center with 1/4 cup mincemeat—about 1 1/2 cups for 6 apples—dot with bit of red currant jelly, add sugar-syrup and bake and baste. Serve warm.

- Fill centers of tart apples with liquid honey, and add a little grated lemon rind, cinnamon and nutmeg. Bake without extra liquid in covered dish until fruit is almost tender; remove cover to finish cooking. Serve warm or chilled.

Wednesday

BREAKFAST	LUNCHEON	DINNER
Grapefruit juice	FRANKFURTERS	CREAMED CHICKEN IN
Hot cereal	AND	PATTY SHELLS
Toast Jelly	SAUERKRAUT	Hot potato chips
Coffee Milk	Rolls	Peas with mint
	Apple	Tossed salad
	Tea Milk	Pineapple BROWNIES
		Coffee Tea Milk

Frankfurters and Sauerkraut

4 frankfurters
Boiling water
1 pound sauerkraut

Place frankfurters in pan of boiling water, cover, remove from heat and allow to stand 7–8 minutes. Remove from water with tongs or spoon, to prevent pricking skins. Simmer sauerkraut in its own juice 15–20 minutes; drain before serving. If less pronounced flavor is desired, juice may be poured off first and sauerkraut barely covered with boiling water, and simmered 20 minutes. Serves 4.

Note: As frankfurters are completely cooked when you buy them, they have only to be heated through. For serving with sauerkraut, they are best heated in boiling water.

Note: Sauerkraut may be bought in cans or in bulk.

Creamed Chicken in Patty Shells

3 tablespoons butter or margarine
3 tablespoons flour
1 3/4 cups milk
1/2 teaspoon salt
Pepper to taste
Paprika to taste
3 cups diced cooked chicken
6 heated patty shells
Chopped parsley

Melt butter or margarine in saucepan over low heat. Stir in flour; blend till smooth and bubbling.

Add milk gradually, stirring to blend. Return saucepan to heat, add seasonings and stir and

cook until sauce is smooth and thickened and there is no taste of raw starch. Add chicken. Keep hot until time to turn into heated patty shells. Sprinkle with chopped parsley before serving. Serves 6.

Note: This recipe starts with a dependable basic procedure for that most versatile menu item, *white sauce*. If you prefer a thicker sauce, use 1 tablespoon *more* of both butter and flour. A good white sauce can also be made by scalding milk, then adding paste made by blending together softened butter or margarine and flour in correct proportions and stirring constantly until mixture thickens and bubbles and there is no taste of uncooked starch. Season to taste. When making white sauce to serve over hot vegetables, use vegetable water (but not from green vegetables) as part of liquid for extra flavor. Add shredded cheese to make cheese sauce.

Brownies

3/4 cup sifted flour
1/4 teaspoon baking powder
1/4 teaspoon salt
1/2 cup shortening
1 cup granulated sugar
2 eggs, beaten
2 (1-ounce) squares unsweetened chocolate, melted
3/4 cup chopped pecans or walnuts
Powdered sugar

Sift together first 3 ingredients. Work shortening with spoon until fluffy and creamy; add sugar slowly, continuing to work until mixture is light. Add eggs and chocolate. Stir in flour mixture with nuts. Turn into a well-greased pan 8″x8″x2″ and bake at 350°F. 30–35 minutes or until done. Immediately cut into 2-inch squares with knife; sprinkle with powdered sugar. Cool; remove from pan with broad spatula. Makes 16.

Thursday

BREAKFAST	LUNCHEON	DINNER
Tomato juice with lemon wedges	Chicken with rice soup	BRAISED VEAL WITH VEGETABLES
FRENCH TOAST with syrup	Egg sandwich Carrot sticks	Noodles APRICOT ICE
Coffee Milk	Tea Milk	Cookies Coffee Tea Milk

French Toast

3 eggs
1/4 teaspoon salt
1/3–1/2 cup milk
3 tablespoons butter or margarine
8 slices stale bread
Cinnamon to taste

Beat eggs until mixed; add salt and milk. Heat butter or margarine in frying pan. Using fork,

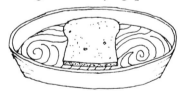

dip each bread slice into egg mixture for thorough moistening. Fry until golden brown, turn-

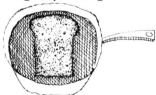

ing once. Dust with cinnamon, and serve with syrup, jam, butter or margarine. Serves 4.

Braised Veal with Vegetables

    1 pound stewing veal
1 1/2 tablespoons flour
    3 tablespoons salad oil
  1/2 cup sliced onions
    1 cup stock or 1 cup water and 1 beef bouillon cube
    1 teaspoon salt
  1/4 cup diced celery
  1/2 cup diced carrots
    2 tablespoons chopped green pepper
  1/2 cup green peas
    8 ounces noodles, boiled
Parsley sprigs

Cut veal into 1-inch cubes. Dredge with flour. Heat oil in large skillet. Add veal, and cook until light brown, turning several times. Add onions, and cook until golden, stirring once or twice. Add stock and salt to veal mixture. Cover pan tightly, and cook over low heat 1 hour, adding vegetables for last 30 minutes. Arrange cooked noodles on platter with veal and vegetables in center, and garnish with parsley. Serves 4–6.

Apricot Ice

    1 egg, separated
  2/3 cup superfine sugar
  3/4 cup pulp of STEWED APRICOTS
  1/2 cup orange juice
    2 tablespoons lemon juice
    2 teaspoons grated orange or lemon rind
    1 cup ice-cold evaporated milk or heavy cream

Beat egg white till fluffy but not dry. Gradually fold in sugar, then apricot pulp, juices and rind. Beat milk in chilled bowl to form softly rounded peaks. Fold in apricot mixture. Put into refrigerator tray, and freeze to mushy consistency. Remove to chilled bowl, and beat quickly with rotary beater until smooth. Return to tray and refreeze. Serves 4.

Note: Superfine sugar is finer than granulated but coarser then confectioners.

Friday

BREAKFAST	LUNCHEON	DINNER
STEWED	WELSH RAREBIT	Vegetable juice
APRICOTS	ON TOAST	TUNA FISH–MUSHROOM
Hot oatmeal	Chilled cherries	CASSEROLE
Bacon Muffins	Cookies	Buttered spinach
Coffee Milk	Tea Milk	GINGERBREAD
		LEMON SAUCE
		Coffee Tea Milk

Stewed Apricots

    1 pound dried apricots
Cold water
1 1/2 cups sugar

Put apricots in saucepan with enough cold water to cover completely. Cover and simmer 30 minutes. Add sugar. Stir to dissolve. Makes 4 cups.

Note: For apricot pulp, force cooked fruit through sieve. If thicker syrup is desired for plain stewed apricots, remove fruit when tender, and simmer juice until reduced by 1/2. Pour over fruit and chill.

Welsh Rarebit on Toast

    2 tablespoons butter or margarine
    2 tablespoons flour
    1 teaspoon dry mustard
  1/4 teaspoon salt

    1 cup milk
    1 teaspoon Worcestershire sauce
Cayenne pepper
  1/2 pound Cheddar cheese, diced
    3 tablespoons beer or ginger ale
 9–12 toast points

Melt butter or margarine in top of double boiler. Add flour, mustard and salt; then stir in milk gradually. Cook over direct heat till mixture thickens. Place over gently simmering water. Add Worcestershire sauce and cayenne; stir in cheese, and continue to stir until cheese is melted. Just before serving, stir in beer. Serve over toast points. Serves 3–4.

Tuna Fish–Mushroom Casserole

    2 (7-ounce) cans (2 cups) coarsely flaked tuna
    2 tablespoons flour
    2 teaspoons Worcestershire sauce
  1/2 teaspoon salt
Pinch pepper
    2 cups milk
  3/4 cup sautéed sliced fresh mushrooms, 1/2 pound raw
    1 cup (approximately 2 1/2 ounces) potato chips, broken up

Measure 2 tablespoons oil from canned tuna into double boiler. Gradually stir in flour, Worcestershire sauce, salt, pepper and milk. Cook over boiling water until smooth and thickened, stirring constantly. Add mushrooms. Cover bottom of greased 1 1/2-quart casserole with 1/4 cup potato chips. Top with 1/3 the tuna, then 1/3 the sauce. Repeat, making 3 layers of each, and top with remaining potato chips. Bake, covered, at 375°F. 20 minutes. Uncover, and bake 5 minutes or until brown. Serves 4.

Gingerbread

    1/2 cup soft shortening
    2 tablespoons sugar
    1 egg
    1 cup dark molasses
    1 cup boiling water
    2 1/4 cups sifted all-purpose flour
    1 teaspoon baking soda
    1/2 teaspoon salt
    1 teaspoon ginger
    1 teaspoon cinnamon

Blend together thoroughly shortening, sugar and egg. Mix molasses and boiling water together, and add to first mixture. Sift together remaining ingredients, and stir in, beating until smooth. Pour into well-greased and floured 9-inch square pan, and bake at 325°F. 45–50 minutes. Cut into 3-inch squares in pan, and serve warm. Serves 9.

Lemon Sauce

    1 tablespoon cornstarch or 2 tablespoons flour
    1/3 cup sugar
    Grated rind of one lemon
    1 cup cold water
    1 1/2 tablespoons butter or margarine
    Juice of 1 lemon, strained

Mix cornstarch, sugar and lemon rind. Slowly add water, keeping mixture smooth. Cook, stirring until sauce is thick and clear. Serve hot, adding butter or margarine and lemon juice just before pouring over gingerbread. Makes 1 1/4 cups sauce.

Saturday

BREAKFAST	LUNCHEON	DINNER
Grapefruit halves	Split-pea soup	Chicken soup
Cold cereal	Watercress sandwiches	PORK CHOP SUEY
Poached eggs	Carrot sticks	FLUFFY RICE
Toast	SPICED FRUIT COMPOTE	Sliced tomatoes
Coffee Milk		Chocolate refrigerator dessert
	Tea Milk	Coffee Tea Milk

Spiced Fruit Compote

    1 cup syrup from fruits
    6 whole cloves
    1 stick cinnamon
    2 tablespoons lemon juice
    2 ripe pears
    1 (1-pound, 1-ounce) can peaches
    1 (1-pound, 1-ounce) can greengage plums
    2 bananas

Place syrup in small saucepan; add spices and lemon juice; simmer uncovered 15 minutes. Strain. Wash and peel pears; thinly slice into serving bowl. Add drained peaches and plums.

Pour hot syrup over. Chill in refrigerator. Just before serving, peel bananas, and slice over top. Serves 4–5.

Pork Chop Suey

    2 tablespoons salad oil
    1/2 cup chopped green pepper
    1/2 cup chopped onion
    2 cups cooked pork, cut in strips
    1 cup chopped celery with leaves
    1 cup canned bean sprouts
    1/2 cup chicken bouillon
    1 tablespoon cornstarch
    1 tablespoon soy sauce
    1/2 cup sautéed or canned mushrooms
    1/2 cup blanched, shredded and toasted almonds

Heat oil in large skillet. Add green pepper and onion; sauté 3 minutes. Add pork, and cook 3 minutes. Add celery, bean sprouts and 1/4 cup chicken bouillon. Make paste of remaining bouillon and cornstarch. Add paste to pork mixture and cook, stirring until thickened. Add soy sauce and mushrooms. Heat thoroughly, turn out on platter and scatter almonds over top. Serves 4–6.

Fluffy Rice

    1 cup raw white rice
    2 1/2 cups cold water
    1 teaspoon salt

Combine rice, water and salt in 3-quart saucepan with tight-fitting lid. Bring to full boil, uncovered, and stir once or twice as water starts rolling. Lower heat to simmer, place lid on pan and cook about 14 minutes without stirring or uncovering. If after you have tested a grain or 2, rice seems not quite tender, replace lid, and continue to simmer 3–4 minutes longer. Fluff rice lightly with fork, stirring a few times from bottom of pan to make sure no moisture remains there. All water should be absorbed by this amount of rice, so that there is no need to drain it. If serving is delayed, let rice stand in covered pan to steam-dry and keep hot. Serves 4.

Sunday

BREAKFAST	LUNCHEON	DINNER
Blended fruit juice	FRENCH ONION SOUP	ROAST BEEF
Puffed wheat	Carrot and celery sticks	Horseradish gravy
SCRAMBLED EGGS with chives	APPLESAUCE	YORKSHIRE PUDDING
	Cookies	OVEN-BROWNED POTATOES
Toast	Coffee Milk	Scalloped tomatoes
Marmalade		PEACHES MELBA
Coffee Milk		Coffee Tea Milk

Scrambled Eggs

6 eggs
1/2 cup milk
1/2 teaspoon salt
1/8 teaspoon pepper
2 tablespoons butter or margarine

Beat eggs, milk and seasonings together lightly in a bowl. Melt butter or margarine in skillet over low-to-medium heat, tipping pan so that sides too are greased. Pour in egg mixture, and cook over low heat. As mixture begins to thicken, gently scrape with spoon from bottom and sides of pan. Continue cooking until mixture is uniformly set but still moist. Serve at once. Serves 4.

Note: If you prefer, eggs may be cooked in top of double boiler; melt butter or margarine first, and scrape and lift mixture as in skillet. Water in lower section should be boiling, but should not touch upper container. This method takes a little longer.

VARIATIONS:

● Add a few sautéed chopped mushrooms, 1 tablespoon grated cheese, 1 tablespoon chopped cooked ham or 1 tablespoon chopped chives.

French Onion Soup

4 or 5 medium-sized onions
1/4 cup butter or margarine
2 (10 1/2-ounce) cans condensed beef bouillon
2 soup cans water
2 tablespoons cognac
Salt and pepper to taste
6 1/2-inch slices French bread
1 cup grated Parmesan cheese

Peel onions, and slice thinly, keeping in rings. Heat butter or margarine in pot. Add onions.

cover and cook slowly until soft. Uncover, increase heat and allow onions to brown. Remove

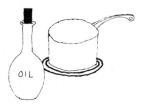

from heat, and add bouillon, water and cognac. Return to fire, and simmer 1/2 hour, adding salt and pepper. Toast French bread. Just before serving time, turn on broiler; ladle soup into fireproof bowls, float toast slice on top of each,

sprinkle with cheese and place under broiler until topping is melted Serves 5 or 6.

This recipe is a simple, easily made version of *soupe à l'oignon*.

Applesauce

6 large tart apples
Cold water
Granulated sugar

Wash apples, quarter, remove stems and blossom ends but leave cores and seeds. Do not peel. Put into saucepan. Add enough water to come not quite to top of the apples, cover and cook over low-to-medium heat 20–30 minutes or until tender. Add sugar to give desired degree sweetness, which will depend on personal taste and tartness of apples. Put through strainer, and cool. Serves 6–8.

Note: In late winter or spring, as apples become older, it may be desirable to add an extra flavor touch, like nutmeg, cloves or lemon juice.

Roast Beef

1 2-rib roast of beef

Place roast, fat side up, on rack in shallow pan. If meat thermometer is used, insert so that tip reaches center without touching fat or bone. Place, uncovered, in 325°F. oven. Do not add water to pan. For rare beef, allow 18–20 minutes per pound; for medium, 22–25 minutes; for well done, 27–30 minutes. Meat thermometer will read 140°F., 160°F., or 170°F. respectively. Let finished roast stand in warm place a few minutes while gravy is being made. Serves 6.

Note: For roast beef at its best, select your cut with care. A standing rib roast is one of the finest cuts for roasting; if you prefer it without bone, buy rolled rib piece. Round-steak roast and rump may also be used for same type of dry-heat roasting in open pan. If possible, allow meat to come to room temperature before putting it in oven; a roast directly from refrigerator requires longer cooking time per pound. For less shrinkage, better flavor and juiciness, do not sear in hot oven, and withhold salt and other seasoning until last 1/2 hour of cooking time.

Yorkshire Pudding

    1 cup sifted all-purpose flour
    1 teaspoon salt
    2 eggs, well beaten
    1 cup milk
    1/4 cup drippings from hot roast beef

Sift flour and salt together; combine eggs and milk, gradually stir into flour and beat with egg beater until smooth. Let stand until roast is done. Remove roast from oven and increase heat to 450°F. Pour hot drippings into preheated 9-inch square pan. Pour batter into pan, and bake 15–20 minutes while you make gravy and carve the roast. Cut into squares, and serve at once with roast beef. Individual greased muffin tins may be used instead, with batter divided into equal parts. Serves 6.

Oven-browned Potatoes

    6 medium potatoes, peeled

About 1 1/4 hours before roast is done, parboil 6 potatoes for 10 minutes. Drain, and arrange around roast in roasting pan. Bake 40–60 minutes or until tender, turning occasionally. Baste with fat in pan. Serves 6.

Peaches Melba

    6 canned peach halves
    1 quart vanilla ice cream
    1 package or pint sweetened mashed raspberries
        (fresh or frozen)

Place one peach half, cut side up, in each of 6 sherbet dishes. Top with ice cream, and add chilled raspberries. Serves 6.

BREAKFAST	LUNCHEON	DINNER
Grapefruit	CREAMED	HOT, SPICED TOMATO
Hot oatmeal	SALMON	JUICE
Bacon Muffins	Toast points	VEGETABLES WITH
Tea Milk	Celery and	LIVER
	carrot sticks	FLUFFY RICE
	PRUNE WHIP	Tossed green salad
	Tea Milk	BANANA SPONGE
		Coffee Tea Milk

Creamed Salmon

    1 (8-ounce) can salmon
    1 cup hot medium white sauce made with cream and
        liquid from fish
    2 teaspoons grated onion
    1/4 teaspoon mace
    2 teaspoons finely chopped parsley
    Toast points

Drain salmon, reserving liquid. Discard dark skin. Flake salmon, mash bones and add to hot white sauce with onion and mace. Heat thoroughly, and serve, sprinkled with parsley, on toast points. Serves 2–3.

Prune Whip

    2 egg whites
    1/3 cup granulated sugar
    1 (5-ounce) jar strained prunes
    2 teaspoons lemon juice

Beat egg whites until stiff peaks form. Gradually add sugar, beating continuously, until mixture forms stiff, dry peaks. Combine prunes and lemon juice, fold into egg whites and chill. As this dessert does not "stand up" well, it should be used within 1/2 hour of preparation. The mixture may be baked in the oven if preferred, at 350°F. about 20 minutes or until lightly browned. Serves 4.

Note: Unused egg yolks can be used in a custard sauce to serve with this prune whip, or they can be used in tomorrow's breakfast omelet.

Hot, Spiced Tomato Juice

    2 quarts tomato juice
    1/4 cup butter or margarine
    1/4 cup lemon juice
    2 tablespoons Worcestershire sauce
    2 teaspoons basil
    1/2 teaspoon pepper
    1/4 teaspoon mace
    12 lemon slices (2 lemons), optional

In a large saucepan, heat tomato juice, butter or margarine, lemon juice, Worcestershire sauce, basil, pepper, mace. Cook gently for 2 minutes. Serve in 8-ounce mugs, cups or glasses. Garnish each with a lemon slice. Makes 12 (6-ounce) servings.

Vegetables with Liver

    2 pounds beef or pork liver, sliced
  Seasoned flour
    3 tablespoons hot fat
    2 medium onions, chopped
  6–8 whole carrots, sliced
  2–3 stalks celery, sliced
  Salt and pepper to taste
  1/2 cup hot water

Remove skin from liver by inserting sharp knife under it and pulling or scraping it away from the meat; snip edges, and slice separately. Carefully cut out tubes with sharp-pointed scissors. Roll each slice separately in seasoned flour, and brown in hot fat, together with onions, carrots and celery. Season. Place in greased casserole, add water, cover, and bake at 350°F. for 45–60 minutes or until vegetables are tender. Serves 6.

Banana Sponge

    1 envelope unflavored gelatin
    2 tablespoons cold water
  1/2 cup boiling water
  1/2 cup sugar
    3 bananas, mashed
    2 teaspoons lemon juice
  1/4 teaspoon salt
    3 egg whites
  1/2 teaspoon sugar
  1/2 cup heavy cream, whipped

Mix gelatin with cold water; set aside 5 minutes. Dissolve in boiling water. Stir 1/2 cup sugar into gelatin mixture until dissolved. Cool. Add bananas and lemon juice. Chill until mixture begins to set. Add salt to egg whites; beat until they form softly rounded peaks. Beat gelatin mixture until frothy, and fold in egg whites. Pour into chilled serving dishes. Add 1/2 teaspoon sugar to whipped cream, and mound on top of banana mixture. Serves 4–5.

Tuesday

BREAKFAST	LUNCHEON	DINNER
Orange juice	Bacon-tomato	CASSEROLE OF LAMB
Dry cereal	sandwiches	WITH VEGETABLES
Omelets	Chilled canned	Pickled beets
Toast	plums	Tossed green salad
Marmalade	Tea Milk	COTTAGE PUDDING
Coffee Milk		CARAMEL SAUCE
		Coffee Tea Milk

Casserole of Lamb with Vegetables

  1 1/2 pounds lean uncooked lamb
  1 1/2 teaspoons salt
  1/8 teaspoon pepper
    2 tablespoons flour
    2 tablespoons shortening
  1/4 cup chopped onion
  Boiling water or broth
    3 medium potatoes, diced
    3 carrots, diced
    1 small white turnip, diced
    2 tablespoons chopped parsley

Cut lamb in 1-inch cubes. Combine seasonings and flour. Toss well with lamb cubes. Heat shortening in frying pan. Add lamb, and cook until light brown. stirring 2 or 3 times. Add onion, and cook until golden, stirring occasionally. Turn into 2-quart casserole, and add enough boiling water to cover lamb. Cover, and bake at 350°F. 90 minutes. Add potatoes, carrots and turnip, and cook 30 minutes longer or until vegetables are tender. Garnish with parsley. Serves 4.

Cottage Pudding

  1/2 cup shortening
    1 teaspoon vanilla
  1 1/2 cups sugar

        1 egg
    1/2 teaspoon salt
      3 teaspoons baking powder
2 1/4 cups sifted all-purpose flour
      1 cup milk

Preheat oven to 350°F. Prepare an 8-inch square pan by lining it with a piece of waxed paper cut to fit over all areas smoothly; grease paper lightly. Using wooden spoon, cream shortening until light and fluffy. Add vanilla. Add sugar little by little, blending and beating after each addition. Add egg, and beat thoroughly into mixture. Sift salt and baking powder with flour. Add dry ingredients to creamed mixture alternating with milk, a little at a time, starting and ending with flour, and beating well after each addition. Pour batter into prepared pan. Place on rack in center of oven, and bake about 45 minutes. Take from oven and let stand a few minutes; then invert pan, and peel paper off cake. Cut into squares for serving. Serves 9.

Note: Cottage pudding is a plain cake, served warm with a dessert sauce. This recipe is for a standard 1-egg cake. Ingredients should be at room temperature before mixing.

Caramel Sauce

    2/3 cup brown sugar
      1 cup boiling water
      1 tablespoon cornstarch
      1 tablespoon cold water
Few grains salt
      1 tablespoon butter or margarine
    1/2 teaspoon vanilla

Melt sugar in small, heavy saucepan over medium heat. When it has colored to a rich brown, add boiling water very carefully, a little at a time, stirring. Dissolve cornstarch in cold water; then stir in a little of the hot mixture, and blend well. Stir cornstarch mixture into sugar mixture, and cook until smooth and thick; simmer a few minutes. Add salt, butter or margarine and vanilla. Serve hot over pudding. Makes approximately 1 cup of sauce.

Wednesday

BREAKFAST	LUNCHEON	DINNER
Tomato juice	Pizza	PORK CHOPS WITH
Oatmeal	Fresh fruit	APPLE RINGS
Toast Jelly	Tea Milk	Mashed potatoes
Coffee Milk		CORN-STUFFED
		TOMATOES
		TAPIOCA PARFAIT
		Coffee Tea Milk

Pork Chops with Apple Rings

      1 tablespoon shortening
      6 lean pork chops

      2 tablespoons flour
      1 cup hot water
      1 tablespoon vinegar
      1 teaspoon salt
    1/2 teaspoon sage
    1/8 teaspoon pepper
      3 tart apples, cored and cut into rings
    1/4 cup brown sugar

Heat shortening in frying pan. Add chops, and cook until lightly browned, turning once. Remove chops to baking dish. Pour out drippings; return 1 1/2 tablespoons drippings to frying pan and place over low heat. Add flour to drippings, stirring until smooth. Add water and vinegar slowly, and continue stirring. Add seasonings, and continue to cook until bubbling. Pour gravy over chops, and bake, covered, 25–30 minutes at 350°F. Place apple rings on chops, and sprinkle with brown sugar. Bake 20 minutes longer. Serves 6.

Corn-stuffed Tomatoes

      6 tomatoes
    1/2 teaspoon salt
      1 (10-ounce) package frozen whole-kernel corn, thawed
      2 tablespoons chopped green pepper
      2 tablespoons chopped celery
      2 tablespoons chopped onion
    1/2 cup bread crumbs
      2 tablespoons corn liquid or cream
      1 tablespoon butter or margarine
Water
      2 tablespoons grated cheese

Scoop out pulp from tomatoes, and salt them inside; then turn upside down to drain a few minutes. Combine other ingredients, except water and grated cheese, and sauté lightly in skillet, turning frequently, until vegetables are partly cooked. Then fill tomato shells with mixture, and set in baking dish with very small amount of water to prevent burning. Sprinkle with grated cheese. Bake 20–30 minutes at 350°F. Serves 6.

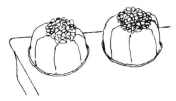

Tapioca Parfait

    1 1/2 cups milk
    1/8 teaspoon salt
      3 tablespoons quick-cooking tapioca
    1/4 cup sugar
      2 eggs, separated
    1/2 teaspoon vanilla extract
    Jam

Combine milk, salt, tapioca and 3 tablespoons sugar in top of double boiler. Cook over boiling water, stirring occasionally, until tapioca becomes transparent and mixture thickens, about 20 minutes. Meanwhile, beat egg whites until stiff but not dry; beat in remaining sugar. Beat egg yolks, add some of cooked tapioca, quickly add egg-yolk mixture and vanilla to double boiler over heat and stir until mixture thickens, about 3 minutes. Remove from heat and cool slightly. Fold in beaten egg whites. Allow to chill thoroughly. To serve, place small teaspoons of jam against side of sherbet or parfait glasses alternately with large tablespoons of pudding. Serves 4.

Thursday

BREAKFAST	LUNCHEON	DINNER
Vegetable juice	Cream of	CRISP ROAST BEEF
Poached eggs	tomato soup	HASH
Toast	MEXICAN SALAD	Buttered turnips
Coffee Milk	Rolls	Green peas
	ANGEL FOOD	LEMON MERINGUE PIE
	CAKE	Coffee Tea Milk
	Tea Milk	

Mexican Salad

      1 (10-ounce) package frozen green lima beans,
        cooked and drained
    1/4 cup FRENCH DRESSING
    1/2 green pepper, cut in strips
    1/4 cup sliced green onion
      2 or 3 fresh tomatoes, diced
    1/2 cup sliced celery
    Mayonnaise
    Lettuce
    1/4 cup sliced olives or 2 sliced hard-cooked eggs

Marinate lima beans in dressing about 1 hour. Combine with next 4 ingredients, adding just enough mayonnaise to moisten. Pile into a lettuce-lined bowl and garnish with olives or sliced eggs. Serves 6.

Crisp Roast Beef Hash

      3 cups diced cooked roast beef
      3 cups diced cold, cooked potatoes
    1/2 cup chopped onion
    1/4 cup chopped green pepper
    Salt and pepper to taste
    Milk or leftover gravy

Combine beef, potatoes, onion, green pepper, salt and pepper. Moisten with milk, and spread evenly in lightly greased hot skillet. Brown thoroughly on 1 side over low heat. Fold over as with omelet. Turn onto hot platter, and serve. Serves 6.

Note: Leftover meat should be diced small but not ground. The cooked potatoes should be diced about the same size as the meat cubes.

Friday

BREAKFAST	LUNCHEON	DINNER
Orange juice	MACARONI AND	BAKED STUFFED FISH
Cornflakes	CHEESE	CUCUMBER SAUCE
Broiled sausages	Crisp relishes	Macédoine of
Coffee Milk	PRUNE COMPOTE	vegetables
	Tea Milk	Baked potatoes
		Grapefruit halves
		Coffee Tea Milk

Macaroni and Cheese

      1 (8-ounce) package elbow macaroni
      3 tablespoons butter or margarine
      3 tablespoons flour
      2 cups milk
    1/4 teaspoon salt
    1/8 teaspoon pepper
      2 cups grated cheese
    1/2 cup dry bread crumbs
      1 tablespoon butter or margarine

Boil macaroni until tender, following directions on package. Rinse and drain in sieve. Prepare

medium white sauce of 3 tablespoons butter or margarine, flour, milk and seasonings; add 2/3 cup cheese, and stir until melted. Put macaroni in 1 1/2–2-quart baking dish, and add sauce.

Sprinkle remaining cheese over macaroni, and add crumbs and 1 tablespoon butter or margarine. Bake at 350°F. 20–30 minutes. Serves 5–6.

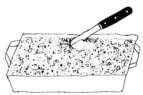

Prune Compote

    1/2 pound packaged tenderized prunes
    2 1/2 cups hot water
    1/4 cup sugar
    1 tablespoon lemon juice

Put prunes in saucepan with hot water, and simmer until tender (10–15 minutes). Remove from stove; stir in sugar and lemon juice. Chill. Serves 4.

Note: Packaged tenderized prunes need no soaking. Orange sections or slices may be added when serving.

Baked Stuffed Fish

    6 medium fresh or frozen haddock fillets
    1 1/2 tablespoons chopped onion
    1/4 cup chopped celery
    3 tablespoons butter or margarine
    2 cups soft bread crumbs
    1/2 teaspoon salt
Few grains pepper
1 teaspoon thyme (or sage or savory)
Milk
Lemon juice
Salt and pepper to taste

If using frozen fish, thaw. For stuffing, brown onion and celery in butter or margarine. Add bread crumbs, salt, few grains pepper and thyme, and moisten with a little milk. Place heaping spoonful of stuffing on each fillet; roll fillet and secure with skewer. Brush with lemon juice, and sprinkle with salt and pepper to taste. Bake in greased shallow pan, uncovered, at 375°F. 30–40 minutes or until tender. Serves 6.

Cucumber Sauce

    1 cup sour cream
1/4 cup unpared, chopped cucumber
    4 radishes, thinly sliced or 1 teaspoon chopped pimento
    2 teaspoons prepared horseradish
    1 teaspoon lemon juice
1/4 teaspoon salt
Dash cayenne
Dash tarragon vinegar

Combine ingredients, and chill 1–2 hours before serving. Makes about 1 1/3 cups.

Saturday

BREAKFAST	LUNCHEON	DINNER
Tomato juice	Beef bouillon	MEAT-STUFFED SQUASH
Pancakes and	Cabbage,	Parsley potatoes
syrup	orange and	Creamed celery
Coffee Milk	date salad	CINNAMON-APPLE
	Cookies	CRISP
	Tea Milk	Coffee Tea Milk

Meat-stuffed Squash

    1/2 small Hubbard squash
Boiling salted water
Soft butter or margarine
Salt to taste
    2 slices bacon, diced
    1/4 cup diced onion
    1/4 cup chopped green pepper or drained pickle relish
    1/3 cup tomato juice or tomato soup
    1 cup bread crumbs or leftover mashed potatoes
    1 egg
    1/4 pound sausage meat or chopped pork
    3/4 pound chopped veal, lamb or beef
1 1/4 teaspoons salt
    1 tablespoon prepared mustard
Mace and sage to taste

Discard seeds and any stringy pulp from squash. Cut off small slice of underside so that it will rest flat. Parboil 10 minutes in boiling salted water. Drain, and dry with absorbent paper. Brush inside with soft butter or margarine, and sprinkle with salt. Sauté bacon until clear, and remove from heat. Combine with all remaining ingredients. Pile mixture into squash cavity, and set in baking dish containing 1/2 inch boiling water. Bake at 350°F. 1 1/4 hours or until squash is tender when tested with fork. To serve, cut in wedges to make equal portions. Serves 6.

Cinnamon-apple Crisp

    4 cups sliced peeled apples
    1 teaspoon cinnamon
    1/2 teaspoon salt
    1/4 cup cold water
    1/2 cup sifted all-purpose flour
    1 cup sugar
    1/3 cup butter or margarine

Place apples in buttered baking dish, preferably of shallow, oblong type. Sprinkle with cinnamon, salt and water. Combine flour and sugar, and rub in butter or margarine to make crumbly mixture. Scatter lightly over apples, and bake at 350°F. 40 minutes. Serve warm with cream. Serves 6.

Hot Weather Menus

Sunday

BREAKFAST	LUNCHEON	DINNER
Fresh berries	Make-your-own	Broiled minute steaks
Cold cereal	sandwiches	Broiled tomato halves
Toast Jam	Watermelon	MASHED POTATOES
Coffee Milk	wedges	Tossed salad
	MILKSHAKES	GLAZED STRAWBERRY–
		CREAM PIE
		Coffee Tea Milk

Simplify for Summer Sundays. Here's a Sunday meal pattern that will appeal to everybody, including the cook. A picnic lunch with milk-shakes, an easy hot dinner, a summer pie, quick to make.

Milkshakes

With chilled milk, a large carton of ice cream and an assortment of flavorings, sauces or crushed fruit, everybody can make his or her favorite shake. For mixing, use a bowl and rotary beater or a portable electric mixer, electric blender, plastic juice shaker or screw-top sealer.

Mocha Shake: 2–3 tablespoons chocolate sauce, 1 teaspoon instant coffee, 1 cup cold milk, 1 scoop vanilla ice cream.

Cherry Shake: 2 tablespoons cherry jam or sauce, dash almond extract, 1 cup cold milk, 1 scoop vanilla ice cream.

Banana Shake: 1/2 banana, crushed; 1–2 tablespoons sugar, 1 cup cold milk, 1 scoop vanilla ice cream.

Glazed Strawberry–Cream Pie

      1 1/2 cups milk
          2 tablespoons cornstarch
      1/4 cup sugar
      1/8 teaspoon salt
          1 egg, slightly beaten
          1 teaspoon vanilla extract
          1 (9-inch) chilled graham-cracker crust
          3 cups fresh strawberries
      1/2 cup sugar
          1 tablespoon cornstarch
          1 tablespoon lemon juice
      Drop red vegetable coloring

Heat 1 cup milk in top of double boiler. Combine remaining 1/2 cup milk with 2 tablespoons cornstarch, 1/4 cup sugar and salt. When mixture is smooth, pour into hot milk, and cook over direct heat until thickened and no starch flavor remains. Stir a little hot mixture into egg; then blend egg into mixture. Cook over hot not boiling water, stirring, about 3 minutes. Remove from heat, and add vanilla extract. Pour into prepared crust and cool.

Wash and hull berries. Drain, and dry on absorbent paper. Slice 1/2 the berries and arrange over custard filling. Crush remaining berries, stir in 1/2 cup sugar and 1 tablespoon cornstarch and cook, stirring constantly, until mixture is thick and clear. Add lemon juice and vegetable coloring. Spread mixture over fresh berries, and chill thoroughly before serving, with whipped cream if desired. Serves 6–8.

Note: To make graham-cracker crust, follow illustrated directions in Chapter 4, omitting cinnamon if you prefer. Chill crust thoroughly without cooking; early preparation of this kind of shell means that it will have time to set.

Monday

BREAKFAST	LUNCHEON	DINNER
Grapefruit juice	Vegetable soup	SUMMER SAUSAGE
Bacon Toast	Crusty rolls	CASSEROLE
Coffee Milk	Celery sticks	Whole new carrots
	and radishes	Lettuce wedges
	Raspberry whip	THOUSAND ISLAND
	Cookies	DRESSING
	Tea Milk	FRESH PEACH
		CRUMBLE with
		cream
		Coffee Tea Milk

Summer Sausage Casserole

      1 pound sausages
      2 slices bacon, cut in small pieces
      1 small onion, chopped
      2 tomatoes, peeled and diced
  1/4 cup chopped green pepper
      1 teaspoon salt
  1/2 teaspoon dry mustard
  Pinch cayenne pepper or 2 drops hot pepper sauce
      2 teaspoons Worcestershire sauce
      1 (15-ounce) can kidney beans
      1 cup soft bread crumbs
  1/2 cup grated Cheddar cheese

Prick sausages, and partly fry over medium heat about 10 minutes; lift out, and drain on paper towels. Add bacon to pan, and fry until transparent. Pour off and reserve all but 1 tablespoon fat. Add onion, tomatoes, green pepper, salt, mustard, cayenne and Worcestershire sauce. Fry 5 minutes over low heat. Add beans with juice, and remove from heat. Mix bread crumbs with cheese and 2 tablespoons reserved fat. Spread 1/2 the crumb mixture in bottom of greased 9"x5"x4" baking dish. Cover with bean mixture, and spread with remaining crumbs. Arrange partially cooked sausages on top, and bake 30 minutes at 350°F. or until brown and bubbly on top. Serves 4–6.

Mayonnaise

      2 egg yolks or 1 egg
      1 cup salad oil
      1 teaspoon sugar (optional)
      1 teaspoon dry mustard
      1 teaspoon salt
      2 tablespoons vinegar or lemon juice
      1 tablespoon hot water

Beat egg yolks until thick, and add salad oil, very gradually, 1 teaspoon at a time. Continue beating until mixture is thick. Add remaining ingredients, and beat until blended. Keep in covered jar in refrigerator. Makes about 1 1/4 cups.

Note: All ingredients *must be* at room temperature. Beat very hard. If mixture "curdles," reconstitute by placing an additional egg yolk in a bowl. Stir it constantly and slowly add "curdled" dressing. Increase the flow as mixture thickens.

VARIATIONS:

Tartar Sauce: Combine 1/2 cup mayonnaise with 2 tablespoons chopped dill pickle, 2 teaspoons chopped pimento, 1 teaspoon each chopped onion and parsley and 1 teaspoon lemon juice.

Cucumber Mayonnaise: Combine 1/2 cup each mayonnaise and diced peeled cucumber; add sprinkle of chopped chives, with extra salt to taste. Prepare only just before serving as cucumber makes mayonnaise watery.

Remoulade Mayonnaise: Combine 1 cup mayonnaise with 1 teaspoon dry mustard and 1 tablespoon each chopped parsley, capers and chopped olives. Add tarragon or horseradish to taste.

Sour-cream Dressing: Use 1/2 cup mayonnaise or "boiled" dressing, and add 1/4 cup sour cream, whipped or plain; 2 teaspoons chopped chives, and dash black pepper.

Curry Mayonnaise: To 1/2 cup mayonnaise, add 1/4 teaspoon curry powder, for use with fish salads, or 1 teaspoon capers and 1/2 teaspoon tarragon vinegar.

Piquant Mayonnaise: Rub bowl with 1/2 clove garlic; add 2 tablespoons each chopped green pepper and pimento, and 1/4 cup each chopped celery, dill pickle and chili sauce; add 1 cup mayonnaise, and combine gently. Serve with green salads.

Norwegian Sauce: To 1 cup mayonnaise add 1 tablespoon prepared horseradish.

Mustard–Cream Dressing: Add 1/4 cup prepared mustard to 1 cup mayonnaise; fold into 1/2 cup heavy cream, whipped. Serve with meat and vegetable salads.

Pimento–Cheese Dressing: Add 1/4 cup pimento-cheese spread, dash of salt and 1 hard-cooked egg, finely chopped, to 1 cup mayonnaise. Serve with vegetable salads.

Russian Dressing: Add 2 teaspoons each chopped green pepper, pimento and chives; 1/2 teaspoon paprika; 3 tablespoons chili sauce, and yolk of hard-cooked egg, sieved, to 1 cup mayonnaise.

Quick Russian Dressing: Combine 1/2 cup mayonnaise with 2 tablespoons chili sauce, 1 teaspoon lemon juice and few drops of hot pepper sauce.

Thousand Island Dressing: Combine 1/2 cup mayonnaise with 1/4 cup chili sauce, 2 tablespoons each chopped onion, green pepper, celery and sweet pickle and 1 chopped, hard-cooked egg.

Honey–Cream Dressing: Blend 1/4 teaspoon dry mustard with 1 tablespoon honey and 1/2 teaspoon lemon juice. Add to 1 cup mayonnaise; season to taste with salt, then fold in 1/2 cup heavy cream, whipped. Serve with fruit-salad plates.

Fresh Peach Crumble

      3 cups peeled sliced fresh peaches
      1/4 cup water
      2 teaspoons lemon juice
      3/4 cup all-purpose flour
      1/8 teaspoon salt
      1 cup brown sugar
      2 tablespoons butter or margarine

Place peaches in greased baking dish, and sprinkle with water and lemon juice. Combine remaining ingredients until mixture resembles cornmeal. Sprinkle over peaches, and bake in moderate oven 350°F. 40 minutes. Serves 4–6.

Tuesday

BREAKFAST	LUNCHEON	DINNER
Orange sections	Chicken noodle	GROUND-BEEF PATTIES
Bran flakes	soup	Parsley new potatoes
SCRAMBLED	Cucumber and	MIXED GREEN SALAD
EGGS with	cream cheese	FRENCH DRESSING
chives	sandwiches	WITH BLUE CHEESE
Toast	Fruit cup	Butterscotch pudding
Coffee Milk	Iced tea Milk	Coffee Tea Milk

Ground-beef Patties

      1/4 cup dry bread crumbs
      1/2 cup evaporated milk or tomato juice
      1 1/2 pounds hamburger
      1 1/2 teaspoons salt
      1/4 teaspoon pepper
      1 egg, slightly beaten
      1/4 cup finely chopped onion
      1 teaspoon prepared mustard

Soak bread crumbs in milk. Mix all ingredients

together lightly; dampen the hands, and shape into 10–12 patties, about 1/2-inch thick. For tender patties, avoid pressing or packing meat too firmly. Fry about 3 minutes on each side. For broiling, brush patties with oil and broil about 3 inches from heat; then turn and continue broiling, 3–5 minutes on each side. Serves 6.

Note: Chopped parsley, Worcestershire sauce and your favorite herbs may be added for flavor variations. Chili sauce makes a good accompaniment.

Mixed Green Salad

                1 medium head lettuce
            1/8 pound chicory
                1 bunch watercress
                1 clove garlic, cut
                2 tomatoes, quartered
                2 green onions, chopped
            1/4 cup FRENCH DRESSING WITH BLUE CHEESE

Discard any wilted lettuce leaves. Wash greens well, drain and chill 1/2 hour. Dry by wrapping in towel. Tear into pieces. Rub salad bowl with cut clove of garlic, letting tiny shreds remain in bowl. Add greens and other vegetables, and toss lightly with dressing, using fork in each hand. Dressing should be added to salad just before serving. Serves 6.

French Dressing

                1 cup salad oil
            1/4 cup vinegar
            1 1/2 teaspoons salt
            1/4 teaspoon pepper
            1/2 teaspoon dry mustard

Measure ingredients into covered jar, and shake well before using.

Note: Add 1 teaspoon sugar for a sweeter dressing.

VARIATIONS:

French Dressing with Blue Cheese: Combine 2 tablespoons crumbled blue cheese with 1/2 cup French dressing, stir and shake well before using.

Italian Dressing: Use olive oil in place of salad oil, and add 1/4 teaspoon oregano or sweet basil and 1/2 clove garlic. Let dressing chill several hours, and remove garlic before serving.

Piquant Dressing: Add 1 clove garlic, cut crosswise; let stand in dressing 1 hour. Remove; add 1 tablespoon sugar and 1 teaspoon each celery seed and grated onion.

Roquefort Dressing: Mash 1/4 cup Roquefort with dash of Worcestershire sauce, and blend into 1/2 cup dressing: cheese may be quickly crumbled in before serving.

Lorenzo Dressing: Add 1 tablespoon chili sauce to 1/2 cup dressing.

Note: There are many possible variations of basic FRENCH DRESSING. For a flavor change, try wine vinegar or tarragon vinegar. Add a pinch of celery seed, a drop of hot pepper sauce or the merest pinch of cayenne pepper for sharpness.

Wednesday

BREAKFAST	LUNCHEON	DINNER
Chilled melon wedges	Fresh asparagus on toast with pimento strips	BAKED ORANGE-GLAZED HAM
Cereal		SCALLOPED POTATOES
Toast Honey	Cucumber sticks	WITH CHEESE
Coffee Milk	Sherbet	SPICED PEACHES
	Cookies	Swiss chard
	Tea Milk	ANGEL FOOD CAKE
		Coffee Tea Milk

Baked Orange-glazed Ham

                1 boned ready-to-eat ham, 6–8 lbs.
                1 teaspoon dry mustard
                3 tablespoons grated orange rind
                2 (6-ounce) cans frozen orange juice concentrate
            1/2 cup confectioners' sugar

Place ham, fat side up, in roasting pan. Mix mustard with 1 tablespoon orange rind, and rub over ham. Spoon 1 can orange juice concentrate over top of ham. Bake in slow oven, 300°F. 25

minutes per pound. If drippings should brown, add small amount water. During last 1/2 hour of baking, baste with remaining can of orange juice and pan drippings. Sprinkle with remaining orange rind, and, just before removing from oven, sprinkle on confectioners' sugar. Turn oven heat to 475°F., and glaze top of ham about 20 minutes. Serves 8–10 with some left over.

Scalloped Potatoes with Cheese

6 medium potatoes
1 onion, thinly sliced
1 teaspoon salt
1/8 teaspoon pepper
2 tablespoons flour
3 tablespoons butter or margarine
1 1/2–2 cups hot milk
1/4 cup grated cheese

Wash, peel and thinly slice potatoes. Butter 1 1/2-quart casserole or baking dish. Place layer of onion slices and layer of sliced potatoes in dish, using about 1/3 of each. Sprinkle with salt, pepper and flour. Dot with butter or margarine. Repeat layers, finishing with potatoes. Pour on hot milk. Sprinkle top with grated cheese. Bake, uncovered, at 375°F. 1 hour or until potatoes are tender and top is lightly browned. Serves 6.

Spiced Peaches

1 cup water
3/4 cup sugar
1/4 cup vinegar
1 broken stick cinnamon
3 or 4 freestone peaches
18 or 24 whole cloves

Simmer water, sugar, vinegar and cinnamon in 8-inch skillet 5 minutes. Peel peaches, and halve, removing stones. Press 3 whole cloves into rounded side of each half, and drop into simmering syrup. Cover pan, turn heat low and gently cook 3–4 minutes. Turn peach halves over, and continue cooking until just tender, about 2 minutes longer. Cool in syrup, drain and serve. Keep leftover syrup in covered jar to use again. Serves 6.

Thursday

BREAKFAST	LUNCHEON	DINNER
Sliced peaches	Grilled	Cold-meat platter
Cold cereal	tomato-cheese	POTATO SALAD
Toast Jam	sandwiches	MARINATED GREEN
Tea Milk	Raw celery	BEANS
	hearts	Carrot sticks
	Chilled melon	GRAPE SHERBET
	Tea Milk	Coffee Tea Milk

Potato Salad

2 cups diced, cooked potatoes
2 tablespoons chopped onion
2 green onions, sliced
1 hard-cooked egg, diced
1 teaspoon salt
Few celery seeds
2 egg yolks or 1 egg, slightly beaten
1/2 cup MAYONNAISE or COOKED SALAD DRESSING
Salad greens
2 tablespoons pimento

Combine potatoes, onion, hard-cooked egg, seasonings, egg yolks and mayonnaise, tossing lightly. Chill. Arrange salad on greens; garnish with pimento. Serves 4–5.

Cooked Salad Dressing

3 tablespoons flour
1 1/2 teaspoons salt
5 tablespoons sugar
2 tablespoons dry mustard
Pinch cayenne pepper
1 1/4 cups milk
2 egg yolks or 1 egg, slightly beaten
1/2 cup vinegar
2 tablespoons butter or margarine
Milk or sweet or sour cream

Combine first 5 ingredients in top of double boiler with 1 1/4 cups milk. Cook over direct heat, stirring, until mixture is thick and smooth. Place over hot water. Beat in egg yolks. Add vinegar and continue cooking 2–3 minutes longer. Remove from heat, and stir in butter or margarine. Taste for seasoning, and add more salt or sugar if necessary. Pour into covered jar, and keep in refrigerator. Beat before using, and dilute with milk to desired consistency. Makes approximately 2 cups.

Note: You may want to add 1/3 cup salad oil for a semi-oil-type dressing when mixture has cooled.

VARIATION:

Honey Fruit-salad Dressing: Blend 2 tablespoons honey into 1/2 cup cooked dressing; then fold in 1/2 cup whipped cream.

Marinated Green Beans

2 tablespoons oil
2 tablespoons vinegar
Salt and pepper to taste
1 pound cooked and chilled green beans

Combine oil and vinegar, season with salt and pepper and pour over beans. Cover, and chill 1–2 hours to absorb flavors. Oil and vinegar can be poured off and used again to dress a salad. Serves 4–5.

Note: Use 1 (1-pound, 1-ounce) can green beans or 2 (10-ounce) packages frozen green beans, cooked.

Grape Sherbet

1 envelope unflavored gelatin
1 cup water
1/2 cup sugar
1 1/2 cups unsweetened grape juice
3 tablespoons lemon juice
1 egg white, stiffly beaten

Heat gelatin, water and sugar in small saucepan. Stir until sugar melts. Cool and add grape and lemon juices. Pour into freezing trays, and freeze until mushy, stirring occasionally after first 15 minutes. Turn into cold bowl, break up with fork and beat until light. Fold in stiffly beaten egg white, and return mixture to freezing tray. Freeze until firm, stirring occasionally. Serves 6.

Friday

BREAKFAST	LUNCHEON	DINNER
Vegetable juice	FRESH FRUIT–	Fried fish fillets
Puffed wheat	CHEESE	TARTAR SAUCE
Toasted fruit	SALAD	New potatoes
bread	Butter tarts	Pickled beets
Coffee Milk	Tea Milk	SPINACH OR BEET
		GREENS
		LEMON SNOW AND
		CUSTARD SAUCE
		Coffee Tea Milk

Fresh Fruit–Cheese Salad

Crisp lettuce
1 small melon, peeled
1/2 pint cottage cheese
1 cup fresh berries
Superfine sugar
2 or 3 oranges, peeled
2 fresh pears or peaches, sliced
1 banana, sliced
Lemon juice
HONEY FRUIT-SALAD DRESSING

Arrange crisp lettuce on 4 serving plates. Cut melon in half, and scoop out seeds. Slice each 1/2 into 4 wedges. Arrange 2 wedges overlapping in center of each lettuce-lined plate, and fill with scoop of cheese. Dip fresh berries in sugar; surround melon with berries, orange and peach slices. Dip pear and banana slices in lemon juice to prevent discoloring and add to salad. Pour on dressing. Serves 4.

Spinach or Beet Greens

3 pounds raw spinach or beet greens
Butter or margarine
Salt and pepper to taste

Discard coarse stems, roots and wilted or discolored leaves. Wash in warm water, then in 2 rinses of cold water. Put greens loosely into saucepan without adding water, cover tightly, bring to quick boil and cook 3–4 minutes, turn-

ing greens just once. Drain thoroughly; add butter or margarine, salt and pepper. Serves 6.

Note: Spinach, beet greens and Swiss chard are at their best when crisply fresh and quickly cooked.

Lemon Snow

3 tablespoons cornstarch
3/4 cup sugar
1 1/4 cups boiling water
Grated rind of 1 lemon
1/2 cup lemon juice
2 egg whites

Mix cornstarch and 1/2 cup sugar together in small saucepan, and stir in boiling water and lemon rind. Place over medium heat, and cook, stirring until thick and clear. Add lemon juice, and bring to boil. Remove from heat. Cool. Beat egg whites until soft peaks form; then add remaining sugar, and beat until stiff. Fold in cooled lemon mixture. Pour into serving dish, and chill thoroughly. Serve with CUSTARD SAUCE. Serves 5–6.

Custard Sauce

1 cup milk
2 egg yolks
2 tablespoons sugar
Pinch of salt
1/4 teaspoon vanilla extract

Heat milk in top of double boiler until small bubbles form around edge. Beat egg yolks, sugar and salt together, and add a little hot milk. Return mixture to double boiler, and turn heat low, so that water in bottom stays hot but not rapidly boiling. Cook mixture, stirring, until it coats a metal spoon. Remove from heat, and add vanilla. If custard curdles, beat with rotary beater until smooth. Cover and chill thoroughly. Makes approximately 1 cup sauce.

Saturday

BREAKFAST	LUNCHEON	DINNER (Outdoor barbecue)
Sliced bananas	Peanut butter-	LAMB SHISH KEBAB
Shredded wheat	crumbled	Potato chips
Soft-cooked	bacon	Mixed green salad
eggs	sandwiches	Watermelon
Toast	RHUBARB–	BROWNIES
Coffee Milk	STRAWBERRY	Coffee Tea Milk
	COMPOTE	
	Tea Milk	

Rhubarb–Strawberry Compote

1 pound rhubarb
3 tablespoons cold water
1 scant cup granulated sugar
1 pint strawberries

Wash rhubarb, cut in pieces and put in saucepan with water over low heat. When fruit has started to soften, add sugar, stirring to dissolve. Cook until tender. Meanwhile wash and hull berries, and cut in half. Remove rhubarb from heat, and immediately add berries. Serves 6.

Note: Choose crisp stalks of rhubarb. They should break easily, and the rosier the skin the better.

Lamb Shish Kebab

        1 1/2–2 pounds lean lamb shoulder
            1/4 cup FRENCH DRESSING
              6 strips bacon
             12 cherry tomatoes
             18 whole mushroom caps
             12 small onions
              1 green pepper, cut in 1-inch squares
    Salt and pepper to taste

Have 6 metal skewers ready. Cut meat into 1–1 1/2-inch cubes, and marinate in dressing 1–2 hours, then divide into 6 parts. Cut each strip of bacon into 4. Thread lamb, bacon, tomatoes, mushrooms, onions, and green pepper on

each skewer. Salt and pepper lightly, and place over hot coals of barbecue grill, to brown on all sides. After 5 minutes, brush with marinade, and broil for 5–10 minutes longer. Turn several times during cooking. Serves 6.

Note: Shish kebabs may be cooked under broiler if preferred, turning to cook all sides.

VARIATIONS:

Chicken Liver Kebabs: Substitute 1 pound fresh chicken livers cut in uniform pieces for lamb, but do not marinate before cooking. Brush livers

with seasoned melted butter or margarine when turning from time to time during grilling.

Scallop Kebabs: Pick over, and wash 1 1/2 pounds fresh raw scallops. Pat dry with paper towels. Dip in melted butter or margarine, then in finely crushed cracker crumbs to which salt and pepper have been added to taste. Thread long slice of bacon on each skewer; add scallop; weave bacon back and forth continuously between another 4 or 5 scallops. Lay prepared skewers on grill (or under range broiler). Turn frequently until evenly browned. Garnish with chopped parsley, and serve with sprinkle of lemon juice.

Meatball Kebabs: To 1 pound hamburger or ground round steak, add 1/2 cup fine dry bread crumbs, 2 tablespoons grated onion, 2/3 cup milk or evaporated milk. Salt and pepper to taste. Form into small balls, and spear alternately with onion and tomato pieces.

Pork and Pineapple Kebabs: Thread alternate pieces of lean pork, marinated in soy sauce, and pineapple cubes. Green-pepper pieces also go well with this combination.

Sunday

BREAKFAST	LUNCHEON	DINNER
Fresh blueberries	Cream of pea soup	STUFFED CHICKEN BREASTS
CORNED BEEF HASH	Crisp raw vegetables	MUSHROOM SAUCE
Whole wheat toast	Cheese	Buttered zucchini
Coffee Milk	Melba toast	Sliced tomatoes
	Tea Milk	FRENCH PADDLE ICE CREAM sundaes
		Sugar cookies
		Coffee Tea Milk

Corned Beef Hash

        2 tablespoons bacon drippings or oil
        1/2 cup chopped onion
    2–2 1/2 cups cooked potatoes, diced
          1 teaspoon dry mustard
          1 teaspoon Worcestershire sauce
          1 (12-ounce) can corned beef, diced
    Salt and pepper to taste

Heat bacon drippings or oil in large, heavy frying pan or skillet, and add onion. Fry slowly until onion begins to color. Add potatoes, mustard, Worcestershire sauce and corned beef. Season with salt and pepper. Cover pan 1–2 minutes or until fat in corned beef begins to melt. Uncover, and scrape mixture up from bottom of pan with spatula. Press down evenly in pan, and increase heat to medium. When the hash begins to brown on bottom, scrape up again with spatula, and turn mixture over. Press down, and continue browning until crusty. Serve 4–5.

Stuffed Chicken Breasts

2 tablespoons butter or margarine
1/2 cup chopped onion
2/3 cup dry bread crumbs
1/2 teaspoon marjoram
1/2 teaspoon mace
1/4 teaspoon salt
1/3 cup milk
1 egg, slightly beaten
8 small single chicken breasts or 4 double breasts
2 tablespoons flour
1/2 teaspoon salt
Salad oil

Melt butter or margarine in small frying pan, and add onion. Fry slowly until onion begins to color. Remove from heat, and add bread crumbs, marjoram, mace and 1/4 teaspoon salt. Combine milk with beaten egg, and stir in. Wipe chicken breasts with damp cloth. Cover rib sides of 4 of

breasts with dressing, and place remaining breasts on top, rib side down. Tie breasts together with string; mix flour and 1/2 teaspoon salt, and sprinkle both sides of breasts. Heat salad oil about 1/4-inch deep in skillet, and brown chicken breasts on both sides. Reduce

heat to medium low, and cover pan. Continue cooking 45 minutes or until tender, turning breasts halfway through cooking. Drain on absorbent paper, and serve with hot mushroom gravy. Serves 4 generously.

Note: If double breasts are used, stuff the cavity; then secure top and bottom edges with toothpicks.

These can be "oven-fried" by baking at 375°F. for 45 minutes. Brush with salad oil occasionally.

Mushroom Sauce

1/4 pound mushrooms, chopped
1 tablespoon butter or margarine
Salt and pepper to taste
1 tablespoon flour
1 cup water or chicken stock

Sauté mushrooms in butter or margarine. Season with salt and pepper, and blend in flour. Gradually add water, and cook until thickened. Pour this sauce into pan in which STUFFED CHICKEN BREASTS were cooked, or serve as is. Makes approximately 1 1/4 cups sauce.

Note: Make quick mushroom sauce by heating 1 can mushroom soup, undiluted, in pan in which chicken was cooked.

French Paddle Ice Cream

4 egg yolks
1/2 cup superfine sugar
1 1/2 cups light cream
1/4 teaspoon salt
1 teaspoon vanilla extract
1/2 pint heavy cream

Beat egg yolks until thick and lemon-colored; add sugar gradually, and continue beating. Stir in light cream and salt, and cook in top of double boiler over hot water until custard thickens. Add vanilla; chill. Whip heavy cream until stiff, and fold in cold custard. Pour into center cylinder of 2-quart hand freezer. Cylinder should be only 3/4 full, to allow for expansion. Cover. Pack rock salt and crushed ice around outside, and put top in place. Crank handle until it becomes difficult to turn. Open freezer and remove paddles. Cover again, repack outer sections with ice and salt. Leave to ripen about 1/2 hour or until serving time. Makes 1 1/2–2 quarts.

Note: This recipe makes a rich, very smooth ice cream. It can also be made in a refrigerator freezing compartment.

Monday

BREAKFAST	LUNCHEON	DINNER
Tomato juice with lemon wedges	Frankfurters	Grapefruit halves
	CORN ON THE COB	POT ROAST OF BEEF WITH VEGETABLES
Cornflakes	Bran muffins	Sponge cake with
Toast	Celery sticks	FRESH LIME CREAM
Conserves	Watermelon	Coffee Tea Milk
Coffee Milk	Tea Milk	

Corn on the Cob

Water
6 cobs fresh corn
Butter or margarine
Salt and pepper to taste

Half fill large saucepan with water, and bring to boil. Add corn. Cover, and bring again to boil. From this point, count cooking time, allowing 5–10 minutes, depending on size of cobs and age of corn. Uncover, and lift out corn with tongs. Serve at once with butter or margarine, salt and pepper. Serves 6.

Note: Flavor of older corn can be improved by adding 1–2 teaspoons sugar to the cooking water.

Pot Roast of Beef with Vegetables

```
        4 pounds beef chuck or round
        3 tablespoons flour
    1 1/2 teaspoons salt
      1/4 teaspoon pepper
      1/8 teaspoon marjoram
      1/8 teaspoon summer savory
      2–3 tablespoons shortening
1/2–3/4 cup water
      6–8 small onions
      6–8 small potatoes, peeled
       12 carrots, scraped
      2–3 celery stalks
Cooking liquid from roast
        2 tablespoons flour
      1/4 cup cold water
```

Wipe beef with clean damp cloth or paper towel. Mix 3 tablespoons flour and seasonings together, and rub into beef. Heat shortening in heavy pan and add beef. Cook slowly until meat is brown on all sides, about 20 minutes. Add 1/2–3/4 cup water, cover and cook slowly 3 hours or until tender. Add vegetables for last hour of cooking. Remove from heat. Arrange meat and vegetables on heated platter, and keep warm. Skim excess fat from top of liquid with spoon. Mix 2 tablespoons flour with 1/4 cup cold water until smooth. Or measure water into small screw-top jar, add flour and cover tightly; shake well. Pour flour mixture into hot liquid, and return pan to heat. Cook, stirring, until thickened. Taste, and add more seasonings if you wish. Pour into gravy boat to serve with meat and vegetables. Serves 6.

Fresh Lime Cream

```
    3 eggs plus 1 egg yolk
    1 cup sugar
1/2 cup butter or margarine, cut in pieces
Juice of 3 fresh limes, strained
```

In top of double boiler, beat eggs and egg yolk slightly; add sugar, butter or margarine and lime juice. Cook over simmering water, stirring frequently, 20–25 minutes until thick and smooth. Chill thoroughly. Use as filling for 2 cake layers or as topping on individual sponge rounds. Serves 6.

Tuesday

BREAKFAST	LUNCHEON	DINNER
Fresh cherries	Sliced tomatoes	SAUTEED LIVER
POACHED EGGS	with fresh	FRIED GREEN
Toast	basil	TOMATOES
Tea Milk	Peanut butter	SUCCOTASH WITH
	sandwiches	PIMENTO
	Green	Crisp raw relishes
	applesauce	Quick-set gelatin
	Iced coffee	Coffee Tea Milk
	Milk	

Poached Eggs

```
    Water
1/2 teaspoon salt
    6 eggs
    6 slices toast
```

Half fill skillet with cold water and bring to boil. Add salt. Break eggs 1 at a time into saucer, and slip each carefully into boiling water. When all are added, cover pan, and remove from heat. Let stand until eggs are set to soft or medium stage, about 3 minutes. Lift eggs out, 1 at a time, with slotted spoon, and set on toast slices. If solid spoon is used, rest edge on absorbent paper for a moment to drain before slipping eggs onto toast slices. If pan does not have cover, turn heat to low and baste eggs with surrounding hot water until yolks are filmed and white is set. Serves 6.

Sautéed Liver

```
1 1/2 pounds baby beef or calves' liver, sliced
  2–3 tablespoons flour
  1/2 teaspoon salt
  1/8 teaspoon pepper
    3 tablespoons shortening
```

Remove skin, veins and membrane from liver, and wipe with damp cloth. Mix flour and seasonings together. Dip liver into flour mixture, coating each piece. Heat shortening in frying pan, and add liver slices. Cook until golden brown or until each piece is tender, turning once. Be careful not to overcook. Drain liver on absorbent paper. It may be served with broiled bacon or fried onions. Serves 4–5.

Note: If skin is difficult to remove, gash edges of liver slices in several places to prevent curling during frying.

Fried Green Tomatoes

```
4 firm green tomatoes
Salt and pepper to taste
```

Wash tomatoes; remove stem ends but do not peel. Cut into 1/2-inch slices, allowing several slices per serving. After removing sautéed liver from pan, put in tomato slices, adding a little more fat if necessary. Turn once. When tender but still shapely, remove, season well with salt and pepper and serve. Serves 4–5.

Succotash with Pimento

1 tablespoon butter or margarine
1 (12-ounce) can whole-kernel corn, drained
1 (1-pound, 1-ounce) can green lima beans, drained
Light cream or milk
Salt and pepper
Pimento, finely chopped

Melt butter or margarine; add vegetables, a little light cream or milk, and salt and pepper. Heat thoroughly. When serving, sprinkle with finely chopped pimento. Serves 5.

Wednesday

BREAKFAST	LUNCHEON	DINNER
Green applesauce	Jellied consommé	DELUXE HAM LOAF with SPICED CHERRY SAUCE
French toast and jelly	HERO SANDWICH	
	Cookies	CORN ON THE COB
Coffee Milk	Milkshakes	Relishes
		COCONUT MACAROONS
		Coffee Tea Milk

Hero Sandwich

1 long loaf Italian bread
Butter or margarine
Mayonnaise
1/2 head curly leaf lettuce
2 large tomatoes, sliced
2 cucumbers, sliced
Mustard
1/2 pound cheese slices
1 Spanish onion, sliced thin
3 dill pickles, sliced thin
1/2 pound corned beef, sliced

Slice bread in 3 lengthwise slices. Butter bottom slice, and spread with mayonnaise. Cover with lettuce, over which arrange alternate slices of tomatoes and cucumbers. Top with buttered center slice, and spread with mustard. Cover with cheese slices, onion, and dill pickle. Add corned beef, and top with buttered crust. To serve, cut through from top to bottom in 1-inch slices, and secure with toothpicks. Serves 5–6.

Note: For small hero sandwich, use 1/2 loaf French bread; use large, crusty rolls for individual hero sandwiches, sometimes called "torpedoes."

Deluxe Ham Loaf

1 pound ground ham
1 pound ground fresh pork
2 eggs, slightly beaten
1 1/2 cups milk
2 teaspoons prepared mustard
1 1/4 teaspoons salt
2 cups seasoned dry bread crumbs
1/2 teaspoon summer savory
1/4 teaspoon sage
1/4 teaspoon dry mustard
Black pepper to taste

Mix ingredients in order given, and pack into deep 9"x5"x3" greased loaf pan. Cover with foil, and bake at 350°F. 1 hour. Uncover, and bake 20 minutes longer. Remove any fat around loaf with baster, and invert on heated platter. Slice. Serves 6–8.

Note: If soft bread crumbs are used, reduce milk to 1 cup.

Spiced Cherry Sauce

1 (15-ounce) can sweetened pitted red cherries
1/3 cup water
Juice of 1/2 orange
2 tablespoons white vinegar
1 stick cinnamon, broken
6 whole cloves
2 tablespoons cornstarch
3 tablespoons cold water

Drain cherries, reserving juice. Mix next 5 ingredients with cherry juice, and simmer gently 20 minutes. Remove spices. Combine cornstarch with water, and add to juice. Cook, stirring, until thickened and clear. Add drained cherries. Serve hot over ham loaf. Serves 6–8.

Coconut Macaroons

1/8 teaspoon salt
2 egg whites
1 cup sugar
1/2 teaspoon vanilla extract
2 cups cornflakes
1 cup shredded coconut

Add salt to egg whites, and beat until stiff but not dry. Fold in remaining ingredients. Drop batter, 1 teaspoonful at a time, well apart on greased cookie sheet. Bake at 350°F. 15–20 minutes. Remove at once from pan, using spatula. If macaroons stick to pan, return to oven to reheat, or place sheet on wet cloth. Serves 6–8.

Thursday

BREAKFAST	LUNCHEON	DINNER
Fresh fruit	COMBINATION	SAVORY BEEF–
Cold cereal	SALAD PLATE	VEGETABLE
Toasted waffles	Hard-cooked	CASSEROLE
with syrup	eggs	Broccoli
Coffee Milk	Sherbet	Crisp relishes
	Cookies	CHILLED BAKED PEARS
	Tea Milk	Coffee Tea Milk

Combination Salad Plate

1/2 cup grated carrot
1/2 cup diced celery
1 1/2 cups shredded cabbage
Drained cooked leftover vegetables (peas, beans, asparagus)
1 tablespoon chopped chives or onion
Mayonnaise
4 lettuce cups
Cucumber slices
Radishes or cherry tomatoes
Hard-cooked egg slices
Cheese strips

Combine first 6 ingredients, and arrange in mounds in centers of lettuce cups. Add a few overlapping cucumber slices to each plate, and garnish with radishes or tomatoes, egg slices and strips of cheese. Serves 4.

Savory Beef–Vegetable Casserole

2 onions, sliced
2 tablespoons bacon drippings
3 or 4 fresh, peeled tomatoes, diced
2 stalks celery, sliced
3 or 4 new carrots, scraped and quartered
1 teaspoon monosodium glutamate (optional)
1/2 teaspoon salt
2 tablespoons catsup
1 bay leaf
1 1/2–2 cups diced leftover pot roast
1/2 cup or more leftover gravy
2–3 cups seasoned diced potatoes
1/2 cup grated Cheddar cheese

Sauté onions in drippings 2–3 minutes. Add tomatoes, celery and carrots. Turn heat low, and cover. Let mixture simmer about 5 minutes. Stir in next 6 ingredients, and heat thoroughly. If necessary, pour in a little water; amount will depend on thickness of gravy, but avoid making mixture too liquid. Taste for seasoning, and re-move bay leaf. Scrape mixture into greased 1 1/2-quart casserole or deep oblong baking dish. Spread potatoes over top, and press down lightly. Sprinkle with cheese, and bake at 350°F. 35–40 minutes or until potatoes brown and meat mixture is bubbly. Serves 6.

Note: Condensed canned mushroom, chicken, vegetable or meat soup may be used instead of gravy.

Chilled Baked Pears

6 large firm pears
12 whole cloves
1/4 cup maple syrup
1/4 cup orange juice

Halve pears lengthwise, peel, core and discard stem and blossom ends. Pierce each half with 2 cloves. Place, rounded sides down, in baking dish. Mix maple syrup and orange juice, and pour over fruit. Cover and bake in oven at 350°F. about 20 minutes or until fruit is tender when tested with fork. Chill before serving. Serves 6.

VARIATION:

Baked pears with Honey: Substitute 1/4 cup each honey and water for maple syrup and orange juice.

Friday

BREAKFAST	LUNCHEON	DINNER
Fresh grapes	BARBECUED	French onion soup
Toasted English	HOT DOGS	PAISLEY RICE
muffins	FRESH FRUIT	Carrot curls
Bacon Jelly	COMPOTE	GINGER–PINEAPPLE
Coffee Milk	Tea Milk	SHERBET
		Coffee Milk Tea

Barbecued Hot Dogs

1/2 cup catsup or chili sauce
1 cup tomato juice
2 tablespoons vinegar
2 tablespoons brown sugar
1 tablespoon prepared mustard
1/2 cup chopped onion
1/4 cup chopped celery
1/4 cup chopped green pepper
1 pound skinless frankfurters
10 hot finger rolls

Combine the first 8 ingredients in skillet or saucepan, and bring to a boil. Cover, and simmer 2–3 minutes. Add frankfurters, and cover again. Cook until frankfurters are thoroughly heated and glazed, about 3 minutes. Lift each frank-furter into heated roll, using tongs or fork, and spoon sauce over each. Serve at once. Makes 10 hot dogs.

Fresh Fruit Compote

       3 firm ripe pears
       1 large peach
       6 fresh apricots
       1 cup sugar
     1/2 cup water
       1 tablespoon or more lemon juice

Thinly peel pears and peach, halve and core. Wash apricots, but do not peel. Halve, and remove pits. Combine sugar. and water in saucepan, and heat to boiling. Put in pears, rounded sides down, and let simmer gently 2–3 minutes. Add peach and apricot halves, and simmer 4–5 minutes more. With slotted spoon, remove cooked fruit to serving bowl. Simmer syrup another few minutes until it thickens slightly. Remove from heat, and add lemon juice, judging amount according to sweetness of fruit syrup. Pour over fruit. Chill thoroughly before serving. Serves 8–10.

Note: Various other fruits may be used in this simple compote. Washed cherries (do not pit) should be simmered 6–7 minutes. With plums, prick skins before adding, and cook until just tender. Strawberries, raspberries, and blackberries should not be cooked on stove. After washing, place in bowl with cooked fruits to mellow in hot syrup.

Paisley Rice

   2 1/2 cups water
       1 chicken-bouillon cube
     1/2 clove garlic, stuck on toothpick
     1/2 bay leaf
       1 cup long-grain rice
       1 tablespoon grated onion
     1/4 cup FRENCH DRESSING
     1–2 teaspoons soy sauce
     1/4 pound fresh mushrooms, sliced
             (1 1/4 cups)
     1/4 cup diced pimento
     1/4 cup slivered black olives
     1/2 cup toasted almonds
       1 cup diced chicken
       1 cup cooked shrimp
   Salt and pepper to taste
   Curly chicory

Bring first 4 ingredients to boil, and stir in rice. Cover, and turn heat low. Allow to simmer until rice is tender, about 20 minutes (the water will be completely absorbed). Stir rice, and make sure bottom of pan is quite dry. Lift out garlic and bay leaf, and stir in onion and dressing. Add next 7 ingredients, and heat thoroughly, but do not cook any further. Season with salt and black pepper. Turn out on serving platter, and garnish with curly chicory. Pass mayonnaise or a bowl of sour cream with chopped chives. Serves 6.

Ginger–Pineapple Sherbet

       1 envelope unflavored gelatin
     1/4 cup cold water
       1 cup boiling water
       1 cup sugar
     1/4 cup lemon juice
       3 cups ginger ale
       1 cup pineapple juice

Soften gelatin in cold water. Combine boiling water and sugar in small saucepan, and heat until sugar is melted. Add gelatin, and stir until dissolved. Cool and add lemon juice, ginger ale and pineapple juice. Pour into freezer trays. Place in refrigerator until mixture is thoroughly chilled. Set in freezer, and freeze until mushy, stirring occasionally. Turn into bowl, and beat until light. Return to freezer trays, and freeze until firm. Serves 6–8.

Saturday

BREAKFAST	LUNCHEON	DINNER
Bing cherries	FLUFFY	Tomato juice
Oatmeal	OMELETS	JELLIED SALMON LOAF
Toast	Crisp relishes	Potato chips
Marmalade	Fresh fruit	PAPRIKA CUCUMBER
Coffee Milk	Cookies	ORANGE TAPIOCA WITH
	Tea Milk	STRAWBERRIES
		Coffee Tea Milk

Fluffy Omelet

       3 tablespoons butter or margarine
     1/2 teaspoon salt
       4 eggs, separated
       2 tablespoons milk
   Pepper to taste

Heat butter or margarine in large skillet over low heat. Add salt to egg whites, and beat to form stiffly pointed peaks. Beat egg yolks (with same beater) until thick. Add milk and pepper to egg yolks, stirring until blended. Fold egg whites gently into yolks. Pour egg mixture into skillet. Cook 5 minutes on top of range, moving skillet gently several times. Put under broiler until omelet is light brown. When set, crease through center, fold 1/2 over with spatula, then roll omelet from skillet to heated platter. Serves 2.

Note: Allow 2 eggs for each serving, and never try to make an omelet using more than 4 eggs.

Jellied Salmon Loaf

       1 envelope unflavored gelatin
     1/2 cup cold water
     3/4 cup Italian-style salad dressing
       2 tablespoons lemon juice
       1 cup chopped celery
     1/2 cup stuffed olives, sliced
       1 tablespoon chopped parsley

1 teaspoon salt
Dash pepper
1 (1-pound) or 2 (1/2-pound) cans salmon
Chicory or lettuce
Olive slices

Soften gelatin in water 5 minutes; then heat in double boiler over hot water until dissolved. Stir in salad dressing, lemon juice, celery, stuffed olives, sliced, parsley, and seasonings. Discard skin from salmon. Mash salmon bones, salmon and juice together, and add to vegetable mixture. Chill, stirring occasionally, until mixture thickens; then scrape into oiled 7"x 4" loaf pan. Unmold on chicory or lettuce, and garnish with olive slices. Serves 4.

Paprika Cucumber

1 cucumber
Wine vinegar
Paprika

Peel cucumber, and slice very thin. Cover with wine vinegar and generous sprinkling of paprika. Chill a few minutes before serving. Serves 2.

Orange Tapioca with Strawberries

1 1/3 cups skim milk
1/3 cup quick-cooking tapioca
1/2 cup sugar
1/4 teaspoon salt
1 1/2 teaspoons grated orange rind
1 teaspoon vanilla extract
2/3 cup chilled evaporated milk
2 tablespoons lemon juice
1–2 cups fresh hulled strawberries, sliced and lightly sweetened

Heat skim milk, and stir in tapioca. Cook 5 minutes, stirring. Remove from heat, and add sugar, salt, orange rind and vanilla. Chill mixture. Beat evaporated milk until fluffy. Add lemon juice, and beat until stiff. Fold tapioca mixture into whipped milk. Chill thoroughly. To serve, spoon strawberries into 6 fruit bowls, and spoon tapioca cream over top. Serves 6.

Pointers on Some Favorite Beverages. For good coffee, start with clean pot, and grind suitable to method used. Measure both coffee and water accurately: for medium strength, 2 tablespoons coffee to 6 ounces water. If your method involves filters, keep them in clean cold water when not in use; replace with new ones every 2 weeks. Avoid buying large quantities of ground coffee or leaf tea; flavor is fresher when supply is regularly renewed and kept closely covered. Don't boil reheated coffee—it will have a bitter taste. For good tea, start with fresh water, never water left in kettle.

Percolator Coffee

Measure cold water into percolator. Measure medium-grind coffee into basket; set basket in water. Cover, and place percolator over medium heat. When coffee begins to "perk," reduce heat, and percolate slowly 7–8 minutes. Remove basket and serve.

Drip Coffee

Hot water is allowed to seep through fine-grained coffee while pot stands in warm place but not over direct heat. Heat lower container first by scalding with boiling water. Set coffee holder in place, and measure coffee into it. Set top compartment in place, and slowly pour in freshly boiling water. Cover, and let stand until all liquid has dripped through.

Vacuum Coffee

Measure cold water into lower bowl of coffee maker. Place filter in upper bowl. Measure correct amount of fine-grind coffee into it; set upper bowl in place over lower bowl, and twist to make airtight seal. Turn heat to medium. When nearly all water has risen, turn off. Stir, to mix coffee and water. Cover, and let stand while brew filters through. Remove upper bowl.

Hot Tea

Allow 1 teaspoon leaf tea or 1 tea bag for each 6 ounces (3/4 cup) boiling water. When water in kettle gets hot, pour a little into teapot; allow pot to heat thoroughly; then empty it. Measure tea into pot and add required amount of fresh boiling water. Brew tea 3–5 minutes, letting pot stand in warm place. Remove tea bags.

Iced Tea

Because ice dilutes the brew, it is necessary to make tea extra strong. Use 4 teaspoons tea leaves for 2 measuring cups boiling water. Make tea in regular pot, and allow to stand in warm place 5 minutes. Pour into tall glasses filled with chipped ice. Serve with lemon wedges, orange slices or sprigs of mint and sugar.

Instant Coffee and Tea

Find brands that suit your taste, and follow directions on labels. Instant powders are particularly useful for making iced coffee and tea in a hurry.

Cocoa

For 6 servings, mix 5 tablespoons cocoa, 5 tablespoons sugar, and a dash of salt in saucepan. Add 1 cup cold water, and mix together; cook, stirring, over medium heat until thickened and bubbling. Stir in 3 1/2 cups milk, keep stirring and heat just to boiling point. Remove pan from heat, and pour into serving cups or mugs. A drop or 2 of vanilla extract may be added.

CALORIE-COUNTING TIPS

Before attempting to reduce your weight, consult your physician. He will advise you on the basis of your age, frame, activities and "ideal" body weight. He will also suggest how much you should limit your calorie intake and give you a diet plan to follow.

In order to lose 1 pound of fat, you must take in about 3500 calories fewer than you need to maintain your weight, which means that if you want to lose 2 pounds a week, you must reduce your caloric intake 1,000 calories a day below your maintenance needs.

Faster weight loss is not usually recommended, for it doesn't give you a chance to reeducate your eating habits so that you won't gain the lost pounds right back.

Do Not Skip Essentials

The basic foods that you are careful to include in the family menus each day should continue to be part of any reducing diet. There should be plenty of lean meat, fish, eggs, milk and milk products; fruits and vegetables in variety, including a little plain baked or boiled potato; whole wheat or enriched cereals, and bread and even a small amount of fat for certain food elements and flavor. Stunt diets, fad foods and pills have no place in sensible weight control.

Enjoy Your Family Meals, But

Omit some of the high-calorie items. Eat your roast beef without gravy, your salad without mayonnaise, your breakfast cereal without sugar. A rich sauce on cooked vegetables can play havoc with your calorie counting; reserve your own portion without sauce before sending the vegetable dish to the table. Have an egg soft-cooked or poached, not fried. Use skim milk, lemon juice for vegetables, commercial low-calorie salad dressings, water-packed tuna, artificially sweetened fruits and beverages.

Keep Servings Small

Avoid large portions generally. Get used to small servings, and eat slowly—and your appetite will be satisfied. Banish second helpings entirely,

and don't eat tidbits of this or that in the kitchen as you put leftovers away. This little routine, perfectly natural though it is, has added unwieldy pounds to generations of homemakers.

Between-meal Nibbles

These snacks can help you stay with a reducing plan, as long as you count the calories and include the extras in the total day's intake. You will be less ravenous for lunch if you have a cup of coffee or an apple in mid-morning. A celery stick or a glass of skim milk or tea with lemon may be just what you need at 4 p.m. But sweet soft drinks or doughnuts should be banned. Be discriminating about your "nibbles."

Avoid These Temptations

Cut out entirely those rich concoctions that are high in starch, fat and sugar content. Cakes and pastry, whipped-cream desserts, candies, jams and deep-fried foods should not be permitted on your dieting program. Artificial sweeteners used in beverages and gelatin desserts or fresh fruit will satisfy your sweet tooth, yet keep your calories within bounds. Avoid alcoholic or malt beverages; they can defeat a reducing plan.

How Is Your Daily Score?

It will help a great deal if you keep a daily score card showing how many calories you are eating each day. At the end of each week weigh yourself, and check your weight against your calorie consumption. Persevere until you have said good-bye to excess pounds. And then determine that you can and will continue to control the kinds and quantities of food you eat.

Menus and Recipes for Calorie Counters

Good basic eating habits will keep you fit while you slim. The measure of a successful reducing diet is whether or not you also learn precisely how much you can eat without gaining weight.

A good breakfast is particularly important for the weight watcher. Take your serving of unsweetened juice or fruit without sugar. Have a small helping of unsweetened cereal with milk. Or, instead of cereal, have a soft-cooked or poached egg. A thin slice of toast lightly buttered may be included, but skip jams and jellies, except the dietetic kind. Coffee or tea adds no calories; use milk instead of cream, artificial sweeteners instead of sugar.

Using this basic breakfast and menus like the following ones for a week's lunches and dinners, you can keep your caloric intake at 1,200–1,500 calories daily, depending on sizes of servings.

- Recipes are given for items printed IN THIS STYLE.
- Use low-calorie salad dressings.
- Use unsweetened or artificially sweetened fruits.
- Add a glass of skim milk at lunch or dinner.

Sunday

DINNER

Roast turkey, 2 ounces	190
Mashed yams, 4 ounces	114
Lettuce wedge, 1/4 head	13
Rye roll and 1 pat butter	115
Lemon ice, 1/2 cup	72
	504

SUPPER

Salami, 1 slice on hard roll	120
Sliced beets (1/3 cup), sliced egg (1/3 cup)	80
APPLE CLOUD, 1 serving	63
	263

Monday

LUNCH

Consommé, 1 cup	26
Hamburger (2 ounces) on roll	251
Coleslaw, 1/2 cup	24
Small banana	85
	386

DINNER

Broiled salmon (7 ounces) with lemon	250
Small baked potato with yogurt	100
GREEN BEANS IN BEER, 1/2 cup	27
Dietetic butterscotch pudding, 1/2 cup	60
	437

Tuesday

LUNCH

Vegetable juice, 1 cup	40
Open-faced grilled cheese sandwich (1 slice cheese)	187
(2 slices cheese)	160
Dill pickle, 1 large	11
Plums, 2 red	50
	288

DINNER

Pan-broiled liver and onions	597
Paprika cauliflower, 1 cup	22
Tossed green salad, 1 cup	15
APRICOT BAVARIAN, 1/2 cup	59
	693

Wednesday

LUNCH

Chicken broth, 1 cup	18
Cottage cheese, 1/2 cup	97
Canned fruit, 1/2 cup	31
Whole wheat roll	85
Small pat of butter	35
Dietetic cherry gelatin, 1/2 cup	59
	325

DINNER

Veal chop, 3 1/2 ounces	220
Peas with mushrooms, 2/3 cup	70
Cucumber salad	18
CINNAMON BAKED APPLE, 1 medium	58
Skim milk, 8 ounces	82
	448

Thursday

LUNCH

Vegetable beef soup, 1 cup	65
Egg salad (2 eggs)	160
Pumpernickel, 1 slice	62
Celery hearts, 2	17
Low calorie dressing, 1 tablespoon	24
Cantaloupe, 1/2	90
	418

DINNER

CURRIED CRAB	144
Rice, 2/3 cup	109
Chopped green pepper, chopped tomato chutney, pineapple chunks, 1 cup	40
Lime sherbet, 1/2 cup	120
	413

Friday

LUNCH

Clear tomato soup, 1 cup	80
Crackers, 2	34
Tuna salad, 1/2 cup	145
Lettuce	9
Grapes, 2/3 cup	67
	335

DINNER

PUFF-BROWNED CHICKEN, 6 ounces	190
Carrots, 2/3 cup	31
Lettuce, 2 leaves	9
Tomato, 1 small	22
Angel food cake, 2-inch slice	108
Skim milk, 8 ounces	88
	448

Saturday

LUNCH

Vegetable soup, 1 cup	64
Frankfurter	153
Roll	118
Mustard	7
Sauerkraut, 1/4 cup	8
Fresh pear, medium	63
	413

DINNER

POACHED HALIBUT WITH HORSERADISH SAUCE, 6 ounces	225
Boiled potato, medium	76
Broccoli, 2/3 cup	26
Strawberry–pineapple cup, 2/3 cup	45
Skim milk, 8 ounces	88
	460

Apple Cloud

    1 envelope unflavored gelatin
1 3/4 cups apple juice
    1/2 teaspoon non-caloric liquid sweetener
    1 egg white, stiffly beaten

Soften gelatin in 1/2 cup apple juice. Heat over boiling water until dissolved, and add remaining juice and sweetener. Chill until syrupy, and fold into egg white. Pile into sherbet glasses. Serves 4–6.

Green Beans in Beer

    1 (1-pound) can green beans
    1/4 cup beer
    2 tablespoons chopped onion
    1/4 teaspoon prepared horseradish
    1/2 teaspoon dry mustard
    1/4 teaspoon salt
    Dash pepper
    Lettuce

Drain green beans, put in bowl. Make mixture of beer, onions, horseradish, mustard, salt and pepper, and pour over beans to cover. Mix well. Cover, and marinate in refrigerator 30 minutes. Drain, and serve beans in lettuce cups. Serves 4.

Apricot Bavarian

    1 envelope unflavored gelatin
    2 tablespoons cold water
    3 (8-ounce) cans dietetic apricots
    2 teaspoons lemon juice
    2 teaspoons liquid sweetener
    1 cup nonfat dry milk solids
    1 cup cold water

In top of double boiler, soften gelatin in 2 tablespoons cold water. Puree apricots in blender, or force through sieve to make 2 cups. Add apricots, lemon juice, and liquid sweetener to gelatin, and cook 5 minutes, stirring as mixture thickens. Remove from heat, cool and chill until syrupy. Beat milk solids and 1 cup cold water together until stiff. Fold into gelatin mixture. Chill in 4-cup mold until firm. Serves 8.

Cinnamon Baked Apples

    4 medium apples
    1 teaspoon liquid sweetener
    1 teaspoon cinnamon

Set oven at 400°F. Core apples, and pare 1/2 inch down from tops. Sprinkle each apple with 1/4 teaspoon liquid sweetener and 1/4 teaspoon cinnamon. Wrap each apple in aluminum foil, and bake in shallow baking dish at 400°F. 25 minutes or until tender. Serves 4.

Curried Crab

    1/4 cup chopped onion
    1 tablespoon butter or margarine
    3 tablespoons flour
    3/4 teaspoon salt
    1/8 teaspoon pepper
    1 teaspoon curry powder
1 1/2 cups skim milk
    2 (6-ounce) cans crabmeat, drained and flaked

Sauté onion in butter or margarine until transparent. Remove pan from heat; add flour, salt, pepper and curry powder. Mix well. Add skim milk, blend well, stir and cook until mixture thickens. Add crabmeat; heat 5 minutes. Serves 4.

Puff-browned Chicken

    1 2-pound broiling chicken
    3/4 teaspoon salt
    1/8 teaspoon pepper
    1 tablespoon lemon juice
    Boiling water

Cut chicken into 8 pieces, and sprinkle with salt, pepper and lemon juice. Cover bottom of shallow pan with aluminum foil. Place chicken in pan, and broil quickly about 5 minutes or until brown. Remove from broiler, turn over and cover bottom of pan with 3/4 inch boiling water. Bake at 475°F. 20–25 minutes or until chicken is tender and skin golden brown and puffed. Serves 4.

Poached Halibut with Horseradish Sauce

    2 cups water
    4 onion slices
    1 tablespoon chopped parsley
    1 bay leaf
    1 teaspoon salt
    4 (1 3/4 pounds) halibut steaks
    1 tablespoon butter or margarine
    1 tablespoon flour
    2 teaspoons prepared drained horseradish

Put water, onion, parsley, bay leaf and salt in a large skillet. Simmer 10 minutes. Put in halibut steaks, and simmer 20–25 minutes or until fish is tender. Remove steaks from skillet; save 1 1/2 cups liquid. Keep fish hot. In a small saucepan melt butter or margarine. Add flour, and stir until smooth. Gradually add 1 1/2 cups liquid saved from poaching, stirring constantly. Still stirring, simmer 10 minutes. Remove from heat; add horseradish, and mix well. Serve sauce over halibut steaks. Serves 4.

PACKING AN APPETIZING LUNCHBOX

What's in a lunchbox? Good food, attractively packed, and perhaps a surprise.

The best sandwiches are those that have generous and substantial fillings between not-too-thick slices of bread that are spread right to the edges with butter or margarine. The spread adds nourishment and also helps to keep the filling from soaking into the bread and making it soggy.

Vary the bread from day to day—whole or cracked wheat, enriched white, dark or light rye, fruit bread, rolls, hot dog or hamburger buns.

Pack fillings with proteins—meat, fish, eggs, cheese, nut butters—and season to taste. Here are some suggestions:

Meat

Use several thin layers of cooked meat rather than 1 thick slice; they make a more generous filling and are easier to eat.

Add a little chili sauce, chopped parsley, grated onion or horseradish to butter for meat-filled sandwiches.

Put raw vegetables (carrots, celery, cucumber, onion or crisp spinach leaves) through food chopper with cooked meat.

Fish

Flake or mash drained canned salmon; include crushed bones for extra food value. Add sliced green pepper, olive, celery or parsley; sprinkle with lemon juice.

Use canned tuna with the same additions.

Leftover fish can be flaked and made into delicious mixtures; moisten with salad dressing or tomato juice.

Eggs

Chopped hard-cooked eggs, seasoned and moistened with cream or salad dressing, are always a favorite. Occasionally add a little grated onion, chopped chives or green onion, chopped crisp bacon, flaked sardine, sliced stuffed olives.

Cheese

There is a wide range of cheese products, and there are many ready-to-use cheese spreads. You can make your own spreads, using either cream cheese or grated Cheddar as bases. Season to taste, and blend to desired consistency with a little milk or cream. Store, covered, in refrigerator—ready for quick spreading with or without additional fillings.

Try cream cheese spread with ground ham, or chopped, dried fruit and nuts.

Use Cheddar spread with hard-cooked eggs or chopped, crisp bacon.

Some Sandwich Combinations

Cold

Salami, Swiss cheese and roasted pepper on Italian bread
Smoked salmon and sliced onion on pumpernickel
Chopped chicken livers, bacon and tomato on rye
Corned beef or pastrami and mustard on rye or pumpernickel
Herring salad on dark bread of any kind
Liverwurst and relish on whole wheat toast
Cold roast pork with horseradish on rye
Cream cheese on date-nut bread
Sliced chicken and Russian dressing on whole wheat bread
Tuna fish salad and sliced egg on roll
Muenster cheese and sliced tomato, sprinkled with oregano, on toasted roll
Sliced frankfurter and beans on rye
Cream cheese and walnuts on raisin bread
Deviled ham, relish and mayonnaise on white bread
Pork roll and mustard on rye bread

Hot

To make a hot sandwich possible in a lunch box, package filling in a wide-mouthed vacuum container. Wrap bread separately.

Meatballs in small amount of spaghetti sauce on toasted Italian bread
Scrambled eggs, sautéed pepper and onion on roll
Eggplant Parmesan on Italian bread
Scrambled egg and bacon on onion roll
Sautéed sweet sausage and peppers on Italian bread
Hamburger on toasted bun
Frankfurter wrapped in bacon on toasted roll
Brown-and-serve sausage patties and scrambled eggs on toasted roll
Chili on toasted bun
Barbecued beef (sliced leftover beef heated in barbecue sauce) on toasted bun

For variety, pack salad-type fillings like chopped meat, flaked fish or hard-cooked eggs in small jars with screw tops or in individual plastic containers. Accompany with buttered buns or sliced bread.

A small container will also carry salads of vegetables or fruits. Lettuce will wilt if it is combined in a salad or sandwich, but a crisp wedge wrapped separately keeps well in the lunchbox. Shredded cabbage with green pepper, pimento, diced apple, well-drained crushed pineapple and a small amount of dressing make a not-too-perishable salad. Grated raw carrot with raisins or chopped dates, moistened with dressing, makes another easily transportable salad.

A cooked chicken leg, cold cooked spareribs, a round of liverwurst on a toothpick, slices of cold meat rolled up and fastened with toothpicks, a deviled egg or a wedge of cheese will carry well when wrapped in aluminum foil or plastic wrap.

Fresh fruit can be included as well as containers of fruit salad, stewed or canned fruit or berries. Raw carrots, turnip strips, radishes, small whole tomatoes, Swiss cheese and celery, stuffed with cheese or plain, can also be included.

Pies, if they have double crusts and are not too juicy, can be carried in individual portions. Use pie-shaped plastic containers, or make triangular "plates" for pie. Cut thick cardboard slightly larger than pie wedge, and cover with aluminum foil. Place piece of pie on it; then cover all with aluminum foil or plastic wrap.

Tarts, turnovers, cakes with firm icing, doughnuts, cupcakes and cookies are always welcome.

The beverage, if it is milk, should be chilled and carried in a vacuum bottle, which is equally useful for hot liquids.

If you prepare lunches the night before, be sure to keep perishables in refrigerator until final packing. Never combine protein foods with salad dressing, but you can put dressing in small plastic container to be added at lunchtime.

Frozen Sandwiches. If you have a home freezer, you can prepare sandwiches weeks ahead. Many kinds freeze perfectly. Taken from the freezer in the morning, they are just right for eating at noon and will be colder and fresher than otherwise. Spread with butter or margarine. Mayonnaise tends to soak into bread as it thaws, so use it sparingly in filling mixtures. Do not freeze lettuce, tomato, cucumber or celery; and remember that cheese and cooked egg white get tough in the freezer.

2
~
Hearty Main Dishes

Dinner is usually the family's big meal of the day. It is a time to be together and a meal to enjoy unhurriedly. A good dinner menu needs planning.

When you start to plan a meal, think first of the members of your family—the foods they like and the amounts they need. Keep in mind which foods are in season and the best buys at that particular time of year. For your sake, as well as theirs, it's wise to plan for wide variety.

The main dish should be decided first and then the accompanying appetizer, vegetables, salad, bread and dessert.

A good starting point when you are choosing the main dish is the "Daily Food Guide," which advises 2 servings per day of meat, fish, poultry, eggs, cheese or dried beans, peas or nuts. You'll be sure then that your family is receiving an adequate supply of essential proteins.

But good, nutritious foods in themselves don't always provide the necessary appetite appeal. So remember that your menu must have color harmony. Visualize the servings together on a plate. You can then foresee that the rich, dark color of beets will lose much of its attraction next to the bright red of tomatoes. And you will realize the need for something brighter than boiled parsnips to offset pale mounds of mashed potatoes.

Flavors, too, should harmonize and complement one another. Avoid 2 strong-flavored foods, like onions and turnips, at the same meal, although each combines well with mild-flavored food.

Keep the meal interesting by avoiding repetition. Shrimp cocktail may be delectable, but it takes a little of the zest out of a main fish dish.

The textures of your foods are important too. Two mashed vegetables should not be served together. Instead, replace one with something that contributes shape and texture. When your main course is a creamed dish or other soft food, offer crisp, raw vegetables in a salad or on a relish tray. Another way to ensure variety is to vary temperatures throughout the meal. Hot soup can be a tempting introduction to a cold main dish, and a chilled dessert is often a delightful climax to a substantial hot meal.

Maintain appetite appeal by serving new and different main courses. And always plan your main dish with thought for the preparation time it requires. Avoid steak or chops, which require watchful last-minute cooking, when you are having a large group for dinner. Instead, choose a roast or a big casserole, which can be started well ahead and allowed to cook slowly. Then, before dinner, you'll be free to enjoy your guests. Casseroles or other specialties that can be prepared at your leisure and stored in the refrigerator or freezer are wise choices for busy days.

Be sure that the main dish fits the type of service you plan. For a casual buffet meal, fork foods, like croquettes, hash or creamed dishes are much easier to serve and eat than is a roast or thick steak.

Whatever you plan for your main course, there is one important rule to follow to ensure that the dish will be at its best: *Always serve hot foods piping hot and cold foods icy cold.* The plates for hot foods should be warm. If you have no warming oven, heat plates by placing them in your oven, turned low, 5 minutes just before serving. Plates for cold foods can be chilled in the refrigerator ahead of time.

POINTS TO KNOW ABOUT CARVING

Good carving depends chiefly on good tools, kept in good condition. A good knife, properly cared for, will last a lifetime, so it's worth investing in quality. The basic carving set consists of a knife with a 9-inch blade, a fork with long tines and a guard to protect the carver's hand and a steel for honing the knife edge.

As well as the standard "carving knife," there are others—the meat slicer, for example, which has a slender flexible blade and is useful for carving poultry and ham, in which there is a lot of bone. Choose your basic "wardrobe" of cutting tools; learn how to use them and how to care for them.

Learn this honing technique: Hold steel in left hand, with thumb *over* handle and steel pointing upward and away from the body. Hold knife in right hand, and place heel of knife blade (the end near the handle) against the far tip of the underside of the steel. Draw knife edge *down and diagonally across* steel, ending stroke with knife point at handle of steel. Repeat motion with *other* side of knife edge against *other* side of steel.

A few such quick strokes before each use of the knife (the way your butcher does it) will keep your knife sharp. Professional sharpening is also necessary occasionally.

Carving Tips: A large roast can be carved more easily when it has stood for a few minutes after cooking. Use a heated platter large enough to leave room for the carved slices, or have another heated platter ready. Heat all plates because meat cools quickly. Cut across the grain—long meat fibers are tough and stringy. Plan servings before you begin so that choicest portions can be divided equally among all. Don't cut second helpings before they are wanted; that way meat will stay hot and juicy. Lay slices with newly cut surfaces up, to save juices, which escape more freely when meat is first cut. Carving is usually easier when the carver is standing up.

Buying and Cooking Meat. Meat is one of the most expensive items in the family food budget. An average family of 4 will eat more than 700 pounds of meat in a year. It is thus to your advantage to know the various kinds and cuts of meat and how best to prepare them to get the most value. To stretch your meat budget, the trick is to balance your purchases of such tender, expensive cuts as porterhouse steaks with some of the cheaper cuts. The latter have the same food values, but may require more time and attention to prepare.

How Much To Buy

Your family's ages and tastes will to some extent affect the amount of meat required in your household. But, when you are estimating how much meat to buy, keep in mind also the amount of bone, fat and gristle in each particular cut. They may account for 10–15 percent of total weight. Shrinkage in cooking can double even this percentage of waste. Here is a guide to the approximate weights of meat to buy for 1 average serving.

Roasts, boneless	1/4–1/3 pound
Roasts, bone in	1/3–1/2 pound
Steaks	1/3–1/2 pound
Chops	1/3–1/2 pound
Stewing meat, boneless	1/4 pound
Stewing meat, bone in	1/2 pound
Ground meat	1/4 pound
Liver	1/4 pound
Kidneys	1/4 pound
Heart	1/4 pound

Safeguards in Selection

Meats with the Federal inspection stamp have been inspected for your protection (see Chapter 1). Your butcher will be glad to show you the purple "U.S. Insp'd & P's'd" stamp on the fat outer side of the various carcasses—beef, pork, veal and lamb (the dye in the stamp is quite harmless, by the way).

Hanging and aging of meat vary with each type. All beef should be properly aged for flavor and tenderness—1–2 weeks or perhaps longer before cutting. Top-quality lamb is sometimes aged a few days only. Pork and veal do not require aging but are merely chilled before cutting.

When buying frozen meats, be sure that they are thoroughly frozen. Check that the wrappings are not broken. Frozen meats that have "freezer burn"—patches that appear white and dry—have received poor storage handling; they will lack flavor and texture.

Success with Seasoning

All fresh meats need some salt to bring out their full flavor. As salt tends to draw out juices, it is best to add it after meat has been cooked, when roasting, broiling or pan-broiling. For braising or stewing, in which the rich flavored

sauce is a main feature, the seasoning can be added to the dredging flour before initial browning of the meat.

Other seasonings, from bottled sauces to herbs, add zest to meat dishes. Experiment, and become familiar with the spices best suited to the meat types and your own taste. Freshly ground pepper and monosodium glutamate (a prepared chemical salt) enhance the flavor of any meat.

Methods of Cooking Meat

Good meats deserve careful cooking. Be sure to use the best method for each particular cut. An expensive oven roast should not be braised in moist heat, whereas a pot roast cut, costing perhaps 1/3 less, should.

Do not pierce meat with fork during cooking, for piercing releases natural juices that are so desirable for the final result. Use tongs and lifter for turning.

You can save juices and pan fat for gravy and sauces. If much fat accumulates in pan, pour it off from time to time.

When braising or stewing, keep liquid at a slow simmer. Boiling toughens meat fibers.

To Roast

Roasting is a dry-heat method for cooking large, tender cuts of meat. For a succulent result, use low-to-moderate temperatures. Do not sear, as it causes dryness and shrinkage.

The size, shape, fat covering and initial temperature of the meat all influence the length of the cooking period. A meat thermometer is the only dependable way to test the doneness of your roast.

1. Wipe meat with damp cloth or paper towel.
2. Place meat, fat side up, on rack in open pan in slow oven (325°F.).
3. Do not add water, do not cover pan.
4. Insert meat thermometer in thickest part of meat; be sure tip is not touching bone or fat.
5. Roast meat until thermometer registers desired internal temperature; internal temperature will rise about 10°F. after roast is removed from oven, so be sure to allow for it in determining when to remove roast.

6. Let roast stand at least 10 minutes in warm place before carving, to make carving easier.
7. Use drippings in pan to make gravy.

Frozen roasts cook more evenly if they are first thawed. Leave meat in wrapping while thawing. Allow 2 hours per pound when thawing at room temperature. Allow 24–36 hours to thaw a 4-pound roast in refrigerator.

Cook immediately after thawing, following same procedure as for fresh meat. Once thawed, meat should not be refrozen.

Frozen meats may be cooked without thawing, but an additional 10–20 minutes per pound should be allowed. To ensure proper doneness, insert meat thermometer midway through estimated cooking period.

To Broil

Broiling is a dry-heat method of cooking small, tender cuts like steaks and chops. The kind of meat, thickness and desired degree of doneness all affect broiling time. Broiled meats will retain less fat than will fried meats, as it drips away during cooking. Manufacturer's directions for using broilers in gas and electric ranges vary. Follow the instructions supplied with your range for preheating broiler, positioning broiler door and so forth.

1. Snip fat around edge of meat with shears or knife to help prevent curling.
2. Place meat on rack of broiler pan at recommended distance from heat.
3. When meat is brown on 1 side, turn with tongs, and broil to desired doneness on other side.
4. Season, and serve.

To Pan-broil

Pan-broiling is a quick, top-of-the-stove method for cooking small, tender cuts of meat. Use heavy frying pan for even distribution of heat.

1. Heat pan, and grease it lightly with piece of fat cut from meat.
2. Snip fat edge of meat with shears or knife to prevent curling.
3. Brown meat on both sides, using tongs to turn; do not prick meat with fork while cooking.
4. Do not add extra fat.
5. Reduce heat, and complete cooking; do not cover pan except for meats like pork chops, which must always be thoroughly cooked.
6. Season, and serve.

To Braise

Braising is a moist-heat method for cooking less tender cuts of meat. They may be large pieces like pot roast or small cuts like shoulder chops. Use a heavy skillet or Dutch oven.

1. Coat meat in seasoned flour. Such boneless pieces as round or flank steak may be pounded to tenderize.
2. Brown meat well on all sides in hot fat.
3. Add small amount of liquid and any additional seasonings desired.
4. Cover kettle tightly to keep steam in during cooking; add more liquid, if needed while cooking.
5. Cook slowly until very tender over low heat on top of stove or in slow oven, 325°F. (if using oven, be sure that kettle and lid have heat-proof handles).
6. Uncover oven-cooked pot roasts for last 1/2 hour of cooking time for better color.

To Stew

Stewing is similar to braising, except that more liquid is generally used in order to provide ample, thick sauce with meat and vegetables. Less costly cuts of lamb, veal and beef are ideal for stewing.

1. Cut meat into small pieces, and dredge in flour according to recipe.
2. Brown in melted fat.
3. Cover with liquid—tomato juice, water, vegetable stock or wine.
4. Cover tightly and simmer until tender (if vegetables are to be cooked with meat, add to simmering stew at proper time, according to their cooking requirements).
5. Thicken stew with smooth paste made from equal parts flour and cold water; allow 2 tablespoons flour for each cup gravy.
6. Season to taste, and serve piping hot.

To Pressure-cook

Pressure-cooking is a fast, moist-heat method for cooking less tender cuts of meat. Follow the manufacturer's directions for each type of pressure saucepan. In general, the following steps apply.

1. Brown meat well on all sides, if directed.
2. Add small amount of liquid; vegetables may also be added at this time.
3. Cover, and cook for specified time.
4. Allow pressure saucepan to cool slowly to prevent juices from being drawn out of meat; but if vegetables were added with liquid, cool quickly.
5. If desired, vegetables may be added at end of cooking time.

Barbecue and Rotisserie

In general, any meat that can be roasted or broiled can be successfully barbecued. Food may be barbecued on a flat grill over hot coals, on a turning spit close to heat source or under regular broiler of your range. Because of the closeness and intensity of the heat, it is important to coat and baste meat with rich, well-seasoned sauce to prevent drying out.

If less tender cuts of meat are to be used, an enclosed, moist-heat method is recommended. Wrap meat, with sauce, fat or such other accompaniments as vegetables in aluminum foil. Allow to cook until tender.

If you are using an oven rotisserie, study and follow directions for your specific equipment. It is particularly important to know maximum weights that your rotisserie motor can handle. Food must be centered correctly on skewer to ensure even rotation. Always set a pan under food to catch drippings. When you are basting with sauce or liquid seasoning, a more desirable color can be obtained if you wait until the last hour of cooking. When very lean meat is to be cooked on rotisserie, tie a layer of suet or other firm fat around piece before cooking.

Beef. Whether it is served as a choice roast for special company dinner or in an everyday stew for hearty family appetites, beef can fill the bill.

Beef in its great variety of cuts is one of the favorite meats. The rich, red color and firm, fine-grained texture of good beef are a constant challenge to the homemaker who enjoys mastering many different methods of preparation. And beef's tempting aroma and hearty flavor can be highlighted by many variations. Among the herbs, basil, thyme, marjoram and rosemary make good beef seasonings.

Beef is available in specific grades, each a different quality.

Know the Cuts

The tenderest cuts in a beef carcass come from the center back, chiefly the loin and ribs. From this area—the least exercised and therefore having the most delicate fiber—the highest-priced roasts and steaks are cut.

As you move towards the more exercised portions of the animal—the rump, shoulders, and shanks—the meat becomes leaner, coarser and less tender. And the cuts become cheaper. The nutritional value of these less tender cuts is as high as that of the tender cuts, but cooking methods must be varied accordingly.

Tender cuts of beef are at their best cooked with dry heat, as in roasting, broiling or panbroiling. Less tender cuts develop full flavor and succulence when cooked with added moisture for sufficient time at low temperatures, as in braising, stewing, or pot-roasting. Other methods of tenderizing these cheaper cuts are grinding, waffling (minute steaks) and applying commercial tenderizer.

Keep in mind that one cut of beef may be purchased in several different ways: as a roast, boned and rolled or with the bone in or sliced as steak, for example. "Bone-in" roasts usually cost less per pound, but a rolled boneless piece has no bone, and the carving will be easier.

Your choice depends on your own personal taste, as cost works out about the same.

Tender Beef Steaks

The tender cuts are spoiled by overcooking, and some cooks like to marinate medium-tender cuts before broiling them.

These choice cuts from the least exercised portion of the carcass should be carefully cooked with a dry heat to retain their delicate texture and flavor. No liquid is added during the cooking period, and they are best cooked uncovered.

There is no such hard-and-fast rule for cooking the moderately tender cuts of beef. They are the cuts (e.g. the rump) that fall between the 2 extremes of tender and least tender. The cooking methods therefore vary with the *grade* of beef from which the cuts come.

The higher-grade, moderately tender cuts may be cooked in the same way as tender cuts, by a dry-heat method. The same cuts from a lower-grade carcass should be cooked with moist heat, at low temperatures and for longer periods.

Quick Tips on Steak

Steaks for broiling to medium or rare must be at least 1 inch thick. Broiling heat will quickly penetrate a thinner steak and cook it well done without browning its surface. Leave the door open if you are broiling it in an electric range and closed if you are using a gas range. Allow about 5 minutes per side or 10 minutes' total broiling time for a rare 1-inch steak, 12 minutes' total time for medium. For well-done steak, place pan farther from heat, and allow 14–16 minutes' total broiling time.

Fry thinner steaks if you like them medium or rare—a hot, lightly greased cast-iron frying pan or an electric pan at "steak" setting will give good results.

Roast Fillet of Beef (Beef Tenderloin)

    1/3–1/2 pound beef fillet per serving
    Fat bacon or salt pork
    Mushroom caps, sautéed

Fillet is the most delicately tender beef and the most costly, in this case bought in a solid piece for oven roasting. Have the butcher lard the meat, or lay strips of fat bacon or salt pork over the top. Place on rack in shallow pan, uncovered, and roast in 325°F. oven. Allow about 22 minutes per pound for rare, 25 for medium rare, 28–30 for well done. Serve on hot platter, garnished with sautéed mushroom caps.

London Broil

    1/2 cup orange marmalade
    1/4 cup soy sauce
    1/4 cup lemon juice
      1 (2–2 1/2 pound) flank steak, about 3/4 to 1 inch thick

In large shallow dish, combine orange marmalade, soy sauce and lemon juice. Marinate steak at least 30 minutes, turning frequently. May be marinated, covered, up to 12 hours, with less frequent turning in refrigerator. Remove steak from marinade and drain. Broil 3 to 4 inches from heat in preheated broiler, allowing 4 minutes per side for medium. Brush with remaining marinade while broiling if steak was marinated only briefly. Heat remaining marinade and serve with steak. Serves 4–6.

Roast Beef Steak

      1 teaspoon peppercorns, finely crushed
      1 (4-pound) sirloin tip steak, about 3 inches thick
      4 cloves garlic
      2 teaspoons salt
      2 tablespoons butter or margarine
      2 tablespoons olive oil (can substitute 1/4 cup butter
        or margarine)

Crush 1 teaspoon peppercorns and run into both sides of steak. Chop 4 cloves garlic fine. In small bowl, using back of small spoon, crush garlic with salt to make a paste. Spread on both sides of meat. Melt butter or margarine in large skillet; add olive oil (or butter or margarine). Cook meat on medium heat 5 minutes per side. Put in 350° oven; roast 30 minutes. Serves 6–8.

Boeuf en Gelée

      2 (10 1/2-ounce) cans beef consommé
    1/2 cup sherry
      2 packages unflavored gelatin
      1 clove garlic
      1 bay leaf
      1 cup thinly sliced carrots
      1 cup thinly sliced onion rings
    1/2 teaspoon salt
      1 pound cooked, sliced roast beef
      2 tablespoons chopped parsley

To consommé and sherry add enough water to measure 1 quart. In large bowl, blend unflavored gelatin with 1 cup of this beef liquid. Let soften 5 minutes. Add garlic and bay leaf. Dissolve by blending in remaining 3 cups boiling beef liquid. Set aside to cool. Discard garlic clove and bay leaf. Meanwhile, in small saucepan, cook carrots and onion rings with salt and 1 cup water. Simmer until just tender. Drain and cool. To assemble: Rinse a 1 1/2-quart mold with cold water. Drain, but do not dry. Pour in 1/2 cup beef liquid. Refrigerate 15 minutes or until set (or put in freezer 10 minutes). Arrange roast beef slices, rolled-up jelly roll fashion, cooked carrots and chopped parsley in layers over set aspic until you have used 1 pound beef slices, 1 cup cooked carrots, 1 cup cooked onions and 2 tablespoons chopped parsley. Fill to top of mold with remaining beef liquid. Refrigerate 2 hours or 30 minutes in freezer until firmly set. Serve unmolded (following above directions) or serve *en terrine* as in France—still in mold cut into chunks, slices or wedges. Serves 6.

Spicy Rump Roast

```
4-pound rump roast
1 teaspoon salt
1 cup vinegar
1 teaspoon cinnamon
1/2 teaspoon pepper
1/2 teaspoon cloves
1/2 teaspoon allspice
1/4 teaspoon nutmeg
```

Wipe roast with clean, damp cloth. Blend all other ingredients into paste-like marinade. Place roast in dish that holds it snugly, and pour marinade over. Cover dish, and set in cool place 5–6 hours or longer, basting and turning meat occasionally. Preheat oven to 325°F. Place roast, fat side up, on rack in open pan. For medium rare, allow about 35 minutes per pound; for well done, 40 minutes. Serves 8.

Steak au Poivre

```
2 tablespoons peppercorns
2–2 1/2 pounds porterhouse or sirloin steak, 1 inch thick
2 tablespoons butter or margarine
2 tablespoons chopped green onions
1/2 cup beef stock or canned beef bouillon
1/3 cup cognac
Watercress
```

Place peppercorns in big mixing bowl, and crush roughly with mallet, or use rolling pin to crush them on aluminum foil. Wipe steak with damp paper towels. Press peppercorns well into each side of steak. Cover with waxed paper, and let stand at least 1/2 hour to let flavor of pepper penetrate meat. Pan-broil steak in lightly greased skillet, and cook to desired doneness. Remove to hot platter, and keep steaks warm. Pour off excess fat in skillet. Add 1 tablespoon butter or margarine and onions. Cook slowly 1 minute, but do not brown. Pour in stock, and cook briskly

until liquid is reduced by 1/2. Add cognac, and boil rapidly to evaporate alcohol. Remove from heat, and gradually add remaining butter or margarine, cut in small pieces. Pour over steak on hot platter, and garnish with watercress. Serves 5–7.

Steak Sauce

```
1/4 cup finely chopped onion
2 tablespoons steak drippings or butter or margarine
1/2 cup boiling water
1 teaspoon Worcestershire sauce
1/2 teaspoon dry mustard
1/2 teaspoon salt
1/8 teaspoon pepper
1 egg, beaten
```

Sauté onion in drippings 5 minutes. Add remaining ingredients, except egg. Cover pan, and simmer 10 minutes. Just before serving steak, strain sauce, and pour slowly over beaten egg, beating constantly. Cook sauce, stirring 1 minute over low heat.

Note: Prepare this sauce while steak is being broiled.

Broiled Porterhouse Steak

```
1 porterhouse steak, 1–1 1/2 inches thick
1 clove garlic, cut
2 tablespoons salad oil
2 tablespoons red wine
1/2 teaspoon Worcestershire sauce
2 thickly sliced boiled potatoes
1 large tomato, halved
1 tablespoon butter or margarine, melted
Salt and pepper to taste
```

Trim excess fat from steak, and gash remaining fat edge to prevent curling. Skewer tail close to steak. Rub each side with garlic. Combine salad oil, wine and Worcestershire sauce, and brush over steak. Leave at room temperature 20 minutes. Preheat broiler 10 minutes, and set broiling rack in place. Center steak on rack. Broil 5–6 minutes about 2 inches from heat. Turn steak with tongs to avoid piercing meat and losing juice. Add potatoes and tomato halves, brush with melted butter or margarine, season and continue broiling 3 minutes. Turn potatoes, brush again with butter, and broil 2–3 minutes longer. Remove steak to heated platter, and season. Garnish with vegetables. Serves 2.

Note: Carve steak in 1/2-inch strips, starting at bone and slicing toward you. Serve a slice of tenderloin and less tender portion to each person.

Fried Steaks (Argentine Style)

```
4 egg yolks
1 1/2 cups sifted flour
1/2 cup milk
```

1 clove garlic, chopped
1 1/2 teaspoons salt
1/2 teaspoon pepper
1/2 teaspoon marjoram
4 egg whites, stiffly beaten
6 fillets of beef or 6 individual boneless sirloin steaks
1 cup cooking oil

Beat egg yolks in bowl, and add flour, beating until smooth. Add milk, garlic and seasonings, and beat again until smooth. Fold in egg whites carefully. Dip steaks in batter, coating well. Heat oil in skillet, and fry steaks 2 minutes on each side. Serves 6.

Less-tender Beef Cuts

There's a special way of cooking less tender cuts to bring out all their flavor and make them fork-tender. A tenderizing method is necessary. There are several. First, the cooking method must be different. Because these less tender cuts come from more used muscular parts of the animal, the fibers are tougher and there is more connective tissue. It takes long cooking in moisture to soften this meat and make it tender. This long, slow cooking, incidentally, adds considerably to the flavor of the meat, especially when subtle herbs and spices are used.

Another way to prepare such meats is with one of the commercial tenderizers, which are made from protein-digesting enzymes and are most effective on steaks and other thin cuts. They should not be used on roasts. Several kinds are available, plain and seasoned. Some methods of moist-heat cooking use marinades that add piquant flavor to meats and sauces to be served with them.

A good basic marinade is standard FRENCH DRESSING, which is of course simply oil and vinegar. You can add soy sauce, a little dry mustard, 1 tablespoon sherry. Let meat stand in this marinade, turning it often, for anything from 1/2 hour to several days, as with SAUERBRATEN. Meat should be refrigerated, covered, for the marinating period.

Every nation has its characteristic ways of using these less tender cuts. What we call "stew" is closely related to what the Hungarians call "goulash" and the French call "ragoût." The differences are in the seasonings; the method remains the same. You will enjoy trying new recipes that provide variety and save you money.

Braised Stuffed Flank Steak

2 cups SAVORY BREAD STUFFING
1 flank steak
2 tablespoons fat
2 cups hot water
1/2 teaspoon peppercorns

1 1/2 teaspoons cider vinegar
Pinch garlic salt
1 beef bouillon cube
2 tablespoons flour
2 tablespoons cold water

Pack dressing over unscored side of steak. Roll up as for long jelly roll; secure with skewers or string. Melt fat in heavy skillet or electric frying pan, and brown steak roll thoroughly over high heat. Reduce heat to simmer, adding 1 cup hot water and peppercorns and sprinkling meat with vinegar and garlic salt. Cover tightly, and simmer until tender—1 1/2–2 hours. Place steak on warm platter, and remove skewers or string. To liquid in pan add an additional cup of hot water and bouillon cube; boil until the latter dissolves. Remove peppercorns. Make smooth paste of flour and 2 tablespoons cold water, and use to thicken liquid. Cook 5 minutes. Serve gravy in separate dish. Serves 4–5.

Note: Have butcher score flank steak on 1 side to improve tenderizing during cooking. Various seasonings may be used, according to your taste. Leftover stewed tomatoes can replace some of the liquid. Bottled meat sauces, a spoonful of chili powder or a pinch or two of powdered herbs make an interesting variation.

Oven-barbecued Round Steak

1 1/2 pounds round steak, 1 inch thick
2 tablespoons salad oil
1/2 cup tomato catsup
1 clove garlic
1/4 cup vinegar
2 tablespoons Worcestershire sauce
1 tablespoon sugar
1 teaspoon paprika
1 teaspoon salt
1 teaspoon dry mustard
1/8 teaspoon pepper

Cut beef into strips or squares. Heat oil in skillet, and brown meat on all sides. Remove to casserole. Pour off excess fat from pan, and make sauce by simmering all remaining ingredients a few minutes. Pour over meat pieces, cover and bake in 325°F. oven about 1 hour or until meat is completely tender to the fork, basting occasionally. Remove garlic before serving. Serves 4.

Pressure-braised Short Ribs or Oxtails

1 tablespoon flour
2 teaspoons salt
1/8 teaspoon pepper
3 pounds short ribs or oxtails, cut in 2-inch pieces
3 tablespoons fat
1 cup tomato juice
1/2 cup chopped onion

Combine flour, salt and pepper, and dredge meat in flour mixture. Heat fat in uncovered pressure saucepan, and brown meat pieces thoroughly over moderate heat. Add tomato juice and onion. Follow manufacturer's directions for using your pressure-cooker. At 15-pound pressure, short ribs should be nicely done in 25 minutes, oxtails in 30 minutes. Allow pressure cooker to cool slowly before removing lid. Serves 5–6.

Tomato Swiss Steak

    1 1/2–2 pounds round steak, 3/4 inch thick
         2 tablespoons flour
         1 teaspoon salt
      1/8 teaspoon pepper
    Suet, drippings or cooking oil
         1 small onion, sliced
    1 1/2–2 cups tomato juice
         1 tablespoon chopped celery
         1 tablespoon chopped green pepper
         1 teaspoon Worcestershire sauce

Snip fat edge of steak to prevent curling. Mix flour, salt and pepper, and, using edge of plate, pound mixture into both sides of meat. Heat small amount of fat in heavy frying pan. Brown steak thoroughly on both sides over high heat. Add onion slices, and cook until brown and softened. Reduce heat, and add remaining ingredients. Cover tightly, and cook slowly about 1 1/2 hours, turning meat once and adding a little more tomato juice or hot water if necessary. Serves 5–6.

Note: Swiss steak may be baked at 325°F. after top-of-the-stove browning.

Northern Stew

    1/4 cup flour
    1/2 teaspoon salt
    Pepper to taste
         2 pounds shank beef, cut in 2-inch pieces
         2 tablespoons melted fat
    Boiling water
    1/2 teaspoon marjoram
    1/2 teaspoon thyme
    1/4 teaspoon celery salt
         6 or 7 small onions, peeled
         6 medium potatoes, peeled
         4 scraped carrots, quartered
         2 tablespoons flour
         2 tablespoons cold water

Mix 1/4 cup flour, salt and pepper, and coat beef pieces thoroughly. Heat fat in good-sized heavy skillet, and brown meat over high heat, browning on all sides. Reduce heat, add boiling water just to cover and add marjoram, thyme

and celery salt. Cover tightly and simmer over low heat about 2 1/2 hours, keeping water level adjusted. Add vegetables, and continue to cook until tender—30–40 minutes. Blend 2 tablespoons flour with cold water, thicken gravy and cook 5 minutes longer. Serves 6–8.

Note: Stew may be cooked in oven at 300°F. after top-of-the-stove browning, in which case vegetables should be allowed at least 1 hour's cooking.

Beef Brisket with Lima Beans

         1 (12-ounce) package dry lima beans
         4 cups water or vegetable juice
         1 pound lean beef brisket
    1–2 tablespoons hot drippings
         2 onions, sliced
    1–2 tablespoons molasses
         1 bay leaf, broken
         1 teaspoon salt
         2 or 3 sliced carrots
    Salt and pepper to taste

Soak beans overnight in water. Brown brisket slowly in drippings until well cooked. Pour off and save fat. Add onions, molasses, bay leaf, salt and water drained from beans. Cover, and simmer 15 minutes. Add beans, and cook until meat and beans are almost tender, about 1 hour. Add carrots, and cook 15 minutes longer. Season with salt and pepper to taste. More water may be added during cooking if necessary. Serves 5–6.

Glazed Corned Beef

         4 pounds rolled corned beef brisket
    Cold water
         2 bay leaves
         6 whole allspice berries
         1 onion, peeled and sliced
      1/3 cup chili sauce
      1/3 cup brown sugar
         3 tablespoons lemon juice
    1 1/2 teaspoons dry mustard
    Whole cloves

Wash meat; place in saucepan, and cover with cold water. Add bay leaves, allspice and onion. Cover and bring slowly to simmering point. After about 1 hour, skim, and continue to cook at low temperature until meat is tender—about 2 hours longer. Remove bay leaves. Meanwhile make glaze by mixing other ingredients, except cloves. Preheat oven to 350°F. Lift meat from its liquid, drain thoroughly and place in shallow roasting pan. Stick whole cloves here and there over surface. Pour glazing mixture over meat, and bake about 1/2 hour, basting with sauce from time to time. Serves 6–8.

Deluxe Hamburgers

2 pounds ground round steak
1/4 cup melted butter or margarine
1/4 cup milk or tomato juice
2 tablespoons catsup
2 tablespoons cracker crumbs
1 tablespoon chopped onion
1 1/2 teaspoons salt
1 teaspoon Worcestershire sauce
Pinch oregano or chervil

Mix all ingredients together thoroughly, and with wet hands shape into 10 or 12 large, flat, round patties. In lightly greased skillet, pan-broil quickly until medium-well done, 1 1/2–2 minutes per side. Centers should still be quite pink; over-cooking makes hamburgers dry and shriveled. Serve on toasted hamburger rolls with Spanish onion and tomato slices lightly sprinkled with salt. Serves 6.

Note: Omit melted butter in mixture if less expensive hamburger or ground beef (containing more fat) is used in place of ground steak.

Hamburgers in Sauce

2 pounds ground round steak
2 tablespoons butter or margarine
2 medium onions, chopped (1 cup)
1/4 lb. mushrooms, chopped (3/4 cup)
1/2 teaspoon salt
1/4 teaspoon thyme
1/4 teaspoon coarse black pepper
Pinch rosemary
1/2 cup sherry
1/2 cup water

With wet hands shape meat into patties, and broil or fry until thoroughly brown on each side. Hamburgers should be slightly pinkish inside for tenderness. While they are cooking, melt butter or margarine in small pan, and add onions, mushrooms and seasonings. Cook gently til golden brown; add sherry and water, bring to boiling point and simmer 2–3 minutes longer. Serve sauce over hamburger patties. Serves 6.

Beef–Rice Balls in Sour Cream Sauce

1 pound hamburger
1/2 cup milk
1/2 cup quick-cooking rice
2 tablespoons chopped onion
1 teaspoon salt
1/2 teaspoon mixed Italian herbs or 1/8 teaspoon nutmeg and 1/8 teaspoon allspice
1/8 teaspoon pepper
1/3 cup flour or dry bread crumbs
1/4 cup bacon drippings
1 1/2 cups rich beef stock or 1 (10 1/2-ounce) can condensed bouillon diluted with 1/4 cup canned mushroom juice

1/4 cup red wine
2 tablespoons tomato paste
1 (3 1/4-ounce) can mushrooms, drained
1/4–1/2 cup sour cream
Salt and pepper to taste
Plain buttered or margarined noodles

Mix the first 7 ingredients together, and form into 40 small balls. Roll in 1/3 cup flour or bread crumbs, and fry slowly in drippings until lightly browned. Lift out meat, and stir in 2 tablespoons flour. Add stock slowly, and cook until smoothly thickened. Mix in wine and tomato paste, and add mushrooms and meatballs. Season. Cover, and simmer slowly about 20 minutes. Stir in sour cream and salt and pepper to taste, and reheat without boiling. Serve over plain buttered noodles; accompany with tossed salad. Serves 4.

Swedish Meatballs

1 1/2 pounds ground round steak or 1 pound beef and 1/2 pound ground veal
1 large onion, diced (1 cup)
1/4 cup cracker crumbs or fine bread crumbs
2 eggs, beaten
1/2 teaspoon ground allspice or mace
Salt and pepper to taste
2 tablespoons butter or margarine
1/2 cup red wine
1/2 cup water
3 tablespoons sour cream or 1 teaspoon flour and 1 tablespoon water

Mix together meat, onions, crumbs, eggs and seasonings. Shape into small balls, about the size of a walnut. Cook gently in butter or margarine in frying pan, turning as they brown until uni-formly colored. Pour in wine and water, and simmer 20 minutes. A little more water may be added if the sauce boils away. Just before serv-ing, stir in sour cream. Serve with hot buttered or margarined noodles, baked potatoes or fluffy rice. Serves 4–5.

Quick Tips—Hamburger

Hamburger lends itself to easy and economical cooking in many different ways: Patties may be pan-broiled in a little fat over medium heat—(for thick patties, allow 4–8 minutes on each side; for thin patties, 2–6 minutes on each side, or cook until done). Or they may be broiled, grilled or barbecued—about 4–6 minutes on each side, about 3 inches from heat (brush with fat or barbecue sauce if desired).

Or hamburger may be browned in skillet in very little fat, then braised with small amount of water, consommé or tomato juice and season-ings to taste (use covered skillet or casserole, and cook slowly 20–30 minutes).

Sweet-sour Meatballs

1 pound ground round steak
1/2 pound pork-sausage meat
3/4 cup fine dry bread crumbs
3/4 cup milk
1/4 cup finely chopped onion
1 egg, slightly beaten
3/4 teaspoon salt
Pinch pepper
2 tablespoons salad oil
2 tablespoons chopped green pepper
1 clove garlic, peeled
1/2 cup pineapple juice
1/2 cup wine vinegar
1/4 cup sugar
3 tablespoons brown sugar
1 teaspoon soy sauce
3/4 teaspoon cornstarch
1 teaspoon cold water

Combine meat, crumbs, milk, onion, egg, salt and pepper. Shape into firm, small balls, using rounded teaspoonful of mixture for each. Heat oil in frying pan, and brown a few balls at a time, turning frequently for even coloring. Transfer to shallow casserole. To remaining fat in frying pan (add more if necessary to make 2 tablespoons) add green pepper and garlic. Cook, stirring, 5 minutes; discard garlic. Add pineapple juice, vinegar, sugar, and soy sauce. Blend cornstarch and cold water. When juice mixture reaches boiling point, stir in cornstarch, cook and stir until smooth. Pour sauce over meatballs. Set covered casserole in 325°F. oven, and cook about 30 minutes. Serve with fluffy rice. Serves 6–8.

Stuffed Green Peppers

6 green peppers
Boiling salted water
2 small onions, chopped (1/2 cup)
1 clove garlic
1 tablespoon olive oil, butter or margarine
1 pound ground round steak
1 (11-ounce) can condensed tomato soup
1 teaspoon salt
1/4 teaspoon pepper
Pinch rosemary
Pinch cayenne
1 tablespoon chopped parsley or 1/4 teaspoon dried
    parsley

Cut off stem ends of peppers, and scoop out seeds and membrane. Parboil peppers 5 minutes in boiling salted water to cover. Reserve liquid. Fry onions and garlic in olive oil until golden brown. Add meat, and fry, stirring constantly, until thoroughly browned. Add 1/2 can of soup with seasonings to mixture, and blend well; pile mixture loosely into pepper cups. Set in shallow baking dish. Dilute remaining soup with a little less than 1 soup can of water in which peppers were parboiled, and pour around stuffed peppers in dish. Bake at 375°F. 30–40 minutes. Sprinkle tops of peppers with chopped parsley. Serves 6.

Ground Beef Casserole

1 pound ground beef
1 large onion, diced (1 cup)
2 tablespoons shortening, melted
2 or 3 potatoes, sliced
1 cup chopped celery
1/2 cup chopped green pepper
1 (1-pound, 1-ounce) can tomatoes
Salt and pepper to taste
Pinch cayenne
1/4 teaspoon garlic salt

Sauté ground beef and onion in shortening until onion is soft and all trace of pinkness disappears from meat. Cover bottom of 2-quart casserole with meat and onions; add layer of potatoes, celery and green pepper. Repeat layers, add seasonings and pour canned tomatoes over. Cook, covered, 45–60 minutes or until potatoes are done. Serves 4.

Gold-topped Beef Loaf

1/2 cup dry bread crumbs
1 cup evaporated milk
1 pound hamburger
1/2 pound sausage meat
2 grated raw potatoes
1 small onion, diced
1 tablespoon dark steak sauce
1 teaspoon salt
1 teaspoon meat extract
1 teaspoon monosodium glutamate
1/2 teaspoon dry mustard
1 recipe CORN BREAD TOPPING

Soak crumbs in milk, and blend in remaining ingredients, except topping, thoroughly. Spread 1/2 topping mixture in bottom of greased loaf pan. Evenly cover with meat, and top with remaining corn bread. Bake at 350°F. 1 hour. Cool slightly, and invert on breadboard; then turn right side up onto heated platter. Serves 8.

Corn Bread Topping

1 cup all-purpose flour
3/4 cup cornmeal
2 1/2 teaspoons baking powder
1 teaspoon sugar
1/2 teaspoon salt
1 cup milk
2 eggs, beaten
1/4 cup salad oil

Combine flour, cornmeal, baking powder, sugar and salt. Blend together milk, eggs and salad oil. Stir into dry ingredients to make smooth batter.

Stuffed Cabbage Rolls

    1 small cabbage
    Boiling water
    3/4 pound ground beef
    1 cup diced onion
    3/4 cup raw (not quick-cooking) white rice
    2 tablespoons melted butter or margarine
    1 teaspoon salt
    1/4 teaspoon pepper
    1/4 pound (1 cup) grated process Cheddar cheese
    1 (1-pound 13-ounce) can or 3 1/2 cups tomatoes

Gently remove 8 cabbage leaves, retaining their shape and size. Simmer, covered, in 1 inch of boiling water, 5 minutes. Drain, and lay out ready for filling. Pan-broil ground beef only until all traces of pinkness disappear. Remove from pan, and combine thoroughly with next 5 ingredients. Fill leaves with mixture; roll up one by one, folding ends toward center. Secure with toothpicks, and place in greased skillet. Sprinkle cheese over rolls, and pour tomatoes around edge. Cover, and simmer 45 minutes or until tender. Remove toothpicks. Serves 8.

Scotch Beef Loaf

        2 pounds hamburger
      2/3 cup rolled oats
        1 cup milk
        2 eggs, well beaten
        3 tablespoons finely chopped onion
        3 tablespoons finely chopped celery
        3 tablespoons Worcestershire sauce
    1 1/2 teaspoons salt
      1/2 teaspoon summer savory
      1/8 teaspoon pepper

Blend meat and oats together thoroughly. Mix milk and eggs, and add to meat. Add remaining ingredients, mixing thoroughly. Turn into lightly greased 9"x 5"x 3" loaf pan large enough to leave about 1/2-inch space at top. Bake about 1 3/4 hours at 350°F. Let loaf stand in pan a few minutes before turning out on serving platter. Serves 6–8.

Note: For an interesting change in flavor, try beef broth or tomato juice in place of milk. Or spread top of loaf with chili sauce or catsup before putting in oven.

Chili in Potato Shell

    1 egg, slightly beaten
    4 cups seasoned mashed potatoes, fresh or instant
    1/4 cup crushed cornflakes
    2 onions, chopped (1 1/2 cups)
    1 or 2 cloves garlic, chopped (optional)
    2 tablespoons fat
    1 pound hamburger
    1 cup canned tomatoes or 1/2 cup tomato juice
    1 tablespoon flour
    1 tablespoon chili powder
    1 (15-ounce) can red kidney beans
    Dash salt or sugar or Worcestershire sauce or herbs or
        cayenne

Stir about 1/2 the egg into potatoes, and mold mixture into nest shape in greased deep pie dish (for free-standing nest, use greased removable bottom of round cake tin). Brush surface with remaining egg, and sprinkle with flakes. Bake 15–20 minutes at 375°F. Meanwhile sauté onions and garlic in fat until tender. Add hamburger and fry, stirring, until meat is brown all through. Stir in tomatoes, flour, and chili powder. Boil 5 minutes. Add beans, stir and continue cooking 5 minutes longer. Taste, and flavor. Pour chili into hot potato shell, and keep hot until serving. Cut in wedges. Serves 6.

Spaghetti with Romano Sauce

        1 pound hamburger
      1/2 pound spicy smoked Italian sausage, sliced
        1 large onion, chopped
        2 tablespoons chopped parsley
        1 or 2 cloves garlic, crushed
        1 (4-ounce) can tomato paste
        3 cups water
        2 or 3 fresh tomatoes, peeled and sliced or 1 cup canned
            tomatoes
        1 or 2 crushed chili peppers
        1 teaspoon chopped mint or 1/4 teaspoon dried mint
      1/2 bay leaf
      1/4 teaspoon oregano
      1/4 teaspoon salt
        1 pound spaghetti, cooked and drained
    Parmesan cheese

Sauté hamburger and sausage together until thoroughly cooked. Pour off fat, and add onion, parsley and garlic. Sauté 5 minutes; add remaining ingredients except spaghetti and cheese. Cook slowly until thickened; taste for seasoning. Remove bay leaf before serving. Serve over hot cooked spaghetti, and pass bowl of Parmesan cheese. Serves 6.

Mild-flavored Veal. *Because of its subtle, delicate flavor, veal needs gentle, slow cooking, with plenty of help from seasonings, sauces and stuffings.*

Veal is the delicately flavored meat of beef cattle 4–14 weeks old. Beef from animals 14 weeks to 1 year old is called "calf," but for practical purposes the term "veal" covers this meat also. As it comes from young animals, veal has little exterior fat and no marbling. Although the muscle fibers are tender, veal does contain considerable connective tissue and thus is as its best cooked slowly to well done. The best cooking methods for veal are roasting, frying, braising and stewing. Because meat contains little fat (some cuts have no fat covering at all), every veal dish is improved by the addition of butter, margarine, and cooking oil. And because its natural flavor is bland, veal becomes more interesting when combined with condiments, tomatoes or other vegetable or soup mixtures. Sage, tarragon, summer savory, rosemary, thyme and basil add a lively tang to a veal dish.

What To Look for

Veal is sold by the same grades as is beef. First, be sure that you are getting government-inspected meat by checking for the Federal inspector's stamp on the carcass or by obtaining your butcher's assurance on this point. Then look for the packer's brand name or Federal grade stamp.

There is considerably less fat in veal than in other meats; what there is may be white, creamy white or tinged with pink.

Veal is most plentiful in the spring and early summer months, but there is generally a supply on the market the year round.

To Cook Veal Roasts and Chops

Many veal cuts can be temptingly prepared by roasting, braising or stewing. All veal should be well cooked, so that meat is pale gray throughout, with no trace of pink. Extra fat should be added at start of cooking; seasonings should be added at halfway point.

To Braise: Brown chops, steaks or cutlets in 2–4 tablespoons fat over moderate heat; allow several minutes on each side. Add seasonings and 1/2 cup liquid. Cover and cook slowly until tender —for 1-inch thickness, 30 minutes on each side; for 1/2-inch thickness, about 20 minutes on each side.

To Bake (Breaded): Dip chops, steaks or cutlets in seasoned flour, then in slightly beaten egg mixture (2 tablespoons water to 1 egg). Roll in fine bread crumbs. Brown in 2–4 tablespoons fat over moderate heat, allowing 3–4 minutes on each side. Use extra fat after turning. Place, uncovered, in oven preheated to 325°F. Bake 1-inch thickness about 40 minutes, turning meat once during cooking.

TIMETABLE FOR ROASTING VEAL*

TYPE OF ROAST	WEIGHT IN POUNDS	MINUTES PER POUND
Leg, bone in	3–8	30–40**
Rump	4–6	40–50
Loin or rib	4–6	35–40
Rolled, boned shoulder	3–5	40–45

*Oven temperature is 325°F.; meat thermometer reading is 180°F.
**The shorter times apply to roasts of heavier weights specified; for smaller cuts, allow longer times listed.

Times given are for roasts taken directly from the refrigerator (40°F.). For unthawed roasts extend cooking period by 1/2 the total time required for same size and cut of fresh veal.

Roast Veal with Pennsylvania Stuffing

    4–6 pound boned shoulder or boned leg of veal
    2 or 3 skinless fresh sausages
Boiling water
    1 recipe BREAD DRESSING
1/2 cup chopped celery
1/2 cup peeled chopped apple
Cream
    4 slices fat bacon or salt pork
Salt to taste
Pepper to taste
Thyme to taste (optional)

Wipe meat, both outside and in the cavity, with clean damp cloth or paper towels. Put sausages in saucepan with boiling water to cover; simmer 10 minutes. Lift out, break up sausage meat, and add to dressing, along with celery and apple. Bind dressing with a little cream. Stuff meat cavity, and skewer or sew opening to hold dressing firmly. If veal is very lean, lay bacon strips over top. Preheat oven to 325°F. Roast, uncovered, on rack in shallow pan, allowing 45–50 minutes per pound if meat is chilled at start of cooking time, slightly less if at room temperature (meat thermometer should indicate an internal temperature of 180°F. for well-cooked roast). After first hour or so of roasting, sprinkle veal with salt, pepper and a little thyme. For even browning, remove bacon strips during last hour of roasting time. Serves 7–10.

Marinated Veal Roast

    4-pound sirloin roast of veal
1/2 cup chopped onion
1/3 cup salad oil
1/4 cup lemon juice
    2 tablespoons thick meat sauce
    2 teaspoons salt
    2 teaspoons monosodium glutamate (optional)
    1 clove garlic, halved
1/2 teaspoon marjoram
1/8 teaspoon basil
    1 cup water

Wipe meat with clean damp cloth. Make marinade of remaining ingredients, except water (for easy removal of garlic later, spike each piece with toothpick). Put meat in container, pour marinade over, cover and let stand in refrigerator or other cool place 7–8 hours. Turn occasionally. Heat oven to 325°F.; place meat on rack in roasting pan equipped with cover. Blend water with marinade, and pour over roast. Cover tightly, and cook about 2 1/2 hours, basting occasionally. Remove cover, and continue cooking another 1/2 hour. Serves 8. (See note on p. 54.)

Note: The marinade plus meat juices make a delicious gravy, thickened with a smooth paste of equal parts flour and cold water and allowed to simmer at least 5 minutes.

Curried Veal

```
1 1/2  pounds veal cutlet
Flour
  1/4  cup butter or margarine
  3/4  cup chopped onion
  3/4  cup chopped tart apple
  2–3  teaspoons curry powder
  1/2  teaspoon salt
  1/2  teaspoon grated lemon rind
Speck cayenne
    1  (10 1/2-ounce) can bouillon
  1/2  cup water
    1  tablespoon lemon juice
    2  cups cooked rice
    1  banana
  1/4  cup shredded coconut, fresh or dried
```

Cut meat into 1-inch pieces, and flour lightly. Melt butter or margarine in heavy skillet, and gently fry meat, turning till all sides are golden. Push meat to one side, and add onion and apple. Continue cooking over low heat a few minutes, stirring and turning. Add curry powder, salt, lemon rind and cayenne. Add bouillon, water and lemon juice, continuing to stir until mixture reaches simmering point. Cover, and simmer about 45 minutes or until meat is tender. Serve over hot fluffy rice, scattering banana slices and shredded coconut on top of curry. Serves 5–6.

Note: The same amount of lamb or beef may be used instead of veal. Simmer 1 1/2 hours.

Veal Wellington

```
    1  cup coarsely grated or chopped raw carrots
  1/2  cup finely chopped celery
    2  tablespoons butter or margarine
    1  (6-oz.) can drained, sliced mushrooms
    1  egg
Heavy cream
    2  teaspoons salt
  1/2  teaspoon thyme
  1/2  teaspoon pepper
    2  pounds chopped veal
```

Crust:

```
1 (8-oz.) package refrigerated, ready-to-bake crescent rolls
1 egg
```

Turn on oven to 400°F. Sauté carrots and celery in butter or margarine until tender (about 15 minutes). With a slotted spoon remove them from skillet and place in large bowl. Add mushrooms and one egg beaten with enough heavy cream to make 1/2 cup liquid. Stir in salt, thyme

and pepper. Using spatula and a light touch, fold in veal. Turn out onto wooden board and shape with fingers into a loaf about 12 inches long, 4 inches wide and 3 inches high.

For crust, use ready-to-bake crescent rolls. They come eight to the package. Open out seven, and wrap around and under the loaf. Brush whole loaf with an egg wash made by beating 1 egg with 1 tablespoon cold water. From the eighth roll, cut small shapes, brush them with egg wash, and use for decoration. (Decorations optional.) Bake loaf for 15 minutes at 400°F. Cover with aluminum foil. Bake 30 minutes longer at 350°F. Lift onto serving platter. Garnish with watercress. Serves 6.

Jellied Veal

```
    2  pounds veal shank or neck
    1  veal knuckle
    2  quarts cold water
    1  large onion, sliced
    1  slice lemon
  2–3  celery stalks with leaves
    1  small bunch parsley
    2  teaspoons salt
    4  peppercorns
    1  bay leaf
    2  tablespoons gelatin dissolved in 1/2 cup cold water
  1/4  cup chopped gherkins
  1/4  cup chopped pimento
  1/4  cup chopped green pepper
Hard-cooked eggs, sliced (optional)
```

Put meat, with all skin and bone, in big saucepan. Cover with water, and add onion, lemon, celery, parsley and seasonings. Heat slowly to simmering point. Simmer until meat is tender and liquid reduced to about 1/3, 2–3 hours. Remove from heat, and cool. Remove bay leaf, strain off hot stock and cool quickly, uncovered. When completely cold, cover, and refrigerate several hours or overnight. Meanwhile remove all skin and bones from meat; chop meat fine or put through grinder. Skim fat off top of stock. If stock jelly is firm enough to cut, it is ready for the second step. If it remains soft after 6–7 hours, boil stock 5 minutes, reduce heat quickly, stir in 1 tablespoon gelatin for every 3 cups stock and chill stock until it begins to thicken. Combine jelly with cold cooked meat. Taste, and add extra seasoning if required. Add gherkins, pimento and green pepper. Pour into loaf mold or individual molds. For an extra decorative touch, pour first a thin layer of jelly, arrange hard-cooked egg slices symmetrically, let set a few minutes and carefully turn in remaining jellied meat. Leave undisturbed until completely firm; turn out on platter for serving. Serves 8–10.

Spanish Veal Casserole

1 1/2 pounds thin veal cutlets
2 tablespoons flour
1/4 cup butter or margarine
1 onion, thinly sliced
1 (10 1/2-ounce) can condensed tomato soup
1 cup canned mixed vegetable juice
1/2 cup sliced stuffed olives
1 teaspoon salt
1/4 teaspoon pepper
1/4 teaspoon ground cloves
1 (10-ounce) package frozen lima beans, thawed
Parmesan cheese, grated

Preheat oven to 375°F. (moderately hot). Coat veal lightly with flour. Brown richly in heated butter or margarine. Place in broad, shallow baking dish. Fry onion until tender, but not browned, in same pan. Stir in soup, juice, sliced stuffed olives, salt, pepper and cloves. Mix in lima beans. Pour over veal; cover baking dish with foil. Bake in preheated oven until veal is tender—about 1 hour. Remove foil and sprinkle meat with grated cheese. Place under broiler a few minutes until cheese is melted and bubbly. Serves 6.

Veal Viennese

1/4 cup bacon drippings or fat
2 pounds lean stewing veal
2 bouillon cubes
1 cup boiling water
1/4 cup finely chopped onion
1 teaspoon salt
1/8 teaspoon pepper
1 cup sour cream
4 thin slices lemon, unpeeled
2 tablespoons flour
2 tablespoons cold water
Parsley, finely chopped

Melt fat in heavy saucepan, and brown meat thoroughly. Dissolve bouillon cube in boiling water, and pour over meat. Add onion, salt and pepper. Stir in sour cream and lemon slices; cover, and simmer until meat is tender, about 1 hour, stirring occasionally and adding more boiling water if necessary. To thicken gravy, make smooth paste of flour and cold water; stir in and cook 5 minutes longer. Garnish with finely chopped parsley. Serves 8.

Breaded Veal Chops

1/3 cup flour
1 teaspoon salt
1/2 teaspoon dry mustard
1/4 teaspoon pepper
Pinch garlic salt
6 thin loin veal chops
3 tablespoons milk
1 1/2 teaspoons salad oil
1 egg, slightly beaten
Fine dry bread crumbs
2–3 tablespoons fat
2 tablespoons hot water

Mix together flour, salt, dry mustard, pepper and garlic salt. Coat chops lightly with this mixture. Combine milk and oil with beaten egg and dip each chop in this mixture; then roll in bread crumbs, coating completely. If there is time, chill chops in refrigerator for 1/2 hour to set coating. Melt fat in heavy skillet over moderate heat. Fry chops slowly turning to brown well on both sides—about 15 minutes. Add hot water, cover pan and cook slowly another 15 minutes or until perfectly tender. Serves 6.

Note: Veal steaks or cutlets may be cooked in same way.

Savory Veal Loaf

2 pounds lean ground veal
1 cup rolled oats
1/2 cup finely chopped onion
2 tablespoons chopped parsley
2 teaspoons salt
1/2 teaspoon pepper
6 slices bacon
2 eggs, slightly beaten
1 cup tomato juice
1 tablespoon bottled thick meat sauce
2 teaspoons prepared mustard
Parsley sprigs
Lemon wedges or slices

Put veal and next 5 ingredients in mixing bowl. Fry bacon until crisp; drain, crumble and add to mixture. Mix lightly together. Combine eggs, tomato juice, meat sauce and mustard; add to meat mixture, and combine thoroughly. Turn into lightly greased 9" x 5" x 3" loaf pan, and bake at 350°F. about 1 1/2 hours. Stand pan on wire rack in warm place 10 minutes; turn meat loaf out on warm serving platter and garnish with parsley and lemon. Serves 8.

Veal Birds with Prunes

1 1/2-pound veal steak, 1/2 inch thick
4 or 5 pitted prunes, uncooked
1 small cube salt pork
1 cup soft bread crumbs
1/4 teaspoon salt
Dash pepper
1 egg yolk
1 tablespoon lemon juice
Meat stock
Salt and pepper to taste
1/2 cup flour
1/4 cup butter or margarine
1 cup light cream

Remove bone from steak, trim off skin and fat, reserving trimmings, and wipe meat with damp cloth. Pound meat with mallet until very thin (or have butcher do it at time of purchase). Cut meat into 12 individual serving pieces. Prepare stuffing by putting through grinder prunes, veal trimmings and salt pork or chop very fine. Mix with crumbs, 1/4 teaspoon salt and dash pepper. Moisten all with egg yolk, lemon juice and a little meat stock (or hot water). Spread stuffing over each portion of veal to within about 1/4 inch of edge, roll and fasten with twine or toothpicks. Sprinkle with salt and pepper to taste, roll in flour and sauté in butter or margarine, turning so that all sides brown. Reduce heat, add cream and simmer, covered, until meat is completely tender—about 30 minutes, depending on the thickness. Lift out meat, and carefully remove twine or toothpicks. Pour sauce around birds arranged on a platter. Serves 6.

Note: Meat rolls, after initial browning, may be baked at 325°F. 45–50 minutes or until tender.

VARIATIONS:

- Instead of prunes use 1/4 cup drained pineapple or same amount seedless raisins.
- A regular bread stuffing or bread-and-apple mixture makes an excellent center for veal birds.

Mexican Veal with Macaroni Shells

        2 onions, chopped (1 cup)
        2 tablespoons bacon drippings
        1 or 2 stalks celery, sliced
        1 (1-pound, 4-ounces) can tomatoes, drained
    Diced leftover veal, pork or lamb
    1/2 cup or more gravy
        1 can (15 ounces) kidney beans
    1–3 teaspoons chili powder
    5–6 cups hot cooked macaroni shells
    Grated Cheddar cheese

Sauté onions in bacon drippings until tender. Add celery, tomatoes, meat and gravy. Cover, and simmer 20 minutes. Uncover, and add kidney beans and chili powder to taste. Season with Worcestershire sauce, garlic and bay leaf to suit your taste. Serve on macaroni shells and sprinkle with cheese. Serves 6–8.

Note: One bouillon cube or 1 teaspoon beef extract dissolved in 1/2 cup boiling water may be used instead of gravy.

Fine-flavored Lamb. When it's time for a special Sunday dinner or when you want a hearty, flavorful casserole, it's time to use a lamb recipe.

Lamb is good all year round, but in the spring it is most plentiful and reasonably priced.

The term "lamb" covers meat from animals up to around 14 months of age. After that, lamb becomes "mutton." Most mutton is used in commercially prepared soups and processed meats; it is not often seen on the retail market. "Spring lamb"—a tender, juicy meat—comes from lambs 3–5 months old.

Be sure to look for the round, purple "U.S. Insp'd & P's'd" stamp and check packer's brand name or Federal grade stamp for quality.

Look for velvet-smooth, fine-grained, pink-to-dark-pink meat and small bones tinged with red. Young lamb bones can be quite easily cut. As animal matures, bones grow larger, whiter and harder to cut and meat becomes redder.

The thin, paper-like covering on lamb is called the "fell." It is usually left on lamb roasts but is generally removed from chops. Mutton "fell" should always be removed before cooking.

Most lamb cuts are sufficiently tender to be cooked with dry heat—roasted, broiled or pan-broiled. The fresh, distinctive flavor of lamb is best when it is served hot or cold, never lukewarm. Lamb is usually cooked to medium or well done, although some people prefer lamb chops and roasts cooked rare.

Two of the finest lamb roasts are the leg and the circular crown roast formed by the tender chops. Both are ideally suited to dry-heat (oven-roasting) preparation. The less expensive cuts are useful in any recipe using the moist-heat (braising) method of cooking. The inexpensive cuts include neck, flank, breast and shank.

Broil or pan-broil lamb chops to desired doneness, which depends on whether you like them rare, medium or well done. Test by slitting next to bone to check color. The lower-price shoulder chops are an excellent value for braising with vegetables in casseroles. Marinating adds flavor when lamb is to be cooked by such dry-heat methods as roasting, broiling and barbecueing. Oil and vinegar or soy sauce contribute flavor and honey-garlic glaze is especially good on a leg of lamb for roasting or barbecueing.

If you want to vary the traditional mint seasoning with lamb, try a little thyme, marjoram, ginger, basil or rosemary. Or rub dry mustard or chili powder over cut surface of lamb roast before you put it in the oven. Another way to season a roast is to make several shallow slits on top before cooking; fill openings with slivers of garlic, mint leaves or parsley.

When you serve your lamb dish at the dinner table, be adventurous with accompaniments. Try your favorite barbecue sauce, whipped grape or currant jelly or a firm mold of green mint jelly.

And for a final dash of color and flavor, garnish with broiled tomatoes, mushrooms, peach halves, pear halves, orange or pineapple slices or watercress.

To Cook Lamb Roasts and Chops

Lamb cuts should be roasted uncovered until meat is medium or well done. Mint or currant jelly may be basted over roast toward end of cooking period.

To Pan-broil Chops: Snip fat edges of chops. Rub hot pan with a little lamb fat. Brown meat over high heat 1 minute on each side. Reduce heat, and cook to desired doneness. Test color by slitting along bone.

To Broil: Place chops on cold rack under preheated broiler, with top about 3 inches from heat. Broil 6–8 minutes on each side for 1-inch chops, 9–11 minutes for 1 1/2-inch chops.

To Bake: After browning chops over high heat, place pan in 325°F. oven. For 1-inch chops bake 12–18 minutes, turning once, depending on desired doneness.

Unthawed frozen lamb chops should be allowed twice as long to cook as are fresh ones.

TIMETABLE FOR ROASTING LAMB*

TYPE OF ROAST	WEIGHT IN POUNDS	MINUTES PER POUND**
Leg	5–8	25–30
Loin	2–3	50–55
Rack	4–5	40–45
Rolled shoulder	3–5	40–50
Cushion shoulder	3–5	30–35

*Oven temperature is 325°F., meat thermometer reading is 180°F. for well done, 175°F. for medium.

**For meat taken from refrigerator (40°F.); for unthawed frozen roasts, extend cooking period by 1/2 the total time required for same size and cut of fresh lamb.

The shorter times apply to roasts of heavier weights specified; for smaller cuts allow longer times listed.

Roast Leg of Lamb

    6-pound leg of lamb
1/4 cup FRENCH DRESSING
  1 teaspoon salt
1/2 teaspoon rosemary
1/2 teaspoon thyme
1/2 teaspoon sweet basil
  2 cups boiling water
4–5 tablespoons flour
1/2 cup cold water
Salt and pepper to taste

Have meat at room temperature. Place in shallow pan lined with greased heavy-duty aluminum foil. Score fat; mix dressing, 1 teaspoon salt and herbs, and brush all surfaces of meat. Pour remaining herb mixture over top. Roast at 325°F. allowing 30 minutes per pound, or until meat thermometer registers 180°F. for well done. Remove meat to hot platter, and keep warm. Skim most of fat from drippings, and add boiling water. Stir to dissolve brown bits, lift out foil and pour drippings into saucepan. Combine flour with cold water and thicken gravy to smooth consistency. Taste, and season. Serves 6–8.

Crown Roast of Lamb

Ground lamb
    4-pound crown roast (7 ribs) of lamb
1/2 pound ground ham or beef
1/2 cup tomato juice
1/4 cup finely chopped onion
1/2 teaspoon salt
1/4 teaspoon thyme
1/4 teaspoon rosemary
1/4 teaspoon sweet basil
1/2 cup soft bread crumbs
  1 egg
Garlic slivers
  1 teaspoon dry mustard
  1 teaspoon salt
1/2 teaspoon rosemary
  7 cubes salt pork

Remove ground lamb packed in center of roast, and mix it with ham, tomato juice, onion, 1/2 teaspoon salt, thyme, 1/4 teaspoon rosemary, and basil. Stir in soft bread crumbs and egg. If beef is used in place of ham, add more salt. Refill crown and insert garlic in meat near base. Make a mixture of dry mustard, 1 teaspoon salt and 1/2 teaspoon rosemary and rub all surfaces of meat. Cover each projecting rib end with cube of salt pork (to prevent charring) or small squares of aluminum foil, and set in open roasting pan. Roast slowly at 325°F. about 3 hours. Lift to hot platter, and remove salt-pork cubes or aluminum foil. Keep roast warm while making gravy. Serves 5–6.

Note: A crown roast is a special-event cut. Your butcher will usually prepare this roast for you if you order ahead of time. Be sure backbone is removed to make carving easier.

Roast Lamb with Herbs

3–4 pound rack or shoulder lamb
  1 teaspoon salt
1/2 teaspoon thyme
1/2 teaspoon rosemary
1/2 teaspoon sweet basil
3/4 cup water (can be water in which vegetables have been cooked)

Cut 1/2-inch gashes in fat of lamb roast. Mix salt, thyme, rosemary and basil and rub into meat. Roast uncovered at 400°F. for 45 minutes. Pour off excess fat; lower heat to 325°F. Add water, cover and continue roasting slowly 2 1/2–3 hours. Baste now and then with pan juices. Lift lamb to hot platter, and make gravy.

Grilled Lamb Chops à l'Anglaise

    1 double loin lamb chop with pocket
    Vegetable oil
    Bread crumbs
    2 strips partly cooked bacon
    2 tablespoons finely chopped ham
    1 teaspoon dry mustard

Brush chop with vegetable oil, and dip in bread crumbs. Combine chopped ham and mustard. Fill pocket with mixture. Encircle with bacon and secure with toothpicks. Broil 10–15 minutes, turning 3 or 4 times. Season, and remove to hot platter. Serves 1.

Casserole Dinner of Lamb Chops

    2 tablespoons fat
    4 lamb-shoulder chops
    4 medium potatoes, halved
    8 small onions
    8 medium, or 4 large carrots, sliced lengthwise
    2 tablespoons butter or margarine
    2 tablespoons flour
    1/4 cup milk
    1 cup sour cream
    Salt and pepper to taste
    1/4 teaspoon powdered ginger
    Paprika

Heat fat in skillet, and brown chops well. Put a layer of potatoes and onions in bottom of deep baking dish, add chops, then another layer of potatoes and onions and top with carrots. Melt butter or margarine, and stir in flour. Remove from heat, and slowly stir in milk, then sour cream. Add ginger, salt and pepper. Return to heat, and cook until smooth and thickened, stirring constantly. Pour over chops, sprinkle with paprika and bake, covered, at 325°F. about 1 1/2–2 hours. Serves 4.

Stewed Breast of Lamb

    1 1/2 pounds breast of lamb
    1/4 pound mushrooms
    1/2 cup chopped onion
    2 tablespoons fat
    1 (10 1/2-ounce) can condensed celery soup
    1 cup light cream
    2 tablespoons flour
    1/4 cup cold water
    1 (10-ounce) package frozen green peas,
        just thawed

Wipe meat with damp cloth or paper towels, and cut into 1-inch cubes. Wash mushrooms, quarter and sauté slowly with onion in fat. Add lamb, soup and cream. Cover, and simmer about 1 1/2 hours or until meat is tender, stirring occasionally. Blend flour and cold water smoothly, and stir into pan to thicken gravy. Simmer another 10 minutes, stirring constantly. Add green peas, and continue slow cooking until just tender. Serves 4–5.

Note: This stew is pale as meat is stewed without initial browning.

Lamb Stew with Mint Dumplings

    2 pounds trimmed stewing lamb (breast or neck)
    2 tablespoons fat
    2 cups water
    1 (10 1/2-ounce) can consommé
    1 tablespoon lemon juice
    1/2 teaspoon salt
    Pinch rosemary
    6 (or more) peeled small potatoes
    6 small onions, peeled
    1/2 cup sliced celery
    1 (10-ounce) package frozen peas and carrots
    2–3 tablespoons flour
    1 recipe MINT DUMPLINGS

Cut lamb in pieces; dredge meat with flour. Brown slowly in fat about 15 minutes, turning now and then to color all sides. Add next 5 ingredients. Cover and simmer 40 minutes. Add potatoes, onions and celery, and continue simmering 15 minutes. Shake in frozen vegetables. Mix 2–3 tablespoons flour with water into smooth paste. When lamb mixture comes to boil, thicken with flour paste. Drop in small mint dumplings, and cover pan tightly. Steam without lifting lid 10 minutes. Serves 6.

Note: For additional flavor, add any or all of the following: pinch sweet basil, Worcestershire sauce, onion flakes, whole clove.

Mint Dumplings

    2 slices white bread
    2/3 cup milk
    1 tablespoon fresh mint
    Dry biscuit mix

Cut crusts off bread; crumble bread into bowl, and add milk and mint. Stir in enough biscuit mix (as it comes from package) to make soft drop dough. Shape lightly into small balls. Makes about 12.

Lamb and Eggplant Ragout

    1 1/2 pounds stewing lamb
    1/4 cup flour
    1 teaspoon salt

1 teaspoon pepper
2 tablespoons fat
1 (1-pound, 13-ounce) can tomatoes, undrained
5 onions, quartered
3/4 cup sliced celery
3/4 cup diced carrot
1/2 teaspoon salt
1/2 teaspoon sugar
1 eggplant
3 tablespoons flour
1/4 cup water

Cut meat into cubes. Combine 1/4 cup flour, 1 teaspoon salt and pepper; then roll meat cubes in seasoned flour. Heat 2 tablespoons fat in skillet, and brown meat; drain off excess fat, add tomatoes, vegetables (except eggplant), 1/2 teaspoon salt and sugar. Cover and simmer 3/4 hour. Peel eggplant, cut into 1-inch cubes and add to ragout. Cover, and simmer 1/2 hour longer. Make smooth paste of 3 tablespoons flour and 1/4 cup water and thicken gravy. Cook 10 minutes longer. Taste, and add extra seasoning if required. Serves 4–5.

Lamb and Kidney Pie

3/4 pound ground stewing lamb
2 tablespoons milk
1 teaspoon salt
1/2 teaspoon rosemary
1/8 teaspoon basil
1/8 teaspoon dried mint
2 tablespoons flour
2 tablespoons bacon drippings
1/2 pound lamb kidneys, diced
1 large onion, chopped (1 cup)
1/2 cup sliced celery
1 sliced carrot
1 (10 1/2-ounce) can thick soup (Scotch broth, minestrone or chicken gumbo), diluted according to label directions
1 chicken or beef bouillon cube
1 tablespoon flour
1 tablespoon cold water
1 deep 9" or 10" unbaked pastry shell
1 1/2 cups shredded or riced cooked potatoes or 9" or 10" pastry top crust
Fresh mint or parsley sprigs

Mix lamb, milk and seasonings together. Roll into walnut-size balls. Dust with 2 tablespoons flour and brown slowly in drippings. Push to one side of pan, and sauté diced kidneys. Add next 5 ingredients, and cover. Simmer 15 minutes. Combine flour and cold water. Stir in soup and flour-water mixture. Taste, and correct seasonings. Pour into pastry shell. Arrange cooked potatoes around top, or cover with pastry circle. Bake at 400°F. 40–45 minutes. Garnish top with fresh mint sprigs. Serves 5–6.

Curried Lamb with Rice

2 tablespoons flour
1 teaspoon paprika
1/2 teaspoon salt
1/4 teaspoon black pepper
2 pounds stewing lamb
1/2 cup chopped onion
2 tablespoons bacon drippings
2 (10-ounce) cans chicken broth
2 tablespoons vinegar
1 tablespoon curry powder
3 cups hot cooked rice

Mix flour, paprika, salt and pepper. Cut lamb into cubes, and dredge in flour mixture. Brown onion in hot bacon drippings. Add meat, and brown slightly. Add chicken broth, vinegar and curry powder, cover pan and bake 1 1/2 hours at 350°F. (If gravy is too thin, stir in 1 tablespoon flour mixed to paste with 2 tablespoons cold water, and cook 10 minutes more.) Serve around mound of rice. Serves 5–6.

Shish Kebab

1 pound lamb patties (about 2 cups ground lamb)
1/4 cup packaged seasoned bread crumbs
1 teaspoon salt
1/4 teaspoon pepper
1 egg
6 lamb kidneys
3 lemons
6 thick onion wedges
6 cherry tomatoes
1 package instant meat marinade

Lightly mix lamb patties with bread crumbs, salt, pepper, and egg. With wet hands, shape into 12 balls. Cook kidneys 5 minutes in 1 quart boiling water. Drain. Have ready lemons, quartered, and 6 thick wedges of onion. Assemble six skewers as follows: first a wedge of lemon, then a lamb meatball, a wedge of onion, a kidney, another meatball, another lemon wedge. To top it all, a cherry tomato. Place the readied skewers on a broiler pan. Brush with packaged instant meat marinade, diluted with water according to package directions. Broil 5 minutes; turn and broil 5 minutes longer. Serves 6.

Buying and Cooking Pork. *Rich in distinctive flavor, pork in its almost endless range of cuts and forms—fresh, smoked, cured—is a most versatile meat and rivals beef in popularity. It is high in essential nutrients and always available.*

Because it has very little connective tissue and is by nature tender, pork can be successfully cooked by dry-heat methods (as for tender beef parts) and in various other ways as well. But there is one hard-and-fast rule basic to all pork preparations: It must be *thoroughly* cooked, that is, there should be no pink color—the meat should be all gray. Underdone pork should never be eaten because of the possible danger of trichinosis.

As with other meats, ask your butcher to show you the "U.S. Insp'd & P's'd" stamp on the carcass or cuts. Because of the uniform age at which the animal is brought to market and therefore the uniform tenderness, pork does not carry a packer's brand name or Federal grade stamp to differentiate quality.

In selecting your cut, look for a good proportion of lean to fat. The lean should be firm and fine-grained—light grayish-pink, a deeper rose in older animals. Fat should be firm and white and bones porous and slightly pink. In pork the proportion of bone to meat is small.

The choicest roasting cuts are the rib, loin, shoulder and leg (the last sometimes known as "fresh ham"). The all-meat tenderloin may be baked or fried. Pork chops and steaks are best braised. Broiling is not recommended because meat is likely to become hard and dry by the time it is well done. Half-inch chops may be pan-broiled successfully. "Pink pork" must never be eaten. Take care that you cook your fresh pork, whatever the cut, until it is grayish-white in color all through.

Pork in roasts, chops, sausages or braised dishes takes agreeably to a wide range of seasonings and accompaniments. When cooking a roast, drop cored apple halves or parboiled onions in pan for last 1/2 hour or so of cooking; or serve it with sauerkraut and caraway seeds. Sage, oregano, paprika and marjoram have an affinity for pork. Garlic, dry mustard or chili powder rubbed over surface adds zest. More than any other fresh meat, pork can support plenty of freshly-ground pepper, in addition to the salt used.

Most pork cuts, no matter what part of the carcass they come from, are tender and therefore suitable for roasting. But shoulder chops and steaks do take well to slower cooking methods, and they give a delicious flavor to vegetables cooked with them.

Because pork is a sweet meat, with a pronounced flavor of its own, it takes very well to a contrasting tart flavor, which is why we so frequently see it combined with applesauce or apple rings or served with sauerkraut. Peaches or pineapple slices make good accompaniments for fresh, smoked or cured pork cuts.

But, in addition to being a valuable standby for varying family menus, pork, because of its own very definite flavor, adds strength to other dishes as a flavor ingredient in a good many recipes in which savory accents provide special touches.

Skewered Pork Cubes

    1/2 cup chopped onion
    1/4 cup lemon juice
    1/4 cup apple juice
    2 tablespoons brown sugar
    1 or 2 cloves garlic, crushed
    2 tablespoons soy sauce
    1 tablespoon prepared mustard
    2 pounds lean pork
    6 preserved kumquats, crab apples or sweet pickles

Combine everything but pork and kumquats. Use blender if you have one, and let ingredients liquefy. Cut pork in 1-inch cubes, and thread on 6 skewers. Brush meat generously with sauce. Place skewered meat in greased baking pan, and refrigerate, covered, 1/2 hour. Put in 375°F. oven, and roast, 20 minutes. Turn skewers, and brush with remaining sauce; continue cooking until meat is tender, about 20 minutes more. Garnish ends of skewers with preserved kumquats, crab apples or sweet pickles. Serves 6.

Sausages with Apple Rings

    Pork sausages
    1 recipe SAUTÉED APPLE RINGS

Place sausages in cold frying pan, and cook slowly over moderate heat until browned on all sides and thoroughly cooked, depending on thickness. Average or medium sausages will take 20–25 minutes. Sausages in casings may first be simmered in a very little boiling water; do not prick casings. After 5–6 minutes, drain off water, and fry slowly. Serve with fried apple rings.

Sautéed Apple Rings

    2 large apples
    2 tablespoons sugar
    1 teaspoon cinnamon
    2 tablespoons butter or margarine

Peel and core apples, and cut each into 4 thick slices. Combine sugar and cinnamon. Dip slices into sugar mixture and sauté gently in butter or margarine in heavy frying pan, browning rings on both sides. Makes 8 rings.

Sweet-and-Sour Pork Wheels

    3/4 cup diced apple
    1 tablespoon butter or margarine
    1/2 cup soft bread crumbs
    1/4 cup raisins

2 tablespoons milk
Salt and cinnamon to taste
10–12 round slices (1/4-inch thick) canned luncheon pork
1 recipe SWEET-AND-SOUR SAUCE

Sauté the apple in melted butter or margarine until tender. Remove from heat, and add bread crumbs, raisins and enough milk or fruit juice to moisten. Season with salt and cinnamon, and spread on half the pork slices; top with remaining pork slices. Place in a greased baking pan, and pour sauce over and around. Bake at 350°F. 25 minutes. Serves 5–6.

Sweet-and-Sour Sauce

1 small onion, chopped
2 stalks celery, chopped
1 (1-pound, 13-ounce) can tomatoes, undrained
2 tablespoons catsup or chili sauce
1 tablespoon brown sugar
1 tablespoon vinegar
Salt and pepper to taste
2 tablespoons flour

Simmer onion, celery and tomatoes with their juice, until tender (about 10 minutes). Add catsup, brown sugar and vinegar. Season to taste, and thicken slightly with flour.

Layered Sausage Loaf

1 pound pork-sausage meat
2 cups soft bread crumbs
2 cups peeled, diced raw apple
2 small onions, peeled and chopped
1/2 teaspoon sage
Salt and pepper to taste

Divide sausage meat into 2 equal parts. Combine crumbs, apple, onions, sage, salt and pepper. Pat out 1/2 sausage meat in bottom of loaf pan(9"x 5"x 3"). Spread dressing on top and press down lightly. Cover with remaining meat in smooth layer. Bake at 350°F. about 45 minutes. Invert onto serving platter. Serves 6.

Pigs in Potatoes

6 small link sausages
1/4 cup water
2 cups cold mashed potatoes
1 egg yolk
1 tablespoon finely chopped onion
1 teaspoon finely chopped parsley
1/4 cup fine dry bread crumbs
1 egg, diluted with 1 tablespoon water or milk
2 tablespoons hot fat

Place sausages in heavy skillet, add water, cover and steam 5 minutes. Drain off water, and continue cooking 20 minutes. Beat together pota-toes, egg yolk, onion and parsley; then coat each cooked sausage with this mixture, roll in bread crumbs, then in diluted egg, then again in bread crumbs. Fry sausages in very hot fat until golden brown. Serves 3.

Hawaiian Pork

3–4 pound pork loin
Salt and pepper to taste
1/2 cup honey
1/2 cup pineapple juice

Score fat surface of pork. Season with salt and pepper and place on rack, fat side up, in roasting pan. Make glaze of honey and pineapple juice. Roast meat 3 hours at 350°F., basting at intervals with glaze. Serve with gravy made from pan juices. Serves 6.

Note: This dish is excellent served cold.

To Cook Pork Roasts and Chops

Any cut of fresh pork of suitable size and shape can be roasted. Use shallow pan, and do not cover; allow sufficient time for slow cooking to bring meat to completely well-done stage, when it will be fork-tender. Season halfway through cooking.

Pork chops and steaks from leg can be pan-broiled, baked or braised. Broiling may be used for loin or rib chops, but thorough cooking is essential. To check doneness, cut slit in meat near bone; if any pink shows, cooking is incomplete.

To Fry Chops: Remove excess fat from chops if desired; snip edges to prevent curling. Use a little fat to rub over hot pan. Brown meat, 3–4 minutes on each side. Reduce heat, cover and cook slowly according to thickness: for 1-inch chops 10 minutes each side, for 1/2-inch chops 4–5 minutes on each side. Pour off accumulation of fat during cooking.

To Bake: After browning each side, place chops uncovered in 325°F. oven, and allow to cook according to thickness: 1-inch chops 10–12 minutes on each side, for 1-inch steaks, 26–28 minutes on each side. Turn as required, and pour off excess fat as it accumulates.

In cooking unthawed frozen chops or steaks, extend cooking period by 1/2 the total amount required for a fresh cut of similar thickness.

If rind is left on roast, it should be scored with very sharp knife before cooking begins. This rind makes crisp "crackling," which some people enjoy very much with pork.

TIMETABLE FOR ROASTING PORK *

TYPE OF ROAST	WEIGHT IN POUNDS	MINUTES PER POUND **
Leg, whole, boned	10–14	25–30
Leg, half, bone in	4–6	35–40
Loin, center	3–5	30–35
Picnic shoulder, rolled	3–5	35–40

*Oven temperature 325°F.; meat thermometer reading 170°F.

**For meat taken from refrigerator (40°F.); for unthawed frozen roasts, extend cooking period by 1/2 total time required for same size and cut of fresh pork. Shorter times apply to roasts of heavier weights specified, for smaller cuts allow longer time listed.

One-dish Creole Chop Dinner

        1/2 pound fresh mushrooms, sliced, 2 cups
        1 medium onion, sliced, 1/2 cup
        1/2 green pepper, sliced, 1/4 cup
        3 tablespoons butter or margarine
        4 shoulder pork chops
        2 tablespoons flour
        1 teaspoon dry mustard
    Dash sage
        1 (12-ounce) can lima beans
        1 (8-ounce) can tomato sauce
        2 tablespoons brown sugar
        1 tablespoon molasses

Sauté green pepper, onion and mushrooms in butter or margarine until just tender but not brown; put in 8"x10" baking dish, reserving fat in pan. Combine flour, mustard and sage and sprinkle mixture on chops. Brown chops lightly in fat left in pan; remove. Rinse pan with 1/4 cup juice from lima beans, and pour contents of pan over fried vegetables. Add drained lima beans, tomato sauce, brown sugar and molasses, and stir until well mixed. Set chops on top of mixture, and cover dish with lid or foil. Bake 25 minutes at 350°F. Uncover, and bake 20 minutes longer or until meat is very tender. Serves 4.

Pork Chops with Rice

        4 pork-shoulder chops, 1 inch thick
        4 slices onion, 1/4 inch thick
        4 rings green pepper
        1/4 cup uncooked rice (not quick-cooking)
        1 (1-pound, 13-ounce) can tomatoes, undrained
        1 cup diced celery

Cut off and fry some pork fat in pan. In this fat, brown chops well on both sides—about 15 minutes total. Place slice of onion on each pork chop and ring of green pepper on top onion, and 1 tablespoon uncooked rice in each ring. Pour tomatoes over meat, and add celery. Cover pan, and simmer 1 hour, or transfer to baking dish, and bake at 350°F. 1 hour. Serves 4.

Stuffed Pork Chops

        6 rib pork chops, 3/4 inch or more thick
        1 cup soft bread crumbs
        1/4 cup celery
        1/4 cup chopped onion
        2 tablespoons chopped parsley
    Milk to moisten
        1/4 teaspoon salt
        1/8 teaspoon paprika
        1/4 cup milk or sour cream

Wipe chops with damp cloth, remove bones and trim off excess fat. Prepare dressing by combining remaining ingredients except 1/4 cup milk. Cut large gash or pocket in side of each chop, and fill with dressing. Sew chops up with coarse needle and thread. Sear in hot skillet; transfer to baking pan. Cover bottom of pan with 1/4 cup milk. Cover pan, and bake chops at 350°F. until tender—about 1 hour. Serves 4–6.

Stuffed Roast Pork

        4–5 pound pork butt or leg, boned
        1 recipe APRICOT DRESSING
        3 tablespoons flour
        3 tablespoons cold water

The roast should be taken out of refrigerator at least 1/2 hour before cooking. Stuff cavity with apricot dressing. Fasten securely with string to hold shape. If rind is still on, score it with sharp knife to facilitate carving. Place meat on rack in roasting pan, and cook, uncovered, until well done—about 3 1/2 hours at 325°F. Let roast stand in warm place 10 minutes while making gravy, to make carving easier. Combine flour and water, and stir into pan juices to thicken, adding additional chicken broth to achieve correct consistency. Remove string from roast before bringing to table. Serves 6–8.

Note: Have your butcher remove bone from roast when you buy it; ask him to leave rind on if you prefer crisp, crunchy top.

Apricot Dressing

        1 cup dried apricots
        1 cup cold water
    Scant 4 cups dry bread crumbs
        1/2 cup chopped celery
        1/4 cup melted butter or margarine
        1/2 teaspoon salt
        1/8 teaspoon pepper

Combine apricots and water in saucepan and bring to boil. Simmer 5 minutes; then drain, reserving liquid, and cut into strips. Mix strips with remaining ingredients, and moisten slightly with water from apricots. Makes 5 1/2 cups.

Note: 1 1/3 cups prunes can be substituted for apricots.

Baked Pork Tenderloin

    2 whole pork tenderloins (1/2–3/4 pound each)
    Bread (or apple) stuffing
    4–6 bacon strips

Split tenderloins lengthwise. Cover 2 pieces with stuffing. Top each with remaining pieces; fasten together with skewers or string. Place bacon over top. Roast on rack in shallow pan in center of moderate oven, 325°F., 1 1/4–1 1/2 hours. Serves 4–6.

Mock Geese

    12 thin slices lean pork tenderloin
    Salt and pepper to taste
     2 apples, each cut into 6 vertical sections
     6 prunes, halved
    1/4 cup grated onion
     2 eggs, beaten
    1/2 cup fine dry bread crumbs
     2 tablespoons butter or margarine
    3/4 cup (approximately) stock, water or sweet cider

Pound meat and rub with salt and pepper. Lay apple section and 1/2 prune on each pork slice. Top each with 1 teaspoon grated onion; roll up, and tie with string. Dip in beaten egg, then in crumbs; brown rolls in butter or margarine in heavy frying pan; add stock to depth of 1/4 inch. Cover, and braise about 1 hour or until meat is tender. Turn rolls once, and baste a few times while cooking, adding more liquid if necessary. Remove string, place rolls on platter and pour a little gravy from pan over them. Serves 4–6.

Baked Spareribs

    2 1 1/2-pound pieces side spareribs
    Bread (or apple) stuffing

Cut ribs into serving-size pieces, 5–6 ribs each. Spread well-seasoned stuffing over each piece, roll up and tie with string. Bake on rack in shallow roasting pan, uncovered, in center of moderately slow oven, 325°F. 2 hours. Serves 4–6.

Note: Spareribs may be cooked for carving at the table. Place 1 long piece, hollow side up, on rack, and spread with stuffing. Cover with second piece, hollow side down, and skewer or tie ribs together.

Pork Hocks with Sauerkraut

     3 pounds pork hocks
    6–8 cups hot water
    1/2 cup sliced onion
     1 tablespoon salt
     1 tablespoon mixed pickling spice
    2 1/2 cups (28 ounces) drained sauerkraut or 1 small cabbage, cut in wedges

Scrub pork hocks thoroughly. Cover with water; add onion, salt and spices. Cover tightly and simmer on top of stove 1 1/2–1 3/4 hours. Skim off fat. Strain cooking liquid. Return 1 cup liquid to saucepan. Arrange sauerkraut or cabbage around hocks. Simmer 10–12 minutes or until cabbage is tender. Drain, and serve hocks surrounded by vegetable on hot platter. Serves 6.

Stuffed Pork Steaks

    2 pounds pork-shoulder steaks
    2 teaspoons lemon juice
    1/2 teaspoon salt
    1/4 teaspoon pepper
    2 cups dry bread crumbs
    3/4 cup cream
    1/2 cup raisins, chopped
    1 teaspoon salt
    2 tablespoons flour
    2 tablespoons fat
    2 bouillon cubes
    1 cup boiling water

Pound steaks to 1/4 inch thickness; cut into 6 oblong serving pieces. Make a mixture of lemon juice, 1/2 teaspoon salt and pepper and rub into meat. Combine next 4 ingredients, and spread over pork slices. Roll slices, and secure with toothpicks or twine. Dredge with flour, and brown well in hot fat. Dissolve bouillon cubes in boiling water, and add to rolls. Cover pan, and simmer 30–40 minutes. Serves 6.

Cured or Smoked Ham

Bacon and ham products are available in a wide variety of forms; there are also many ways to serve them.

Hams—the cured, smoked legs of pork—are available in almost bewildering variety today; uncooked, partially cooked, completely cooked, boneless or bone in; whole or in various small sections; canned or in dry wrap. The price rises according to the amount of pre-preparation. Most packers identify each type of ham and suggest home procedures on wrapper or tag. Always follow these directions for best results. If such information is missing and your dealer can't supply it, you would be wise to *treat the ham as uncooked.*

Nowadays hams are very mildly cured, as compared with earlier times, when cold storage was inadequate and strong brines had to be used as preservatives. Today's hams should be stored in the same way as fresh pork—refrigerated until just before cooking.

Bacon comes sliced or in slabs. It has a high proportion of fat to lean—the former white and firm, the latter deep pink to reddish-brown. Canadian-style bacon comes from the loin and is leaner and more expensive. It's sold sliced or by the piece.

All bacon is best started in a cold pan, cooked over low to moderate heat and turned frequently. High heat toughens and hardens meat.

Bacon or ham can be useful as a flavor emphasis in other cooked dishes, or can perk up otherwise bland dishes. They combine well with many other ingredients—fish, cheese, eggs, vegetables, dried beans and other meats.

Here are a few suggestions. Fry bacon until crisp, and crumble into cream soups. Cut slices into 1-inch pieces and scatter over tops of such casserole dishes as macaroni and soufflés. Add small bacon pieces to any savory crumb topping. Strips of bacon or ham about 1/2 inch wide, fried until crisp and drained of any fat, can be scattered over the top of cooked green peas or beans at the last minute, in which case 1 teaspoon or so of chopped onion may be fried with bacon.

Bacon can add flavor to soups, stews, and casseroles. When you make a meat loaf, place strips of bacon across top of loaf before putting it in oven.

Ham and bacon also can lend variety to salads. Add crumbled bacon or cubes or strips of cooked ham to potato salad. Crumbled bacon adds a novel touch to any green salad, and cubes of ham and cheese add protein to make it a main-dish attraction. Then, of course, there are many uses for these meats in snacks and sandwiches.

To Cook Cured and Smoked Pork

Many of the cured, smoked pork cuts on today's market are packaged with full instructions for home preparation, according to the degree of tenderizing or cooking that has already been done by the processor. These directions should be followed for best results.

In general, hams should be baked, uncovered, in a moderately slow oven. Casing should be left on until cooking is completed, then removed before glazing or other finishing. The casing on a boned, rolled ham is easier to remove before cooking.

Cooking in Water: Hams and picnic shoulders may be cooked in simmering water on top of the stove. Add water to cover meat, spices and raw vegetables for flavor; cover kettle and cook until tender. Allow about 30 minutes per pound for medium ham (longer for smaller pieces); 30–35 minutes for 5–7 pound picnic shoulder; 35–40 minutes for boneless picnic shoulder.

To Cook Ham Steaks: Ham steaks may be baked in preheated 325°F. oven, allowing 50–55 minutes for 1-inch thickness and 1–1 1/4 hours for 1 1/2-inch thickness; pour 1/2 cup milk or fruit juice over them during cooking.

To Pan-broil: Brown over high heat for a few minutes on each side; cover, and cook slowly, allowing 8–10 minutes on each side for 1-inch steak, 6–8 minutes on each side of a thinner slice.

To Broil: Place on cold rack under preheated broiler, with meat 3 inches from heat. Broil 9–10 minutes on each side for 1-inch steak, 4–5 minutes on each side for 1/2-inch slice.

To Bake Bacon: If you have to cook a large amount of bacon at one time, use oven instead of frying pan. Place slices, with fat edge of each overlapping lean edge of next slice, on rack in shallow pan or broiler pan. Bake in oven preheated to 400°F., allowing 12–15 minutes or until bacon is crisp. There is no need to turn or drain.

To Broil Bacon: Place slices of bacon on rack of preheated broiler about 3 inches from heat. They take only 1 or 2 minutes on each side and should be turned once. Watch carefully, as they cook very rapidly.

Note: To separate bacon with speed, put whole layer of sliced bacon in pan without separating slices, as bacon heats, slices can be easily separated.

TIMETABLE FOR BAKING HAM*

TYPE OF HAM	WEIGHT IN POUNDS	MINUTES PER POUND**
Whole ham	10–14	18–20†
Ham (boneless)	7–10	22–25
Half ham	5–7	22–25
Picnic shoulder	5–8	35
Picnic shoulder (boneless)	3–5	45

*Oven temperature is 325°F., meat thermometer reading is 160°F.
**Times are for hams taken directly from refrigerator (40°F.).
†Shorter times apply to roasts of heavier weights specified, for smaller cuts allow longer times listed.

Glazed Baked Whole Ham

The mildly cured, high-grade hams of today usually come in packers' wraps with complete cooking instructions for each specific product. For best results it is wise to follow the method and timing suggested. As a general rule, a fine whole raw ham needs no presimmering; it is baked uncovered on rack in roasting pan, without added moisture, in moderately slow oven (325°F.). Minutes per pound depend on total weight and initial temperature of meat. If taken from refrigerator just before cooking, allow 20 minutes per pound for large, heavy ham; 25 minutes for 10–12 pounds. If a meat thermometer is used, internal temperature should register 160°F. to indicate doneness. At the end of cooking period take ham from oven, and remove rind by loosening with sharp knife and lifting off gently, leaving smooth white fat. Cut gashes 1/4-inch deep in long diagonal lines to form diamonds. Stick clove in center of each diamond. Spread with 1 of the following glazes, covering all fat. Return meat to oven, with heat increased to 425°F., and allow glaze to brown, about 15 minutes. Baste once or twice.

GLAZES:

Sugar Glaze: Mix 1 1/2 cups brown sugar, 2 teaspoons dry mustard, 3 tablespoons flour; blend in 1/4 cup cider vinegar.

Marmalade Glaze: Mix 1/2 cup orange marmalade, 3/4 cup brown sugar, 1 tablespoon flour, 2 teaspoons dry mustard and sufficient orange juice to make thick paste.

Pineapple Glaze: Mix 1 1/2 cups brown sugar and 3/4 cup crushed pineapple that has been thoroughly drained of its juice and 2 teaspoons dry mustard.

Note: A simple finish can be given by basting with maple syrup, liquid honey or beaten apple jelly.

Ham Rolls

1 1/2 cups cooked rice
1/4 cup toasted almonds
2 tablespoons chopped parsley
2 tablespoons butter or margarine, melted
8 thin slices cooked ham
1 (10 1/2 oz.) can condensed cream of chicken soup
1/2 soup can water

Mix first 4 ingredients, and place rounded tablespoon of mixture on each ham slice. Roll, fasten with toothpicks and place in baking dish. Mix soup and water, and pour over ham rolls. Bake at 350°F. 20 minutes. Serves 4–6.

Ham–Noodle Scallop

1/2 package (4 ounces) broad noodles
1/4 pound mushrooms (1 cup)
2 tablespoons butter or margarine
2 cups diced cooked ham
2 teaspoons prepared mustard
2 cups medium white sauce
2 tablespoons finely grated cheese
2 tablespoons fine dry bread crumbs

Cook noodles as directed on package; drain, and rinse with cold water. Chop mushrooms, and sauté in butter or margarine. Combine noodles, mushrooms, ham and mustard with white sauce in greased casserole. Mix bread crumbs and cheese and use resulting "cheese crumbs" to top casserole. Serves 5–6.

Cauliflower–Ham Scallop

1 medium head cauliflower, cooked
3 cups medium white sauce
2 cups diced cooked ham
1/4 cup almonds, blanched
2 tablespoons butter or margarine
1 cup cracker crumbs

Cauliflower may be left whole or broken apart. Arrange it in baking dish. Combine white sauce, ham and almonds, and pour over cauliflower. Melt butter or margarine, stir in crumbs and use to top cauliflower mixture. Bake at 350°F. until crumbs brown and dish is heated through—about 30 minutes. Serves 6–7.

Roast Ham

2–3 pound picnic ham
1/2 cup apple juice or cider

Set ham on heavy-duty foil in roasting pan, folding up sides and ends of foil to make narrow container to fit ham with just 1 inch to spare. Pour apple juice over the meat, and bake at 375°F. at least 45 minutes (meat thermometer should register 170°F.).

Note: The secret of success here is to have the pan fit the meat, so that the apple juice gently flavors the meat and you don't have to baste it.

Broiled Ham Steaks

Preheat broiler 5 minutes. Snip fat edges of raw ham steaks, and place on cold rack of broiler pan so that meat is 3 inches from heating unit. For 1-inch steaks, broil 9–10 minutes on each side, for 1/2-inch steaks, 4–5 minutes on each side. After turning, glaze with your favorite ham glaze, or baste several times during cooking, using maple syrup, honey, apple jelly or fruit juice.

Ham with Cranberries

2 cups cranberries
2 1-inch slices raw smoked center-cut ham
1 cup brown sugar
Whole cloves

Wash and chop cranberries. Place 1 slice ham in baking dish, and cover with 1/2 the berries and 1/2 the sugar. Place other ham slice on top, and cover with remaining berries and sugar. Stud fatty edges of ham with whole cloves, and

Spicy Pot Roast

                2 tablespoons fat
    4 1/2–5 pounds chuck or rump
                1/2 teaspoon salt
    Pepper to taste
                1 cup hot water
                1 onion, sliced
                3 bay leaves
                3/4 teaspoon thyme
                1/4 teaspoon powdered ginger
                8 small potatoes, peeled
                12 carrots, halved
                1 tablespoon flour
                2 tablespoons cold water

Use a Dutch oven, deep-well cooker, roasting pan or any large, heavy, covered kettle. Melt fat and brown roast thoroughly on all sides. Turn with spatula, rather than fork, which would pierce meat and allow juices to escape. Sprinkle with salt and pepper. Add hot water, onion and spices. Cover and simmer about 3 hours. Add potatoes and carrots. Cover, and cook another 45 minutes or until vegetables are tender. Remove pot roast to platter, and surround with potatoes and carrots. Keep warm; blend flour and cold water, and thicken liquid. Serve gravy separately. Serves 8.

Note: This recipe can be used with any suitable "less tender" cut of beef—chuck, fresh brisket, rump or heel of round. A roast of this size makes a dozen or more generous servings. Leftovers can be used in any way suitable for roast beef: sliced for sandwiches, reheated in gravy, cut up and added with canned-soup sauce to lightly cooked vegetables for a quick casserole dish, used in hash with chopped cooked potatoes and raw onions or ground up for SHEPHERD'S PIE.

Hungarian Goulash

                2 pounds stewing beef
                1 tablespoon bacon drippings or fat
                5 tablespoons flour
                1 small onion, peeled and sliced
                1 tablespoon Worcestershire sauce
                2 teaspoons salt
                1 teaspoon paprika
                1 teaspoon caraway seeds (optional)
            1/8 teaspoon pepper
        3 1/2 cups hot water
            1/2 cup sour cream

Cut meat into neat 1-inch cubes. Melt fat in heavy skillet. Brown meat cubes on all sides; sprinkle with flour, and stir again to brown further. Add onion, Worcestershire sauce and dry seasonings. Add hot water, and continue stirring. Reduce heat, cover tightly and simmer until meat is very tender—about 2 hours. Stir in sour cream just before serving. Drained boiled noodles

are a traditional accompaniment with the spicy goulash. Serves 4.

Beef Strips with Raisins

                1/2 cup seedless raisins
                1/2 cup red wine
                    1 good-sized minute steak (1 lb.)
        1 1/2 tablespoons flour
        Salt and pepper to taste
        1 1/2 tablespoons salad oil
        Boiling water
        Bay leaf
        Pinch thyme
        Fluffy rice

Pick over, wash and drain raisins. Put to soak in wine. Prepare steaks by cutting into strips about 1/2" x 2". Combine flour, salt and pepper and coat strips. Heat oil in frying pan until it begins to sputter. Put in flour-coated meat, and brown thoroughly. Reduce heat to simmer; add wine with raisins and only enough boiling water to barely cover. Add bay leaf and thyme. Cover tightly and simmer 1 hour or less or until meat is very tender. Remove bay leaf before serving over fluffy rice. Serves 2.

About Ground Beef. Ground beef may either be ground round steak, ground chuck or beef trimmings ground with some of the less tender cuts like flank, shank or neck. "Ground round" and "ground chuck" are always labeled as such and cost more than the other, which is known variously as "hamburger" or "ground beef." Hamburger contains more fat and therefore, loses more weight during cooking.

Ground beef is one of the most versatile meat purchases. It may be pan-broiled, broiled, braised or baked. It is economical, particularly as it lends itself well to "stretching" with various other ingredients to make interesting main courses. Ground beef is ideal for use in a hearty sauce for spaghetti or rice; in baked pies with pastry, biscuit or potato toppings; teamed with kidney beans in chili con carne, or as stuffing with such baked vegetables as peppers and squash.

Do not overcook ground beef or expose it too long to dry, high temperatures which cause meat to harden and lose flavor.

Warning: Ground beef is very perishable. It should be refrigerated and used within 1–2 days. For a longer period, it should be wrapped in freezer paper and frozen.

If you are freezing a quantity of ground meat to be used later in patties, shape patties before freezing. Separate with layers of waxed paper; then wrap for the freezer.

bake 1 hour at 300°–350°F., basting occasionally with liquid in pan. Serves 4–5.

Baked Ham with Potatoes and Onions

2-pound slice (1/2 inch thick) raw smoked ham
6 medium potatoes, peeled and sliced
1/4 cup flour
2 onions, peeled and sliced
(approximately 1 1/2 cups)
1 cup milk (approximately)

Place ham in casserole, and cover with layer of potato slices. Sprinkle with flour, and add layer of onion. Repeat layers, ending with potatoes. Pour in milk until it is halfway up the dish. Cover, and bake at 350°F. 1 hour. Uncover during last few minutes to brown. Serves 4–6.

Paprika Ham

2 tablespoons butter or margarine
1 small onion, sliced (1/4 cup)
2 cups cooked ham, cubed
1 (8-ounce) can tomato sauce
2 tablespoons French mustard
1 teaspoon paprika
1 cup sour cream

Melt butter or margarine, and sauté onion till transparent. Add ham. Mix together tomato sauce, mustard and paprika. Stir into ham, and simmer 30 minutes. Just before serving, stir in sour cream; heat, but do not boil. Serve with rice. Serves 4.

Ham with Tarragon Sauce

6 scallions or 1 small onion, chopped (1/4 cup)
1 teaspoon dried tarragon
1/2 cup wine vinegar
2/3 cup heavy cream
1/3 cup chicken bouillon
2 egg yolks
2 tablespoons butter or margarine
Salt and pepper to taste
4 slices baked or boiled ham

Simmer onions with tarragon in vinegar until reduced by 1/2. Place in top of double boiler over hot water, and add cream, bouillon and egg yolks. Cook, stirring, until mixture thickens, taking care not to boil. Stir in butter or margarine and salt and pepper. Pour over baked or boiled ham. Serves 4.

Variety Meats. "Variety Meats" are the edible parts of an animal that are not classified as flesh: liver, kidney, tongue, heart, sweetbreads, brains, tripe, oxtail. Most are rich in minerals and vitamins and inexpensively add variety to your menus. They must be handled with care and speed, for they spoil very quickly. Be sure they are fresh when you buy them and use them within 1 day of purchase; or freeze in proper wrapping, and use within 3–4 months.

Liver

Calf or veal liver is the choicest and costliest kind. It has the lightest reddish-brown coloring; it is mild-flavored, tender and very suitable for sautéing or broiling. Beef and pork liver are stronger in flavor and less tender. Braising makes them more tender and the liquid added may provide tempting flavor.

Thin, even slices of liver are desirable for uniform cooking. Allow about 1/4 pound for each serving. Cook calf liver only to desired doneness; overcooking toughens it.

Kidney

Allow about 1/4 pound of fresh kidneys per serving. This meat requires careful preparation to ensure good flavor and tenderness. Cut away membrane, fat and tubes, and slice meat in neat pieces. The strong flavor of beef and pork kidneys can be diminished by soaking uncooked meat in salted cold water (1 teaspoon salt to 1 cup water) in refrigerator for 1 hour or so.

Heart

All heart meat is close-textured and muscular and must therefore have long cooking at low temperatures. Choose hearts that are smooth, shiny and well rounded. One beef heart will serve 8–10; one veal or pork heart makes 2–3 servings; small lamb hearts yield 1 serving each. Before cooking, wash heart thoroughly, and trim away any fat, tubes or coarse fibers.

Tongue

Tongue is not so tender as are most of the other variety meats and requires long, slow cooking in moist heat.

Calf and veal tongues are usually sold fresh. Lamb and beef tongues are available either fresh or pickled. Pork tongues usually come in cans or jars as "lunch tongue." The cooking method is the same for fresh and pickled types, but pickled tongue should be soaked for a minimum of 2 hours beforehand in cold water.

Allow about 1 pound for 4 servings.

Sweetbreads

Sweetbreads are the pinkish-white thymus glands of young cows, calves and lambs. They are delicate in flavor and generally considered gourmet food. Allow 1/4 pound of sweetbreads for each serving.

Nowadays sweetbreads are usually sold frozen because of their high perishability. After thawing, sweetbreads should be precooked. To achieve firmer texture, parboil in water with a little vinegar or lemon juice and salt, drain quickly, chill in fresh water and slip off membrane with fingers. The sweetbreads may then be heated in a cream sauce, fried, broiled or braised.

Brains

Another tender and delicate-flavored specialty, brains should be parboiled and recooked in the same way as sweetbreads. Allow 1/4 pound per serving.

Tripe

Tripe comes from the muscular inner lining of the stomach of cattle, is creamy yellow in color and is either smooth or honeycombed. All tripe is cleaned and partially cooked before it is sold; nevertheless additional cooking is required to tenderize. Cover, and simmer until tender, about 1 1/2 hours.

Much of the tripe on the market is used commercially in canned meat products, soups and so forth.

Liver–Onion Hot Pot

    1/2 pound beef liver
    1/4 cup seasoned flour
    1/2 pound sausages
    1–2 tablespoons bacon drippings
  1 1/2 cups consommé or tomato juice
      1 bay leaf
      3 or 4 medium potatoes, peeled and sliced
      2 sliced onions
    1/4 cup flour
  Salt and pepper to taste
    1/4 teaspoon Worcestershire sauce
      2 tablespoons bread crumbs, buttered

Dip liver in seasoned flour. Fry liver and sausages together in bacon drippings until lightly cooked; remove from pan. Put consommé and bay leaf in pan; stir to dissolve brown bits. Cut liver and sausage into 1-inch pieces. Grease 1-quart baking dish, and add alternate layers of potatoes, onions, liver and sausage, ending with potatoes. Between layers, sprinkle 1/4 cup flour, salt, pepper and Worcestershire sauce. Pour in consommé and sprinkle top with buttered crumbs. Cover, and bake at 350°F. 30 minutes. Uncover, and continue baking 30–40 minutes. Serves 3–4.

Note: This dish is just as tasty made with leftover liver and sausage.

Liver–Bacon Croquettes

    3/4 pound pork liver
  Salted water
    1/2 small onion
      1 (1-pound) can tomatoes or tomato juice
    1/2 cup dry bread crumbs
      2 teaspoons prepared mustard
  Salt and pepper to taste
    1/4 cup dry bread crumbs or flour
      5 or 6 slices bacon
      1 tablespoon melted drippings

Cover and cook liver in salted water about 10 minutes. Drain and cool. Chop liver and onion together; add tomatoes, 1/2 cup crumbs, mustard and seasonings. Form into 5 or 6 cylindrical croquettes. Roll each in crumbs or flour, and encircle with bacon. Secure with toothpicks, brush with melted drippings and bake at 400°F. about 20 minutes or until bacon is crisp. Serves 4.

Fried Liver

Coat liver slices with seasoned flour, melt small amout of fat in pan (if serving liver with bacon, fry bacon first, and cook liver in hot bacon fat). Turn heat to high. Cook just 1 minute to brown on both sides; reduce heat to medium, and cook 2–3 minutes longer, turning sides once or twice. Partial covering of pan at this stage will keep liver tender and juicy.

VARIATION:

Fried Kidney: Use sliced or halved kidneys, but cook over medium heat a few minutes longer or until all red color at center of meat has disappeared. Avoid overcooking.

Kidney Stew

      2 beef kidneys (about 1 1/2 pounds)
      1 quart cold salted water
    1/4 cup seasoned flour
    1/4 cup chopped onion
      2 tablespoons hot fat
      2 (10-ounce) cans beef consommé
      1 teaspoon salt
    1/8 teaspoon pepper
      2 tablespoons vinegar

Split kidneys, and remove all fatty tissue. Cut into 1-inch pieces, and soak 1 hour in cold salted water. Drain, dry on paper towels. Roll kidneys in seasoned flour, and brown with onion in fat. Add beef consommé, and simmer, covered, about 1 1/2 hours. If necessary, thicken with 1 tablespoon flour mixed with 2 tablespoons water. Season with salt and pepper; add vinegar last. Serves 6.

Oxtail–Kidney Ragout

1 oxtail, cut in pieces
1/2 pound beef kidney, diced
1/4 cup flour
2 tablespoons fat
2 tablespoons Worcestershire sauce
1 teaspoon salt
1 beef bouillon cube
1 (1-pound, 13-ounce) can tomatoes
2 bay leaves
4 small onions, peeled
1/2 cup sliced celery
1/2 cup diced turnip
3 tablespoons flour
3 tablespoons water

Dredge oxtail and kidney in flour, and brown slowly in fat until all sides are colored. Add Worcestershire sauce, salt and bouillon cube, tomatoes and bay leaves. Cover, and simmer 45 minutes; then add onions, celery and turnip. Cook 30 minutes longer or until meat and vegetables are tender. Remove bay leaves. Make smooth paste of flour and 3 tablespoons water; use to thicken cooking liquid. Serves 4.

Braised Chicken Livers

1 pound chicken livers
1/2 cup flour
3/4 teaspoon salt
Pinch pepper
3 tablespoons fat
2 tablespoons chopped onion
2 tablespoons chopped green pepper
2 cups hot water or 1 (13 1/2-ounce) can chicken broth
1/2 teaspoon Worcestershire sauce

Cut away any stringy portions from livers. Wash meat in cold water, and dry with paper towels. Mix flour and seasonings (varying latter if desired); put in paper bag, add livers and shake to coat all surfaces. Melt fat in frying pan. Brown meat in fat, add onion and green pepper and cook 1 minute. Add all water and Worcestershire sauce. Simmer, covered, about 10 minutes or until livers readily break apart with fork. Serves 6.

VARIATION:

Braised Chicken Giblets: Substitute 1 pound mixed giblets—hearts, gizzards, livers—for chicken livers. Before cooking, cut away membranes, fat and so forth and slice gizzards. Serve over boiled noodles or fluffy rice.

Liver Loaf

1 1/2 pounds beef or other liver
1 1/2 cups boiling water
1/4 pound salt pork
3/4 cup rolled oats
1 medium onion
2 eggs
1/2 teaspoon thyme
Salt and pepper to taste
6 bacon strips
6 tomato slices

Cover liver with boiling water, and let stand 10 minutes. Drain off liquid, and grind liver with salt pork, oats and onion. Add eggs and seasonings, mix well and pack mixture into greased casserole. Garnish with bacon strips and tomato slices and bake 1 hour at 350°F. Serves 6.

Chicken Livers Supreme

1 pound chicken livers
2 tablespoons butter or margarine, melted
1 (7-ounce) can steak sauce with mushrooms
1 tablespoon flour
1 tablespoon chopped onion
1/2 teaspoon salt
Dash hot pepper sauce
3 tablespoons sherry
24 melba toast points

Halve chicken livers, and sauté slowly in butter or margarine until lightly browned. Stir in steak sauce, flour, onion, salt, and pepper sauce. Cover, and cook until livers are tender, about 10 minutes. Remove from heat, and add sherry. Pour into serving dish, and keep hot. Serve over points of melba toast. Serves 6.

Savory Hearts

2 veal or lamb hearts
1 tablespoon flour
2 tablespoons hot shortening
1 small onion, sliced
2 bouillon cubes
2 cups boiling water
1/4 cup vinegar
2 tablespoons sugar
1/2 teaspoon salt
1/2 teaspoon mixed herbs, crushed
1/4 teaspoon pepper

Clean hearts, removing membranes and large veins. Cut into cubes, dredge with flour in paper bag, and brown in hot fat over medium heat. Add onion. Crumble bouillon cubes in boiling water, and combine with remaining ingredients. Pour over meat in skillet. Cover and simmer 1/2 hour or until tender. Serves 4.

Oven-braised Stuffed Heart

    1 tablespoon fat
    1 tablespoon chopped onion
    1 tablespoon chopped celery
    2 cups soft bread crumbs
    1 teaspoon sage
    1/2 teaspoon salt
    1/8 teaspoon pepper
    1 beef heart (about 3 pounds)
Salt and pepper to taste
    1/4 cup seasoned flour
    1 tablespoon hot fat
    3/4 cup hot water or vegetable stock

Melt 1 tablespoon fat, and cook onion and celery until lightly colored. Add to bowl with next 4 ingredients, and mix well. Wash heart, dry, hollow out a cavity for stuffing and sprinkle with salt and pepper. Stuff heart, fasten with skewers and tie firmly in place with string. Roll heart in seasoned flour, and brown in 1 tablespoon hot fat, turning to color all surfaces. Place heart in oven pan or casserole that can be tightly covered. Rinse out searing pan with hot water and pour over heart. Cover and cook in oven at 300°F. until tender—3–4 hours. Serves 4.

Herbed Tongue

    1 fresh beef tongue, 3–4 pounds
    2 stalks celery, sliced
    2 carrots, sliced
    1 medium onion, sliced
    3 bay leaves
    1 tablespoon mixed pickling spice
    1 clove garlic, cut
    1 tablespoon salt
    2 peppercorns
10–12 cups hot water

Scrub tongue thoroughly. Put in pan with vegetables and seasonings; pour hot water over. Cover tightly, and simmer slowly until tender, about 60 minutes per pound. Tongue is done when it can be readily pierced with fork and the skin comes off easily. Lift out tongue, and while still hot, remove skin and any ragged glands, gristle, fat and bones from root end. Serve hot with suitable sauce, or allow to cool thoroughly and serve sliced in sandwiches or accompanied by other cold meats and salad. Serves 4–6.

VARIATION:

- Substitute 1 pickled for fresh tongue, and soak in cold water at least 2 hours before cooking. Omit salt, and cook about 45 minutes per pound.

Poultry. *Poultry, always available, is a year-round favorite.*

Because it is rich in protein, minerals and vitamins, poultry is an ideal alternate for animal meats and as a main course often costs considerably less. When buying ready-to-cook whole chicken or turkey, look for a tag indicating "U.S. Insp'd & P's'd" and the grade mark (see Chapter 1 for explanation of poultry grading).

Turkey

Before buying, estimate your special requirements. For each serving of roast turkey, you will need 1/2 pound very large turkey, or 1 pound small turkey. When making stuffing, allow 3/4 cup for every pound of turkey's weight.

Estimate your oven capacity as well. A huge king-size bird that crowds an oven, blocking heat circulation, will require extra cooking time. Unless you are preparing for a big occasion with guests, you would be better advised to choose a smaller bird. The recently developed 6–8 pound turkey, plump and delicate in flavor, is ideal for average family use the year round, and there is no long-drawn-out leftover problem.

Turkey can be cooked by methods used for chicken: simmered or stewed, oven-broiled or fried in covered skillet on top of stove. Have turkey cut up—in most cases it is an advantage to cut it into serving-size pieces, which will reduce total cooking time necessary to bring meat to perfect tenderness.

Chicken

This familiar term now covers a sizable group of fowl, most bred and finished for special culinary use. Rock Cornish hens are tiny birds, averaging 1 pound and never more than 2 pounds. They may be roasted or broiled, and a larger bird makes 2 servings. Broiler-fryer chickens, 1 1/2–3 1/2 pounds, are excellent for roasting, broiling or frying; allow 1/4–1/2 bird per serving. With roasters (more than 3 1/2 pounds) and capons—the plump, desexed males, weighing as much as 8 pounds—stuffing and roasting or oven-frying is the ideal treatment. Allow 3/4 pound per serving. Stewing fowl is the market name for laying hens; they must be cooked in moist heat as in stewing, to make them tender. The weight of stewing fowl varies from 2 1/2–6 pounds, 1/2–3/4 pound is about right for each serving.

Cut-up chicken is readily available and offers many advantages. You may purchase legs, breasts or wings separately, according to your family's tastes or your preferred method of preparation: frying, oven-frying, braising, fricasseeing and so on.

Ducks and Geese

These birds are quite different from chickens and turkeys. Their meat is dark, they have distinctive flavors not unlike those of wild game and they have high proportions of fat. Always look for a duck or a goose that is not too fat. Estimate at least 3/4–1 pound per serving.

Ducklings are young ducks, 8–12 weeks old and weighing up to 5 pounds. Geese vary from 4–14 pounds. As their meat is tender and delicate, these birds may be roasted or cut up and broiled.

Because ducks and geese contain so much fat themselves, fat is never applied to them when roasting. Boiling water is sometimes used to "baste" a fat bird, or fruit juices to counteract richness and add flavor. A well-seasoned bread stuffing may be used. Or stuff cavity with sliced apple, onion, celery bits and poultry seasoning. Discard apple stuffing before serving, as bird will have absorbed flavors during cooking.

It is unwise to keep fresh poultry, even under refrigeration, longer than 1–2 days before cooking. Loosen wrappings, and store in coldest part of refrigerator. If you do not plan to cook it within the next 2 days, freeze it. Giblets should be washed and cooked immediately or wrapped in a separate package and frozen.

To Freeze, tie wings and legs close to body. Wrap in freezer paper, aluminum foil or plastic wrap. If using plastic bag, put bird in bag, and submerge 3/4 of it in pan of warm water. The water will collapse bag firmly around bird and expel air. Twist top of bag, and close tightly over bird. Mark with weight and date. Stored at 0°F., turkey should be used within 6 months; whole chicken or stewing fowl within 12 months at the most.

Never freeze home-stuffed poultry, either before or after cooking, as it carries the risk of food poisoning. The heat to be applied later cannot penetrate quickly enough to the center of the chilled dressing to ensure that possibly harmful food organisms are destroyed. (Commercially stuffed and frozen raw birds are protected by "stabilizers" in their preparation. Simply follow instructions on the package.)

Home-prepared poultry should be stuffed just before cooking. If you prepare stuffing ahead, store it in shallow pan, covered, in refrigerator until ready to use.

Frozen poultry must be thawed before cooking. Do not remove freezer wrap. Allow 5 hours per pound when thawing in refrigerator. For speedier thawing, place bird in cold water in sink or big kettle. Change water frequently. Room-temperature thawing requires about 1 1/2 hours per pound—less if cool air from electric fan is directed on bird while thawing.

Note: Certain frozen poultry purchased stuffed "ready for the oven" should be roasted *unthawed* as indicated on package.

Cooking

Most poultry on the market today is ready to cook, but if the bird has not been drawn (entrails removed), here is the procedure.

Place bird on its back. Make an incision through skin along line from end of keel to vent. Do not cut vent. Lift out intestines located at left side of bird, but do not detach. Place left forefinger under intestines close to vent. Make incision around vent so that entrails (intestines, gizzard, heart, lungs, liver, kidneys, crop and windpipe) may be removed intact. Grasp gizzard, located at right side and to rear of body cavity, and remove. All entrails must be completely removed, including red, spongy lung bits adhering to ribs. Detach giblets (heart, liver and gizzard) from entrails.

Remove any pinfeathers with tweezers. The oil sac (a small nodule under skin at back of bird, close to tail) should be cut out. It will produce a strong flavor if left in.

Ask your butcher to remove leg tendons on large birds like turkeys.

If necessary, singe off hairs by rotating bird over flame. Wash outside of bird thoroughly. Rinse body cavity with plenty of cold water. Drain well. Dry with soft cloth. Sprinkle cavity with salt, and fill lightly with stuffing. Allow room for expansion during cooking; otherwise stuffing may become soggy. To close slit, use poultry pins, and lace with cord—or sew with darning needle and coarse white thread.

Because a cooked bird looks better and is moister if legs and wings are kept close to body, poultry should always be trussed after dressing.

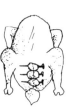

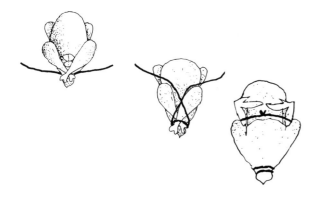

WEIGHT IN POUNDS**	APPROXIMATE TIMES†
4–8	3–4 1/2 hours
6–12	3 1/2–5 hours
12–16	5–6 hours
16–20	6–7 1/2 hours
20–24	7 1/2–9 hours

*Oven temperature 325°F.
**For eviscerated, ready-to-cook birds.
†For stuffed birds; shorter times apply to smaller weights.

Before putting bird in oven, insert meat thermometer into inside thigh muscle (thermometer must not touch bone). Cook until reading is 185°F. If thermometer is inserted through center of bird, having tip surrounded by stuffing, reading should be 165°F.

If you do not have a thermometer, make the drumstick test. If the bird is properly done, the leg will move freely at the hip socket, and the meat will feel soft.

Follow timetable for each kind of fowl for approximate cooking periods. Remember that size and shape of uncooked bird influences length of time necessary to roast it.

Keep cooked bird in warm place 10 minutes before carving to allow juices to be absorbed, so that meat will stay moist and carving will be easier.

Roast Turkey

Sprinkle body cavity with salt. Lightly fill both neck and body cavities with dressing; do not pack. Truss. Place bird on rack in shallow pan, breast side up. Dip double thickness of cheesecloth into pan of melted fat; place cloth on top of turkey. Or brush bird generously with fat, and cover loosely with aluminum foil, putting the shiny surface next to the skin to reflect the heat. Have extra melted fat ready for occasional remoistening of cloth or for basting. Always remember that tender, succulent roast turkey is the result of a steady, moderate temperature. If heat is too high, meat will dry out and skin will scorch and blister. If oven door is opened frequently, cooking temperature will drop, with risk of underdone turkey.

Roasting in aluminum foil shortens total cooking time by about 1/2 hour for birds up to 12 pounds and by about 1 hour for larger turkeys. The prepared bird is laid on the *shiny* side of well-greased heavy-duty foil, which is then folded around bird, completely enclosing it. It is not sealed airtight. Oven temperature is 450°F. Foil should be opened for last 1/2 hour to brown bird.

Roast Half-turkey

Tie leg to tail, and skewer wing flat against body. Place, skin side up, on rack in roasting pan. Completely cover with cheesecloth dipped in melted fat, or rub bird with fat and cover loosely with foil. Roast at 325°F., allowing 3 1/2–4 hours for 5–8 pounds. Dressing may be cooked under bird if foil is placed over rack; or bake it separately in greased casserole.

Broiled Half-turkey

Have 4–6 pound turkey split in half by butcher. Wipe clean. Skewer wing close to side. Rub skin with lemon, oil, salt and melted fat. Place, skin side down, in pan without rack. Broil 8–10 inches from heat about 40 minutes or until nicely browned. Turn skin side up, and baste with pan drippings. Broil until brown and done, about 40 minutes longer.

Broiled Chicken Halves

Have butcher split in half lengthwise a tender young chicken—2 1/2 pounds or less. Fold wing tip back onto cut side, exposing thick breast area. Place in broiler pan without rack. Brush all chicken surfaces with melted fat, and season with salt and pepper. Arrange skin side down, place pan under broiler 6–9 inches directly below heat source. Let halves cook slowly; they should just begin to brown lightly after 10 minutes. Turn halves skin side up for even broiling; brush with fat several times. Test for doneness after 20 minutes or so, when drumstick should twist out of thigh joint readily. Serve pan drippings over chicken.

Fried Chicken

    1/2 cup flour
      2 teaspoons paprika
 1 1/2 teaspoons salt
    1/4 teaspoon pepper
      4 pounds chicken pieces (legs, wings, breasts and so
        forth)
Fat

Mix flour with seasonings, and put in paper bag. Add chicken pieces, a few at a time, and shake to coat. Save remaining flour for gravy. Heat fat in heavy frying pan—enough for at least 1/4 inch depth. Fat is at right temperature when a drop of water sizzles in it. Put in thickest chicken pieces first, turning frequently until evenly and lightly browned; continue till all pieces are nicely browned—15–20 minutes. Cover pan tightly, and cook until meat is tender—20–25 minutes longer. For crispy coating, uncover pan for last 10 minutes of cooking, and turn pieces once. Serves 8.

Note: Other seasonings may be used as desired: thyme, oregano, garlic powder, rosemary, ginger or curry powder.

VARIATIONS:

Oven-fried Chicken: After browning in frying pan, remove to shallow roasting pan. Melt 1/4 cup butter or margarine, and spoon over chicken. Bake uncovered at 350°F. 30–40 minutes, turning pieces once for even crisping.

Deep-fried Chicken: Use deep fryer or pot, and heat 2–3 inches of fat to about 350°F. Place some of chicken in frying basket, leaving space between pieces. Immerse in fat and fry at about 325°F. until golden brown on all sides and tender—about 15 minutes. Lift out, and drain on crumpled paper towels in warm oven. Continue until all pieces are cooked; hold fat at steady temperature throughout.

Crumb-coated Fried Chicken: For thicker, richer coating dip flour-coated chicken pieces in mixture of 2 teaspoons water to 1 beaten egg and roll in fine bread or cornflake crumbs. Cover pieces completely, and allow to set a few minutes before frying by any of the methods outlined.

Chicken Fricassee

        1 4-pound stewing fowl, whole or cut up
        2 teaspoons salt
        2 peppercorns
        1 stalk celery
        1 onion
        1 carrot
        1 bay leaf
    Boiling water
        2 tablespoons flour
    1/4 cup water

Wash chicken thoroughly inside and out. Place with spices and vegetables in deep kettle; barely cover with boiling water. Cover tightly, and simmer 2–3 hours or until meat is tender. Lift out chicken. Strain stock. Measure 3 cups for gravy,

and set remainder aside to cool quickly (it makes an excellent soup for next day). Blend flour and 1/4 cup water to smooth paste. Thicken 3 cups stock with paste. Cook 5 minutes, adding extra seasoning to taste. If fowl is cooked whole, cut into serving pieces, arrange on platter, and pour gravy over. Serve with hot fluffy rice. Serves 4–5.

TIMETABLE FOR ROASTING CHICKEN*

WEIGHT IN POUNDS**	APPROXIMATE TIME†	
1 1/2–2 1/2	1 1/4–2	hours
2 1/2–3 1/2	2–3	hours
3 1/2–4 3/4	3–3 1/2	hours
4 3/4–6	3 1/2–4	hours

*Oven temperature 325°F.
**For eviscerated, ready-to-cook birds.
†For stuffed birds; shorter times apply to smaller weights.

Roast Goose

Have your butcher draw goose. Make sure oil sac at base of tail is removed. Pull out pinfeathers and singe to remove any down. Check body cavity for bits of lung and so forth. Wash very thoroughly inside and out under cold running water. If bird is very fat, wash in cold water to which a little baking soda has been added; then rinse in clear water. Dry thoroughly. Rub body cavity with salt. Stuff bird with highly seasoned bread dressing, to which chopped raw apple may be added if desired. Skewer or sew up vent; truss. If goose is very fat, prick through skin into fat around legs and wings to encourage fat to drain off during cooking. Rub salt over skin. Place bird, breast side up, on rack in roaster. If using meat thermometer, insert in breast to rest in stuffing. Add 1 cup boiling water, and cover pan tightly (if roaster has no lid, use heavy aluminum foil, shiny side down). Roast at 325°F. 1 hour. Pour all liquid from pan, and continue roasting, uncovered, until done. A little apple juice makes a flavorful addition to pan juices for basting during last cooking period. A 5–7 pound goose (eviscerated weight) will take approximately 3–4 hours. The meat thermometer should register 165°F. when bird is done.

Roast Duckling

        4–5 pound drawn duckling
        1 small orange, quartered
    Juice of 1/2 lemon
    1/2 teaspoon salt
    1/2 cup ginger ale
    1/4 cup sherry

Wipe duckling inside and out with damp cloth. Fill cavity with orange quarters. Roast, breast side up, uncovered, 3/4 hour at 375°F. Drain off all fat. Sprinkle with lemon juice and salt. Add ginger ale and sherry. Cover pan, and reduce heat to 325°F. Continue roasting 1 1/2 hours or until drumstick separates easily from thigh bone. Baste several times during roasting. Make gravy of pan drippings. Serves 4.

Cooking Wild Game. *Each type of game has its own characteristics and requires specific handling in the kitchen.*

Venison

Venison is the flesh of deer. A young animal, which has not run too much, will be tender, with delicate, fine-grained meat. An older animal may be rather tough and should be cooked with moist heat.

Venison cuts are similar to those of mutton. The fat is similar too, in that it is hard and must be served piping hot to be palatable. The leg, rump, saddle and loin are the best cuts for roasts, steaks and cutlets. The less tender flank, shank and neck portions should be stewed. Tender venison cuts suitable for broiling and roasting may be served rare . . . "the blood follows the knife," as the saying goes.

Marinating venison will make it moist and tasty but won't, as is sometimes thought, counteract the strong, gamey flavor. This taste comes from the fat; therefore as much fat as possible should be cut away before cooking.

During cooking period, replace natural fat with mild-flavored lard, shortening or bacon fat, so that meat will not dry out but will stay moist and juicy. Never try to disguise the flavor of venison with strong herbs and spices. Properly cooked venison has a good natural flavor that is adequately highlighted and complimented by salt, freshly ground pepper and monosodium glutamate.

Larding is a process for introducing fat directly into meat to increase tenderness and flavor. Cut meat with sharp knife or steel larding needle, making gashes deep enough to hold strips of bacon fat or fat pork. Close gashes by tying roast in several places with twine. When venison roast is larded, it is not necessary to add any other fat during cooking period.

Wild Fowl

Partridge are small, tender birds; they may be broiled or roasted and served with wild rice or mushrooms. One partridge may serve 2 people. Allow about 1 pound, drawn weight, for each serving. Partridge should be prepared in the same way as chicken (see poultry section in this chapter for directions for how to clean, draw and singe).

The delicious tender meat of edible wild ducks —canvasback, mallard, teal, redhead and black duck—may be roasted to your own taste, rare or well done. If you prefer it rare, use shorter cooking period; increase time if you prefer it well done.

Rabbit

Rabbits generally have tender meat that tastes best when broiled, fried, fricasseed or roasted. Before cooking, soak rabbit overnight or at least several hours in marinade or in salt water, vinegar and water. During cooking period, add fat for browning or basting, as very little natural fat remains after rabbit has been skinned.

Rabbits have small waxy scent glands that must be removed before cooking. They are located under the forelegs and on either side of the spine, in the small of the back and between the shoulders. If these glands have not been removed beforehand, be sure to lift them out, taking care not to cut them.

Venison Loin Roast

    1 3–4 pound deer loin
    1/4 pound fat, suet or pork fat
    Salt and pepper to taste
    1 cup red currant jelly
    1/2 cup water
    2 medium onions, quartered

Wipe roast with damp paper towel or clean damp cloth. Trim off all fat. Place on rack in shallow roasting pan, skin side up. Cut suet in pieces, and lay on top of roast. Roast in 325°F. oven 1/2 hour. Season with salt and pepper. Add other ingredients to pan. Continue roasting until done, about 1 hour longer. Baste every 15 minutes. Allow 20–25 minutes per pound roasting time. Do not overcook venison. Serves 6–8.

Note: The saddle roast may also be prepared in this way.

Roast Leg of Venison

    1 4-pound venison leg roast
    4 cups cold water
    1 cup tomato juice
    1 cup sliced celery
    1/2 cup wine vinegar or red wine
    1/4 cup sugar
    2 bay leaves
    2 cloves garlic, crushed
    1/4 lemon, sliced
    1/2 teaspoon salt

Wipe roast, and place in bowl. Make marinade of next 9 ingredients and pour over. Marinade should come at least halfway up roast. Cover bowl, and place in refrigerator. Turn roast frequently. Allow roast to soak in marinade 1–2 days. Before roasting, drain and dry roast, put on rack in open pan; then proceed as for VENISON LOIN ROAST, using marinade for basting.

Note: The leg roast is better if it is marinated before roasting; the marinade makes it moist and flavorful.

To broil venison steaks or to make stew with flank, neck or shank, follow any recipe for similar cooking methods with beef, remembering to trim away as much fat as possible before cooking and to replace natural fat with other milder fat for cooking.

Broiled Partridge

    1 2 1/2-pound partridge
    2 tablespoons soft butter or margarine
    Salt and pepper to taste

Singe, draw and clean partridge. Wash inside and out. Dry. Split, allowing 1/2 bird per serving. Rub outside well with soft butter or margarine. Place on broiler rack, skin side down, and broil 15–20 minutes. Season with salt and pepper; turn halfway through cooking. Serves 2.

Roast Partridge

    1 2 1/2-pound partridge
    1 tablespoon lemon juice
    4 strips bacon

Singe, draw and clean partridge. Wash inside and out. Dry. Rub with lemon juice. Push legs toward breast, and secure with skewer pushed through middle of bird. Cover with strips of bacon. Roast, uncovered, at 325°F. 50–60 minutes or until tender. Baste several times during roasting. Serve with red currant jelly. Serves 2.

Note: Two tablespoons brandy, heated and set afire, may be poured over roast on platter at serving time, for distinctive flavor.

Roast Wild Duck

    1 wild duck
    1/4 cup olive oil
    1/2 teaspoon salt
    1/8 teaspoon pepper
    1 apple, peeled and sliced
    3 strips bacon

Singe, draw and clean, wash inside and outside thoroughly. Dry. Combine olive oil, salt and pepper, and rub bird all over with mixture. Insert apple in cavity, and place bird, breast side up, on rack in open shallow pan. Arrange bacon strips over breast, securing with toothpicks if necessary. Roast bird 50–60 minutes at 325°F., basting several times during cooking. Good accompaniments for wild duck are candied sweet potatoes and apple-celery salad with sliced-orange garnish.

Note: Allow 1 pound wild duck, drawn weight, per serving.

Fried Rabbit

    1 1 1/2-pound drawn rabbit
    1 1/2 cups cold water
    1/4 cup cider vinegar
    1 clove garlic, halved
    1 teaspoon salt
    1/8 teaspoon pepper
    1/3 cup flour
    1/2 teaspoon salt
    1/4 cup fat or bacon drippings
    2 tablespoons flour
    1 cup milk or light cream
    1 teaspoon grated onion
    Salt and pepper to taste

Clean rabbit, and remove scent glands; if any shot parts remain, cut out with sharp pointed knife. Wash thoroughly inside and out under cold water. Cut into serving pieces, and place in bowl. Make marinade by combining next 5 ingredients. Pour over rabbit, cover and soak several hours in refrigerator. Remove rabbit, drain and pat dry with paper towel. Combine 1/3 cup flour and 1/2 teaspoon salt; use to coat meat surfaces. Melt fat in heavy frying pan over moderate heat; add rabbit pieces, brown on all sides, cover and cook over slightly reduced heat. Turn occasionally, and cook until tender, about 1 1/4 hours. Remove meat to platter, and keep warm. Add 2 tablespoons flour to remaining fat in skillet; mix thoroughly. Then stir in milk to make smooth sauce; simmer 5 minutes. Add grated onion and extra seasoning to taste. Serve very hot with cooked rabbit. Serves 3–4.

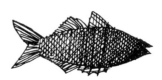

Use Fish for Variety. *Fish is a protein food, rich in important nutrients and an excellent alternative to meat.*

Fat fish and fish livers provide abundant supplies of essential vitamins A and D. For nutrition, variety and economy, include fish often in your menus. Learn interesting new ways to use the various forms so readily available—fresh, frozen, dried, canned.

How to Select Fish

The flesh of fresh fish should always be firm and should adhere firmly to bone. The odor should be distinctly fresh and mild. Fresh fish is marketed in a number of ways. "Whole, round" means fish are exactly as they came from the water. The eyes should be clear, the gills bright

red and the skin shiny with tightly clinging scales. Allow 1 pound per serving. "Dressed or pan-dressed fish" are fish with scales and entrails removed and usually also with head, tail and fins removed. Allow 1/2 pound per serving. "Drawn" is applied to whole fish with only entrails removed. "Steaks" are ready-to-cook cross-sectional slices of large fish, which may also be divided by cutting through backbone. Allow 1/3–1/2 pound per serving. "Fillets" are ready-to-cook sides of fish cut lengthwise from backbone. They are practically boneless. Allow 1/4–1/3 pound per serving.

Frozen fish should be solidly frozen with no discoloration in the flesh. There should be no air between fish and moisture-vapor proof wrappings; the presence of air indicates long storage or poor condition. Frozen fish is usually sold in fillets, in individually wrapped packages or 1-pound cartons. Frozen whole fish is seldom wrapped but is coated with a glaze that prevents discoloration.

Smoked and dried fish include cod, haddock, salmon, sturgeon, herring, eels and whitefish. Dried salt fish has a distinctive flavor; and, although the salting process delays spoiling for a time, it does not preserve fish indefinitely.

Many kinds of fish can be bought canned. Some may be bought in several qualities, each priced accordingly. For instance, the price of canned salmon is determined largely by its color. Red sockeye is the choicest and the highest-priced; the pinks, ranging from cohoe to the palest chum, cost less on a diminishing scale. Tuna is also sold in several varieties. "White tuna meat" costs more than the darker type. Tuna flakes are cheaper than are the solid-pack cans and are a sensible buy for sandwich spreads or casseroles.

Fresh fish is very perishable, and should be refrigerated or frozen as soon as possible after purchase. Wipe thoroughly with clean damp cloth. Wrap loosely in waxed paper, and place in tightly covered container to prevent odor from spreading; then refrigerate. If fish is whole, clean and scale it before storing.

Frozen fish should ideally be kept solidly frozen at a constant temperature of 0°F. This low temperature is difficult to maintain in home freezer units, and it is therefore wise to use frozen fish within a reasonably short period. Once fish thaws, it must be treated as fresh fish and cooked immediately. *Never refreeze fish.*

Smoked fish should be handled and stored in the same way as fresh fish, as the smoking process is not sufficient to preserve it.

Freshly caught fish may be stored whole, filleted or in steaks in the home freezer. Eviscerate and thoroughly wash fish as soon as possible after taking from the water. If unable to freeze immediately, pack carefully in ice, and refrigerate. Before freezing, rinse well in cold salt water (2/3 cup salt to 1 gallon water). Then wrap airtight in heavy moisture-vapor proof wrap or aluminum foil, and place in freezer. Use within a few weeks.

Fish has little connective tissue; it should be cooked quickly at moderate temperature, just until translucent flesh becomes opaque. Cooked fish should flake easily. If overcooked, it falls apart.

There are 4 basic methods for cooking fish—frying or broiling with a little added fat; baking; poaching in liquid (or steaming over water), and deep frying.

Basic Cooking Methods

1. *To Fry*: This method is particularly good for small whole fish, steaks, or fillets. Cut into serving pieces and coat with seasoned flour or bread crumbs (partially thaw frozen fish for easier handling). Heat fat in heavy pan. Fry fish quickly on 1 side; turn and fry on other. Fish should flake easily with fork.

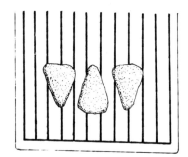

To Broil: Sprinkle with salt and pepper. Place on greased broiler rack 2–3 inches from heat, and brush with melted fat (place frozen fish farther from heat to prevent burning before it is cooked through). Broil 5–10 minutes, depending on thickness. Turn and broil until fish flakes easily with fork.

2. *To Bake*: Cut 2 pounds fish fillets into serving portions. Season on both sides or bread by dipping in 1/2 cup milk to which 1 teaspoon salt has been added, then rolling in fine bread crumbs. Place in greased baking dish and dot with butter or margarine. Bake in moderate oven, 350°F. 20–30 minutes or until fish flakes easily with fork. Remove at once, and serve.

To bake whole fish; prepare fish as for fillets, and stuff loosely with dressing, using string to tie fish in shape. Place in greased pan and brush with fat or oil. Bake in moderate oven, 350°F. 10–15 minutes per pound or until fish flakes easily with fork. (Fish may also be baked in greased aluminum foil, which should be folded tightly over it, so that steam cannot escape. Add 5 minutes to cooking time to allow heat to penetrate foil.)

3. *To Poach*: Poaching is a good method for whole fish or fillets to be used in salads, fish cakes, casseroles or creamed dishes. Place on greased, double-thickness, heavy aluminum foil; season with salt, pepper, chopped celery, chopped onion. Fold over, and secure open edges with double fold to make watertight. Place in rapidly boiling water. When water returns to boiling, cover pan, and cook 5–10 minutes or until fish flakes with fork. Also see court-bouillon method, page 77.

4. *Deep frying*: This method requires a deep pan, allowing at least 3 inches between boiling fat and rim. Allow 1 quart salad oil for 3-quart kettle. Heat fat to 375°F. Always thaw frozen fish before deep frying. Cut fish into uniform serving pieces, season and dip in batter. Lower gently in frying basket, or carefully use egg lifter or kitchen tongs. Fry until golden brown. Drain on paper towel.

Deep-fried Fillets in Pancake Mix

Use your favorite packaged pancake mix, and make batter according to manufacturer's directions. Use slightly more liquid than specified and if you like a very crisp coating, substitute water for milk. Frying kettle should be 1/2 full of fat heated to 375°F., at which point a small cube of bread will brown in 60 seconds. Cut fish fillets into uniform pieces no more than 1/2 inch thick, sprinkle with salt, coat in batter and lower carefully into hot fat to avoid dangerous splashing. A frying basket is useful, but do not crowd it. Fry until golden brown, 5–7 minutes. Drain on paper towels; keep warm while remaining fillets are cooking. Frying a few pieces at a time permits fat to retain its hot frying temperature.

Homemade Batter for Fried Fish

        1 1/2 cups all-purpose flour
          3 teaspoons baking powder
          1 teaspoon salt
          1 cup milk
          2 eggs, well beaten

Mix and sift dry ingredients. Add milk to eggs. Pour liquid into dry mixture, and beat until smooth. Dip fish pieces into this mixture and fry in deep fat until golden brown.

Fried Smelts

          2 pounds smelts
          2 eggs, beaten
          2 tablespoons milk
          1 teaspoon salt
        1/2 cup flour
        1/2 cup fine cracker crumbs
        Hot fat

Cut off heads and tails of smelts; eviscerate fish, and wash thoroughly inside and out. Drain

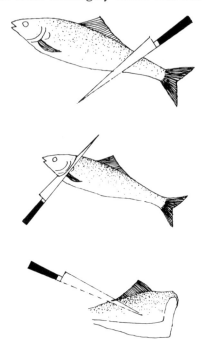

on paper towels and pat as dry as possible. Combine egg, milk and salt. Mix flour and crumbs together. Dip fish in liquid, then in dry mixture. Have about 1/4-inch depth of hot fat in frying pan. Fry smelts quickly on 1 side; turn, and brown on other side. Cooking time should be about 10 minutes per inch of thickness. Serves 4–5.

Broiled Salmon Steaks

```
    2 pounds salmon steaks, 1 inch thick
1/4 cup butter or margarine
1/2 teaspoon salt
1/8 teaspoon pepper
```

Wipe fish with clean, damp cloth. Melt butter or margarine. Preheat broiler. Place steaks on greased broiler pan. Brush with melted butter or margarine and position 2–4 inches from heat. When top side is browned, sprinkle with 1/4 teaspoon salt and dash pepper; turn with lifter, brush with melted butter and complete broiling and seasoning. Steaks should be done in about 10 minutes. Serves 4.

Note: Any fish fillet or steak may be prepared as above. A piece 3/4–1 inch thick is ideal for broiling, as it is sufficiently thick to retain moisture. Another easy way, especially when it comes to turning, is to use an old-fashioned wire toaster with handle. Lay it over broiler pan; when fish is browned on one side, turn toaster, protecting hand with oven mitt. In broiling unthawed frozen fish, it is best to place it farther from heat source and to double cooking time.

Baked Fillets in Lemon Butter

```
    2 pounds fish fillets, fresh or thawed
1/4 cup melted butter or margarine
    2 tablespoons lemon juice
    2 tablespoons chopped parsley
1/2 teaspoon salt
1/8 teaspoon pepper
```

Grease shallow baking dish and arrange single layer of fillets in it. Combine remaining ingredients and pour over fish. Place in 450°F. oven, and allow 10 minutes' cooking time per 1-inch thickness of fillets. You will know fish is done when it becomes opaque, flakes readily and can be easily pierced with a fork. Serves 6.

Baked Fillets with Cream

```
    2 pounds fish fillets
    2 tablespoons butter or margarine
3/4 cup chopped onion
    1 tablespoon flour
    1 teaspoon salt
1/8 teaspoon pepper
    1 cup light cream
Paprika to taste
Curls lemon rind
```

Cut fillets into uniform pieces suitable for serving. Arrange in greased baking dish. Melt butter or margarine in saucepan and sauté onion gently until tender but not browned. Add flour, salt and pepper; blend. Then stir in cream slowly. Simmer sauce until smooth; pour over fish. Sprinkle top with paprika. Bake in 350°F. oven 30 minutes or until fish is cooked. Garnish with curls of lemon rind. Serves 6.

Note: Fillets and steaks and solid chunks may also be boiled or baked odorlessly in double-thickness, heavy aluminum foil, in which case seasonings are wrapped with fish. Sprinkle fish with salt and place on sheet of dampened parchment or greased foil. Estimate thickness of fish. Add a little chopped onion, parsley and celery. Wrap securely, preferably in pouch fashion and tie with string to make watertight. Place parcel in rapidly boiling water, and cover. Time cooking period after water returns to boiling point. Allow 10 minutes per inch thickness for fresh fish; double the amount for unthawed frozen fish. The parcels are ready to serve and there is no pan to clean.

Poached Fish

```
    2 pounds fillets or 1 solid piece fish (salmon, halibut
        or cod)
    5 cups boiling water
1/2 cup vinegar
1/4 cup sliced onion
    1 tablespoon salt
    1 stalk celery
    1 bay leaf
    2 or 3 peppercorns
```

Tie fillets in double thickness of clean cheesecloth. Prepare court bouillon by boiling remaining ingredients 10 minutes. Drop in fish, cover and, when liquid bubbles again, reduce heat to simmer. Cook about 10 minutes per inch thickness. Test fish for doneness; when it flakes easily with toothpick, remove it at once. Double the time for unthawed frozen fish. Serves 6.

Poached Trout in White Wine Sauce

```
    3 (10-ounce) packages frozen trout (6 trout)
    1 teaspoon salt
1/2 teaspoon pepper
    2 cups white wine
1/2 cup thin onion rings
1/4 cup parsley sprigs
    1 or 2 cloves garlic, slivered
    2 bay leaves
    2 sticks celery, sliced
1/8 teaspoon thyme
    1 (2-ounce) package white-sauce mix
    2 egg yolks
```

Butter a large, shallow pan. Arrange frozen trout evenly in pan. Sprinkle with salt and pepper. Mix together white wine, onion rings, parsley, garlic, bay leaves, celery, and thyme. Pour white wine sauce over fish.

Bake at 350°F. 20–25 minutes or until fish is tender when tested with fork. Spoon juices over fish 2 or 3 times during baking.

Lift fish with slotted spoon or spatula. Arrange on large warmed serving platter. Cover with foil. Keep warm.

Strain fish broth. Measure 1 1/2 cupfuls into medium saucepan. Add white-sauce mix. Bring to boil over medium heat, stirring constantly. Remove from heat. Beat 2 egg yolks. Add a little of the sauce to egg yolks and then turn mixture into the sauce and beat again. Makes about 2 cups sauce. Serve sauce with fish. Serves 6.

Crunchy Baked Haddock

        1 pound fresh or frozen haddock fillets
        1 egg, slightly beaten
        3 tablespoons Worcestershire sauce
        1 cup crushed cereal crumbs
        1 tablespoon butter or margarine, melted
        2 cups CURRIED CREAM SAUCE

Cut fish into 5 or 6 pieces. Combine egg and Worcestershire sauce, and dip fish in mixture. Coat with crumbs; then dip again in egg mixture and again in crumbs. Place in greased dish and drizzle with melted butter or margarine. Bake at 450°F. 15–20 minutes. Serve with cream sauce, quickly cooked spinach garnished with hard-cooked egg slices and fluffy whipped potatoes. Serves 4.

Curried Cream Sauce

        Salt and pepper to taste
        1 tablespoon curry powder
        2 cups medium cream sauce

Add seasoning and curry powder to cream sauce.

Finnan Haddie Poached in Milk

        1 cup milk
        2 pounds smoked haddock fillets
        1 tablespoon butter or margarine
        Pepper to taste

Heat milk in saucepan, add fillets and allow to simmer until fish flakes readily at touch of fork. Transfer fillets to serving platter and dot with butter or margarine and pepper. Serves 6.

Note: Cooking milk can be thickened with flour and butter rubbed together and served as sauce.

Cod with Tomatoes

        2 tablespoons butter or margarine
        1 carrot, sliced
        1 stalk celery, thinly sliced
        1 small onion, thinly sliced
        1 (10 1/2-ounce) can tomato soup
        2 tablespoons water
        1 pound frozen cod fillets
        1/2 cup buttered bread crumbs
        1/2 cup grated cheese

Melt butter or margarine in small saucepan, and add carrot, celery and onion. Sauté 2 minutes; cover, and cook 3 minutes. Add soup and water. Arrange fillets in greased baking dish, cover with vegetable mixture. Sprinkle with bread crumbs and cheese. Bake in hot oven, 400°F., about 15 minutes. Serves 4.

Cod Soufflé

        1/2 pound salt cod
        Cold water
        4 slices bacon, diced
        2/3 cup chopped onion
        1/4 cup diced green pepper
        1/4 cup chopped pimento
        1 tablespoon flour
    1 1/4 cups milk
        1/4 teaspoon thyme
        1/4 teaspoon pepper
        2 eggs, separated

The salt cod should first be freshened by soaking overnight in cold water to cover. Drain, and put in pan with fresh water to cover. Place over low heat, and bring to simmer. Drain. Fish should now be ready to use, but if still too salty, repeat simmering procedure, and drain. Flake fish. Fry bacon bits till crisp; lift out and gently cook next 3 ingredients in bacon fat. Sprinkle flour over vegetables, and add 1 cup milk gradually, stirring and cooking until thickened. Add flaked fish, bacon and seasonings. Beat egg yolks and 1/4 cup milk, add carefully to mixture and cook gently 2–3 minutes. Beat egg whites until stiff but not dry, and fold into hot mixture. Turn into greased baking dish, and bake at 350°F. about 20 minutes or until soufflé is high, firm and lightly browned. Serves 4–5.

Salmon Puff

        1 envelope (4 serving size) instant potatoes
        1 (8-ounce) can red salmon
        2 eggs, separated
        2 tablespoons mayonnaise
    1–2 tablespoons chopped parsley
        1/2 teaspoon salt
        1/2 teaspoon grated lemon rind
        1 (10 1/2-ounce) can tomato soup
        1/4 cup tomato juice
        2 tablespoons sherry

Prepare instant potatoes according to directions. Discard skin from salmon and add salmon and juice from can to potatoes. Mix egg yolks with mayonnaise, and stir into potatoes. Add parsley, salt and lemon rind. Stiffly beat egg whites, fold into potatoes and spread in greased baking dish. Bake in a pan of water at 375°F. 30 minutes or until set and puffed. Heat soup, tomato juice and sherry together; spoon over salmon puff. Serves 6.

Mushroom–Tuna Soufflé

> 3 eggs, separated
> 1 (7-ounce) can flaked tuna, drained
> 1 tablespoon lemon juice
> 1 (10 1/2-ounce) can mushroom soup

Beat egg yolks until thick, and stir in drained tuna, lemon juice and soup. Stiffly beat egg whites, and fold into tuna mixture and scrape into buttered 1 1/2-quart baking dish. Bake at 325°F. 35–45 minutes or until center is set. Serves 4–6.

Salmon Loaf

> 2 (7-ounce) cans salmon
> 3/4 cup (approximately) milk
> 1 1/2 cups soft bread crumbs
> 2 tablespoons chopped sweet pickle
> 2 teaspoons lemon juice
> 1 teaspoon salt
> 1/4 teaspoon pepper
> 1 egg, slightly beaten

Drain salmon, reserving liquid. Add sufficient milk to liquid to make 1 cup in all. Remove skin, and flake salmon, mashing bones. Combine all ingredients well and turn mixture into small greased loaf pan. Bake at 375°F. 1/2 hour or until loaf is nicely browned with crust on top. Serve hot with suitable sauce—egg, parsley or cucumber, for example. Loaf is also delicious chilled, sliced and served with potato salad or in sandwiches. Serves 4–5.

Note: Finely chopped onion may be substituted for sweet pickle for a slightly different flavor.

30-Minute Baked Fish Dinner

> 1 1/2–2 pounds frozen halibut
> 1/4 cup evaporated milk
> 3 tablespoons bottled dark steak sauce
> 3/4 cup crushed crackers
> 6 small unpeeled potatoes, quartered
> 1/4 cup salad oil
> Salt to taste
> 2 (10-ounce) packages frozen mixed vegetables
> 1/4 cup butter or margarine
> 1 1/2 cups MUSTARD SAUCE

Preheat oven to 425°F. Spread halibut in foil-lined pan, mix evaporated milk and steak sauce, and spread over fish. Sprinkle with crackers. Dry potato quarters, and dip in salad oil. Sprinkle generously with salt, and make layer in second baking dish. Unwrap frozen vegetables, and place on 2 squares heavy-duty foil. Sprinkle with salt, and top each with 2 tablespoons butter or margarine. Wrap each block separately, to be airtight. Set potatoes and vegetables in oven, and bake 10 minutes. Turn vegetable packages over; put pan of fish in oven. Continue baking 20 minutes. Serve fish steaks, mixed vegetables and potatoes on individual plates, and pass mustard sauce. Serves 6.

Mustard Sauce

> 1 cup tartar sauce
> 1/2 cup diced cucumber
> 2 tablespoons prepared mustard
> 1 tablespoon lemon juice

Combine all chilled ingredients. Makes 1 1/2 cups.

Seafood

Molluscs or Crustaceans. The edible parts of the various "molluscs" (oysters, scallops, clams and mussels) and of the "crustacean" group (including lobster, crab and shrimp) have a delicacy of texture and special flavors that most gourmets enjoy. One reason is that these seafoods take so well to sauces, seasonings and complementary touches. And the fact that they do so makes them economical for they can be "stretched" with such inexpensive items as rice, noodles, breadstuffs, vegetables, milk and eggs.

The flesh of shellfish becomes tough if cooked too long, so it is important to remember that only a few minutes' cooking is necessary.

The cooked meat adds a great deal to salads.

Lobster

Live lobsters vary in size from 1 to 3 pounds. A healthy lobster is very active, with a color that is deep blue to shades of green and brown (the handsome red color comes during cooking). If you buy lobster cooked in the shell, you can check that it was alive and healthy when cooked by straightening the tail; it should spring back into curled position. A 1-pound lobster serves 1.

When you buy frozen cooked lobster meat, thaw in refrigerator overnight, or open container at room temperature (this way a 14-ounce can will thaw in about 6 hours). Before serving lobster, whether home-cooked or canned, check carefully through claw meat to remove any thin pieces of cartilage that might be present.

Shrimp

You can take your pick when buying shrimp, choosing either the very small variety or the good-sized meaty jumbo shrimp. Though they may be gray or green at this stage, all shrimp turn pink when cooked. One pound of raw or "green" shrimp will give you enough meat for about 3 servings in a main course.

Peel off shells, then with small, sharp knife cut along outside curvature and lift out dark vein running length of body. Rinse under cold water, and drain. Raw shrimp should be immersed in boiling salted water (1 tablespoon salt per 1 quart water). Frozen shrimp need not be thawed. When water has returned to boiling point, reduce heat, and simmer. Allow 2 minutes for small shrimp, 5 minutes for large jumbo shrimp. Drain and cool. Shrimp are ready for use in a variety of dishes.

Crab

Live crabs survive only a short time out of water and when purchased should be promptly cooked by being plunged, head first into rapidly boiling salted water (1 tablespoon salt per 1 quart water). Cover and simmer 15–20 minutes. Cool quickly in cold water; shell, clean and refrigerate till serving time. Allow 2 crabs per serving.

In some localities you may buy cooked and frozen whole and half-crabs in plastic bags; you can also buy cooked and shelled frozen crabmeat. Check carefully through canned crabmeat, and remove any small bits of cartilage and shell.

To shell and clean cooked crab, hold it with your left hand and pull off top shell from rear (discard shell, or use it as a serving plate, after scrubbing well to remove yellow fat that clings to it). Lift off gills on either side of back, and discard. Turn crab on its back. Break off mouth parts, and tailpiece apron. Turn crab over again. Scrape out center fat and entrails. Flush cavity thoroughly under cold running water. Hold crab with both hands, and crack body shell in half over edge of sink. Shake out body meat from each 1/2 shell by crushing shell and knocking it against edge of bowl. Hold legs curved side down, and hit sharply with loosely held mallet. Break off. Pull out movable pincer claws and

sharp inside shell. Extract meat from shell. Rinse meat in salt water, and drain.

Clams

Live clams have tightly closed shells, which may be steamed opened or pried apart with a knife. Allow about 6 per serving. Raw clams are also available shucked by the pint or quart. Canned clams may be bought whole or minced.

Oysters

Oysters are available in the shell by the dozen. Use soft brush to clean oyster shells under cold, running water. Do not let oysters stand in water. Hold each scrubbed oyster with deep part of shell down, and insert a strong blunt oyster knife near hinge. Pry shells apart with twisting motion. To prevent knife from slipping, wear heavy glove, or hold oyster in folded cloth. Sever muscle that holds shell together and under-muscle holding oyster to shell. Take care to retain as much salty-flavored juice as possible.

If you do not intend to serve your oysters raw on the half-shell, drain them and strain juice to remove particles of shell. Store oysters with juice in tightly covered container, and refrigerate. Raw oysters are also available shucked, by the 1/2-pint, pint or quart. Use within 24 hours.

Scallops

Tender white scallops are packaged and sold by the pound, both fresh and frozen. They need no shelling as they are "shucked" as soon as they are harvested from the sea. Always wipe scallops with clean, damp cloth before using. Frozen scallops should be sufficiently thawed to separate before cooking. Allow 1/4–1/3 pound per serving.

Shellfish, which used to be special treats to be enjoyed near their coastal habitats, are now available almost everywhere, fresh, canned or frozen. Experimenting with the various types is bound to be rewarding.

Fried Rice Ring with Shrimp

    2 cups boiling water
    1 (8-ounce) package frozen ready-to-cook shrimp
1/4 cup butter or margarine
1/2 cup chopped green pepper
1/4 cup chopped onion
1 1/3 cups quick-cooking rice
1/4 teaspoon salt
1 1/3 cups chicken bouillon
    1 (10 1/2-ounce) can shrimp soup, undiluted
    2 teaspoons cornstarch
1/2 cup milk
    1 (10-ounce) package frozen peas

Pour boiling water over shrimp to separate. Drain well. Cook shrimp lightly in butter or margarine; lift out, and cut into 1/2-inch pieces. Put green pepper and onion in frying pan, and cook until transparent. Add rice, stir and cook until lightly browned. Add salt, bouillon and shrimp. Bring to boil, pour into greased 5–cup ring mold. Cover and set in pan of boiling water 10 minutes. Heat soup in top of double boiler until defrosted. Mix cornstarch with milk, add to soup and cook until thick and smooth. Cook frozen peas according to directions on package. Unmold rice ring on hot platter. Fill center with hot cooked peas. Top with hot shrimp sauce. Serves 6.

French-fried Shrimp

        1 1/2 pounds large shrimp, fresh or frozen
        3/4 cup flour
          1 teaspoon baking powder
        1/2 teaspoon salt
        3/4 cup milk
          1 egg, beaten
    Salad oil

If using frozen shrimp, allow to thaw. Peel shrimp, and cut almost through lengthwise. Remove veins, wash and drain. Make batter by sifting dry ingredients together; combine milk with beaten egg, and add liquid to dry ingredients, stirring until smooth. Heat salad oil in skillet until very hot (375°F. if using thermometer). Use enough oil to cover shrimp completely. Dip shrimp in batter and fry until golden brown—5–7 minutes. Drain on paper towels. Serve plain or with TARTAR SAUCE. Serves 5–6.

Lobster Newburg

        1/4 cup butter or margarine
        1/4 cup flour
        1/2 teaspoon salt
        1/8 teaspoon pepper
    1 1/2 cups milk
          2 cups cooked lobster meat or 2 (5-ounce) cans lobster
              cut into bite-size pieces
          2 tablespoons sherry or lemon juice
          6 toast slices or patty shells

Make a white sauce, using butter or margarine, flour, seasonings and milk. Add lobster meat, and heat thoroughly. Add wine just before serving. Serve on toast or in patty shells. Serves 6.

Lobster–Grapefruit Mold

          2 cups bite-sized pieces cooked lobster meat or 2 (5-ounce) cans lobster, drained
          1 tablespoon lemon juice
    1 1/2 teaspoons gelatin (1/2 envelope)
        2/3 cup sweetened, canned grapefruit juice
          1 cup mayonnaise

          1 cup canned grapefruit sections, diced
          1 teaspoon salt

Sprinkle lobster pieces with lemon juice. Soak gelatin in 1/3 cup grapefruit juice 5 minutes; then melt by setting container in hot water. Combine remaining grapefruit juice with mayonnaise; add dissolved gelatin, stirring thoroughly. Add grapefruit and salt. Fold in lobster, mix and pour into 1 1/2 qt. mold rinsed in cold water. Chill until firm and unmold on bed of salad greens. Serves 6.

Note: Or use small individual molds instead of 1 large one.

Boiled Fresh Lobster

Fill deep kettle with sufficient water to cover lobsters, adding 1/4 cup salt for each quart water. Bring water to fast boil; plunge each lobster in, grasping it by the back, behind head.

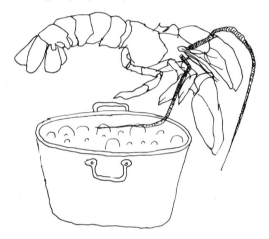

Allow water to return to gentle boil, cover container and cook 18 minutes from the time they were put in water. Lobsters weighing less than 1 pound will cook in 15 minutes. Lift out and cool immediately by holding under running water; then drain.

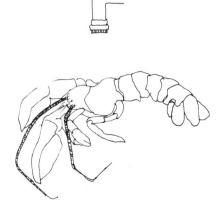

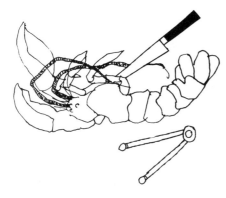

Note: Turn lobster on its back, and split lengthwise down center, using sharp knife or kitchen scissors. Remove meat, and discard dark vein, small sac at back of head, and spongy green tissue on each side of back. Do not discard bright green liver or red roe (if present) as these are delicious tidbits. Crack large claws with nutcracker. Repack body shell. If to be served hot, put lobster in very slow oven to heat through; serve with melted butter or margarine and lemon wedges. Or serve cold with lettuce garnish, mayonnaise and lemon slices.

Stuffed Broiled Lobster

        1 2–3 pound lobster
        2 tablespoons butter or margarine, melted
        5 tablespoons soft bread crumbs
        2 tablespoons chopped parsley
    1/4 teaspoon salt
    Dash pepper

Split lobster in 2 and lay open as far as possible. Discard vein and spongy green tissue on each side of back. Crack big claws. Place lobster, top-shell side up, on broiler rack 3 inches from heat. Brush with 1/2 the butter or margarine, broil 8 minutes under medium heat. Turn lobster. Combine remaining ingredients, and place mixture in lobster cavity. Broil 4 minutes or until crumbs are golden brown. Serves 1–2.

Deep-fried Scallops

        1 pound scallops
    Salt to taste
    1/4 cup flour
        1 egg, beaten
    3/4 cup fine, dry bread crumbs
        1 cup salad oil or fat

Sprinkle scallops with salt. Roll each in flour, dip in egg, and roll in bread crumbs. Heat fat over low heat until very hot (375°F. if using thermometer), using just enough to cover an uncrowded single layer of scallops in frying basket. Lower basket, and fry scallops until golden brown on all sides—3–4 minutes. Drain on paper towels and serve with lemon wedges or TARTAR SAUCE. Serves 3.

Scallop Casserole

        1 pound scallops
    Salt to taste
        2 tablespoons butter or margarine
    1 1/2 cups chopped celery
        1 cup sliced mushrooms
        1 cup chopped green pepper
    1/2 cup chopped onion
    1/4 cup butter or margarine
    1/4 cup flour
        1 teaspoon salt
        2 cups milk
        2 tablespoons butter or margarine
        2 cups soft bread crumbs
    1/4 cup finely grated cheese

Sprinkle scallops with salt to taste. Melt butter or margarine in skillet, and gently fry scallops with vegetables until partially cooked but not limp, about 10 minutes. Make white sauce with 1/4 cup butter or margarine, flour, 1 teaspoon salt and milk; when thickened, add scallops and vegetables. Combine thoroughly, and transfer to greased 1 1/2-quart casserole. Melt remaining 2 tablespoons butter and moisten bread crumbs. Scatter buttered crumbs over top of casserole; then sprinkle grated cheese over crumbs. Bake uncovered at 375°F. about 20 minutes or until sauce is bubbling and crumbs lightly browned. Serves 6.

Spicy Oyster Stew

    1/4 cup butter or margarine
        2 dozen raw oysters, with liquid
        1 tablespoon Worcestershire sauce
        1 teaspoon celery salt
    3/4 teaspoon salt
    1/4 teaspoon paprika
    1/8 teaspoon pepper
        1 quart milk
        4 small lumps butter or margarine

Heat 1/4 cup butter or margarine in skillet, but do not brown. Add oysters with liquid and

next 5 ingredients. Heat only until edges of oysters curl slightly; then add milk. Heat quickly,

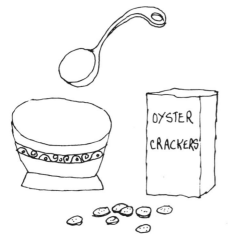

but do not boil. Serve with additional dash of paprika and lump of butter or margarine in each bowl. Serve with oyster crackers and small dish of sliced dill pickles. Serves 4.

Broiled Oysters

    1/2 pint oysters
    Salt to taste
      3 tablespoons melted butter or margarine
    1/2 cup dry bread crumbs

Drain oysters, and sprinkle lightly with salt. Dip in melted butter or margarine and roll in bread crumbs. Place on greased rack about 4 inches from heat, and broil approximately 2 minutes on each side, turning once. Bread crumbs will be lightly browned. Serves 1–2.

Note: To bake, place breaded oysters in greased, shallow baking dish, and bake at 450°F. 10–12 minutes or until lightly browned.

Steamed Clams

Scrub clams well under running cold water to remove sand. Cover bottom of large skillet with 1/2 inch water, add clams, cover tightly and steam until shells start to open—about 10 minutes (or place clams in steamer). Top shells can be removed for serving if desired. Serve clams hot

with side dishes of melted butter or margarine. If desired, liquid remaining in pan after cooking may be added to butter or margarine for dipping.

Manhattan-style Clam Chowder

    2 slices bacon, diced
    1 medium onion, thinly sliced, approximately 1/2 cup
    1 cup diced raw potato
    1 small bay leaf
    1 (1-pound, 4-ounce) can tomatoes
    1 pint clams and liquid or approximately 20 ounces canned clams
    1 teaspoon salt
    1/8 teaspoon pepper
    1/8 teaspoon thyme

Fry bacon until crisp; add onion, and fry until tender, about 5 minutes. Add potato, bay leaf and undrained tomatoes. Simmer 10–15 minutes until potato is tender; then add remaining ingredients. Heat until piping hot, but do not allow to boil. Remove bay leaf before serving. Serves 6.

Fundy-style Clam Chowder

    2 tablespoons finely diced bacon
    1/2 cup chopped onion
    1 cup diced raw potato
    2 cups water
    1 pint clams and liquid or approximately 20 ounces canned clams
    1 (16-ounce) can evaporated milk
    3 tablespoons butter or margarine
    1 teaspoon salt
    1/4 teaspoon white pepper

Fry diced bacon until crisp; remove from pan, and save for garnish. Sauté chopped onions in bacon fat until tender but not brown. Combine potato and cooked onion in deep saucepan, add water, bring to simmering point and simmer until potato is cooked, about 15 minutes. Stir in clams, clam liquid, milk, butter or margarine and seasonings, and heat until piping hot. Do not boil. Garnish with crisp diced bacon. Serves 6.

Clam–Potato Cakes

    2 (7-ounce) cans minced clams (drained)
    2 cups cooked mashed potatoes
    2 tablespoons butter or margarine
    1 tablespoon lemon juice
    1/2 teaspoon salt
    1/4 teaspoon nutmeg
    2 eggs

Combine drained minced clams with remaining ingredients, except eggs. Beat eggs slightly; add to mixture, and mix well. Shape into 12 patties, and fry in hot fat until lightly browned on both sides. Serves 6.

Crab Creole

    2 tablespoons butter or margarine
    1 cup diced celery
    1/2 cup chopped onion
    2 cloves garlic, finely chopped
    1 (1-pound, 13-ounce) can tomatoes
 1 1/2 teaspoons Worcestershire sauce
    1 teaspoon salt
    1/2 cup raw rice
    2 cups fresh cooked crabmeat or 2 (6-ounce) cans
        crabmeat
    1/4 cup chopped parsley

Melt butter or margarine in skillet, and gently fry celery, onion, and garlic until tender. Add tomatoes, Worcestershire sauce and salt; bring to boil. Add rice, mix well and cover skillet. Simmer 20 minutes or until rice is cooked, stirring occasionally. Add crabmeat and chopped parsley, and heat through. Serves 6.

Crabmeat Alaskan

    3 cups cooked fresh, frozen or canned crabmeat
    1 egg yolk, beaten
    1/2 cup heavy cream
    1/2 teaspoon salt
    1/8 teaspoon pepper
    6 slices bread
    3 tablespoons melted butter or margarine
    1/2 cup soft bread crumbs
    1 tablespoon melted butter or margarine

Flake crabmeat, and combine with next 4 ingredients. Brush bread slices on 1 side with 3 tablespoons butter or margarine. Then fry on buttered side until golden brown. Heap crab mixture on unbuttered side; combine bread crumbs with 1 tablespoon butter or margarine and sprinkle over crab. Garnish with parsley and bake at 400°F. 10 minutes. Serves 6.

Deviled Shrimp

    2 cups (1 pound frozen) shrimp or 2 (5-ounce)
        cans shrimp
    2 tablespoons chopped onion
    1/4 cup melted butter or margarine
    1/4 cup flour
    1/2 teaspoon dry mustard
    1/2 teaspoon Worcestershire sauce
    2 cups milk
    1 (10-ounce) package frozen peas, cooked
   24 toast points
 Paprika to taste

If using large shrimp, cut in half, set aside. Sauté onion in butter or margarine until tender, not brown. Blend in flour, seasonings and Worcestershire sauce. Gradually add milk, and cook over very low heat until thickened, stirring constantly. Add reserved shrimp and peas; heat through. Serve piping hot on toast points or unsweetened waffles; sprinkle with paprika. Serves 6.

Shrimp in Curry Mayonnaise

    2 cups (1 pound frozen) cooked shrimp or
        2 (5-ounce) cans shrimp
    1/2 cup diced red-skinned apple
    1/2 cup celery leaves
    1/4 cup diced green pepper
    1/2 teaspoon salt
    1/2 teaspoon curry powder
    1/4 cup mayonnaise
   12 lettuce leaves

Combine shrimp with next 3 ingredients. Add salt and curry powder to mayonnaise, combine with salad mixture and toss lightly. Arrange in chilled lettuce cups. Serves 6.

Seafood Cocktail

    1 pound cooked crabmeat or 3 (6-ounce) packages
        frozen crabmeat
    1/2 pound cooked lobster, cut up or 1 (9-ounce) package lobster tails, cooked
    3 avocados, peeled and cut up (brush with
        lemon juice)
 Lettuce leaves
    1 cup ripe olives
 1 1/2 cups cocktail sauce (or 1 1/2 cups chili sauce plus
        2 tablespoons horseradish and 4 drops hot-
        pepper sauce)

Arrange crabmeat, lobster and avocados, brushed with lemon juice, all cut up, on lettuce leaves along with olives. Chill well. Serve with cocktail sauce (or use combination of chili sauce, horseradish and hot-pepper sauce). Serve in individual shell plates. Serves 6.

Alternatives to Meat. *It's a good idea to vary your menu with fish, eggs, cheese, lentils or other legumes and nuts.*

Although every well-balanced meal should be built around a protein-rich main course, it does not always have to be meat, poultry or even fish. A number of other foods make a variety of attractive substitutes possible. These "meat alternates" are good as well as inexpensive.

Eggs

Eggs are the most versatile and nutritious of the alternatives to meat providing quality pro-

London Broil. *Credit: Bernard Gray.*

Trout in Wine.
Credit: Arthur Beck.

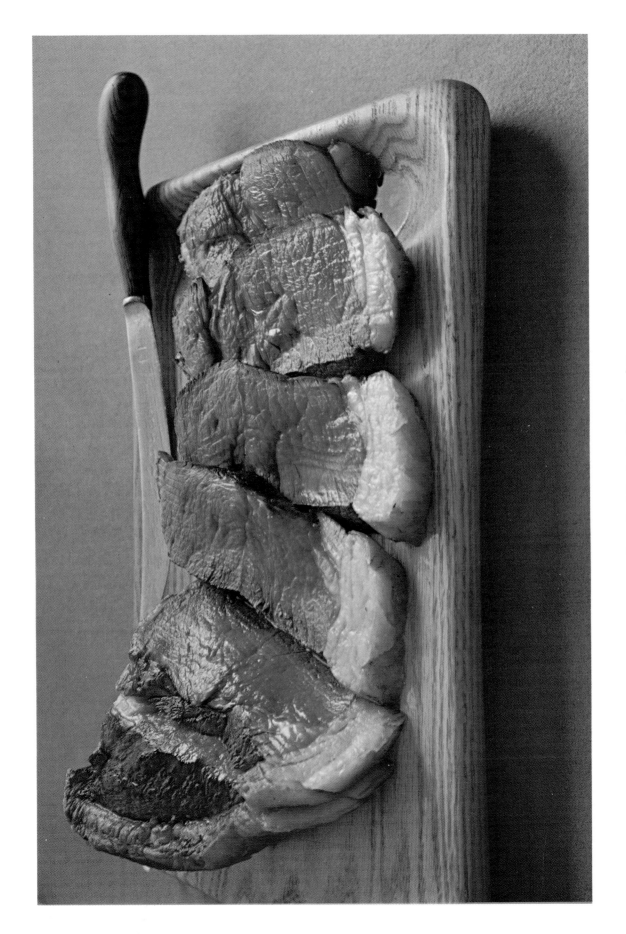

Roast Beef Steak. *Credit: Bernard Gray.*

Port Wine, Crème de Menthe, Burgundy Wine, and Ginger Beet jellies packaged for Christmas gifts. *Credit: Bernard Gray.*

Crêpes Gismonda. *Credit: Bernard Gray.*

A Thanksgiving Turkey Dinner. *Credit: Bernard Gray.*

Tomato Juice, but with a difference—buttered, spiced, served hot. *Credit: Bernard Gray.*

Cheese Bread. *Credit: Bernard Gray.*

Roast Beef surrounded by carrots, onions, and potatoes. *Credit: Bernard Gray.*

Roast Ham. *Credit: Bernard Gray.*

Shish Kebab. *Credit: Elbert Budin.*

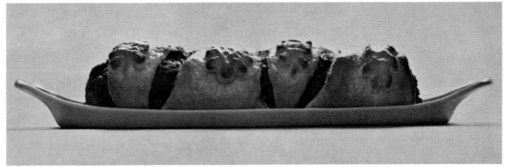

Veal Wellington. *Credit: Bernard Gray.*

Boeuf en Gelée. *Credit: Richard Jeffery.*

Three-Bean Salad, Lentils Hiding in Tomatoes,

Italian Bean and Artichoke Salad, Wax Bean Vinaigrette, and Curried Sikh Salad. *Credit: Elbert Budin.*

A Fall table featuring baked ham and acorn squash with mushrooms and lime. *Credit: Ben Somoroff.*

tein, essential vitamins and iron. They are sold by grade: grade AA, grade A, grade B, grade C.

Grade A is the top quality most commonly sold, and there are 5 classifications according to size and weight: jumbo (minimum weight 30 ounces per dozen), extra large (27 ounces), large (24 ounces); medium (21 ounces); small (18 ounces) and peewee (15 ounces). The first and last classes are not often found in the stores.

Always store eggs, covered, in the refrigerator and wash them right before using.

It is worthwhile to master a range of egg specialties for the basic ingredient is always available and the results always popular. Eggs should never be cooked at high temperatures, as texture toughens and gives an unattractive appearance.

Cheeses

All cheese is rich in protein, calcium, riboflavin and vitamin A. In buying cheese you have a wide variety from which to choose, for most food markets stock many types at many prices.

One of the most economical buys is Cheddar—mild, sharp or very sharp. A constant supply of Cheddar is never wasted. Cottage cheese, too, is worth buying regularly—and using up quickly, as it is perishable. The various process cheeses and cheese spreads have an important place in every kitchen today; they are easy to use in toppings, sauces, grilled or plain sandwiches and so forth. Through cheese, the whole world is practically at your door—Gruyère and Swiss from Switzerland; Edam and Gouda from Holland; Brie, Camembert and Roquefort from France; Romano, Parmesan and Mozzarrella from Italy and numerous others.

Keep cheese tightly wrapped, and store covered in refrigerator. To enjoy the full flavor, always serve cheese, except cottage cheese, at room temperature.

When cooking cheese, use low heat so that it will melt smoothly. Too long cooking or too high heat will make cheese stringy and tough.

Dried Beans and Peas

Dried beans and peas make possible a considerable range of low-cost, high-protein dishes. However, some animal protein, like that in cheese and milk, should be included in the menu. When bought in ready-to-eat form like canned pork and beans, these legumes are a dependable convenience item.

To prepare at home, dried beans and peas require time. One cup raw dried beans or peas will give you 2–3 cups cooked beans; 1 pound (2 1/4–2 1/2 cups) dried beans or peas after cooking gives 10–11 cups. Soak beans overnight; then add more water and seasonings, and cook. Soybeans taste best when cooked in meat stock.

If you are preparing beans for same-day use, here is a quick trick that shortens the preliminaries. Boil 2 cups beans in 6 cups water 2 minutes. Remove from heat, and soak 1 hour. Return to stove, and cook in same water until beans are just tender.

Quick-cooking beans are available today. Follow label directions for cooking.

Generally in good supply on the market are lima beans, navy beans, lentils, kidney beans, pinto beans, soybeans, black-eyed peas and split peas.

Nuts for Protein

Nuts contain valuable proteins. Aside from their appeal as garnishes and between-meal nibbles, nuts in large amounts in salad can be a main dish for luncheon.

Peanuts are from the legume family but are treated as nuts. They are the most economical of "nuts" and have a variety of uses: in soups, sauces, sandwich fillings, salads, vegetable dishes, main-dish casseroles, cookies, cakes, pies and puddings.

A bowl of nuts brought to the table for dessert adds extra nutrients to meals.

Cheese Soufflé

        3 tablespoons butter or margarine
        3 tablespoons flour
        1 cup milk
        4 egg yolks
        1/4 teaspoon salt
    Dash cayenne
        5 egg whites
        3/4 cup grated sharp cheese

Melt butter or margarine in saucepan, add flour and cook until mixture is bubbling. Remove from heat, and add milk all at once. Return to heat and cook, stirring constantly, until thick and smooth. Allow to cool slightly; then beat in egg yolks with seasonings. Beat egg whites until stiff but not dry; lightly fold 2 mixtures together with grated cheese. Pile lightly into buttered 1 1/2-quart soufflé dish and bake at 375°F. about 30 minutes or until soufflé is well puffed and firm. Serve at once. Serves 4–5.

Cheese Mousse

        1 envelope powdered gelatin
    3/4 cup cold water
        1 (10 1/2-ounce) can condensed tomato soup
        2 (3-ounce) packages plain cream cheese
    1/2 cup finely chopped celery
    1/2 cup grated carrot
    1/2 cup shredded cabbage
    1/4 cup finely chopped green pepper or 1 green pickle,
            finely chopped
        1 tablespoon grated onion
    1/8 teaspoon mace
    Dash cloves
        1 cup mayonnaise

Soften gelatin in water. Heat soup in top of double boiler, and stir in gelatin to dissolve. Remove from heat, and add cheese. Beat with electric mixer or hand beater until smoothly blended. Cool, and, when mixture begins to thicken, add all remaining ingredients, except mayonnaise. Pour into oiled ring mold. Chill until firm. Unmold, and spread with mayonnaise. Serve in slices. Serves 6–8.

Cheese–Celery Loaf

    1/2 cup chopped celery
    2 tablespoons chopped onion
    2 tablespoons butter or margarine
    3 cups cooked elbow macaroni
    1 (10 1/2-ounce) can cream of celery soup
    1/2 cup skim milk
    1 egg, beaten
    1 1/2 cups grated cheese

Sauté celery and onion in butter or margarine until tender. Remove from heat, and stir in macaroni, soup, milk and egg. Alternate layers of macaroni mixture and cheese in greased 9″x5″x3″ loaf dish, ending with cheese. Cover with foil, and place in pan of hot water. Bake at 350°F. 1 hour or until center of loaf is set. Invert on heated platter. Serves 6–8.

Curried Eggs and Mushrooms

    1/2 pound sliced fresh mushrooms (2 cups)
    2 tablespoons butter or margarine
    1/2 teaspoon lemon juice
    Salt and pepper to taste
    2 cups milk
    1 chicken bouillon cube, crumbled
    1/4 cup soft butter or margarine
    1/4 cup flour
    2 teaspoons curry powder
    1/4 cup mayonnaise
    1/4 teaspoon salt
    1/8 teaspoon pepper
    Dash cayenne
    Dash nutmeg
    2 egg yolks
    2 tablespoons sherry
    6 hard-cooked eggs, quartered
    1/4 cup chopped parsley
    6 slices hot toasted French bread, buttered
    Bacon curls

Sauté mushrooms in 2 tablespoons butter or margarine. Season lightly with lemon juice, salt and pepper. Set mushrooms aside, but keep them hot. Heat milk and bouillon cube in top of double boiler, but over direct heat. Make smooth mixture of flour and butter or margarine, add to milk. Whisk until smoothly thickened. Add mushrooms, curry powder and mayonnaise; season to taste with salt, pepper, cayenne and nutmeg. Mix together egg yolks and sherry, and stir in. Keep mixture hot over boiling water, or

make it earlier in the day, refrigerate and reheat. Just before serving, add hard-cooked eggs and parsley. Heat thoroughly and spoon over hot French bread. Garnish with bacon curls. Serves 6.

Baked Meringue Eggs

    6 slices buttered toast
    1 (10-ounce) can asparagus soup
    6 egg whites
    Pinch salt
    6 individual egg yolks
    1/4 cup grated cheese

Spread toast with undiluted soup. Place slices side by side on cookie sheet. Beat egg whites and salt together until stiff; then mound egg whites on toast, being careful to cover each slice completely. Make depression in center of each mound, and drop in 1 egg yolk. Sprinkle with grated cheese. Bake at 350°F. until egg whites are set and cheese melts, about 10 minutes. Serve with hot tomato sauce or additional asparagus soup diluted and heated with a few tablespoons cream. Serves 4–6.

Mushroom Soufflé in Green-pepper Cups

    4 large green peppers
    3 egg yolks
    1 (10 1/2-ounce) can condensed mushroom soup
    1/2 cup grated sharp cheese
    3 egg whites
    Pinch salt

Slice tops off peppers and remove seeds and pith. Beat egg yolks and blend well with soup and grated cheese. Beat egg whites until stiff but not dry, adding salt. Lightly fold soup mixture into egg whites. Place peppers close together for support in greased baking dish, and fill each with egg mixture. Bake at 350°F. about 30 minutes or until knife inserted in soufflé comes out clean. Serves 4.

Note: Tomatoes may be used in place of green peppers. Cut tops off tomatoes, remove pulp and invert to drain.

Rice Ring with Creamed Vegetables

    2 cups water
    3/4 teaspoon salt
    1 cup rice (not quick-cooking type)
    1/2 teaspoon grated nutmeg
    1/4 cup butter or margarine
    3/4 cup blanched almonds, coarsely chopped
    2 cups creamed or buttered vegetables

Bring water to rolling boil; add salt, then rice. Cover, let come to high boil again, reduce heat and simmer 20–30 minutes, removing cover last 5 minutes and shaking pan to separate grains. Season with nutmeg; then place in well-greased 4-cup ring mold. Melt butter or margarine and pour over mold, sprinkle with almonds. Set mold in pan of hot water and bake 20 minutes at 350°F. Loosen edges, invert on platter and fill center with vegetables. Serves 6.

Macaroni and Cheese à la King

    4 cups cooked and drained elbow macaroni
    2 cups grated Cheddar cheese
    1 (10 1/2-ounce) can cream of mushroom soup
    1 cup commercial sour cream
    1/2 green pepper, chopped
    1/4 cup diced pimento
    2 tablespoons pimento juice
    1 teaspoon salt
    1/2 teaspoon pepper
    1/2 teaspoon dry mustard
    3/4 cup crushed bacon-flavored crackers

Combine all ingredients except crackers, and spread mixture in a greased baking dish. Add about 1/2 cup milk if you want a moister consistency. Sprinkle with crackers, and bake at 350°F. 35–40 minutes. Serves 8.

Tomatoes and Macaroni with Cheese

    2 cups uncooked elbow macaroni
    4 quarts boiling salted water
    3 tablespoons butter or margarine
    1/2 cup chopped onion
    1 green pepper, cut in strips
    1 (1-pound, 4-ounce) can tomatoes
    1 cup grated cheese
    2 tablespoons salt
    1/8 teaspoon pepper
    1 egg, beaten
    1/4 cup CHEESE–CRUMB TOPPING

Cook macaroni in boiling water until tender. Drain; rinse in cold water. Melt butter or margarine in skillet, and sauté onion and green pepper until soft. Remove from pan, and combine with tomatoes, cheese and seasonings. Stir in egg. Pour over macaroni in greased casserole, and sprinkle with topping. Bake at 350°F. 30 minutes. Serves 4–6.

Cheese–Crumb Topping

    1 tablespoon butter or margarine
    2 tablespoons dry bread crumbs
    2 tablespoons grated cheese

Melt butter or margarine and combine with bread crumbs and cheese.

Easy Cheese Bake

    3 cups uncooked elbow macaroni
    6 quarts boiling salted water
    2/3 cup milk
    2 (10 1/2-ounce) cans cream of chicken soup
    12 slices process cheese
    4 tomatoes, sliced

Cook macaroni in boiling water until tender; drain and rinse. Stir milk into soup; heat, and combine with cooked macaroni. Place in buttered shallow baking dish. Top with alternate slices of cheese and tomatoes, ending with layer of cheese. Bake at 325°F. until cheese is melted and golden brown, about 25 minutes. Serves 6.

Luncheon Rarebit

    2 tablespoons butter or margarine
    2 tablespoons flour
    3/4 cup milk
    1/8 teaspoon baking soda
    1 (1-pound) can tomatoes, drained
    1–1 1/2 cups shredded Cheddar cheese or 1/2 pound
            diced nippy processed cheese
    1/2 teaspoon dry mustard
    1/4–1/2 teaspoon salt
    6 slices toasted French bread, buttered
Bacon curls

Melt butter or margarine and stir in flour. Remove pan from heat, and gradually stir in milk. Return pan to heat, and whisk until thick and smooth. Mix soda with tomatoes, and add to white sauce. Stir in remaining ingredients, and heat until cheese melts. Spoon over French bread and garnish with crisp bacon curls. Serves 6.

Savory Luncheon Custard

    2 tablespoons butter or margarine
    2 cups thinly sliced onion
    6 eggs
    1 1/2 cups milk
    1 1/4 teaspoons salt
Dash pepper

Melt butter or margarine in skillet, and sauté onions until tender. Beat eggs lightly, and add milk, salt and pepper. Place onion slices in greased casserole; pour egg mixture over. Set casserole in pan of warm water, and bake at 350°F. 50 minutes. Serves 4.

Baked Cheese Fondue

    2 cups whole wheat bread, cut in 1/2-inch cubes
    1 cup grated cheese
    2 cups milk
    2 eggs
    2 tablespoons butter or margarine, melted
    2 teaspoons salt
Pinch pepper

Grease casserole. Arrange bread cubes in layers with grated cheese between, ending with bread on top. Beat milk, eggs, butter or margarine and seasonings together; pour mixture over bread. Let stand about 20 minutes. Set casserole in pan containing hot water to at least 1-inch depth. Bake in 350°F. oven 35–40 minutes. Serves 3–4.

Cheese Chiffon Pie

    1 1/3 cups unsifted all-purpose flour
    1/2 cup mayonnaise
      2 tablespoons water
      1 (8-ounce) package processed cheese
    1/2 cup milk
    1/8 teaspoon cayenne
      3 egg yolks, well beaten
      3 egg whites

Stir flour into mayonnaise and water to form firm dough. Knead slightly, and roll out to fit deep 9-inch pie plate. Bake at 425°F. 12 minutes. Meanwhile, melt cheese in milk in top of double boiler, and, when creamy-smooth, remove from heat. Stir in egg yolks and cayenne. Beat egg whites until stiff but not dry, and gently fold into cheese mixture. Scrape into pastry shell, and bake at 300°F. 30 minutes. Serve in wedges with fresh tomato slices. Serves 6–8.

Onion–Mushroom Bake

      8 medium onions, peeled
    1 1/2 cups salted water
    1/2 pound mushrooms, sliced
    1/3 cup melted butter or margarine
    1/3 cup flour
    1/2 teaspoon salt
    1/2 teaspoon paprika
    1/4 teaspoon celery salt
      2 cups milk
      1 cup shredded Cheddar cheese
      3 tablespoons butter or margarine
      1 cup soft bread crumbs

Parboil onions in salted water 25 minutes. Drain well, and place in a shallow baking dish. In medium saucepan sauté mushrooms in 1/3 cup butter or margarine until tender. Blend in flour and seasonings. Stir in milk gradually, and cook until mixture thickens, stirring constantly. Remove from heat and stir in cheese, and pour sauce over onions. Melt 3 tablespoons butter or margarine and combine with bread crumbs. Sprinkle over sauce, and bake at 350°F. 30–35 minutes. Serves 8.

Lentils Baked in Honey

      2 cups dried lentils
      4 cups cold water
      1 cup water
      6 slices bacon, diced
      1 medium onion, finely chopped (3/4 cup)
    1/4 cup chutney
      1 teaspoon salt
      1 teaspoon dry mustard
    Dash pepper
    1/2 cup honey

Preheat oven to 325°F. Put lentils in large saucepan, add 4 cups cold water, and bring to boiling point. Reduce heat and simmer, covered, 1 hour. Drain, reserving 1 cup liquid. Add to lentils reserved liquid plus 1 cup water, bacon, onion, chutney, salt, mustard and pepper. Turn into baking dish and pour honey over top. Bake, covered, 45 minutes. Remove cover, and continue baking 30 minutes. Serves 6–8.

Spiced Beans

      1 pound dried pinto beans
      3 cups cold water
      1 teaspoon whole cloves
      1 medium onion, sliced (1/2 cup)
    1/4 pound salt pork, cut into bits
      2 teaspoons salt
      1 (8-ounce) can tomato sauce
      2 tablespoons molasses
      1 tablespoon Worcestershire sauce

Put beans in deep kettle, and cover with 3 cups cold water; adjust lid and leave in cool place overnight. Next day drain, and add enough fresh water to barely cover beans. Tie cloves in small square of cheesecloth. Add cloves, onion, salt pork, and salt to beans. Bring mixture to boiling point; reduce heat to low, cover and simmer about 2 hours or until beans are tender. Stir several times during cooking. Remove bag of cloves, and add tomato sauce, molasses and Worcestershire sauce, mixing thoroughly. Let simmer another 30 minutes. Serves 6–8.

Mexican Kidney Beans

      1 pound dried kidney beans
      3 cups cold water
    1/4 pound salt pork, cut into bits
      3 cloves garlic, finely chopped
    1/2 cup chopped onion
      2 tablespoons chili powder
    3 1/2 cups canned tomatoes
    1/4 cup tomato paste
    1 1/2 teaspoons salt
    1/2 teaspoon oregano
    Pinch cumin
    Dash pepper

Put beans in deep kettle, and cover with cold water; cover and leave in cool place overnight. Next day drain, and add enough fresh water to barely cover beans. Bring to boiling point; reduce heat to low, and simmer, covered, about 1 hour. Drain off any remaining liquid. In small saucepan sauté salt pork until quite crisp; add garlic and onion, and cook until just golden. Scrape contents of pan into beans; add all remaining ingredients, combining thoroughly. Let cook, covered, over very low heat about 1 1/2 hours or until beans are tender, stirring several times during cooking period. Serves 6–8.

Note: Second phase of preparation may be done in oven, using covered casserole.

Lima Beans in Sour Cream

        1 pound dried lima beans
        3 cups cold water
        3 teaspoons salt
        1/4 cup butter or margarine
        3/4 cup finely chopped onion
        1/2 pound mushrooms, sliced
                (approximately 2 cups)
        1 tablespoon flour
        1 tablespoon paprika
        2 cups commercial sour cream
        2 tablespoons chopped parsley

Cover beans in kettle with cold water; leave to soak, with lid on, overnight. Drain; add 1 teaspoon salt and enough fresh water to barely cover beans. Bring to boiling point, reduce heat and simmer about 1 1/2 hours or until beans are tender, stirring several times during cooking. Drain well (save liquid for soup). Melt butter or margarine in large skillet and sauté onion until just golden; add mushrooms, and cook 5 minutes. Stir in flour and paprika; cook until bubbling. Add drained beans, remaining salt and sour cream. Heat thoroughly, but do not boil. Garnish with parsley. Serves 6–8.

Lima Bean Casserole Deluxe

        1 pound dried lima beans
        4 cups cold water
        1/4 cup salad oil
        1 small onion, chopped (1/4 cup)
        1/2 teaspoon salt
        1/4 cup green pepper, diced
        2 teaspoons sugar
    Pinch cayenne
        1 (2-pound, 3-ounce) can tomatoes, drained
    Salt and pepper to taste
        1 teaspoon sugar
        1 cup grated Parmesan cheese

Cover beans with cold water and let soak, covered, in cool place overnight. Simmer until tender and drain. Heat salad oil, and sauté onion until just golden. Put beans in shallow casserole, and add oil and onion, scraping pan thoroughly. Add green peppers, salt, 2 teaspoons sugar, and cayenne. Combine well, so that beans glisten with oil. Top mixture with canned tomatoes, sprinkle lightly with sugar, salt, and pepper; finish with grated cheese. Bake uncovered in oven at 350°F. about 35 minutes. Serves 6–8.

Old-fashioned Baked Beans

        4 cups pea or navy beans
        3 cups cold water
        3/4 pound fat salt pork
    Strip of pork rind
        1/2 cup boiling water
        1 medium whole onion (optional)
        1 cup dark molasses
        3 tablespoons brown sugar
        1 tablespoon salt

        1/2 teaspoon dry mustard
        2 cups boiling water

Wash and pick over beans, and soak overnight in cold water to cover. Before cooking, add more water if necessary barely to cover beans. Heat slowly, keeping water under boiling point. Cook until bean skins begin to burst and peel back; test by removing a few beans on spoon tip and blowing on them. Drain beans. Wash pork, scald in 1/2 cup boiling water, and scrape if necessary. Put a thick slice pork at bottom of a bean pot. Turn beans into pot. For extra flavor, bury whole onion in center of mass. Make gashes in rind meat, place piece, rind-side up, on top of beans. Mix molasses, sugar, salt, and mustard; dissolve in 1 cup boiling water, and pour over beans. Add more boiling water to cover contents of pot completely. Put on lid, and place in center of oven, at 250°F. Bake 6–8 hours. Check about every hour, and add more water as needed; liquid should be visible at least 4 hours of cooking period. Remove pot lid for last hour of baking to brown and crisp pork rind. Serves 6–8.

Note: If bacon or other smoked pork is used instead of salt pork, decrease amount of salt to 1 teaspoon.

French Omelet

        2 eggs
        1 tablespoon water
        1 tablespoon butter or margarine
    Pinch salt
    Dash pepper

Break eggs into bowl. Add water. Beat until frothy. Heat small omelet pan until drop of water dances when dropped in center of pan. Put butter or margarine in pan, and tilt so that all surfaces are coated. Pour in eggs, and stir with tines of fork until edges begin to set. Allow omelet to cook until surface becomes shiny; then fold in half or roll and slide onto warm plate. Season with salt and pepper. Serves 1.

VARIATIONS:
Fillings should be arranged over 1/2 the cooked omelet before folding it.

Bacon Omelet: Crumble 6 slices crisp, cooked bacon.

Cheese Omelet: Sprinkle 1/3 cup grated cheese over omelet as it cooks; or add 1/2 the cheese to egg mixture before cooking, and sprinkle rest over as it cooks.

Chicken-curry Omelet: Melt 2 tablespoons butter or margarine, and sauté 1 tablespoon chopped onion. Add 1 cup diced cooked chicken, and heat through, add 1/2 teaspoon salt and 1/4 teaspoon curry powder.

Herb Omelet: Add 1/4 teaspoon thyme or sage, 1/4 teaspoon chopped marjoram or savory and 1 teaspoon minced parsley to egg mixture before cooking.

Mushroom Omelet: Scatter 1 cup sautéed sliced mushrooms on omelet as it cooks.

Jelly Omelet: Omit pepper and 1/2 the salt from egg mixture; add 1 tablespoon sugar, spread omelet with jelly before folding.

Hearty Main-dish Soups

Sometimes a favorite soup can be the *pièce de résistance*. Here are some you'll enjoy. If the menu is nicely balanced, a hearty soup, perfectly seasoned and served steaming hot, can be readily substituted for the more familiar type of main course.

A thick soup made with dried legumes—beans of various kinds, peas or lentils—is a good source of protein. The meal should also include some milk or cheese. For example, a crisp vegetable salad with cottage cheese.

Old-fashioned vegetable soup, slowly cooked with a beef bone; MULLIGATAWNY, with its generous pieces of chicken and its whiff of curry; cream soups; potato or corn chowder and oyster stew can also be main attractions for luncheon, dinner or supper. Individual portions should be ample—served in chowder bowls or big soup plates—and you should be prepared to offer second helpings as well as crisp crackers, melba toast, hot French bread, and hot rolls.

Follow a main-dish soup with a change of texture, taste and color—a crisp salad, raw relish platter or hot fresh asparagus. A dessert, of the type that is perhaps too heavy or rich for a meat-and-vegetable menu, is appropriate. Consider baked-apple dumplings, dessert pancakes, ice-cream waffles with sauce.

The many excellent commercial soups are ready for the table in minutes. They lend themselves to experimenting too—as in quick PUREE MONGOLE with CROUTONS, which blends cream of green pea with cream of tomato; in leftover creamed celery added to cream of celery, and in many other combinations.

Canadian Pea Soup

```
    2 cups dried whole yellow peas
    8 cups water
    2 onions, chopped (1 1/2 cups)
    1 stalk celery, chopped (1/2 cup)
    1 cooked ham bone or 4 slices bacon, cut in pieces
    2 teaspoons salt
1/2 teaspoon pepper
1/8 teaspoon thyme (optional)
```

Pick over and wash peas. Soak overnight in water, using large cooking kettle. In morning, add onions, celery and ham bone. Put kettle on medium heat, bring to boil, reduce heat and simmer 3–4 hours. More water may be needed, but remember that the famous pea soup of French Canada should be quite thick. Taste soup, and season; salt needed will depend on ham bone's contribution. Serves 6–8.

Lentil Soup

```
1 1/2 cups dried lentils
    2 quarts cold water
    1 smoked ham hock or bone left from baked ham
    1 large onion, chopped fine (1 cup)
    2 large stalks celery, chopped fine (1 cup)
    2 bay leaves
Salt and pepper to taste
1/4 cup sherry
1/4 cup cream (optional)
```

Soak lentils in cold water at least 6 hours, preferably overnight. Drain and measure 2 quarts liquid, adding cold water if necessary. Add ham bone and liquid to lentils, with onion, celery and bay leaves; bring to boil, and simmer 4 hours. Remove bone and bay leaves; skim fat. Cut meat off bone, chop into tiny pieces and return to soup. Stir well, taste and add salt unless ham has salted it enough; add pepper and sherry. If soup becomes too thick during simmering, more water may be added. A little cream may be stirred into soup to "sweeten" it just before serving. Serves 6.

Mulligatawny

```
1/4 cup butter or margarine
    1 medium onion, sliced (1/2 cup)
    1 green pepper, diced (1/2 cup)
    1 stalk celery, diced (1/2 cup)
    1 carrot, diced (1/2 cup)
    1 tart apple, sliced 1/4 inch thick (1/2 cup)
    2 tablespoons flour
    2 cups boiling water
    1 (1-pound) can tomatoes
    2 chicken bouillon cubes
    1 teaspoon curry powder
    1 teaspoon salt
Sprig parsley
    2 cloves
Pinch mace
    3 cups milk
    1 cup cooked chicken
```

Melt butter or margarine in deep kettle, and sauté next 5 ingredients, stirring frequently, until onion is tender but not browned. Stir in flour, then remaining ingredients except milk and chicken. Cover, and simmer 1/2 hour. Just before serving, add milk and chicken, and heat through. Serves 4–6.

Borsch

1 1/2 pounds beef, neck or shin
2 1/2 quarts salted water
1 large onion (1 cup approximately)
2 tablespoons butter or margarine
1/3 cup tomato paste
6 beets
4 stalks celery
1 small head of cabbage
1 tablespoon sugar
1 bay leaf
1 tablespoon salt
4 potatoes, finely diced
(2 cups approximately)
1/2 cup sour cream

Put beef into salted water, boil 15 minutes and skim; simmer 2 hours longer. Strain. Cut onion into julienne strips, sauté in butter or margarine until tender but not brown. Add tomato paste and mix into beef broth. Slice beets, celery and cabbage in fine strips, and add to soup, with sugar and seasonings. Allow soup to simmer 1 1/2 hours; 1/2 hour before serving, add potatoes, and continue cooking. Serve in deep soup plates, stirring into each 1 large tablespoon sour cream. Serves 6.

Note: Canned beef broth, diluted to 2 1/2 quarts liquid, can be substituted for beef cooked in water. Strained borsch may be served ice-cold in the same way.

Beef–Vegetable Soup

1 pound shin beef with bone
3 1/2 quarts water
2 cups shredded cabbage
1 cup cut-up green beans
1 cup diced carrots
1 (1-pound, 4-ounce) can tomatoes
3/4 cup diced celery
2/3 cup fresh peas
1/2 cup chopped onion
1 1/2 teaspoons salt
1 clove garlic, chopped
1/8 teaspoon pepper
Chopped parsley

Place beef and bone in large kettle, cover with water and add salt. Cover kettle, bring to boil and skim. Simmer 4 hours; then remove bare bone. Add remaining ingredients, except parsley, cover, and simmer 1/2 hour. Garnish with parsley. Serves 8–10.

Oxtail Soup

1 1/2 pounds oxtail, cut in small pieces
1 tablespoon melted butter or margarine
1 1/2 quarts water
4 teaspoons salt
3/4 cup diced raw carrots
1/2 cup sliced onions
1/2 cup diced raw celery
2 tablespoons rice (not quick-cooking variety)
1 (1-pound) can tomatoes

Brown oxtails in butter or margarine. Add water and salt; cover, and simmer 2 hours. Add carrots, onions, celery and rice, and simmer 1/2 hour longer. Skim fat off surface, add tomatoes and heat thoroughly. Serves 4.

Clam–Tomato Bisque

1 (2-pound, 3-ounce) can tomatoes
1/2 cup water
1 onion, chopped (1/2 cup)
2 stalks celery, chopped (1/2 cup)
1/4 cup chopped green pepper
1 bay leaf
2 tablespoons chopped parsley
1 teaspoon sugar
Dash thyme
Salt and pepper to taste
Juice of 1/2 lemon
1 (6-ounce) can clams
1/2 cup whipped cream, slightly salted

Put tomatoes in heavy saucepan with water, onion, celery, pepper and bay leaf. Cover tightly, and simmer 20 minutes. Remove bay leaf. Add parsley, sugar, seasonings, lemon juice and clams. Serve topped with whipped cream. Serves 4–5.

Green-and-Gold Chowder

4 slices salt pork, diced
1 1/2 cups water
1 cup diced peeled potatoes
2 chicken bouillon cubes
1 (1-pound, 1-ounce) can cream-style corn
1 (1-pound, 1-ounce) can kernel corn
1/4–1/2 cup sliced green onions including some tops
3 tablespoons flour
1/2 cup cold water
Dash cayenne
Pinch mace
1 pint hot milk

In deep saucepan fry salt pork slowly until crisp; don't allow it to burn. Add 1 1/2 cups water, potatoes and bouillon cubes. Simmer about 15 minutes; add both cans corn, and onions. Simmer 2 minutes. Make smooth mixture of flour and 1/2 cup water, and stir into corn. Add cayenne and mace. Bring to boil. Stir in milk and reheat thoroughly, but do not boil. Serves 5–6.

Chicken–Meringue Soup

1 quart strong chicken broth
1 carrot, grated (approximately 1/2 cup)
1/4 cup onion, chopped
2 tablespoons minute tapioca
2 cups hot milk

2 egg yolks, well beaten
1/2 cup cream
1/2 cup diced cooked chicken (optional)
2 tablespoons chopped parsley
Salt and pepper to taste
2 egg whites
1/2 teaspoon salt
1/2 cup grated Parmesan cheese

Heat chicken broth with carrot and onion until vegetables are tender. Add tapioca, and simmer gently until tapioca is transparent. Add milk. Mix egg yolks with cream. Add cream-and-egg mixture to soup. Cook slowly until soup is slightly thickened, do not boil. Add salt, pepper, chicken and parsley. Beat egg whites with 1/2 teaspoon salt until stiff. Place soup in oven-proof casserole or individual pottery bowls. Cover top with beaten egg whites, sprinkle with cheese and brown quickly under hot broiler. Serve at once. Serves 6–8.

Minestrone

1 slice day-old bread
1/2 cup red wine or tomato juice
1 pound fresh-ground meat
1 egg, lightly beaten
2 tablespoons chopped onion
1 teaspoon salt
1/4 teaspoon marjoram
1/4 teaspoon sweet basil
1/4 teaspoon garlic salt
1 cup dried navy beans
5 cups water
1 teaspoon salt
1/4 cup hot oil
1/2 cup diced celery with leaves
1/2 cup shredded cabbage
1/2 cup diced turnip
1 clove garlic, crushed
2 cups beef broth or bouillon
2 sliced onions
1 (1-pound, 13-ounce) can tomatoes
    (strained if you wish)
1 bay leaf
1 clove
1 cup tiny macaroni shells or elbow macaroni
2 quarts boiling salted water
1/4 cup grated Parmesan cheese

Crumble bread into wine; add next 7 ingredients. Form into small balls, the size of hazelnuts, and refrigerate until needed. Wash beans and soak overnight in 5 cups water. Next morning add 1 teaspoon salt, and simmer 30 minutes. Sauté meat balls in oil; when richly browned, drain and set aside. Pour off 1/2 the fat, and add celery, cabbage, turnip and garlic to pan; fry, stirring, 5 minutes. Scrape into large saucepan, and add next 5 ingredients and undrained beans. Cover, and simmer 1 hour or until beans are almost tender, stirring occasionally. Meanwhile,

cook macaroni in boiling water until almost tender. Drain. Add macaroni and meat balls to soup. Cover, and simmer 20 minutes. Taste for seasoning. Serve in deep bowls, sprinkled with cheese. Serves 10.

Gazpacho

1 small onion, chopped
1 cup fresh tomatoes, peeled and diced
1/2 cup diced green pepper
1/2 cup diced celery
1/2 cup diced cucumber
1/2 clove garlic
3 cups tomato juice
1/3 cup FRENCH DRESSING
1 tablespoon lemon juice
Salt and cayenne to taste

Place all vegetables and garlic in blender with 1 cup tomato juice. Blend until mixture is smooth. Add French dressing, lemon juice, salt and cayenne with remaining tomato juice. Chill thoroughly. Serve very cold with small bowls of cubed tomato, celery, green pepper and cucumber, to be sprinkled over soup. Serves 5–6.

Cold Cream of Asparagus Soup

1/2 pound fresh asparagus
1 1/2 cups water
1 sliced onion
2 chicken bouillon cubes
2 tablespoons quick-cooking tapioca
1 (10 1/2-ounce) can cream of chicken soup
1/2 cup light cream
Salt and pepper to taste

Wash asparagus, and discard tough ends. Simmer in water with onion and bouillon cubes 10 minutes. Add tapioca, and simmer 5 minutes. Pour into blender, and blend 30 seconds. Add soup and cream, and blend 10 seconds. Season to taste, and chill well.

Ideas for Leftovers. Do plan to have leftovers so that you can put meals together quickly at times and extend the enjoyment of a fine roast or a whole fish over several meals, each individually distinctive and tempting.

Cooked roast beef, pot roast or steak can be ground or chopped and used in casseroles, expanded with macaroni and vegetables. Or substitute it for raw meat in spaghetti sauce. Mixed with thick cream sauce, it can become croquettes, fried delicately brown, with a little cooked rice, it can stuff cabbage rolls, peppers and tomatoes, to be baked with sauces of canned soup, for example. Beef bones can form the basis of a good soup, with onions, carrots, and barley added.

Cooked lamb roast or chops can be used as the basis of lamb curry, in a meat and macaroni casserole or in pot pie. Leftover lamb stew needs only a can of lima beans, a handful of frozen peas and some curry power to become a version of curried lamb.

Cooked pork can be used in any of the same ways as beef and lamb, or as the basis for small or family-size pork pies. The meat is ground and mixed with onions and a little seasoning. Or cut it into thin strips and use it in Chinese fried rice, pork chop suey, and so forth.

Baked or boiled ham bones can go into lentil, lima bean or dried-pea soup. Dice any remaining meat, and serve it with cream sauce or in ham omelet. Ground, it can be mixed with a little salad dressing for deviled-ham sandwiches. Mixed with diced onion and cooked rice, it can stuff peppers or tomatoes.

Roast, broiled or fried chicken can be used in Chinese fried rice or chop suey; it can also form the basis for a chicken casserole, made with cream of chicken soup, frozen peas and carrots and a biscuit crust. It is excellent of course, in chicken salad, chicken à la king or croquettes. Or try making toast cups: Trim crusts from fresh bread, press each slice into muffin cup and toast in oven, fill with creamed chicken mixture to make a quick snack.

Even the smallest amounts of cooked vegetables can be used to advantage. Mashed potatoes go into sautéed fish cakes with an egg to bind the mixture. Leftover carrots, turnips or spinach combined, puréed and added to thin white sauce, make a delicious cream of vegetable soup.

Casserole of Turkey Slices

      1/4 cup chopped onion
        1 tablespoon melted butter or margarine
        1 cup tomato catsup
      1/2 tablespoon prepared mustard
      1/2 cup chopped celery
      1/4 cup water
      1/4 cup lemon juice
        3 tablespoons Worcestershire sauce
        2 tablespoons brown sugar
    Dash pepper
    Dash cayenne
        6 thick slices cooked turkey (2 pounds)

Sauté onion slowly in butter or margarine until golden; do not brown. Add remaining ingredients, except turkey, and simmer, covered, 15 minutes. Adjust seasoning to taste. Pour sauce over turkey slices in casserole, cover and heat about 20 minutes at 350° F. Serves 6.

Jellied Turkey Salad

        1 (3-ounce) package lime or lemon gelatin
        1 cup boiling water
        1 cup less 2 tablespoons cold water
        1 tablespoon lemon juice

        1 cup diced cooked turkey
      1/2 cup finely chopped cabbage
      1/4 cup diced green pepper
        2 tablespoons chopped pimento or sliced radishes
        1 tablespoon chopped chives or green-onion tops
        1 tablespoon diced sweet pickle

Dissolve gelatin powder in boiling water; add cold water and lemon juice. Chill in refrigerator until syrupy. Oil 6 1-cup individual molds (or 1 6-cup mold). Thoroughly combine remaining ingredients, and divide among molds. Pour chilled gelatin over contents, and chill until set. Serves 5–6.

Chicken–Almond Casserole

        3 tablespoons fat or drippings
      2/3 cup chopped celery
      1/3 cup chopped onion
      1/4 cup chopped green pepper
        2 tablespoons flour
        2 chicken bouillon cubes dissolved in 1 1/2 cups
           hot water or chicken stock
        1 (10-ounce) can chicken gravy
      1/2 teaspoon salt
      1/4 teaspoon dry mustard
    1 1/2 cups diced cooked chicken
      1/2 cup toasted almonds
    2 1/2–3 cups cooked noodles
      1/2 cup buttered bread crumbs

Melt fat in frying pan; add celery, onion and green pepper. Sauté until vegetables are lightly colored. Stir in flour. Add bouillon, gravy, salt and mustard, and cook until mixture thickens. Alternate layers of diced chicken, almonds, sauce and noodles in greased 2-quart casserole, ending with noodles. Sprinkle with buttered crumbs and bake at 350° F. 30–40 minutes. Serves 6.

Note: Any leftover poultry or cooked meat may be substituted, so don't be afraid to experiment. Most dishes specifying finely cut or chopped meat can be varied.

Deviled Beef Ribs

    Cooked beef ribs
    Prepared mustard
    Bread crumbs
        2 teaspoons dry mustard
        1 cup medium white sauce

Smear ribs with thick layer of prepared mustard; then coat thoroughly with bread crumbs. Place in broiling pan under broiler until crumbs are browned; turn off broiler, and let meat heat through completely in warm oven. Make sauce of dry mustard and white sauce and pour over.

Note: Deviled ribs are a delicious Tuesday luncheon dish with leftovers from Sunday's standing rib roast. Leave 1/4 inch meat on bones when first carving the roast. Allow 2 ribs for each serving. For a variation, save bones in same way, but spread generously with barbecue sauce, and brown under broiler.

Brunswick Stew

    3 cups mixed leftover cooked meats (roast beef, pork
        or veal)
    1 (10 1/2-ounce) can condensed consommé
    1 (1-pound, 13-ounce) can tomatoes
    3 tablespoons white wine
Salt and pepper to taste
    1 (10-ounce) package frozen lima beans
    6–8 potatoes, peeled
    1 (1-pound, 1-ounce) can kernel corn, drained

Cut meat into bite-size pieces, and place in saucepan. Cover with consommé, and add tomatoes. Bring just to boil. Add wine and seasonings, and reduce heat to simmer. Meantime cook frozen lima beans separately, following package directions, and boil potatoes. When beans are almost tender, drain, and add to meat mixture. When potatoes are done, drain, cube, and add to stew, together with corn. Heat thoroughly, and add further seasonings if necessary. Serves 6–8.

Fish in Aspic

    2 envelopes powdered gelatin
    1 3/4 cups cold fish stock or 2 chicken bouillon cubes
        dissolved in water
    2 tablespoons capers
    1 tablespoon caper juice
    1 tablespoon lemon juice
Salt and pepper to taste
Paprika
    4 1/4 cups cooked flaked fish
    1 cup mayonnaise
    2 tablespoons chopped chives
    2 tablespoons chopped parsley
    2 tablespoons diced cucumber

Soak gelatin in 3 tablespoons cold fish stock. Heat remaining stock, and dissolve gelatin in it. Add capers and caper juice. Season stock well with lemon juice, salt, pepper and paprika. Chill until mixture begins to thicken; place layer of aspic in 8-cup rinsed mold. Mix flaked fish with rest of aspic and pour into mold. Chill well, and serve very cold with mayonnaise to which chopped chives, chopped parsley and diced cucumber have been added. Serves 6.

Scalloped Fish with Cheese

    1/2 cup butter or margarine
    1/2 teaspoon salt
    2 tablespoons chopped green pepper
    1 tablespoon chopped onion
    2 tablespoons flour
    1 cup milk
    1 teaspoon bottled thick meat sauce
    1 1/2 cups flaked cooked fish

    1/3 cup grated Cheddar cheese
    1/2 cup soft bread crumbs

Melt butter or margarine in double boiler over direct heat. Add salt, green pepper, onion, and cook until tender. Stir in flour, and slowly add milk and meat sauce. Cook over boiling water until smooth, stirring constantly. Arrange alternate layers of fish and sauce in buttered casserole or individual ramekins. Combine cheese and crumbs and spread on top. Bake at 400° F. until brown. Serves 4.

Quick Vermicelli Supper

    8 ounces long vermicelli
    3 quarts boiling salted water
    1/4 cup fat
    4 medium onions, sliced
        (approximately 2 cups)
    2 green peppers, chopped
        (approximately 1 cup)
    2 cloves garlic, finely chopped
    2 tablespoons flour
    1 can (1 lb. 4 oz.) tomatoes
    2 cups diced leftover beef
    2 1/2 teaspoons salt
    1 teaspoon thyme
    1/4 teaspoon powdered cloves
    1/4 cup Parmesan cheese, grated

Boil vermicelli in salted water. While it cooks, melt fat in good-sized skillet. Add raw vegetables and garlic, and cook until tender. Push vegetables to one side. Add flour, and stir into fat thoroughly, letting bubble for 1–2 minutes. Gradually add tomatoes, stirring constantly until well mixed. Add meat and seasonings. Drain vermicelli, and arrange in deep serving dish. Pour sauce over, and sprinkle with cheese. Serves 4–6.

Shepherd's Pie

    3 cups ground cooked beef
    1/4 cup leftover gravy or bouillon
    1 tablespoon bottled thick meat sauce
    2 1/2 cups mashed potatoes
    2 tablespoons finely chopped onion
    1 egg, beaten
Salt and pepper to taste
    2 tablespoons butter or margarine

Combine meat with enough leftover gravy and condiment sauce to moisten well and hold mixture together. Turn meat into baking dish; pat level. Combine mashed potatoes, onion, egg, salt and pepper. Cover meat with potato mixture, and smooth. Dot with butter or margarine, and bake at 375°F. 25–30 minutes or until potato topping is puffed and lightly browned. Serves 6.

Note: When preparing beef, remove hard bits and gristle, but put some of the fat through the grinder with the lean.

Speedy Chow Mein

1/4 cup fat
2 cups cooked pork or beef cut in 1/4-inch strips
2 cups sliced celery
2 cups sliced mushrooms
2 cups sliced onion
1/2 cup sliced green pepper
1/2 cup chicken broth
1 tablespoon cornstarch
2 teaspoons Worcestershire sauce
1 teaspoon salt
1 (1-pound, 12-ounce) can bean sprouts,
     drained and rinsed
1 tablespoon soy sauce
1 teaspoon preserved ginger, finely chopped
1 package ready-to-use Chinese fried noodles, heated

Melt fat in skillet, and gently sauté meat, celery, mushrooms and onion about 8 minutes. Add green pepper, and sauté 2–3 minutes longer. Mix chicken broth with cornstarch; add Worcestershire sauce and salt. Stir this mixture lightly into meat and vegetables, add bean sprouts and toss mixture lightly with fork. Never stir chow mein vigorously as such handling makes it mushy. Cover pan, and heat 5 minutes. Add soy sauce, scatter ginger over top; then sprinkle noodles over all. Accompany with hot rice. Serves 6–8.

Half-hour Veal Creole

1 cup sliced onion
1/4 cup salad oil
2 cups cubed cooked veal
1 (1-pound, 13-ounce) can tomatoes
1 cup diced green pepper
1 cup sliced mushrooms
2 teaspoons salt
2 teaspoons sugar
2 whole cloves
1 bay leaf
Dash pepper
1/4 cup flour
1/3 cup water

Sauté onions in hot oil until just tender. Add all except last 2 ingredients. Cover, and simmer 25 minutes. Make smooth paste of flour and water, and thicken veal mixture. Cook another 5 minutes, stirring constantly. Serves 5–6.

Ham–Bean Casserole

1 (20-ounce) can lima beans
1 (20-ounce) can red kidney beans
1 cup diced cooked ham
1 (10 1/2-ounce) can cream of mushroom soup
1 teaspoon Worcestershire sauce
1 medium green pepper, thinly sliced
     (approximately 1/2 cup)
1 small onion, thinly sliced (approximately 1/4 cup)

Drain both cans beans, reserving liquid from kidney beans. Combine beans and ham, and place in casserole. Blend soup with Worcestershire sauce and 1/4 cup kidney-bean liquid; pour over beans and ham. Arrange rings of pepper and onion over top, and bake at 350° F. 35 minutes or until bubbling hot. Serves 8.

Creamed Ham with Mushrooms

3 tablespoons butter or margarine
1/4 pound fresh mushrooms, sliced
1/4 cup flour
1 1/2 cups milk
1/4 teaspoon salt
Speck pepper
1 1/4 cups diced cooked ham
1/4 teaspoon bottled thick meat sauce

Melt butter or margarine, and sauté mushrooms till tender. Stir in flour, add milk and seasonings, and cook over boiling water until smooth and thickened, stirring constantly. Add ham and meat sauce. Heat 5 minutes longer. Serve over split and buttered corn bread, tea biscuits, or toasted English muffins. Serves 4.

VARIATION:

Diced cooked chicken may be used instead of ham; meat sauce should then be omitted and sweet paprika or curry powder added to taste: serve over tea biscuits or toast or in toast cups.

Fish Timbale

2 cups flaked cooked fish
1/4 cup butter or margarine, melted
3/4 cup bread crumbs
3 egg yolks, lightly beaten
3 egg whites
2 teaspoons lemon juice
Salt and pepper to taste

Combine first 4 ingredients in mixing bowl. Beat egg whites until stiff, and fold into mixture. Add lemon juice and seasonings. Place in greased 4-cup mold, and steam 1 hour. Serve with cream sauce spiked with dash of Worcestershire sauce. Serves 6.

Jellied Deviled Tongue

2 envelopes powdered gelatin
1/2 cup cold water
1 3/4 cups boiling water
1/4 cup mayonnaise
2 tablespoons bottled horseradish
1 tablespoon prepared mustard
1 teaspoon salt
1/4 teaspoon pepper
2 cups chopped cooked tongue
2 hard-cooked eggs, chopped
1/4 cup chopped sour pickle

Soften gelatin in cold water 5 minutes. Add to boiling water, and stir until dissolved. Let stand till almost cool; then beat in next 5 ingredients. Chill until thick and syrupy. Add tongue, eggs and pickle. Rinse loaf pan with cold water, pour in mixture and chill until firm. Unmold and slice. Serves 8.

Ham–Rice Pompoms

        1 1/2 cups cooked rice
        1 1/2 cups ground cooked ham
        1/2 cup chopped Brazil nuts
        1/4 cup chopped onion
            2 tablespoons butter or margarine, melted
            2 eggs, beaten
            1 tablespoon prepared mustard
            1 tablespoon flour
    Salt to taste
        1/2 cup fine dry bread crumbs
        1 1/2 cups pineapple juice

Combine first 9 ingredients and form into 12 croquettes (the variation in salt depends on the mildness of ham). Roll in crumbs, and place in well-greased baking pan. Pour pineapple juice around croquettes. Bake uncovered at 350° F. 30–40 minutes, basting now and then with juice. Serve with MUSHROOM SAUCE.

Note: Any leftover cooked, smoked or pickled pork, free of fat and bone, may be substituted.

Stuffed Baked Potatoes

            6 medium potatoes
            2 tablespoons drippings or butter
            1 cup chopped cooked meat
            1 tablespoon butter or margarine
            1 tablespoon cream
            1 tablespoon finely chopped onion
            1 tablespoon finely chopped parsley
        1/2 teaspoon salt
        1/4 teaspoon pepper
        1/4 cup stock or gravy
            2 tablespoons Worcestershire sauce
        1/4 cup grated cheese

Choose well-shaped potatoes of even sizes. Scrub well, pat dry and grease lightly with drippings or butter. Bake at 350° F. about 1 hour or at 450° F. about 40 minutes. Larger potatoes require more time. When potatoes are done, cut thin slice off flat side of each, and remove as much potato as possible without breaking skin. Combine potato lightly (do not mash) with next 9 ingredients, using fork, then moisten with stock, and season with Worcestershire sauce. Fill potato skins with mixture, and heap tops. Sprinkle each with grated cheese, and brown in 400° F. oven or under broiler. Serves 6.

Note: Baked potatoes may be filled with leftover fish, vegetables and so forth in any palatable combination, in cream sauce or merely buttered. Interesting additions to leftover mixtures are chopped bacon, sautéed sliced mushrooms, chopped chives, browned, chopped onion.

Good Companions. *Main dishes have maximum appeal when accompaniments help to create balanced flavors, colors and textures.*

In planning meals, the most important factor of course is your choice of meat or alternative. Accompaniments, though, should be thoughtfully chosen. There are many combinations that can add different looks and flavors to main courses.

Color, texture and flavor are the points that will decide what goes with what, which is why the blandness of veal, for instance, is offset by a spicy tomato sauce or a savory herb dressing.

There are certain accompaniments—spiced fruit with ham, the well-known stuffings and cranberry sauce with turkey, currant jelly or mint sauce with lamb, applesauce with pork, crisp relishes with almost any cooked meat, dumplings with beef stew—that add special notes to many a meal. And garnishes are not always strictly ornamental. The sprigs of parsley and lemon wedges you serve with fish add flavor, as well as color.

Sometimes an ordinary meal can win you extravagant compliments, and the difference may lie in a little added note, something you have done to point up the flavors or something you serve with your main dish to take it right into the class of very special cooking.

Never be afraid to be adventurous. Something that's completely new with you may in time become a tradition. Do look to other lands for examples: to the Chinese, with their sweet-and-pungent accents, or to the French, with their simple green salads and epicurean sliced tomatoes.

Affinities with Herbs

You can point up the natural flavor of your meat with herbs. For lamb use the time-honored touch of mint or rosemary, savory or dill. Beef takes well to basil, thyme, marjoram, savory or rosemary. Veal goes with sage, tarragon, summer savory, thyme or basil. Monosodium glutamate, a prepared chemical salt long known to the Chinese, enhances the flavor of meat. And if you haven't yet tried freshly ground pepper, you'll find that it adds piquancy to any dish.

Gravies and Sauces

The most appetizing gravy takes only a few minutes to make, and, when you've mastered the basic method, you can apply your skill with virtually all meats.

You need a thickener (flour or cornstarch) and a separating ingredient (melted fat or cold water) to prevent lumping when boiling water or stock is added to the mixture. Flour will give you a more opaque gravy than will cornstarch, which produces a thick, clear gravy. When you use cornstarch, remember that it has about double the thickening power of flour so that you need only 1/2 as much. Choose all-purpose flour (rather than the pastry type) when you use water as the separating ingredient.

If the drippings in your roasting pan are not brown enough when the flour is blended with them, brown them further by cooking and stirring over medium heat. Remember, gravy will not brown any more after you have added water or stock. Gravy made from beef drippings seldom needs additional color or flavor, but you might like to add bouillon cubes or liquid bouillon when you make gravy from pork, lamb or veal drippings.

Vary the flavor of your gravies by experimenting with seasonings. Two teaspoons of chopped or instant dry onion or a couple of tablespoons of sliced mushrooms can be added to brown gravy or if you prefer the fresh sweet taste of celery use 1 teaspoon dried celery flakes or 2 teaspoons finely chopped fresh celery.

Some meat dishes and many types of fish dishes taste best when served in smooth, creamy white sauce. Like brown gravy, white sauce needs only the simplest ingredients—fat, flour, liquid. Butter or margarine is the best fat to use in white sauce; the liquid can be milk, light cream or a mixture containing the nutritious stock from mild-flavored vegetables.

If you use 1 tablespoon butter or margarine and 1 tablespoon flour to 1 cup liquid, you will have a thin sauce ideal for cream soups. Increasing the flour and butter to 2 tablespoons each for the same amount of liquid will make the sauce thicker and richer for your meat and fish dishes, poultry and vegetables. For croquettes and soufflés you will need an even thicker sauce; increase the butter or margarine and flour measurements to 3 tablespoons of each, again keeping liquid constant. Season your white sauce with salt and freshly ground pepper. If cream sauce is not to be served immediately, it must be covered with a tightly fitting lid to prevent a skin from forming on top, and placed in refrigerator. Cream sauce taken off the heat and kept at room temperature 2 hours or longer is hazardous to use because of bacterial growth. If use is to be long delayed, reheat refrigerated sauce to gentle boil for several minutes before serving.

Horseradish Sauce

        1 tablespoon butter or margarine
    1/4 cup prepared horseradish
        1 tablespoon all-purpose flour
        1 tablespoon lemon juice
        1 teaspoon sugar
    1/8 teaspoon salt
        1 bouillon cube
    1/4 cup boiling water
    1/2 cup commercial sour cream

Melt butter or margarine. Blend in flour, salt, sugar, lemon juice and horseradish. Dissolve bouillon cube in boiling water, and add to sauce. Cook, stirring, over medium heat until thickened. Simmer 10 minutes. Remove from heat, and allow to cool 3 minutes. Stir in sour cream. Makes 1 cup.

Note: Serve with beef, tongue, steak, veal or meat loaf; it is a very smooth sauce but with a tang.

Chicken Gravy

    3 tablespoons fat remaining from frying chicken
    3 tablespoons flour
    2 cups hot meat juices, stock, water or milk
    Salt and pepper to taste

Pour off fat and juices that remain after cooking chicken; leave all brown residue in pan. Measure fat back into pan, and stir in flour. Cook over low heat, stirring constantly, until mixture bubbles; continue cooking to brown flour-fat mixture as desired. Pour in hot liquid, and cook, stirring constantly, and scraping bottom and sides of the pan to blend brown particles into gravy. Simmer about 5 minutes till uniformly thickened, season and serve very hot. Chopped, cooked giblets may be added to gravy. Makes 1 pint.

Mustard Sauce

        2 tablespoons dry mustard
        2 tablespoons flour
        1 teaspoon sugar
    1/4 teaspoon salt
    3/4 cup boiling water
        1 bouillon cube
        2 tablespoons vinegar
        2 egg yolks, slightly beaten
        1 teaspoon butter or margarine

Combine mustard, flour, sugar and salt in top of double boiler. Combine water and bouillon cube, and add to mustard mixture. Stir in vinegar. Add egg yolks and butter or margarine. Cook over hot water until thickened, stirring constantly. Serve hot or cold, with ham, tongue or corned beef. Makes 1 cup.

Curry Sauce

          1 tablespoon butter or margarine
          1 small onion, chopped
                (approximately 1/4 cup)
          1 tablespoon all-purpose flour
     1 1/2 teaspoons curry powder
          1 (8-ounce) can crushed pineapple
        1/2 cup water
          1 teaspoon lemon juice
     Salt to taste
     Dash cayenne

Melt butter or margarine. Add onion; cook, stirring over medium heat until tender. Stir in flour and curry powder. Add and mix in pineapple. Add water, and simmer 15 minutes. Stir occasionally. Add lemon juice, salt and cayenne. Serve hot or cold with lamb or chicken. Makes 1 cup.

Note: Meat or vegetable stock can replace some or all of the liquid called for.

Garlic Cheese Sauce

          1 tablespoon butter or margarine
          1 clove garlic, halved
          1 cup evaporated milk
          1 cup grated Canadian Cheddar cheese
        1/2 teaspoon salt
        1/4 teaspoon pepper

Melt butter or margarine in top of double boiler. Add garlic; cook 5 minutes. Remove garlic; add milk and heat. Stir in cheese until melted. Season with salt and pepper. This sauce is good with macaroni, vegetables (especially asparagus) or poached eggs on toast. Makes 1 3/4 cups.

Mint Sauce

        1/4 cup hot water
        1/4 cup vinegar
          3 tablespoons sugar
        1/4 cup finely chopped mint leaves

Combine water, vinegar and sugar. Stir until sugar is dissolved. Pour over mint leaves. Set in warm place 1/2 hour. Serve with lamb. Makes 1/2 cup sauce.

Raisin Sauce

        1/2 cup brown sugar
          2 teaspoons cornstarch
        1/4 cup water
        1/2 cup seedless raisins, washed and drained
     1 1/2 tablespoons vinegar
          1 tablespoon butter or margarine
     Juice and grated rind of 1 orange
        1/2 teaspoon salt

Combine sugar and cornstarch in saucepan. Stir in water. Cook, stirring, over medium heat

5 minutes. Add raisins. Cook, stirring, 5 minutes longer. Add next 4 ingredients. Serve with ham or pork. Makes approximately 1 cup sauce.

Cranberry Sauce

          2 cups sugar
        1/2 cup water
          1 pound (about 4 cups) cranberries

Measure sugar into saucepan. Add water. Bring to boil, stirring constantly. Lower heat. Cook, stirring 5 minutes over low heat. Pick over and wash cranberries. Remove any tiny stems. Add cranberries to sauce, and cook over low heat until berries are tender, a few minutes only. This sauce is traditional with poultry. Makes 3 cups.

Cranberry Jelly

          1 pound (about 4 cups) cranberries
          1 cup water
          2 cups sugar

Pick over and wash cranberries, removing any stems. Put cranberries in saucepan. Add water. Cook until cranberries stop popping and are very soft. Press through sieve. Add sugar, and stir until sugar is dissolved. Return to medium heat, and cook 5 minutes. Pour into 5 (8-ounce) jelly glasses and chill. Serve with poultry.

Easy Hollandaise Sauce

          3 egg yolks
        1/4 teaspoon salt
          2 tablespoons lemon juice or vinegar
        1/3 cup butter or margarine, melted
        1/4 cup boiling water

Beat egg yolks slightly; add salt and lemon juice. Stir in melted butter or margarine and add boiling water. Place over hot but not boiling water. Cook, stirring, until thickened, about 5 minutes. Serve immediately, or set aside, and reheat when needed. Makes 3/4 cup.

Tomato Sauce

          2 tablespoons chopped onion
          2 tablespoons butter or margarine
          2 tablespoons flour
          1 teaspoon sugar
          1 teaspoon salt
        1/8 teaspoon pepper
          6 peppercorns
          1 bay leaf
          1 (1-pound, 4-ounce) can tomatoes

Cook onion in butter or margarine until tender. Stir in flour and cook until bubbly. Add sugar and seasonings. Slowly add tomatoes, and cook, stirring, until thickened. Simmer 5 minutes. Remove peppercorns and bay leaf before serving. Makes 2 cups.

Barbecue Sauce

      1/2 cup chopped onion
      1/2 cup tomato catsup
      1/3 cup water
      1/4 cup vinegar
        2 tablespoons sugar
      1/2 teaspoon chili powder
      1/2 teaspoon salt
      Few drops hot pepper sauce

Combine all ingredients in saucepan. Bring to boil, lower heat and simmer 5 minutes. Serve with spareribs, lamb, meat patties, pork chops, wieners or use to baste any barbecued meats. Makes about 1 1/4 cups.

Drawn Butter Sauce

        1 cup butter or margarine
      1/4 cup fresh lemon juice
      1/2 teaspoon salt
      1/4 teaspoon pepper

Blend all ingredients together and heat.

VARIATIONS:

Parsley Sauce: Add 1 tablespoon finely chopped parsley.

Caper Sauce: Add 2 tablespoons drained pickled capers.

Lemon Sauce for Fish

      1/4 cup mayonnaise
        2 tablespoons flour
        1 cup milk
        1 tablespoon lemon juice
        1 teaspoon grated lemon rind
      1/4 teaspoon salt
        1 tablespoon chopped parsley

Blend mayonnaise and flour. Add milk. Cook until thickened. Add lemon juice slowly. Mix in grated rind and salt. Add parsley. Makes enough for 6 servings of fish (1 1/3 cups).

Seafood Cocktail Sauce

        3 tablespoons catsup
        1 tablespoon mayonnaise
        2 teaspoons lemon juice
        1 teaspoon horseradish
      1/4 teaspoon prepared mustard
      1/4 teaspoon barbecue sauce
        2 drops hot pepper sauce

Mix ingredients until well blended. Makes 1/4 cup.

Egg Sauce

        1 cup white sauce or DRAWN BUTTER SAUCE
        1 hard-cooked egg, coarsely chopped or sliced

To sauce add egg, and mix well. Makes 1 cup.

Parsley Butter or Maître d'Hôtel Sauce

      1/4 cup soft butter or margarine
        1 tablespoon chopped parsley
        2 teaspoons lemon juice
      1/2 teaspoon salt

Cream butter, and blend in other ingredients. Shape into tiny pats or balls, and chill. Dot over steak before serving.

Stuffings. Stuffing for meat, fish or poultry fills the cavity with an aromatic mixture of seasonings and at the same time absorbs some of the juices that would otherwise evaporate (and of course the juices absorbed in turn add flavor to the dressing).

For best results, bread should be a few days old, so that, having lost some of its own moisture, it will be more uniform in bulk and will absorb more flavor and juice. The bread may be treated in different ways: Some cooks prefer to soak stale bread in beaten egg, then stir bread and add onions, herbs and other ingredients; you can stir chopped onions and bread cubes or crumbs into foaming butter in frying pan and sauté them lightly before adding other ingredients, or you can brown bread or melba toast slowly in oven, which adds an almost nutlike flavor.

Stuffing should be packed into cavity very lightly. Remember, bread will swell during cooking, so leave plenty of room. Remember too that dressing absorbs some of the juices, so it should be fairly dry to start with. Allow about 3/4 cup stuffing for each pound of bird, drawn weight.

It isn't necessary to take the word "stuffing" too literally. Most people like it for its own texture and flavor and it can be served apart from the roast or fowl: cooked in a baking dish, in aluminum foil, in individual muffin cups. It can be rolled lightly into balls about the size of a golf ball and baked in a separate pan. Such methods are best, though, with dressings that contain egg for binding ingredients together.

It is important that stuffing for poultry be completely cooled before inserting in bird.

Basic Bread Stuffing

      1/4 cup chopped onion
        2 tablespoons fat
        2 cups soft stale bread crumbs
        2 tablespoons chopped parsley
      1/2 teaspoon salt
      1/8 teaspoon pepper

Brown onion lightly in fat. Add bread crumbs and seasonings, and heat slightly. Makes about 2 cups.

Note: For use with beef, as in rolled flank steak, add 1/2 teaspoon savory or marjoram. For veal, spice should be thyme or savory. For pork, use sage or savory, plus 2–3 tablespoons chopped tart apple. For lamb add 4 tablespoons chopped fresh mint or 1/2 teaspoon thyme.

Old-fashioned Poultry Stuffing

    8 cups fine fairly dry crumbs
    3/4 cup finely chopped onion
    1/2 cup melted butter or margarine
    2 tablespoons finely chopped celery leaves
    2–3 teaspoons poultry seasoning or combination of savory
             and sage
    1/2 teaspoon salt
    1/8 teaspoon pepper

Combine ingredients thoroughly. Taste, and adjust seasonings. Stuff lightly into neck and body cavities of turkey, and close openings. Increase or reduce recipe to suit size of bird to be stuffed. (Makes about 8 cups or enough for a 12–15 pound bird.)

Caribbean Rice Stuffing

    3 cups cooked rice
    1 (8-ounce) can crushed pineapple, drained
    1/3 cup melted butter or margarine
    1 teaspoon cinnamon
    Salt and pepper to taste

Combine crushed, drained pineapple, cooked rice, butter or margarine, seasonings, and pineapple. Mix well. Stuff body and neck cavity. Makes enough for 5-pound chicken. Delicious with pork, too.

Southern Stuffing

    2 cups fine bread crumbs
    1/2 cup butter or margarine, melted
    1/2 cup pecans
    2 tablespoons finely chopped onion
    2 tablespoons diced celery
    1/2 teaspoon salt
    1/2 teaspoon rosemary
    1/4 teaspoon ginger
    1/4 teaspoon savory

Mix ingredients, tossing lightly but thoroughly. Adjust seasonings to taste. Stuff lightly into neck and body cavities of bird. Makes about 2 1/2 cups or enough for a 4-pound bird.

Note: If baking chicken breasts, arrange stuffing in mounds on baking pan, cover with breasts, skin side up, and sprinkle with lemon juice, salt, pepper and melted butter or margarine; bake in moderately hot oven 375°F. 50–60 minutes. Cover chicken breasts with aluminum foil for first 35 minutes of cooking period.

Cranberry Stuffing

    1/4 cup butter or margarine, melted
    4 cups bread crumbs (3–4 day-old bread)
    1 cup canned whole-cranberry sauce
    1/4 cup water
    1/4 cup raisins
    2 tablespoons sugar
    2 teaspoons grated lemon rind
    1 teaspoon salt
    1/4 teaspoon cinnamon

Blend butter or margarine and bread crumbs. Add cranberries and other ingredients. Toss lightly until well mixed. Stuff bird.

Note: 1 cup fresh cranberries, chopped, and 2 additional tablespoons sugar may be substituted for canned cranberry sauce.

Potato Stuffing

    6 cups fluffy mashed potatoes
    1 1/2 cups soft bread crumbs
    1/4 cup finely chopped onion
    1/4 cup butter or margarine, melted
    3 tablespoons cream or top milk
    2 egg yolks
    1–2 teaspoons poultry seasoning
    1 teaspoon salt
    1/4 teaspoon pepper

Combine potatoes, butter or margarine, onion, egg yolks, crumbs and cream. Add seasonings a little at a time, to taste. Pile stuffing lightly into neck and body cavities of chicken. Do not pack. The amount is approximately enough to fill a 6-pound chicken, allowing some extra to be baked separately during final hour of roasting.

Rice–Raisin Stuffing

    1 cup rice
    1 (10 1/2-ounce) can boiling bouillon, diluted, or 2 1/2
             cups boiling stock
    2 tablespoons butter or margarine
    1 cup finely chopped celery
    1/4 cup chopped onion
    1 cup seedless raisins
    2 tablespoons chopped parsley
    1 teaspoon poultry seasoning
    1/4 teaspoon nutmeg or cinnamon (optional)
    Salt and pepper to taste

Add rice to boiling bouillon, and cook until rice is tender and stock absorbed, about 20 minutes. Melt butter or margarine, and sauté celery and onion. Add with remaining ingredients to cooked rice. Mix lightly, and use to stuff boned leg of veal, roasting chicken or small turkey. Makes approximately 5 cups.

Credit: Gommi.

Lemon–Rice Stuffing

      1/3 cup butter or margarine, melted
        1 cup chopped celery
      1/3 cup chopped onion
    1 1/2 cups water
      1/4 cup lemon juice
        1 tablespoon grated lemon rind
        1 teaspoon salt
      1/4 teaspoon thyme
      1/8 teaspoon pepper
        2 cups quick-cooking rice

To butter or margarine, add celery and onion, and cook until tender, about 5 minutes. Add remaining ingredients, except rice, and bring to boil. Add rice and mix just to moisten. Cover and remove from heat. Let stand 10–15 minutes. Makes 3 cups—enough for 3–4 pound dressed fish.

Whole Wheat–Pecan Stuffing

      2 cups fine soft whole wheat bread crumbs
    1/4 cup chopped pecans
    1/4 cup butter or margarine, melted
      2 tablespoons chopped onion
      2 tablespoons chopped celery
    1–3 teaspoons poultry seasoning
    1/2 teaspoon salt

Combine all ingredients. Adjust seasonings to taste. Yields enough stuffing for a 4-pound chicken (makes approximately 2 1/2 cups).

Almond Stuffing

      1/3 cup butter or margarine
      1/4 cup chopped almonds
      3/4 cup chopped celery
      1/4 cup chopped onion
        3 cups coarse soft bread crumbs
      3/4 teaspoon salt
      1/8 teaspoon pepper
        1 egg, slightly beaten

In large pan, melt butter or margarine. Fry almonds until golden. Stir in celery and onion, and cook until almost tender. Add bread crumbs, and sprinkle with salt and pepper. Stir in egg. Use to stuff 3–4 pound dressed fish for baking. Makes about 4 cups.

Rice–Gherkin Stuffing

      1/4 cup butter or margarine
        1 cup diced celery
      3/4 cup chopped onion
    1 1/3 cups cooked rice
        1 cup chopped gherkins
      1/4 teaspoon salt
      1/4 teaspoon pepper
      1/4 teaspoon dried sage
      1/4 teaspoon dried thyme

To melted butter or margarine, add celery and onion and cook until tender. Add remaining ingredients. Use to stuff 4–5 pound dressed fish. Makes about 3 cups.

Fruits as Accompaniments

Fruits balance the dryness of meats, as you know from using applesauce with pork, cranberry sauce with turkey. But there are so many more combinations—oranges, sliced in their skins and served with roast or fried chicken; spiced cherries with ham; red currant jelly with lamb—all worth adding to your repertoire.

Cinnamon Apples: Core and peel small firm sour apples. Cook till tender in syrup made with 1 cup sugar and 1 cup water, flavored with about 1/4 cup tiny red cinnamon candies. Serve hot or cold with pork or ham.

Cinnamon Apple Rings: Cook gently in syrup as for cinnamon apples, slice apples thickly.

Spiced Peaches: Make syrup by boiling liquid from 1 can peaches, and adding 3 tablespoons brown sugar, 1 tablespoon wine vinegar (or vinegar from jar of sweet pickles of any kind), 4 or 5 cloves, 1/2 teaspoon cinnamon and 1/4 teaspoon ginger or few slices of preserved ginger. Simmer mixture until it is reduced and slightly thickened; then add peach halves, and heat gently. Serve over broiled ham steaks.

Spiced Pears: Follow procedure for SPICED PEACHES. Spiced crabapples, spiced plums and spiced pineapple rings are made in the same way.

Garnishes for the Main Dish. A garnish is primarily a means of making a dish look appealing, so it's wise to keep it simple. The herbs, fruits or vegetables that you use should be fresh, perfect in shape, eye-catching—and usually edible. The paper frills used to cover the unattractive exposed bones of Frenched lamb chops or crown roasts after cooking are an exception.

Do make the most of color, texture, flavor and attractive arrangement.

13 Garnish Suggestions

● Peel oranges, slice thinly, stick clove in center of each; serve with ham, duck, pork.
● Use pineapple slices and attach maraschino cherry to center of each; serve with ham, pork, veal.
● Serve lemon boats or baskets with fish, veal cutlets.
● Peach or pear halves can be filled with mint jelly, red currant jelly, cranberry sauce; serve with roast lamb, grilled or baked ham.

- Very thin slices of white turnip can be rolled into cones to represent calla lilies, with julienne carrot sticks as stamens and secured with toothpicks.
- Radish roses, celery fringed or stuffed with cheese, and olives are good garnishes.
- Cucumber slices are excellent with fish.
- Tomatoes, cut into 8 wedges each with a sprig of parsley in each wedge, accompany steak, veal cutlets, pork chops.
- Make flowers of hard-cooked eggs, halved, then cut into wedges; the whites make petals, the crumbled yolks flower centers.
- Use candied or maraschino cherries, cut in sections, to form petals, with blanched almonds as centers.
- Or use blanched almonds as petals, and maraschino cherry halves as centers.
- Spanish-onion slices, crossed with strips of pimento, are good with beef.
- Alternate onion and green-pepper rings with beef.

Main Dishes for 2. Everything has to be scaled down when you are cooking for 2, but that's no reason why meals can't be prepared efficiently and well.

You don't always have to divide recipes in half. You can save work by preparing enough stew and spaghetti sauce or similar foods for 2 meals; such dishes even improve in flavor with refrigeration and reheating.

Make the most of compact, canned and packaged staples—soups, dehydrated milk, canned or instant potato—and keep ample supplies of condiments and flavorings for finishing touches. Have a good-size Sunday roast—an excellent starting point for casserole, croquettes and hash later in the week.

6 Menus for 2. Recipes are given for items printed IN THIS STYLE.

SEAFOOD NEWBURG	BARBECUED SPARERIBS	Chilled tomato-clam juice with lemon
Rice	Spinach	
Tossed green salad	Baked potatoes	CURRIED EGGS AND MUSHROOMS
Toasted French bread	Grapefruit salad Jelly roll	Lima beans Hot corn muffins
Chilled fruit cup Ginger wafers		APPLE CRISP
Cream of corn soup	SKILLET MEAT LOAF with	CHICKEN WITH ALMOND-CREAM SAUCE
BAKED TROUT NORMANDE	CREOLE LIMA BEANS	Noodles
Sautéed cucumbers	Broiled tomatoes Endive and	Asparagus with lemon butter
Boiled new potatoes	baby-beet salad Biscuits	Baked peaches with puréed
Fresh fruit and cheese	Lemon pie	raspberries

French Toast Ham Sandwich with Rarebit Sauce

    3/4 cup chopped canned ham
    Mayonnaise or salad dressing
      1 teaspoon pickle relish, drained (optional)
      4 slices French bread, buttered
      1 egg, slightly beaten
    1/4 cup milk
    Dash barbecue sauce
      2 tablespoons butter or margarine, melted
    RAREBIT SAUCE

Mix meat with enough mayonnaise to moisten, and add relish. Makes 2 generously filled sandwiches of bread and meat mixture. Mix egg, milk and barbecue sauce. Dip sandwich quickly in mixture. Fry in melted butter on both sides until golden. Cut diagonally and serve covered with rarebit sauce. Serves 2.

Rarebit Sauce

      1 tablespoon butter or margarine
      1 tablespoon flour
    1/2 cup milk
    1/4 pound processed cheese, diced or 1/2 cup grated cheese
    2–3 tablespoons beer or ale
    Salt and pepper to taste

Melt butter or margarine in small saucepan, and add flour and milk. Cook until smoothly thickened; then stir in cheese. Heat until cheese melts, and stir in beer. Season to taste. Makes approximately 1 cup sauce.

Seafood Newburg

      1 (10 1/2-ounce) can shrimp or oyster soup
      2 tablespoons flour
      2 tablespoons soft butter or margarine
    1/4 cup dry sherry
      1 egg yolk, slightly beaten
    1/2 cup light cream
      1 teaspoon onion juice
      1 (6-ounce) can crabmeat plus juice or 1 (5-ounce) can lobster, plus juice
    Salt and black pepper to taste
    Chopped parsley (optional)
    1/2 (10-ounce) package frozen asparagus tips
      1 teaspoon salt
      1 package frozen waffles, toasted and buttered
      1 tablespoon chopped parsley

Melt soup in top of double boiler over boiling water. Make smooth mixture of flour and butter, and stir into hot soup. Combine next 4 ingredients, add to soup and cook until smoothly thickened. Fold in crabmeat and juice, with salt and pepper. Drop frozen asparagus tips into bottom part of double boiler, and add 1 teaspoon salt. Set top part of pan in place, and cook until asparagus is tender. Spoon seafood mixture over toasted waffles. Sprinkle with parsley, and serve with drained asparagus. Serves 2.

New England Boiled Dinner
(Pressure-cooker Method)

1 1/2–2 pounds corned beef or smoked or pickled pork
3 cups cold water
1 bay leaf
1/2 clove garlic
1 1/2 cups water
6 small whole potatoes
4 small peeled onions
2–3 scraped carrots
1/2 cabbage (cut in wedges)
MUSTARD–CREAM SAUCE

Cover corned beef with 3 cups cold water, and refrigerate overnight, or set to soak in the morning before cooking for evening meal. Drain. Place corned beef on rack in pressure cooker, and add bay leaf, garlic and 1 1/2 cups water. Cover, and pressure-cook about 40 minutes. Cool, and remove cover. Add vegetables, and replace lid. Continue cooking 8 minutes. Slice meat, and arrange on heated platter surrounded by vegetables. Serve with sauce. Serves 2.

Note: Smoked or pickled pork doesn't need soaking. Cook 30 minutes only before adding vegetables.

Mustard–Cream Sauce

Prepared mustard
1/2 cup medium-thick cream sauce

Stir mustard into cream sauce. Serves 2.

Barbecued Spareribs

1 tablespoon fat
1 1/4 pounds spareribs, cut in pieces
1 medium onion (1/2 cup chopped)
1 (8-ounce) can tomato sauce
1 teaspoon salt
1/4 teaspoon pepper
Dash Worcestershire sauce

Melt fat in frying pan over medium heat. Brown spareribs and onions in fat; then turn heat low, and add remaining ingredients. Continue cooking over low heat 1 1/4 hours. Serves 2 generously.

Baked Trout Normande

1 (10-ounce) package frozen rainbow trout or
2 fresh brook trout
Salt and black pepper to taste
1/4 cup butter or margarine
2–3 tablespoons white wine
2 teaspoons chopped parsley
2 teaspoons chopped onion
Generous pinch chervil
Generous pinch tarragon
2 tablespoons heavy cream
2 tablespoons buttered crumbs

Remove heads and tails from trout, and wipe inside and out. Sprinkle with salt and pepper.

Place each trout in center of 8"x 6" oblong of heavy-duty foil and cup foil edge. Heat butter, wine, parsley, onion, chervil and tarragon together, and spoon over each trout. Cover with oblongs of foil, crimping upper and lower edges together to seal. Bake on cookie sheet at 425°F. 12–15 minutes. If fish is frozen, allow 5–10 minutes longer. Slit top of each package, and pull edges back from fish. Spread fish with cream, and sprinkle with crumbs. Broil 1–2 minutes. Serve in foil.

Chicken with Almond–Cream Sauce

3 tablespoons fat
2 servings chicken pieces
1/2 lemon
1 tablespoon flour
1/2 teaspoon salt
Dash black pepper
1/4 cup slivered almonds
2 tablespoons flour
3/4 cup chicken broth
1/2 cup light cream or 1/4 cup milk and 1/4 cup evaporated milk
1 teaspoon sherry
1 tablespoon chopped parsley
Salt and pepper to taste

Melt fat in skillet. Rub chicken all over with lemon; sprinkle with 1 tablespoon flour, 1/2 teaspoon salt and dash pepper. Brown chicken pieces on both sides about 10 minutes. Remove chicken, and brown almonds lightly in same pan. Stir in 2 tablespoons flour, then broth and cream. Cook until thick and smooth. Add chicken, and turn in sauce. Cover pan, and lower heat. Simmer 20 minutes. Lift chicken to heated platter, and add chopped parsley and sherry to sauce. Whisk until smooth; then season to taste. Pour over chicken. Serve with potato puffs and glazed carrots. Serves 2.

Skillet Meat Loaf with Creole Lima Beans

1/2 cup soft bread crumbs
1/2 can or 2/3 cup onion soup
1/2 can luncheon meat, finely chopped
1/2 pound hamburger or ground fresh pork
1/4 cup dry bread crumbs
1 egg
1/2 teaspoon salt
Pinch sage
Pinch thyme
2 tablespoons salad oil
3 slices bacon
1 (1-pound, 1-ounce) can lima beans in tomato sauce
1/4 cup diced green pepper

Soak crumbs in onion soup a few minutes; then mix in next 7 ingredients. Shape meat into small loaf and roll in crumbs. Heat salad oil in covered skillet over low heat. Place strips of bacon close together in pan. Set meat loaf on bacon, which will add flavor and prevent bottom of loaf from cooking too quickly. Cover, and cook slowly, about 10 minutes. Turn meat loaf and add lima beans and green pepper. Cover, and continue cooking 10–15 minutes.

Chipped Beef Scramble

             3 tablespoons butter or margarine
             3 or 4 fresh mushrooms, sliced or 1 peeled diced
                tomato
             1 or 2 green onions, sliced
             4 eggs, slightly beaten
       1/3–1/2 cup shredded chipped beef
           1/4 cup sweet or sour cream
             2 slices buttered toast
             1 teaspoon grated Parmesan cheese

Heat butter or margarine in chafing dish or frying pan and add mushrooms and onion. Fry slowly, stirring until onion is tender. Mix next 3 ingredients, and pour into pan. Scramble softly, using metal spoon. Serve on toast. Sprinkle with Parmesan cheese.

Pick Your Utensils

Make do with 1 saucepan for your dinner vegetables. There's no danger of mingled flavors if you wrap one seasoned vegetable in airtight foil and drop it into boiling water containing potatoes. Use both sections of your double boiler at once: hard-cooked eggs below, and sauce above.

Try making up standard-lot sauces, salad dressings and so forth once a week. Store each, covered in refrigerator, ready for use. Use your freezing compartment for shaped meat patties that are ideal for a quick dinner, for sliced turkey left over from company occasions, the second 1/2 of layer cake recipe and so forth. Make use of leftovers, and remember that even 2 tablespoons of cooked vegetables will provide the character ingredient for 2 servings of cream soup the next night.

When you divide a cake recipe or mix that normally required 1 egg, simply use the whole egg in 1/2 the amount; you will not endanger the result. Here is a meal that you can cook all at once in a 9-cup muffin tin. Oil 6 muffin cups and leave 3 unoiled but fill with water while baking.

Meal in a Muffin Tin

       1/2 pound ground lamb
           2 tablespoons dry bread crumbs
           1 tablespoon catsup
           1 teaspoon chopped fresh mint or 1/2 teaspoon dried
              mint
       1/2 teaspoon salt
   Pinch crumbled rosemary
           1 large potato, cut in half
           4 tablespoons canned fruit cocktail or 2 canned peach
              halves or 4 canned apricot halves
           2 teaspoons brown sugar
           2 teaspoons lemon juice
       1/3 cup biscuit mix
           2 teaspoons sugar
           1 teaspoon soft butter or margarine
           3 tablespoons milk or cream
   Dash vanilla or almond extract
           1 cup frozen peas
           2 teaspoons butter or margarine
           2 teaspoons water
       1/8 teaspoon salt

Minted Lamb Cups: Combine lamb with first 5 ingredients, and spoon into 2 muffin cups.

Baked Potato: Prick potato halves, and place, cut side down, in 2 cups.

Fruited Upside-down Cake: Place spoonful of fruit cocktail, peach half or 2 apricot halves in 2 muffin cups. Sprinkle brown sugar and lemon juice over. Spoon biscuit mix into a 1-cup measuring cup and add sugar, 1 teaspoon butter, 3 tablespoons milk and vanilla. Stir quickly until quite smooth, and spoon over fruit. Bake all together at 350°F. 35 minutes.

Buttered Peas: Wrap frozen peas, 2 teaspoons each butter and water, plus 1/8 teaspoon salt in foil, and place in unoiled cups for last 20 minutes of baking time.

Menus Featuring Dishes From Chapter 2

BEEF

BRAISED STUFFED FLANK STEAK
Potatoes
Baked whole carrots
Coleslaw
Rice–raisin pudding

DELUXE HAMBURGERS
Spanish onions and tomato slices
Hot buttered rolls
Fresh fruit bowl
Cheese tray

STUFFED CABBAGE ROLLS
Kernel corn with green pepper
Toasted French bread
ZABAGLIONE

BROILED PORTERHOUSE STEAK
HORSERADISH SAUCE
Lyonnaise potatoes
Peas
Fresh fruit
CUSTARD SAUCE

SCOTCH BEEF LOAF
Browned potatoes
String beans
Pickled beets
Butterscotch meringue pie

LAMB

ROAST LEG OF LAMB
Mint jelly
MASHED POTATOES
VEGETABLE MACEDOINE
Relish platter
Fresh pumpkin pie

CASSEROLE DINNER OF LAMB CHOPS
Green peas
Celery hearts
Individual tea-biscuit shortcakes with strawberries

CURRIED LAMB WITH RICE
Pineapple rings
Tossed salad with orange sections
Maple nut sundae

GRILLED LAMB CHOPS A L'ANGLAISE
Broiled tomatoes halves and mushrooms
Boiled potatoes
Mint sprinkle
Trifle with orange garnish

BARBECUED LAMB
Rice
Tossed green salad
FRENCH DRESSING
Cottage cheese
Cherry upside-down cake

VEAL

VEAL VIENNESE
Boiled noodles
Red cabbage
LEMON SNOW with CUSTARD SAUCE

ROAST VEAL WITH PENNSYLVANIA STUFFING
Baked potatoes
Tossed green salad
Raspberry whip
Ladyfingers

BREADED VEAL CHOPS
Whipped potatoes
Green limas
Celery stuffed with cheese
Half grapefruit

JELLIED VEAL
POTATO SALAD
Tossed greens
Chilled stewed rhubarb
Cheese-cracker tray

CURRIED VEAL
Rice
Garnishes
Cooked vegetable salad
MAYONNAISE
Doughnuts
Coffee

PORK

LAYERED SAUSAGE LOAF
Baked sweet potatoes
Zucchini
Lemon gelatin
Icebox cookies

BARBECUED SPARERIBS
SCALLOPED POTATOES
Broccoli
Mélange of fruits in meringue pie shell

SKEWERED PORK CUBES
BAKED EGGPLANT WITH RICE STUFFING
Sliced tomatoes
Herb dressing
Devil's food cake
Marshmallow sauce

GOLDEN HAM ROAST
Scalloped sweet potatoes
Creamed onions
Celery sticks
Cucumber fingers
APPLE CRISP
CARAMEL SAUCE

BROILED HAM STEAK
SAUTEED APPLE RINGS
Succotash
Mixed salad in lettuce cups
Coconut cream pie

POULTRY

ROAST TURKEY
CRANBERRY SAUCE
Whipped potatoes
Broccoli
Celery
Olives
Steamed fruit pudding

Cream of green pea soup
Turkey, celery and nut salad
Jelly roll and cranberry filling

OVEN-FRIED CHICKEN
Shoestring potatoes
Baked stuffed tomatoes
Chocolate blanc mange

CHICKEN FRICASSEE
Fluffy rice
Grapefruit, orange and prune salad
Cheese wedges

ROAST DUCKLING
Boiled wild rice
Harvard beets
Jellied raw vegetable salad
Blueberry tarts

FISH AND SEAFOOD

Vegetable juice cocktail
DEEP-FRIED FILLETS IN PANCAKE MIX
Mashed potatoes
Scalloped tomatoes
Vanilla pudding

SPICY OYSTER STEW
Heated crackers
Cabbage, onion and apple salad
Gingerbread with hot lemon sauce

MUSHROOM SOUFFLE
Asparagus with cream sauce
Carrot sticks
Celery curls
Lemon chiffon pie

Corn chowder
LOBSTER-GRAPEFRUIT MOLD on salad greens
Peach shortcake
Whipped cream

Tomato juice cocktail
FINNAN HADDIE POACHED IN MILK
Baked potatoes
Spinach
Fresh apple pie
Cheese

VARIETY MEATS

LIVER—ONION HOT POT
Baby beets
Beet greens
Orange sherbet
Chocolate-chip cookies

BRAISED CHICKEN GIBLETS
FLUFFY RICE
Mixed garden vegetables
Ice cream with caramel sauce
Cupcakes

HERBED TONGUE
Baked potatoes
Baked squash
Jellied tomato salad
Angel food cake

BRAISED CHICKEN LIVERS
Boiled noodles
Minted green peas
Fresh fruit cup
Cheese tray
Apple juice

OVEN-BRAISED STUFFED HEART
Whipped potatoes
Brussels sprouts
Poached pears

ALTERNATES

MEXICAN KIDNEY BEANS
Apple, celery and nut salad
Chilled baked custard

Hot consommé
Crackers
CHEESE MOUSSE
Lettuce wedges
FRENCH DRESSING
APPLESAUCE
Cookies

LUNCHEON RAREBIT
Toasted French bread
Celery curls
Gherkins
Jellied fruits
Nuts

Tomato juice cocktail
MUSHROOM SOUFFLE in GREEN PEPPER CUPS
Potato chips
Parsleyed carrots
Raisin pie

Cream of potato soup
BAKED MERINGUE EGGS
Buttered broccoli
STUFFED BAKED APPLES

Good menu planning involves using several kinds of meat (beef, pork, lamb, veal), as well as the variety meats, fish, cheese, eggs and legumes. You'll thus be able to vary your main dishes with different kinds of protein.

3
~
The Wonder World
of Fruits and
Vegetables

It is important to note all the forms in which fruits and vegetables are available, to consider food value in relation to price and to learn the methods for storing, cooking and serving. Impulse buying can be costly.

Prepare your shopping lists from definite menus drawn up for the next few days. Keep in mind substitutions that can be made when price makes substitution profitable. For example, canned tomato juice may replace orange juice for breakfast—but double the amount; lettuce greens with dressing may replace fresh asparagus for dinner.

If adequate home storage is available, take advantage of specials on canned and frozen items by purchasing in larger quantities.

When comparing costs of fresh fruits and vegetables with those of frozen or canned fruits and vegetables, consider amount of waste from fresh items. Remember also that out-of-season and long-stored raw products may not be as high in food values as those that were processed and packed where they were grown.

Buy fresh fruits and green vegetables in amounts to be used within a few days. Patronize a dealer who has quick turnover and proper facilities for keeping his produce in good condition in order to ensure more food value. Oranges, for instance, that have been kept on display for weeks in a sunny store window offer less than constantly replenished supplies.

Discard any spoiled or inedible portions immediately after purchasing; store according to kind—in your refrigerator, or, with roots and apples, in a cool, dark place.

Know the various grades on the market—government grades, Federal inspection stamps,

manufacturers' or retailers' brands—check weights, and in buying fresh produce, purchase by weight whenever possible; usually the heavier a fruit or vegetable for its size, the more value you receive.

Always wash fresh fruits and vegetables thoroughly before using, even if you intend to peel them.

Vegetables provide almost endless food value.

The *carbohydrate* (sugar and starch) content in vegetables varies, depending on water content and variety of vegetable. The actively growing parts (leaves, stems, flowers, fruits) contain high amounts of water and are therefore lower in carbohydrates.

Parts of the plant used for storage (roots, tubers, pods and seeds) contain less water and more carbohydrates. Dried vegetables like dried beans and peas do not have all their water restored, even in soaking and cooking, so they remain higher in carbohydrates than do fresh vegetables.

Most vegetables have more starch and less sugar than fruits have. As vegetables ripen, sugar decreases, and starch increases, which accounts for the greater sweetness of young green peas and new potatoes.

Because of their carbohydrate contents, tubers and some roots are valuable sources of energy.

The amount of *protein* in vegetables also varies, and in most cases it is not of top nutritional quality. The only vegetables considered really valuable sources of protein are the legumes (dried beans, peas and lentils), especially soybeans. The protein in potatoes is good in quality, even though the amount is low.

Vegetables are relatively free of *fat* and are therefore valuable in low-fat diets. They also can provide a large part of the day's *mineral* requirements.

The green leafy vegetables are valuable, among other things, for their *calcium* content, particularly broccoli, chard, collards, kale, mustard greens and turnip tops. Another good source of calcium is dried beans. Spinach, although it tests high in calcium, contains oxalic acid, which

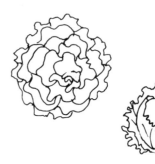

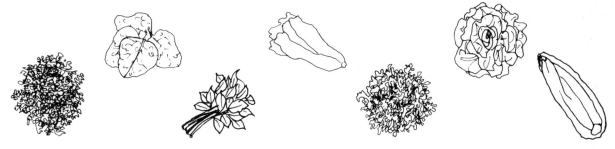

changes calcium in the body so that it cannot be assimilated.

Green leafy vegetables have high *iron* content, especially asparagus, beet greens, broccoli and chard. In general, the greener the leaf, the higher the iron content. Also valuable for iron are dried beans, mushrooms and potatoes.

Vegetables grown near the coast absorb *iodine* from the soil, though more dependable sources of iodine are seafoods and iodized salt. And soils rich in *fluorine* and *manganese* transfer these minerals to their vegetable crops.

A knowledge of *vitamin* values helps to explain the importance of daily consumption of green and yellow vegetables, tomatoes and potatoes.

Yellow and green vegetables, in general, are high in vitamin A. Among yellow vegetables, the deeper the color, the higher in vitamin A; white potatoes are very low and sweet potatoes very high. Carrots, the yellow varieties of squash and tomatoes are high. And green varieties of cabbage, lettuce and the like are much higher than are the white varieties.

Although whole grains are the most dependable sources of *thiamine* (vitamin B1) in the diet, vegetables provide a useful supplementary supply, especially fresh asparagus, corn, lima beans, dried navy beans, raw mushrooms, peas (fresh or dried) and potatoes.

Leafy greens score high among vegetable sources of *vitamin B2* (riboflavin). Fresh asparagus, broccoli, Brussels sprouts, dandelion greens and spinach are especially good. Legumes (beans, peas and lentils), mushrooms and winter squash also contribute.

Tomatoes are the best vegetable source of *vitamin C.* Also valuable are beet greens, broccoli, Brussels sprouts, cabbage (especially raw), cauliflower, chard, green peppers, spinach, turnips and turnip greens. Potatoes are a good regular source, though the amounts are not high. Cooking and exposure to air decrease the quantity of vitamin C, and the fresher the vegetable, the higher its vitamin C content.

Meats, fish and other high-protein foods are the most dependable source of *niacin,* but dried beans, peas and other legumes provide supplementary amounts.

One of the most important contributions of vegetables is "bulk" or "roughage" (cellulose) which has a regulating effect on the digestive system. Cellulose, however, can upset digestive systems that are unable to stand irritation—those of ulcer patients, and others on bland diets.

Certain vegetables must be cooked before serving to render them digestible; others are simply more appealing if cooked before serving hot or cold. Make full use of the many cooking methods to ensure variety.

To retain maximum nutrients, any cooking method that permits leaving the vegetable whole in its skin is best. If paring is to be done, remove a minimum of skin. A vegetable's minerals and vitamins can be drawn out by lengthy immersion in water or by cooking in too much water. So avoid peeling ahead of time and holding raw vegetables in cold water, and cook them in as little water as possible. Nutrients will also be lost if vegetables are cut finely or chopped before cooking. Whole vegetables or large pieces are best for boiling, and carrots should be cut lengthwise to preserve more nutrients.

Besides retaining food values, correct cooking procedures will ensure maximum appeal. Methods that develop and retain flavor, attractive color and good texture are desirable, even if a little food value is sacrificed. For example, a family that refuses to eat turnips with the strong flavor brought about by cooking them in a waterless cooker may readily accept the same vegetable boiled in water to cover, with the resulting milder taste.

Cooking Fresh Vegetables. First, 2 groups are frequently referred to—"mild-flavored," which include asparagus, beans (all types, fresh or dried), beets and beet greens, carrots, celery, chard, corn, cucumber, young dandelion greens, eggplant, lettuce, mushrooms, okra, peas, potatoes, squash and tomatoes, and "strong-flavored," which include broccoli, Brussels sprouts, cabbage, cauliflower, kale, onions, rutabagas, spinach and turnips.

To Bake

Baking is the best method for retaining food values, especially if vegetable is baked whole in its skin.

Suitable for uncovered baking are cucumbers, potatoes (sweet or white), squash (all varieties), onions, peppers (generally stuffed) and tomatoes. Place on rack or in open pan. Squash should be halved or cut in pieces, and the seeds removed.

Many vegetables can be baked covered, although such baking is not generally recommended for strong-flavored vegetables and greens. Vegetables may be left whole in their skins (beets, for example) or peeled and cut in pieces. Use covered casserole, add a little water or brush with oil, season and bake covered until tender. Some vegetables can be cut in pieces, covered with sauce and baked uncovered.

Baking temperatures: 350°–400°F. for all vegetables (except tomatoes, which should bake at 425°–500°F.).

To Boil

Boiling is the most common and convenient method and one suited to all vegetables. Correct procedure keeps loss of food values to a minimum.

Bring water to rapid boil before adding raw vegetables, return quickly to boiling point, reduce heat and allow vegetables to simmer gently until just tender. Drain immediately, and serve. Salt should be added at beginning of cooking period or halfway through. More important is the *amount of water* used and the care taken to avoid overcooking. Mild-flavored vegetables should be boiled, covered, in very little water, just enough to prevent burning. Strong-flavored vegetables will also retain their maximum food value when cooked in minimum amounts of water, but their flavors may be unpleasantly strong.

To retain good color in green vegetables, cook uncovered. *Do not add baking soda* for it destroys vitamin values. To leave mild green vegetables uncovered during cooking is best for preservation of color, but there will be a slight decrease in vitamin C. A compromise for both green and strong-flavored vegetables is to let them remain uncovered until they boil, and then to cover them and reduce heat.

To Braise

Braising is best for celery, cucumbers, summer squash and the like. Melt 2 tablespoons oil or fat in frying pan; add 2 cups prepared raw vegetables plus 2 tablespoons water or consommé.

Cover, and cook slowly until just tender, seasoning at midway point. Flavor and food values are retained in braising, but color may fade.

To Broil

Broiling is handy for eggplant slices, mushrooms, summer squash, halved tomatoes, parboiled carrots or potatoes when broiler is being used for other foods. Brush with oil, melted fat or French dressing. Broil 3–5 inches from heat, and turn once during cooking, or put canned or cooked vegetables in tray under rack while broiling meat; they will heat through nicely and will absorb meat juices.

To Fry

Diced or thinly sliced young vegetables like vegetable marrow, summer squash and green tomatoes may be fried. Melt fat in frying pan, and, when hot, add vegetable. Cover tightly, and cook at moderate heat, turning as necessary and seasoning to taste.

To Deep-fry

Deep-frying is not a method that retains full food values, but potatoes, vegetable croquettes and vegetables like onion rings in batter taste good deep-fried.

Use at least 1 1/2 inches of fat in pan. Prepare vegetables as required; for instance, potatoes, in fingers or julienned, should be soaked 10 minutes in ice water, then dried on towel. Fry enough food at a time to cover surface of fat.

Drain on absorbent paper, and serve very hot. A deep-fat thermometer ensures correct tempera-

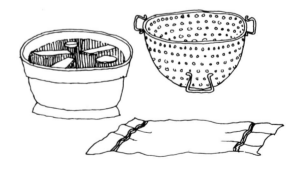

ture and is especially useful in cooking potatoes by the "blanch-and-brown" method, which involves prefrying potatoes at 365°F. until they are soft but not brown. They are then removed from fat, set aside and drained. Just before serving time, quickly brown at 390°F. In place of thermometer, the crumb test may be used: Drop 1-inch cube of day-old bread into fat; it should brown in 1 minute at first temperature. A similar bread cube should brown in 20 seconds at second temperature. When deep-frying potatoes in one operation, have fat at 385°F., hot enough to brown a cube of bread in 40 seconds.

Onion rings and other batter-fried foods are best cooked at 365°F.

To Parboil

Parboiling is a first step toward further cooking; boil only until half-tender.

To Pressure-cook

Food values are well preserved by pressure cooking, as only a small amount of water is used and the cooking is done very quickly. Pressure-cooking results in a "steamed" flavor, and strong vegetables retain their full characteristic taste. It is most important to follow the manufacturer's directions exactly and to avoid overcooking. Pressure-cooked green vegetables have a tendency to change color. Leafy greens develop a mushy consistency, and an ordinary saucepan is generally preferable for them.

To Steam

Steaming is appropriate for almost all vegetables; it is slow, but results in high food values. Use a 2-section steamer, placing vegetables in perforated upper pan, or place vegetables on rack over boiling water in saucepan. Cover tightly, and make sure water does not boil away.

To Roast

Roasting is a variation of baking. Suitable vegetables like carrots, parsnips and potatoes—either raw or parboiled—are placed around meat and roasted in fat and juice until tender. They should be turned several times and seasoned to taste.

Waterless Cooking

This method requires no special equipment. After thorough washing, thin leafy greens like spinach can be cooked in water that adheres to leaves. Cover pot, and gently boil greens, turning once; drain well, and serve.

To Barbecue

For barbecueing, put small whole raw vegetables, pieces or combinations of both (Frenched green beans, tomato wedges and onion slices for example) on a square of heavy aluminum foil, dot with butter or margarine, add salt and pepper, wrap foil into airtight parcel and cook over gray-hot coals about 40 minutes. Several parcels of individual servings are handy, plates will not be needed.

To Scallop

To scallop cooked or partially thawed frozen vegetables, place in greased casserole, and pour over them 1 cup medium white sauce. Sprinkle bread crumbs, croutons or coarsely crushed potato chips on top, dot with butter or margarine and bake at 350°F. about 20 minutes.

Potatoes. Actually, although it contains energy-giving material in the form of starch, an average potato supplies only 100 calories, which is about equal to 1 serving of cooked cereal, a fair-sized apple or 1/2 pint skim milk. It's the butter or gravy that should be watched by calorie counters.

Potatoes keep best in a cool, dark place with rather high humidity, the same conditions that existed in the old-time root cellars. After storage at 40°F., quality is improved by bringing potatoes into warm room for a few days before using.

Note that warm *dry* air causes potatoes to shrivel in storage whereas warm *moist* air may cause sprouting. Exposure to light causes greenish patches, which give a bitter flavor. Apartment dwellers should buy supplies sufficient only for a week or so, and they may find it best to store potatoes in the refrigerator.

Baked Potatoes

6 medium or large potatoes
2 tablespoons butter or margarine or drippings or salad oil

Scrub potatoes thoroughly, using cool water and vegetable brush. Rinse well. If soft skin is preferred, rub potatoes all over with butter, margarine, bacon drippings or salad oil. Otherwise skin will bake crisp, which many people prefer. Place on rack in preheated oven. For light, mealy potatoes, use oven temperature of 425°–500°F., but for convenience when baking complete oven dinner, temperatures as low as 375°F. may be used. Allow about 1 hour for medium potatoes. At very high heat they will be ready sooner, of course. When potatoes are baked, prick tops, or cut a cross on each. Squeeze potatoes to allow steam to escape, making potatoes fluffier. Serve with butter or margarine and sprinkle of paprika, with commercial sour cream mixed with chopped chives or with butter mixed with crumbled blue cheese.

Note: Select sound potatoes of even sizes. Medium or large potatoes bake better than do small ones. New potatoes do not bake well. To retain maximum vitamin C, it is best that potatoes *not* be pricked with a fork before baking. Pricking before baking does, however, prevent potatoes from bursting in oven, and it may result in drier baked potatoes. If desired, potatoes may be wrapped in aluminum foil for baking; potatoes are then actually oven-steamed, which keeps skins soft.

Boiled Potatoes

6 potatoes
Boiling water
Salt to taste

Scrub potatoes thoroughly, and remove any blemishes. Do not peel. Drop potatoes into smallest amount of rapidly boiling water that can do the job, possibly only 1-inch depth. Add salt, return rapidly to boil, cover and reduce heat to a gentle simmer. Cook until potatoes are just tender, about 25 minutes. Drain at once; then shake pan, uncovered over low heat to evaporate moisture. Serve in skins or peel quickly before serving. Serves 6.

Note: Select potatoes of even size.

Whipped Potatoes

6 medium potatoes
2 tablespoons butter or margarine
Salt and pepper to taste
1/4–1/3 cup hot milk
1 tablespoon butter or margarine
Paprika

Boil potatoes, peel quickly, and return to saucepan. Place over low heat. Mash quickly until free of lumps. Add 2 tablespoons butter and seasonings. Gradually stir and beat in milk. Whip until fluffy. Serve in heated dish. Dot with 1 tablespoon butter or margarine and sprinkle with paprika. Serves 6.

Note: If potatoes are very dry or if they are to stand briefly before using, add extra milk. New potatoes are not satisfactory for whipping. More nourishment is retained when potatoes are boiled

in their skins, but peeling before cooking makes whipped or mashed potatoes whiter. Serves 6.

Oven-roasted Potatoes

The familiar method is to place peeled potatoes in drippings about 1 1/2–2 hours before meat is to finish cooking. But potatoes need *high* temperatures for best results, whereas beef and other roasts develop juicy tenderness in a fairly *slow* oven. The compromise is to give potatoes a fast parboiling before placing in oven. About 45 minutes before meat is to finish cooking, boil required number of peeled medium potatoes 10–15 minutes. Drain. Arrange in juices around meat; continue cooking at correct temperature for roast. Turn potatoes once or twice to coat and brown all sides. Sprinkle lightly with salt just before serving.

Fried Raw Potatoes

4 or 5 medium potatoes
2 onions
4 tablespoons fat (butter, margarine or salad oil or 2 tablespoons fat plus 2 tablespoons bacon drippings)
1 teaspoon salt
1/8 teaspoon pepper

Peel potatoes and onions, slice fairly thin. Melt fat in large frying pan over medium heat. Put in about 1/2 the potatoes, next the onions, then remaining potatoes; sprinkle seasonings over. Cover pan, and cook about 10 minutes, at which time bottom layer will be lightly browned and potatoes almost tender. Turn potatoes, using wide spatula. Let cook uncovered another 15–20 minutes, turning once or twice for even browning. Serves 4.

VARIATIONS:

Both baked and boiled potatoes may be used in following recipes. Estimate 1 medium cooked potato per serving. For fat, use butter or margarine, bacon or beef drippings or salad oil. Allow about 2 tablespoons fat for 3 cups prepared potato.

Hash-browned Potatoes

Melt fat, add finely-chopped potatoes and sprinkle lightly with salt and pepper; add a little chopped onion (optional). Using spatula, press down potatoes until they are a compact mass. If very dry, add a little top milk. Let cook, uncovered, over low heat about 20 minutes or until brown crust is formed on bottom. Do not stir during cooking. Fold as with omelet; lift out to hot platter.

Potatoes O'Brien

To diced or chopped potatoes add chopped onion, green pepper and pimento, allowing about 1 tablespoon each for 3 cups potatoes. Cook in melted fat over low-to-medium heat, stirring occasionally, until mixture is piping hot and potatoes delicately browned. Season to taste.

Potato Cakes

Use leftover mashed potatoes. For extra richness, add a lightly beaten egg yolk to potatoes. Dip hands in flour, and shape mixture into little flat cakes about 2 inches across. Brown on both sides in hot fat in frying pan. Serve very hot.

Broiler Fried Potatoes

        4 medium potatoes
        Cold water, lightly salted
        1/4 cup salad oil
        Salt to taste

Scrub potatoes; peel and slice about 3/4 inch thick and then into lengthwise strips. Soak in cold water, about 30 minutes. While broiler is preheating, drain potatoes, and dry between paper towels. Put potatoes in broiler pan (do not use rack); add salad oil, and stir to coat all potatoes. Broil 3 inches below heat 15–20 minutes, stirring frequently. When potatoes are golden brown on all sides, sprinkle with salt, and serve. Serves 4.

New Potatoes with Peas

    8 small new potatoes
    1 cup freshly cooked peas, drained
    1/2 cup hot thin cream, seasoned with salt and pepper
    Chopped parsley or chives

Scrub potatoes, leave unpeeled and boil. When just tender, drain; skins may be quickly peeled off or left on. Place in heated vegetable dish, and add peas. Pour seasoned cream over all. Sprinkle with chopped parsley or chives. Serves 4.

Herbed New Potatoes

        8 small new potatoes
        1/2 cup soft butter or margarine
        3 tablespoons chopped parsley
        3 tablespoons chopped chives
        1 teaspoon fresh dill
        Pinch thyme
        Pinch salt

Boil potatoes without peeling. Drain; if desired, remove skins. Combine butter or marga-rine, parsley, chives, dill, thyme and salt; add to potatoes. Set pan over very low heat 5–10 minutes; stir potatoes carefully to coat with melted herb butter. Serves 4.

Spanish Scallop

        4 medium potatoes, sliced
        1 teaspoon salt
        2 tablespoons flour
        1/2 green pepper, diced
        1 onion, sliced
        1 1/2 cups tomato juice
        3 tablespoons butter or margarine

Place layer of potatoes in bottom of greased 1-quart casserole. Sprinkle with a little of the salt and flour. Cover with layer of green pepper and onion slices. Repeat layers until all vegetables, seasonings and flour are used, ending with remaining potatoes. Pour tomato juice over, and dot with butter or margarine. Bake at 375°F. until potatoes are quite tender and top is nicely browned. Serves 4.

Mashed Potatoes in Sour Cream

    2/3 cup commercial sour cream
    1 cup water
    1/2 teaspoon salt
    2 tablespoons butter or margarine
    1 cup instant mashed potato flakes
    Dab commercial sour cream
    Chopped chives or bacon bits or chopped parsley or
        chopped green onion

Bring water, salt and butter or margarine to boil. Stir in mashed potato flakes as directed on package. Beat in 2/3 cup sour cream. Top with dab sour cream and chives. Serves 2.

Potato Pancakes

        6 medium potatoes
        1 small onion
        1 tablespoon flour
        1 egg
        1/2 teaspoon salt
        Cooking oil

Peel potatoes, and grate on medium grater. Peel onion, and chop very fine. Add onion to potatoes, and quickly add flour, egg and salt, mixing well. Pour into heavy frying pan enough cooking oil or fat to cover the bottom to depth of about 1/2 inch, and heat to frying temperature. Spoon potato mixture into hot pan, spreading each cake with tip of spoon so that it will be as thin as possible, not heaped up. Cook cakes until golden brown on one side; then turn with spatula, and brown on other side. Remove cakes from pan and drain on absorbent kitchen paper to eliminate greasiness. Serve as soon as possible, or pancakes will become soggy. Serve with applesauce or sour cream. Serves 6.

Potato Puffs

2 cups cold mashed potatoes
2 tablespoons butter or margarine
1/2 cup grated cheese
1/2 teaspoon salt
Few grains cayenne
2 tablespoons cream
2 egg yolks
Hot fat

Mix first 7 ingredients, and beat well until light. Shape into balls and chill well. Fry in deep hot fat until golden brown. Serve at once. Serves 4–6.

Scalloped Potatoes

6 potatoes
2 onions
Salt and pepper to taste
3 tablespoons butter or margarine
Water or stock

Slice onions and potatoes very thin and spread in large shallow baking dish, making layer about 1/2-inch thick. Add seasonings, dot butter or margarine generously over top and pour in enough water or stock to come almost to top of potatoes. Bake at 400°F. about 1 hour or until well browned on top. Serves 6.

Top-of-the-stove Potatoes au Gratin

1/2 cup boiling water
1 1/2 teaspoons salt
4 cups diced raw potatoes
1/2 cup chopped onions
1/2 cup milk
1/2 cup grated Cheddar cheese
Pepper to taste
Few sprigs parsley

To boiling water and salt in saucepan add potatoes and onion, cover, and boil 10 minutes. Remove lid, and, stirring several times, let mixture simmer until water is almost evaporated. Add milk, cheese and pepper. Heat thoroughly. Turn into warm dish, and garnish with parsley. Serves 4–5.

Packaged Potatoes

Potatoes ready to cook, to heat or to use are available in various forms and can be a boon when you are busy. The forms include instant "mashed" potatoes, instant diced or sliced potatoes for "hashed brown" treatment, specially prepared scalloped or potato-salad mixtures, frozen small whole potatoes for cooking, frozen French

fries and canned cooked white and sweet potatoes and yams. The nutritional level may vary with the type of preparation (as in home cooking of raw potatoes), but fast factory processing and laboratory controls have tended to safeguard the potato's food values in these packaged forms. Cost per serving compared with home-prepared potatoes is high.

Quick Potato Soup

1 beef-bouillon cube
1 1/4 cups boiling water
2 1/2 cups milk
3/4 teaspoon salt
Few grains pepper
1 tablespoon chopped onion
1/2 cup mashed potato flakes
1/2 cup grated Cheddar cheese
2 tablespoons chopped parsley
1 tablespoon butter or margarine

Crumble bouillon cube into boiling water. Add milk, salt, pepper and onion. Heat to boiling. Remove from heat. Mix in instant potato, cheese, parsley and butter or margarine. Cook, stirring, over low heat until cheese is melted. Serves 6.

Curried Chicken Pie with Potato Topping

2 tablespoons butter or margarine
1 tablespoon flour
1 teaspoon curry powder
1 (10 1/4-ounce) can chicken gravy
1/2 cup sliced mushrooms, drained
1/2 cup cooked peas
1 1/2 cups diced cooked chicken
1/4 teaspoon salt
1/8 teaspoon black pepper
2 tablespoons sherry
1 (4-serving size) package mashed
   potato flakes

Heat oven to 350°F. Melt butter or margarine and stir in flour and curry powder. Gradually add chicken gravy. Cook, stirring constantly, until mixture thickens. Stir in mushrooms, peas, chicken, seasonings and sherry. Pour into casserole. Prepare instant mashed potato flakes according to package directions. Press through pastry tube to form decorative potato border, or drop in rough mounds over chicken mixture. Bake 15–20 minutes or until potatoes are delicately browned. Serves 4–6.

Sweet Potatoes or Yams

Sweet potatoes and yams are interchangeable in menus and recipes. They are generally cooked by baking or boiling, as with white potatoes, but will be finished in about 3/4 the time. Peel after cooking. One medium-to-large potato is allowed per serving. In various recipes calling for parboiled sweet potatoes or yams, the canned product can be substituted conveniently.

Sweet Potatoes with Apples

    4 boiled sweet potatoes
    1 cup sliced tart apples
    1/4 cup tightly packed brown sugar
    3 tablespoons butter or margarine
    1 teaspoon salt

Peel and slice boiled potatoes. Place layer in greased baking dish, cover with 1/2 the other ingredients; continue layers, and finish with potato slices and few dots butter or margarine. Bake, covered, in 375°F. oven 30 minutes; uncover, and continue cooking until apples are perfectly tender and top potatoes nicely browned. Serves 4.

Note: With apples that have little juice, it may be advisable to add 2 tablespoons water before baking.

VARIATIONS:

Sweet Potatoes with Pineapple: Instead of apples use drained canned pineapple tidbits, plus 2 tablespoons pineapple juice, and reduce brown sugar to 2 tablespoons.

Sweet Potatoes with Tangerines or Oranges: Make syrup by simmering together 1/4 cup each butter or margarine and water and 1/2 cup corn syrup. Pour over potatoes as substitute for other ingredients. Bake, covered in medium oven 30 minutes. Remove cover. Arrange on top thin slices from 2 tangerines, peeled, or from 1 large navel orange, leaving rind on 2 or 3 slices for extra flavor. Baste fruit with hot syrup, and slide dish under broiler 4–5 minutes to glaze and heat.

Yam and Ham Dinner for 2

    2 medium yams
    1 tenderized ham steak (not more than 1/2 inch thick)
    3 tablespoons butter or margarine
    4 canned pear halves
    1 (10-ounce) package frozen asparagus spears
    Salt to taste
    1/4 cup honey or corn syrup
    3 tablespoons pear juice
    2 slices processed cheese, cut in strips

Parboil yams 25 minutes. Peel, and slice thickly lengthwise. Gash fat edge of ham in several places. Melt butter or margarine in large covered skillet or electric frying pan. Add ham slice and potatoes; sauté 3–5 minutes over low heat; turn contents over. Arrange pear halves on top of ham slice, and between them neatly pile asparagus. Lightly salt vegetables, and brush potatoes with honey. Pour pear juice around them. Cover pan, keep heat low and cook 10–15 min-

utes or until asparagus is tender. Top asparagus with cheese strips and keep covered 1 minute till cheese melts. Serves 2.

Sweet-potato Puffs

    2 sweet potatoes
    1/4 teaspoon salt
    1/8 teaspoon pepper
    1 tablespoon butter or margarine
    2 eggs
    2 tablespoons warm milk

Boil, peel and mash potatoes. Add salt, pepper and butter or margarine. Add eggs and beat vigorously until potatoes are perfectly smooth and fluffy. Add milk, and continue to beat. Mixture should be quite moist. Turn into buttered casserole, and bake at 450°F. about 15 minutes or until rough crest of potatoes shows brown points. Serves 2.

Vegetables in Menus. *A wide choice is always available—fresh, canned, frozen, dried or pickled. Vary your cooking methods and add sauces and last minute touches.*

Herbs. Use fresh chives (easily grown in pot on kitchen windowsill) and parsley. Add just a dash of 1 other zesty herb—dill, fresh or dried, marjoram, thyme, rosemary, oregano, mint or nutmeg.

Seasonings. Experiment with a sprinkle of celery seed, mustard seed or curry powder over hot vegetables or coleslaw. Keep garlic and other seasoned salts handy. Try horseradish over hot buttered beets, a dusting of ground ginger on carrots. To enhance the flavor of winter root vegetables, add 1 teaspoon sugar towards the end of cooking time or while mashing.

Miscellaneous "go-withs." Other possibilities range from lemon or lime touches, plain or herbed vinegars, grated cheese and diced firm jelly to swirls of thick sour cream and toasted nuts. Scatter fried bacon bits over chopped cooked spinach. Sprinkle hot croutons over buttered vegetables. Strew a few seedless raisins over creamed cabbage or Brussels sprouts.

Sauces. The popular white or cream sauce is best when it emphasizes the character of the vegetable that it accompanies; substitute vegetable water for some of the milk, unless it has too strong a flavor for your taste. For 2 cups drained cooked vegetables you will need 1 cup medium white sauce. If you use condensed canned soup (celery, mushroom, asparagus) for sauce, mix 1/2 can with 1/3 cup water. Blend and heat thoroughly before pouring over 2 cups of hot vegetables.

Melted butter or margarine brings out flavor of hot cooked vegetables. Add a few drops of lemon juice occasionally. For mashed squash, use orange juice plus a sprinkle of brown sugar and nutmeg.

In choosing vegetables, aim for harmony of color, texture and flavor in total meal. Beef is compatible with almost any vegetable, with the possible exception of cucumber. Pork takes to beets, carrots, cauliflower, red cabbage, greens, squash, leeks and onions. Ham teams well with sweet potatoes or yams, peas, corn, beans of all kinds, asparagus, broccoli, Brussels sprouts and zucchini. With lamb serve beets, carrots, peas, cauliflower, yellow turnips, winter squash, sweet green or red peppers and tomatoes. Veal is best with Harvard beets, scalloped tomatoes and mushrooms. Chicken and turkey have many affinities, but if you are serving roasted whole fowl, it is best not to duplicate any vegetable used in the stuffing, onions and celery for example.

Asparagus with Mushrooms

    1 pound fresh asparagus tips
    3 tablespoons salad oil
    1 (4-ounce) can sliced mushrooms, and liquid
    1 small onion, chopped
Salt and pepper to taste
    1/4 cup light cream
Chopped parsley

Wash and trim asparagus under cold water. Combine oil with 1/4 cup mushroom liquid, and bring to boil in skillet. Add asparagus, onion and seasonings. Cook, covered, 8–10 minutes or until asparagus is tender, shaking skillet occasionally. Add mushrooms and light cream; heat thoroughly. Garnish with parsley. Serves 3–4.

Green Beans Lyonnaise

    1 pound green beans, Frenched, or 2 (10-ounce)
        packages frozen Frenched green beans
Salted water
    1 medium onion, chopped
    2 tablespoons butter or margarine or oil or bacon fat
1/4 teaspoon sweet basil
Salt and pepper to taste
    2 tablespoons toasted slivered almonds or sliced Brazil
        nuts

Gently boil beans in salted water. Drain as soon as tender. Sauté onion in fat until lightly browned; add basil, salt and pepper to taste. Pour over hot beans in serving dish, and garnish with nuts. Serves 6.

Savory Lima Beans

    1 (10-ounce) package frozen lima beans
    1 chicken-bouillon cube
    3 green onions, sliced
    2 tablespoons butter or margarine
    1 tablespoon flour
    1/4 teaspoon paprika
    1/4 teaspoon basil
    1/2 teaspoon salt
Dash pepper

Cook lima beans as directed on package, adding chicken-bouillon cube to boiling water. Drain, reserving 1/2 cup liquid. Simmer onions in melted butter or margarine 2 minutes, stir in flour. Add bean liquid, and cook, stirring, until thickened. Add beans and remaining ingredients, and heat through. Serves 4–6.

Harvard Beets

    1/2 cup sugar
    1 tablespoon cornstarch
    1/2 teaspoon salt
    1/4 cup vinegar
    1/4 cup water
Rind of 1 orange, grated
    2 tablespoons orange juice
    2 tablespoons butter or margarine
    4 cups hot sliced or diced cooked beets

Blend sugar, cornstarch and salt in saucepan, stir in vinegar, water and orange rind. Cook, stirring until sauce is smoothly thickened and clear. Add orange juice, butter or margarine and beets. Keep hot over low heat 15–20 minutes. Serves 5–6.

Broccoli with Olives

    1 bunch broccoli (approximately 1 pound)
    3/4 cup boiling salted water
    1/4 cup FRENCH DRESSING
Pinch basil
    1 tablespoon lemon juice
    1/2 cup chopped ripe olives

Clean and wash broccoli; cut off tough stem ends. Cook stalks in boiling salted water about 8 minutes. Drain well. Combine French dressing with basil and lemon juice, pour over hot broccoli and add olives. Heat thoroughly. Serves 4.

Parmesan Brussels Sprouts

    2 pounds fresh Brussels sprouts or 1 (10-ounce) package
        frozen
Boiling salted water
    2 tablespoons butter or margarine
1/2 clove garlic, crushed
1/3 cup grated Parmesan cheese

Trim off stems of Brussels sprouts, and remove any loose or discolored leaves. Put into small amount boiling salted water, and cook, covered, about 8 minutes. Drain. Heat butter or margarine and garlic together until bubbly; strain over sprouts, turning and coating them well with sauce. Pile on heated serving dish, and sprinkle with cheese. Serves 6.

Creamed Scandinavian Cabbage

                5 cups finely shredded cabbage
                1/2 cup boiling salted water
                1/2 cup sour cream
                1/2 cup chopped dill pickles
                1/2 teaspoon caraway seeds
                Salt and pepper to taste

Cook cabbage in boiling water until almost tender, 5–6 minutes. Drain, and add remaining ingredients to pan. Heat through. Serves 4.

Cabbage with Onion Rings

                2 small onions, peeled and sliced
                1/2 cup milk
                Salt and pepper to taste
                1/4 cup fine dry bread crumbs
                1/4 cup butter or margarine
                4 cups shredded cabbage
                1/2 teaspoon salt
                Juice of 1/2 lemon
                2 tablespoons water

Separate onion slices into rings. Season milk with salt and pepper to taste. Dip onion rings into milk, then into dry bread crumbs to coat well. Melt butter or margarine in skillet over medium heat. Sauté onion rings until crisp and golden brown; lift out and keep hot. Put shredded cabbage in same pan, sprinkle with salt, water, and lemon juice. Cover tightly and cook 3–4 minutes over low heat, turning once. Toss with 1/2 the onion rings, and garnish with remainder. Serves 4–5.

Chinese Cabbage with Tomatoes

                5 cups shredded Chinese cabbage
                Boiling salted water
                1/2 cup canned tomatoes
                1 small onion, finely chopped
                1 teaspoon sugar
                Salt and pepper to taste
                Pinch marjoram
                1/2 bay leaf

Parboil cabbage 5 minutes and drain. Combine tomatoes with onion, sugar and seasonings. Pour over cabbage, and cook slowly, covered, until cabbage is tender, 15–20 minutes. Remove bay leaf before serving. Serves 5–6.

Corn Fritters

                2 (10-ounce) packages frozen kernel
                    corn, thawed
                3 eggs
                1/2 teaspoon salt
                1/4 teaspoon pepper
                1 tablespoon chopped onion
                1/4 cup all-purpose flour
                1/3 cup fat

Drain corn of excess moisture; then measure 1 3/4 cups. Separate eggs; beat yolks until light and frothy. Add corn, seasonings, onion and flour. Beat egg whites until stiff but still glossy; fold into corn mixture. Heat fat in skillet, and drop mixture in by generous spoonfuls. Cook over medium heat until well browned; turn, and continue frying until thoroughly cooked. Fritters are especially good with chicken, ham or crisp bacon. Accompany fritters with maple syrup or honey. Serves 4–6.

Sautéed Cucumber

                2 firm medium cucumbers
                2 tablespoons butter or margarine
                1 teaspoon sugar
                1 teaspoon paprika
                1 teaspoon curry powder
                Salt and pepper to taste

Peel and dice cucumbers. Melt butter or margarine in skillet, and sauté cucumber over medium heat 1 minute. Turn heat low, sprinkle vegetable lightly with sugar, paprika, curry powder, and salt and pepper. Cover pan, and cook slowly about 4 minutes. Use as accompaniment for baked sausages, meat patties and the like. Serves 4.

Creamed Mushrooms with Spinach

                1 pound mushrooms, washed
                1/3 cup butter or margarine
                2 1/2 tablespoons flour
                1/2 teaspoon salt
                1/8 teaspoon pepper
                1 1/2 cups milk
                2 pounds spinach, thoroughly washed
                2 teaspoons salt
                Paprika to taste

Separate caps from stems of mushrooms. Melt butter or margarine in skillet, add stems and cook gently for 1 minute. Add caps, turning to cook both sides lightly until just tender; avoid heavy browning. Blend in flour; add 1/2 teaspoon salt, pepper and milk gradually, stirring constantly until sauce is smooth and thick. Keep hot over low heat. Put spinach into saucepan, and cook in its own moisture 3–4 minutes, adding 2 teaspoons salt, and turning vegetable once. Drain well. Arrange hot spinach around sides of serving dish, and fill center with hot creamed mushrooms. Shake paprika over mushrooms. Serves 6–8.

Carrots with Green Grapes

    1/2 cup butter or margarine
    4 cups carrots, cut in 2-inch strips
    1 cup seedless green grapes
    2 tablespoons honey
    1 tablespoon lemon juice
    Salt to taste
    3 or 4 mint leaves, chopped

Melt butter or margarine in heavy pan, add carrots and turn over and over until well coated with butter or margarine. Cover, and cook until almost tender, about 25 minutes. Add grapes, honey and lemon juice, and cook slowly 10 minutes. Add salt, and scatter mint leaves over just before serving. Serves 6.

Celery Braised in Consommé

    2–3 small heads celery
    1 medium onion, chopped
    2 tablespoons butter or margarine
    Dash pepper
    1 (10-ounce) can beef consommé
    1 tablespoon chopped parsley

Scrub celery, remove top leaves and cut each head lengthwise through heart, making 4 or 5 slender sections. If very long, cut in half crosswise. Place onion in casserole, and arrange celery on top. Dot with butter or margarine and sprinkle with pepper. Add undiluted consommé, cover and bake 1 hour at 375°F. Sprinkle with parsley before serving. Salt may be needed, depending on strength of consommé. Serves 6.

Jerusalem Artichokes

    1 1/2 pounds Jerusalem artichokes
    1/2 cup boiling water
    2 tablespoons butter or margarine
    1 teaspoon mild vinegar or white wine
    1 tablespoon chopped parsley
    2 drops hot pepper sauce

Wash and scrape artichokes, and cook in boiling water, covered, until just tender. Do not cook beyond this point, or artichokes will become tough again; test with toothpick after 15 minutes. Drain well. Melt butter or margarine, combine with remaining ingredients, and pour over cooked vegetable. Serves 4–6.

Instead of seasoned butter, cream vegetable in 1 cup medium white sauce. Slice cooked artichoke, and sauté in butter.

Acorn Squash with Mushrooms and Lime

    3 medium acorn squash (approximately 3 pounds)
    1 1/2 teaspoons salt
    1/2 teaspoon pepper
    1/2 teaspoon nutmeg
    3/4 cup butter or margarine
    4 cups button mushrooms (1 pound)
    6 slices lime

Wash acorn squash. Dry, cut in half lengthwise and remove seeds. Sprinkle each squash with salt, pepper, and nutmeg. In each hollow, place 1 tablespoon butter or margarine. (Save rest for later.) Place on a shallow baking tray. Cover with foil. Bake at 400°F. for 40 minutes or until tender. Drain any butter sitting in hollows of squash into a skillet. Add rest of butter to this. Sauté mushrooms until tender, approximately 5 to 7 minutes. Fill each squash half with about 3/4 cup of the mushrooms. Garnish each serving with 1 slice lime. Serves 6.

Roast Corn

    5 or 6 ears corn
    1/4 cup butter or margarine, melted
    Salt and pepper to taste
    Water

Pull back husks of corn; remove silks. Brush cobs with butter or margarine, and salt and pepper. Replace husks, and twist ends together as tightly as possible. Wrap individually in heavy foil, and place on rack over glowing embers. Roast about 30 minutes, turning several times with tongs. Serves 4–6.

Mashed Parsnip Patties

    3 cups mashed cooked parsnips
    1 tablespoon finely chopped onion
    1 tablespoon finely chopped parsley
    3/4 teaspoon salt
    Pinch poultry seasoning
    1 egg, well beaten
    1/2 cup coarse bread crumbs
    1/2 cup fine bread crumbs
    2 tablespoon bacon drippings or salad oil

To parsnips, add onion, parsley and seasonings; stir in egg and coarse crumbs. Shape into 8 patties, and roll in fine crumbs. Heat drippings in frying pan, and sauté until crisply brown on both sides. Serves 4.

Vegetable Soufflé

    1 cup cooked vegetables (peas, turnips, onions, carrots,
        broccoli, asparagus, mushrooms, or mixture of
        several)
    1 cup thick white sauce
    2 tablespoons finely chopped onion
    1 tablespoon lemon juice
1/2 teaspoon salt
Dash pepper
Dash Worcestershire sauce
    2 egg yolks, beaten
    2 egg whites
1/4 teaspoon cream of tartar

Purée vegetables in blender, mash or chop fine. Combine with white sauce, onion, lemon juice, seasonings, Worcestershire sauce and egg yolks. Cool. Beat egg whites stiffly with cream of tartar. Fold into vegetables. Turn into a greased 1 1/2-quart casserole, and bake at 325°F. 1 hour. This soufflé is a good accompaniment for creamed ham or chicken. Serves 6.

Scalloped Tomatoes

    2 tablespoons butter or margarine
    2 tablespoons finely chopped onions
1 1/2 cups soft bread crumbs
    1 (1-pound, 4-ounce) can tomatoes, drained
    1 teaspoon sugar
1/2 teaspoon salt
Dash celery salt (optional)
1/4 teaspoon pepper

Melt butter or margarine, add onion, cook till tender. Combine with bread crumbs, mixing well. To tomatoes add sugar, salt, celery salt and pepper; mix through. Pour 1/2 the tomatoes into greased casserole; top with layer of crumb mixture using a little more than 1/2. Add remaining tomatoes, and cover with remaining crumb mixture. Bake at 375°F. about 45 minutes. Serves 4–5.

VARIATIONS:

● Instead of celery salt add 1/4 cup chopped celery to tomatoes; increase salt to taste.
● Peel and core 1 large tart apple; slice into tomatoes before cooking; increase sugar and salt to taste.

Turnip–Potato Casserole

    1 turnip (about 1 pound)
Boiling salted water
    4 or 5 potatoes
Boiling salted water
1/4 cup finely chopped onion
    2 tablespoons cream
    1 egg, beaten
Salt and pepper to taste
1/2 teaspoon dry mustard

Peel turnip, slice, and boil in salted water until tender but not too soft, about 15 minutes; drain, and mash. Cook potatoes in salted water in separate saucepan. Drain well, mash and combine with mashed turnip. Add remaining ingredients, and whip with egg beater or electric beater. Turn purée into buttered casserole, and bake uncovered at 400°F. 20 minutes or until firm, puffed and lightly browned on top. Serves 4–6.

Note: Grated cheese may be sprinkled over top a few minutes before removing from oven.

Sweet-and-Sour Red Cabbage

    1 small firm red cabbage (4 cups shredded)
Boiling salted water
    2 medium tart apples, cored, peeled and sliced
1/4 cup brown sugar
1/4 cup cider vinegar
    1 tablespoon butter or margarine

Discard core and tougher white ribs of cabbage. Shred coarsely. Cook, covered, in boiling salted water, about 10 minutes. Add apples, and cook until tender, about 10 minutes more. Drain. Dissolve brown sugar in vinegar, stir into cabbage mixture and add butter or margarine. Cover, and keep hot over low heat a few minutes before serving. Serves 4–5.

Eggplant Italian Style

1/4 cup tomato paste
    1 (2-pound, 3-ounce) can Italian-style tomatoes, drained
Pinch salt
    1 large or 2 small eggplants
    1 cup hot water
    3 tablespoons hot salad oil
Salt and pepper to taste
    2 cups soft bread crumbs
1/2 cup grated Parmesan cheese
    1 tablespoon chopped parsley
    1 clove garlic, chopped, or 2 tablespoons finely
        chopped onion
1/2 pound mozzarella cheese, cut in thin strips

Blend tomato paste with canned tomatoes; add pinch salt, and simmer 5 minutes. Meanwhile, wash, dry and slice eggplant crosswise into 1/2-inch slices; do not peel. Place in bowl, cover with hot water and let stand 5 minutes. Drain slices, and pat dry with paper towel. Fry in hot oil until tender and light brown, about 3 minutes each side. Sprinkle with salt and pepper to taste. Mix crumbs, Parmesan, parsley and garlic. Add spoonful of hot oil from pan. Arrange layer of eggplant slices in baking dish; cover with 1/2 crumb mixture, then with 1/2 the tomatoes. Top with another eggplant layer, remaining crumbs and tomatoes. On final eggplant layer, place mozzarella cheese. Bake in moderate oven (350°F.) until cheese is bubbly and slightly colored. Serves 5–6.

Sweet-sour Zucchini

6 medium zucchini
1/2 cup salad oil
Salt and pepper to taste
3 tablespoons cider vinegar
1 tablespoon sugar
1/2 clove garlic (optional)
1/2 teaspoon sweet basil
Chopped parsley

Wash zucchini, and scrape lightly. Cut each into 2 or 3 lengthwise slices. Fry in salad oil about 3 minutes each side or until squash is lightly browned and tender. Sprinkle with salt and pepper. Remove from skillet, and place in hot serving dish. Mix vinegar and sugar, and add with garlic and sweet basil to remaining oil in skillet. Simmer slowly 2 minutes, remove garlic and pour sauce over zucchini. Garnish with parsley. This dish may be served hot or chilled. Serves 4–5.

Herbed Onion Casserole

2 pounds onions
1 teaspoon salt
1 teaspoon paprika
1 teaspoon celery seed
1/4 teaspoon pepper
1/4 teaspoon basil or sage
1/2 cup consommé or bouillon
3/4 cup crushed potato chips

Peel onions, and slice thick. Combine seasonings. Place layers of sliced onion in shallow greased casserole, sprinkling seasonings between layers. Add consommé, cover casserole and bake 1 hour at 400°F. Remove cover; scatter crushed potato chips over onions; cook another 5–10 minutes until topping is crisp and browned. Serves 4–5.

Fireside Chicken–Vegetable Stew

4–5 pound stewing fowl
1/2 lemon
1/4 cup butter or margarine, melted
Bouquet garni
5–6 cups water
2 chicken-bouillon cubes
1 teaspoon salt
1/2 cup sliced celery
6 small carrots, scraped
6 or more potatoes, peeled
1 (10-ounce) package frozen lima beans
1 cup cream or milk
1/4 cup soft butter or margarine
1/3 cup flour
1 (1-pound) can small onions, drained
Chopped parsley

Wash chicken, wipe and cut in serving pieces. Run cut surface of lemon over meat surfaces. Sauté legs, wings and breast sections slowly on both sides in melted butter or margarine until golden, watching that butter doesn't burn. Add remaining chicken pieces, including giblets from which all fat has been cut away. Add bouquet garni, water, bouillon cubes and salt. Cover tightly and simmer until chicken is just tender, about 1 1/2–2 hours. Add raw vegetables, and simmer 20 minutes longer. Lift out, and discard large bones and pieces of skin. Pour cream and stock from chicken into double boiler. Make roux by blending butter or margarine with flour and stirring into stock until thickened. Pour over cooked chicken, vegetables and drained onions. Heat until bubbly, and sprinkle with chopped parsley. Serves 6.

Note: Make a bouquet garni from 1/2 teaspoon thyme, slice of onion, few peppercorns, celery leaves, parsley sprigs and tie all in cheesecloth bag. If chicken is fat, strain cooking stock into bowl and chill until fat comes to top, then skim. If preferred, use 1/4 cup chicken fat in place of butter or margarine for thickening stock. Cut-up frying or roasting chicken may be used in place of boiling fowl and will require less cooking time; 35 minutes for preliminary simmering or 10 minutes in pressure cooker.

Whole Cauliflower Polonaise

1 medium head cauliflower
Boiling water
3 tablespoons melted butter or margarine
1 teaspoon chopped parsley
2 tablespoons toasted fine bread crumbs
1 hard cooked egg yolk, sieved

Trim off leaves, and cut from cauliflower as much of core as possible without harming flowerets. Gently boil 15–18 minutes. Drain. Place in serving dish; then, combine melted butter or margarine and parsley, and pour over cauliflower Sprinkle with bread crumbs and egg yolk. Serves 4–5.

Vegetable Chowder

1 cup diced carrots
1/2 cup finely chopped onion
2 1/2 cups boiling salted water
2 1/4 cups chopped cabbage
2 tablespoons butter or margarine
2 tablespoons flour
1 cup milk
2 teaspoons salt
1/8 teaspoon pepper
1 cup cooked peas
2 tablespoons chopped parsley

Cook carrots and onion in boiling water until almost tender. Add cabbage and continue cooking until all vegetables are tender. Drain, and save liquid (approximately 1 1/2 cups). Melt butter or margarine in pan. Add flour, milk, 1 teaspoon salt, pepper and 1/2 cup vegetable liquid. Stir until smooth. Add remaining 1 cup vegetable liquid. Stir, and cook over boiling water until sauce thickens. Add cooked vegetables and parsley. Keep hot over simmering water till serving time. Serves 6.

Accompaniments for Vegetables. Special seasonings, sauces and other interesting touches can enhance plain vegetables.

Flavored Butters

Melt butter or margarine for boiled or steamed vegetables, using 3 tablespoons to 4–6 servings. Before pouring over vegetables, stir into butter 1 of the following: 1–1 1/2 teaspoons lemon juice; 1 teaspoon thick meat sauce; 1 tablespoon grated dry cheese; 1/4 teaspoon dry mustard; 1 tablespoon chopped nuts; 1/4–1/2 teaspoon Worcestershire sauce; 1/4–1/2 teaspoon beef bouillon; 1 teaspoon spaghetti sauce; 1 teaspoon chopped parsley or green onions.

From the Salad Shelf

For 4–5 servings of hot cooked vegetables, toss lightly with 1 of the following: 2–3 tablespoons FRENCH DRESSING; 1–2 tablespoons herb vinegar; 1 tablespoon MAYONNAISE thinned with lemon juice.

Bread Accompaniments

Buttered Crumbs: Allow 1/3 cup melted bacon dripping or butter for 1 cup fine dry bread crumbs. Sauté crumbs until hot, and scatter over hot vegetable for serving. Or to buttered crumbs or croutons add 1 of the following: sprinkle of grated cheese, spoonful of finely chopped onion or scallion, diced cooked bacon, dash of curry powder, dash of paprika.

Stuffing: For 1 halved acorn squash or 4–5 onions or tomatoes, use 1 cup soft bread crumbs seasoned with grated cheese, crisp bacon pieces, grated onion or salt and pepper along with a pinch of mixed herbs or 1 favorite like oregano.

Bread Croustades: Remove crusts from sliced bread. Brush one side with melted butter or margarine, press buttered sides into muffin tins. Toast in 350°F. oven 15 minutes or until golden. Remove from tins, keep hot and fill with creamed vegetables at serving time.

Sauce for Creamed Vegetables (White Sauce)

2 tablespoons butter or margarine
2 tablespoons flour
1 cup milk or 1/2 cup milk and 1/2 cup vegetable water
Salt and pepper to taste

Melt butter or margarine, and blend in flour. Stir in liquid slowly. Cook until smooth, stirring constantly, until no taste of raw starch remains. Season to taste. Makes 1 cup.

VARIATIONS:

To basic cream or white sauce, add 1 of the following, according to kind of vegetable and to your own taste: celery salt, 1 teaspoon onion juice, 1 teaspoon sherry, 1 teaspoon lemon juice, dash Worcestershire sauce, 1/2 teaspoon curry powder, 2 teaspoons capers or chopped sweet pickle, 2 tablespoons chopped chives or parsley.

To plain creamed vegetables in serving dish, add a last-minute grating of nutmeg, or sprinkle 2 chopped hard-cooked eggs over top.

Canned-soup Sauce: Use condensed cream soup of suitable flavor—chicken, mushroom, tomato, or celery. Dilute with 1/2 liquid required for soup. Heat, and pour over cooked vegetables.

Au Gratin Vegetables: Add cream sauce to hot vegetable; sprinkle with fresh or dry bread crumbs, and dot with butter, margarine or grated cheese. Heat under broiler 2–3 minutes.

Sour Cream–Horseradish Sauce

1 cup commercial sour cream
1/2 teaspoon prepared mustard
1/2 teaspoon horseradish
Salt and pepper to taste

Combine ingredients, adding more horseradish if desired. Serve cold in sauceboat with hot spinach.

Glazed Vegetables

Leave parboiled, peeled vegetables like sweet potatoes, parsnips, carrots and squash, whole or in large pieces. Place in buttered baking dish. Drizzle 1 of the following glazes over pieces. Bake, basting with syrup, at 350°F. 20–30 minutes.

Sugar Glaze

1/2 cup sugar
1/2 cup brown sugar
1/2 cup boiling water
2 tablespoons butter or margarine

Mix all ingredients.

Honey Glaze

        1/2 cup honey
          1 tablespoon butter or margarine, melted
        1/2 teaspoon mint

Combine all ingredients.

Orange Glaze

        1/2 cup sugar
          1 tablespoon orange juice
        Dash cinnamon

Combine all ingredients.

FRUITS

A minimum of 2 servings of fruit or juice per day—1 of them a citrus fruit or tomato juice—is recommended. The 2 servings are specified because of vitamin C requirements, but oranges and tomatoes contain vitamin A as well. The mild, natural acids that such fruits provide help digestion.

In season, cantaloupe and strawberries are perfectly acceptable as the day's vitamin C ration. A normal serving of 1/2 cantaloupe supplies as much of this dietary essential as 1/2 cup fresh orange juice; in addition, the melon contains more vitamin A than does any other fruit.

There is no difference in nutritive value between canned juices and diluted frozen citrus juices; selection can be made on the basis of taste or price. To avoid a "tinny" taste, opened cans of citrus fruits and juices should be poured into another type of container, covered and kept in the refrigerator. Canned or bottled juices develop maximum flavor when aerated by pouring several times from one container to another.

All fresh, cooked, canned and frozen fruits provide a variety of vitamins, and, served whole or as unstrained juice, they provide bulk for the digestive tract and some energy, which is of course increased when sugar is added.

Fruits are low in protein and fat, except for avocados and ripe olives. With few exceptions, they are also low in minerals.

Often canned and frozen fruits and juices are less expensive than are fresh ones. And you can use the juices from canned or frozen fruits, preferably without additional cooking.

Always remember that frozen fruits must be kept at 0°F. and should not be refrozen after thawing, especially if the package has been opened.

Special Canned Fruits. *Fruit nectars* are thicker than juices. They contain some sieved pulp and pectins, which provide bulk not present in strained liquid. Sugar has generally been added, and vitamins are fewer per serving than in unsweetened juices. Fruit nectars are best used in mixed beverages or in recipes.

Don't forget that all "baby foods" are *strained* and "junior foods" *chopped*. Both can be used for special diets, recipes and elderly people. "Baby foods" are low in bulk because they are strained. Yet they have the same food value as do regular sweetened canned fruits.

Dietetic canned fruits offer the same food values as do other canned fruits but are processed without added sugar, or with addition of non-caloric sweeteners.

Dried Fruits. Because large amounts of liquid have been removed, dried fruits are high in sugar content and therefore are an energy source. They have valuable mineral contents but are usually low in vitamins. Prunes, dates and figs encourage elimination.

Dried fruits are available the year round, are comparatively low in cost and go well with other fruits.

Prunes, raisins, apples, peaches, apricots, and pears are most common in this group; others are dates, figs and currants.

Packages labeled "tenderized" have moisture content and thus more weight. Large prunes have larger percentages of edible pulp than do smaller ones, but the volume packs of the latter are often more economical.

The three varieties of raisin most widely available are golden raisins, dark raisins, and seedless (muscats).

Preparation Tips. To halve orange or grapefruit, cut crosswise; cut between flesh and membranes of each section. Run sharp knife or curved grapefruit knife around edge to separate flesh from white inner rind. Center pith may be removed with scissors or knife.

To section orange or grapefruit, slice top and bottom rind just to flesh. Stand fruit upright. With very sharp knife, slice off skin all around, top to bottom. Trim off rind bits. Turn fruit over, and complete trimming. Cut sections free of membrane.

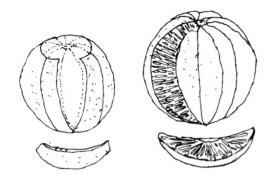

To prepare citrus fruit juice, halve and squeeze chilled fruit. Remove seeds, but do not strain (except for low-bulk diet). Juice for breakfast may be prepared night before, covered and refrigerated. There is little loss of vitamins, but flavor may be decreased.

The small berries, particularly raspberries, need care to avoid bruising. Spread on flat surface to pick over; remove any moldy or overripe fruit. Place in colander, and dip colander in pan of very cold water to wash fruit thoroughly. Drain; then stem or hull.

To skin peaches, work at kitchen sink. Place fruit in colander set in pan. Pour boiling water over to cover all fruit. Let stand 1 minute, put colander with fruit under tap and run cold water over for 1 minute. Skins can then be slipped off readily.

Lemon rind and juice are often called for in recipes. It is best to grate rind before halving fruit. When "a few drops" of juice are wanted, it is convenient to pierce whole lemon with a skewer and even more convenient to use frozen or bottled lemon juice.

Remove apple core with an apple peeler (a slotted, rounded knife) and peel by pulling peeler toward you, holding apple over bowl. If apples are very juicy, it may be advisable to pare by pushing peeler away from you.

In making melon balls, be sure to press special scoop firmly, to its full depth, into flesh, thus ensuring well-rounded ball.

The edible part of a pomegranate is the juicy pink pulp containing the seed clusters; remove with fork. Use for garnish or fruit cups.

A pineapple needs special attention. Slice off ends. With sharp knife, pare off skin top to bottom. To remove deep "eyes" make wedge-shaped cuts along their diagonal line. Cut pineapple in crosswise slices; then quarter slices and remove hard inner core point.

Uncooked Fruit Dishes

3-Fruit Juice

> 2 cups orange juice
> 1 cup apple juice
> 1 cup pineapple juice

Mix, and keep covered in refrigerator. Use with any fresh-fruit appetizer or dessert to enhance flavor and prevent discoloration of cut fruits—or drink plain or with chilled soda water and ice cubes. Serves 4–5.

Melon–Ginger Mélange

> 1/4 cup fresh lime juice
> 1/4 cup orange juice
> 3 cups cantaloupe balls
> 1/3 cup preserved ginger, chopped
> 1 banana, sliced
> Sugar to taste

Add juices to cantaloupe balls. Just before serving add ginger, banana and sugar. Serves 4–5.

Honeydew Rings with Fruit

> 1 ripe honeydew melon
> 2 cups canned pineapple chunks, drained
> 1 cup cantaloupe balls
> 1 cup pitted sweet cherries
> 1 cup raspberries
> 1 pint lemon sherbet
> 8 sprigs fresh mint

Peel melon, discard all seeds and slice crosswise into 8 1-inch thick rings. Arrange 1 ring on each individual dessert plate. Chill all other fruits ready for serving time. Place scoop of sherbet in center of each melon ring, and scatter cantaloupe balls, pineapple chunks, sweet cherries and raspberries over. Garnish with mint sprigs. Serves 8.

Watermelon Fruit Basket

1/2 watermelon
1 pint fresh berries
1 dozen fresh apricots, halved
1 cup cantaloupe balls
1 banana, sliced
1/4 cup superfine sugar
2 tablespoons cherry liqueur or Cointreau (optional)
8 sprigs fresh mint

Watermelon half may be left as cut or notched for sawtooth edge. Scoop out some of the melon center, and save removed pulp for next day's fruit cup. In hollow, arrange other fruits. Sprinkle fruit with sugar. Cherry liqueur may be drizzled over. Just before serving, decorate watermelon basket with mint sprigs. To serve, start cutting from 1 end of basket, making thick slices, and spoon mixed fruits onto each slice. Serves 8–10.

Strawberry Ice-cream Soda

2 tablespoons mashed strawberries
2 tablespoons sugar
1 tablespoon cream
1 scoop vanilla ice cream
3/4 cup chilled soda water

Use blender, or mix in bowl with hand beater. To mashed fresh or barely thawed frozen berries add sugar and cream. Mix together, add ice cream and beat till thoroughly blended. Pour into serving glass, fill with chilled soda water and serve at once. Serves 1.

Applesauce Delight

2 egg whites
1/4 teaspoon salt
1 tablespoon lemon juice
1 (1-pound) jar applesauce, chilled
1/2 cup crushed almond macaroons

Beat egg whites with salt until stiff and glossy. Gradually add lemon juice and applesauce. Continue beating until mixture is very fluffy. Turn into dessert bowls, and sprinkle tops with fine macaroon crumbs. Serves 4.

Fresh Lemonade

4 lemons
3/4 cup sugar
1 tray ice cubes
2 cups cold water
4 maraschino cherries with stems

With sharp knife, slice 3 lemons very thin crosswise. Discard seeds and end slices. Put lemon slices into large bowl or sturdy pitcher. Add sugar. With wooden spoon or potato masher, muddle until sugar is dissolved and slices are broken. Strain; then add ice cubes and cold water. Stir until very cold. To serve, pour lemonade into glasses; garnish each glass with 1 whole slice from remaining lemon and 1 cherry. Makes 4 tall glasses.

VARIATION:

Apricot Lemonade

Reduce sugar to 1/2 cup, and put 2 or more tablespoons chilled apricot nectar into each glass. Fill with lemonade, and garnish with cherry.

Banana Whip

1 egg white
1/2 cup sugar
1/2 cup mashed banana
Juice of 1/2 lemon
1/8 teaspoon salt
1 teaspoon red currant jelly

Beat first 5 ingredients together with an eggbeater or blender until mixture is very light and fluffy. Heap in sherbet glasses, and garnish each with dot of jelly. Serves 2–3.

Cherry Swirl

1 (3-ounce) package vanilla-pudding mix
Few drops almond extract
1 cup cherry jam

Prepare vanilla pudding according to package directions, adding almond flavoring, and allow to thicken partially. To achieve attractive diagonal stripes with red jam, proceed as follows:

Hold parfait glass at an angle, spoon in some jam, then a layer of partially thickened pudding, then another spoonful of jam and so on, ending with layer of pudding. Chill, and garnish with more jam before serving. Serves 3–4.

Banana–Pineapple Milkshake

1 1/4 cups milk
1 (4 3/4-ounce) can strained bananas with pineapple
1/4 cup pineapple juice
2 scoops vanilla ice cream

Measure all ingredients into blender; mix 1 minute. Pour into tall glasses. Serves 2.

Citrus–Plum Compote

1 (1-pound) can plums in heavy syrup
1 fresh lime
3 oranges, peeled and sectioned
2 bananas, sliced

Put plums and juice into serving bowl; then grate rind of lime directly over them. Peel, and discard all white skin from lime; cut into small sections, and add to plums. Chill 5–6 hours. Just before serving, add fresh orange sections and sliced bananas. Serves 6.

Pears Helene

1 can (1 pound 13 ounces) Bartlett pears
1 pint vanilla ice cream
1/2 cup chocolate sauce

Chill pears. At serving time, drain off juice. Allow 2 pear halves for each serving; place in individual dish with scoop of ice cream between

halves. Drizzle chocolate sauce over ice cream and pears. Serves 4.

Cranberry Whip

2 cups (1 pound) canned cranberry sauce
3 egg whites, beaten
1 teaspoon grated orange rind
1 teaspoon lemon juice
12–18 ladyfingers

Put sauce through sieve. Beat egg whites until very stiff but not dry; fold in cranberry purée, orange rind and lemon juice. Continue beating until completely blended and mixture stands in glossy peaks. Arrange 2 or 3 ladyfingers upright in each sherbet glass, and pile whip in center. Serves 6.

Crystal Grapes

1 large bunch seedless green grapes
1 egg white
1/4 cup finely granulated sugar

Cut off small clusters of firm grapes from large bunch, leaving them attached to their stems. Beat egg white slightly. Dip grapes in it, then sprinkle generously with sugar. Let dry on cake rack at room temperature.
Note: These easy-to-make novelties are great for garnishing cold-meat platters, salad plates, or cheese trays. Do not make on a humid day.

Frosted Fruit Compote

1 (3-ounce) package cream cheese
1/2 cup mayonnaise
2 bananas
1 cup raspberries
1 (8-ounce) can pineapple tidbits
1/2 pound midget marshmallows
1/2 pint heavy cream
3 tablespoons sugar

Cream cheese with fork until softened. Blend in mayonnaise, and beat until smooth. Cut bananas into small pieces. Pick over, wash and thoroughly drain raspberries. Drain pineapple tidbits. Combine all fruits and marshmallows; then add to cheese. Whip cream until stiff, add sugar and gently fold in cheese and fruit mixture. Freeze in refrigerator trays. Thaw slightly before serving. Serves 6–8.

Fresh Fruit Whip

2 egg whites
1/4 teaspoon cream of tartar
1/4 cup sugar
1 1/2 cups fresh fruit (peaches, pears, apples)

Beat egg whites with cream of tartar until stiff but not dry. Gradually add sugar, and beat until stiff peaks can be formed. Fold in well-drained fruit, and spoon into serving dishes. Accompany with whipped cream. Serves 4.

Note: Canned fruit or cooked prunes may be substituted if desired, and you can save drained juice for later use.

Orange–Brittle Ambrosia

2 large slabs peanut brittle
1 cup heavy cream
2 cups fresh orange, peeled and cut into small pieces

Crush with rolling pin until fine and powdery sufficient peanut brittle to make 1/2 cup. Beat cream until stiff; combine with crushed brittle. Just before serving, fold in fresh chilled orange pieces. Serves 4.

Note: Ambrosia also makes a nice topping for plain cake.

Rice Cream with Cherries

1 (1-pound, 5-ounce) can cherry pie filling
Few drops almond flavoring
1 cup heavy cream
1 cup cold cooked rice
1 tablespoon sugar

Sprinkle cherries with almond flavoring. Whip cream until stiff, sweeten lightly and combine with cold rice and sugar. Place spoonful of cherries at bottom of each of 4 dessert bowls, cover with thick layer of rice cream and top with remaining cherries. Chill. Serves 4.

Fruit Candy Bars

1/2 pound dried apricots or dates or seedless raisins
1 or 2 pieces preserved ginger
3/4 cup confectioners' sugar
1/4 cup soft butter or margarine
2 tablespoons orange juice
1/2 cup crushed vanilla wafers
1/4 cup confectioners' sugar

Put fruit and ginger through grinder; it should be finely ground. Add 3/4 cup sugar, butter or margarine and orange juice, blending thoroughly. Gradually stir in enough wafer crumbs to make mixture sufficiently stiff to form into fingers. Coat fingers with 1/4 cup sugar. Wrap in waxed paper, and chill in refrigerator. Makes about 3 dozen bars.

Do consider the following ideas for fruits and their juices.

Freeze them in refrigerator trays. A chilled drink becomes more tempting when there's a wedge of pineapple, lemon or orange or a whole cherry, berry or grape imprisoned in each ice cube. To hold fruit neatly in position in cube, fill tray to 1/4 depth with water, partially freeze, add the berry or piece and freeze till almost firm. Fill tray to usual level, and finish freezing. Keep temperature control at regular setting throughout; the garnished cubes may cloud with fast freezing. Fruit juices—grape, orange, berry—take to the freezing compartment as easily as does water.

Fruit sodas and milkshakes are popular among the young crowd as after-school snacks. Make milkshakes quickly with electric beater or blender, shake in cocktail mixer or stir vigorously in tall glass. For each serving use 1 scoop ice cream, 2–3 tablespoons crushed fruit or juice (not lemon) and 1 cup milk. Make fruit soda in tall glass, using peach or apricot halves or berries over ice cream, then pouring in carbonated soda water. Stir, and serve.

For garnishing, suit fruit to course: pineapple slices dipped in chopped parsley and topped with mint jelly for roast lamb; cloved canned pear or peach halves with ham, and fried apple rings prepared by cutting in 1/2-inch slices, coring and gently cooking in hot sausage fat until tender with baked or fried sausages.

Sauces for Fruit Desserts. Although the various creams, plain, whipped, ice cream, commercial sour cream are always available, there are other excellent accompaniments as well. Choose a sauce to complement the dish's flavor; a bland sauce for a tart pudding, a sauce with special character for a mild-flavored dish.

Vanilla Sauce

1/2 cup sugar
1 tablespoon cornstarch
Dash salt
Dash nutmeg
1 cup boiling water
2 tablespoons butter or margarine
1 teaspoon vanilla extract

Mix first 4 ingredients in small saucepan. Gradually add boiling water, stirring to blend, and cook over low heat until thick and clear. Add butter or margarine, and vanilla. Makes 1 1/3 cups.

Sherry–Custard Sauce

4 egg yolks
1/4 cup sugar
1/4 teaspoon salt
1/4 cup sherry

Beat yolks until thick and lemon colored; then beat in sugar and salt. Cook over hot (not boiling) water 5 minutes, beating constantly. Remove from heat, and stir in sherry. Serve warm or cold over fresh fruit pieces. Makes 1 3/4 cups.

Hard Sauce

1/2 cup butter or margarine
2 cups confectioners' sugar
1 teaspoon vanilla extract or lemon or orange juice plus
    1/4 teaspoon grated rind or brandy

Cream butter or margarine very thoroughly; add sugar, a little at a time, blending after each addition, add flavoring. Beat well. Mound sauce on serving plate, and chill at least 1 hour. Serve with hot puddings. Makes 1 2/3 cups.

Chocolate Sauce

1/2 cup light corn syrup
1 cup sugar
1 cup water
3 ounces unsweetened chocolate
1 teaspoon vanilla extract
1 cup evaporated milk

Mix first 3 ingredients in saucepan, and boil (236°F.) until 1 drop of mixture forms a soft ball in cold water. Remove from heat, stir in chocolate until melted and add vanilla. Add milk slowly, stirring vigorously. Serve chilled with ice cream, sherbets, baked pears. Makes 2 1/2 cups.

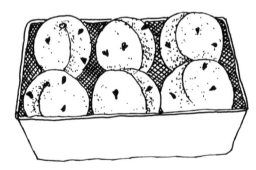

Cooked Fruit. Some fruits should be cooked to be palatable. Green apples, rhubarb, hard little Seckel pears, quinces and red or black currants are examples. Cooking and sweetening develop the full flavors of these fruits; correct procedures make them softer and more digestible. Cooking also prevents spoilage of perishable raw fruits and extends their many possibilities. (For long-term storage, of course, fruit must be specially handled—sterilized and sealed as in canning or simply frozen.)

Simple Fruit Sauces

Applesauce is always a favorite when well made. To achieve maximum flavor and a smooth, thick consistency, it is important to cook apples in a minimum of water and to wait until fruit is soft before adding sugar. If sugar is added at the start, more is needed and more time too, as sugar has a tendency to toughen fruit flesh and skin, thus delaying softening. Place quartered, unpared apples in saucepan with just enough water to prevent burning. Cover pan, and over medium or higher heat begin the cooking quickly; then reduce heat, and cook fruit until soft. Press through sieve at once; then stir in sugar to taste. Apples past their prime need more water than does juicy fall crop. For extra flavor add a few drops of lemon juice or a sprinkle of cinnamon or nutmeg.

Stewed rhubarb is best when prepared without water, but some water is added at the start to draw out the abundant natural juices of this fruit. Wash rhubarb stalks, and cut in uniform 1–2 inch lengths. Use about 1/2 as much sugar as fruit. Sprinkle about 1/3 the total quantity of sugar over fruit in a saucepan, cover and cook over low heat. Do not stir. As juice is drawn out, add more sugar; when fruit is almost tender, add remainder.

Poaching

To poach fruit, stew gently, either whole or cut in fairly large pieces. The aim is to keep shape intact; the fruit is put into steadily simmering sugar-and-water syrup, a little at a time, cooked till just tender, carefully lifted out and replaced by another small batch. The smallest pieces and the softest fruits require the shortest cooking time and are added last. When all fruit is cooked, syrup is usually reduced by boiling and poured over fruit before chilling and serving.

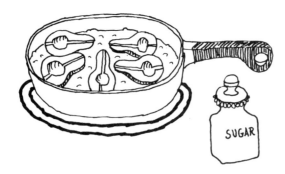

Baked Fruits

Apples are the most frequently baked fruit, but other fruits can be baked as well. Peeled pears or peaches are baked whole or in cored halves in shallow baking dish containing a few tablespoons of water. Sprinkle sugar over fruit, dot with butter or margarine and bake in slow oven. Peeled whole bananas are baked without water. Place in greased dish; sprinkle with lemon juice, sugar and a few grains of salt; dot with butter or margarine and bake uncovered about 20 minutes.

Special Equipment

A pressure cooker can produce a variety of interesting cooked fruit desserts. Always follow manufacturer's directions exactly for quantities and timing particularly with fruits that tend to froth and sputter, as do apples and cranberries.

With an electric blender, raw fruit can be pulverized for quickly assembled whips and shortcake fillings. In less than 1 minute of blending, quartered raw apples can be transformed into very good applesauce, without heat.

Deep-dish Fruit Pie

> 1 1/4 cups all-purpose flour
> 1/4 teaspoon salt
> 1/3 cup shortening
> 2–3 tablespoons cold water
> FRUIT FILLING

Sift together flour and salt; cut in the shortening, using pastry blender or 2 knives; continue cutting in until mixture is in particles the size of peas. Add cold water very gradually, moistening dry areas in turn; use only enough water to bind dough. Wrap dough in waxed paper, and chill in refrigerator a few minutes while preparing filling. Roll out pastry about 1/8-inch thick on lightly floured cloth or board; make circle large enough to allow 1/2-inch margin for rim. Cut 2 or 3 small gashes in center to allow steam to escape. Lay pastry over filling in baking dish or deep pie plate; take care not to stretch it. Fold overhang under outer rim of dish, and press into place with floured fork. Start pie in hot oven, 425°F. After 15 minutes reduce heat to 350°F., and bake about 30 minutes longer. Serves 5–6.

Fruit Fillings

Apple Pie Filling: Pare, core and thinly slice 6–8 tart apples. Place in 1-quart buttered dish, and sprinkle with mixture of 2 tablespoons flour, 1 cup sugar, 1/2 teaspoon salt, pinch nutmeg, and pinch cinnamon. Dot 2 teaspoons butter or margarine over top before covering with pastry.

Blueberry Pie Filling: Use 4 cups fresh or just-thawed frozen berries. Follow procedure for APPLE PIE FILLING using 1 1/2 tablespoons flour and 3/4 cup sugar.

Peach–Cream Pie

> 1 cup all-purpose flour
> 1/2 teaspoon salt
> 1/3 cup shortening
> 1/4 cup blanched almonds, ground
> 2–3 tablespoons cold water
> 1/3 cup flour
> 1/3 cup granulated sugar
> 1/8 teaspoon salt
> 1 (20-ounce) can sliced peaches and juice
> Water
> 3 egg yolks, slightly beaten
> 2 teaspoons lemon juice
> 2 teaspoons butter or margarine
> 1/2 teaspoon vanilla extract
> 1/4 teaspoon almond extract
> 3 egg whites
> 1/3 cup granulated sugar
> 1 teaspoon lemon juice

Sift together 1 cup flour and 1/2 teaspoon salt. Cut in shortening until quite fine; add almonds. Sprinkle cold water over until dough is moist enough to hold together. Chill; roll dough out on lightly floured board, and ease it into 9-inch pie pan. Flute edge, and bake 12–15 minutes at 450°F. Allow to cool while making filling.

Combine 1/3 cup flour, 1/3 cup sugar and 1/8 teaspoon salt in top of double boiler. Stir in peach juice, adding enough water to make 2 cups, and cook over direct heat until thickened. Add a little hot filling to egg yolks, and return to hot mixture. Cook 2 minutes longer over hot water; then cool. Add lemon juice, butter, vanilla and almond extract. Turn 1/2 the mixture into cooled pastry shell, arrange peaches over filling, and add remainder of filling.

Beat egg whites until stiff; add 1/3 cup sugar, 1 tablespoon at a time, beating after each addition until all sugar is blended in. Add lemon juice. Spread meringue evenly over filling. Bake at 350°F. about 15 minutes or until meringue is golden brown. Serves 6.

Honey Fruit Cake

```
2 cups dried prunes
1 cup dried apricots
Boiling water
1 cup seedless raisins
1 cup slivered blanched almonds
1 cup coarsely chopped walnuts
1 pound mixed candied fruit, diced
1 cup shortening
1 cup honey
4 eggs
2 cups sifted all-purpose flour
1 teaspoon salt
1 teaspoon baking powder
1 teaspoon cinnamon
1 teaspoon allspice
1/4 teaspoon cloves
1/4 teaspoon mace
1 recipe HONEY-GLAZED FRUIT
2 tablespoons chopped nuts
```

Cover prunes and apricots with boiling water and let stand 10 minutes. Drain and cool, remove pits and chop finely. Combine all dried fruits, nuts and candied fruit. Cream shortening, and add honey, then eggs, 1 at a time, beating well after each addition. Sift together flour, salt, baking powder and spices. Add to creamed ingredients, and blend well. Pour batter over fruit–nut mixture, and combine thoroughly but lightly. Turn mixture into 9-inch tube pan lined with 2 thicknesses of greased brown paper and 1 of greased waxed paper. Set pan in shallow container of hot water, place on bottom rack in very slow oven (about 250°F.) and bake 3 1/2–4

hours or until a cake tester inserted in center comes out clean. When cake has almost cooled decorate top with HONEY-GLAZED FRUIT and sprinkle of chopped nuts.

Honey-glazed Fruit

```
3–4 prunes
3–4 dried apricots
Water
1/4 cup sugar
1/4 cup honey
```

Gently simmer prunes and apricots in water 10 minutes; lift out fruit. Measure 1/4 cup liquid, add sugar and honey and simmer fruit until well glazed. Allow to cool slightly before arranging on top of cake.

Cinnamon Pear Mold

```
1/3 cup sugar
2 cups water
1 tablespoon red cinnamon candies
Juice of 1/2 lemon
5 fresh firm pears
1 (3-ounce) package lemon gelatin
1 teaspoon plain gelatin
1 (3-ounce) package coconut-, banana-, or vanilla-
   pudding mix (not instant variety)
1 cup whipped cream or whipped topping
```

Simmer first 4 ingredients together 10 minutes. Peel, core and quarter pears; add to syrup; cover pan, and simmer until just tender. Drain, reserving syrup; dissolve gelatin powder in syrup. Slice 8 pear quarters into oiled baking dish, and cover with gelatin mixture. Allow to set. Meanwhile, add plain gelatin to pudding powder, and follow package directions for pudding. Cool to room temperature, and spread over jellied pears. Chill in refrigerator at least 1 1/2 hours, then unmold. Garnish with remaining pear quarters and whipped cream. Serves 4–6.

Ginger Baked Apples

```
6 large tart apples
10 gingersnaps, crushed
1 (8-ounce) jar mixed candied fruits, diced
1/4 teaspoon salt
2 tablespoons butter or margarine
1 cup ginger ale
3/4–1 cup brown sugar
```

Wash apples, core but do not peel. Place in buttered baking dish snug enough to keep apples upright and close together. Combine gingersnaps and glacé fruits, and add salt and butter or margarine. Fill each apple center with mixture.

Prick apples at several points to prevent bursting of skin. Pour ginger ale into pan, and sprinkle brown sugar over and around apples. Bake at 375°F. 1 hour or until tender, basting frequently. These baked apples are at their best when allowed to cool and served with cream. Serves 6.

Apple Brown Betty

    1 1/2 cups bread crumbs
        3 tablespoons melted butter or margarine
        4 tart apples, sliced
    3/4 cup brown sugar
    1/4 teaspoon salt
    1/4 cup seedless raisins
        1 tablespoon lemon juice
        1 tablespoon water

Mix crumbs with melted butter or margarine, and scatter 1/3 mixture over bottom of greased baking dish. Cover with about 1/2 the sliced apples, sprinkle 1/2 the brown sugar and salt over apples and add 1/3 more crumbs. Make another layer sliced apples, add raisins and remainder of sugar and salt and sprinkle with lemon juice and water. Top with remaining crumbs, cover dish and bake at 350°F. about 40 minutes or until apples are tender when pierced with a fork. Uncover dish, and bake another 10–15 minutes to brown top. Serve warm with SPICY VANILLA SAUCE or cream. Serves 4–5.

Apple Crisp

        4 large tart cooking apples
    Lemon juice (optional)
    1/2 cup flour
    1/2 cup rolled oats
    1/2 cup brown sugar, firmly packed
    1/2 cup butter or margarine

Peel and core apples, and place in greased shallow baking dish. If apples are dry and not at their prime flavor, sprinkle with a little lemon juice. Combine flour, rolled oats and sugar, and blend in butter or margarine (with 2 knives or with fingers). Mixture will have rough, crumbly appearance. Cover apples with this topping, and bake, uncovered, at 375°F. 30–40 minutes or until fruit is quite tender and top crisp and nicely browned. Serve warm with cream or ice cream. Serves 5–6.

VARIATIONS:

Use 4 cups diced rhubarb or sliced peaches or 3 cups blueberries or blackberries.

Baked Rhubarb Compote

    1/4 cup sugar
    1/4 cup boiling water
        2 tablespoons orange juice
    1–2 drops red vegetable coloring (optional)
        4 cups rhubarb, washed and diced

Dissolve sugar in water in casserole. Add orange juice and vegetable coloring. Add rhubarb, cover dish and bake at 350°F. about 20 minutes. This dish is best served chilled. Serves 4.

Broiled Grapefruit Halves

        4 grapefruit halves
    1/4 cup brown sugar or honey
        4 teaspoons butter or margarine

Prepare grapefruit as for serving raw, loosening flesh from inner white rind and segment membranes. Sprinkle each half with 1 tablespoon sugar, and top with 1 teaspoon butter, cut into small pieces. Place fruit in pan 3–4 inches below preheated broiler. Broil about 15 minutes until topping is completely melted, skin edges begin to brown and pulp is heated through. Serve as hot appetizer in place of soup or as dessert. Serves 4.

Key-lime Sponge

        1 (3-ounce) package lime-flavored gelatin
    1/2 cup hot water
    Thin strip green lime rind
    1/2 cup lime juice
        2 eggs, separated
    1 1/3 cups sweetened condensed milk
    Few drops green vegetable coloring

Place first 3 ingredients in electric blender, cover and blend at high speed 20 seconds. Add lime juice and egg yolks, cover and resume high speed a few seconds. Add milk and coloring; blend again. Beat egg whites until very stiff, and fold lightly into lime mixture. Chill in 6 parfait glasses in refrigerator until firm; or turn immediately into 9″ baked pie shell, and chill. Serves 6.

Grape Mallow

        1 cup grape juice
    20 marshmallows, quartered
    1/2 cup heavy cream, whipped
        1 (8-ounce) can mandarin orange sections

Heat grape juice, add marshmallows and stir until melted. Cool, and when syrupy fold in whipped cream. Set in individual molds; chill until firm. Unmold, and garnish with drained orange sections. Serves 4.

Fresh Berry Charlotte

1 1/2–2 cups washed strawberries, raspberries or
    blackberries
1 1/2 cups soft white bread crumbs
1/2–3/4 cup sugar
3/4 cup orange juice
1/3 cup butter or margarine, melted
2 egg yolks, slightly beaten
2 egg whites
Pinch salt
2 tablespoons sugar

Combine first 3 ingredients; combine orange juice, butter or margarine and egg yolks, and stir into berries. Spread in greased 1 1/2-quart casserole dish. Beat egg whites and salt together until soft peaks form; then beat in 2 tablespoons sugar gradually. Spread meringue evenly over fruit mixture. Bake at 350°F. about 35 minutes. Serve warm with cream or CUSTARD SAUCE. Serves 6–8.

Mincemeat Puffs

1 (14-ounce) package raisin-bran muffin mix
1 1/2 cups mincemeat

Prepare batter according to package directions. Grease 8 6-ounce deep custard cups, and spoon 2–3 tablespoons mincemeat into each. Pour in batter to 2/3 depth. Distribute remaining batter among greased muffin pans and bake the 2 batches according to package directions. Invert warm puffs on individual plates, and pass hot sauce. Serves 8.

Note: By preparing full package of muffin mix you will have enough batter for 8 dessert puffs plus several plain muffins that will be useful at next day's breakfast or in the lunchbox.

Datebread Pudding

2 cups cubed day-old bread
2 cups warm milk
3/4 cup pitted dates, chopped
1/2 cup apple juice
1/2 cup sugar
1/4 teaspoon salt
3 eggs
1/2 teaspoon nutmeg
1/4 teaspoon cinnamon

Soak bread cubes 10 minutes in warm milk. Add chopped dates, apple juice, sugar and salt. Beat eggs well, and stir in lightly with fork. Turn mixture into greased baking dish, and sprinkle nutmeg and cinnamon over top. Set dish in shallow pan of hot water, and bake at 350°F. about 1 hour. Serve warm with cream or HARD SAUCE. Serves 5–6.

Bananas Alaska

4 or 5 medium-firm ripe bananas
4–5 tablespoons red currant jelly
1/2 pint heavy cream, whipped
3 egg whites
1/3 cup sugar
1/2 teaspoon lemon juice
1/4 teaspoon cream of tartar
1/4 cup chopped walnuts

Split bananas lengthwise, spread with jelly, and put together sandwich-fashion. Arrange in square, shallow baking dish, and spread thickly with whipped cream. Beat egg whites until very stiff but not dry; gradually add sugar, lemon juice, and cream of tartar, beating continuously. Completely cover cream-coated bananas with meringue mixture. Sprinkle with chopped nuts, and put immediately into very hot oven—500°F. —for just 6–7 minutes until meringue is golden brown. Serves 4–5.

Double Strawberry Shortcake

1 quart strawberries
3/4 cup granulated sugar
2 cups sifted flour
3 teaspoons baking powder
1/2 teaspoon baking soda
1/4 teaspoon salt
1/2 cup milk
1/3 cup corn oil
2 eggs, separated
2 tablespoons lemon juice
Grated rind of 1 lemon or 1 teaspoon dehydrated grated
    lemon peel
Few drops almond extract
Pinch salt
1/4 cup sugar
1/2 cup whipped cream or topping

Wash, hull and sort strawberries. Pick out and slice any that are soft or underripe. Add enough sliced good berries to make 1 cup, and spread in well-greased 8- or 9-inch pan. Sprinkle with 1/4 cup sugar. Halve remaining berries. Sweeten to taste with 1/2 cup sugar and refrigerate. Sift next 4 ingredients together in bowl. Combine milk, corn oil, egg yolks, lemon juice, rind and almond extract, and stir into dry ingredients. Beat until blended; then pour over berries in prepared pan, and bake at 450° F. 25 minutes. Invert shortcake on cookie sheet. Beat egg whites and pinch salt until soft peaks form. Add 1/4 cup sugar gradually, and continue beating until stiff. Spread over shortcake, and bake at 350°F. 5–6 minutes. Serve warm with reserved sweetened berries and whipped cream. Serves 8.

Homemade Biscuit Shortcake

1 1/2 cups all-purpose flour
1 tablespoon sugar
2 teaspoons baking powder
1/4 teaspoon salt
1/4 cup butter or margarine
1/2 cup (approximately) milk
2 tablespoons soft butter or margarine
STRAWBERRY SHORTCAKE FILLING or other fruit filling
1 cup whipped cream

Preheat oven to 425°F. Sift flour, sugar, baking powder and salt into bowl. Cut in butter or margarine using pastry blender or 2 knives; add milk gradually, stirring quickly. Use sufficient milk to make dough that is light and soft but not sticky. Put dough on flour-sprinkled cloth, and use palms of hands to knead lightly until smooth (takes less than 1 minute). Divide dough into halves, and pat or roll each into circle about 1/2 inch thick. Brush top of 1 round with 1 tablespoon soft butter or margarine. Set on baking sheet, top with other round and bake 15–20 minutes. To serve, separate layers, spread lower half with 1 tablespoon butter or margarine, add 1/2 fruit filling and replace top 1/2 of cake. Cover with remaining fruit filling, and garnish with whipped cream. Serves 4.

Note: Individual shortcakes may be made by using cutter to shape small rounds of dough, about 3 inches in diameter, before baking.

Strawberry Shortcake Filling

1 quart strawberries
1/3 cup sugar

Wash and hull strawberries, reserving a few large ones for garnish. Slice or crush remainder, add sugar, let stand till sugar is dissolved and just before serving, spread as directed over warm shortcake.

VARIATIONS:

Raspberry Shortcake Filling: Raspberries or other suitable small berries may be used instead of strawberries.

Peach Shortcake Filling: For strawberries substitute ripe peaches thinly sliced and sweetened.

Rhubarb Shortcake Filling: Thick stewed rhubarb makes appropriate and tasty shortcake filling in the spring.

Applesauce Shortcake Filling: Tart applesauce makes a good filling any time of year.

Cranberry Sherbet

4 cups cranberries
2 1/2 cups cold water
2 cups sugar
1 envelope powdered gelatin
1/2 cup cold water
Juice of 2 lemons

Cook berries in 2 1/2 cups water until they stop popping. Strain, add sugar to juice and simmer until sugar is dissolved. Soften gelatin in 1/2 cup water, and add to syrup, stirring well. When mixture is cool, add lemon juice. Pour into refrigerator tray, and freeze, stirring occasionally, 2–3 hours. Serves 6.

2-in-1 Custard Cream for Fruit

2 1/4 cups milk
1/3 cup evaporated milk
2 eggs, beaten
1/3 cup sugar
3 tablespoons flour
2 tablespoons cornstarch
1 teaspoon vanilla
1/4 teaspoon salt

Heat milk and evaporated milk in top of double boiler over hot water. Combine remaining ingredients in small bowl and beat until smooth. Pour into hot milk, and cook, stirring until smoothly thickened. Makes about 3 cups.

Note: This recipe makes enough thick custard to accompany dessert at 2 meals. Pour 1/2 the custard into bowl, and cover with waxed paper; chill in refrigerator. To serve, fold in 1 or 2 sliced bananas or 1 cup drained, cut-up fresh or canned fruit. For following day's use, this basic custard may be diluted with a little milk or thin cream and reheated to serve with hot dessert like APPLE CRISP or FRESH BERRY CHARLOTTE. Or use chilled without diluting over fruit-flavored molded gelatin.

SALADS

Arabs and Greeks in the pre-Christian era used to serve mixtures of greens and herbs, with simple dressings. The Romans of Caesar's time dipped raw greens in salt ("sal") and dubbed them "salata" (salted). From these beginnings developed an ever-expanding group of tempting variations.

Appetizer salads are usually mixtures of fresh greens tossed with flavorful French or other thin dressings. They should be light and appetizing, to stimulate rather than satisfy the appetite and could precede hot main courses.

Mixed fruits with their juices served in sherbet or dessert glasses, are properly called "fruit cocktail" or "fruit cup," rather than "salad." Fruit salads, however, may be served as appetizers.

Accompaniment salads go with hot main dishes and should be served on separate salad plates or in individual salad bowls. With cold meats, fish, cheese and eggs, they may be placed on dinner plates. At a formal dinner, the salad sometimes becomes a separate course, following the main dish and preceding dessert.

Variety can be almost endless, but the accompaniment salad should suit the main course. When the main part of the meal is light, a satisfying salad may be used: for instance, potato salad with stuffed eggs or cold cuts; to accompany a substantial main dish, the salad should be as light as an appetizer salad. Suitable types include tossed greens or coleslaw, raw-vegetable salads (sliced raw tomatoes, cucumbers, green pepper rings), asparagus tips in lettuce cups, colorful fruit salads, jellied fruit or vegetable salads.

Main course salads should include protein foods (meat, fish, seafood, eggs, cheese, nuts or dried beans). They should also be substantial enough to satisfy and provide energy material.

Dessert salads are fresh, light and satisfying without providing too many calories. They are usually made of fruits, thoroughly drained and carefully arranged in lettuce cups or on greens. The fruits may be folded lightly together and piled in lettuce cups or served as jellies in large or individual molds. Dressings may be French, special sweet fruit-salad dressing, thick dressings, folded into whipped cream or commercial sour cream.

Arranged Salads

Whole or carefully cut pieces of food are set out on beds of greens. The dressing is poured carefully over the top, spooned into tiny lettuce cups at sides or passed in a bowl. Decorative placement of the food is in itself the garnish. Fruit salads are usually "arranged" on individual serving plates. Sometimes arranging is done after "folding."

Folded Salads

For these salads the ingredients are usually very carefully cut—diced, sliced or julienned. They are combined in a large bowl, dressing and seasonings are added and all are "folded" together *lightly* so that the shapes of the pieces are retained. Sometimes the ingredients are gently lifted with 2 forks from the bottom of the bowl, the procedure being repeated until a uniform combination is achieved. Meat, fish and potato salads are usually prepared this way and some fruit mixtures too.

Tossed Salads

Torn or shredded greens and other items, well chilled, are sprinkled with dressing and seasonings, then lightly but thoroughly tossed with 2 forks or fork and spoon until every particle has its touch of dressing. Tossed salads are at their best when served immediately after assembling.

Jellied Salads

Many interesting mixtures can be molded in jelly form, a "make-ahead" convenience appreciated by the busy hostess. Gelatin powder (made tart and flavorful with the addition of vinegar or lemon juice and seasonings) or plain unflavored gelatin is used to set the mixture. In preparing a large shape for dividing into servings at the table, the solids in the mixture are finely cut or chopped. For individual jellied salads there is much greater flexibility in the sizes of cooked or raw items to be featured.

Selecting and Preparing. Buy salad greens only in quantities that can be used up within a few days. Long-stored greens become soft and watery, with a tendency to "rust" or otherwise discolor.

Look over your purchases as soon as you bring them from the store, and discard any bruised or stale parts. Wash greens well under cold running water. Do not soak. Keep bunches or heads intact until ready to use. Drain well, dry and store in refrigerator—in crisper or in plastic bags or aluminum foil. To prevent yellowing of parsley, store it well drained in tightly-covered container in refrigerator.

Before Serving. Be sure that all your salad ingredients, including dressings, are thoroughly chilled. If possible, chill salad plates too. If your cold salad course features cooked vegetables like potatoes, beets or green peas, start preparing in time to allow complete chilling. Such extra garnishes as ripe olives, anchovies and hard-cooked eggs should also be refrigerated ahead of time.

Wash, separate and chop or shred raw salad materials, according to kind of salad planned. To make lettuce cups for individual servings, cut out core at base of lettuce head and holding it upside down, allow cold water from tap to pour over cut area. The leaves will separate under force of the water. Drain, and shake or pat dry with towel, taking care not to break shape.

Added Dressing. Try to have all greens free of excess moisture after their final washing. Remember that an oil-base dressing cannot properly adhere to wet greens and water in the salad bowl will thin any type of dressing. Of course, your choice of dressing will depend on the type of salad, but, unless the recipe directs otherwise, add dressing just before serving. Use just enough to season and blend ingredients.

There is a dressing to make every salad taste better. Keep several kinds ready, covered: basic FRENCH DRESSING plus the variations your family likes best; MAYONNAISE (refrigerated) and your favorites from among the various excellent commercial products. All these dressings store well. Homemade cooked or "boiled" dressings, however, should be used up quickly because of their milk-and-egg bases.

Note: 1/2 cup dressing of any kind is usually enough for 6 servings.

Dressings for Fruit Salads

Lemon French Dressing: Replace vinegar in FRENCH DRESSING with lemon juice, and increase sugar to taste.

French Dressing for Fruit Salads: For use with fruit salads, omit strong flavors like garlic and onion, and experiment instead with touches of herbs and spices—mint, sweet basil, marjoram, poppy seeds, sesame seeds, curry powder.

Ruby Dressing: Beat 2 tablespoons red currant jelly until smooth; add 1/4 cup each lemon juice and salad oil and 3/4 teaspoon salt. Beat again.

Mayonnaise–Cream Dressing: Combine 1/2 cup each mayonnaise and heavy cream, whipped.

Hawaiian Dressing: Add 2 tablespoons canned pineapple juice to 1/2 cup mayonnaise.

Orange Whip Dressing: To 1 cup mayonnaise or "boiled" dressing, add 1/2 cup heavy cream, whipped; 2 tablespoons grated orange rind, and a little sugar.

Velvet Dressing: Mash 1 (3-ounce) package cream cheese; blend in 1 tablespoon lemon juice and 3 tablespoons currant jelly. Whip 1 cup heavy cream, fold into cheese mixture and chill.

Hearty Salads

Potato Salad: Allow 1 medium potato per serving. Scrub, boil in skins and do not peel until cooked unless recipe directs otherwise.

Potato Salad with Bacon Bits: Slice potatoes into bowl lined with lettuce or other greens, and sprinkle each layer with chopped onion, crumbled crisp bacon and finely chopped parsley.

Pour over just enough FRENCH DRESSING to moisten. Sprinkle freshly ground black pepper over top, and garnish with parsley.

Potatoes in Mayonnaise: Prepare required quantity of diced potatoes. For each cupful allow 1/2 cup chopped celery and 1 teaspoon chopped mild onion. Combine with MAYONNAISE to moisten. Serve on lettuce leaves, and garnish with such color contrasts as sliced stuffed olives, pimento or green pepper strips, and sliced or chopped hard-cooked eggs. For an interesting touch, place a spoonful of chilled cooked new peas in tiny lettuce cup at side of each serving; sprinkle with FRENCH DRESSING.

Potato Salad Vinaigrette

    1/3 cup white-wine vinegar
    1/2 teaspoon salt
    1/2 teaspoon dry mustard
    1/4 teaspoon celery seed
      6 medium potatoes, boiled and cubed
      2 tablespoons chopped onions or chives
      2 tablespoons salad oil
      2 tablespoons chopped parsley

Heat together vinegar, salt, mustard and celery seed. Pour over 6 hot coarsely cubed potatoes. Stir in onion. Let mixture cool; add salad oil and parsley. Serves 6.

Ham–Potato Salad

    2 cups diced cooked ham
    2 cups diced cooked potatoes
    2 green onions, chopped
    4 gherkins, chopped
    1 cup mayonnaise
    Salt and pepper to taste
    Crisp salad greens
    3 hard-cooked eggs, sliced

Mix first 4 ingredients together, blend in mayonnaise lightly, season with salt and pepper and arrange on bed of crisp salad greens. Garnish with slices of hard-cooked eggs. Serves 6.

VARIATIONS:

Replace 1 cup cooked ham with diced cooked chicken or turkey. Use 2 cups diced cooked corned beef in place of other meat. One cup chopped celery may be added to any of these variations.

Shrimp Salad

    2 (4 1/4-ounce) cans shrimp, chilled, or
        1-pound frozen or fresh shrimp,
        cooked and chilled
    1 cup cooked peas, chilled
    1/2 teaspoon salt
    Few grains pepper

1/2 cup chopped celery
 1 tablespoon chopped parsley
 1 tablespoon chopped green pepper
 1 tablespoon chopped green onion
1/4 cup FRENCH DRESSING
Salad greens
 2 hard-cooked eggs, sliced

Rinse shrimp under cold running water, and halve if large. Combine with peas. Sprinkle with salt and pepper, and stir lightly with fork. Add celery, parsley, green pepper and onion to dressing. Pour over shrimp mixture, and toss lightly with fork. Serve on crisp greens, garnished with slices of hard-cooked egg. Serves 4.

VARIATION:

Omit French dressing, and mix first 5 ingredients with 1/4 cup mayonnaise. Garnish individual salads with remaining ingredients.

Tuna Salad in Tomato Cups

 1 (7-ounce) can solid tuna
 1 cup chopped celery
1/2 cup chopped cucumber
 1 tablespoon grated onion
1/4 teaspoon salt
Dash pepper
1/3 cup mayonnaise
 4 large firm tomatoes
Watercress or other crisp greens

Drain liquid from tuna. Flake fish, and combine with celery, cucumber, onion, seasonings and enough mayonnaise to hold mixture together. Slice off stem ends of tomatoes, remove a little of the pulp to make "cups" and invert for a few minutes to drain. Pile tuna salad into tomatoes on individual salad plates, and surround with watercress. Serves 4.

VARIATION:

Canned lobster, salmon or shrimp may be substituted for tuna in tomato cups or piled on salad greens. Garnish with twist of lemon peel, hard-cooked egg wedges and green pepper rings.

Chef's Salad

 1 quart torn salad greens
 3 or 4 tomatoes, peeled and quartered
1/2 cup sliced radishes
 1 green pepper, cut in strips
 1 peeled avocado, diced
1 1/2 cups chicken or ham, in julienne strips
 6 hard-cooked eggs, sliced
1/2 pound Swiss cheese, in strips
1/2 cup ITALIAN DRESSING

Wash greens thoroughly, pat dry and place in wooden bowl rubbed with garlic. Add tomatoes and all remaining ingredients. Toss together lightly but thoroughly with dressing.

Note: For a good chef's salad choose at least 3 of the following greens: leaf or head lettuce, romaine, chickory, spinach, escarole, watercress.

Curried Chicken Salad

1/2 cup chopped raw or canned water chestnuts
 4 cups diced cooked chicken
1/2 cup chopped celery
1/2 cup diced green pepper
2/3 cup MAYONNAISE
 2 tablespoons light cream
 1 tablespoon vinegar
 1 teaspoon salt
 1 teaspoon curry powder
 6 lettuce cups
 6 pickled peaches or 1/2 cup apple jelly

Chop water chestnuts coarsely. Combine with chicken, celery and green pepper. Blend mayonnaise, cream, vinegar, salt and curry powder, and combine with chicken mixture. Chill until serving time. Serve in lettuce cups on individual salad plates. Garnish with peaches. Serves 5–6.

Vegetable Salads

Relish Tray

Simple crisp relishes can be served as soon as prepared. Relishes like carrot curls and celery fans, however, should be made at least 1 hour ahead and refrigerated in ice water so that they will hold their shapes.

Carrot Curls: With vegetable parer, shave lengthwise strips from peeled long, straight carrot. Shape each strip around forefinger to make curl, secure with toothpick and place each tight curl in ice water 1 hour.

Celery Fans: Cut each large tender stalk of celery into 3-inch lengths; then make several slits in each end, almost to the center. Refrigerate in ice water until ends curl.

Marinated Tomatoes: Peel ripe tomatoes. (To peel, hold each tomato on fork over flame till skin wrinkles and splits; then pull off. Or dip tomatoes first in boiling then in cold water, before peeling.) Slice into shallow dish. Using scissors, snip scallions over tomatoes until latter are lightly covered. Sprinkle with a little salt and dried basil. Pour FRENCH DRESSING over all (about 1/2 cup of dressing for each 1 1/2 pounds tomatoes). Chill 1 hour. Before serving, drain off excess moisture.

Coleslaw

1/2 cup MAYONNAISE
1/4 cup commercial sour cream
1 tablespoon lemon juice
1 tablespoon sugar
1 tablespoon white vinegar
1 teaspoon celery seed
1/2 teaspoon dry mustard
1/4 teaspoon salt
1/8 teaspoon pepper
6 cups finely shredded cabbage
8 green pepper rings
2 pimentos, finely diced

Combine mayonnaise, sour cream, lemon juice, sugar, vinegar, celery seed, mustard, salt and pepper. Chill well. Put shredded cabbage into large serving bowl, pour mayonnaise mixture over and toss lightly. Garnish with green pepper rings, sprinkle with diced pimento. Serves 6–8.

Coleslaw with Fruits

2 cups finely shredded cabbage
1 cup canned pineapple tidbits
3/4 cup seedless raisins
2/3 cup cooked dressing
8 large lettuce leaves
Paprika to taste

Combine cabbage, pineapple, seedless raisins and 1/3 cup dressing. Blend lightly. Garnish 4 plates with lettuce, and top with salad mixture and remaining dressing. Sprinkle with paprika. Serves 4.

Garden Salad

1 cup grated carrot
1 cup grated cabbage
1 cup chopped celery
1 cucumber, diced
1/3 cup sliced radishes
1/2 cup (approximately) MAYONNAISE
3 tablespoons thick chili sauce
6 lettuce cups
12 sprigs watercress

Toss first 5 ingredients together lightly. Combine mayonnaise and chili sauce, and pour over vegetables, adding only enough to moisten vegetables well. Toss lightly again. Serve in lettuce cups, and garnish with sprigs of watercress. Serves 6.

Savory Salad

6 cups torn-up salad greens (lettuce, romaine, chicory, raw spinach leaves and the like)
6 anchovies—chopped
1/4 cup chopped pimento
3 tablespoons chopped onion
1/2 cup French dressing
8 large lettuce leaves

Combine first 4 ingredients. Pour dressing over mixture, and refrigerate 1 hour. Serve on lettuce leaves. Serves 4.

Bean Salads

Three-bean Salad

1 cup dried fava or lima beans, cooked
1 cup white beans, cooked
1 cup pinto or cranberry beans, cooked
1/2 cup chopped onion
1/2 cup chopped and drained bread and butter pickles
1/2 cup chopped parsley
1/2 cup salad oil
1/4 cup apple cider vinegar
1 teaspoon salt
1/4 teaspoon pepper
2 cups fresh spinach leaves

Toss together fava or lima beans, white beans, and pinto or cranberry beans with onion, pickles and parsley. Pour on dressing made from salad oil, cider vinegar, salt and pepper. Chill covered for about an hour in the refrigerator or for no more than 20 minutes in the freezer. Serve on a bed of fresh spinach leaves. Serves 6.

Lentils Hidden in Tomatoes

Check the directions on your lentil box before fixing this salad.

1 cup (1/2 pound) lentils
1/4 cup chopped onions
1/4 cup coarsely chopped radishes
2 cloves garlic, crushed
1/2 cup olive or salad oil
2 tablespoons wine vinegar
1 1/2 teaspoons salt
1/8 teaspoon pepper
3 large tomatoes
Watercress

Cook lentils according to label directions. Drain well. While still hot, combine with onion, radishes. Stir in garlic, olive oil, vinegar, salt and pepper. Chill at least 1 hour.

Cut tomatoes crosswise. Scoop out seeds and pulp. Chill. At serving time, fill each of 6 tomato halves with about 1/2 cup lentil salad. Place on platter. Garnish with watercress. Serve any remaining lentil salad separately in a bowl. Serves 6.

Italian Bean and Artichoke Salad

Be careful not to marinate the beans and artichokes more than half an hour, or the green color will turn dull.

2 (9-ounce) packages frozen Italian-style green beans, cooked
1 (9-ounce) package frozen artichoke hearts, cooked

1/4 cup diced pimentos
1/2 cup olive or salad oil
1/4 cup red wine vinegar
1 teaspoon onion juice
1/2 teaspoon salt
1/2 teaspoon powdered oregano
1/4 teaspoon crushed rosemary
1/8 teaspoon pepper

To green beans and artichoke hearts, cooked separately according to label directions, then drained and cooled, add pimentos. Cover and chill. Make dressing separately by combining olive oil with wine vinegar, onion juice, salt, oregano, rosemary and pepper. Lightly toss and chill well. To serve: drain beans and artichoke hearts from the dressing, using a slotted spoon. Mound on serving platter. Serve extra dressing alongside, if desired. Serves 6.

Wax Beans Vinaigrette

3 (1-pound) jars wax beans, drained or 4 pounds fresh wax beans, cooked (about 4–5 cups)
1 cup sliced fresh mushrooms
1/2 cup thinly sliced green-pepper rings
1 cup Italian-style salad dressing
2 small heads Bibb lettuce

Place cooked and cooled wax beans, drained, in a large bowl. Toss with mushrooms, green-pepper rings and salad dressing. Let chill at least 1 hour in refrigerator or 15 minutes in the freezer. To serve: drain dressing from beans. Place on shallow serving platter surrounded by Bibb lettuce leaves. Serves 6.

Curried Sikh Salad

2 (1-pound) cans pork and beans
4 cups cooked rice, cooled
1/4 cup chopped onions
Dressing:
1 cup MAYONNAISE
1 teaspoon curry powder
1 teaspoon salt
1/4 teaspoon pepper
Garnish:
1/2 cup shredded coconut, toasted
12 lime slices (approximately 2 whole limes) cut in halves

Drain pork and beans very well. Rinse with cold water. Drain again. Place in a large bowl together with cooked, cooled rice and chopped onion. Toss gently. Fold in mayonnaise, curry powder, salt and pepper. Mound evenly on a shallow platter. Sprinkle toasted coconut to make a border around the edge. Garnish edge of platter with overlapping halved lime slices. Chill in refrigerator for at least 1 hour or in freezer for 15 minutes. Serves 6.

Fruit Salads

Caribbean Salad

1 head endive
2 cups salted water
3 oranges, peeled and sliced
1 large Spanish onion, thinly sliced
1/2 cup FRENCH DRESSING
2 avocados, peeled, halved and sliced

Separate endive leaves; trim off and discard hard white ends. Put in cold water, and let stand to reduce characteristic bitter taste. Place orange and onion slices in bowl, and pour over enough dressing to cover. Chill in refrigerator. Just before serving time, drain and dry endive, and arrange on individual plates. For each serving arrange 2 or 3 orange slices with 1 onion slice on endive; surround with 1/2 slices of avocado dipped in dressing. Serves 4–5.

Florida Citrus Salad

2 large grapefruit
2 navel oranges
Salad greens
1 (3-ounce) package cream cheese
2 tablespoons orange juice
1/4 teaspoon grated orange rind
12 cooked prunes, chilled
1/2 cup FRENCH DRESSING made with orange juice or MAYONNAISE-CREAM DRESSING

Prepare grapefruit and oranges by removing peel and white rind and cutting into natural sections between membranes. Arrange on crisp salad greens on individual plates, alternating grapefruit and orange sections. Blend cream cheese with juice and grated rind. Pit prunes, and stuff with cheese, allowing 2 to each plate. Serve with dressing. Serves 5–6.

VARIATION:

Instead of prunes, use large sweet grapes, sliced and seeded, then stuffed with cheese mixture, or fresh or canned apricot halves piled with the stuffing.

Stuffed Pear Salad

1 (3-ounce) package cream cheese
1 cup cottage cheese
1/4 cup chopped nuts
1/4 cup chopped dates
1 tablespoon chopped maraschino cherries
Salad greens
8 cooked pear halves
1/3 cup MAYONNAISE
2 tablespoons pear syrup
1/2 teaspoon lemon juice

Soften cream cheese with fork, and mix with cottage cheese. Blend in nuts, dates and maraschino cherries. Arrange salad greens on four plates, and place 2 pear halves on each. Heap with cheese mixture. Thin mayonnaise with syrup and lemon juice. Serve with salad. Serves 4.

VARIATION:

This cheese mixture may also be used to stuff canned peach halves, or with pineapple slices as base.

Fruit-salad Platter

```
1/2  large ripe cantaloupe, seeds removed
  2  cups cottage cheese, drained
  2  cups fresh strawberries, raspberries or blackberries,
       dipped in finely granulated sugar or 1 cup
       fresh or canned pineapple wedges
  2  cups watermelon balls
  8  fresh orange slices
  8  banana fingers, dipped in mayonnaise and rolled
       in shredded coconut
Fresh mint leaves
```

Slice melon down part way to expedite serving in wedges, and place in center of platter. Fill hollow center with cottage cheese. Heap berries in mounds at intervals around melon. Between mounds arrange separate grouping of various other fruits. Garnish platter with fresh mint leaves. Serves 8.

Citrus–Cream Dressing

```
  2  eggs
1/4  cup sugar
1/4  cup lemon juice
  2  tablespoons orange juice
1/2  teaspoon dry mustard
1/4  teaspoon salt
Few grains cayenne
  1  tablespoon butter or margarine
1/2  cup heavy cream, whipped
Pecans, coarsely chopped
Kumquats, coarsely chopped, or candied orange peel,
       coarsely chopped
```

Beat together in saucepan eggs, sugar, fruit juices, spices and butter or margarine. Cook, over low heat, stirring, and bring just to boiling point; then remove from stove. When cool, fold in whipped cream. Turn into serving bowl, and garnish with pecans and kumquats or candied orange peel.

Waldorf Salad

```
  1  cup diced tart apples
Few drops lemon juice
  1  cup diced celery
1/2  cup walnuts, coarsely chopped
3/4  cup "boiled" dressing or MAYONNAISE
4-6  lettuce cups
4-6  maraschino cherries
```

Apples may be peeled or left with skins on for color. Sprinkle with lemon juice. Combine apples, celery and walnuts; fold in dressing and serve in individual lettuce cups. Top each with maraschino cherry. Serves 4–6.

VARIATION:

- Add 1/2 cup seedless raisins for extra flavor and nutrition.
- Substitute generous spoonful peanut butter for walnuts at side of plate, and sprinkle coarsely chopped peanuts over it.

Minted Fresh-fruit Salad

```
  4  slices fresh or canned pineapple
  2  cups whole fresh strawberries
Honey or sugar
  1  cup heavy cream, whipped
```

If fresh pineapple is used, sprinkle slices with sugar or honey, and let stand at least 2 hours to absorb sweetness. Halve whole fresh berries, sprinkle with honey or sugar and let stand to absorb sweetness and draw out juice. Just before serving, mound serving of strawberries on each pineapple slice, and top with whipped cream. Serves 4.

Note: Sliced bananas may also be combined with strawberries. Sprinkle with lemon and chopped fresh mint to preserve color; do not sweeten.

Jellied Salads
Waldorf–Cider Salad

```
  1  envelope unflavored gelatin
  2  tablespoons lemon juice
1 3/4  cups apple cider
Dash salt
  1  red apple
3/4  cup diced celery
1/2  cup fresh or canned apricots, diced and drained
Salad greens
```

Soften gelatin in lemon juice. Heat cider to boiling, and dissolve gelatin in it. Stir in salt, and cool until slightly thickened. Core and dice unpeeled apple. Fold apple, celery and apricots into gelatin mixture. Rinse 6 individual molds with cold water, and fill with mixture. Chill until firm, and serve unmolded on greens. Serve with mayonnaise or with equal parts mayonnaise and commercial sour cream beaten together. Serves 4.

Cucumber Mousse

        2 cucumbers
        1 envelope unflavored gelatin
    1/2 cup cold water
        1 (3-ounce) package lime-gelatin
    1 1/4 cups boiling water
    1/2 cup lemon or lime juice
        2 teaspoons onion juice
    3/4 teaspoon salt
    1/8 teaspoon cayenne
    1/2 cup chopped celery
    1/4 cup chopped parsley
    1/2 pint heavy cream, whipped
    Fish salad

Peel cucumbers, remove seeds and grate coarsely. Soften gelatin in cold water. Dissolve lime gelatin powder in boiling water, and stir in plain-gelatin mixture, lemon juice, onion juice, salt, cayenne and prepared cucumbers. Chill until thickened; then fold in celery, parsley and lastly whipped cream. Pour into large oiled ring mold, and chill in refrigerator until set. Unmold, and fill center with fish salad. Serves 6–8.

Tomato Aspic

        2 envelopes unflavored gelatin
        4 cups sieved canned tomatoes or tomato juice
        1 bay leaf
        1 celery stalk
        1 tablespoon sugar
        1 tablespoon vinegar
    3/4 teaspoon salt
    Salad greens

Soften gelatin in 1/2 cup tomato. Heat remaining tomato with bay leaf and celery, and bring to boiling point. Discard bay leaf and celery. Stir softened gelatin into hot tomato until completely dissolved. Add sugar, vinegar and salt. Pour into 1 large or 6 individual molds, rinsed with cold water, and chill in refrigerator until firm. Turn out on crisp salad greens, and serve with MAYONNAISE.

Note: If ring molds are used, fill centers with one of the following: cottage cheese mixed with coarsely chopped nuts, chopped celery and cucumber mixed with thick mayonnaise, diced cooked chicken and diced celery mixed with mayonnaise. Serves 6–8.

Frozen Cheese Salad

        2 (8-ounce) packages cream cheese
    1/2 cup stuffed olives, chopped
    1/2 cup toasted almonds, chopped
    1/4 cup lemon juice
    1/2 teaspoon salt
    1/2 cup heavy cream, whipped
    Salad greens
    1/2 cup FRENCH DRESSING
    Fresh mint

Mash cream cheese with fork. Add olives and almonds, and stir in lemon juice and salt. Fold whipped cream into mixture. Spoon into refrigerator tray, and freeze without stirring. Cut into squares, and serve on salad greens with dressing; garnish with mint. Serves 6–8.

Orange–Cranberry Salad

        1 envelope unflavored gelatin
    1/4 cup cold water
        4 cups cranberries
        2 small oranges
        1 cup sugar
    1/4 cup hot water
        1 (3-ounce) package lemon gelatin

Soak unflavored gelatin in cold water until dissolved. Meanwhile, wash cranberries, and cut oranges into pieces, leaving skins on but removing seeds. Put oranges and cranberries through meat grinder or blend in electric blender. Reserve juices from chopping. Add sugar to hot water; add lemon gelatin, softened plain gelatin and stir until gelatin is dissolved. Stir in minced oranges and cranberries and reserved juices. Mold in wet ring mold or individual molds, and chill until firm. Serves 6.

Pineapple–Cucumber Salad

        1 envelope unflavored gelatin
        2 tablespoons cold water
    1/4 cup boiling water
    1/2 cup lemon juice
    1/3 cup sugar
    1/8 teaspoon salt
        1 or 2 drops green vegetable coloring (optional)
        1 (8-ounce) can crushed pineapple
        1 small cucumber

Soak gelatin in cold water, and dissolve in boiling water. Add lemon juice, sugar, salt and coloring. Mix well with pineapple. Peel cucumber, quarter lengthwise and remove seeds. Grate cucumber, and add to mixture. Pour mixture into wet mold or individual molds, and chill thoroughly. Serves 4.

Jellied Avocado Salad

1 envelope unflavored gelatin
2 tablespoons cold water
1 cup boiling water
Juice of half a lemon
1 cup mashed avocado
1/4 teaspoon celery salt
1 teaspoon salt
1/2 teaspoon Worcestershire sauce
Few drops hot pepper sauce
2 tablespoons chopped pimento

Soak gelatin in cold water; then dissolve in boiling water. Add lemon juice and other ingredients, blend well together, pour into wet mold or individual molds and chill until firm. Serves 4.

Jellied Beet Salad

1 (3-ounce) package lemon gelatin
1 cup boiling water
3/4 cup beet juice
3 tablespoons vinegar
1 tablespoon chopped onion
1 tablespoon horseradish
1/2 teaspoon salt
1 cup finely diced cooked beets
1 tablespoon finely chopped celery
Shredded lettuce

Dissolve gelatin in boiling water, and add all other ingredients except beets and celery. Chill mixture until it just begins to set. Fold in beets and celery, and turn the mixture into wet mold or individual molds. Chill until very firm, and serve on shredded lettuce. Serves 4.

12 Luncheon Menus Starring
Vegetables and Fruits—recipes for items printed IN THIS STYLE can be found by consulting the index.

Hamburgers in buns
MUSTARD PICKLES
APPLESAUCE DELIGHT
Cookies

TUNA SALAD IN TOMATO CUPS
Hot bran muffins
CITRUS–PLUM COMPOTE
Cheese tray

Toasted-cheese sandwiches
COLESLAW
FRESH-FRUIT WHIP
Sponge cake

3-FRUIT JUICE COCKTAIL
Poached egg on chopped spinach
RICE CREAM WITH CHERRIES

CHEESE OMELETS
Brown-and-serve sausages
HARVARD BEETS
Celery hearts
Raspberry ice and vanilla ice cream

Vegetable soup
Crusty bread
WALDORF SALAD
BROWNIES

QUICK POTATO SOUP
Frankfurters in buns
STUFFED PEAR SALAD
Cookies

VEGETABLE SOUFFLE
Crisp bacon
Melba toast
Baked apples with cream

Cream of asparagus soup
Sardine—lettuce sandwiches
Fresh fruit cup
Gingersnaps

Creamed chicken and celery on toast points
Carrot sticks
Chilled stewed rhubarb

Browned corned beef hash
Tossed green salad
CINNAMON—PEAR MOLD

Toasted peanut butter–chopped bacon sandwiches
FRUIT-SALAD PLATTER
CITRUS—CREAM DRESSING

12 Well-Balanced Dinners

BROILED GRAPEFRUIT HALVES
Casserole of beef and mushrooms
Fluffy rice   Parsleyed carrots
Vanilla ice cream with maple syrup

OVEN-FRIED CHICKEN
SWEET POTATO PUFFS   Green beans
Raw relish platter
Strawberries and cream

Roast lamb
Minted potatoes
Asparagus
Crisp raw relishes
FRESH BERRY CHARLOTTE

Minute steaks
BAKED POTATOES
Buttered onions
Pickled beets
Apricot upside-down cake

Pot roast of beef
SOUR CREAM-HORSERADISH SAUCE
Riced potatoes
Baked zucchini
CRANBERRY WHIP

Oyster stew with crackers
CHEF'S SALAD with diced ham
GINGERBREAD with LEMON SAUCE

Chilled vegetable juice
Sautéed calf's liver
BAKED POTATOES   String beans
Melon balls   Brown-edge cookies

Salmon steaks with TARTAR SAUCE
AU GRATIN POTATOES
Head lettuce with ROQUEFORT DRESSING
KEY-LIME SPONGE

CHILI CON CARNE
Cornbread sticks
Tossed green salad
Banana–Cream pie

Breaded pork chops
Lyonnaise potatoes
SWEET-AND-SOUR RED CABBAGE
Lemon sherbet

Curry of lamb
Rice   Pineapple rings
Green peas with almonds
Ice cream   Coffee

Tomato juice
Swiss steak with mushroom gravy
MASHED POTATOES   Brussels sprouts
ORANGE–BRITTLE AMBROSIA

PRESERVING FRUITS AND VEGETABLES

Making Jams and Jellies. *Do conserve the fruits of summer in jams and jellies—to serve on breakfast toast, with dinner meat, on snack-time crackers.*

Unlike canning, which is generally done speedily at the peak of the crop and in sizable quantities, making jams and jellies is best in small batches throughout the season. Or, if unsweetened fruit is first frozen, they can be made at any convenient time during the year. Blueberries, gooseberries, currants, peaches, plums and rhubarb are good choices for freezer storage preliminary to being made into jam. Measure fruit into cartons, and mark amounts on lids. To use, defrost almost completely; then follow any desired recipe for jams or jellies.

This type of preserving is really easy.

Jams

Jams are made by cooking together crushed or chopped fruits and sugar until thickened or set. Some jams are best with the liquid part still fluid; others have their greatest appeal when firm, as is jelly.

Conserves

Conserves are a variation of jam, generally combining several fruits, including such dried varieties as raisins. Unsalted nuts are frequently added.

Marmalade

Marmalade is the specific term for jam made with thinly sliced citrus fruit with rind (oranges, grapefruit, lemons, limes, kumquats, tangerines or any mixture of them), though some call jam made with any type of fresh fruit prepared in thin slices "marmalade." When citrus fruit with rind is combined with other types of fruit, the product is called either "conserve" or "marmalade."

Jellies

Jellies are made from the juice extracted from prepared fruit. Juice is boiled with sugar and then chilled to set or "jell."

All jellies must be set so that they retain their shapes when turned out for serving. They should be clear and quivery and should cut easily with a spoon, giving a smooth, clean edge.

For perfectly set jellies and for firm jams, there are 3 essentials: pectin, fruit acid and sugar, all in proper proportion to one another. With fruits containing enough natural pectin and fruit acid, a set jam or jelly can be produced simply by boiling fruit or juice with sugar until mixture reaches jelling point. When fruit is deficient in either pectin or acid, jelling cannot be achieved without adding correct quantities of either.

Pectin. Pectin is a substance in fruits that, when combined with fruit acid and sugar and heated, causes juice to set. It is found in generous amounts in the fruits long known to housewives as "good for jellying"—apples, sour blackberries, crab apples, cranberries, currants, gooseberries, grapes, quinces, plums and citrus fruits (especially their rinds). Pectin content is highest when fruit is underripe; it decreases as fruit ripens. The fruits naturally low in pectin include apricots, cherries, peaches, raspberries and strawberries, plus most other varieties when they reach an overripe state.

If you are in doubt about the natural jelling capacity of any fruit, heat a little extracted juice to boiling point. Pour into alcohol away from heat. If juice does not form thick clot but looks weak and stringy, you should boil a fresh batch of juice and retest, *do not taste*. Or supplement with pectin from another fruit, or use commercial pectin.

A fruit lacking in pectin is often combined with another that has good pectin content. For example, raspberry juice, poor by itself, makes excellent jelly when teamed with red currant juice. Don't use fresh pineapple at all.

Commercial pectin (usually processed from underripe apples) can be combined with virtually any fruit for quickly made jellies or jams. For best results, always use quantities and times outlined by manufacturer. One advantage of commercial pectin is that fruits can be used at their full ripeness, when flavor is best but natural pectin receding.

Fruit Acids and Sugar. The acids naturally present in fruits enhance flavor and setting quality for jams and so forth. When preparing such low-acid fruits as peaches and sweet blackberries, add 1 tablespoon lemon juice to each cup fruit juice, or follow exact proportions specified in recipe.

Make a point of measuring or weighing sugar carefully. To hasten dissolving, heat sugar in shallow pan in 250°F. oven 15 minutes.

Equipment. Equipment that permits you to cook in quantities calling for no more than 5 cups fruit or juice at a time is best. In specific recipes, do not double amounts.

An electric blender crushes fruits in seconds, but if you don't have one, a potato masher can be used. For some jams, fruit can be put through food chopper.

Use wide kettle, which will allow mixture to boil freely and also will allow quick evaporation.

Use standard measuring equipment, and be accurate with measurements.

A long-handled ladle with a small bowl is useful for filling jars. Leave 1/4-inch space at tops of jars.

Sterilize all jars. Wash in sudsy water, and rinse well. Stand jars upside down in kettle containing 2 inches clean water. Bring to boil, drain and keep jars in 275°F. oven until required for filling. Or sterilize in dishwasher. If you are using cup for pouring, sterilize it along with the jars. If using ladle, scald it.

Always use fresh paraffin for sealing. Heat in small container placed in or over hot water. As paraffin is highly inflammable, *never heat over open flame or electric element*.

Cover jams and jellies while hot with 1/8-inch layer of hot paraffin. When wax is set, seal around edges with additional hot paraffin. Avoid thick layer of wax, as it causes jams and jellies to "break" and "weep."

Label and date all jars. Store jams and jellies in cool, dark, dry place. Apartment dwellers will find that the coolest shelves are at the bottom of the cupboard.

Easy Methods

No-cook Method

Simply crush fruit, add sugar and pectin, pack in handy containers and store in freezer, in frozen-food section of your refrigerator or on

refrigerator shelves. Jams and jellies keep perfectly up to 3 months on refrigerator shelves, up to 8 months in freezer.

Quick-cook Method

Boil fruit for very few minutes before pouring into sterilized jars, sealing with paraffin, capping and storing in any cool spot in the home.

Foolproof Method

Bring jams and jellies to specified temperatures (using candy or deep-frying thermometer) during cooking, resulting in perfect consistency every time.

Choose your favorite fruit or berries, and pick recipe that suits your taste.

To Test Jams and Jellies. For jam in which commercial pectin is not used, lift wooden spoonful of boiling mixture into saucer, and place in freezer until cold; meanwhile remove jam from heat. Within 2–3 minutes, cooled sample should set as will finished jam. If it is not sufficiently thick, further cooking of jam is necessary.

For jelly in which commercial pectin is not used, lift wooden spoonful of boiling mixture, and pour slowly back into kettle. If mixture separates at edge of spoon into *two* slow-moving clots or drips, it is ready for bottling (the saucer test may be used for jelly too).

No-cook Red Cherry Jam

2 1/2 cups crushed pitted cherries
4 cups sugar
2 tablespoons lemon juice
1 (1 3/4-ounce) package powdered pectin
3/4 cup water

Measure cherries into bowl. Stir in sugar and lemon juice. Let stand 20 minutes, stirring occasionally. Boil pectin and water together 1 minute, and remove from heat. Stir in fruit mixture, and continue stirring 2 minutes. Ladle into 6–8 jelly glasses or freezer cartons. Let stand at room temperature 24 hours or overnight; then cover with waxed paper and metal or cardboard lids. Store in freezer or refrigerator. Makes 6–8 jelly glasses.

VARIATION:

No-cook Blueberry Jam: Use 3 cups crushed blueberries, 5 cups sugar, 1/4 cup lemon juice and 1 package powdered pectin boiled with 1 cup water.

Quick-cook Red Currant Jelly

3 quarts fully ripe red currants
1 cup water
6 cups sugar
Juice of 1 lemon
1/2 (6-ounce) bottle liquid pectin

Wash and stem currants. Crush in blender, in fruit press or with stainless potato masher. Add water, and cover. Simmer about 8 minutes. Pour into jelly bag, and squeeze out juice with back of wooden spoon. (The ready-made type jelly bag, standing on metal supports, is very convenient. Otherwise make bag of cotton flannel or several layers of cheesecloth; tie securely at top after filling.) For clearer jelly, let jelly bag drip overnight in cool place. Measure 4 cups juice into saucepan (if necessary, make up amount with water). Stir in sugar and lemon juice. Bring to full rolling boil, stirring constantly. Add pectin, and boil hard 1 minute. Remove from heat, and skim. Pour into 8–10 sterilized jelly glasses or jam jars. Seal with paraffin immediately. When cool, store in cool place.

Note: If you have more than 4 cups juice, add remainder to cooling summer drinks.

Foolproof Grape Jelly

10 cups (about 4 pounds) Concord grapes, 1/2 underripe and 1/2 ripe
1/2 cup water
3 1/2 cups sugar

Crush grapes with stainless-steel potato masher in large saucepan, and add water. Cover, and simmer about 10 minutes. Pour into moistened jelly bag, and strain juice into glass bowl in cool place overnight; then strain through cheesecloth to remove tartrate crystals (which sometimes cause grape jelly to form sugar crystals around top). Measure 5 cups juice into saucepan, and add sugar. Stir and cook to boiling point. Insert candy or fat thermometer, and stir until temperature reaches 218°F., or use the "pour test" for jelly. Remove from heat. Stir and skim; then pour into 6–8 sterilized jelly glasses. Seal at once with paraffin.

No-cook Red Currant Jelly

2 quarts red currants
5 cups superfine sugar
1/4 cup lemon juice
1 (1 3/4-ounce) package powdered pectin
3/4 cup water

Crush currants in blender for speed. Otherwise a fine sieve works well. Strain, and measure 3 cups juice into bowl; mix in sugar and lemon juice. Let stand 20 minutes, stirring occasionally. Boil pectin and water together 1 minute; remove from heat, and stir in fruit-juice mixture. Stir 2 minutes, and pour into 6–8 jelly glasses, jam jars or freezer cartons. Leave at room temperature 24 hours. Cover with waxed paper and metal or cardboard lid. Store in freezer or refrigerator.

Note: To use pulp, add 2 cups water to remaining currant pulp, and bring to boil. Simmer 5 minutes, and strain. Add sugar to sweeten. Bring again to boil, and pour into screw-top jars. Keep refrigerated, and use in combination with soda water or other carbonated beverages for cool drinks.

Crab Apple Jelly

4 pounds crab apples
2 cups cold water
Sugar

Wash crab apples, remove stems and blossom ends and cut into halves. Put into kettle, and add only enough cold water to be visible under top layer of fruit. Bring to boil, and boil until apples are completely soft, 20–25 minutes. Put hot contents of kettle into moistened jelly bag. Allow juice to drip through for several hours, into large container underneath. For sparkling, clear jelly, do not squeeze bag. Measure strained juice, and heat to boiling. Measure correct amount granulated sugar, allowing 1 cup per 1 cup juice. Add sugar to boiling juice, and continue rapid boiling until jelly stage is reached (see saucer and pouring tests at beginning of section). Remove from stove, and let stand 30 seconds. Skim off scum, and pour the jelly into hot sterilized glasses. Let cool slightly. Seal.

Note: With tart apples or crab apples, a second extraction from pulp may be made. Measure pulp, add equal amount water and cook slowly for 15–20 minutes; proceed as with first batch of juice. If less-clear jelly is acceptable, press bag with 2 wooden spoons, or squeeze and twist; flavor will still be good, but jelly will be slightly cloudy. For spiced jelly, add cinnamon stick and a few whole cloves, tied loosely in cheesecloth bag, to boiling juice.

Quick-cook Cherry Conserve

        2 cups pitted cherries
        2 cups gooseberries
        7 cups sugar
    1/2 (6-ounce) bottle liquid pectin
        1 cup shredded almonds

Put fruit through mincer, or blend 2 minutes. Combine sugar and fruit in deep saucepan, and stir until sugar is dissolved. Heat to full rolling boil, and boil 1 minute. Remove from heat, stir in pectin, skim and stir 1 minute. Mix in almonds. Pour into jars immediately, and seal with hot paraffin.

Quick Orange Juice Jelly

    3/4 cup (6-ounce can) frozen orange juice
        1 (1 3/4-ounce) package powdered pectin
        2 cups water
    3 1/2 cups sugar

Thaw orange juice. Place pectin crystals and water in deep saucepan, and mix well. Place over high heat, and bring to full rolling boil. Boil 1 minute, stirring constantly. Reduce heat to low; then add thawed orange-juice concentrate and sugar. Stir until sugar is completely dissolved. Do not boil. Remove from heat, and skim if necessary. Pour into 6 or 7 sterilized jelly glasses, and cover with hot paraffin.

Port Wine Jelly

        3 cups sugar
        2 cups port wine
    1/2 (6-ounce) bottle liquid pectin

In the top of a double boiler, over rapidly boiling water, combine sugar and port wine. Mix well and stir until dissolved—approximately 2 minutes. Remove from heat. Stir in liquid fruit pectin immediately, mixing well. Skim off any foam. Pour into hot, sterilized jars. Seal with 1/3 inch melted paraffin. Makes 4 cups.

Crème de Menthe Jelly

    2 1/2 cups sugar
        1 cup crème de menthe liqueur (rose or green)
        1 cup water
    1/2 (6-ounce) bottle liquid pectin
  Mint sprigs

In the top of a double boiler, over rapidly boiling water, combine sugar, crème de menthe liqueur and water. Stir until sugar is dissolved—approximately 2 minutes. Remove from heat; stir in liquid fruit pectin. Skim off foam if necessary. Place 1 sprig of mint, which has been plunged in boiling water for one minute, in each of the hot, sterilized jars. Pour jelly into jars. Seal with 1/3 inch melted paraffin. Makes 4 cups.

Burgundy Wine Jelly

        6 cups sugar
        4 cups Burgundy
        1 (6-ounce) bottle liquid fruit pectin

In the top of a double boiler, over rapidly boiling water, combine sugar and Burgundy. Mix well and stir until dissolved. Remove from heat. Stir in liquid fruit pectin immediately, mixing well. Skim off any foam. Pour immediately into hot, sterilized jars. Seal with 1/3 inch melted paraffin. Makes 8 cups.

Ginger Beet Jelly

        3 cups juice drained from canned beets
    1/4 cup fresh lemon juice
        1 (1 3/4-ounce) package powdered pectin
        4 cups sugar
        1 teaspoon ground ginger

In a large saucepan combine juice from beets, lemon juice and powdered pectin. Stir over high heat until the mixture boils hard. Stir in sugar. Bring to a full rolling boil, boil hard for 1 minute, stirring constantly. Remove from heat; skim off any foam. Stir in ginger, and pour immediately into hot, sterilized jars. Seal at once with 1/3 inch melted paraffin. Makes 5 cups.

Quick-cook Plum Jam

        5 cups crushed yellow plums, 1/2 ripe and sweet,
                1/2 sour
    1/2 cup water
        7 cups sugar
    1/2 (6-ounce) bottle pectin

Cut plums from stones, and crush in blender, or chop fine. Measure fruit into saucepan, and add water. Cover, and simmer 5 minutes, stirring occasionally. Add sugar, and bring to full rolling boil. Boil 1 minute, stirring constantly. Remove from heat, and add pectin. Stir and skim 2–3 minutes. Cool slightly, and ladle into 8–10 sterilized jam or jelly glasses. Seal at once with paraffin. When cold, store in cool place.

Ripe Cucumber Marmalade

      2 cups prepared ripe cucumbers
      4 cups sugar
    1/3 cup lemon juice
      2 tablespoons grated lemon rind
    1/2 (6-ounce) bottle liquid pectin

You will need 1 1/2–2 pounds of fully ripe yellow cucumbers. Peel, cut flesh in strips and discard all seeds. Chop cucumber very fine, or put through grinder. Measure 2 cups into large saucepan. Add next 3 ingredients, and mix well. Bring to full rolling boil, and boil hard 1 minute, stirring constantly. Remove pan from heat, and stir in pectin. Skim. Cool slightly; then ladle into jelly jars. Cover with melted paraffin. Makes about 6 (6-ounce) glasses.

Grape Conserve

      1 (6-quart) basket Concord grapes
    Sugar
      1 orange (grated rind and juice)
      1 lemon (grated rind and juice)
    1/2 pound broken walnuts

Wash grapes, and remove stems. Squeeze pulp and grape juice into saucepan. Save skins. Cover saucepan, and simmer about 10 minutes or until seeds float free. Remove seeds by pressing mixture through sieve or fruit press. Mix pulp and skins together and measure by cups into saucepan. Add equal amount of sugar; stir, bring to boil and continue boiling 10 minutes. Add rind and juice of orange and lemon and nuts. Boil 5 minutes; then skim. Stir constantly while mixture cools slightly. Ladle into jelly glasses, and cover with melted paraffin. Makes 24 small jars.

Spiced Pickled Fruits

      1 pound dried prunes
      2 cups firm sweet or Montmorency cherries
      7 cups granulated sugar
      4 cups cider vinegar
      3 cups water
      4 (3-inch) pieces stick cinnamon
      1 tablespoon whole cloves
      1 tablespoon allspice
    12–16 firm peaches, peeled, halved and pitted

Soak prunes in cold water several hours, and drain; pick over cherries, and wash. Combine next 3 ingredients in large kettle; tie spices in cheesecloth bag, and add. Bring to boil, and simmer 5 minutes. Add all fruit to kettle; simmer gently 15 minutes. Remove from heat, cover kettle and let stand overnight. Next morning bring to boil; remove peaches carefully, and pack in hot sterilized jars; add prunes and cherries to fill spaces around peaches. Boil syrup hard 20 minutes; discard spice bag, and pour liquid into jars, covering fruit completely. Seal. Store in cool dry place.

Peach–Raspberry Jam

      1 (12-ounce) package frozen raspberries
      2 pounds (approximately) ripe peaches
      6 cups sugar
    1/4 cup lemon juice
    1/2 (6-ounce) bottle liquid pectin

Thaw berries according to package directions. Peel, pit and crush peaches. Measure thawed berries, and add enough crushed peaches to make 4 cups fruit. Place in kettle; add sugar and lemon juice, mixing thoroughly. Bring to full rolling boil over high heat, and boil hard 1 minute, stirring constantly. Remove from heat, and add pectin, stirring vigorously. Stir and skim alternately about 5 minutes. Ladle quickly into hot sterilized glasses; cover with melted paraffin. Makes about 10 medium jars.

Strawberry Jam

      3 pints mixed ripe and underripe strawberries
      4 cups sugar
      2 tablespoons lemon juice

Crush fruit, using blender, food press or stainless-steel potato masher. Measure 4 cups into large saucepan, and stir in sugar and lemon juice. Bring to boil, stirring constantly. Continue stirring and boiling until thick, about 15 minutes. Remove from heat, and skim and stir alternately 3–4 minutes. Ladle into hot jelly glasses, and cover with melted paraffin immediately. Makes about 6 (6-ounce) jars.

Red Tomato Preserves

    12 pounds red tomatoes
     6 pounds granulated sugar
     1 (16-ounce) can crushed pineapple
     3 oranges (put through grinder)

Scald tomatoes, and peel. Cut up fine. Place all ingredients in preserving kettle, and boil gently 2 1/2 hours. Pour into sterilized jars.

Note: A delicious soft marmalade for September, when local tomatoes are best.

Tomato Marmalade

      4 oranges
      2 lemons
      1/2 cup cold water
      8 tomatoes
      Scalding water
      Sugar

Peel oranges and lemons. Cut away white pith, and discard. Cut peel in thin strips; cover with 1/2 cup water, and bring to boil. Simmer 15 minutes; drain. Dip tomatoes in scalding water, and peel. Halve peeled oranges and lemons, and discard pits. Mince fruit pulp and tomatoes together. Add cooked peel, minced fruit pulp and tomatoes; cover, and simmer about 20 minutes. Boil uncovered 15 minutes. Measure, and add equal amount of sugar. Simmer uncovered, stirring occasionally, until ready to jell (use drip test described at beginning of section). Ladle into sterilized jars; cover with melted paraffin.

Apricot Conserve

      1 (1-pound, 13-ounce) can pineapple chunks,
         drained
      3 oranges
      1 1/4 cups water
      1 (6-ounce) bottle maraschino cherries and juice
      1/2 pound blanched almonds, halved
      6 cups chopped unpeeled apricots
      3 cups sugar

Juice oranges, and grind peel. Mix pineapple, orange juice and rind, 1 1/2 cups water and cherry juice in saucepan. Cover and simmer until rind is tender, about 15 minutes. Add apricots and sugar. Bring to boil, stirring occasionally. Insert candy or fat thermometer, and cook, stirring until it registers 216°F., about 20 minutes; or use saucer test. Add cherries and almonds. Simmer 5 minutes. Skim, and ladle into 10–12 sterilized jelly glasses or jam pars. Cool slightly, and seal with paraffin.

Note: Heat mixture to 219°F.–220°F. for firm jam, 216°F.–217°F. for softer texture. Note temperature for consistency you like best for another year.

Rhubarb–Pineapple Jam

      8 cups rhubarb, cut in 1-inch pieces
      1 (1-pound, 13-ounce) can pineapple chunks,
         drained
      4 cups sugar

Put rhubarb and pineapple into kettle. Place over low heat, and cook until juice starts to flow. Bring to boil, and continue boiling, uncovered, 15 minutes, stirring to prevent sticking. Add sugar, stir, bring to boil again and cook at same heat, uncovered, to jam stage, about 25 minutes. Watch carefully, and stir frequently after adding sugar. Pour into 5 or 6 hot sterilized jars; seal when slightly cooled.

Note: If rhubarb is not very juicy, 1/4 cup water should be added during first cooking. If rhubarb lacks color, a few drops of red vegetable coloring may be incorporated.

Orange–Lemon–Grapefruit Marmalade

      1 thin-skinned grapefruit
      2 large navel oranges
      1 large thin-skinned lemon
      12 cups water
      8 cups sugar

Peel grapefruit, scrape white pulp from rind and discard pulp. Cut yellow rind into very thin strips. Cut grapefruit into sections (removing membrane). Prepare oranges and lemon in same way, and remove any seeds. Combine fruits and rinds in water, and let stand overnight. Boil 10 minutes; set aside to cool. Stir in sugar. Boil again, stirring frequently, over low heat until jelly test is satisfactory or candy thermometer reads 218°F. Pour into sterile jars, and cover with paraffin.

Green Tomato Marmalade

      9 whole green tomatoes
      5 1/2 cups sugar
      Grated rind and juice of 2 lemons
      1/3 cup chopped candied or preserved ginger

Wash and stem whole tomatoes, leaving unpeeled. Put through meat grinder, using coarse blade, and measure into kettle. Add sugar, stir mixture thoroughly and let stand overnight. Bring to boil, reduce to slow heat and cook uncovered about 30 minutes. Add lemon rind and juice and ginger. Increase heat to full rolling boil, and continue cooking, uncovered, until jam stage is reached, about 15 minutes. Pour into 6 or 7 hot sterilized jars, and seal.

Pickling. A wide variety of vegetables and fruits is suitable for pickling. Frequently items that are less than perfect for canning or freezing find their way into pickle jars. But in this area, as in others, the fresher the raw product, the better the result. Sound, firm vegetables and slightly underripe fruits are preferable for all pickles, with the exception of tomato catsup, chili sauce and "butters," in which the necessary boiling down plus liberal addition of seasonings may justify the use of substandard raw products.

Salt is used either for pre-preparation of ingredients or in sauce or vinegar mixtures for finishing. Coarse or pickling salt is the best choice. Iodized salt may be used, but as most packaged salt contains a "free-flowing" conditioner that can cause cloudiness in pickles, it is advisable to buy old-fashioned, untreated salt for pickling use.

In making brine for soaking vegetables, always follow proportions exactly. If too little salt is used, pickles may become soft, with a slimy tendency; too much salt may shrivel and toughen pickles. In addition to keeping vegetables firm throughout processing and storage, the soaking procedure reduces possible bitterness.

Vinegars of good quality and standard strength make pickling results very certain. Remember that vinegars are stronger today than they were 20 years ago; in spite of the charm of grandmother's pickle recipes, it is better therefore to follow up-to-date proportions and procedures and to use exactly the amounts of vinegar called for.

There are 4 basic types of vinegar on the market. Cider vinegar is frequently specified in fruit pickles because of its superior flavor. White vinegar is often preferred when a light color is important, as in pickling onions, cauliflower and the like. Herbed vinegar, a mixture of herbs and cider or white vinegars, is especially good, but expensive for pickling purposes and for all-round use. Red wine vinegar, the darkest and strongest in flavor, is excellent in pickling.

It is unwise to dilute vinegar for a recipe, as weakening the solution may cause stored pickles to turn soft or spoil.

Sugar in pickle recipes is generally of the standard white type, although brown may occasionally be specified for added flavor.

Spices should be purchased in fresh supply for pickling. Once opened, packaged spices can quickly lose their effectiveness.

Whole spices are frequently required in recipes. They yield excellent flavor and have the advantage of not darkening the mixture as ground seasonings do. For convenience, tie stick cinnamon, whole nutmeg, allspice berries, and so forth in a little cheesecloth bag loosely enough so that boiling syrup completely penetrates. Remove and discard bag and its contents before bottling pickles.

Follow spicing directions carefully. When ground spices are called for, use exact level measurements. Overspicing is one of the commonest errors in home-pickling. Always be cautious with such strong flavors as allspice, cloves, cayenne and the like. Add only at point specified in recipe; do not boil too long in vinegar, or flavor may be overpowering, even bitter, and pickles will darken.

Equipment for Pickling

No elaborate utensils are needed. The kitchen's usual measuring equipment and mixing bowls, a large saucepan or preserving kettle (preferably of enamel or stainless steel to preserve color of pickles), a long-handled spoon, an earthenware crock for brining if necessary and containers for bottling and storing are the items you will require.

Sealers of the type used for canned fruits are generally preferred for storage. Certain thick relishes like MUSTARD PICKLES can be stored in sterilized small glass jars and covered with hot paraffin, but this method is not so satisfactory as sealing in standard airtight containers. Sterilizing of jars is a worthwhile precaution, although it is true that pickles containing high proportions of vinegar and sugar will generally keep acceptably in well-washed and dried jars. Earthenware crocks are seldom employed for storage in the modern household because their use entails a more complicated operation and because a continuously cool atmosphere is hard to ensure. In crock storage the pickles are left in a cool place, and they should be completely covered with their own liquid to prevent spoilage. A plate or other cover that fits inside the crock should be placed over pickles and weighted down to keep them immersed. The only appropriate storage place is the refrigerator.

Small Batches in Variety

Pickles and relishes can be highly individual in character and in preparation; it is therefore better to make half-a-dozen kinds of pickles in small batches than a monotonous overlarge quantity of 1 kind.

Pickled Silver-skin Onions

> 2 quarts silver-skin onions
> 1 pint boiling water
> 1 cup salt
> 3 pints cold water
> 1 quart milk
> 2 sweet red peppers, cut in thin strips
> 1 quart white-wine vinegar
> 1 pound white sugar

Skin onions; heat boiling water and salt together until salt is dissolved. Add cold water. When brine is cold pour over onions, and let stand 24 hours. Add milk, and bring to boil. Drain, and pack in sterilized jars, adding a few strips red pepper between layers. Boil vinegar and sugar together 2–3 minutes, and pour over onions. Seal. Makes 4 pints.

Note: It is the milk that keeps the onions white.

Sour Silver-skin Onions

Peel skins from onions. Soak 48 hours in strong salt water (1 tablespoon salt to 1 quart water). Drain and pack in clean jars. Fill jars with boiling white vinegar, and seal according to manufacturer's directions. Leave in a cool place a month or 2 before using.

Dark Hot Chili Sauce

```
 18 large ripe tomatoes
  4 green peppers
  2 large onions
  2 cups cider vinegar
1/2 cup brown sugar
  2 tablespoons salt
  2 tablespoons ginger
  2 tablespoons cinnamon
  1 tablespoon allspice
  1 tablespoon nutmeg
```

Peel and cut tomatoes coarsely. Chop peppers and dice onions. Combine vegetables with remaining ingredients, and bring to boil. Simmer uncovered about 1 hour, stirring occasionally, especially as mixture thickens. Ladle into sterilized jars, and seal. Makes 6 pints.

Note: If tomatoes are overripe or juicy, drain off some juice before cooking. Otherwise simmering time will have to be considerably extended before sauce reaches right thickness. You can use drained juice in jellied salads, gravies and the like.

Pickled Mushrooms

```
    1 cup white-wine vinegar
    1 cup water
  1/2 cup salad oil
2 1/4 teaspoons basil
   12 peppercorns
    1 clove garlic
    1 teaspoon chili powder
    1 bay leaf
  1/2 teaspoon salt
    2 pounds tiny button mushrooms, washed and dried
```

Place liquids and seasonings in saucepan; add mushrooms. Bring to boil; reduce heat, and simmer 15 minutes. Remove from stove, and cool in saucepan. Pour into sterilized jars, and process in boiling water bath 15 minutes. (See p. 156.)

Spiced Watermelon Rind

```
  3 pounds watermelon rind (from approximately 1/2 melon)
  3 quarts cold water
1/3 cup salt
  3 quarts cold water
  5 cups sugar
  2 cups vinegar
  1 cup water
  1 lemon, sliced
  1 tablespoon whole cloves
```

```
  1 tablespoon allspice
  1 tablespoon ginger
  1 cinnamon stick
```

Pare and discard outer skin of melon rind, and cut rind into 1-inch pieces. Make brine of 3 quarts water and salt. Soak rind in brine overnight. In morning, drain thoroughly. Cover rind with 3 quarts fresh water, and simmer until almost tender, about 30 minutes. Drain. Combine sugar, vinegar, 1 cup water, and lemon slices; tie spices loosely in cheesecloth bag, and add to liquids. Bring to boil; simmer, stirring 5 minutes. Add rind; cook gently, stirring, until rind becomes transparent, about 5 minutes. Discard spice bag, ladle pickles into sterilized jars and cover with hot syrup. Seal at once.

Apple Chutney

```
    3 pounds (approximately 8 medium) tart cooking apples
    4 cups cider vinegar
    3 cups brown sugar, firmly packed
    4 or 5 large chopped onions
    1 pound sultana raisins
    6 chili peppers, crumbled
  1/4 pound chopped preserved ginger or 3 tablespoons
        ground ginger
    2 tablespoons salt
    1 tablespoon mustard seed
    1 or 2 crushed garlic cloves
```

Peel and dice apples into large heavy saucepan (5–6 quart size). Add remaining ingredients, and bring to boil. Cover, and turn heat low. Let mixture simmer 1 hour. Uncover, and continue cooking until thickened, stirring occasionally to prevent sticking. The time will depend on consistency you prefer; a thickish mixture will require about 3 hours. Ladle into hot sterilized preserving jars, and seal immediately; or ladle into jelly jars, and seal with melted paraffin. Makes about 4 pints or 9–10 (8-ounce) glasses.

Note: Taste mixture halfway through cooking, and if you like sweeter chutney, add 1 cup brown sugar.

4-Fruit Chutney

```
      3 pounds (about 10) tart apples
1 1/2 pounds (about 6 large) peeled onions
      1 pound (about 4 large) carrots, scraped
      2 oranges
      1 lemon
      4 cups vinegar
      4 ounces crystallized ginger
      1 or 2 cloves garlic
      3 or 4 chili peppers, crumbled, or 3 hot pickled
          banana peppers
      4 cups brown sugar
1 1/2 cups seedless raisins
      2 tablespoons salt
    1/2 teaspoon cinnamon
    1/2 teaspoon allspice
    1/2 teaspoon cloves
```

Quarter apples, onions, carrots, oranges and lemon and grind with coarse blade of food chopper; or use blender, grinding small quantities at a time, adding some of vinegar with fruit and vegetable quarters. Grind or chop ginger and garlic. Grind hot peppers if you use them in place of chili peppers. Mix all ingredients in large saucepan, and bring to boil. Simmer until mixture thickens, stirring occasionally to prevent sticking, about 1–1 1/2 hours. Ladle into sterilized jars, and seal. Makes 10–12 (8-ounce) jars.

Mustard Pickles

```
    5 or 6 cucumbers
    3 cauliflowers
    2 quarts silver-skin onions
    3 quarts cold water
3/4 cup salt
    3 sweet red peppers, diced
    5 cups brown sugar
    1 cup flour
1/2 cup dry mustard
    1 tablespoon turmeric
    1 tablespoon salt
    1 tablespoon celery seed
    3 quarts cider or white vinegar
```

Dice cucumbers without peeling to make 2 quarts, and cut cauliflowers into small flowerlets. Peel onions. Mix all together, and cover with cold water. Sprinkle with 3/4 cup salt, stir well and leave overnight. In morning scald by bringing to boil in same brine. Drain, and add red peppers. Make mustard by mixing sugar, flour, mustard, turmeric, 1 tablespoon salt and celery seed until thoroughly blended. Add vinegar very gradually, stirring until smooth after each addition. Place over low heat, and bring to boil, stirring constantly as moisture thickens. Simmer 2–3 minutes to ensure complete cooking of flour. Drain any accumulated moisture off scalded vegetables; combine with mustard sauce. Ladle into sterilized jars, and seal. Makes 12–14 pints.

Note: For lighter yellow color, use 4 1/2 cups white sugar in place of brown.

Bread-and-Butter Pickles

```
    6 quarts small crisp cucumbers, about 1 inch in
          diameter
    1 quart small white onions
    4 green peppers
    1 sweet red pepper
1 1/2 cups pickling salt
    9 cups boiling water
    8 cups white wine vinegar
    4 cups sugar
    1 teaspoon celery seed
    1 teaspoon mustard seed
    1 tablespoon turmeric
```

Wash vegetables. Peel and slice onions. Slice cucumbers thin. Seed and dice peppers. Dissolve salt in boiling water, and, when cool, pour over vegetables. Let stand overnight. Drain thoroughly. Make pickling syrup of vinegar, sugar and spices, and as soon as it boils add vegetables. When completely heated (not boiling), pack into hot sterilized jars, and seal. Makes about 6 quarts.

Pickled Seckel Pears

```
    8 pounds (6 quarts) Seckel pears
    3 quarts boiling water
   10 sticks cinnamon
    2 tablespoons whole cloves
    2 tablespoons whole allspice
    8 cups sugar
    1 quart cider vinegar
    1 quart water
```

Seckel pears are small, hard and rather tough-skinned. Rub off blossom ends, but leave stems and skins intact. Cover with boiling water; simmer 10 minutes, and drain. Tie spices in bag, and add to sugar, vinegar and 1 quart water. Stir, and bring to boil. Simmer 5 minutes. Drain accumulated moisture from pears; pour hot syrup over them, bring to simmer and cook 15 minutes. Turn contents of pan into crock, and cover. Let stand overnight. In morning, drain, discarding spice bag. Pack pears in sterilized jars, reheat syrup and fill jars with it. Seal. Makes about 8 pints.

VARIATION:

Pickled Crab Apples

Use 8 pounds crab apples in place of pears. Do not parboil, but add raw to hot vinegar syrup. If deeper tone is desired, add a little red vegetable coloring to syrup before pouring over apples in jars.

Winter Chili Sauce

```
    2 (20-ounce) cans tomatoes
    1 cup chopped onions
    1 cup chopped celery
    1 medium green pepper, chopped
1/2 cup cider vinegar
1/4 cup sugar
    3 tablespoons salt
Few grains cayenne
```

Turn all ingredients into large saucepan or kettle. Bring to boil, reduce heat and simmer 30–40 minutes or until thickened. Pour into hot sterilized jars, and seal. Makes 3–4 pints.

- For spicier sauce, add 1 stick of cinnamon, 3 allspice berries and 2 cloves, tied in cheesecloth bag; remove before packing.
- Add 1 teaspoon dry mustard and 1 tablespoon Worcestershire sauce.

Wax Beans in Mustard

```
            6 quarts wax beans
            2 quarts boiling water
            3 tablespoons salt
            6 cups brown sugar
        2/3 cup dry mustard
        1/2 cup flour
            2 tablespoons turmeric
            2 tablespoons celery seed
            6 cups white-wine vinegar
```

Trim beans, and cut in 1-inch lengths. Cover with boiling water, and add 1 tablespoon salt. Bring to boil, and simmer 15 minutes. Drain. In the meantime, mix remaining salt with brown sugar, mustard, flour and seasonings until well blended. Add vinegar gradually, stirring to keep mixture free of lumps. Put sauce over low heat, and cook, stirring constantly, until thick and smooth. Add drained beans, and cook 5 minutes, stirring occasionally. Ladle into sterilized jars, and seal. Makes 8 pints.

Corn Relish

```
        6 ears corn, uncooked, or 2 (10-ounce) packages
            frozen kernel corn
        2 cups chopped cucumber
        2 cups chopped ripe tomatoes
        2 cups chopped celery
    1/2 cup chopped green pepper
    1/2 cup chopped sweet red pepper
        2 cups chopped onions
  1 1/2 teaspoons turmeric
  2 1/2 cups vinegar
  1 1/4 cups brown sugar
```

Cut corn from raw cobs, removing all bits of silk and green parts, measure 3 cups corn into kettle (or thaw and drain frozen corn), and add other vegetables. Add all remaining ingredients, and mix very thoroughly. Bring just to boiling point, reduce heat and simmer, uncovered, about 50 minutes or until thickened, stirring frequently. Turn into hot sterilized jars; seal. Makes about 4 pints.

Sweet Green Tomato Pickles

```
        8 pounds (about 32) green tomatoes
        6 large onions
        3 cups vinegar
        3 cups brown sugar
        1 tablespoon salt
        1 teaspoon cloves
        1 teaspoon cinnamon
        1 teaspoon mace
```

Chop or grind tomatoes and onions, and bring to boil in their own juices. Turn heat low, and simmer 30 minutes. Add remaining ingredients, and simmer about 1 hour, stirring occasionally. Ladle into hot sterilized jars, and seal. Makes 8 pints.

Prune–Apple Chutney

```
        2 pounds dried prunes
        3 cups peeled, chopped onions
        2 cups peeled, chopped tart apples
        3 cups blended vinegar
        1 lemon, thinly sliced
  1 1/2 cups brown sugar, firmly packed
    1/2 cup seeded raisins
        2 teaspoons salt
        1 teaspoon mustard seed
        1 teaspoon cayenne
        1 teaspoon ground ginger
```

Soak prunes overnight in water to cover. Drain, remove pits and cut prunes into coarse pieces. Turn all ingredients into preserving kettle, bring to boil, reduce heat and simmer, uncovered, at least 2 hours. Stir from time to time, especially when mixture starts to thicken. Ladle into hot sterilized jars, and seal. Makes 3–4 pints.

Rhubarb Relish

```
        6 cups rhubarb, cut fine
        4 cups (about 16) minced onions
        4 cups brown sugar
        1 quart vinegar
        4 teaspoons salt
        1 teaspoon cinnamon
        1 teaspoon cloves
        1 teaspoon ginger
        1 teaspoon allspice
    1/4 teaspoon cayenne
```

Mix all ingredients together and cook until thick, about 1 hour, stirring from time to time. Ladle into hot sterilized jars, and seal. Makes 8 pints.

Sweet Pepper Relish

```
        1 dozen large sweet red peppers
        1 dozen large green peppers
        1 dozen medium onions
        4 cups white-wine vinegar
        1 cup sugar
        2 tablespoons salt
        1 tablespoon dry mustard
        1 tablespoon celery seed
        1 teaspoon mustard seed
```

Wash and stem peppers; remove seeds and white membrane. Peel onions. Put vegetables through meat grinder, using coarse blade. Cover with boiling water, and let stand 5 minutes. Drain thoroughly. Add remaining ingredients, bring to boil, reduce heat and simmer, stirring several times, until vegetables are tender, 10 minutes, Pack in hot sterilized jars, and seal. Makes about 6 pints.

Celery Relish

> 1 quart ripe tomatoes
> 3 large onions
> 2 bunches celery, sliced
> 2 hot red peppers
> 2 1/2 cups white sugar
> 2 cups vinegar
> 1/4 cup salt
> 1/4 cup whole mixed pickling spices

Peel tomatoes and onions, and cut into coarse pieces in preserving kettle. Add celery, discarding all leaves. Chop hot red peppers (protect your hands with rubber gloves or oven mitts), and add to kettle. Tie spices in cheesecloth bag, with remaining ingredients to kettle. Bring to boil, reduce heat and simmer until desired consistency is reached. Remove spice bag. Ladle into sterilized jars, and seal. Makes about 10 pints.

Home Freezing of Fruits. Know the capacity of your freezer. At the beginning of summer, make a rough plan of the foods you intend to freeze, so that you can make full use of your equipment and leave space for items available late in the season.

Label each package with full information—date, kind, sugar, no sugar, and so forth. Hang an inventory pad and pencil on the wall near the freezer, and cross off all items as they are taken out.

Keep thermometer in center of freezer, and check often to see that it registers the correct 0°F. In case of power failure, remember that even a well-filled freezer requires 2–3 days to raise the temperature to a dangerous level. Thawed fruits can be refrozen if temperature has not gone above 40°F. (Never refreeze thawed vegetables).

As fruits cannot "improve" during storage, select only choice ripe products for freezing. Some fruits, notably pears and apples, do not freeze well. See Freezing Guide for Fruits in this section, for dependable varieties.

As *fast* freezing is always desirable, freeze in reasonably small quantities at one time, using small rather than large packages. Distribute containers here and there until contents are solid. Place against cold walls of freezer chest, or on metal shelves of upright freezer cabinet. Group packages later for convenience.

Most home freezers can, in 24 hours, freeze 2–4 pounds of foodstuffs for each cubic foot of freezer capacity.

Which Packaging Materials? The importance of proper packaging cannot be overemphasized. The fresh flavor, color, texture and nutritive value of foods that are frozen will reach the table only if they are properly protected during storage. Packaging materials must permit no exchange of moisture or air between frozen food and atmosphere in freezer cabinet. In other words, packaging must be "moisture-vapor proof". Ordinary waxed paper and ice-cream cartons will not do as moisture can seep through.

Here is a list of various satisfactory containers for home freezing of fruits: firm polyethylene containers with snap-on or squeeze-in lids; heavily waxed cartons (although round shapes waste freezer space); plastic containers (more costly but reusable, with the additional advantage of transparency); polyethylene freezer bags (excellent for dry-packing fruits); and folding cartons (best for vegetables but sometimes used for dry-packing fruits).

Suit size of container to contents and use. Pint packages are good for sliced strawberries, small boxes for perfect whole berries to be used as garnishes. Packaging in different sizes according to purpose permits you to thaw only what you need.

Pack with or without Sugar. Fruits can be packed in any of 4 ways, depending on variety and intended use.

Dry Sugarless Pack

Some fruits (blueberries, cranberries, raspberries, whole strawberries and so forth) can be frozen without sweetening. Berries intended for later jam making should be frozen without sugar.

Wet Sugarless Pack

For special diets in which sugar is restricted, this method is useful. Use fully ripe fruit; crush enough fruit to extract sufficient juice to cover fruit in container; then pour crushed fruit over cut-up pieces to fill package to correct level. If diet permits a calorie-free sweetener, it may be added.

Dry Sugar Pack

Sift sugar over small amounts of fruit at a time, using bowl and stirring carefully so as not to break fruit. Or add sugar by the tablespoon, in alternate layers with fruit. Use this guide for proportions:

1 pound sugar to 5 pounds blueberries
1 pound sugar to 3–5 pounds sour cherries

1 pound sugar to 4 pounds peaches or plums
1 pound sugar to 4 pounds strawberries (a little more sugar for 4 pounds raspberries)

Syrup Pack

Use firm containers only. Suit sweetness to specific fruit and to personal taste. Prepare syrup the day before, and chill overnight. Allow 1 cup syrup for pint carton, 1 1/2 cups for quart carton. Place fruit in containers, and cover with syrup, leaving 1 inch space at top. Place crumpled clean waxed paper on fruit to keep it under syrup.

For proportions of sugar to water in thin, medium and thick syrups, see recipes for canning later in chapter.

To Prevent Darkening. Vitamin C (ascorbic acid) can be used to prevent darkening of frozen apples, apricots and peaches. Buy it at drugstore or locker plant, and follow instructions on package. Generally 1/4 teaspoon of ascorbic-acid power is allowed for each pint of fruit. Sprinkle it in with sugar, or add to syrup. With applesauce, mix in just before packaging.

Important: In packaging sweetened fruits for freezing, work quickly. Never let filled packages stand more than 10 minutes at room temperature, as fruit will develop "cooked" flavor. Transfer immediately to freezer, or place in refrigerator until all packages are ready.

Using Frozen Fruits. As thawed fruit quickly deteriorates, it should be used at once. It may be thawed at room temperature or in refrigerator; the latter is better when fruit is to be served cold. Or container may be placed in lukewarm water and fruit removed as soon as it has defrosted.

FREEZING GUIDE FOR FRUITS

FRUIT	NOTES	TO PREPARE FOR FREEZING
Sliced apples	Slice apples into weak brine (1 teaspoon salt to 1 quart cool water); drain well.	Parboil two minutes; cool quickly over ice; pack and label.
Blackberries	Must be fully ripe; otherwise they change color and become sour.	Crush gently with dry sugar, and seal; or pack in thin-to-medium syrup, and label.
Cantaloupe and watermelon	Use fully ripe, deep-colored fruit.	Slice, seed, peel and dice in 1/2- or 3/4-inch cubes, or use melon-ball cutter; pack, cover with thin syrup and label.
Sour cherries	Frozen cherries make an excellent pie filling.	Pit, and sugar; stir frequently until all sugar is dissolved; pack, press waxed paper over and seal.
Blueberries	Pick over, wash and drain carefully.	Pack dry, or add thin syrup to cover.
Red and black currants	Good for later jelly making.	Pack sugarless in freezer bags; label with exact quantities.
Cranberries		Use dry sugarless method, label freezer bags.
Gooseberries	Do not use underripe fruit.	May be frozen "as is" or in dry sugar pack, or in medium-to-heavy syrup.
Grapes	Freeze for jelly later on if desired.	After stemming, freeze "as is."
Peaches	Note variety, for next season's guidance.	Scald, cool and peel; halve, pit and pack; cover with thin, medium or heavy syrup; add ascorbic acid; seal.
Plums	Must be fully ripened.	Remove pits; pack, and cover with light syrup; add 1/4 teaspoon orange juice (optional). Seal.
Raspberries	Only first-quality fruit should be used.	Dry-pack, with or without sugar.
Rhubarb	Use tender stalks.	Cut into 1-inch pieces; freeze "as is," in dry sugar pack or stewed for table use.
Strawberries	Wash under very cold water; drain well, and hull.	Slice each berry into 2 or 3 pieces; use dry sugar pack.

FREEZING GUIDE FOR SPECIAL FRUIT DISHES

FRUITS	PREPARATION FOR FREEZING	NOTES ON USE
Baked apples	Select best varieties for baking, and bake as usual; cool quickly in basin surrounded by cold water; pack in container with 2 pieces of foil between apples.	Do not thaw; reheat in 350°F. oven.

Applesauce, cranberry sauce, and the like	Prepare and sweeten as for immediate use, cool, pack and label.	Thaw at room temperature.
Uncooked jams	See instructions in section on jams and jellies.	
Purees (fresh apricots, cantaloupe, berries, peaches, plums)	Choose well-ripened fruit; puree in electric blender; 1 1/2 cups sugar to 6 cups fruit; or simmer fruit until soft, add sugar, cool and pack in containers.	For dessert sauces.

Note: For full freezing instructions, see Freezing Guide for Fruits. Do not overcook fruits for freezing, and do not refreeze.

Freezing Vegetables. Freezing has a number of advantages over other methods of long-term storage of vegetables. With a home freezer, preparation is quick and convenient and calls for little equipment beyond that usually available in the kitchen. Vegetables retain fresh color and flavor, and, when freshly gathered and quickly and correctly processed, their high food value is also retained.

For best results, use only highest-quality fresh vegetables, and follow instructions carefully.

Freeze Only the Best. Vegetables that freeze with greatest success include asparagus, broccoli, corn, green peas, squash (cooked), spinach and similar greens. Green and wax beans also freeze well, although the flavor tends to be weak.

Celery, cucumbers, lettuce, radishes and whole and cut-up tomatoes are not suitable for freezing. (Tomato juice, however, freezes well.)

Choose fresh, high-quality vegetables that are tender and succulent, just right for table use. Not-quite-ripe vegetables soften and are rather flavorless after freezing. Overripe vegetables tend to become tough.

Blanching Before Freezing. Rules given for home-freezing fruits apply equally to vegetables, except that, whereas fruits are usually frozen raw, vegetables must be "blanched," that is scalded in boiling water, before packing.

Blanching destroys enzymes that would otherwise affect quality during storage. It also "sets" natural colors, partially sterilizes vegetables and softens them for closer packing.

You will need a kettle (at least 6-quart) and a long-handled sieve or wire basket or a large double square of cheesecloth. Blanch only about 1 pound of prepared vegetables at a time, so that water can be quickly brought back to boil after vegetable is added. Have at least 1 gallon of water boiling rapidly over high heat (2 gallons for 1 pound of leafy vegetable). Place vegetable in sieve, basket or cheesecloth. Immerse vegetable in water, bring very quickly to boil again and start counting the blanching time. Watch a clock with a second hand, or set a timer—*blanching time must be exact* (see tables for specific vegetables). Move container of vegetable through water to help heat penetration.

Immediately after blanching, lift container of vegetable to tray, and transfer to sink. Turn vegetable into colander under running cold water, or immerse in ice water. Vegetable takes as long to cool as to blanch. To check, bite a piece; it should not feel hot to the tongue.

Drain quickly and thoroughly. The vegetable is now ready for packaging.

The Right Packaging Materials. As for all frozen foods, packaging material for vegetables must be moisture-vapor proof.

Suitable containers for home freezing of vegetables include polyethylene or plastic-film freezing bags; heavily waxed rectangular cardboard cartons with heat-sealed inner bags or heat-sealed overwraps; and firm polyethylene containers with snap-on or squeeze-in lids.

The first 2 mentioned are probably the most convenient for home use, as they are easy to handle and take relatively little freezer space. Remember, smaller containers freeze more quickly, thus giving better results. For convenience at serving time, a container that holds the right amount for your family at 1 meal is ideal. If larger quantities are stored in freezer bags, it is important to remove needed amounts quickly; then tie down wrap, or secure it with rubber band to exclude air from remainder while stored in the freezer.

Step-by-Step Procedure

1. Plan to freeze only amount of vegetable that will be used in 1 season.

2. Assemble necessary utensils and equipment. Be sure to have on hand right sizes, types and number of containers and labels, as well as an inventory pad.

3. Select best vegetable variety for freezing. If in doubt about varieties, pack small sample, freeze overnight and test next day.

4. Reorganize freezer to leave space for scattering packages through it against the metal walls or shelves. Plan also where packages will be assembled after they are completely frozen.

5. Make space in refrigerator, if necessary, to "hold" packages briefly before you transfer them to freezer.

6. Vegetables should be frozen the day they are bought or gathered, preferably within a few hours of gathering. If preparation must be postponed, put vegetables in refrigerator. Or place in pan or pail, cover and immerse in larger container of ice water up to level of vegetables.

7. Sort vegetables, setting aside any of inferior quality for immediate use.

8. Prepare carefully and quickly. Wash very thoroughly, remove bruised or blemished parts and, when necessary, cut in serving sizes (prepare as for table use). Be sure to have clean hands, clean utensils and frequent changes of clean water, as the next step, blanching, does not heat the product sufficiently to sterilize before freezing.

9. Blanch, cool and drain vegetables as already outlined.

10. Pack in moisture-vapor proof containers. Place vegetables neatly to save space and facilitate later use; leave 1-inch space at top to allow for expansion in freezing.

Neither salt nor brine is used, as they delay freezing and thawing.

11. Seal, according to type of container employed; with moisture-vapor proof bags, press out as much air as possible. Twist top, and secure with metal or paper closures or with rubber band.

With rectangular cartons, press air out of inner container. If carton has heat-sealed inner bag, seal bag, and close the carton. If the carton has heat-sealed outer wrap, close carton, wrap closely and heat-seal. Use your electric iron set at "warm" to heat-seal; press top inch of container edges together with iron.

With polyethylene containers, adjust covers, and, if desirable, seal with freezer tape.

12. Label cartons with names of vegetables, special details of preparation and date of freezing.

13. Store each group of 2 or 3 packages in the refrigerator as it is filled and labeled, or place in freezer immediately if convenient.

14. Freeze promptly at 0°F. or lower temperature. If packages are to be taken to a freezer plant, place in carton lined with newspaper.

15. Make complete inventory listing, which you will keep handy to freezer.

16. Postpone stacking of home-frozen vegetables for 1–2 days. Remember, do *not* refreeze after thawing.

Home-canned Fruit. Home canning of fruits is most satisfying and profitable when fresh, fully ripened fruit is readily obtainable. Avoid overripe or underripe products, and plan to can fruit as quickly as possible to ensure maximum flavor and texture.

It is necessary to destroy organisms that cause ripening and, if allowed to continue working, produce spoilage. You must also provide a perfect seal, which will prevent entrance of spoilage-producing organisms. You can destroy the organisms and provide a perfect seal by heat sterilization and by airtight sealing of filled jars or cans.

Unlike non-acid vegetables, fruits (including tomatoes) may be home canned even without the aid of a pressure cooker, for fruits and tomatoes contain organic acids that help prevent spoilage. Also, fruits are usually sweetened, which further helps preservation. (Vinegar and spices, when suitable, are additional aids in preventing spoilage of home-processed foods.)

Equipment for Home Canning. Check carefully the day before canning, and be sure your supplies are in satisfactory condition.

Jars

Jars must be sound, airtight and free of slightest crack, chip or dent. Styles in jars have changed slightly over the past years, but the types listed here are basic and include those now generally available. Jars with 3-piece tops are the familiar containers that are closed with rubber rings, glass covers and metal sealing rings. Jars may be squat or tall. Today's Mason jar has sides of rounded-square shape and a 2-piece top, consisting of a metal cover with a rubber gasket and a metal screw-on ring. Variations of these 2 types may be on the market in some localities.

Rubber Rings

Never use old or once-used rubber rings; they lose their springiness and provide poor protection. If your jars require separate rings, buy as required, and be very sure that they are the right size for the jars you use. Be sure they are of the current year's production, but do not test by stretching.

Screw Tops

Screw tops should be free of corrosion and should perfectly fit jars.

Metal Cans

If you process large amounts of home-canned fruits and vegetables, you will probably find metal cans useful and convenient. For most products, plain tin cans are satisfactory. Enameled cans are recommended for some fruits and vegetables (red berries, red and black cherries, plums, rhubarb and pressure-canned corn, beets, pumpkin and winter squash). Enamel lining prevents discoloration of food; it is not essential for safety.

Kitchen Utensils

The following utensils are required: 2 large bowls, large kettle, saucepan and dependable container—hot water bath or steam-pressure cooker. For various reasons, including the danger of exploding jars, oven canning is no longer recommended. Open-kettle canning is now also considered less efficient than other methods.

A colander or large sieve will be needed, as well as measuring cups, towels, potholders, a wide-mouthed funnel, pie plate, long knife, peeler and spoon. Handy additions to your canning equipment are paper toweling, small brush, jar lifter and metal tongs.

Water-bath Processor

Use large clean kettle or other container with cover. If container lacks lid, you may use double layer of heavy foil, fitted over rim, in place of cover. Container should be deep enough to allow 2 inches or more space above tops of jars. To keep jars off bottom of container, a rack, preferably of wire or wood, is essential. Overlapping cake coolers or 3 thicknesses of perforated *heavy* foil may be used.

Pressure Canner

For the general procedure, see section on pressure canning. Always consult instructions given by manufacturer. If you have a pressure saucepan large enough to take several jars at 1 time, it can substitute for large canner. Consult your instruction booklet for specific use.

Preparing Jars and Rings

1. Test seal. Put about 2 inches of water in jar; fit with rubber ring and glass top, and invert. If water leaks out, it is not airtight and should be refitted or discarded.

2. Wash jars and glass lids (except those with sealing compound) in hot sudsy water. Rinse, and scald.

3. Sterilize jars and lids (except those with sealing compound) in kettle of water, dishwasher or oven. Place jars in kettle, half-fill with water and cover with glass lids, if latter are to be used. Pour around them 3 inches or more warm water. Add 1 tablespoon vinegar (to prevent lime coating). Bring water to boiling, and leave jars in water until ready to fill. Or place empty jars on rack in cold oven. Cover each with its glass top, if latter is to be used, or with foil.

Heat oven slowly to 200°F. Remove jars as needed, and place on folded paper or dry cloth for filling.

Dip rubber or metal rings in boiling water just before using. To use sealing compound, follow instructions of the manufacturer.

Preparing Metal Cans. See that cans, lids and gaskets are perfect. Discard any that are bent, dented or rusted or have damaged gaskets. To protect lids from dust and moisture, leave in paper packing until required.

Just before using, wash cans in sudsy hot water, and rinse in boiling water. Invert to drain until required. Do not wash lids, as washing damages gaskets; simply wipe with damp cloth if dirty before putting on cans.

Follow manufacturer's sealing instructions.

Use only standard enamel cans for tomatoes or fruits.

It will speed your canning preparations if you know how to do quick translation of pounds or quarts into cups. You should also have a good approximate idea of the number of pint or quart containers that will be needed for a given quantity of the finished product.

CONVERSION TABLE FOR FRUITS

FRUIT	AS PURCHASED	QUANTITY
Apricots, small	1 pound	18 apricots
Blackberries	1 quart	1 3/4 pounds or 4 1/2 cups
Blueberries	1 quart	1 3/4 pounds or 4 1/2 cups
Blue grapes	1 quart	2 pounds or 5 cups
Cherries	1 quart	1 3/4 pounds or 4 1/2 cups
Gooseberries, whole	1 pound	1 heaping pint or 2 cups or 1 3/4 cups crushed
Plums, small yellow	1 pound	18 plums
Peaches	1 pound	4 medium peaches
Strawberries	1 quart	1 1/2 pounds or 4 1/2 cups or 2 1/2 cups crushed
Tomatoes	1 pound	4 medium-large tomatoes

TABLE OF YIELDS FOR FRUITS

FRUIT	QUANTITY RAW	YIELD IN QUART JARS
Apricots	15 pounds	9
Berries, general	12 quarts	12
Strawberries	12 quarts	9–10
Cherries	6 quarts	5
Peaches	6 quarts	4
Plums, pears	6 quarts	5

Before proceeding with either cold- or hot-pack methods, it is necessary to know the type of syrup required for particular fruit and estimate amount needed. For type of syrup best suited to canning each type of fruit, see charts with discussions of packs.

To Make Syrup. Measure sugar and water according to type of syrup specified (see following list of proportions). Stir in saucepan until sugar dissolves; then heat to boiling. Should scum form, skim it off. Always use syrup boiling hot in either cold- or hot-pack procedures.

For 2 1/2 cups thin syrup, 1 cup sugar to 2 cups water

For 2 cups moderately thin syrup, 1 cup sugar to 1 1/2 cups water

For 1 1/2 cups medium syrup, 1 cup sugar to 1 cup water

For 1 1/4 cups heavy syrup, 1 cup sugar to 3/4 cup water

Allow ample syrup. For cold-pack method, you should estimate 1–1 1/2 cups syrup for each quart of raw berries, strawberries, cherries or rhubarb; 1 1/2–2 cups syrup for larger fruits like apricots, peaches, plums and pears. The size of the fruit or cut pieces has a bearing on the amount of syrup. For example, 12 cups of syrup may be sufficient to do a crate of good berries, whereas 10 cups may be needed for a 6-quart basket of peaches, especially if they are prepared in halves.

The hot-pack method uses less syrup than does the cold-pack method. Allow about 1/2 less syrup for each quart of raw fruit to be canned in this way.

Sort fruit under a good light. Set aside and refrigerate for jam, relish or similar purposes any with blemishes or spots, cutting out bad patches. Carefully wash small amounts of sound fruit in sieve under gently running water. Fruits like raspberries and cherries should be lifted from 1 rinse to another.

To skin peaches or tomatoes, first scald by pouring boiling water over them; let stand 1 minute. Drain, cover with cold water and peel.

Lemon-water dip will prevent peaches, pears, and apples from darkening during preparation. As fruits are peeled, slip pieces into lemon-water, made with 1 cup lemon juice to 5 cups cold water. Put only enough fruit for 3 jars in lemon-water at a time, and work quickly. Lift out fruit, and drain well before precooking or packing. Change water if it becomes discolored.

A special powdered ascorbic acid can be purchased to mix into water to prevent discoloration of fruit. Use according to manufacturer's directions.

BOILING BATH METHOD

FRUIT	PREPARATION	MINUTES OF PROCESSING[°]	
		PINTS	QUARTS
Apples	Use thin syrup. Hot pack: Wash, peel, core and slice or quarter; drop in brine bath; drain; bring to boil in syrup, and simmer 3 minutes; pack hot in hot jars, leaving space at top.	15	15
Applesauce	Make applesauce as usual; pack hot in hot jars, leaving space at top.	15	15
Apricots	Use moderately thin syrup. Cold pack: Wash, but do not peel; halve and pit, or leave whole; pack "cups" down if halved; add boiling syrup, leaving space at top.	20	25
	Hot pack: Prepare fruit; bring to boil in syrup, simmering 2–3 minutes; pack hot, leaving space at top.	15	15
Small berries	Use thin syrup for blueberries, blackberries, raspberries; moderately thin or medium syrup for raspberries; medium or heavy syrup for gooseberries or loganberries. Cold pack: Wash, and pick over (remove ends of gooseberries); pack, cover with boiling syrup, leaving space at top.	15	20
Strawberries	Use moderately thin or medium syrup. Cold pack: Wash, and hull; bring slowly to boil in syrup, and simmer 1 minute; cover, and let stand off heat 1 hour; pack, leaving space at top.	15	20
	Hot pack: Add hulled berries to boiling syrup; cover, and let stand off heat 1 hour; bring to boil; pack, leaving space at top.	10	10
Cherries	Use thin syrup for sweet cherries; medium or heavy for sour cherries. Cold pack: Wash, stem and pit (or not); pack, and cover with boiling syrup, leaving space at top.	20	25
	Hot pack: Wash, stem	15	15

[°]If you live at an altitude over 2,000 feet, the processing times for canning by boiling-bath method will have to be increased by 1/5 for each additional 1,000 feet. For example, if processing time is listed in this chart as 20 minutes, add 4 minutes, if you live at an altitude 2,000–3,000 feet; above 3,000 feet add 2/5 of 20 minutes, or 8 minutes, to processing time.

	and pit (or not); bring to boil in syrup, and simmer 3 minutes; pack hot, leaving space at top.		
Peaches	Use moderately thin syrup.		
	Cold pack: Peel, and pit after blanching 1 minute or less and then cold-dipping; drop in brine; drain; pack as slices or halves, the latter "cup" down; add boiling syrup, leaving space at top.	20	25
	Hot pack: Prepare fruit as for cold pack; bring slices or halves to boiling point in syrup, and simmer 3 minutes; pack hot, leaving space at top.	15	15
Pears	Use thin syrup.		
	Cold pack: Wash, peel, and core; halve or quarter; drop in brine, and drain; pack halves "cup" side down; cover with boiling syrup, leaving space at top.	20	25
	Hot pack: Prepare fruit as for cold pack; bring to boil in syrup, simmering 3–5 minutes, depending on hardness of pears; pack hot, leaving space at top.	10	10
Plums	Use moderately thin syrup for tart plums; thin syrup for prune plums.		
	Cold pack: Wash, and leave whole, or halve and pit; pack, and cover with boiling syrup, leaving space at top.	15	20
	Hot pack: Prepare fruit as for cold pack; bring to boil in syrup, simmering 2 minutes; pack hot, leaving space at top.	10	10
Tomatoes	Cold pack: Peel, and cut out stem ends, after blanching 1/2 minute and then cold-dipping; pack, and add 1 teaspoon salt per quart, 1/2 teaspoon per pint; cover with heated tomato juice; leave space at top. Or press down on tomatoes in jar until covered with their own juice; add salt, leaving space at top; and add extra 5 minutes to processing time.	25(30)	30(35)
	Hot pack: Prepare tomatoes as for cold pack; heat, whole or quartered, to boiling point;	15	15
	pack hot, adding 1 teaspoon salt per quart; leave space at top.		
Grape juice	Hot pack: Wash grapes, stem and crush well; add 2 1/2 cups water per 6-quart basket; bring to boil, and simmer, covered, 15 minutes; strain through moistened jelly bag; add sugar if desired; heat to boiling point, and pour into hot jars, leaving space at top.	10	10
Tomato juice	Hot pack: Wash tomatoes, cut out ends and cut in pieces; bring to boil; simmer, covered, 5 minutes; press through sieve; heat to boiling point; and pour into hot jars, leaving space at top; add 1/2 teaspoon salt per pint. Or obtain juice by using juice extractor; bring juice to boiling point, and pour into hot jars, leaving space at top; salt as in first method.	15 15	15 15

Cold-pack Method. Fill sterilized jars with cold raw fruit (see recipe chart for specific fruits). Cover with boiling syrup. Leave a 1/2-inch space at top. Adjust tops correctly, according to type of jar (see jar-closure directions that follow). Process in hot-water bath.

The cold pack is often preferred because with it fruits (especially berries, though not strawberries) retain their shapes and food values better. The disadvantages of the cold pack are the higher proportion of syrup to fruit in each jar and the sometimes excessive space between processed fruit and lid, although the latter does not affect the keeping qualities.

Hot-pack Method. By this method the fruit is precooked in syrup for a few minutes (see recipe chart). It is then packed in sterilized jars and covered with hot syrup, leaving 1/2-inch space below rims. Tops are correctly adjusted (see jar closures), and jars are ready for processing in hot-water bath. The hot-pack method has certain advantages. It prevents floating fruit, especially strawberries; more fruit may be packed in each jar; processing time is shorter; fruit color stays truer. The chief disadvantage is that more preparation time is required because of precooking.

To Fill Containers. Do not fill more containers than your hot-water processing bath will hold. With the hot-pack method, precook only sufficient fruit to fill 3–5 jars at 1 time.

Place hot empty jars on trivet or cake rack, covered with folded newspaper or towels, to prevent cracking glass.

Fill each container to within 1/2 inch of rim (or 1/4 inch, when using tin cans and sealing machine). Insert knife to bottom of jar to let out air bubbles or tilt jar before sealing. Work quickly.

Adjusting Jar Closures. Two of the most familiar types of jars are sealed only partially before processing. They are the standard glass design with 3-section top and the bail or spring-type jar.

For 3-section top, dip new rubber ring into boiling water; then fit onto jar. Fill jar with fruit and syrup (if necessary, wipe ring and rim clean; a spilled bit of fruit will break seal). Place on glass cap, and screw on metal band firmly as far as it will go; then turn band back about 1/2 inch to allow for expansion.

With bail or spring-type closure, click longer wire into place over glass cup, but leave shorter wire *up*.

In other types of containers—those with flat metal lids or tin cans for machine sealing—sealing is completed before processing. Follow manufacturer's instructions carefully in each case.

Processing in Hot Bath. Have your big kettle ready with several inches of hot—not boiling—water. To prevent cracking of glass, temperature of water should be as close as possible to that of filled jars. Carefully lower jars into water. They should be standing upright, not touching and supported on rack or in basket to permit water to circulate underneath and around. Add enough hot water to cover jars by at least 2 inches. Cover kettle, and place over heat. Count processing time from minute water is actually boiling vigorously. Keep water boiling, and boil only so long as specific recipe directs (see chart).

Remove jars at end of processing time. (A large baster or small dipper is handy to scoop out excess water; canning basket with handles is also ideal at this point.) Place hot jars on layer of newspapers or crumpled towels. When contents have ceased bubbling, *complete seal* on regular or bail-type jars. Screw metal ring tight on 3-section tops. Push short wire down on spring-top jars.

Do not touch top again until opening for table use. To retighten top after jar has cooled can break seal and spoil contents. Do not be concerned about empty space at the top, as everything inside the container has been sterilized. Never attempt to open a jar after processing in order to "fill it up."

Let jars cool in upright position; do not cover them. Let tin cans cool in cold water, and keep adding cold water to hasten cooling.

When cool, test for leakage by inverting each screw-top or spring-top jar for 2–3 minutes. If a jar leaks, do not attempt to reprocess, but use contents within a few days. On the vacuum-type jar a complete seal is identified by a ringing sound when the lid is tapped with a spoon.

Wipe all containers with a damp cloth; then dry and label.

Store in cool, dark place. Cover canned fruit with pad of newspaper if necessary to absorb dampness in the atmosphere and to keep out light. With this protection, the metal bands will not corrode, and the fruit will not fade.

In home canning do not use canning compounds, sulphur compounds, chemicals like boracic acid or salicylic acid or saccharine. Such additions can be harmful.

Vitamin C (ascorbic acid) is sometimes used in canning peaches and pears, in order to prevent discoloration in canned fruit during storage. This additive is obtainable from the drugstore. Place powder or tablet in bottom of each jar before filling with fruit and syrup. Allow 1/16 teaspoon powder or one 25-milligram tablet for each jar (pint or quart).

Pressure Canning. *Pressure canning is the only safe way to preserve the nonacid vegetables, because it ensures a high enough temperature to destroy organisms.*

The warning cannot be repeated too often: *do not* attempt home canning of nonacid vegetables without a pressure cooker. It is true that tomatoes, because of their high acid content, may be safely processed in jars in a hot-water bath (see preceding section for full directions). But such vegetables as asparagus, beans, corn, peas and squash must be raised to temperatures above that of boiling water; otherwise harmful microorganisms that can cause illness, and even death, may continue to live and grow in the stored product. A pressure cooker, properly used, gives temperatures necessary to assure destruction of harmful organisms in nonacid vegetables.

A few jars at a time may be canned in the regular pressure saucepan, but homemakers who wish to can frequently and in quantity would be wise to invest in a pressure canner.

In addition to pressure equipment, you will need some of the utensils outlined for home canning of fruits.

Choose fresh, firm, tender vegetables, free from blemishes. Wash, and sort for size and quality; then peel, trim, shell or husk. Cut, and precook according to kind (see chart on Pressure Canner Method).

Packing

Have hot sterilized jars ready. Pack hot vegetables quickly, and cover with boiling water, leaving 1/2–1 inch space at top—the larger allowance for corn and peas, the lesser for other vegetables (in using tin cans, allow 1/2 inch space at top for corn and peas, 1/4 inch for other vegetables). Add 1 teaspoon salt to each quart container, 1/2 teaspoon to each pint. Work out air bubbles by running knife blade around inside of jar.

Pressure Canning Procedure

1. Check cleanliness of petcock and safety valve by running toothpick around them. Do not put gauge in water: Make sure gasket fits snugly; replace when necessary.

2. Pour 2 inches hot water into canner. Place filled containers on rack, allowing space around each. If canning only 4 or 5 jars, add 3 extra cups hot water. You must have 2 quarts water in the canner.

3. In using machine-sealed tin cans, a second row of tin cans may be added, preferably on a cake rack and arranged for uneven distribution (not directly on top of one another).

4. Fasten lid on securely. Keep petcock open until steam escapes in steady stream with hissing sound, 5–10 minutes.

5. Close petcock, and allow pressure to rise slowly until gauge indicates required pressure, usually over medium or low heat (not high). Set a "minute minder" as soon as desired pressure is reached.

6. Turn heat low, but not off, to maintain constant pressure.

7. At end of specified canning time, move canner to a board, and allow pressure to drop gradually to 0.

8. Slowly open petcock. Let canner cool about 2 minutes longer.

9. Remove lid, tilting it away from face. Place towel over canner to absorb excess steam 2 minutes; then remove towel.

10. Leave containers in canner until bubbling ceases; lift out, and complete jar seals. Let cool. Label and store. (Tin cans should be placed in cold water immediately. Leave cans in cold water until cold. Label and store.)

A pressure saucepan equipped with accurate indicator or gauge for controlling pressure at 10 pounds (240°F.) may be used as a steam-pressure canner for processing vegetables in pint jars or 20-ounce tin cans. *If you use a pressure saucepan, add 20 minutes to processing times listed on Pressure Canner Method chart for pint containers.*

Never place pressure pan or cooker in cold water to reduce pressure.

All home-canned vegetables except tomatoes should be opened and boiled 10 minutes before they are tasted and served.

PRESSURE CANNER METHOD

VEGETABLE	PREPARATION	MINUTES OF PROCESSING*	
		PINTS	QUARTS
Asparagus	Wash, and break off tough ends of stalks; remove scales if necessary to help wash away sand; cut into lengths to fit containers; tie in uniform bundles, and stand upright in sufficient boiling water to come 1/2 way up stalks; cover, bring to boil and boil 3 minutes; pack hot, all tips up except a few in center, to help keep stalks upright.	30	35
Beans, green or wax	Wash young tender beans; trim ends and string if necessary; leave whole or cut in pieces; cover with boiling water; bring to boil and boil, covered, 3 minutes; pack hot; add salt; cover with hot cooking liquid from beans, leaving space at top.	30	35
Beets	Wash small young beets; leave on roots and 2 inches of stem; cover with boiling water; bring to boil, and boil, covered until skins slip off easily, about 20 minutes; remove skins and roots;	30	35

*At 10-pound pressure; increase pressure 1 pound for each additional 1,000 feet after 2,000 feet above sea level.

	pack hot, adding salt; cover with boiling water, leaving space at top.		
Greens: spinach, chard, beet tops	Wash thoroughly; cook, covered, in very little water until thoroughly wilted, 5–8 minutes, turning several times during cooking; pack hot, loosely; cut greens crosswise with sharp knife to bottom of container; add salt; cover with boiling water, leaving space at top.	50	60
Peas	Shell and wash young tender peas; cover with boiling water; bring to boil, and boil, covered,	40	45

	1 minute; pack hot, loosely; add salt; cover with hot cooking liquid from peas, leaving space at top.		
Pumpkin and squash	Cut or break apart; remove seeds and stringy fibers; cut into pieces; steam, bake or boil in small amount of water until tender; scrape from skins, and mash or sieve; bring to boiling point, adding little water, if necessary, to prevent scorching; pack hot, leaving space at top.	70	80
Tomatoes	See Boiling-Bath Method chart.		

4
~
Creative Baking

Baking is the test of delicate cookery—an imaginative art and a careful science.

Today's kitchen makes baking easier than ever before. And, with freezers, what you bake today can be stored for later use.

If you don't have time to bake a fancy cake all at once (which means baking cake, making filling, making icing—3 distinct operations) you can make a batch of fillings and icings 1 day, and refrigerate them. Another day, you can make cake layers. Or turn out a recipe of tiny tart shells or some *vol-au-vent* shells which can be filled with either sweet or savory mixtures. But whenever you do bake make sure you measure accurately and time carefully. Recipes offer directions for achieving perfect products, so follow them.

Ingredients. *Know the characteristics of various flours, fats, leaveners and liquids; how to measure each, and how to adjust for substitution.*

Flour is the essential ingredient of all baked products, and there are different flours suited to different types of baking. Flour made from soft wheat is excellent for cakes.

Hard-wheat flour contains the strong gluten necessary for yeast products but may also be used for cakes and pastry when coarser texture is sought. As it can be used for all baking, it is sold as *all-purpose flour*.

Self-rising flour (found only in some areas), as its name indicates, contains a leavening agent; to use it successfully the specific recipes accompanying the package must be followed. In following any baking recipe, the most satisfactory results will be achieved if you use the type of flour called for. If it is necessary to substitute all-purpose for cake flour, reduce quantity, using 7/8 cup sifted all-purpose flour for 1 cup sifted cake flour. (A quick and easy way to measure 7/8 cup of flour is to fill 1 cup level and then to remove 2 level tablespoons.) But if possible it is best to avoid such substitutions. For accuracy, flour should be sifted before measuring. For convenience, sift over sheet of waxed paper; then lightly spoon flour into standard dry measuring cup, heaping slightly above rim. Then level with straight-edged knife or spatula. The important point to remember is *never* to pack flour into measuring cup or to bang cup on table to shake down flour.

Use granulated *sugar* for most baking. Superfine sugar is used when an extremely fine texture is desired, for instance in angel food cake. Brown sugar is somewhat moist, and measurements are given for "firmly packed" amounts. To pack firmly, press down enough so that sugar holds its shape when turned out of cup. As confectioners' sugar packs down and lumps easily, it should be sifted before measuring.

Leavening action causes dough to rise, making it lighter, more digestible and more palatable. Rising may be achieved in several ways. One is by incorporation of air, as in beating egg whites for angel food cake in which no other leavening is used. Another is by quick formation of steam, as in popovers or cream puffs. A third is by addition of baking powder, baking soda or yeast.

There are 2 kinds of *baking powder*: quick acting and double acting. The first starts its function on contact with the moisture in the mixture and slowly continues its action. The second, as its name implies, works in 2 stages: first, on contact with liquid ingredients and, second, when subjected to heat. Nevertheless these 2 types of baking powder are usually interchangeable in practically all kinds of home baking. Baking powder should be stored covered and dry in cool place. A combination of moisture and heat will cause it to deteriorate in leavening ability.

Yeast is a tiny living plant that produces carbon dioxide gas, causing dough to rise. There are 2 kinds of yeast available today: active dry yeast, granulated in form, and cakes of compressed fresh yeast. Dry yeast needs no refrigeration, but it should be used before expiration date printed on each package. The 2 kinds of yeast may be used interchangeably. One envelope of active dry yeast is equal to 1/2 ounce of compressed fresh yeast. To substitute fresh yeast for active dry yeast, crumble yeast cake over water as directed on package.

Skim and whole *milk* may be used interchangeably. When using instant nonfat dry milk, follow manufacturer's directions. Sometimes dry milk is reconstituted with water before adding to mixture, or it may be preferable to combine it with dry ingredients and stir in water later. Sour milk and buttermilk are interchangeable. Add 1 tablespoon vinegar to each cup of fresh milk, and let stand a few minutes before using, to sour.

To measure liquids accurately, use liquid measuring cup. Set measuring cup at eye level, and fill it exactly to measuring mark. Do not dip measure *into* honey, molasses or other thick liquids; instead, pour from container into measuring spoon or cup. If you lightly grease or wet measure, sticky liquids will not cling.

Shortening is often used as a general term for any type of fat. When specified in a recipe however, it refers to emulsified shortening, which may be all vegetable or a mixture of vegetable and animal. Lard, which is not emulsified, is usually used only for pastry. Butter and margarine may be used interchangeably, but if you substitute shortening for butter or margarine, use 7/8 cup of shortening for each cup of butter, and add 1/2 teaspoon of salt.

There are several ways to measure shortening:

1. Press fat (at room temperature) firmly into standard measuring cup or individual measures.

2. Use water-displacement method when shortening is cold and hard. To measure 1/2 cup shortening, fill 1-cup measure to the 1/2-cup mark with water. Add shortening in pieces until water reaches 1-cup level.

3. The 1-pound packages of various emulsified shortenings generally have printed measuring marks, and they are helpful. Remember that whereas 1 pound of butter, margarine or lard measures 2 cups, the same weight in modern shortenings yields 2 1/3 cups.

Recipe for Successful Baking

1. Assemble all necessary ingredients and utensils.

2. Preheat oven to required temperature. The oven heat specified in a recipe must be used from first moment of baking.

3. Measure out quantities of each ingredient in advance, to expedite proper combining at the right moment in your recipe.

TABLE OF MEASURES

1 pint	=	16 ounces* (2 cups)
1 quart	=	32 ounces* (4 cups)
1 gallon	=	128 ounces* (16 cups)
1 tablespoon	=	3 teaspoons
16 tablespoons	=	1 cup
1 cup	=	8 ounces*
1/2 cup	=	8 tablespoons
1/3 cup	=	5 1/3 tablespoons
1/4 cup	=	4 tablespoons
1 pound	=	16 ounces (dry measure)

TABLE OF EQUIVALENTS*

Butter, margarine	1 pound = 2 cups
	1 ounce = 2 tablespoons
Cheese, shredded	1 pound = 4 cups
Cornmeal	1 pound = 3 cups
Heavy cream, unwhipped	1 cup = 2 cups whipped
Currants, seedless raisins	1 pound = 3 cups
Dates, pitted and chopped	1 pound = 2 cups
Egg whites	8–11 = 1 cup
Egg yolks	12–14 = 1 cup
Flour, cake and pastry, sifted	1 pound = 4 cups
all-purpose, sifted	1 pound = 3 3/4 cups
whole wheat, unsifted	1 pound = 3 2/3 cups
Lemons, juice from 1 medium	= 3 tablespoons
grated rind from 1 medium	= 1 tablespoon
Almonds, shelled	1 pound = 3 1/2 cups
Walnuts, whole, shelled	1 pound = 4 cups
finely chopped	1 pound = 1 3/4 cups
Marshmallows	8 ounces = 32 large
Sugar, brown, lightly packed	1 pound = 3 cups
granulated	1 pound = 2 1/4 cups
confectioners', sifted	1 pound = 3 1/2 cups

*Equivalent amounts are approximate.

SUBSTITUTIONS*

1 teaspoon baking powder = 1/4 teaspoon baking soda plus 1/2 teaspoon of cream of tartar

1 ounce (1 square) chocolate = 3 tablespoons cocoa plus 3/4 tablespoon fat

1 tablespoon cornstarch = 2 tablespoons flour or 2 tablespoons quick-cooking tapioca (for thickening)

1 cup all-purpose flour = 1 cup plus 2 tablespoons cake and pastry flour

1 whole egg = 2 egg yolks (in custards) or 2 egg yolks plus 1 tablespoon water (in cookies)

1 cup whole milk = 1/2 cup each evaporated milk and water or 4 tablespoons powdered milk plus 1 cup water

1 cup sour milk = 1 cup milk plus 1 tablespoon lemon juice or vinegar (allow to stand)

1 cup honey = 1 cup sugar plus 1/4 cup liquid

*As mentioned previously, it is best to use the ingredients called for in the recipe.

Quick Breads. "Quick" breads are so called because they are made with quick-acting leavening agents: baking powder, baking soda or steam as distinct from those leavened with yeast. There are many varieties and many different methods of cooking. Quick breads may be baked in the oven, as with muffins, popovers, baking-powder biscuits and tea breads; deep-fried, as with fritters and doughnuts; steamed, as with dumplings, Boston steamed bread and steamed puddings; cooked on griddle, as with pancakes; cooked in a frying pan, as with crêpes, or cooked on waffle iron as with waffles. All can be made quickly, shortly before the meal, and served hot, except for the tea breads which are better if sliced cold.

The packaged convenience items—mixes for muffins, breads, pancakes and biscuits; refrigerated biscuits, ready to slice and bake, frozen biscuits, waffles and doughnuts—are very good.

Biscuits

The dough has many uses. It may be the foundation for berry shortcakes or fruit cobblers. You can use it to make topping for savory meat pie, either whole topping or cut into rounds, or to cover individual casseroles or meat pies. And you can vary the flavor to complement other foods served. To make biscuits and toppings light and flaky *cut* rather than mash shortening into flour mixture. Add liquid *all at once*, and stir mixture quickly with fork to make soft, unsticky dough. Knead dough very gently on lightly floured surface to distribute ingredients. Roll or pat dough gently to desired thickness—good biscuits will double in height during baking.

Baking-powder Biscuits

> 2 cups all-purpose flour
> 4 teaspoons baking powder
> 1 teaspoon salt
> 1/3 cup shortening
> 3/4 cup milk

Sift flour, baking powder and salt in mixing bowl. Cut in shortening with pastry blender or 2 knives until mixture has texture of quick-cooking oatmeal. Add milk; stir with fork to make soft dough. An extra tablespoon of milk may be used if mixture seems too stiff. Place on lightly floured board, and knead gently 8–10 times. Roll or pat dough to desired thickness, and cut with floured cutter. Pat leftover dough together, and cut

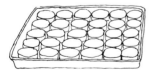 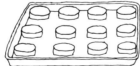

again. Place biscuits on ungreased baking sheet, close together for soft-sided biscuits or about 1 inch apart for crusty ones. Bake 12–15 minutes at 450°F. Makes 18–20 biscuits, (approximately 1 3/4 inches in diameter).

VARIATIONS:

Sour-milk Biscuits: Replace milk with sour milk or buttermilk; substitute 1/4 teaspoon baking soda for 1 teaspoon baking powder.

Savory Biscuits: Add 1 teaspoon poppy seeds, 1/2 teaspoon sage and 1/4 teaspoon dry mustard to flour mixture.

Cheese Biscuits: Add 3/4 cup grated Cheddar or Swiss cheese to flour mixture.

Vegetable Sticks: Add 1 teaspoon celery salt and 1 teaspoon parsley flakes to flour mixture. Roll dough 1/4 inch thick, cut into fingers 5 inches long, 1/2 inch wide. Place on ungreased baking sheet. Brush with butter or margarine. Sprinkle with sesame seeds before baking.

Drop Biscuits: Add 1/3 cup additional milk. Drop dough from tablespoon onto greased baking sheet.

Butterscotch Pinwheels: Cream 1/3 cup butter or margarine, blend in 2/3 cup brown sugar. Set aside. Roll out dough into 9-inch square. Spread sugar mixture over it; roll up as for jelly roll. Dampen edges to seal. Slice into 3/4-inch pieces; place, cut side down, in greased muffin pans. Bake in preheated 450°F. oven 12–15 minutes. To remove, invert pan immediately. Makes 12 biscuits.

Fruit Pinwheels: Add 1/2 cup currants or raisins to brown-sugar mixture when making BUTTERSCOTCH PINWHEELS.

Whole Wheat Biscuits: Substitute 1 cup whole wheat or graham flour for 1 cup all-purpose flour, and mix with dry ingredients.

Scones

> 1 3/4 cups all-purpose flour
> 1 tablespoon baking powder
> 1 tablespoon sugar
> 1/2 teaspoon salt
> 1/4 cup shortening
> 1/2 cup currants or raisins
> 2 eggs, beaten
> 1/2 cup milk or cream

Sift flour, baking powder, sugar and salt in large bowl. Cut in shortening with blender or

2 knives until mixture resembles coarse oatmeal. Add currants. Reserve 2 tablespoons of beaten egg, and mix remainder with milk. Make well in dry ingredients, and add milk mixture. Stir quickly with fork. Place dough on lightly floured surface. Knead gently 8–10 times. Divide dough

in 1/2. Pat or gently roll each 1/2 until 3/4 inch thick and circular in shape. Transfer to cookie

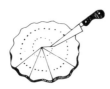

sheet or layer pans. Brush with remaining egg. Score into wedge-shaped pieces. Bake 10–12 minutes at 450°F.

Sweet Biscuit Dough

    1 cup all-purpose flour
    1 tablespoon sugar
    2 teaspoons baking powder
    1/4 teaspoon salt
    3 tablespoons shortening
    1 egg, beaten
    1/3 cup milk

Sift dry ingredients and cut in shortening with pastry blender or 2 knives till mixture is fine grained. Add egg and milk, and stir with fork to make drop batter. Makes 1 dozen.

Note: Use this dough for fruit cobblers.

Orange-glazed Biscuits

    1/4 cup butter or margarine
    1/2 cup orange juice
    1/2 cup sugar
    2 teaspoons grated orange rind
    2 cups all-purpose flour
    1 tablespoon baking powder
    1/2 teaspoon salt
    1/4 cup shortening
    3/4 cup milk
    2 tablespoons melted butter or margarine
    1/3 cup sugar
    1/2 teaspoon cinnamon

Combine first 4 ingredients and cook 2 minutes; pour into 9 greased muffin cups. Sift to-

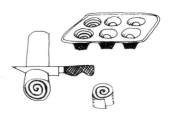

gether flour, baking powder and salt; cut in shortening. Add milk, and stir with fork to make soft dough. Place on lightly floured board, and knead gently 4 or 5 times. Roll out to 1/4 inch thick. Brush with melted butter or margarine; mix sugar and cinnamon, and sprinkle over dough. Roll up as for jelly roll, cut in 1-inch slices and place, cut side down, over orange mixture in muffin pans. Bake at 450°F. 20–25 minutes.

Popovers, Corn Bread, and Similar Batters

Popovers

    1 tablespoon melted shortening
    1 cup all-purpose flour
    1/4 teaspoon salt
    3 eggs
    1 cup milk
    1 tablespoon vegetable oil or melted shortening

Preheat oven to 425°F. Brush muffin pans well with 1 tablespoon melted shortening, and heat pans in oven while preparing batter. Put flour and salt in large bowl. Beat eggs well; then stir in milk and vegetable oil. Make well in flour, pour in egg mixture and beat until smooth. Pour batter into hot pans, filling them 1/3 full. Bake at 425°F. 20 minutes; reduce heat to 325°F. and bake 15 minutes longer. Serve at once. Makes 6–8 popovers.

Note: To prevent sogginess, remove baked popovers from pans as soon as they come from oven, and insert knife in side of each to let out steam. They should be served at once.

VARIATION:

Yorkshire Pudding: Remove roast beef from pan, and keep warm. Raise oven temperature to 475°F. Pour 3 tablespoons beef drippings into an 8″ x 11 1/2″ x 2″ baking pan, and heat in oven while preparing batter. Pour popover batter into hot pan; bake at 475°F. 15 minutes. Reduce heat to 350°F., and bake 15 minutes longer. Cut in squares, and serve immediately with roast beef.

Corn Bread (Johnnycake)

    3/4 cup all-purpose flour
    1/4 cup sugar
    4 teaspoons baking powder
    1/2 teaspoon salt
    1 cup yellow or white cornmeal

1 egg, beaten
1 cup milk
1/4 cup vegetable oil or melted shortening

Preheat oven to 375°F. Combine flour, sugar, baking powder and salt. Mix in cornmeal, and make well in center. Combine egg, milk and veg-

etable oil; then stir quickly into dry ingredients until combined. Pour into greased 8-inch square cake pan. Bake 25–30 minutes at 375°F. Cut into squares. Or bake in corn-stick pans 15 minutes. Serve warm. Makes 16 squares.

VARIATION:

Ham–Corn Bread: Add 1/2 cup finely diced ham to batter.

Pancakes, Waffles and Crêpes

The general term "pancakes" includes 3 basic types. The thin, rich pancakes that the French call "crêpes" are usually served as dessert, with sugar sprinkled over them and wedges of lemon, rolled up with jam or with various sauces. For crêpes suzette, pour a liqueur sauce over pancakes and set aflame.

We are more familiar with the kind called "hotcakes" ("griddle cakes," "flapjacks"), which are a heartier version of the Scottish griddle cake. Then there are waffles, which are lighter and crisper, made from thinner batter in an iron designed to expose more of the surface to the heat and develop more crustiness.

All these pancakes are made with pouring batters, made by adding liquids to dry ingredients and beating only until flour is incorporated. The batter may be lumpy. Waffle and French pancake batters, however, should be beaten until smooth.

To bake pancakes, heat griddle or electric frying pan to 380°F. or until a drop of cold water will "dance" across it. Grease lightly with unsalted fat, unless you have a special grill that does not require greasing. Bake pancake on the first side until its top is covered with bubbles and edges start to lose their gloss. Using spatula, turn cake, and bake other side until golden brown. If batter thickens as it stands or if a very thin pancake is preferred, add more liquid.

To keep pancakes hot, place between folds of a towel in a warm oven as soon as they are cooked. Do not stack pancakes while you keep them hot; stacking causes sogginess.

For waffles, preheat waffle iron as directed (greasing is usually not necessary), and pour required amount of batter in center. Close iron, and bake until waffle stops steaming. Lift out carefully with fork. A 9-inch square waffle iron requires about 1 cup batter; a 7-inch round iron takes about 1/2 cup batter. To keep waffles warm, place on cookie sheet (do not stack) in warm oven.

Pancakes

1 1/2 cups all-purpose flour
2 tablespoons sugar
1 tablespoon baking powder
1/2 teaspoon salt
1 egg, beaten
1 1/2 cups milk
2 tablespoons vegetable oil or melted shortening

Mix flour, sugar, baking powder and salt together in bowl. Combine egg, milk and oil. Make well in dry ingredients, and pour in egg mixture. Beat only until combined. Heat griddle or frying pan to 380°F. or until drop of cold water will "dance" across the surface. Grease with unsalted oil or shortening if necessary. Allow about 1/4 cup batter (use individual measure) for each 4-inch pancake. Bake until top of pancake is covered with bubbles and edges begin to lose their gloss. Turn cakes, and bake until golden brown. Makes 12–14 pancakes.

VARIATIONS:

Corn Pancakes: Add 1/2 cup well-drained corn kernels to batter.

Nut Pancakes: Add 1/4 cup chopped nuts to batter.

Ham Pancakes: Omit sugar, and add 1/2–1 cup chopped ham to batter.

Blueberry Pancakes: Fold 1/2 cup fresh blueberries into batter.

Pineapple Pancakes: Add 1/2 cup drained crushed pineapple to batter. Serve with butter or margarine and honey.

Sour-milk Pancakes

```
        1  egg
1 1/4  cups sour milk
  1/2  teaspoon baking soda
1 1/2  cups all-purpose flour
    1  teaspoon baking powder
    2  teaspoons sugar
  1/2  teaspoon salt
    2  tablespoons vegetable oil or melted shortening
```

Beat egg well. Stir sour milk and soda together, and add mixture to egg, blending well. Mix flour with sugar, baking powder and salt, and stir into milk mixture; add shortening. Beat mixture well until smooth, pour from tablespoon onto griddle, and bake as directed above. Makes 12–14 pancakes.

Fluffy Breakfast Pancakes

```
    3  egg yolks
1 1/2  cups sour milk or buttermilk
    1  teaspoon baking soda
1 1/4  cups all-purpose flour
    2  teaspoons sugar
    1  teaspoon baking powder
  1/2  teaspoon salt
    3  tablespoons softened butter or margarine
    3  egg whites
```

Beat egg yolks well; stir sour milk and soda together, and stir into egg yolks. Mix flour with sugar, baking powder and salt, and add to milk mixture. Then beat in butter or margarine. Beat egg whites until they hold stiff peaks, and fold into batter. Drop from tablespoon onto hot griddle and bake as directed above. Yield: 14–16 pancakes.

Waffles

```
1 1/2  cups all-purpose flour
    2  tablespoons sugar
    1  tablespoon baking powder
  1/4  teaspoon salt
    2  eggs, separated
1 1/2  cups milk
  1/2  cup vegetable oil or melted shortening
```

Heat waffle iron. Sift flour, sugar, baking powder and salt into bowl. Beat egg whites to form soft peaks. Beat yolks; add milk and oil, and beat to blend. Make well in flour mixture, pour in

milk mixture and beat until smooth; then fold in beaten whites. When waffle iron is hot enough, pour batter into center of griddle and cook, following manufacturer's directions. Do not raise cover until waffle stops steaming. When done, loosen waffle with fork, and serve hot with butter or margarine and warm maple syrup. Makes about 6 7-inch waffles.

VARIATIONS:

Apple Waffles: Fold 1/2–1 cup grated apple into batter. Serve with sausages or alone.

Cheese Waffles: Add 1/2 cup shredded aged Cheddar cheese to batter. Serve topped with creamed ham and mushrooms or creamed asparagus.

Spice Waffles: Add 1 teaspoon cinnamon and 1/2 teaspoon nutmeg to dry ingredients. Serve topped with ice cream and BUTTERSCOTCH SAUCE.

Crêpes

```
      4  eggs
1 1/2  cups milk
1 1/3  cups all-purpose flour
      2  tablespoons sugar
  1/4  teaspoon salt
  1/4  cup butter or margarine, melted and cooled
      1  teaspoon vanilla extract
1/2–1  teaspoon grated orange or lemon rind
      1  teaspoon butter or margarine
Sifted confectioners' sugar
```

Beat eggs in small bowl and stir in dry ingredients. Add milk and next 3 ingredients. Strain and allow batter to stand at least 30 minutes or as long as 2 hours. Melt 1 teaspoon butter or margarine in frying pan of 5-inch diameter; when hot, pour in about 2 tablespoons batter or enough to cover thinly the bottom of the pan. Cook 1 minute; then turn, and cook other side. Lift out and keep warm; sprinkle with sifted sugar. Proceed until all batter is used. Accompany with crushed or sweetened fresh fruit and whipped cream. Makes approximately 16–18 crêpes. (Allow 3 or 4 to a serving).

Note: These French dessert pancakes have a characteristic texture: delicate, almost like custard; and because they roll or fold without cracking they are often served with filling. Be careful to beat batter just until smooth, as overbeating toughens mixture. To cook crêpes evenly, use heavy small pan that is flat on bottom. Cook just 1 crêpe at a time in butter heated until bubbly but not allowed to burn dark. Tilt pan after adding measured batter, so that crêpes will be uniformly round. Turn them just once. Keep warm until all are cooked and ready to serve. Crêpes freeze well and can be quickly defrosted and reheated in dessert sauce. To freeze, leave flat or fold as desired; let cool completely. Then stack with waxed paper between layers. Wrap airtight and freeze.

VARIATIONS:

Crêpes Suzette: Cream together 2/3 cup sifted confectioners sugar, 1/3 cup soft butter or margarine, 1/2 cup orange juice, 3 tablespoons curaçao and 1 teaspoon grated orange rind. Heat until bubbly before adding the crêpes. Sprinkle with 1 teaspoon sugar, pour 1 ounce heated brandy on top and ignite.

Crêpes with Apricot Sauce: Combine in saucepan 1 cup apricot nectar, 1/4 cup sugar, 1 tablespoon each lemon juice and brandy. Heat crêpes in this mixture.

Crêpes with Jam: When each pancake is cooked,

spread with jam, roll as for jelly roll, dust with

confectioners' sugar and keep hot. Or spread each pancake with jam, do not roll but stack 6 or 8. To serve, cut back into wedges as you would a pie.

Crêpes Gismonda

2-ounce package white sauce
  2 tablespoons grated cheese
  2 (10-ounce) packages thawed, drained frozen spinach
  2 tablespoons chopped onion
  2 tablespoons butter or margarine
  1 cup sliced mushrooms
 12 8-inch crêpes
1/4 cup grated Swiss cheese

Prepare the package of white sauce according to directions, adding at least 2 tablespoons grated cheese. To the frozen spinach, add the chopped onion, sautéed in the butter or margarine. Add the sliced mushrooms. Cook 5 minutes. Fill the crêpes. Arrange seam-side down in shallow buttered baking dish. Coat with sauce. Sprinkle with grated Swiss cheese. Bake at 350° 10 minutes or until cheese is golden. Serves 6.

Chicken Crêpes

1/4 cup butter or margarine
1/2 cup all-purpose flour
  2 cups milk
1/2 teaspoon salt
  2 cups diced cooked chicken
  1 cup diced sautéed mushrooms
 12 thin crêpes made without sugar, vanilla extract and orange rind
  2 cups seasoned cooked spinach
  1 cup whipped cream
1/2 cup grated Parmesan cheese

Melt butter or margarine in saucepan, and stir in flour. Mix well, and add milk gradually. Add salt, and stir constantly until mixture comes to a boil; then stir quickly, and cook over low heat 10 minutes or until thick and smooth. Divide sauce in 1/2. Mix chicken and mushrooms with 1/2 the sauce. Spread each crêpe with chicken mixture, and roll up. Butter 12-inch baking dish, and spread bottom with bed of cooked spinach. Set filled pancakes on spinach, and spread with remaining sauce. Top with thin layer of whipped cream, and sprinkle with Parmesan cheese. Bake at 450°F. 10 minutes; then broil quickly until top is glazed. Serves 8.

Hot Milk Pancakes

  1 cup milk
  2 tablespoons butter or margarine
  2 eggs, beaten
1/2 cup all-purpose flour
  2 teaspoons sugar
  1 teaspoon baking powder
1/2 teaspoon salt
Jelly (optional)
Confectioners' sugar

Heat milk and butter or margarine in saucepan, and cool slightly. Add eggs, and beat well.

Sift next 4 ingredients together, and add to egg mixture. Use small frying pan about 5 or 6 inches across. Pour in only enough batter to coat bottom of pan thinly, tipping frying pan so that batter runs around. Cook each side 1 minute, and turn cakes again if not sufficiently browned. Makes 14–16. Serve rolled, with jelly filling if desired, and dusted with confectioners' sugar.

Doughnuts

The secret of achieving a crisp, though tender, golden outer crust and a fluffy, dry interior lies in the temperature of your cooking fat; if it's too low, hot fat will permeate the food and make it soggy and less digestible. To maintain the correct temperature, an electric control is best. Doughnuts and fritters can be cooked easily in an electric frying pan and even better in an electric deep-fryer. But even without these conveniences, your deep-frying can be successful if you maintain correct frying temperature of 375°F. throughout the process. When you put cold, uncooked foods into hot fat, the temperature immediately falls. If you have temperature slightly over 375°F. *before* you start frying and remember to put only a few pieces at a time into fat, temperature will not fall below 375°F. during the frying.

Doughnuts

    2 eggs, separated
    1 cup sugar
    3 tablespoons shortening
    3/4 cup sour milk or buttermilk
 3 1/4 cups all-purpose flour
    2 teaspoons baking powder
    1 teaspoon baking soda
    1 teaspoon salt
    1/4 teaspoon nutmeg
    1/2 teaspoon cinnamon

Beat egg whites until stiff; set aside. Beat egg yolks well. Beat in sugar and shortening, and stir in sour milk. Sift dry ingredients together. Stir 1/2 dry ingredients into egg-yolk mixture until smooth. Fold in beaten egg whites; then stir in remaining dry ingredients. Cover, and chill 1/2 hour. Turn dough onto lightly floured board, and roll to 3/8-inch thickness. Cut out with floured doughnut cutter. Fry in deep fat at 375°F. about 1 minute on each side. Drain on absorbent paper. Makes 28 doughnuts (2 1/2-inch cutter size).

Note: To sugar, shake while still warm in brown paper bag with 1/2 cup sugar and 1/2 teaspoon cinnamon. *To glaze*, gradually add 1/3 cup boiling water to 2 cups sifted confectioners' sugar, mixing well; dip one side of warm doughnut into glaze, and set on cake rack to drain.

Fritters: Savory or Sweet

Fritters are made by coating fruit or vegetable pieces in thin batter and frying them in deep fat. Similar batters may be used to coat seafoods or chicken pieces for deep frying. Sometimes a thicker batter is used, and chopped foods mixed into it, to make a sort of fritter that may serve as a main-course item. You will probably see the similarity to dumplings, and in fact we have included dumplings in this section because they are similar in consistency, though of course they are cooked by steaming over hot liquids and fritters by immersion in hot fat.

Savory Fritter Batter

    1 cup all-purpose flour
    2 teaspoons baking powder
    1 teaspoon salt
    2 eggs
    2/3 cup milk
    1 tablespoon vegetable oil or melted shortening

Sift together flour, baking powder and salt. Beat eggs; add milk and oil. Make well in dry ingredients, blend in liquid, and beat well until smooth. Use as directed to coat foods for deep-frying. Makes 2 1/3 cups.

VARIATIONS:

Chicken in Batter: Partially cook chicken pieces by simmering. Cool and pat dry. Dip each piece in batter and fry in deep fat at 375°F. for 6–8 minutes, or until crisp and golden brown.

Shrimp in Batter: Clean 1 pound fresh or frozen shrimp and pat dry. Use 1/2 the recipe for SAVORY FRITTER BATTER for this amount of shrimp, and proceed as for chicken in batter, cooking only 3–4 minutes.

Note: It is important not to overcook shrimp.

French-fried Cauliflower: Cook 1 medium cauliflower until just tender; cool, and separate into flowerets. Prepare 1/2 SAVORY FRITTER BATTER recipe, dip cauliflower pieces in batter and fry at 375°F. 3–4 minutes or until evenly browned. Serve as is or with cheese sauce.

French-fried Onion Rings: Slice medium-sized onions about 1/3 inch thick, and separate into rings. Prepare 1 recipe SAVORY FRITTER BATTER, less if only a few onions are to be used. Dip each ring into batter, shaking gently to remove excess; fry a few at a time in deep fat preheated to 375°F. Drain well, and keep warm (place rings on cake rack to prevent steaming).

Sweet Fritter Batter

    1/2 cup all-purpose flour
      1 tablespoon sugar
      1 teaspoon baking powder
    1/4 teaspoon salt
      1 egg
    1/3 cup milk
  1 1/2 teaspoon vegetable oil or melted shortening

Combine flour, sugar, baking powder and salt. Beat egg; add milk and oil. Make well in dry ingredients, blend in liquid mixture and beat until very smooth. Use as directed to coat foods for deep-frying. Makes about 1 cup.

Note: Halved bananas and fresh or canned (drained) peaches or pears in suitably sized pieces may be cooked in this batter.

Apple-ring Fritters

    4–5 apples, unpeeled and cored
      1 tablespoon lemon juice
    1/4 cup sugar
      1 recipe SWEET FRITTER BATTER
      1 tablespoon sugar
      1 teaspoon cinnamon

Slice apples crosswide 1/4–1/3 inch thick. Sprinkle with lemon juice, and let stand while preparing batter. Dust slices with 1/4 cup sugar; dip each in batter. Shake off any excess batter, and drop in deep fat preheated to 375°F. Cook 3–4 minutes, turning so that slices brown evenly. Keep fritters warm in 300°F. oven until all apple rings are cooked. Sprinkle with 1 tablespoon sugar and cinnamon, and serve as accompaniment for meat or as a dessert with LEMON SAUCE or cream. Makes 4–5 servings.

Note: Canned pineapple rings or apricot halves can be substituted for apples.

Soufflé Fritters

    1/4 cup butter or margarine
    1/2 cup cold water
  1 1/2 teaspoons sugar
  Pinch salt
      1 cup all-purpose flour
      3 large eggs
    1/2 teaspoon vanilla extract or other flavoring
    1/4 cup confectioners' sugar

Cut butter or margarine into pieces, combine with water, sugar and salt in saucepan. Bring to boil, remove from heat and add flour. Stir vigorously until smooth paste is formed; return pan to heat, and stir until paste begins to dry and forms a ball without sticking to bottom of pan. Remove from heat once more, and stir in eggs 1 at a time, beating each well into mixture before adding next. The stirring and beating will produce a light paste. Add flavoring. Next, shape paste with hands into small balls about size of walnuts.

Drop them into deep fat preheated to 375°F., and cook until golden. Balls swell a great deal while cooking, so leave plenty of space for them to rise. Lift out each fritter as it is done, and drain well on absorbent paper; roll each in confectioners' sugar and serve at once. Makes 5–6 servings.

Muffins

The secret of good muffins lies in the mixing. Start by combining dry ingredients, making a well in center. Then add liquids, mixed together, all at once. Stir *only until flour is lightly incorporated*–the batter should be lumpy. Overmixing causes unevenly shaped muffins with peaks or knobs on top and large tunnels inside. Line muffin pans with paper baking cups, or grease well. Fill cups only 2/3 full with batter. The variation of 5 minutes or so in baking times in the following recipes allows for difference in muffin pan sizes. The yield from each recipe will also vary depending on size of your muffin tins.

To keep muffins warm, tilt baked muffins in pans (to prevent sogginess) and place in warm oven.

To reheat, put in brown paper bag, sprinkle bag with water and warm in oven. Or wrap in foil.

Any muffin pans not filled with batter must be filled with water to achieve even baking.

Plain Muffins

      2 cups all-purpose flour
      2 tablespoons sugar
      4 teaspoons baking powder
    1/2 teaspoon salt
      1 egg, beaten
      1 cup milk
    1/4 cup melted shortening, or vegetable oil

Sift flour, sugar, baking powder and salt in bowl. Combine egg, milk and shortening. Make well in flour mixture. Add liquids all at once; stir quickly only until flour is absorbed. Fill lined or well-greased muffin cups 2/3 full. Bake 20–25 minutes at 425°F. Makes about 12 muffins.

VARIATIONS:

Bacon Muffins: Omit sugar, and add 1/4 cup diced crisp bacon to dry ingredients. Bacon fat can be used in place of oil or melted shortening, or partially cooked thin bacon can be used to line muffin pans before pouring batter in.

Fruit Muffins: Add 1 cup currants, raisins or chopped dates to dry ingredients, or fold 1 cup fresh blueberries into batter.

Whole Wheat Muffins: Decrease flour to 1 cup; increase sugar to 1/4 cup. Add 1 cup whole wheat flour to sifted dry ingredients, and blend.

Orange Muffins: Increase sugar to 1/4 cup; add 2 teaspoons grated orange rind to dry ingredients; decrease milk to 3/4 cup; add 1/4 cup orange juice with liquid ingredients.

Date Muffins: Add 1 cup chopped dates to dry ingredients.

Cinnamon Muffins: While muffins are hot, dip tops in mixture of 1/2 cup sugar and 1 teaspoon cinnamon.

Streusel-topped Muffins: Sprinkle mixture of 1 cup chopped walnuts, 1/2 cup brown sugar, 2 tablespoons each flour and melted butter or margarine and 1 teaspoon cinnamon over batter in tins.

Pineapple Muffins

    1 cup canned unsweetened pineapple juice
    1 egg, slightly beaten
1/4 cup melted shortening
1 3/4 cups all-purpose flour
1/4 cup sugar
    4 teaspoons baking powder
1/2 teaspoon salt
    2 tablespoons sugar
    1 teaspoon grated orange rind

Beat pineapple juice into slightly beaten egg. Add shortening. Sift flour with 1/4 cup sugar, baking powder and salt, and add to egg mixture. Stir quickly until dry ingredients are just moistened. Fill greased muffin pans 2/3 full. Mix 2 tablespoons sugar and orange rind and sprinkle over muffins. Bake at 400°F. 20–25 minutes. Makes 10–12 muffins.

Oatmeal Muffins

    1 cup all-purpose flour
1/4 cup sugar
    1 tablespoon baking powder
1/2 teaspoon salt
    3 tablespoons shortening

    1 cup rolled oats
1/3 cup seedless raisins or currants
    1 egg, beaten
    1 cup milk

Sift together flour, sugar, baking powder and salt, and cut in shortening. Stir in rolled oats and raisins, and add egg and milk, stirring just enough to dampen dry ingredients. *Do not over-stir.* Fill greased muffin cups 2/3 full, and bake at 425°F. 15–25 minutes. Makes 12–14 muffins.

Spiced Apple Muffins

    2 cups all-purpose flour
1/3 cup sugar
    4 teaspoons baking powder
    1 teaspoon cinnamon
3/4 teaspoon salt
1/4 teaspoon nutmeg
3/4 cup finely chopped peeled apple
    1 egg, beaten
    1 cup milk
1/4 cup melted shortening

Sift together first 6 ingredients; stir in apple. Make well in center. Combine egg, milk and shortening, and add to dry ingredients. Stir only until combined; the batter should be lumpy. Fill greased muffin pans 2/3 full, and bake at 400°F. 20–25 minutes. Makes 14–16 muffins.

Bran Muffins

    2 tablespoons shortening
1/4 cup sugar
3/4 cup milk
    1 egg, well beaten
    1 cup bran
    1 cup all-purpose flour
2 1/2 teaspoons baking powder
1/2 teaspoon salt
1/2 cup chopped candied or dried fruit

Work shortening with spoon until creamy and fluffy. Add sugar gradually, continuing to work with spoon until light. Add milk and egg, and beat well. Add bran, and let stand 20 minutes to soak up moisture. Sift together flour, baking powder and salt, and add to first mixture. Fold in chopped fruit. Fill well-greased muffin cups 2/3 full, and bake at 400°F. 30 minutes. Makes 10–12 muffins.

Quick Loaves

The method of mixing these breads varies with the recipe, but many recipes call for the muffin method of combining ingredients with a minimum of stirring. It is important to use pan the exact size and shape specified in recipe. To prevent cracking along top of the loaf, after pouring batter into pan, let stand about 20 minutes before baking.

Nut Bread

2 cups all-purpose flour
1/2 cup sugar
4 teaspoons baking powder
1 teaspoon salt
1 cup finely chopped walnuts
1 egg, beaten
1 1/4 cups milk
4 tablespoons melted shortening

Sift flour, baking powder, sugar and salt into mixing bowl. Add nuts. Combine egg, milk and shortening. Make well in dry ingredients, and add egg mixture. Stir quickly until flour is absorbed. Pour into greased 9″ x 5″ x 3″ loaf pan, and bake 50–60 minutes at 350°F. Makes 1 loaf.

Date–Nut Loaf

2 cups chopped dates
1 teaspoon baking soda
3/4 cup boiling water
3/4 cup sugar
2 tablespoons shortening
1 egg, beaten
1 teaspoon vanilla extract
1 3/4 cups all-purpose flour
1/2 cup chopped walnuts
1/2 teaspoon salt

Combine dates and baking soda, cover with boiling water and let stand until cool. Cream sugar and shortening together, add egg and vanilla and beat until combined. Add cooled date mixture, flour, walnuts and salt; stir until just combined. Do not beat. Pour mixture into greased 9″ x 5″ x 3″ loaf pan, and bake at 350°F. 60–70 minutes. Makes 1 loaf.

Banana Bread

1/3 cup shortening
2/3 cup sugar
2 eggs, well beaten
1 3/4 cups all-purpose flour
2 teaspoons baking powder
1/2 teaspoon salt
1/4 teaspoon baking soda
1 cup well-mashed bananas (3 or 4 bananas)

Cream shortening well, gradually beat in sugar, add eggs and combine well. Combine dry ingredients, and add to first mixture alternately with bananas. Beat well after each addition. Pour into greased 9″ x 5″ x 3″ loaf pan, and bake at 350°F. 50–55 minutes. Makes 1 loaf.

Cherry Bread

2 cups all-purpose flour
2 teaspoons baking powder
1/2 teaspoon salt
1 cup lightly packed brown sugar
1/4 cup shortening
1 egg, beaten
2/3 cup milk
1/3 cup maraschino syrup
1/2 cup drained maraschino cherries, quartered
1/2 cup chopped walnuts

Combine dry ingredients. Cream brown sugar and shortening, add egg and beat well. Combine milk and syrup. Add dry ingredients alternately with milk mixture to creamed mixture. Mix after each addition, but do not beat. Carefully fold in cherries and walnuts, and pour into greased 9″ x 5″ x 3″ loaf pan. Bake at 350°F. 55–65 minutes. Makes 1 loaf.

Orange Bread

2 1/4 cups all-purpose flour
7/8 cup sugar
2 teaspoons baking powder
3/4 teaspoon salt
1/2 teaspoon baking soda
3/4 cup chopped nuts
1/2 cup raisins
2 tablespoons grated orange rind
1 egg, well beaten
1/2 cup milk
1/2 cup orange juice
2 tablespoons shortening, melted

Sift dry ingredients together. Add nuts, raisins and orange rind. Combine egg with milk, orange juice and shortening, and stir into flour mixture. Turn batter into greased 9″ x 5″ x 3″ loaf pan, and bake at 350°F. 60 minutes or until done. Makes 1 loaf.

Apricot Bread

3/4 cup dried apricots
Warm water
1/2 cup boiling water
1/4 cup orange juice
1/3 cup raisins
Peel from 1/2 orange
1 3/4 cups all-purpose flour
3/4 cup sugar
1 1/2 teaspoons baking powder
1/2 teaspoon salt
1/4 teaspoon baking soda
1 egg, beaten
2 tablespoons melted shortening

Soak apricots in warm water 1/2 hour. Combine boiling water and orange juice, and cool to lukewarm. Drain apricots, and put through grinder with raisins and orange peel. Sift together dry ingredients, add ground fruit and combine. Make well in center, and pour in orange-juice mixture, egg and shortening. Stir only until combined; pour into greased 9″ x 5″ x 3″ loaf pan, and bake at 350°F. 60 minutes. Makes 1 loaf.

Peanut Butter Bread

2 cups all-purpose flour
1/2 cup granulated sugar
1 tablespoon baking powder
1/2 teaspoon salt

1/2 cup peanut butter
2 eggs, well beaten
1 cup milk
1 teaspoon grated lemon rind or orange rind
1/3 cup chopped salted peanuts
1 tablespoon butter, melted, or corn syrup

Place first 4 ingredients in bowl. Rub in peanut butter until mixture is crumbly. Combine eggs, milk and lemon rind, and stir quickly into flour mixture. Pour into greased 9″ x 5″ x 3″ loaf pan. Sprinkle with peanuts. Bake at 325°–350°F. 50–60 minutes. While still hot, brush top with melted butter. Cool, and remove from pan. Slice second day. Makes 1 loaf.

Cranberry Bread

1 cup sugar
1 beaten egg
Juice and grated rind of 1 orange
1 cup chopped raw cranberries
2 cups all-purpose flour
1 1/2 teaspoons baking powder
1/2 teaspoon baking soda
1/2 teaspoon salt
1/2 cup chopped walnuts
2 tablespoons salad oil
3/4 cup less 2 tablespoons boiling water

Cream together sugar, egg and orange juice and rind. Mix in cranberries. Sift together next 4 ingredients, and stir into sugar mixture. Add walnuts. In measuring cup put salad oil; then fill to 3/4-cup mark with boiling water, and stir liquid into batter. Grease 9″ x 5″ x 3″ loaf tin well, and pour in batter. Bake 60 minutes at 325°F., allow to cool well in pan before turning out. Makes 1 loaf.

Onion Quick Bread

1 1/2 cups all-purpose flour
1 cup whole wheat flour
1 tablespoon baking powder
1 1/2 teaspoons salt
1 teaspoon baking soda
1 1/2 cups buttermilk or sour milk
1/2 cup light molasses
1/4 cup liquid shortening
1/2 cup finely chopped onion
2 teaspoons caraway seeds or sesame seeds

Combine dry ingredients, and add buttermilk, molasses and shortening. Mix thoroughly but lightly. Add onion; sprinkle 2 teaspoons caraway seeds over batter, and fold in. Scrape into well-greased 9″ x 5″ x 3″ loaf pan. Top may be sprinkled with additional caraway and sesame seeds. Bake at 350°F. 60 minutes or until done. Unmold on rack. Serve when still slightly warm with butter and cottage cheese, sliced apples, pears or bunches of grapes. Makes 1 loaf.

Note: If well wrapped, bread will keep moist for days, and freezes extremely well.

Baking Bread. Baking bread is easier than you think. Here are the basic ingredients. You can buy cakes of compressed fresh yeast or, more commonly, packages of activated dry yeast. The two may be used interchangeably. To substitute fresh yeast for dry yeast, crumble yeast cake over required amount of *unsweetened* lukewarm water, and let stand 10 minutes, remembering that 1 (2-ounce) package fresh yeast equals 4 envelopes activated dry yeast. Yeast works best at about 80°F. For very fast results the temperature can be 110°F., but no higher. A lower temperature slows down production of gases, and too high a temperature kills yeast. All ingredients must therefore be lukewarm during mixing and rising of dough. A constant room temperature, with no drafts in vicinity of dough, is ideal.

Sugar: Sugar provides food for the yeast, whereas *salt* helps to control the action of the yeast. Both ingredients must be used in the right proportions.

Liquid: The liquid may be milk, water, potato water or a mixture of them. Milk gives finer crumbs and more tender crust. When fresh milk is used, it must first be scalded to destroy enzymes that would otherwise interfere with the yeast.

Flour: Hard-wheat or all-purpose flour must be used for bread, as it contains the 2 proteins necessary to make gluten, and gluten gives bread dough its elastic quality, enabling it to hold gases produced by the yeast and to expand or rise. Such other flours or cereals as whole-wheat or rye flour and rolled oats may be used for bread, but the flour content of the recipe must include about 50 percent all-purpose flour, in order to supply necessary gluten.

Yeast Dough

There are 3 basic methods for making yeast breads.

Sponge Method: A batter, made from yeast, lukewarm liquid, sugar and some flour, is allowed to rise until light and bubbly; texture resembles that of sponge. Then the remaining flour and other ingredients are added, and dough is allowed to rise as directed in recipe. Next it is divided into loaves or rolls and left again to rise before baking.

Straight-dough Method: This method is now the most commonly used. The softened yeast is combined with sugar, salt, liquids and shortening. Flour is then added to make soft but not sticky dough, which is kneaded and allowed to rise according to requirements of recipe. When it is ready, the dough is shaped into loaves or rolls and allowed to rise again before baking.

Quick Method: To make rolls or sweet dough quickly, ingredients are combined and beaten, rather than kneaded. A fairly high proportion of yeast is used in batter-type recipes, as well as more liquid. The finished product has a lighter, more open texture, but it lacks the keeping quality of breads made by the straight-dough method. As dough is soft enough to be beaten by electric mixer, however, there is some saving of time and effort. No kneading is required because beating serves to develop gluten sufficiently.

Basic Steps for Making Bread

A firm working of dough with your hands is essential (except in quick method) to develop gluten and to distribute gas bubbles evenly throughout dough. Kneading is a simple, 3-step action. First, fold far side of dough toward you. Then push dough away from you, pressing it firmly with "heels" of your hands. Finally give dough a 1/4 turn. Repeat this folding, pressing and turning with rhythmic motion until dough is satin-smooth and elastic. Kneading usually requires 8–10 minutes for bread, about 5 minutes for sweet dough. Use only enough flour on board to keep dough from sticking. Flour your hands, too, to prevent sticking.

The First Rising: Place kneaded dough in lightly greased bowl. Grease top of dough slightly to prevent dry crust from forming. For white bread and rolls, allow dough to rise until it has doubled in bulk, which takes about 1 1/2 hours. To test dough, push 2 fingers deep into it and withdraw them at once. If indentations remain, dough has risen enough. For dark bread and rolls, dough must rise only until it is 1/2 more than its original volume, as whole wheat, rye, and similar cereals make a heavier mixture.

Rising times will vary, depending on amount of yeast and whether or not dough is kept at fairly constant temperature of 80°F. To keep temperature constant, set bowl of dough in pan of lukewarm water, and cover it with cloth. Always keep dough away from direct heat and cold drafts.

Once dough has risen enough, punch it down to expel air. Allow it to rise again if recipe requires it. Otherwise, divide dough into required portions, shape into smooth balls, cover with cloth and allow to "rest" about 15 minutes, in order to make dough easier to shape into loaves or rolls.

To Shape Loaves: On a lightly floured board, press or roll each ball of dough into rectangle 8″ x 10″. Press out any large air bubbles. First fold far side of the dough into center. Then fold near side into center. Press to seal center seam and to force out any trapped air bubbles. Press dough enough to make it uniform in thickness. Then fold ends in so that they meet in middle, rather like squared parcel. Press out air bubbles once again. Fold dough over, and pinch edges together to seal. Place in greased 9″ x 5″ x 3″ pans with the sealed edges at bottom. Grease tops of loaves lightly.

Second Rising: Place pans in warm place free from drafts or direct heat. Cover with cloth. For white bread, let dough rise until it fills pan and center is rounded slightly above top edge, about 1 hour. To test, press dough gently with fingertips. If slight impression remains, dough is ready for oven. For dark bread, dough should be allowed to rise until rounded center of loaf is about level with top edge of pan. This rising time for bread in pan varies with recipe and room temperature.

To Bake: A hot oven is needed, especially at the beginning. Bread is sufficiently baked when loaves lift free from the pan and when they sound hollow if tapped on bottom crust. Remove baked bread from pans at once, and stand on rack to cool. Keep them away from drafts to prevent crust cracking. For softer crusts, brush warm loaves with softened butter or margarine.

The following recipes can be halved. Use 1/2 the ingredients called for, but otherwise prepare dough exactly as directed for full recipe, allowing same rising and baking times. Shape into 2 loaves when 4 are given in recipe, 1 loaf when 2 are given.

White Bread

    2 cups milk
    1/4 cup sugar
    1/4 cup shortening
    1 tablespoon salt
    2 cups lukewarm water
    2 (1/4-ounce) packages active dry yeast
    2 teaspoons sugar
    9 1/2–10 cups all-purpose flour

Scald milk, and add 1/4 cup sugar, shortening and salt. Stir in 1 cup lukewarm water, and cool until whole mixture is lukewarm. Sprinkle yeast into other cup lukewarm water with 2 teaspoons sugar (if yeast cakes are used, omit sugar). Let stand 10 minutes. Stir yeast, and mix into milk mixture. Add 1/2 the flour, and beat until almost smooth. Add remaining flour gradually, mixing thoroughly. Use enough to prevent dough clinging to bowl. When dough is stiff, turn out on lightly floured board, flour your hands and knead about 10 minutes. Shape into ball, and place in greased bowl. Grease top slightly to prevent crust from forming. Cover, and let rise in warm place until dough doubles in bulk. Punch dough, and fold into center. Turn onto lightly floured board, and shape dough into mound. Cut into 4 equal pieces, and shape each into 2 balls. Cover balls with clean tea towel, and let rest 10 minutes. Shape into 4 loaves. Place in greased 9″ x 5″ x 3″ loaf pans, and bake at 425°F. 15–20 minutes; reduce heat to 375°F. and continue baking 25–30 minutes. Makes 4 loaves.

VARIATIONS:

Bran Bread: Use 2 cups molasses in place of sugar. Use 2 cups bran in place of 2 cups flour plus a little extra flour if necessary.

Cheese Bread: Mix in 1 cup finely shredded Cheddar cheese with last 3 cups flour. Cheese bread rises quickly and requires less time to double in bulk than does white bread.

Rye Bread: Substitute brown for granulated sugar. Mix in 6 cups all-purpose flour and enough rye flour (about 4 cups) to make dough that comes clean from bowl and is not sticky.

Whole Wheat Bread

    1 1/2 cups milk
    1/2 cup brown sugar
    1/2 cup shortening
    2 teaspoons salt
    3 1/4 cups lukewarm water
    2 teaspoons sugar
    2 (1/4-ounce) packages active dry yeast
    6 cups whole wheat flour
    4 1/2–5 cups all-purpose flour

Scald milk, and pour into large mixing bowl. Add brown sugar, shortening and salt, and stir until shortening melts. Stir in 2 1/4 cups lukewarm water, and cool until whole mixture is lukewarm. Dissolve white sugar in 1 cup lukewarm water, sprinkle yeast over it and let stand 10 minutes at about 80°F. Stir yeast mixture with fork, add to lukewarm milk mixture and stir again. Beat in whole wheat flour gradually; then add all-purpose flour, working in all flour. Turn dough onto floured board and knead 8–10 minutes. Shape into smooth ball. Place dough in lightly greased bowl, and grease top a little to prevent crust from forming. Cover, and allow to rise in warm place until almost doubled in bulk, about 1 1/4 hours. Punch down, and turn out again on floured board. Cut into 4 equal portions, and form each into a smooth ball. Cover balls, and allow to rest about 15 minutes before shaping into loaves. Place loaves in greased 9″ x 5″ x 3″ loaf pans, grease tops lightly, cover and let rise 1 hour or until nearly doubled in bulk. Bake at 425°F. 20–25 minutes; then reduce heat to 375°F. and continue baking 25 minutes longer.

VARIATION:

Molasses–Whole Wheat Bread: Instead of brown sugar, use 1/2 cup light molasses, and mix it with salt and shortening in 2 instead of 2 1/4 cups lukewarm water.

Plain Bread

    1 teaspoon sugar
    1 1/4 cups lukewarm water
    1 (1/4-ounce) package active dry yeast
    2 tablespoons soft shortening
    2 tablespoons sugar
    2 teaspoons salt
    3 cups all-purpose flour

Add 1 teaspoon sugar to water in mixing bowl. Dissolve yeast in this water, and let stand 10 minutes. Add shortening, 2 tablespoons sugar, salt and 1 1/2 cups flour. Beat 2 minutes in electric mixer at medium speed or 300 strokes by hand. Scrape sides and bottom of bowl frequently. Add remaining flour, and beat with spoon until smooth, about 1 1/2 minutes. Scrape batter from sides of bowl frequently. Cover bowl with cloth and let rise in warm place (80°F.) until doubled in bulk, about 1/2 hour. Beat down, about 25 strokes. Spread batter evenly in greased 9″ x 5″ x 3″ loaf pan. Smooth top by patting into shape with floured hands as batter will be sticky. Let rise in warm place until edge of batter is within 1/4 inch of top of pan, about 40 minutes. Bake at 375°F. 45–50 minutes. When baked, remove from pan, and brush top with melted butter or margarine. Makes 1 loaf.

VARIATIONS:

Herb Bread: Into first 1 1/2 cups flour, mix 1 teaspoon caraway seeds and 1/2 teaspoon each nutmeg and powdered sage.

Plain Whole Wheat Bread: Substitute firmly packed brown sugar for 2 tablespoons granulated sugar and 1 cup whole wheat flour for 1 cup all-purpose flour. Add 1/2 cup whole wheat flour in first 1 1/2 cups flour; add remaining 1/2 cup whole wheat flour at the end of the mixing.

Festive Bread: To second 1 1/2 cups flour add 1/4 cup each chopped candied peel, raisins and nuts and 1/2 teaspoon each almond and vanilla extracts. Spread batter in 2 greased 1-pound coffee cans. Let rise until batter is 1/2 inch from top. Bake about 40 minutes.

Easy Oatmeal Bread

    1 teaspoon sugar
    1/4 cup warm water
    1 (1/4-ounce) package active dry yeast
    3/4 cup boiling water
    1/2 cup rolled oats
    1/4 cup molasses
    2 tablespoons soft shortening
    2 teaspoons salt
    1 egg
    2 3/4 cups all-purpose flour

Add sugar to warm water, and sprinkle yeast over; let stand 10 minutes. Mix boiling water, oats, molasses, shortening and salt in large mixing bowl, and let mixture cool to lukewarm. Add yeast mixture, egg and 1 1/2 cups flour to lukewarm mixture. Beat 2 minutes in electric mixer at medium speed or 300 strokes by hand. Scrape sides and bottom of bowl frequently. Add remaining flour and blend with mixing spoon until smooth. Spread batter evenly in greased 9″ x 5″ x

3″ loaf pan. Smooth top of loaf with floured hands, and pat into shape. Let rise in warm place (80°F.) until batter is 1 inch from top of pan, about 1 1/2 hours. Bake at 375°F. 50–55 minutes. Crust will be dark brown. To test, tap bottom crust; it should sound hollow. After removing from pan, brush top with melted butter or margarine. Makes 1 loaf.

Cheese Pan Bread

    1/2 cup milk
    1/2 cup butter or margarine
      3 teaspoons sugar
      1 teaspoon salt
    1/2 cup lukewarm water
      1 teaspoon sugar
      1 (1/4-ounce) package active dry yeast
      3 eggs, well beaten
  2 3/4 cups (approximately) all-purpose flour
    1/2 cup grated Parmesan or Romano cheese
    1/4 teaspoon dry mustard
  Few grains pepper

Scald milk; stir in butter or margarine, 2 teaspoons sugar and salt. Cool to lukewarm. Meanwhile, measure lukewarm water into large bowl; stir in 1 teaspoon sugar. Sprinkle with yeast. Let stand 10 minutes; then stir. Stir in lukewarm milk mixture, eggs and 1 3/4 cups flour. Beat until smooth and elastic. Combine cheese, mustard and pepper, and stir into batter. Work in sufficient additional flour to make thick batter, about 1 cup more. Cover with damp towel. Let rise in warm place, free from drafts, until doubled in bulk, about 1 1/4 hours. Stir down batter. Divide between 2 greased 8-inch layer-cake pans, and spread evenly. Cover loosely with waxed paper or plastic wrap. Let rise until almost doubled in bulk, about 45 minutes. Bake at 375°F. 25–30 minutes. Makes 2 round loaves.

Challah (Egg Bread)

    1/3 cup warm water
      2 tablespoons sugar
      1 (1/4-ounce) package active dry yeast
      1 cup lukewarm scalded milk
    1/4 cup soft butter or margarine
      2 eggs, unbeaten
      2 teaspoons salt
  5–5 1/2 cups all-purpose flour
      1 egg yolk
      2 tablespoons water

Combine water, sugar and yeast in warm mixing bowl, and stir until dissolved. Add lukewarm milk, butter or margarine, 2 eggs, salt and 2 1/2 cups flour. Using electric mixer, beat slowly at first until ingredients are well combined; then increase speed to medium, and beat until smooth. Continue adding flour until batter begins to creep up beaters. Remove, scrape beaters, and work in as much remaining flour as you can with wooden spoon, then by hand. Turn dough onto floured board, and knead until smooth, working more flour in until dough loses its stickiness. Place in lightly greased bowl, and oil top. Cover, and let rise until doubled in bulk. Punch down, and cut dough into 2 pieces, one slightly smaller than the other. Cut larger piece into 3 equal parts, and shape each into a strand about 12 inches long and 1 inch in diameter. Roll back and forth on board to form evenly shaped ropes. Make 3 strands 10 inches long out of remaining dough. Braid longer strands loosely on greased cookie sheet, and tuck ends under neatly. Braid shorter strands, and center on top of first braid, tucking ends under. Brush with salad oil, and cover with damp cloth. Let rise 40 minutes or until doubled in bulk. Beat egg yolk with 2 tablespoons water, and brush over loaf. Bake at 425°F. 25 minutes; reduce heat to 350°F. and bake 10 minutes longer. Makes 1 loaf.

Onion Bread

      1 (1/4-ounce) package active dry yeast
    1/2 cup lukewarm water
      1 cup scalded milk
      2 tablespoons sugar
      2 tablespoons shortening
      2 teaspoons salt
      3 cups all-purpose flour
      3 tablespoons chopped onion
      5 teaspoons caraway seeds
  1 1/2 cups (approximately) unsifted rye flour

Dissolve yeast in lukewarm water. Mix milk, sugar, shortening and salt together, and cool to lukewarm. Add yeast mixture, and stir in all-purpose flour. Mix until smooth. Add onion and caraway seeds, then enough rye flour to make firm dough. Knead until smooth on rye-floured board. Brush top with salad oil, and cover. Let rise until doubled. Knead again until free of large air bubbles, and shape into 2 small loaves or 1 large one. Place in 2 small or 1 9″ x 5″ x 3″ well-greased loaf pan, and brush tops with oil. Let rise again until doubled, and bake in a 350°F. oven 45–50 minutes. Makes 2 small loaves or 1 large loaf.

Dill Bread

    1/2 cup lukewarm water
      2 packages (1/4 ounce each) active dry yeast
      2 cups creamy cottage cheese
    1/4 cup chopped onion
    1/4 cup melted butter or margarine
      2 teaspoons salt
      2 eggs
      5 cups sifted flour
      2 tablespoons dried dill weed
      2 thin slices onion

Pour water into jar of electric blender. Add dry yeast, stir, and let stand 5 minutes. Blend at high speed 10 seconds. Add cottage cheese, onion, butter or margarine, salt and eggs; blend at high speed 20 seconds. Sift flour into large mixing bowl; add dill. Add blender mixture. Mix with spoon until dough falls away from sides of bowl. Place in a large, lightly greased bowl, cover with a damp cloth and let rise until double. Punch down. Put into 2 well-greased 9 x 5 x 3-inch pans. Separate onion slices into rings and arrange over top of loaf. Let rise again until double. Preheat oven to 350°F. Bake 1 hour, 15 minutes.

Saint's Loaf

        1 1/2 cups boiling water
        1/2 cup honey
        1/3 cup vegetable shortening
        1 tablespoon salt
        2 packages (1/4 ounce each) active dry yeast
        1/2 cup lukewarm water
        2 eggs
        1/2 cup wheat germ
    2 3/4 cups flour
    1 3/4 cups whole wheat flour
        1 cup coarsely chopped walnuts
        1/4 cup water
        1/4 cup sugar
        1/4 cup coarsely chopped walnuts

In large bowl of an electric mixer, combine water, shortening, honey and salt. Stir until shortening melts. Cool to lukewarm. Dissolve yeast in lukewarm water. Add to honey mixture along with eggs, wheat germ and 1 1/2 cups flour. Beat with mixer 2 minutes at medium speed. Stir in remaining flour, whole wheat flour, and 1 cup coarsely chopped walnuts. Mixture will be sticky. Shape into 2 loaves and place in 2 well-greased 9 x 5 x 3-inch loaf pans. Cover with a damp cloth and let rise until one inch from top of pans.

Preheat oven to 375°F. Bake loaves 40–50 minutes. Meanwhile make topping: in small saucepan combine 1/4 cup water and 1/4 cup sugar. Boil until slightly syrupy (about 2 minutes). Brush tops of loaves with syrup and sprinkle with coarsely chopped walnuts, after loaves are done baking.

Garlic Puffs: A new departure in garlic bread.

        1 package (13 3/4 ounces) hot-roll mix
        1 clove garlic, crushed
        1 tablespoon coarse crystal salt
        Egg wash: 1 egg, 1 tablespoon water

Prepare dough from hot-roll mix, following package directions through first rising. Punch dough down and roll out into 4 x 18-inch oblong.

Cut in half lengthwise, making two strips, then cut each strip into nine 2-inch squares. Form each square into a ball; place in well-greased muffin pans. Brush with egg wash made by beating 1 egg with 1 tablespoon water. Mix 1 clove crushed garlic with 1 tablespoon coarse crystal salt and sprinkle over tops of rolls. Let rise until double. Preheat oven to 375°F. Bake 15–18 minutes. Makes 18 puffs.

Quick Brioches

        1/3 cup warm water
        1 teaspoon sugar
        1 (1/4-ounce) envelope active dry yeast
        1/2 cup all-purpose flour
        1 bowl lukewarm water
        4 eggs
        3/4 cup soft butter or margarine
        1 tablespoon sugar
        3/4 teaspoon salt
        1/2 teaspoon lemon extract (optional)
    2 3/4 cups all-purpose flour
        1 egg yolk, slightly beaten
        2 tablespoons water

Measure 1/3 cup water and sugar into small bowl, and add yeast. Let stand 10 minutes or until dissolved; stir in 1/2 cup flour. Knead slightly until smooth, and shape into soft ball. Gash top, and drop into bowl of lukewarm water. Let dough rise to top of water before removing from water and adding to other ingredients. Meanwhile, beat 4 eggs slightly in large bowl. Add next 4 ingredients, and beat in 1 1/2 cups flour and risen yeast ball. Scrape and remove beaters, and add remaining flour with wooden spoon and then by hand. Knead slightly just until smooth, about 1 minute. Dough will be soft. Place in warm oiled bowl, and cover. Let rise until puffy (about 1 hour); stir down, and scrape into oiled 8-inch square pan. Chill in freezer 30 minutes or until dough is firm enough to handle. Oil 2 1/2 dozen fluted tart pans or muffin pans. Cut off small pieces of dough, and turn edges under to form smooth balls 1/3 the size of the tart pans. Press thumb or finger into center of each ball; mold tiny balls of dough, and place in the depressions. Cover, and let rise about 45 minutes or until doubled in bulk. Make solution of egg yolk, and 2 tablespoons water, and brush carefully over brioches. Bake at 400°F. 15–20 minutes, depending on size. Makes 2 1/2 dozen.

Oatmeal–Honey Bread

        1/2 cup warm water
        1 teaspoon sugar
        1 (1/4-ounce) package active dry yeast
        1 cup commercial sour cream
        1 cup quick-cooking oats
        3 tablespoons honey

1 teaspoon salt
1/4 teaspoon baking soda
2 1/3 cups all-purpose flour
1 tablespoon honey

Combine warm water, sugar and yeast in mixing bowl, and stir or let stand 10 minutes to dissolve. Heat sour cream until warm, but not hot, and remove from heat. Stir in oats, 3 tablespoons honey, salt and baking soda. When cooled to lukewarm, add yeast mixture and 1 cup flour, and beat well. Mix in 1/2 cup flour with wooden spoon. Knead lightly on board to work in remaining flour until dough is smooth, about 5 minutes. Place ball of dough in warm oiled bowl, and turn it over once to oil top. Cover, and let rise 30 minutes. Punch down and shape into round loaf. Place in greased round pan, 7 inches in diameter and 3 inches deep. Cover, and let rise until dough fills pan. Bake at 400°F. 15 minutes; then reduce heat to 350°F., and bake 35 minutes. Brush with 1 tablespoon honey while loaf is still hot. Makes 1 round loaf.

French Bread

1 1/2 cups warm water
2 (1/4-ounce) packages active dry yeast
1 teaspoon sugar
4–6 cups all-purpose flour
1 1/2 teaspoon salt
1 egg white
1 tablespoon water

Measure 1 1/2 cups water into large bowl, and add yeast and sugar. Stir, and let stand until yeast is dissolved. Sift 1 1/2 cups flour with salt and add to yeast. Beat until mixture is smooth. Stir in more flour (about 2 cups) with wooden spoon, then by hand. Knead in remaining flour until dough is smooth and elastic (about 6 minutes). Place ball of dough in warm oiled bowl, turning it over once to oil top. Let rise until doubled (about 1 hour). Punch down, and roll into 2 rectangles—6″ x 10″. Roll each tightly as for jelly roll, using long side. Dampen and seal edges. Roll back and forth to lengthen loaf and taper ends. Loaves should be about 12 inches long and 2 1/2 inches thick. Place side by side 2 inches apart on lightly greased 15″ x 10″ cookie sheet that has been sprinkled with cornmeal. For appearance, gash tops in several places, cutting 1/4 inch deep. Brush with cold water, and let stand uncovered in warm place 1 hour or until doubled. Brush again with water and bake at 375°F. 15 minutes. Beat 1 egg white slightly with 1 tablespoon water and brush 1/2 of mixture over loaves. Continue baking 10 minutes. Brush again with egg-white mixture, and bake until golden brown (about 10 more minutes). Makes 2 loaves.

Note: The secret of the crustiness so characteristic of French bread lies in slower baking than usual. If you bake at 25°F. less than temperature given in recipe, you will have an even thicker crust. Those who have experimented with French bread say that you should always bake it a little longer than you think necessary, for maximum crustiness.

Rolls

The dough for rolls is prepared and allowed to rise in the same way as bread dough. When dough has been punched down after first rising, divide it into smooth balls, and let rest a few minutes. Then proceed according to shape desired.

As with bread, after shaping, rolls are left to rise again. Press them with a finger. If a slight impression remains, rolls are ready for oven.

Dark rolls are ready for oven when they have risen to 1/2 more than their original size. White rolls are allowed to double in bulk before they are baked.

As with any yeast dough, rising should take place in warm room (75°–80°F.) free from drafts.

A 375°F. oven is usually best for sweet rolls, as the sugar in them makes them brown more quickly. Rolls made from bread dough may be baked along with bread. Rolls are done when they are light and nicely browned. If you have more rolls than you can bake at 1 time, place oven-ready rolls in refrigerator while baking first batch. You may also keep rolls this way if you wish to serve them hot from the oven at dinnertime.

If you wish to postpone baking for more than a short time, it is best to use a refrigerator-dough recipe. Because cold retards action of yeast, dough may be kept refrigerated 2–3 days before baking. Special proportions of sugar and salt help to control yeast during waiting period. Regular dough should not be refrigerated, as it does not have these proportions.

Shaping Rolls

Mold rolls into any shape you wish. Then cover again, and allow to rise until doubled in bulk once more. Rising will take 45–60 minutes.

As size of rolls will vary according to shapes you decide to make, baking times will also vary. Generally, they will take 18–30 minutes. Oven temperature should be uniformly 375°F.

Pan Rolls: Form each ball of dough into cylindrical shape about 1 1/2 inches in diameter. Cut into 1-inch lengths and form into balls, tucking under any uneven edges. Place 16 rolls in each greased 8- or 9-inch square pan, and brush with melted butter or margarine. Cover with cloth, let rise and bake at 375°F. 25–30 minutes.

Cloverleaf Rolls: Shape balls of dough into cylinders, about 1 1/2 inches in diameter. Cut into 1-inch lengths, then cut each into 3 parts again. Form each small piece into a ball, tucking edges under. Brush with melted butter or margarine, and place 3 balls in each greased medium-sized muffin cup. Cover, let rise and bake at 375°F. 18–20 minutes.

Parker House Rolls: Roll balls of dough to 1/4-inch thickness. Cut with floured 2-inch round or oval cutter. Brush with melted butter or margarine. Crease each deeply, just off center, with back of knife. Fold each over, with wider half on top. Lightly press edges together. Turn over, and place on greased baking sheets, cover, let rise and bake at 375°F. 10–20 minutes.

Crescent Rolls: Roll balls of dough into circles, about 8 inches in diameter and about 1/4-inch thick. Cut each into 8 triangular wedges. Roll up each wedge, as shown, toward pointed end. Place on greased baking sheet, with point underneath. Brush with melted butter or margarine, and curve each slightly, to form crescent shapes. Cover, let rise and bake at 375°F. 18–20 minutes.

Dinner Rolls: Divide dough into 8 equal parts. Roll each piece into cylindrical shape. Then taper each end to make roll lemon-shaped. Brush with melted butter or margarine, and place on cookie sheet. Cover, and let rise. Bake at 375°F. 25–30 minutes.

Butter Rolls: Roll dough to 1/8-inch thickness, forming into oblong about 9 inches wide. Spread dough with softened butter or margarine. Cut 6 long strips about 1 1/2 inches wide. Stack strips on top of one another, and cut straight down through all layers at about 1-inch intervals. Place each 1-inch section, cut side down, in greased muffin cups, cover and let rise; bake at 375°F. 15–20 minutes.

Twisted Rolls: These rolls may take many shapes, but you begin by rolling out dough to a little less than 1/2-inch thickness, making an oblong about 12 inches wide. Spread dough with soft butter or margarine and fold in half over butter or margarine. Trim edges to make corners even, and cut into strips, each 1 1/2 inches wide and about 6 inches long. Make figure 8s by holding 1/2 end of each strip, twisting other end and stretching it so that when the 2 ends are brought together on greased baking sheet, a figure 8 is formed. Make whirls by holding 1 end of each strip on baking sheet and winding strip around it in circles. Tuck other end of strip under.

Make knots by first rolling each strip of dough lightly under hands, then tying each into a knot, and pulling end through. Cover, and let rise. All these "twists" should be baked on a greased baking sheet at 375°F. 18–20 minutes.

Basic Sweet Rolls

```
1 1/2  cups milk
  1/3  cup sugar
  1/4  cup shortening
    2  teaspoons salt
    1  teaspoon sugar
  1/2  cup lukewarm water
    1  (1/4-ounce) package active dry yeast
    2  eggs, well beaten
5 1/2–6  cups all-purpose flour
```

Scald milk, and pour into large bowl. Add 1/3 cup sugar, shortening and salt, and stir till shortening is melted. Cool to lukewarm. Meanwhile, dissolve 1 teaspoon sugar in water and sprinkle yeast over. Let this mixture stand 10 minutes, being sure that temperature remains at about 80°F. Stir it with fork, and add with eggs to lukewarm milk mixture. Stir well; then beat in 3 cups flour. Add remaining flour, working in the last of it by hand. Turn dough onto lightly floured board. Knead until smooth, about 5 minutes. Shape dough into ball, and place in lightly greased bowl. Grease top slightly to prevent drying, cover, and let stand in warm place until doubled in bulk, about 1 1/2 hours. Punch dough down after it has risen, and turn onto lightly floured board. Divide into 4 equal parts. Form each into 2 smooth balls, cover and let rest for 10 minutes to make dough easier to work. Shape, let rise and bake according to previous directions.

3-Day Refrigerator Rolls

```
1 3/4  cups hot water
  1/2  cup granulated sugar
  1/3  cup butter or margarine
    1  tablespoon salt
  1/2  cup lukewarm water
    2  teaspoons granulated sugar
    2  (1/4-ounce) packages active dry yeast
    2  eggs, well beaten
8 1/2  cups (approximately) all-purpose flour
```

Measure hot water into large bowl. Stir in 1/2 cup sugar, butter or margarine and salt. Cool to lukewarm. Meanwhile, measure lukewarm water into very large mixing bowl. Stir in 2 teaspoons sugar, and sprinkle with yeast. Let stand 10 minutes; then stir well. Stir in butter mixture and eggs. Stir in 4 cups flour, and beat until smooth and elastic. Stir in sufficient additional flour to make soft dough. Work dough in bowl with floured hands to make ball. Grease top. Cover tightly with foil or plastic film and refrigerate. To bake, use 1/3 the dough on each of 3 ensuing days. Form portion of dough into smooth ball on lightly floured board. Form ball of dough into 12-inch roll, and cut crosswise into 1-inch lengths. Shape each length into smooth ball and place in greased muffin cup, 1 ball to each. Grease tops, cover and let rise in warm place, free from drafts, until doubled in bulk. Rising time will depend upon temperature of dough. Bake in hot oven, 400°F. about 15 minutes. Makes 3 dozen.

Homemade Brown and Serve Rolls

            1/2 cup milk
            3/4 cup cold water
              3 tablespoons sugar
              1 (1/4-ounce) package active dry yeast
              2 tablespoons soft shortening
              2 teaspoons salt
              1 egg, well beaten
          4 1/2 cups all-purpose flour

Scald milk; add cold water. When milk and water are lukewarm, stir in 1 teaspoon sugar, and sprinkle yeast on top. After 10 minutes, stir, and add remaining sugar, shortening, salt and egg. Add flour, and stir until liquid is absorbed. By hand, mix dough in bowl to a ball. Knead on greased board until smooth (5 minutes). Place in greased bowl. Cover, and let rise at warm temperature until double in bulk. Punch down. Divide dough in 2 and let rest 15 minutes. Cut each portion into 16 pieces and form each piece into 2 balls. Space evenly in 2 well-greased 8-inch square pans. Cover with greased waxed paper, and let rise in warm place until doubled. Bake in slow oven, 275°F. 40 minutes. Remove from pans, and cool on wire racks. When cold, wrap securely. To brown and serve, heat in hot oven 450°F. about 7 minutes.

Note: 2 tablespoons dried milk may be sifted with flour and 1 1/4 cups lukewarm water used instead of milk and water.

Hot Cross Buns

            3/4 cup milk
              1 tablespoon sugar
              1 teaspoon sugar
            1/2 cup lukewarm water
              1 (1/4-ounce) package
                   active dry yeast
    3 1/2–3 3/4 cups all-purpose flour
            1/4 cup butter or margarine
            1/2 cup sugar
              1 egg, beaten
            1/2 teaspoon salt
            1/2 teaspoon cinnamon
            1/2 teaspoon cloves
            1/2 cup currants
              1 egg white
              1 teaspoon water

Scald milk, put it in large bowl and add 1 tablespoon sugar. Cool until lukewarm. Dissolve 1 teaspoon sugar in lukewarm water, and sprinkle yeast over it. Let stand 10 minutes at temperature of about 80°F. then stir with fork, combine with lukewarm milk mixture and stir again. Add 1 1/2 cups flour, and beat until mixture is smooth. Cover, and leave to rise about 45 minutes, when mixture will be bubbly.

Cream butter or margarine, and add 1/2 cup sugar, blending well. Add this mixture to dough. Add egg. Sift salt and spices into remaining flour, add currants and stir mixture into dough, working in the last of the flour by hand.

Turn dough onto floured board and knead until it becomes smooth and elastic, which will take about 5 minutes. Shape dough into a ball, place in lightly greased bowl and grease top a little. Allow it to rise, covered, about 1 hour or until dough is doubled in bulk, keeping temperature around 80°F. and guarding against drafts.

Punch down dough, turn it out on floured board and divide it into 2 equal parts, shaping each into a ball. Cover, and let rest 10 minutes. Divide each ball into 8 or 9 parts. Shape each piece into round buns; flatten a little. Set buns on greased baking sheet, leaving about 2 inches between, and allow to rise until doubled in bulk, about 45 minutes. Beat egg white slightly with

1 teaspoon water, and brush over buns. Mark a cross on top of each bun before placing in oven. Bake at 400°F. 15–18 minutes. While they are still hot you can use frosting made with confectioners' sugar and milk, to follow shape of crosses marked on buns. Makes 16–18 buns.

French Croissants

    1 cup milk
    2 tablespoons sugar
    2 tablespoons shortening
    1 teaspoon salt
    1 (1/4-ounce) package active dry yeast
    1 teaspoon sugar
    1/2 cup lukewarm water
    2 eggs, beaten
    1 teaspoon grated lemon rind
    5 cups all-purpose flour
    1 cup butter or margarine
    1 egg yolk
    2 tablespoons cream

Scald milk; add 2 tablespoons sugar, shortening and salt, and stir until shortening is melted. Cool to lukewarm. Sprinkle yeast and 1 teaspoon sugar over water; let stand to dissolve, and add to milk mixture. Add eggs and lemon rind, and stir well. Add flour to make soft dough, turn onto floured board and knead lightly. Dough should be smooth but not elastic; kneaded too long, croissants will not be tender. Place dough in refrigerator 10 minutes. Shape butter or margarine into flat brick, roll it in some of remaining flour to keep it from sticking and place it between 2 sheets of waxed paper. Then roll it out into a square 1/4-inch thick. Divide square in 2 oblong pieces. Wrap in waxed paper, and chill. Take dough from refrigerator, and roll out on well-floured cloth until you have a rectangle about 3 times longer than its width. Brush off any excess flour; then place on it 1 slab of chilled butter or margarine. Fold right edge of dough over butter or margarine. Place other slab of butter or margarine on top of this flap of dough, and fold left edge of dough over butter or margarine. Press edges together to seal. Place dough on cloth so that short end is toward you. Roll out into long rectangle as before. Brush off excess flour, fold each side in to meet center. Then fold once more, in half, to make a "book" of 4 layers. Press all edges together again, wrap dough in waxed paper and chill 1 hour. Place dough again on floured cloth, again with short end toward you. Roll out dough into rectangle, and fold, as before. Wrap dough, and chill again, this time 2–3 hours at least. Cut dough into 4 parts. Roll out each piece separately until it is 1/8-inch thick. Cut into strips about 5 inches wide, and divide strips into triangles. Roll triangles, starting with widest edge and working toward point. Roll fairly tightly, stretching dough a little to make them longer. Chill rolls in freezing compartment 1/2 hour.

Take rolls from freezer no more than 1/2 dozen at a time so that they can stay well chilled. Roll them on the pastry cloth under palm of 1 hand until they are thinner and firmer in shape. Place rolls on greased baking sheet, and curve into crescent shapes. Chill again until very cold

before placing in oven. Brush with egg yolk and cream, and bake at 475°F. 5 minutes; reduce heat to 400°F., and bake about 8 minutes longer or until golden brown. Makes 3–4 dozen.

Note: If frozen immediately after cooling, croissants will keep for months. The recipe may be halved, but follow chilling and baking times exactly as specified for full amount.

Sour Cream Twists

    1 (1/4-ounce) package dry yeast
    1/4 cup lukewarm water
    4 cups all-purpose flour
    1 teaspoon salt
    1 cup butter or margarine
    3/4 cup sour cream
    2 eggs, well beaten
    1 teaspoon vanilla extract
    1/2 teaspoon grated lemon rind
    1 3/4 cups granulated sugar

Dissolve yeast in water. Combine flour and salt; cut butter or margarine in with pastry blender. Add dissolved yeast, sour cream, eggs, vanilla and lemon rind, and stir thoroughly. Cover with damp cloth, and refrigerate 2 hours or overnight. Roll 1/2 the dough out on well-sugared board (use 3/4 cup) into rectangle 8″ x 16″. Fold ends toward center, and sprinkle with 1 tablespoon sugar. Repeat rolling and sprinkling twice. Roll about 1/4-inch thick, and cut into strips 1″ x 4″. Twist ends in opposite directions, stretching dough slightly. Place in shape of horseshoes on greased cookie sheets. Repeat with remaining dough. Cover, and let rise until doubled in bulk. Bake at 400°F. about 15 minutes. Remove from pans immediately. Makes 5 dozen twists.

Festive Breads. Many festive breads come to us from other countries. Each recipe should be followed carefully, but once you have experimented a little you can, if you wish, use a basic dough, either plain or rich, and vary the way you shape it. Most of these doughs may be either baked in pans or shaped in special ways and baked on cookie sheets.

Sweet Bread Dough

    1 cup milk, scalded
    1/2 cup shortening
    1/3 cup sugar
    1 1/2 teaspoons salt
    1 teaspoon sugar
    1 (1/4-ounce) package active dry yeast
    1/2 cup warm water
    1 egg, well beaten
    4–4 1/2 cups all-purpose flour

To scalded milk add shortening, 1/3 cup sugar and salt. Sprinkle 1 teaspoon sugar and yeast over water and let stand 10 minutes in warm place (80°F.). Stir yeast briskly, and add to milk mixture. Add egg. Beat in 2 cups flour. Combine remaining flour with batter by stirring with hand. Turn dough onto lightly floured board, and knead 5 minutes or until elastic. Shape into smooth ball, place in greased bowl and grease top slightly. Cover, and let rise until doubled in bulk, about 1 1/2 hours. Punch down, and turn onto lightly floured board. Divide into 2 pieces. Form each into a ball. Cover, and let rest 10 minutes. Use 1 ball of dough for each variation.

VARIATIONS:

Swedish Tea Ring: Roll out 1 ball of dough to make rectangle about 9″ x 16″. Brush with melted butter or margarine to within 1/2 inch of edge. Combine 1/2 cup chopped nuts, 1/3 cup brown sugar, 1/4 cup raisins and 1/2 teaspoon cinnamon. Sprinkle this mixture over dough, and roll as for jelly roll. Seal edges well, and shape into circle on greased baking sheet. Dampen, and seal seam. With scissors, snip dough about 3/4 of the way through at 1-inch intervals. Turn each section on its side. Cover, and let rise about 45 minutes, or until doubled in bulk. Bake at 375°F. 25–30 minutes. Glaze, and serve warm. To make glaze, add sufficient milk (about 2 teaspoons) to 1 cup sifted confectioners' sugar to bring the mix to spreading consistency. Flavor with 1 teaspoon vanilla and a few grains salt. Makes 1 tea ring.

Cinnamon Buns: Combine 1/3 cup butter or margarine, melted and 1/2 cup brown sugar. Spread in pan about 8 inches square. Sprinkle with pecan halves. Roll dough to rectangle about 8″ x 13″. Brush with melted butter or margarine, and sprinkle with mixture of 1/3 cup granulated sugar, 1/3 cup chopped walnuts or pecans and 1 teaspoon cinnamon. Roll as for jelly roll, and seal edges. Cut with sharp knife into 12 1-inch slices, and place, cut side down, in prepared pan. Cover, and let rise until doubled in bulk. Bake at 375°F. 25–30 minutes. Turn out and serve at once, with sugary topping up. Makes 1 dozen.

Fruit Braid

3/4 cup lukewarm water
2 teaspoons sugar
2 (1/4-ounce) packages active dry yeast
3 eggs, well beaten
4 1/2 cups all-purpose flour
1/3 cup sugar
1/2 teaspoon salt
1/2 cup chopped nuts
1/4 cup raisins
2 tablespoons chopped candied peel
1 1/3 cups butter or margarine, chilled

Combine water, 2 teaspoons sugar and yeast, and let stand 10 minutes until dissolved. Add eggs. Sift flour, 1/3 cup sugar and salt into separate bowl, and add nuts and fruit. Cut in butter or margarine with pastry blender, and mix well with fork. Make well in center, and add yeast mixture. Stir and knead in bowl. Cover with damp cloth, and let rise in warm place about 2 hours. Divide dough in half, and roll each piece into a long rectangle; cut each into 3 strips, leaving about 1 inch uncut at 1 end. Braid each group of 3 strips together, and place on greased baking sheet, forming into a circle and fastening ends together well. Cover and let rise in warm place until light and puffy, about 1/2 hour. Bake at 350°F. 30 minutes. Makes 1 braid.

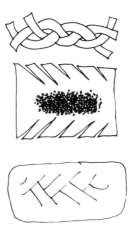

VARIATION:

Fruit-filled Braid: Instead of cutting dough into strips and braiding, roll each large piece into a rectangle about 9″ x 14″. Place on baking sheets, and spread fruit filling down center. For fruit filling, mix 1 1/3 cups chopped peeled apple, 2/3 cup each chopped cooked prunes and brown sugar with 1/2 cup water, 1 tablespoon vinegar, 1/2 teaspoon cinnamon, and 1/4 teaspoon salt. Boil gently until mixture is thick, about 8 minutes; cool before spreading on dough. Slash dough at 1-inch intervals, diagonally, from outer edge in, not quite as far as filling. Fold strips over filling, first 1 side, then the other. Cover, and let rise; then bake.

Apricot–Almond Savarin

1/2 cup chopped blanched almonds
2 (1/4-ounce) packages active dry yeast
1 tablespoon sugar
3/4 cup lukewarm milk
3/4 cup soft butter or margarine
1/2 cup sugar
4 eggs
1 teaspoon vanilla extract
1 teaspoon grated lemon rind
3/4 teaspoon salt
3 1/2 cups all-purpose flour, sifted
2–3 tablespoons chopped orange peel
2–3 tablespoons raisins
1 recipe RICH APRICOT GLAZE
Toasted almond halves
Candied fruits or cherries

Butter 9-inch ring mold generously, and sprinkle bottom and sides with 1/2 cup blanched almonds. Dissolve yeast and 1 tablespoon sugar in milk for about 10 minutes. Cream butter or margarine, remaining sugar and eggs together, and beat until fluffy. Stir in vanilla, lemon rind, salt and yeast mixture. Add sifted flour, and beat until smooth. Fold in orange peel and raisins. Scrape into prepared tube pan, and set in bowl of warm water. Cover with warm wet cloth, and let rise until batter almost fills pan. Bake at 350°F. 30 minutes. Remove cake from pan, and pour 1/2 the glaze over bottom of pan. Return cake to pan, and pour remaining glaze over top and sides. Let marinate several hours. Invert on serving plate, and stick with toasted almonds. Garnish with candied fruits. Slice, and serve plain, or fill hollow with sauce made by blending 1 package frozen raspberries (without defrosting) and folding in 1 cup whipped cream. Savarin may be baked, marinated, cooled, wrapped and frozen. Makes 16 servings.

Rich Apricot Glaze

1/2 cup apricot jam
1/2 cup water
1/2 cup dry sherry, rum or brandy
1/4 cup sugar

Combine all ingredients in saucepan, and simmer about 3 minutes. Makes 1 1/2 cups.

German Apple Cake

1 (1/4-ounce) package active dry yeast
1/2 cup lukewarm water
1 teaspoon sugar
2 eggs
2 tablespoons sugar
1 teaspoon salt
1 teaspoon grated lemon rind
2 3/4 cups all-purpose flour
1/3 cup butter or margarine
1 cup granulated sugar
1/3 cup flour
2 teaspoons cinnamon
6 peeled, cored and sliced cooking apples
1/2 cup butter or margarine, melted

Sprinkle yeast over water, and add 1 teaspoon sugar. Let stand 10 minutes, then stir with fork. Beat eggs in large bowl until light. Stir in 2 tablespoons sugar, salt, lemon rind, dissolved yeast and 1 1/2 cups flour. Beat until smooth; add and beat in 1/3 cup butter or margarine. Work in more flour to make soft dough, about 1 1/4 cups. Turn onto floured board, and knead until elastic; place dough in greased bowl, grease top and let rise, covered, until doubled in bulk (about 1 1/4 hours). Punch down; turn onto floured board and knead. Roll out 1 inch larger than jelly-roll pan. Lift dough into pan; pat and press edges up around sides. Grease top of dough, cover and let rise until almost doubled in bulk, about 45 minutes.

Combine 1 cup sugar, 1/3 cup flour and 2 teaspoons cinnamon. Arrange apple slices over dough, and brush generously with melted butter or margarine. Mix remaining melted butter into flour and sugar mixture, and sprinkle over apple slices. Bake in 375°F. oven 25–30 minutes, covering with foil for first 1/2 of cooking period to soften apples.

Rich Refrigerator Dough

2 1/4 cups lukewarm water
2 (1/4-ounce) packages active dry yeast
1/2 cup sugar
8 cups all-purpose flour
2 teaspoons salt
1/3 cup soft butter, margarine or vegetable
   shortening
3 eggs, well beaten

Measure 1 cup lukewarm water into small bowl; over it sprinkle yeast, and add 2 teaspoons sugar. Let stand 10 minutes to dissolve; then stir with fork. Measure flour into large mixing bowl, and make well in center. To remaining lukewarm water add remaining sugar, salt and butter or margarine into beaten eggs. Add dissolved yeast, and mix thoroughly. Pour mixture into center of flour, and stir until liquid is absorbed, about 1/3 minute. With 1 hand mix dough in bowl, using swinging rotary motion. Gradually form dough into smooth ball; knead in bowl 2 minutes. Transfer dough to greased bowl, large enough to allow at least 1/3 free space for rising (which will take place in refrigerator). Brush top with melted butter, and cover bowl with well-greased waxed paper and tight-fitting lid or refrigerator-bowl cover to prevent formation of crust. Place in refrigerator. Dough may be used after 8 hours or any time within 1 week. If dough rises too much in refrigerator, punch down occasionally. When ready to bake, remove just enough dough from bowl for your recipe. Form piece into ball, turning cut surface under to prevent escape of gases, and allow to rest at room temperature 15 minutes. Then shape according to recipe instructions. Cover remaining dough as before, and store immediately in refrigerator.

Streusel Coffee Cake

        1/4 recipe RICH REFRIGERATOR DOUGH
          1 egg yolk
          2 teaspoons milk
        1/3 cup brown sugar
        1/3 cup flour
        1/2 teaspoon cinnamon
          3 tablespoons butter or margarine, melted

You will need an 8″ x 8″ x 2″ square pan or 8″ x 2″ round pan. Using greased rolling pin, roll out rested ball of dough into square or round to fit nicely into pan. Cover with dampened cloth, with dry cloth over that, and allow dough to rise at warm room temperature, until doubled in bulk (up to 2 hours). When risen, prick top lightly with fork. Combine egg yolk and milk, and brush over dough. Mix brown sugar, flour and cinnamon; add butter or margarine, and combine thoroughly with fork. Sprinkle mixture over dough; then put to rise under damp and dry cloths another 30 minutes. Meantime heat oven to 375°F. Bake coffee cake 25–30 minutes. Loosen edges with spatula, and lift carefully onto cooling rack. Serve warm, cut in squares or wedges. Makes 1 cake.

Butterscotch Rolls

        3/4 cup brown sugar
        1/4 cup butter or margarine, melted
          3 teaspoons water
        1/3 cup whole pecans or walnuts
        1/4 recipe RICH REFRIGERATOR DOUGH

Grease 12 medium-size muffin cups (2 1/2 inches top diameter). Cover bottom of each with 1 1/2 teaspoons brown sugar, 1/2 teaspoon melted butter and 1/4 teaspoon water. Place 3 or 4 nut meats on each. Using greased rolling pin, roll out rested ball of dough to make rectangle 9″ x 12″. Brush last of butter or margarine over top; sprinkle with remaining brown sugar. Roll dough lengthwise as for jelly roll. Seal edge of roll firmly with fingers. Using sharp knife, slice roll into 12 1-inch pieces. Place, cut side down, in prepared muffin tins. Cover pans with dampened cloth, with dry cloth over that. Allow to rise at warm temperature, 75–80°F., away from any drafts until doubled in bulk (about 2 hours). About 20 minutes before rolls are ready to bake, heat oven to 375°F. When rolls have risen almost level with tops of containers, bake 15–20 minutes. Invert tins on cake rack; let stand

5 minutes so that butterscotch mixture will run down over each roll. Turn out rolls, and serve warm or cold. Makes 1 dozen rolls.

Hungarian Coffee Cake

        1/4 recipe RICH REFRIGERATOR DOUGH
          3 tablespoons butter or margarine, melted
        1/3 cup granulated sugar
          1 teaspoon cinnamon
          3 tablespoons chopped walnuts or pecans
          5 maraschino cherries, sliced
          3 tablespoons whole seeded raisins, washed and dried

A tube pan 9 inches in diameter is required. Grease pan thoroughly. Form dough into ball, cover and let stand until other ingredients are ready. Have ready several small bowls, 1 for melted butter, 1 for combined sugar and cinnamon, 1 for chopped nuts, 1 for cherries and raisins. Strew a few chopped nuts, cherries and raisins in bottom of greased pan. Roll dough with hands to form cylinder about 20 inches long. Cut dough with greased knife into 20 1-inch pieces. Form pieces into little balls. Brush each all over with melted butter or margarine, using pastry brush; then dip into sugar and cinnamon mixture. Place some balls in bottom of pan; they should barely touch one another. Strew 1/2 nuts over, and add a few raisins and cherries in spaces between balls, pressing fruit in slightly. Add second layer of dough balls, covering lower spaces. Strew remaining nuts over, and add rest of raisins and cherries, pressing slightly as before. Cover pan with damp cloth, and top with dry towel. Allow dough to rise at warm temperature, 75°–85°F. until doubled in bulk, about 2 hours. Bake in preheated 375°F. oven about 35 minutes. When cake comes from oven, use spatula to loosen it from sides of pan. Invert in pan on rack; cool 10 minutes before removing. Serve warm, breaking cake apart with two forks. Makes 1 cake.

German Coffee Cake

          1 (1/4-ounce) package active dry yeast
          1 teaspoon sugar
        1/3 cup lukewarm water
        1/3 cup soft butter or margarine
        1/3 cup fine sugar
          2 eggs
    2 1/4 cups all-purpose flour
          1 teaspoon grated orange rind
        1/2 teaspoon salt
        1/2 teaspoon ground cardamom
        1/8 teaspoon mace
        2/3 cup lukewarm milk
        1/2 cup chopped almonds
        1/4 cup raisins
        1/4 cup chopped candied fruit peel
          2 tablespoons confectioners' sugar
        1/2 cup whole blanched almonds, split

Dissolve yeast and 1 teaspoon sugar in water. Leave about 10 minutes. Beat next 3 ingredients together, and beat in 1 cup flour. Add orange rind, flavorings, yeast mixture, milk, almonds, raisins, peel and remaining flour. Beat until smooth. Cover, and let rise 45 minutes. Line buttered gugelhupf mold (a 2-quart ring mold or small angel food cake pan will do) with split almonds. Beat dough down, and pour into mold. Cover, and let rise until mixture fills pan, about 1 hour. Bake at 350°F. 45 minutes. Unmold, and dust with confectioners' sugar. Makes one 9" cake.

Chelsea Buns

        1/4 recipe RICH REFRIGERATOR DOUGH
        1/4 cup butter or margarine, melted
          1 cup brown sugar, lightly packed
        1/2 teaspoon cinnamon
        1/3 cup seedless raisins, washed and dried
        1/3 cup chopped nuts

Grease pan and rolling pin. Roll dough to form rectangle about 3/8 inch thick. Brush top surface with a little butter or margarine. Mix 1/2 cup brown sugar with cinnamon, and sprinkle evenly over dough. Strew raisins over sugar. Roll dough as for jelly roll. Seal edge of roll firmly, pinching with fingers. Using sharp knife, slice into 8 or 12 pieces (see Note following recipe). Combine last of butter or margarine and brown sugar with nuts. Spread mixture over bottom of greased pan. Arrange dough slices on top, cut side down. Cover with damp cloth, and top with dry towel; allow buns to rise at warm temperature, 75°–85°F., until doubled in bulk, about 2 hours. Pre-heat oven to 375°F. Bake buns 30 minutes. Remove, and invert pan on cooling rack; let stand 10–25 minutes to allow syrup to run down over buns. Turn out. Serve warm or cooled. Makes 8 large or 12 medium buns.

Note: An 8-inch square or round pan may be used; depth should be 2 inches for medium buns, 3 inches for large ones.

Stollen

          3 (1/4-ounce) packages active dry yeast
    1 1/2 cups lukewarm scalded milk
          6 cups all-purpose flour
    1 1/2 cups butter or margarine
        3/4 cup sugar
          3 eggs
        3/4 teaspoon salt
        3/4 teaspoon grated lemon rind
    1 1/3 cups seedless raisins, washed and dried
          1 cup blanched almonds, chopped
          3 tablespoons butter or margarine, melted
          1 cup confectioners' sugar
          2 tablespoons boiling water
          1 teaspoon lemon juice

Dissolve yeast in milk. Add 1 cupful flour; cover, and let rise in warm place several hours. In large bowl, beat butter or margarine until soft, and add sugar, blending until very creamy. Add eggs, 1 at a time, beating well after each addition. Add salt and grated rind. Turn into risen dough, and beat to incorporate. Sprinkle a little of the remaining flour over raisins and almonds; then add remaining flour gradually to main mixture. Knead in bowl until dough is smooth and elastic. Add raisins and nuts. Cover dough, and let rise until doubled in bulk. Remove to floured board, divide into 3 or more parts and shape each into uniform loaf. Place each in greased loaf pan, and brush with melted butter or margarine. Again let rise until doubled. Bake in preheated 350°F. oven about 45 minutes. Let stand about 15 minutes; then remove to cooling rack. When loaves are quite cool, spread icing on tops and sides. Makes 3 loaves.

To 1 cup confectioners' sugar add boiling water and lemon juice to make icing.

Note: Stollens are old-fashioned European yeast and raisin cakes, always topped with icing.

Danish Pastries. The rich yeast dough used for Danish pastry is prepared and rolled to about 1/4-inch thickness. Sweet butter shortening, or regular butter or margarine, washed free of salt, is then dotted over dough. Or paste can be made by mixing shortening with flour, which is the method used in the following recipes. The dough is then folded over, rolled and chilled. This process of rolling, dotting with fat, folding, rolling and chilling is usually repeated 3 or 4 times, so that finally many layers of pastry are built up. The butter or shortening must be soft enough to roll between layers of dough without breaking through, but not soft enough to soak into dough. When all fat has been used, dough is chilled thoroughly before shaping, rising, baking.

Danish Pastry

    1 1/2 cups butter or margarine
        1/3 cup all-purpose flour
          1 (1/4-ounce) package active dry yeast
          1 teaspoon sugar
        1/2 cup lukewarm water
          1 cup lukewarm scalded milk
          1 egg, beaten
        1/4 cup sugar
    3 1/2 cups all-purpose flour
          1 cup applesauce, jam or preserves
          1 egg, beaten

Prepare butter dough by cutting butter into 1/3 cup flour until grains are the size of marbles. Chill. Combine yeast, 1 teaspoon sugar and water according to directions on yeast package; let stand until dissolved. Beat milk, 1 egg and 1/4 cup sugar together. Stir in enough flour to make batter. Add yeast, and beat until foamy. Add remaining flour to make stiff dough. Shape into loaf, and chill 1 hour. Then roll dough into oblong 1/4 inch thick and twice as long as it is wide. Sprinkle 1/4 chilled butter crumbs over 2/3 the length of yeast dough. Fold unsprinkled piece over middle section, then over again. Roll out again as before. Sprinkle with 1/4 butter crumbs, fold in 3 lengthwise and chill 1 hour. Repeat this rolling and folding process until all butter crumbs have been used. Chill pastry at least 3 hours. Roll dough thinly, and cut in 4-inch squares. Place 1 tablespoon of applesauce in center of each. Bring corners into center, pressing edges to make them stay in place. Brush with beaten egg. Let rise on greased baking sheet in cool place. Bake at 425°F. 10 minutes; reduce heat to 300°F. until done, 10–15 minutes. Makes 2 dozen.

Note: To serve, cover with lemon-cream icing or apricot glaze (1 cup sieved apricot jam, heated to boiling and spread hot over baked pastries).

Cake Making. Basically, there are 3 types of cakes.

Butter cakes include all those made with a solid fat—butter, margarine, lard or shortening. A simple 1-egg cake and an extravagant 3-tiered wedding cake both belong in this category, and there are dozens of other versions—dark and light, rich and plain—ranging between the 2 extremes. All butter cakes, however, have a common richness of flavor and moist texture because of the ingredients they share.

The usual method for preparing butter cakes involves creaming shortening and sugar together until very light and fluffy. It's quite possible though to *overbeat* these ingredients, especially if you are using an electric mixer, so be sure to follow manufacturer's instructions on correct time and speed for your equipment. These instructions generally save an extra step by adding unbeaten eggs to creamed butter-sugar mixture. If you are mixing by hand, however, eggs should

be beaten before they are added, unless the individual recipe specifies otherwise. If yolks and whites are beaten and added separately, the cake texture will be softer and fluffier. Dry ingredients are mixed and sifted together, so that salt and baking powder (or soda) will be evenly distributed throughout batter. A further means to achieve smooth texture is to alternate the addition of dry ingredients and liquids, preferably beginning and ending with the dry.

An electric beater is almost a must, unless you have a strong arm and patience, for several minutes' continuous beating by hand, at 150 strokes a minute, are required, plus careful scraping down of bowl at intervals. With an electric beater, however, the 1-bowl method can produce a very good cake.

For butter cakes grease inside bottom of baking pan, and sprinkle about 1 teaspoon flour lightly over grease; to insure a smooth surface on your cake turn pan upside down to dislodge any surplus. Or cover pan bottom with greased wax paper, cut to fit smoothly. Unsalted shortening or oil is best for greasing.

Butter cakes should be allowed to cool in pan on cake rack 10 minutes for air circulation. Run knife around edge, and carefully remove cake. Cool completely on cake rack before frosting or storing.

Sponge cakes contain no fat. They consist of flour, sugar, eggs and flavorings; the principal leavening agent is air beaten into the eggs. Yellow sponge and angel food are the leading types, but there are also "modified" sponge mixtures, which supplement the leavening with baking powder and the like. Sponge cakes of any type bake best in a rather slow oven—300°–325°F.

Chiffon cakes, a mid-20th century development, are the result of the perfecting of liquid shortenings. As they also have fairly large amounts of beaten egg whites incorporated into the batter, they are often grouped with sponge cakes under the general heading "foam-type cakes." All such types should be baked in *ungreased pans*.

General Hints

Whatever type of cake you plan to make, it is important to have a well-proportioned recipe, with measurements, procedures and baking time carefully spelled out. Study recipe, check ingredients and bring all ingredients to room temperature before starting to mix.

It is not generally advisable to substitute ingredients or to double a recipe, as this may prevent proper blending. A special cake flour milled from soft wheat is best unless recipe specifies differently. All-purpose flour gives coarser texture and slightly smaller volume, but it is quite often preferred for cakes that contain high proportions of fruit.

Before you begin to mix your cake, preheat oven to required temperature. Be sure it has reached correct temperature before cake goes in. Place cake pan as near as possible to center of oven. *Do not open door* until at least 2/3 the recommended baking time has elapsed. Check cake for doneness at minimum time specified in recipe; that is, if recipe says "Bake 25–30 minutes," it is advisable to check at the 25-minute point. If inserted cake tester or toothpick comes out with sticky crumbs adhering, the cake needs an extra 5 minutes. This leeway of 5–10 minutes in recipe baking times is simply a safeguard to allow for differences in oven settings.

To store fruitcakes wrap each cake in a clean cloth dipped in brandy or wine; overwrap in foil or plastic wrap; place in tightly covered container like a breadbox, and store in cool dry place. Remoisten cloth as necessary. Fruitcake stores well in refrigerator and also in freezer.

Cake Pans

It is important to use correct-size pan. The batter itself should fill pan approximately 1/2 full. Some pans have measurements embossed in the metal, which is helpful. If yours doesn't, measure across top to check size.

Shiny metal gives a better result than darkened, warped pans. To prevent uneven browning, be sure your pans have not lost their protective coating.

Glass is great for baking, but requires an oven temperature about 25° lower than specified in recipe.

When making cupcakes, grease muffin cups or line with paper cups or liners. Fill each cup only about 2/3 full of any butter-type cake batter. Bake at 375°F. about 20 minutes. A cake recipe containing 2 cups flour will yield about 18 medium cupcakes.

Generally speaking, pan size specified in recipe is ideal for that particular cake. But it is possible in many cases to use a pan other than the one called for. The amount of batter for 2 8-inch layer pans of shallow depth will generally be successful in 1 8-inch square pan, with extra baking time. A recipe specifying a loaf pan 9″ x 5″ x 3″ can be baked in a 9″ x 9″ x 2″ square pan. Note that for pound cake, though, such a substitution is not advisable: This fine cake should be baked in loaf or tube pan. The shape and size of a tube pan has been designed with angel food cake in mind, but other sponge cakes may be baked in it if you follow guide to approximate capacities at end of this chapter.

Basic Butter Cake

In the practical art of baking, the best way to learn is not only by "doing" but also by knowing some of the reasons for the various steps that you take toward your goal, which is the perfect butter cake.

The following basic steps for 2-EGG CAKE are taken from the first recipe following. You'll be able to follow any recipe for a cake calling for solid shortening, whether butter, margarine, modern packaged lard or vegetable shortening.

1. Read through recipe, and obtain all the ingredients. For this 2-EGG CAKE you'll need butter or other shortening, sugar, eggs, suitable flour, salt, baking powder, milk and flavoring.

2. Assemble necessary utensils. You'll need the right kind of baking pan, in this case an 8-inch square pan or 2 matching round pans 8 inches across by 2 inches deep. You'll also need a large mixing bowl, measuring cups (1 for liquids, nesting set for dry ingredients), measuring spoons, a flour sifter, a wooden spoon, a narrow spatula and a wire rack for cooling cake after baking.

3. All ingredients should be at room temperature to facilitate mixing, so take eggs, butter and milk from refrigerator well in advance. Assemble other ingredients too.

4. Set your oven at temperature specified in recipe to insure even baking, in this case 350°F.

5. Grease bottoms of your cake pans lightly. As salted butter may make cake stick to bottom, use bland shortening. Sprinkle a little flour over greased bottom, then shake pan to distribute flour evenly. Turn pan upside down, and tap it on sides to dislodge any surplus flour. Do not grease sides of pan; your cake will rise better when it can "climb" the sides. As an alternative, cut a piece of waxed paper about 1/4 inch smaller than pan bottom; lay it smoothly in pan and grease over it.

6. Measure butter or shortening into large bowl. Using back of wooden spoon, "paddle" and work it to soft, creamy consistency.

7. Measure sugar. Add it, not more than 2–3 tablespoons at a time so that sugar will dissolve, to butter. Continue to work with back of spoon to keep mixture light and creamy. When all sugar is absorbed, stir and beat vigorously for 1–2 minutes. Add flavoring, in this case vanilla extract.

8. At this point egg yolks or whole eggs, according to individual recipe, are added. For 2-EGG CAKE eggs are added whole, 1 by 1. Combine each thoroughly with butter-sugar mixture, beating vigorously with wooden spoon.

9. Using your dry-measure cup, measure 2 cups sifted flour into sifter. Add baking powder, measured very carefully by leveling off each exact spoonful with straight knife edge; add to flour as you measure, *and count spoonfuls aloud* to avoid making a mistake at this critical point. Measure salt, and add. Sift these dry ingredients together onto another sheet of waxed paper or into a dry bowl.

10. To creamed mixture in large bowl add alternately sifted dry ingredients and measured milk, a little at a time. Using rubber scraper, scrape down bowl and spoon occasionally. Beat to keep batter smooth after each addition, but *do not overbeat* at this stage. In butter cakes requiring separated eggs, the addition of beaten egg white is usually made at this point. The stiff but glossy froth is folded into batter as quickly and lightly as possible, with a down-across-up motion. Batter must not be beaten after this addition, or the air bubbles in the whites will be broken down, and your cake won't be as light as it should be.

11. Pour batter immediately into pan(s) you have prepared. For layer cakes, divide mixture as evenly as possible in order to have layers of uniform depth. Use scraper to remove all batter from bowl. Use spatula to spread batter slightly, with a little more height at sides of pan than in center, which compensates for the tendency of cake to rise in the middle and make an uneven top.

12. Put pan(s) in oven without delay. Set square pan on rack as near center of oven as possible. Set layer pans similarly, but leave some free space around each.

13. Do not open door until minimum baking time in recipe is almost reached. At this point you may test quickly for doneness. Cake is done when it has drawn away from sides of pan, when the top surface springs back when pressed lightly with a finger or when toothpick or metal tester inserted into middle of cake comes out clean, with no dough adhering to it. If the cake needs a few minutes more, shut oven door, and continue for full time specified in recipe.

14. After removing from oven, stand pan on wire cake-cooling rack 10–15 minutes. Circulating air cools the cake and prevents further cooking against pan bottom.

15. To turn cake, run spatula around between cake sides and pan. Place clean towel over top of the cake, and quickly invert covered pan over cake rack. Lift off pan gently. Strip away any lining paper, being careful not to tear cake. Cake may be turned right side up for cooling; or, if cake bottom appears more level than top, you

may decide to make it your surface for filling or icing.

Checking the Finished Cake

Is the cake of uniform depth all around? If not, perhaps batter was not spread evenly; or your oven may not be heating properly.

Is the texture fine and even throughout? Unevenness of texture, with some large air holes, is generally caused by failure to cream butter and sugar sufficiently or to mix in other ingredients thoroughly at the proper time.

Is there heaviness or thickening near bottom of cake? It could mean that sugar was coarse or that butter-sugar mixture was not sufficiently worked to dissolve sugar. Or your oven temperature may have been too low.

Did your cake crack on top? Cracking may be traced to the wrong kind of flour or too much flour. Or the oven temperature may have been too high.

2-Egg Cake (Basic Butter Cake)

> 1/2 cup shortening
> 1 cup sugar
> 1 teaspoon vanilla extract
> 2 eggs, unbeaten
> 2 cups sifted pastry or cake flour
> 2 1/2 teaspoons baking powder
> 1/2 teaspoon salt
> 3/4 cup milk

Cream shortening until very light and fluffy; add sugar gradually, and continue to cream and beat. Add vanilla. Add eggs, 1 by 1, beating thoroughly after each addition. To sifted flour, add baking powder and salt, and sift again. Add sifted ingredients alternately with milk to creamed mixture, beginning and ending with flour and beating to keep batter smooth after each addition. Bake in preheated 350°F. oven. If using 1 8-inch square pan, bake approximately 45 minutes; if using 2 8-inch layer pans, bake

25–30 minutes. Makes one 8″ square cake or 2 8″ round cakes.

VARIATIONS:

Spice Cake: Add 1 teaspoon cinnamon and 1/2 teaspoon each allspice and nutmeg to dry ingredients when sifting.

Nut Cake: Add 1/2 cup finely chopped walnuts to sifted dry ingredients when incorporating with creamed mixture.

Chocolate-fudge Cake: Melt 3 1-ounce squares unsweetened chocolate; beat into creamed mixture after adding eggs; increase milk to 1 cup.

Silver Cake

2/3 cup butter or margarine
2 cups sugar
1 teaspoon almond extract
3 cups sifted cake flour
1/4 teaspoon salt
3 tablespoons baking powder
1 cup water
4 egg whites

Cream butter or margarine and sugar together thoroughly; add almond extract. Sift together flour, salt and 2 teaspoons baking powder. Add to creamed mixture alternately with water, beating well after each addition. Beat egg whites with remaining teaspoon of baking powder until stiff; fold into first mixture. Pour batter into 2 9-inch layer-cake pans, and bake at 350°F. for 30 minutes. Fill and frost.

Gold Cake

1/2 cup butter or margarine
1 cup sugar
3 egg yolks
2 cups sifted cake flour
3 teaspoons baking powder
1/4 teaspoon salt
3/4 cup milk
1 teaspoon grated orange rind
1 teaspoon vanilla extract

Cream butter or margarine, gradually add sugar and beat until mixture is light and fluffy. Beat egg yolks until very thick and lemon-colored; add to creamed mixture, beating thoroughly. Sift together flour, baking powder and salt 3 times; add dry mixture alternately with milk to creamed mixture, beating well after each addition. Stir in orange rind and vanilla. Pour into 2 8-inch layer pans, and bake at 375°F. 25–30 minutes or until cake tests done. Fill and frost.

VARIATION:

Orange Mace Layer Cake: Omit vanilla. Add 1/4 teaspoon mace to dry ingredients before sifting. Replace 1/4 cup milk with fresh orange juice. Fill layers with sieved orange marmalade; frost sides and top with boiled butter icing.

Rich Butter Cake

1 cup butter or margarine
2 cups sugar
4 eggs, separated
1 teaspoon vanilla extract
3 cups all-purpose flour
3 teaspoons baking powder
1/4 teaspoon salt
1 cup milk

Cream butter or margarine, add sugar gradually and continue to blend and beat until very smooth and creamy. Beat egg yolks until thick and lemon-colored; combine with butter mixture. Stir in vanilla, and beat well. Sift together dry ingredients, and add, a little at a time, alternately with milk; beat after each addition except the last, which should be the last of the flour. Beat egg whites until stiff but not dry; fold them into mixture. Divide batter among 3 8-inch layer-cake pans; bake in preheated 350°F. oven 30 minutes. Or bake in rectangular pan, 15″ x 10″ x 2″, about 40 minutes or until toothpick or tester comes out clean.

Apricot–Pecan Torte (Electric Mixer Method)

2 1/2 cups all-purpose flour
2/3 cup finely chopped pecans
1 1/2 cups sugar
1 1/2 teaspoons baking powder
1 teaspoon baking soda
1/2 teaspoon salt
2/3 cup soft shortening
2 (5-ounce) jars strained apricots
2 large eggs
1/2 teaspoon almond extract

Stir 2 tablespoons flour into nuts; set aside. Combine remaining flour, sugar, baking powder, baking soda and salt in large mixer bowl. Add shortening and 2/3 the apricots. Beat at medium

speed 1 1/2 minutes. Add eggs, remaining apricots and flavoring. Beat another 1 1/2 minutes. Fold in floured nuts. Pour batter into 2 deep

9-inch round cake pans lined with greased waxed-paper circles. Bake in 350°F. oven 35–40 minutes. Loosen edges of cake, and cool in pans. The cake may be filled and frosted with orange-flavored boiled icing, or with CARAMEL–CHEESE FROSTING which will require that cake be refrigerated until serving time.

Caramel–Cheese Frosting

1/2 cup sugar
1/4 cup hot water
  1 (8-ounce) package cream cheese
1/2 teaspoon grated orange rind
  4 cups (or slightly more) sifted confectioners' sugar

Melt sugar in small frying pan over low heat until it turns rich golden brown. Add hot water, heat and stir until smooth. Cool. Blend cream cheese with 2 tablespoons cooled syrup; add orange rind, and blend in confectioners' sugar.

Crumb Cake

3/4 cup butter or margarine
  1 cup sugar
  2 cups sifted all-purpose flour
  1 teaspoon cinnamon
1/4 teaspoon nutmeg
1/4 teaspoon powdered cloves
1/4 teaspoon salt
  1 teaspoon baking soda
  2 eggs
3/4 cup sour milk

Prepare 9-inch square pan. Cream butter or margarine, and gradually blend in sugar, beating until light and fluffy. Sift together flour, spices and salt; add to creamed mixture by cutting in with pastry blender or 2 knives. Mixture should be worked until it resembles cornmeal. Measure 1 cup flour mixture, and set aside. To remainder add baking soda, stirring in thoroughly. Beat eggs until foamy; then beat in sour milk. Make well in center of baking-soda mixture, add liquid and combine very thoroughly. Pour batter into prepared pan. Sprinkle reserved crumbs over top, and lightly press into cake top. Bake in 350°F. oven 40–50 minutes. No icing is required.

Butterscotch Coffee Cake

1/4 cup butterscotch sundae topping
1/4 cup brown sugar
  2 cups all-purpose flour
1/3 cup sugar
  4 teaspoons baking powder
1/2 teaspoon salt
1/2 teaspoon nutmeg
1/3 cup butter or margarine
  1 egg, beaten
  1 cup milk
  1 teaspoon vanilla extract
  1 recipe STREUSEL FILLING
1/4 cup chopped walnuts
Candied cherries, sliced (optional)

Grease 8-inch square pan; spread butterscotch topping and brown sugar on bottom of pan. Sift together next 5 ingredients. Cut in butter or margarine. Combine egg with milk and vanilla, and stir into dry mixture. Drop 1/2 the batter by the tablespoon into prepared tin. Sprinkle streusel filling over batter; cover with remaining batter. Bake at 400°F. 30 minutes. Cool in pan 5 minutes; invert cake on rack. Decorate butterscotch surface with nuts, plus sliced candied cherries if desired. Makes 1 8-inch square cake.

Note: The European type of coffee cake is generally made with yeast, but a very satisfactory quick version can be produced with baking powder, as in this recipe.

Streusel Filling

1/3 cup brown sugar
1/4 cup chopped walnuts
  2 tablespoons flour
  1 teaspoon cinnamon
  2 tablespoons butter or margarine, melted

Combine all dry ingredients. Sprinkle melted butter or margarine over. Toss to combine.

Quick Coffee Cake

  2 cups biscuit mix
1/4 cup sugar
1/2 teaspoon cinnamon
1/4 cup milk
  1 (5-ounce) jar strained apricots
  1 egg, beaten
1/2 cup raisins
1/3 cup brown sugar
1/3 cup melted margarine
  2 tablespoons flour

Grease 8-inch square cake pan. Combine biscuit mix, sugar and cinnamon. Combine milk, apricots and egg, and stir into dry ingredients. Spread batter in prepared pan. Combine remaining ingredients, and spread over batter. Bake at 400°F. 25 minutes; let coffee cake cool before cutting and serving. Makes one 8-inch square cake.

Orange Cake

1/4 cup butter or margarine
1/2 cup superfine sugar
  1 egg plus 1 egg yolk
Grated rind of 1/2 orange
1/4 teaspoon salt
1 1/2 cups sifted cake flour
1/2 teaspoon baking powder
1/2 teaspoon baking soda
1/2 teaspoon cream of tartar
1/2 cup milk
1/2 cup sugar
1/4 cup orange juice
  2 tablespoons lemon juice

Cream butter or margarine and 1/2 cup sugar together; add egg and egg yolk, and beat until mixture is very light. Add orange rind. Sift dry ingredients together, and add alternately with milk to creamed mixture. Scrape into well-buttered 8-inch angel-food cake pan, and bake at 350°F. 30–40 minutes. While cake is baking, make syrup of 1/2 cup sugar and juices. Pour over hot cake fresh from oven. Let cake stand until syrup is absorbed; then invert cake onto serving plate. Serve warm or cold.

Pineapple Upside-down Cake

        1/4 cup plus 1 tablespoon shortening
        1/4 cup brown sugar, firmly packed
          6 canned pineapple slices
          8 maraschino cherries
        3/4 cup granulated sugar
          1 egg, beaten
      1 1/4 cups all-purpose flour
      1 1/2 teaspoons baking powder
        1/4 teaspoon salt
        1/2 cup milk
        1/2 teaspoon almond extract
      Grated rind of 1 orange

Melt 1 tablespoon shortening (or butter) in bottom of an 8″ x 8″ x 2″ cake pan, and sprinkle with brown sugar. Arrange pineapple slices, either whole or cut in halves or wedges, with cherries in pattern over brown sugar. Cream 1/4 cup shortening with spoon; add granulated sugar gradually, continuing to work mixture with spoon until fluffy. Add egg, and beat well. Sift next 3 ingredients together. Combine milk and almond extract. Add flour and milk mixtures alternately beating after each addition. Add orange rind. Pour over fruit, and spread evenly. Bake at 350°F. 40 minutes. To serve, turn out, fruit side up, and cut in squares. Can be served warm or cold, with or without cream. Serves 6.

VARIATIONS:

Peach or Apricot Upside-down Cake: Substitute canned peaches or apricot halves for pineapple.

Applesauce Cake

        1/2 cup shortening
      1 1/2 cups brown sugar, lightly packed
          2 eggs
          1 teaspoon lemon extract
      1 2/3 cups all-purpose flour
          3 teaspoons baking powder
          1 teaspoon cinnamon
          1 teaspoon nutmeg
        1/2 teaspoon salt
          1 cup thick applesauce, sweetened and sieved

Prepare 2 round layer-cake pans, 8 or 9 inches across top. Cream shortening thoroughly. Add brown sugar very gradually, creaming and beating after each addition, to make mixture as light and fluffy as possible. Add eggs and lemon flavoring; again beat thoroughly. Sift dry ingredients together, and add alternately with applesauce to creamed mixture, adding just a little at a time and blending well after each addition. Divide batter evenly between pans. Bake in 350°F. oven 30–40 minutes.

Banana Cake (Electric Mixer Method)

      2 1/4 cups all-purpose flour
      1 1/4 cups sugar
      2 1/2 teaspoons baking powder
        1/2 teaspoon baking soda
        1/2 teaspoon salt
        1/2 cup vegetable shortening
          2 eggs
      1 1/2 cups (4–5) mashed bananas
          1 teaspoon vanilla extract

Prepare 2 8-inch layer-cake pans or 1 9-inch square pan. Sift together flour, sugar, baking powder, baking soda and salt in large mixer bowl. Add shortening, eggs and 1/2 cup banana pulp. Beat 2 minutes at medium speed. Scrape bowl often. Add remaining banana and vanilla. Beat 1 minute. Turn into pan(s). Bake in preheated 350°F. oven 30–35 minutes for layers or 50–55 minutes for square cake. Cool. Fill and frost as desired. Or top with sweetened whipped cream and sliced bananas.

Maple-syrup Gingerbread

          2 eggs
          1 cup sour cream
          1 cup maple syrup
        1/2 cup firmly packed brown sugar
        1/2 cup shortening, melted
      2 1/2 cups pastry flour
          3 teaspoons ground ginger
          2 teaspoons cinnamon
          1 teaspoon baking soda
          1 teaspoon baking powder
        1/2 teaspoon salt
        1/2 teaspoon ground cloves
        1/2 teaspoon nutmeg
          1 tablespoon finely chopped candied orange peel

Beat eggs until light, and add sour cream, syrup, brown sugar and shortening. Sift dry ingredients together, add to egg mixture and beat until smooth. Add orange peel. Batter will be thin. Grease deep 8 1/2–9-inch square pan, and line bottom with waxed paper. Pour batter in, and bake at 350°F. for 35–40 minutes or until center is set. Serve with chilled applesauce and whipped cream.

Lemon Cheesecake

                36 chocolate wafers, crushed
               1/3 cup superfine sugar
               1/3 cup soft butter or margarine
                 1 teaspoon grated lemon rind
                 4 (8-ounce) packages cream cheese
           1 1/2–2 cups finely granulated sugar
                 5 eggs, separated
               1/3 cup sifted cake flour
      Juice of three lemons
               1/4 cup heavy cream
               2–3 teaspoons grated lemon rind
                 1 tablespoon superfine sugar
      Shaved chocolate or chocolate curls

Mix wafers, 1/3 cup sugar, butter or margarine and 1 teaspoon lemon rind together, and press thinly onto bottom and halfway up sides of 9- or 10-inch spring-form pan. Bake at 325°F. 10 minutes to prevent sogginess. Let cheese soften at room temperature; then beat until creamy in large mixing bowl. Beat in 1 1/2–2 cups sugar, egg yolks, flour, lemon juice, heavy cream and 2–3 teaspoons lemon rind. Beat egg whites with 1 tablespoon sugar until stiff, and fold into cheese mixture very gently. Batter will be thick. Pour into prepared crust. Bake in preheated oven at 250°F. 1 1/2 hours. Turn heat off, and leave cake in oven 1 hour. Cool at room temperature 4–6 hours. Chill in refrigerator overnight. Before serving, sprinkle top with shaved chocolate or chocolate curls. Cut in small wedges with sharp knife, wiping knife after each cut. Serves 16.

Note: To halve recipe, use same-size pan and all the crumb-crust mixture. Follow procedures for full recipe, using 1 pound cream cheese, 3/4 cup sugar, 3 eggs, 2 tablespoons flour, juice of 1 1/2 lemons, 2 tablespoons heavy cream, 1 1/2 teaspoons grated lemon rind and 1 1/2 teaspoons sugar. Bake 1 hour at 250°F.

Old-Fashioned Pound Cake
(Electric Mixer Method)

                 2 cups (1 pound) butter or margarine
                 4 cups all-purpose flour
               1/2 teaspoon salt
                 2 cups sugar
                 9 eggs
                 1 teaspoon vanilla extract
               1/2 teaspoon mace

Let butter or margarine soften at room temperature. Sift flour and salt together. Following manufacturer's specific instructions for your mixer, cream butter very thoroughly, using largest bowl. Add sugar, a very little at a time, continuing beating and creaming action. Scrape bowl often. After all sugar has been added, beat 1 minute at high speed. Add eggs, 1 at a time, beating 1 minute after each addition. When all eggs have been incorporated, scrape bowl, and

beat 1 minute. Add vanilla and mace. Trickle dry mixture in very slowly, operating mixer at lowest speed. When last of flour has been only just incorporated, pour batter at once, with no further beating, into 2 9″ x 5″ x 3″ loaf pans lined with greased heavy waxed paper. (For convenience in removing cake, let paper extend over sides of pan.) Bake in preheated 325°F. oven 1 hour or until cake has drawn away from sides of pans. Let pans stand on rack 20 minutes; turn out cakes carefully to finish cooling. Store cakes in covered container at least 24 hours before cutting.

Note: This cake freezes well.

VARIATIONS:

Seed Cake: Add 2 teaspoons caraway seeds before turning batter into pan.

Special-occasion Cake: Add 2 tablespoons brandy with vanilla and mace and 1 cup finely chopped candied cherries and pineapple, dusted with a little flour, just before pouring batter into pans.

Christmas or Wedding Cake

                 1 pound seedless black raisins
                 1 pound seedless raisins
                 1 pound currants
               1/2 pound butter or margarine
               1/2 pound shortening
                 2 cups sugar
                 1 tablespoon vanilla extract
                 1 tablespoon almond extract
                12 eggs
                 1 cup brandy or grape juice
               1/2 cup honey
             4 1/2 cups all-purpose flour
                 2 teaspoons cinnamon
                 2 teaspoons baking powder
                 1 teaspoon baking soda
                 1 teaspoon salt
                 1 teaspoon nutmeg
               1/2 teaspoon ground cloves
               1/2 pound pitted dates, cut up
                 1 pound chopped mixed candied peel
                 1 pound candied cherries, halved
               1/2 pound blanched almonds, halved

Use 2 tube pans 10″ x 4″ each, or 5 8 1/2″ x 4 1/2″ loaf pans or 3 graduated cake pans, round or square, plus 1 loaf pan. Line pans with 2 or 3 thicknesses brown or waxed paper; grease well with unsalted shortening.

Wash raisins and currants; dry thoroughly between paper towels. Let butter or margarine and shortening soften at room temperature. Cream together very thoroughly; when smooth and fluffy, add sugar gradually, beating continuously. Blend in vanilla and almond extract. Add eggs, 1 at a time, beating after each addition. Beat brandy and honey; they may cause batter to appear separated, but it will not affect results. Sift together remaining dry ingredients. Put prepared fruits and almonds into large mixing bowl; add sifted dry ingredients, and mix well to coat pieces. Scrape egg-and-butter mixture into bowl, and, using hands, combine very thoroughly. Fill each pan 3/4 full. Preheat oven to 275°F. Bake cakes 2 1/2–3 1/2 hours, depending on size of pans used. After first hour or so, place pan of water on bottom of oven to prevent cakes from drying out. When cakes test done, remove from oven, and let pans stand on racks until contents are completely cooled. Remove from pans, and peel off paper linings. Let ripen 4–5 weeks before serving. See beginning of cake section for storage information.

Note: This recipe makes dark moist cake, rich with fruits and mingled flavors of spices, honey, brandy, and the like. If desired, recipe may be halved with good results.

Foam-type Cakes. The cakes that follow should be cooled completely in pans to prevent shrinkage. Turn pan upside down on cake rack or, if more convenient, suspend from 2 even supports at sides. To remove, run long thin spatula around edge of cake; then tap pan sharply to loosen from pan.

Basic Sponge Cake

> 4 egg whites
> 1/4 teaspoon cream of tartar
> 1/4 teaspoon salt
> 2/3 cup sugar
> 4 egg yolks
> 2 teaspoons lemon juice
> 1/2 teaspoon grated lemon rind
> 3/4 cup all-purpose flour

Beat egg whites with cream of tartar and salt until very stiff but not dry; gradually beat in 1/3 cup sugar and set aside. Beat egg yolks until thick and lemon-colored; then beat in 1/3 cup sugar, lemon juice and rind. Fold this mixture into beaten whites, only until just combined. Sift 1/3 cup flour over fluffy mass, and fold until flour is absorbed; add remaining flour in same manner. Pour into ungreased tube pan 8 or 9 inches in diameter. Bake 45–55 minutes in 325°F. oven. Invert pan until cake is cooled; then remove.

VARIATION:

Spice Sponge Cake: To flour add 1 teaspoon cinnamon and 1/4 teaspoon each nutmeg and allspice. Omit orange juice and rind.

Angel Food Cake

> 1 cup cake flour
> 1 3/4 cups sugar
> 12 egg whites (1 1/2 cups)
> 1 1/2 teaspoons cream of tartar

> 1/4 teaspoon salt
> 1 1/2 teaspoons vanilla extract
> 1/4 teaspoon almond flavoring

Use 1 10-inch tube pan. Sift flour and 1 cup sugar together 3 times. Measure egg whites, cream of tartar and salt into large mixing bowl; beat until foamy. Gradually add 3/4 cup sugar, sprinkling 1 tablespoon at a time over froth. Continue beating until meringue will hold stiff peaks. Fold in flavorings. Gradually sift flour-sugar mixture over meringue. Fold in gently, just until flour is absorbed. Pour batter into ungreased pan. Gently cut through batter with knife to remove any air pockets. Bake at 375°F. 30–35 minutes, until top springs back when touched lightly. Invert pan, cool completely and remove cake.

VARIATIONS:

Coconut Angel Food Cake: Fold 1 cup shredded coconut into meringue when adding flour-sugar mixture.

Mocha Angel Food Cake: Omit almond flavoring. Substitute 1/4 cup cocoa and 2 teaspoons instant coffee for 1/4 cup flour, and sift with sugar and remaining flour.

Cherry Angel Food Cake: Pat dry 1/3 cup finely chopped maraschino cherries, and fold into batter before pouring into pan.

Chiffon Cake

> 2 1/4 cups sifted cake flour
> 1 1/3 cups sugar
> 1 tablespoon baking powder
> 1 teaspoon salt
> 1/2 cup vegetable oil
> 5 egg yolks (3/8 cup)
> 3/4 cup cold water
> 2 teaspoons vanilla extract
> 2 teaspoons grated lemon rind
> 7 or 8 egg whites (1 cup)
> 1/2 teaspoon cream of tartar

Use 1 10-inch tube pan. Sift flour, sugar, baking powder and salt into bowl. Make well in center, and add, in order, oil, yolks, water, vanilla and lemon rind. Beat with spoon until smooth. Measure egg whites and cream of tartar into large mixing bowl; beat until stiff peaks are formed. Pour yolk mixture gradually over beaten whites, folding with rubber scraper just until blended. Pour into ungreased pan. Bake at 325°F. 60–75 minutes. Invert pan until cake is cool. Loosen with spatula to remove from pan.

VARIATIONS:

Confetti Chiffon Cake: Add 1/2 teaspoon cinnamon to dry ingredients. Before pouring batter into pan, sprinkle in 3/4 cup finely chopped red and green cherries and 1/4 cup finely chopped candied fruit peel. Fold in gently with a few strokes.

Candy-stripe Chiffon Cake: Omit lemon rind and vanilla. Add 1 teaspoon peppermint flavoring. Shake in 3 or 4 drops red vegetable coloring during final folding to give striped effect.

Dot Chiffon Cake: Omit lemon rind. Fold 1/2 cup chopped semisweet chocolate bits into batter with egg yolk mixture.

Pink Chiffon Cake: Omit vanilla. Substitute 1/4 cup maraschino cherry juice for 1/4 cup water. Fold in 1/2 cup finely chopped maraschino cherries (first patted dry) and 1/4 cup finely chopped pecans with egg yolk mixture.

Cocoa Chiffon Cake

      1/4 cup cocoa
      1/3 cup boiling water
      7/8 cup sifted cake flour
      7/8 cup sugar
  1 1/2 teaspoons baking powder
      1/2 teaspoon salt
      1/4 cup cooking oil
      4 egg yolks
      1/2 teaspoon vanilla extract
      4 egg whites
      1/4 teaspoon cream of tartar

Mix cocoa with boiling water, and set aside to cool. Sift together into mixing bowl flour, sugar, baking powder and salt. Make well in center, and pour in oil, unbeaten egg yolks, and cooled cocoa. Add vanilla, and beat until mixture is smooth. In large bowl beat egg whites with cream of tartar until very stiff and dry. Pour first mixture gradually over top of egg whites, and gently fold until 2 mixtures are completely blended. Pour into ungreased 9-inch tube pan or 9″ x 5″ x 3″ pan, and bake at 325°F. 50–55 minutes or until cake tests done. Remove from oven, invert immediately on cake rack and let hang until cooled.

Génoise

      1/2 cup sweet butter or margarine
      4 eggs
      1/2 cup finely granulated sugar
      1 cup sifted cake flour
      1/2 teaspoon baking powder
      1/4 teaspoon salt
      1 teaspoon vanilla extract
      1/2 teaspoon grated lemon or orange rind

Oil bottom of 9-inch tube pan. Preheat oven to 350°F. Melt butter or margarine slowly until it froths; remove from heat, and set aside. Beat eggs at high speed 25 minutes or until very thick. Then add sugar, and continue beating about 10 minutes. Meanwhile sift flour, baking powder and salt together. Fold into egg mixture 1/4 at a time. Fold in vanilla and lemon rind. Pour butter or margarine in last, drizzling it over batter slowly, folding as you pour. Stop when you reach sediment and water at bottom of pan (about 2 tablespoons), and discard them. Lift batter up each time you fold to be sure butter or margarine has not settled to bottom. Scrape into prepared pan, and bake 35–40 minutes or until set. Cool upside down; loosen edges with knife, and remove from pan. Slice horizontally through center, and fill and frost with your favorite butter cream frosting. Serves 12.

Chocolate–Rum Sponge Cake

  1 3/4 cups sifted cake flour
      1/4 cup cornstarch
      2 teaspoons baking powder
      1/4 teaspoon salt
      4 eggs, separated
      2 cups finely granulated sugar
      1 teaspoon vanilla extract
      1 cup milk
      2 teaspoons butter or margarine
  1/3–1/2 cup light rum
      1 recipe CHOCOLATE CREAM FILLING
      1/4 cup toasted almonds

Grease and line bottom of deep 9″ x 13″ x 3″ pan with waxed paper. Sift first 4 ingredients together. Beat egg whites until stiff; gradually add 1 cup sugar, and continue beating until very stiff, about 15 minutes. Set aside. Beat egg yolks until thick, and add remaining sugar and vanilla. Continue beating until smooth and cream-colored. Scald milk and butter or margarine together; fold alternately with sifted ingredients into egg yolk mixture, using wire whip or spatula. Fold into egg whites. Scrape into pan, and bake at 350°F. 50–55 minutes. Cool 5 minutes, and run spatula around edge of pan. Invert, and cool completely. Slice cake horizontally through center to make 2 layers. Sprinkle each layer with rum. Fill and frost with filling. Sprinkle with toasted almonds, and refrigerate until serving time (cake can be made the day before serving).

Chocolate Cream Filling

      4 squares semisweet chocolate
      1/4 cup sugar
      1/4 cup milk
      1/8 teaspoon salt
      2 egg yolks, slightly beaten
      1 teaspoon vanilla extract
  1 1/2 cups stiffly beaten cream
      2 egg whites, stiffly beaten

Combine chocolate, sugar, milk and salt in top of double boiler. Heat and stir until blended. Add egg yolks, and cook, stirring, 3 minutes.

Remove from heat, and add vanilla. Stand in bowl of ice cubes, and stir occasionally until cool and thick. Fold in stiffly beaten cream and egg whites. Chill to spread easily.

Cookies. For best results use bright, shiny baking sheet to reflect heat. Darkened metal lets cookies brown too quickly. Grease sheets with shortening to prevent sticking. Place baking sheet in oven so that 2 inches of oven rack show all around it, for proper circulation of heat. The oven rack should be placed almost in center of oven. If 2 racks are used, divide oven into thirds, and stagger baking sheets so they are not directly above one another. When 2 baking times are listed, always check to see if cookies are done at shortest time given. Let delicate cookies cool slightly before lifting, and cool them thoroughly on cake rack.

Soft cookies keep best in airtight containers. Crisp ones need a little air circulation around them and are thus best stored in loosely covered containers.

Unbaked cookie doughs freeze well as do baked cookies if properly packed.

Drop Cookies

Drop cookies are easily and quickly made; the mixture is simply dropped from tip of spoon onto greased cookie sheet. Space cookies about 2 inches apart to allow for spreading. Some drop cookies have soft cake-like texture, others may be firm and macaroons (which are part of this group) have their own distinctive consistency.

Rich Drop Cookies

> 1/2 cup shortening
> 1 cup brown sugar
> 2 eggs, beaten
> 1/2 teaspoon vanilla extract
> 1 3/4 cups all-purpose flour
> 1 teaspoon baking powder
> 1 teaspoon baking soda
> 1/2 teaspoon salt
> 1/3 cup sour milk
> 1/2 cup raisins

Cream shortening, and add sugar. Add eggs and vanilla, and beat until fluffy. Sift flour, baking powder, baking soda and salt together; add alternately with sour milk. Fold in raisins. Drop by teaspoonfuls onto greased cookie sheet, about 2 inches apart. Bake about 12 minutes at 350°F. Makes 4 dozen.

VARIATIONS:

Hermits: Add 1 teaspoon cinnamon, 1/2 teaspoon cloves, 1/2 teaspoon nutmeg with dry ingredients. Fold in 1 cup chopped nuts with raisins.

Date–Almond Drop Cookies: Add 1/2 teaspoon almond flavoring with vanilla. Add 1 1/2 cups chopped dates, and 1/2 cup chopped almonds in place of raisins.

Christmas Drop Cookies: Add 1 cup light golden raisins, 1 cup finely chopped cherries, 1/2 cup sliced blanched almonds, 1/2 cup finely chopped orange peel and 1 teaspoon almond flavoring.

Marmalade Drop Cookies: Add 1/2 cup thick orange marmalade, and reduce sour milk to 1/4 cup.

Cereal Drop Cookies: Use 1/4 cup less flour. Add 1 cup crushed ready-to-eat cereal, 1 cup chopped dates, 1/2 cup chopped walnut meats and 1/4 teaspoon cinnamon.

Coconut Drop Cookies: Add 1 cup shredded coconut.

Chocolate Dot Cookies

> 1/2 cup shortening
> 1/2 cup white sugar
> 1/4 cup brown sugar, lightly packed
> 1 egg, beaten
> 1 teaspoon vanilla extract
> 1 cup all-purpose flour
> 1/2 teaspoon salt
> 1/4 teaspoon baking soda
> 1 cup (6-ounce package) semi-sweet chocolate pieces
> 1/2 cup chopped walnuts

Cream shortening, add all sugar and continue to cream until thoroughly blended. Add egg and vanilla; beat mixture. Sift flour, salt and baking soda together, and add to creamed mixture, combining well. Fold in chocolate bits and walnuts. Drop by teaspoonfuls onto greased baking sheets. Bake in 350°F. oven 10–12 minutes. Makes 3 dozen cookies.

Nut Meringues

        1 1/2 cups finely chopped dates
            1 cup finely granulated sugar
            2 egg whites
        1 3/4 cups finely chopped Brazil nuts

Combine dates and 1/2 cup sugar. Beat egg whites until softly peaked, and add remaining sugar very gradually, beating until very stiff. Fold in dates and nuts. Drop by teaspoonfuls onto baking sheets covered with brown paper. Bake in 275°F. oven 12–15 minutes. Cool on paper; then peel off. Makes 4 dozen meringues.

Note: Nut meringues are delicate little morsels for party use.

Molasses Cookies

            3 cups all-purpose flour
        1 1/2 teaspoons baking soda
            1 teaspoon ginger
            1 teaspoon cinnamon
        1/2 teaspoon salt
        1/2 cup butter or margarine
            1 cup sugar
            1 egg
        1/2 cup dark molasses
            1 cup buttermilk or sour milk
        1/2 teaspoon vanilla extract

Combine flour, soda, spices and salt. Cream butter or margarine until fluffy, and add sugar gradually, continuing to cream. Add egg, and beat well. Stir in molasses. Add sifted dry ingredients alternately with buttermilk, a little at a time, incorporating thoroughly after each addition. Add vanilla. Place bowl of batter in refrigerator 1–2 hours to firm dough. Drop by teaspoonfuls onto lightly greased sheets. Bake in 400°F. oven 8–10 minutes. Makes about 6 dozen cookies.

Coconut Macaroons

            3 egg whites
        3/4 cup sugar
        1 1/2 cups shredded coconut
            1 teaspoon vanilla extract

Beat egg whites to soft peaks; gradually beat in sugar. Place bowl over hot water, and stir until crust begins to form on bottom of bowl. Remove from heat, and stir in coconut and vanilla. Drop by teaspoonfuls onto cookie sheet lined with ungreased brown paper. Bake at 350°F. 10–12 minutes. Makes 3 dozen macaroons.

VARIATIONS:

Date Macaroons: Omit coconut, and add 3/4 cup each chopped dates and chopped walnuts.

Cornflake Macaroons: Omit coconut, and add 1 cup each cornflakes and chopped nuts.

Chocolate Orange Cookies

            1 cup shortening (part butter or margarine)
            1 (3-ounce) package cream cheese
            1 cup sugar
            2 eggs
            2 cups all-purpose flour
            1 tablespoon grated orange rind
            1 teaspoon vanilla extract
            1 teaspoon salt
            1 cup (6-ounce package) semisweet chocolate
                pieces
            1 recipe ORANGE ICING

Cream shortening and cheese together. Add sugar, then eggs, beating until light and fluffy. Stir in flour, orange rind, vanilla and salt, mixing well. Fold in chocolate chips. Drop by teaspoonfuls about 1 inch apart on lightly greased cookie sheet. Bake at 350°F. about 15 minutes. Cookies should be only very lightly browned. While warm, frost with icing. Makes 5–6 dozen.

Orange Icing

            2 teaspoons butter or margarine
            1 cup sifted confectioners' sugar
            2 teaspoons orange juice
        1/8 teaspoon grated orange rind
        Dash salt

Cream butter or margarine with 1/4 cup sugar. Add orange juice, orange rind and salt. Stir in remaining sugar. Beat until smooth. If mixture is too dry, add a few drops more orange juice. A very small amount will glaze top of each cookie.

Fruit–Crumb Cookies

        1 3/4 cups chopped dried apricots
        1 3/4 cups water
            1 cup chopped dates
            1 tablespoon lemon juice
            2 cups all-purpose flour
            1 teaspoon baking soda
        1/4 teaspoon salt
            2 cups quick-cooking oats
        3/4 cup dark brown sugar, firmly packed
        3/4 cup butter or margarine, melted
        1/4 cup corn syrup
            1 teaspoon vanilla extract
        Glacé cherries, sliced dates or nuts

Soak apricots in water overnight, or simmer 1 hour. Add dates, and simmer until very thick, about 20 minutes. Add lemon juice; cool. Sift flour, baking soda and salt into bowl; add oats and sugar. Combine butter or margarine, syrup and vanilla, and stir into flour mixture, which will then consist of coarse crumbs. Drop cooled fruit mixture by teaspoonfuls into crumbs. Roll until well coated. Arrange on greased cookie sheet, and decorate with glacé cherries. Bake at 375°F. 15 minutes or until golden brown. Makes 5 dozen.

Anytime Cookies

1 cup margarine or butter
1 cup light brown sugar, firmly packed
2 eggs
2 teaspoons rum extract
Grated rind of 1 orange
1 cup finely chopped dates
Juice of 1 orange
1/2 cup chopped walnuts
1/2 cup fancy molasses
1/2 cup peanut butter
2 cups sifted all-purpose flour
1 teaspoon baking powder
1 teaspoon salt
1/2 teaspoon baking soda
2 cups bran

Cream butter or margarine and sugar together. Add eggs, rum flavoring and orange rind. Soak dates in orange juice a few minutes, and add to butter mixture. Add nuts, molasses and peanut butter. Sift next 4 ingredients together, and add with bran. Drop from teaspoon onto greased cookie sheets. Bake at 375°F. 10 minutes. Makes 6 dozen.

Ragged Robins

1 cup soft butter or margarine
2 cups lightly packed brown sugar
3 cups sifted all-purpose flour
1 cup chopped walnuts
1/2 cup finely chopped mixed candied fruit
2 eggs
2 tablespoons water
2 teaspoons baking soda
1 teaspoon vanilla extract
1/2 teaspoon salt
1/2 cup chopped glacé cherries

Cream butter or margarine with sugar. Add all ingredients (except cherries) together. Drop by spoonfuls onto greased cookie sheet, center each with cherry and bake at 350°F. 12 minutes or until light brown. Makes 8 dozen or more, depending on size.

Melting Moments

2/3 cup soft butter or margarine
2/3 cup superfine sugar
2 eggs
1 cup sifted all-purpose flour
1/2 cup cornstarch
2 teaspoons baking powder
1 teaspoon grated lemon rind or vanilla extract
1 cup flaked coconut or chopped roasted almonds

Beat butter or margarine, sugar and eggs together until very fluffy. Sift dry ingredients together and stir in butter mixture. Add lemon rind and coconut. Grease cookie sheets with salad oil or unsalted fat to prevent burning, and drop mixture 2 inches apart by small teaspoonfuls. Bake at 350°F. 10–12 minutes or until centers are set and edges golden brown. Makes 6 dozen. *Note*: For fruit-flavored drops, add 1/2 cup finely chopped candied fruit or 1/2 cup coconut.

Refrigerator Cookies

Any cookie dough stiff enough to hold its shape may be formed into a long roll and refrigerated for baking at a later time. Wrap securely in waxed paper, and store in refrigerator. It will keep 3–4 weeks. If you freeze wrapped dough, it will keep 6 months.

In slicing refrigerator cookies, always use a sharp thin or serrated knife. Dip in hot water, and wipe dry; the warm metal will cut more easily.

Cookies sliced very thin will be crisp; thicker slices tend to be softer after baking. Always allow 2–3 minutes' additional baking time for thicker ones.

Cherry Refrigerator Cookies

1/2 cup shortening
1 1/4 cups granulated sugar
2 eggs, well beaten
Juice and grated rind of 1/2 lemon
1/4 teaspoon almond extract
2 1/4 cups sifted all-purpose flour
1 1/2 teaspoons baking powder
1/2 teaspoon salt
2/3 cup chopped candied cherries
1/2 cup chopped almonds or filberts
1/3 cup chopped candied pineapple (optional)

Cream shortening and sugar together. Add eggs, lemon juice, rind and almond extract. Sift dry ingredients together, and stir in; add fruit and nuts. Mix well. Chill dough. Form into 1 1/2-inch rolls. Wrap in waxed paper; chill again. Slice 1/4 inch thick, and place on greased cookie sheets. Bake at 400°F. 10 minutes. Makes 5 dozen.

Butterscotch Cookies

1/2 cup butter or margarine
2 cups brown sugar, lightly packed
2 eggs, beaten
1/2 teaspoon vanilla extract

    3 cups all-purpose flour
    1 teaspoon baking soda
    1/2 teaspoon cream of tartar
    1/4 teaspoon salt
    1/2 cup chopped walnuts

Cream butter or margarine until soft and fluffy; add brown sugar, continuing to cream. Add eggs and vanilla. Sift dry ingredients together. Blend into egg mixture gradually. When mixture is smooth, add walnuts. Have ready several layers of waxed paper; turn dough onto paper, and shape into roll of uniform thickness, about 2 inches in diameter. Wrap tightly in waxed paper, and store in refrigerator. When ready to bake, preheat oven to 375°F. Cut slices from chilled dough, arrange on greased cookie sheet, leaving space between, and bake. Slices 1/4 inch thick will bake in 5–7 minutes. Keep remainder of dough well wrapped in refrigerator. Makes 5 dozen.

Orange Cookies

    1 cup shortening
    1 cup sugar
    1 egg, beaten
    1/3 cup orange juice
    2 tablespoons grated orange rind
    1/2 teaspoon vanilla extract
    2 3/4 cups all-purpose flour
    1 1/2 teaspoons baking powder
    1/2 teaspoon salt

Cream shortening, add sugar and continue creaming until fluffy. Add egg, orange juice, orange rind and vanilla; beat mixture until smooth. Sift together flour, baking powder and salt; blend into first mixture thoroughly. Place dough on waxed paper, and shape into 1 or more rolls about 2 inches in diameter. Wrap securely. Refrigerate until needed. Slice 1/4″ thick, and place on greased cookie sheets. Bake at 400°F. 10 minutes. Makes about 5 dozen.

VARIATIONS:

Orange–Nut Cookies: Add 1 cup finely chopped nuts to dough before shaping.

Chocolate–Orange Pinwheels: Divide dough in 1/2. To 1 portion add 1 square unsweetened chocolate, which has been melted and cooled. Roll each piece of dough to a uniform oblong. Place chocolate dough on top of plain dough, and roll together firmly. Chill very thoroughly before slicing.

Rolled Cookies

Roll out on lightly floured pastry cloth or board; then cut into desired shapes. The dough should be well chilled; otherwise more flour will be needed, and cookies will be heavier. Part of

dough may be rolled out as needed and remainder left in refrigerator for later use.

Roll dough about 1/4 inch thick. Cut out with floured cutter in plain rounds or use fancy cutter shapes. Gather up remaining scraps of dough, combine, roll out again, and cut. Second and third rollings will result in somewhat less tender cookies.

Sugar Cookies

    2/3 cup shortening
    1 1/2 cups sugar
    2 eggs
    1 teaspoon vanilla extract
    3 3/4 cups all-purpose flour
    2 1/2 teaspoons baking powder
    1/2 teaspoon salt
    1 tablespoon milk
    2 tablespoons cream or 1 egg white

Cream shortening, and add sugar gradually, continuing to cream. Add eggs and vanilla; beat until light and fluffy. Sift dry ingredients together. Blend into creamed mixture thoroughly; add milk. Chill dough. When ready to bake roll dough 1/4 inch thick for soft cookies and about 1/8 inch thick for crisp cookies. Cut in any desired size or shape. Use broad spatula to trans-

fer cookies to greased baking sheet. Leave about 1/2 inch between cookies. Brush lightly with cream. Decorate as desired with nutmeats, sprinkles of colored sugar and the like. Bake in 400°F. oven 8–10 minutes. Makes about 6 dozen cookies.

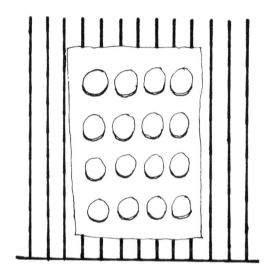

VARIATIONS:

Lemon Sugar Cookies: Omit vanilla. Add 2 tablespoons finely grated lemon rind and 1 tablespoon lemon juice.

Butterscotch–Almond Cookies: Use brown sugar in place of white sugar. Add 1/3 cup finely ground blanched almonds.

Chocolate Sugar Cookies: Add 3 squares unsweetened chocolate, melted and cooled, to creamed shortening egg mixture.

Old-timers

        3/4 cup lard
        3/4 cup granulated sugar
        3/4 cup molasses
        3/4 cup sour cream
          2 eggs, well beaten
    4 1/2 cups sifted all-purpose flour
          2 teaspoons baking soda
          2 teaspoons cinnamon
    1 1/2 teaspoons salt
          1 teaspoon ground ginger

Cream lard and sugar together well. Add molasses and cream, then eggs. Sift dry ingredients together, and stir in. Dough will be soft. Chill in refrigerator overnight. Use 1/2 the dough at a time. Roll out lightly, 1/4 inch thick, on floured cloth. Cut rounds 2 1/2–3 inches in diameter. Place on greased cookie sheets, and bake 15–20 minutes. These cookies are good warm, spread with butter or eaten with cheese. Makes 4 dozen.

Crisp Oatmeal Cookies

          1 cup shortening, butter or margarine
          1 cup brown sugar
          2 eggs, beaten
          2 cups all-purpose flour
          1 teaspoon baking soda
      1/2 teaspoon salt
          2 cups rolled oats
          1 teaspoon vanilla extract

Cream shortening, add sugar and continue creaming. Beat in eggs. Sift together flour, baking soda and salt; add to egg mixture. Stir in oats and vanilla; blend well. Chill. Divide dough into sections for easy handling, and roll out very thin on floured pastry cloth. Cut with 2 1/2-inch floured cookie cutter, and place on lightly greased sheet. Bake at 375°F. 6–8 minutes. Cooled baked cookies can be put together in sandwich fashion with jam or date fillings. Makes 6 dozen single cookies.

Scotch Shortbread

          1 cup butter or margarine
      1/2 cup brown sugar, lightly packed
          1 egg yolk
          1 teaspoon vanilla extract
          2 cups all-purpose flour
          1 teaspoon baking soda

Cream butter or margarine. Add brown sugar, and continue to cream thoroughly. Add egg yolk and vanilla, and beat mixture until light and fluffy. Sift together flour and soda; add gradually to creamed mixture, and combine completely. Turn out dough onto lightly floured board. Roll 1/4-inch thick. Cut in strips, squares or fancy shapes. Bake on ungreased sheet in 300°F. oven 18–20 minutes.

Note: If desired, decorate shortbread tops with halved nuts, candied cherries, angelica, and the like.

Coffee Shortbread Fingers

          1 cup soft butter or margarine
      2/3 cup firmly packed brown sugar
          1 teaspoon instant coffee
    2 1/2 cups sifted cake flour
          1 egg white, slightly beaten
          1 cup finely chopped nuts

Cream butter or margarine and sugar together. Blend in coffee, add flour gradually and mix thoroughly. Chill dough. Roll out 1/2 inch thick, and cut into fingers. Dip fingers in egg white; then roll in finely chopped nuts. Place on ungreased baking sheets. Bake at 300°F. 20–25 minutes. Cool, store in covered tin, with waxed paper between each layer of cookies. Makes about 4 dozen.

Squares, Bars and Molded Cookies

Apricot Dream Squares

> 1 cup crushed graham crackers
> 1 cup sifted all-purpose flour
> 1 cup shredded coconut
> 1 cup brown sugar, packed
> 1/2 teaspoon salt
> 1/2 cup butter or margarine, melted
> 1 cup dried apricots
> 1 cup water
> 2 eggs
> 1 cup brown sugar, packed
> 1 tablespoon lemon juice
> 1/3 cup sifted all-purpose flour
> 1/2 teaspoon baking powder
> 1/4 teaspoon salt

Combine first 5 ingredients. Add butter or margarine and mix well. Reserve 1 cup mixture for topping. Pack remainder in bottom of 9-inch square cake pan. Bake 10 minutes at 350°F. Cover apricots with water. Simmer until tender, approximately 15 minutes. Drain, chop, and set aside. Beat eggs until light, and add brown sugar and lemon juice. Sift remaining ingredients together, and stir into eggs; add apricots. Spread over bottom layer. Sprinkle with topping. Bake 30–35 minutes at 350°F. Cool. Cut into 20 squares.

Marshmallow–Fudge Squares

> 2 cups graham cracker crumbs
> 1/2 cup chopped walnuts
> 3 squares unsweetened chocolate, melted
> 1 (14-ounce) can sweetened condensed milk
> 1/2 teaspoon vanilla extract
> Pinch salt
> 18 large marshmallows, halved
> 1 package chocolate frosting mix, made according to directions

Mix first 6 ingredients together, and spread in greased 8-inch square pan. Bake at 325°F. 25 minutes. Cover with marshmallows, cut sides down, and cool. Drizzle with frosting. When completely cold, cut into 30 small squares.

Fruit Squares

> 1/2 cup soft butter or margarine
> 3 tablespoons brown sugar
> 1 cup sifted all-purpose flour
> 1/2–3/4 cup raspberry jam
> 1/3 cup butter or margarine
> 1/2 cup sugar
> 1/2 teaspoon salt
> 2 eggs
> 1 1/2 cups stale white-cake crumbs
> 1/2 cup raisins

> 1/2 cup chopped mixed candied fruit peel
> 1/4 cup milk
> 1/2 teaspoon rum extract
> 1/4 cup chopped walnuts

Cream first 2 ingredients together, add flour, and spread in greased 8-inch square pan. Bake at 350°F. 10–12 minutes. Remove from oven, and spread with jam. Beat next 4 ingredients together until fluffy, and stir in all remaining ingredients except nuts. Spread over jam. Sprinkle with nuts. Bake at 350°F. 40–45 minutes. When thoroughly cool, cut into 24 squares.

Chocolate–Prune Bars

> 1 cup pitted cooked prunes
> 1/3 cup granulated sugar
> 1/4 cup water
> 1/4 cup orange juice
> 1 cup sifted all-purpose flour
> 1 cup brown sugar, firmly packed
> 1/2 teaspoon salt
> 1/4 teaspoon nutmeg
> 1/2 cup soft shortening
> 1 1/2 cups uncooked rolled oats
> 1 cup (6-ounce package) semisweet chocolate pieces
> 1 tablespoon orange rind
> 1/4 cup milk

Combine first 4 ingredients, and cook in saucepan until mixture thickens, about 10 minutes. Cool. Measure flour, sugar, salt and nutmeg into bowl, and cut in shortening until texture is that of coarse meal. Add oats, chocolate pieces, rind and milk. Mix lightly. Pack 1/2 the oat mixture into greased 8-inch square pan. Cover with prune mixture, and spread remaining oat mixture over top. Press down well, and bake at 325°F. 50–60 minutes. Cool, and cut in bars. For thinner bars use 8″ x 10″ pan, and bake at 350°F. 35–40 minutes.

Cherry–Nut Treats

> 1/2 cup shortening
> 1/4 cup granulated sugar
> 1 egg, separated
> 1 1/2 teaspoons grated lemon rind
> 1 teaspoon grated orange rind
> 1/2 teaspoon vanilla extract
> 1 tablespoon lemon juice
> 1 cup sifted cake flour
> 3/4 cup chopped walnuts
> 6 candied cherries, coarsely chopped

Cream shortening and sugar together until fluffy. Beat egg yolk and add to shortening with lemon juice, lemon rind, orange rind and vanilla. Add flour, and mix well. Wrap in waxed paper, and chill several hours. Roll into small balls. Beat egg white slightly, and dip balls in it, then

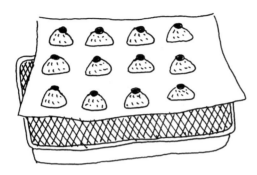

in chopped nuts. Place on greased cookie sheet. Press small piece of cherry into each. Bake at 350°F. 12–15 minutes. Makes approximately 3 dozen.

Salted Peanut Sticks

    1/2 cup soft butter or margarine
      1 cup brown sugar, firmly packed
      1 egg
      1 teaspoon vinegar
      1 teaspoon grated lemon rind
    1/2 teaspoon allspice
      2 cups all-purpose flour
  1 1/2 cups salted peanuts, chopped

Cream first 4 ingredients together until fluffy. Add lemon rind and allspice. Work in flour and peanuts. Press mixture firmly and evenly into 8-inch square pan lined with waxed paper. Chill in freezer until firm. Remove from pan, and peel off paper. Cut square in half; then slice each rectangle into 1/4-inch slices to make fingers 4 inches long and 1/2 inch wide. Place on oiled cookie sheets, and bake at 325°F. 25–35 minutes or until lightly browned. Makes 5 dozen.

Date Squares

      1 cup butter or margarine
      1 cup brown sugar, firmly packed
  1 3/4 cups all-purpose flour
      1 teaspoon salt
    1/2 teaspoon baking soda
  1 1/2 cups rolled oats
      1 recipe DATE FILLING

Cream shortening and sugar well. Sift flour, salt and baking soda together, and stir in. Mix in rolled oats. Place 1/2 mixture in greased 13″ x 9″ cake pan, and pat down firmly. Spread with filling. Cover with remaining crumb mixture, and pat lightly. Bake at 400°F. 25–30 minutes or until lightly browned. Cut in squares while warm, and remove from pan. Makes 2 1/2 dozen medium bars or 4 dozen smaller ones.

Date Filling

      3 cups dates, cut up
  1 1/2 cups boilng water
    1/4 cup brown sugar

Combine all ingredients in saucepan, cook about 10 minutes until mixture takes on consistency of jam and cool thoroughly.

Molded Peanut Butter Cookies

      1 cup shortening
      1 cup brown sugar
      1 cup white sugar
      2 eggs
      1 cup peanut butter
      1 teaspoon vanilla extract
  2 1/2 cups all-purpose flour
      1 teaspoon baking soda
      1 teaspoon baking powder

Cream shortening; add all sugar, and continue creaming until fluffy. Beat in whole eggs. Stir in peanut butter and vanilla; beat mixture very thoroughly. Sift together flour, baking soda and baking powder. Add dry ingredients, a little at a time, to batter, and mix until well blended. Place dough in refrigerator 1–2 hours to firm. Pinch off pieces of dough, and roll into balls the size of walnuts. Arrange on greased baking sheet, and flatten each ball by pressing with fork; let tines make criss-cross pattern. Bake in 375°F. oven 10–12 minutes. Makes about 6 dozen cookies.

Dream Bars

    1/3 cup shortening
    1/3 cup confectioners' sugar
      1 teaspoon vanilla extract
      1 egg yolk
  1 1/3 cup all-purpose flour
    1/4 teaspoon salt

Cream shortening and 1/3 cup confectioners' sugar together; stir in 1 teaspoon vanilla and egg yolk. Add 1 1/3 cups flour and 1/4 teaspoon salt; mix well. Press dough into 1 8-inch square pan lined with waxed paper. Bake at 350°F 12 minutes.

    1/2 cup strawberry jam
      1 egg plus 1 egg white
      1 cup brown sugar
      2 tablespoons flour
    1/2 teaspoon salt
    1/4 teaspoon baking powder
      1 cup chopped nuts
    1/2 cup flaked coconut
      1 teaspoon vanilla extract

Spread jam over baked crust. Beat egg and egg white until light, add brown sugar and beat until thick. Sift together 2 tablespoons flour, 1/2 teaspoon salt and baking powder; add to egg mixture. Fold in nuts, coconut and vanilla. Spread over jam, bake 25–30 minutes.

> 1 cup confectioners' sugar
> 2 tablespoons hot milk
> 1/4 teaspoon vanilla extract

Combine 1 cup confectioners' sugar, milk and 1/4 teaspoon vanilla. Frost baked bars in pan while still warm, and cool in pan. Cut into 24 squares or bars.

Cherry Meringue Squares

> 1/2 cup butter or margarine
> 1/4 cup brown sugar
> 1 cup all-purpose flour
> 1/2 teaspoon baking powder
> 1/2 teaspoon salt
> 1 (6-ounce) jar maraschino cherries, drained and quartered
> 2 egg whites
> 1/4 teaspoon cream of tartar
> 1 1/4 cups sieved brown sugar
> 1/2 teaspoon vanilla extract

Cream butter or margarine and 1/4 cup brown sugar together. Sift flour, baking powder and salt, and blend thoroughly with sugar mixture. Pat into 8-inch square pan, and bake at 350°F. 15 minutes. Sprinkle with quartered maraschino cherries. Beat egg whites until frothy; add cream of tartar, and beat until soft peaks form. Gradually add 1 1/4 cups brown sugar, and continue beating until stiff. Fold in vanilla. Spread meringue evenly over baked layer, and bake 25 minutes at 350°F. When cool cut into 24 squares.

Variety Bars

> 2/3 cup shortening, butter or margarine
> 2 1/4 cups brown sugar
> 3 eggs
> 2 1/3 cups all-purpose flour
> 2 1/2 teaspoons baking powder
> 1/2 teaspoon salt
> 1/4 cup mixed maraschino cherries and drained crushed pineapple
> 1/2 cup mixed grated semisweet chocolate and chopped walnuts
> 1/4 cup mixed chopped dates and chopped almonds

Cream shortening and brown sugar thoroughly. Add eggs 1 at a time, beating after each addition. Sift flour, baking powder and salt; mix gradually into egg mixture. Divide batter among 3 bowls. Add cherries and pineapple to 1, chocolate and walnuts to another and dates and almonds to the third. Pour into 3 well-greased 8-inch square pans. Bake at 350°F. 25–30 minutes. Cut into 6 dozen bars.

Dutch Cookies

> 2 2/3 cups unsifted cake flour
> 1 teaspoon cinnamon
> 1/2 teaspoon baking soda
> 1/4 teaspoon salt
> 1 cup butter or margarine
> 1 cup brown sugar
> 1/2 teaspoon almond extract
> 1 small egg
> 1 teaspoon cold water
> 1/2 cup blanched almonds, chopped or slivered
> 1/3 cup sugar

Sift first 4 ingredients together, and knead in butter or margarine and brown sugar. Add almond extract. Divide dough in half, and press out very thinly on 2 ungreased 15" x 10" cookie sheets (press out to edges of pans with sides or 1/2 inch from edge on flat sheets). Beat egg, and add water. Brush over dough. Sprinkle with almonds and white sugar. Bake at 350°F. 15–17 minutes. Cool 2 minutes; cut into 4" x 2" rectangles. Makes 6–7 dozen.

No-bake Confections

Fruit Balls

> 1 1/2 cups mixed dried fruits
> 1/2 cup dried figs
> 1/2 cup sultana raisins
> 1/4 cup walnuts
> 2 tablespoons honey
> 1/2 teaspoon almond extract
> 1 cup toasted coconut

Wash fruits and dry well. Put fruits and walnuts through food grinder. Combine with honey and almond flavoring, mixing well. Shape into balls about the size of walnuts. Roll in toasted coconut. Chill at least 1 hour. Makes 3 dozen balls.

Brandy Balls

> 1 cup (6-ounce package) semisweet chocolate pieces
> 1/2 cup sugar
> 3 tablespoons corn syrup
> 2 1/2 cups (about 5 dozen) finely crushed vanilla wafers
> 1 cup finely chopped walnuts
> 1/2 cup brandy
> 1/4 cup superfine sugar

Melt chocolate in top of double boiler over hot (not boiling) water. Remove from heat. Stir in 1/2 cup sugar and corn syrup. Blend in wafer crumbs and nuts; add brandy. Mix thoroughly. Form into 1-inch balls. Roll in fine sugar. Let ripen in covered container 2–3 days. Makes about 4 1/2 dozen.

Tips on Frostings and Fillings. If you use a cooked filling, let it cool a little. Spread it over bottom layer; then let filling set a while before placing second layer on top. Butter icings are easy to make and use. Be sure to sift confectioners' sugar, so that frosting will be smooth and creamy. Cooked icings will be perfect every time if syrup is cooked to exact temperature specified in recipe. You can test with a candy thermometer.

It is best to ice sides of cake before doing top. Swirl icing lightly upward from bottom edge to top to assure well-shaped finished cake. A tablespoon or spatula is good for swirling. If you like tinted icing, add only a few drops of vegetable coloring.

Cake crumbs won't get mixed in with creamy frosting if you brush them off with a soft pastry brush beforehand.

For smooth icing on which you plan to write "Happy Birthday" or similar message, make a special effort to hold spatula straight while applying. Use plenty of icing mixture, and scrape it over contours of cake; then dip knife in hot water, and smooth any ridges or dents.

Double-boiler icings sometimes lose their smooth appearance while you are busy with the first spreading. Just beat them up again over hot water, and continue.

Frostings made with butter or shortening will stiffen to good spreading consistency if you place them over a bowl of ice and beat them well.

For really fast finishing touches, decorate iced cake with thin, colored fondant patties cut in half, crushed peppermint candies, crushed and sifted peanut brittle, small marshmallows dipped in delicate food coloring and cut in half or halved thin chocolate wafers stuck into frosting at an angle to make an attractive pattern.

If you have a cookie press, use it for finishing touches. Prepare a thick butter-type frosting of about the same consistency as cookie dough. Put it into press, and produce star, wreath or petal shapes, keeping gadget upright just as you would when pressing out cookies. If basic frosting is sticky, it is best to press shapes out on waxed paper, and let them set a little; then with a knife lift them to positions on the cake. Bits of candied fruit or gumdrops may be dropped onto the various shapes.

For tinted coconut or sugar crystals, half-fill a small jar; then add a few drops of food coloring, cover and shake well.

Dip blanched almonds in vegetable coloring or melted chocolate, and allow to dry. They make attractive touches as edgings around a cake or as "petals" when arranged in flower formations.

Large curls of Brazil nuts make an impressive garnish on chocolate or mocha frosting. To prepare them, use a sharp vegetable scraper or peeler, and pull it toward you the full length of the nut. Try to have each curl about 1/8 inch thick. For chocolate curls, let 1 square semisweet chocolate soften slightly; then scrape with vegetable peeler in the same way.

For swirls on fluffy frostings, drop a little thick butterscotch or chocolate ice cream sauce here and there on the topping; swirl each blob gently with back of spoon.

For the easiest possible garnish, try fruit-flavored gelatin powder straight from the package, sprinkled on a plain whipped-cream topping.

Plain Butter Icing

> 1/4 cup butter or margarine
> Dash salt
> 2 cups sifted confectioners' sugar
> 3 tablespoons cream or milk
> 1 teaspoon vanilla extract

Cream butter or margarine until very fluffy. Add salt and, very gradually, about 1/2 cup sugar, continuing to cream. Add remaining sugar alternately with cream, beating after each addition. When mixture is smooth, add vanilla. Spread on 8-inch square cake or over top and sides of 2–8″ layers.

Butter Cream Icing

> 1/4 cup butter or margarine
> 2 cups sifted confectioners' sugar
> 1 egg yolk
> 1 teaspoon vanilla extract
> 1 tablespoon cream

Thoroughly cream butter or margarine with 1 cup sugar. Stir in unbeaten egg yolk and vanilla. Add remaining sugar and cream. Beat until spreading consistency is achieved. Spread on top and sides of 9-inch square cake.

VARIATIONS:

Chocolate Butter Cream Icing: Add 1 1/2 squares melted unsweetened chocolate to butter after first 1/4 cup sugar has been added. Beat until well blended before adding remaining sugar.

Lemon–Banana Butter Cream Icing: Substitute 3 tablespoons mashed bananas and 1 tablespoon lemon juice for cream and vanilla.

Orange Butter Cream Icing: Substitute orange juice for cream and 1 teaspoon grated orange peel for vanilla.

Mocha Butter Cream Icing: Sift 3 tablespoons cocoa and about 1/4 teaspoon instant coffee with sugar.

Seven-minute Frosting

    1 1/2 cups sugar
        2 egg whites
      1/3 cup cold water
    1 1/2 teaspoons light corn syrup or 1/4 teaspoon cream
            of tartar
        1 teaspoon vanilla extract
Few grains salt

Place all ingredients except vanilla in top of double boiler. Beat 1 minute with electric mixer or rotary beater. Set over boiling water, and beat constantly with rotary or electric beater until mixture forms peaks, about 7 minutes. Remove from heat, and add vanilla. Beat until mixture is of spreading consistency. This amount will frost top and sides of 2 9-inch layers or 1 10-inch tube cake. For smaller amount, halve all ingredients, and cook about 4 minutes. This amount will frost top of average loaf cake, top and sides of 8-inch tube cake or 8–10 cupcakes.

VARIATIONS:

Chocolate Seven-minute Frosting: Fold 3 (1-ounce) squares melted unsweetened chocolate into finished frosting; do not beat.

Ivory Seven-minute Frosting: Substitute 1/4 cup brown sugar for 1/4 cup granulated sugar.

Peppermint Seven-minute Frosting: Add 2 drops of peppermint and 4 drops green vegetable coloring.

Pineapple Seven-minute Frosting: Substitute canned pineapple juice for water. Omit vanilla; add 1 teaspoon grated lemon rind. Tint yellow if desired.

Broiled Frosting

      1/2 cup brown sugar
      1/3 cup soft butter or margarine
        2 tablespoons evaporated milk or cream
      1/2 cup chopped nuts or coconut

Beat first 3 ingredients together. Fold in nuts. Spread on top of warm 9-inch square cake. Place on broiler rack so that top is 4 inches from heat. Broil 3 minutes or until frosting bubbles.

VARIATION:

Broiled Peanut Butter Frosting: Add 1/3 cup peanut butter and extra 1/4 cup chopped peanuts.

Pastel Icing for Petits Fours

        2 tablespoons red currant jelly
        Sifted confectioners' sugar
        1–2 drops red vegetable coloring

Heat jelly in small saucepan until melted. Remove from heat, and stir in enough sugar to make smooth, runny consistency. Add coloring for a pretty shade. Have ready your little petits fours; cut in squares or diamonds about 1-inch thick. Put 1 small cake on fork, and spoon icing over it. Let drip for a moment. If icing runs off completely, letting cake show through, add a little more sugar to the mixture. Keep icing soft over hot water while you frost. If it thickens, add a few drops boiling water. Set each frosted cake, as done, on a rack over waxed paper to catch drips that can be reused. Decorate tops with candied cherries, halved almonds and so forth.

Note: To vary color and flavor, substitute mint, apple, cherry or grape jelly for red currant jelly.

Orange Glaze

        1 cup sifted confectioners' sugar
        2 tablespoons orange juice
        1 teaspoon lemon juice
        1 teaspoon grated orange rind
        1 teaspoon grated lemon rind

Mix all ingredients, blending to a smooth, spreading consistency. Use on sponge cake, angel food cake, tea breads and the like.

Cream Filling

      1/4 cup sugar
        3 tablespoons sifted all-purpose flour
      1/4 teaspoon salt
        1 cup milk
        1 egg, slightly beaten
      1/2 teaspoon vanilla extract

Combine sugar, flour and salt. Scald milk, and carefully pour and stir into dry ingredients. Cook in top of double boiler over hot water 15 minutes or until thick. Add a little hot mixture to egg; then stir back into hot mixture. Continue cooking 3 minutes, and add vanilla. Cool. Makes about 1 cup.

VARIATIONS:

Butterscotch Filling: Use 1/3 cup brown sugar in place of white sugar. Add 2 tablespoons butter or margarine at end of cooking.

Chocolate Filling: Melt 1 square unsweetened chocolate in milk, and increase sugar to 1/2 cup.

Pineapple Filling: Substitute 1/2 teaspoon lemon juice for vanilla. Add 1/3 cup drained crushed pineapple to cooled filling.

Lemon Filling

      3/4 cup sugar
        2 tablespoons cornstarch
    Few grains salt
        1 egg yolk, slightly beaten
      3/4 cup water
        3 tablespoons lemon juice
        1 tablespoon butter or margarine
        1 teaspoon grated lemon rind

Mix sugar, cornstarch and salt; blend in egg yolk, water and lemon juice. Cook in double boiler over hot water until thick, stirring constantly. Remove from heat, and add butter or margarine and lemon rind. Cool before spreading on cake. Makes about 1 1/2 cups.

Orange Filling

      3/4 cup sugar
        2 tablespoons cornstarch
    Few grains salt
      3/4 cup orange juice
        1 tablespoon lemon juice
    1 1/2 tablespoons grated orange rind
        1 tablespoon butter or margarine
        2 egg yolks, beaten

Combine sugar, cornstarch and salt. Add juices gradually, and blend well. Add orange rind and butter or margarine. Cook over medium heat, stirring constantly, until thick and clear. Add small amount of hot mixture to egg yolks, and stir back into hot mixture. Cook over low heat about 3 minutes, stirring constantly. Cool before using. Makes about 1 cup.

Tutti-frutti Filling or Frosting

        1 cup plus 2 tablespoons sugar
      1/2 cup water
        2 egg whites
      1/3 cup finely chopped candied pineapple
      1/3 cup finely chopped candied cherries
      1/2 teaspoon rum extract

Cook sugar and water to soft-ball stage (236°F.). Beat egg whites until stiff, and pour sugar syrup over them, beating constantly. Continue beating until mixture is of spreading consistency; then fold in fruits and rum extract. Makes enough to fill and frost a 9-inch layer cake.

Fruit–Nut Cake Filling

      3/4 cup sugar
        1 cup water
      1/3 cup chopped dates

      1/3 cup seeded raisins
      1/2 cup chopped walnuts
        1 cup orange juice
        1 tablespoon butter or margarine
        1 teaspoon grated orange rind

Combine water, sugar, dates and raisins, and cook over low heat 15 minutes, stirring constantly. Cool, and add remaining ingredients. Fill one 8″ or 9″ layer cake.

Swiss Frosting

        3 squares unsweetened chocolate
      1/4 cup sugar
        3 tablespoons cornstarch
        1 teaspoon instant coffee powder
      1/4 teaspoon salt
        1 egg
      3/4 cup water
        2 cups sifted confectioners' sugar
      1/2 cup butter or margarine
        1 teaspoon vanilla extract

Grate chocolate, and mix with next 4 ingredients. Beat egg, and add to water. Add liquid to chocolate mixture, and mix until smooth. Cook

over low heat until thickened and all starch taste disappears (about 8–10 minutes). Remove from heat, and cool completely. Meanwhile cream confectioners' sugar with butter or margarine until light. Add vanilla, and beat in chocolate custard. Refrigerate until completely cold and butter or margarine starts to stiffen. If necessary add additional sifted confectioners 'sugar to achieve spreading consistency. Fill layer cake, and swirl remaining icing over top and sides.

French Mocha Frosting

    3 squares sweet chocolate, melted
    2 teaspoons instant coffee powder
    1 tablespoon hot water
    3/4 cup confectioners' sugar
    2 eggs
    1/2 cup soft butter or margarine

Mix chocolate, coffee and water in small beater bowl. Beat in sugar and eggs; add butter or margarine, 2 tablespoons at a time, and continue beating until mixture is thick. Chill to spreading consistency. Fill and frost an 8- or 9-inch layer cake. Chill until icing is set.

Thick Butter Cream

    1/2 cup soft sweet or lightly salted butter
        or margarine
    1/3 cup cold SIMPLE SYRUP
    1/2 teaspoon vanilla

Put in blender, and add syrup and vanilla. (Add pinch of salt if using sweet butter or margarine.) Blend until smooth. Stop blender, and

scrape sides once or twice. Use as filling and frosting or to decorate icing for cakes that are not rich. Chill after spreading.

Note: Butter cream freezes well.

VARIATION:

Chocolate Butter Cream: Add 2 squares melted semisweet chocolate and 2 egg yolks to blender with syrup. Makes 1 1/3 cups.

Simple Syrup

    1 1/4 cups sugar
    1/3 cup corn syrup
    2/3 cup water

Put sugar, corn syrup and water into small sauce pan. Bring to boil, and cover. Simmer 5 minutes; uncover, and simmer 4 minutes longer. Cool, pour into screw-top jar and refrigerate. Makes about 1 1/4 cups.

Sauces

Baked or steamed puddings often have their own sauces, the fruit or sugar mixture in the bottom of pan or mold. But often you will wish to serve a separate sauce, one that complements the pudding. A plain pudding can take a rich sauce; a rich pudding needs a simple bland sauce. There are creamy custard sauces, fruit sauces and sugar sauces, and you can experiment with different flavors in all of them. Try adding a few drops of any liqueur to whipped cream: crème de menthe for a cool minty flavor, rum for a rich one.

Orange Sauce

    2 eggs, separated
    1/2 cup orange juice
    1 teaspoon lemon juice
    1/2 teaspoon grated lemon rind
    1/2 teaspoon grated orange rind
    1/3 cup sugar
    Pinch salt
    1/2 teaspoon vanilla extract

Beat egg yolks. Combine juices and rinds with sugar and egg yolks, and stir over low heat until slightly thickened. Remove pan from the heat, and cool slightly. Beat egg whites until stiff; add with salt and vanilla to pan. May be served hot or cold. Makes about 1 cup.

Brandy Sauce

    1/4 cup butter or margarine
    1 cup finely granulated sugar
    2 tablespoons brandy
    2 eggs, separated
    1/2 cup light cream

Cream butter or margarine in top of cold double boiler; add sugar gradually, continuing to cream and incorporate thoroughly. Add brandy, a few drops at a time to prevent curdling. Beat egg yolks, and add with cream. Place mixture over hot (not boiling) water; cook, stirring until thickened. Beat egg whites until stiff. Pour hot mixture gradually over egg whites. This sauce is best when used warm with hot pudding. Makes about 1 1/4 cups.

Note: Rum may be used in place of brandy.

Brandied Cream Sauce

    1/2 pint light cream
    5 egg yolks, beaten
    1/4 cup sugar
    1/8 teaspoon salt
    1/4 cup brandy
    1/2 teaspoon vanilla extract
    1/2 pint heavy cream, whipped

Mix first 4 ingredients together in top of double boiler. Cook, stirring over hot, not boiling, water until mixture coats spoon. Remove from heat, and stir in brandy and vanilla. Cover, and chill. Fold in whipped cream just before serving. Makes 3 1/2 cups.

Easy Chocolate Sauce

    1 1/4 cups instant chocolate milk powder
    3/4 cup milk
    1/4 cup granulated sugar

In saucepan combine all ingredients. Bring to boil; lower heat. Cook 3 minutes, stirring constantly. Cool, and pour into jar and cover. This sauce keeps well in refrigerator. Use evaporated milk for richer sauce. If sauce is too thick after standing, dilute slightly with fresh milk. Makes about 1 cup syrup.

Sabayon Sauce

    6 egg yolks
    1/2 cup granulated sugar
    1/2 cup dry white wine
    Pinch salt

Beat egg yolks until thick, and add sugar gradually. Continue to beat until sugar is melted. Add wine and salt. Pour into top of double boiler, and set over hot water; water must not touch bottom of top section. Beat until mixture is light and creamy. Serve over hot puddings and baked fruit dishes. Makes about 1 cup.

Special Cake Decoration. You should have a cake-decorating set, consisting of a cloth or plastic bag and variously shaped metal tips that make rosettes, shells, leaves, flowers, ruchings, swags and so on. Full instructions for use are packed with bag; follow them closely, and be sure to practice first on an inverted pie plate or cake pan, preferably.

Icing and decorating a large cake of possibly 2 or 3 tiers should not be rushed; if possible spread work over several days. If layer of almond paste is to be used, order it well ahead of time.

First spread very slightly beaten egg white over top and sides of cake. Roll out mound of almond icing to about 1/2-inch thickness (on board sprinkled with confectioners' sugar). Lay this mound over cake like a blanket, press corners to seal and trim bottom edge neatly. Let stand at least 24 hours; the egg white will dry and hold almond paste in position.

The basic icing, which is an egg white, confectioners' sugar and shortening mixture, is to be spread over entire surface. Avoid using any milk, as it tends to turn icing ivory color on standing. If cake is in 2 or more tiers, stack them carefully before starting this basic icing, which is to cover all the exposed almond paste surfaces, top to bottom. Let iced cake stand another 24 hours before decorating.

A special frosting will be needed, soft enough to press through pastry bag and assume desired shapes yet sufficiently stiff to hold form.

Pastry-tube Frosting

    1/4 cup vegetable shortening
    2 cups sifted confectioners' sugar
    1/2 teaspoon vanilla extract
    1/4 teaspoon salt
    3 tablespoons water

Cream shortening, and gradually add 1 cup sugar, continuing to cream and beat after each addition. Add vanilla and salt. Add remaining sugar, alternately with water. Use just enough water to ensure mixture suitable for bag use. After each addition, beat until smooth. Makes 3/4 cup.

All About Pastry Making. The "pyes" of Merrie England were, for the most part, filled with meat, "fysche or fowle," until a certain June day in Elizabeth I's reign, when the Queen ordered fresh stewed cherries baked in a pie. The sweet pie was thus launched.

Basically, pastry is a mixture of flour, fat, salt and liquid. Sometimes other ingredients are specified—egg yolks, baking powder and sugar—for particular textures. The character of the finished product and its success will depend upon proportions of various ingredients, methods of mixing and handling and baking times and temperatures.

Flours

There are 2 modern flours suitable for pastry making: cake flour and all-purpose flour. The first will produce a very light tender crust, whereas all-purpose flour tends to give a flakier pastry. Puff pastry, made with a high proportion of shortening, requires the elastic qualities of all-purpose flour for best results.

In substituting all-purpose flour in recipe designating cake flour, reduce each cup called for to 7/8 cup. Simply measure out sifted all-purpose flour to 1 even cup; then remove 2 level tablespoons flour, and proceed.

Fats

Various types may be used: shortenings, which may be all-vegetable or combinations of vegetable and animal fat; lard, which is wholly derived from fat; liquid cooking oils, or butter or margarine.

Liquids

Cold water is a requisite for most pastries, the one exception being HOT WATER PASTRY, which is made with boiling water. Many of today's recipes are deliberately not specific about the amount of liquid to add, simply because the moisture content of the various flours on the market varies considerably, and this factor has an important influence on the liquid used. If your recipe gives a quantity range like "5–6 tablespoons water," use only *minimum* amount stated, and then judge whether the mixture is moist enough to form into a ball or needs a few drops more.

Utensils

In addition to standard measuring cups, mixing bowl and the like, you will need a board, which provides an even surface for rolling pastry. A canvas pastry cloth and a stockinette cover for the rolling pin are also helpful; they will ensure that only a minimum amount of extra flour need be sprinkled on surface to prevent dough from sticking during rolling.

There are other handy small gadgets to speed the job. A pastry wheel for cutting out rounds for tarts, turnovers, top crusts and lattice-top strips is easy to use and makes attractive edgings. A pastry brush is helpful for glazing.

The most satisfactory materials for pie plates are oven glass, enamelware and aluminum. The most popular sizes are the 8-inch and 9-inch plates—former dividing into 4–6 portions, the latter 6–8.

Basic Pastry

Plain pastry is the most frequently used for dessert pies, tarts, toppings for savory mixtures, and turnovers. (Puff pastry, sweet pastry and certain others are generally reserved for specific dessert purposes other than the family-size pie.) The standard method can be mastered with practice, and the hot-water method is especially recommended for beginners.

Success requires following directions—altering fat content according to type of flour, adding water sparingly as advised, chilling dough if possible before rolling out and handling lightly during rolling and shaping.

Plain Pastry

USING CAKE FLOUR

    2 1/4 cups sifted cake flour
    1 teaspoon salt
    2/3 cup shortening
    4–5 tablespoons cold water

USING ALL-PURPOSE FLOUR

    2 cups sifted all-purpose flour
    1 teaspoon salt
    3/4 cup shortening
    4–5 tablespoons cold water

Measure sifted flour into bowl, and blend in salt. Add shortening. Cut in with pastry blender

or 2 knives until mixture resembles oatmeal, with some pieces slightly larger. Add water, 1 table-

spoon at a time. Sprinkle over surface of the flour

mixture, and mix lightly after each addition until

mixture is dampened. Turn onto piece of waxed paper, and form into a ball, using the paper to press pastry firmly together. Chill 1 hour if time permits, but let pastry stand at least 5 minutes for ease in rolling.

Lightly and evenly flour pastry cloth and rolling-pin cover. To make 2 single shells or a batch of tart shells, cut chilled ball of dough in even halves. For double-crust pie, cut ball into 2 slightly unequal pieces, the larger to be rolled

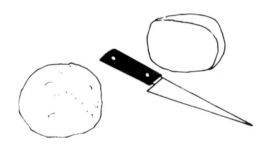

out for the bottom crust. Flatten larger piece into round disc; then, using lightest possible pressure, roll with the floured pin, rolling away from you. Roll from center to edge each time. Lift pastry

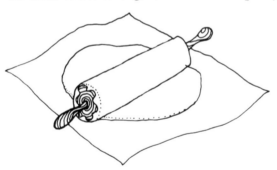

occasionally during rolling process to make sure that dough is not sticking. An extra sprinkle of flour may be needed on pastry cloth or board, but *avoid excessive flouring* as flour could be absorbed by pastry with resultant toughening. When rolled circle is about 1 inch larger than pie plate and about 1/8 inch thick, it is ready for next step.

Fold circle of pastry in half, and transfer quickly to center of pie plate. Or roll circle around pin; place pin over pie plate, and unroll circle of dough. In either case, unfold dough carefully, and ease into plate; then press lightly to exclude any air bubbles.

Do not stretch pastry, either while rolling it or while fitting into plate. Stretched pastry will shrink during baking and spoil the appearance of your pie.

Trim pastry in pie plate flush with edge, using knife. Roll out second ball of dough to size about 1 inch more than width of pie plate, rim to rim. Cut out with knife or pastry wheel; fold over, and make decorative slits at center to allow steam to escape during baking.

Fill pastry-lined plate with fruit filling or other desired mixture. Moisten edge of bottom crust. Place folded pastry circle over filling; or roll it around pin, and set in position. Unfold, and fit cover evenly over filling. Trim off any ragged edges neatly, and fold overhang *under* edge of bottom crust. Seal by pressing 2 crusts together against edge of pie plate, using tines of fork or crimping between finger and thumb. Bake according to the directions in your recipe.

Note: 1 recipe for plain pastry makes 2 9-inch shells, double-crust 9-inch pie, 12–14 medium shells or 20–24 small tart shells.

VARIATIONS:

Single Unbaked Pie Shell: Line pie plate with pastry, leaving an overhang of 1/2 inch. Fold pastry overhang back and under, making it stand upright. Flute edge with fingers. *Do not prick.* Pour in filling. (An unbaked shell is usually used for pumpkin, custard, pecan or any kind of pie in which filling and pastry should be baked together.) To avoid spills between work surface and oven, fill shell 3/4 full, and pour in remainder when pie plate is on oven rack. Bake as directed in recipe.

Single Baked Pie Shell: Line pie plate with pastry. Prick with fork at 1-inch intervals. Bake at 450°F. 10–12 minutes. If, after 5 minutes' baking, pastry puffs up, prick it again. Another way to avoid shrinkage is to set empty pie plate the same size in pastry shell before baking. Bake as usual, but remove empty pie plate 3–4 minutes before end of baking time to allow inside of shell to brown lightly. Cool shell. Fill as directed in recipes.

Flaky Pastry: To make rich pastry with flaky texture, use additional fat. Roll out entire pastry 1/4-inch thick, making shape as square as possible. Cut 2 tablespoons well-chilled fat into small pieces. Dot these pieces over 1/2 the square of pastry, keeping fat 1/2 inch away from edges. Fold other 1/2 of pastry over to cover fat. Dot on 2 more tablespoons of fat, and fold in half once more. Then roll pastry into square, 1/4-inch thick. Fold in half and then in half again, to make quarters. Chill well before using. Divide pastry into parts, roll out 1/2 for bottom crust and other 1/2 for top; bake as 2 pie shells, or use for tart shells.

Flavored Pastry: To measured flour (before cutting in fat) add 3 tablespoons finely ground nuts for pumpkin or squash fillings; 2 tablespoons finely grated mild cheese for apple pie; 1/2 teaspoon finely chopped mint for chicken pie. Or add with cold water 1/4 teaspoon almond extract for cherry pie; 4 tablespoons orange juice and 1/2 teaspoon grated orange rind for custard pies.

Packaged Pie-crust Mix: Add only water before rolling out; for single-shell pie, use 1/2 the amount in package plus 1/2 the suggested proportion of water.

Hot Water Pastry

USING CAKE FLOUR

> 2 1/4 cups sifted cake flour
> 1 teaspoon salt
> 1/2 teaspoon baking powder
> 2/3 cup shortening
> 1/3 cup boiling water

USING ALL-PURPOSE FLOUR

> 2 cups all-purpose flour
> 1 teaspoon salt
> 1/2 teaspoon baking powder
> 3/4 cup shortening
> 1/3 cup boiling water

Sift flour, salt and baking powder together. Melt shortening in boiling water over very low heat. Cool and beat in sifted dry ingredients. Turn dough onto waxed paper, and form into ball. Chill thoroughly at least 2 hours. Roll out as directed for PLAIN PASTRY. Use in any recipe requiring plain pastry.

Easy Pastry Shell

> 1 cup all-purpose flour
> 3/4 teaspoon salt
> 1/3 cup cooking oil
> 1 1/2 tablespoons cold milk

Sift flour and salt into pie pan. Mix oil and milk, stir and pour into flour all at once. Stir

with fork until all ingredients are blended; shape crust by patting and tamping dough with your fingers so that it comes up around sides of pan. Bake at 425°F. 12–15 minutes, and cool before filling. The texture will be crumbly rather than flaky.

Note: This recipe is a time-saver, as it requires no rolling out.

Double-Crust Pies

These pies usually have fillings of fruits (fresh, canned or dried) by themselves or combined. They may be stored, covered, at room temperature. If desired, give them a fresh-baked texture by reheating in slow oven about 15 minutes before serving.

Apple Pie

> 1 recipe PLAIN PASTRY
> 2/3 cup sugar
> 1/2 teaspoon cinnamon or nutmeg (optional)
> 1/4 teaspoon salt
> 6 cups sliced apples, peeled and cored
> 1 tablespoon butter or margarine

Prepare pastry as for double-crust pie, and line 9-inch pie plate. Set oven at 400°F. Mix together sugar, spices and salt. Place 1/2 the apples in lined pie plate. Sprinkle with 1/2 the dry mixture. Add remaining apples, heaping higher at center of pie. Sprinkle remaining dry mixture over, and dot with butter or margarine. Cover with pastry, seal edges and bake at 400°F. 40–50 minutes or until pastry is golden and apples perfectly tender.

Note: If apples are tart, increase sugar to 1 cup. If they are juicy, as with August types, add 1 tablespoon flour to sugar. If fruit is quite dry, as with some winter-stored apples, sprinkle with 1–2 tablespoons water; a dash of lemon juice will help sharpen the flavor.

Berry Pie

    1 recipe PLAIN PASTRY
    4 cups fresh strawberries, raspberries, blackberries or
        loganberries, washed and hulled
    2 tablespoons all-purpose flour or 1 1/2 tablespoons
        quick-cooking tapioca
    3/4 cup sugar
    1/4 teaspoon salt
    1 tablespoon butter or margarine

Prepare pastry as for double-crust pie, and line 9-inch pie plate. Set oven at 400°F. If using flour for thickening, add it to sugar and salt, and proceed in same manner as for APPLE PIE, alternating layers of fruit and dry ingredients. If using tapioca, add to sugar, or sprinkle over bottom crust before turning in berries. Bake as for APPLE PIE.

VARIATIONS:

Blueberry Pie: Add 2 teaspoons lemon juice and 1/2 teaspoon lemon rind to sugar mixture.

Cherry Pie: Stem and pit cherries; increase sugar to 1 1/3 cups or more, depending on tartness of fruit.

Rhubarb Pie

    1 recipe PLAIN PASTRY
    4 cups diced rhubarb
    1 1/2 cups sugar
    1/3 cup all-purpose flour
    1/8 teaspoon salt
    1 tablespoon butter or margarine

Prepare pastry as for double-crust pie, and line 9-inch pie plate. Set oven at 400°F. Place 2 cups rhubarb on pastry. Combine sugar, flour and salt, and sprinkle 1/2 the mixture over rhubarb. Add remaining rhubarb. Top with remaining sugar, and dot with butter. Cover with rolled pastry top, and seal edges. Bake at 400°F. 40–50 minutes.
    Note: Frozen rhubarb, partially thawed and drained, may be used instead of fresh. If rhubarb has been sweetened before freezing, reduce sugar to 1/3 cup.

Raisin Pie

    2 cups seedless raisins
    1 cup brown sugar, lightly packed
    2 tablespoons all-purpose flour or 1 1/2 tablespoons
        quick-cooking tapioca
    1/8 teaspoon salt
    2 cups boiling water
    3 tablespoons lemon juice
    2 teaspoons grated lemon rind
    1 recipe pastry for double-crust pie

Wash and drain raisins. In saucepan mix sugar, flour and salt until well blended. Add raisins, and pour in boiling water gradually, stirring while adding. Bring to boil, and continue to stir until mixture is thick and smooth and raisins nicely plumped. Remove from heat, and add lemon juice and rind. Let cool. Meanwhile line 9-inch pie plate with pastry. Turn in cooled filling. Add top crust, seal and bake in 400°F. oven 35–45 minutes.

Mincemeat Filling

    8 cups chopped tart apples
    4 cups seedless raisins
    4 cups white sugar
    3 cups pineapple juice
    2 cups chopped prunes
    1 1/2 cups chopped mixed candied fruit
    1 cup brown sugar, lightly packed
    1/2 cup cider vinegar
    1 sliced lemon
    1 sliced orange
    3 cups ground suet
    3 cups water
    1/4 cup red wine
    1/4 cup dark molasses
    4 teaspoons cinnamon
    2 teaspoons salt
    1 1/2 teaspoons ground cloves
    1 teaspoon nutmeg
    1 teaspoon allspice
    1/2 teaspoon pepper

Put first 4 ingredients into large kettle; let come to boil, and simmer 1/2 hour. Lift out cooked fruit slices with slotted spoon, and discard. To hot liquid, add remaining ingredients; bring to boil and keep at bubbling simmer 30–40 minutes. Pack in hot sterilized jars, seal tightly and store in cool dry place. Makes 3–4 quarts or enough for 5 pies.

Mince Pie

    3 cups mincemeat filling or (1-pound, 4-ounce)
        jar mincemeat
    1 cup drained crushed pineapple or applesauce
    1 recipe pastry for double-crust pie

Combine mincemeat and pineapple. Line 9-inch pie plate with 1/2 pastry; fill; adjust top pastry cover, and seal edges. Bake in 400°–425°F. oven about 30 minutes or until pastry is golden brown.
    Note: To reheat, place in 300°F. oven about 20 minutes.

Cranberry Pie

    4 cups raw cranberries
    2 cups sugar
    1/3 cup water
    1 teaspoon grated lemon rind

Dash salt
1 tablespoon butter or margarine
1 recipe pastry for double-crust pie

Pick over, wash and drain cranberries. Heat next 4 ingredients in saucepan; when simmering, add fruit, and cook, covered, until skins pop. Remove from heat, add butter or margarine and let mixture cool to lukewarm. Line 9-inch pie plate, turn filling into shell and cover with pastry top. Bake in 425°F. oven about 30 minutes.

Single-Crust Pies

There are several kinds of single-crust pies. With pumpkin, custard and certain fruit fillings, shell and contents are baked together. Other types, notably lemon pie, require a pre-baked and cooled shell. A deep-dish fruit pie uses a top cover only, which, of course, is baked along with the filling.

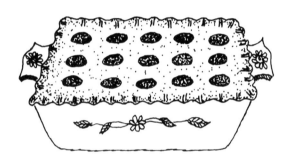

Deep-dish Fruit Pie

1–1 1/2 cups sugar
2 tablespoons quick-cooking tapioca or
3 tablespoons all-purpose flour
1 1/2 teaspoons grated lemon or orange rind
1/4 teaspoon salt
6 cups prepared fruit (apples, peaches, berries or plums)
1 tablespoon butter or margarine
1/2 recipe PLAIN PASTRY or FLAKY PASTRY

Combine sugar, tapioca, grated rind and salt. Grease baking dish or casserole 7 inches in diameter. Turn in prepared fruit, and stir in sugar mixture until well distributed. Add water or lemon juice if necessary. Dot with butter or margarine. Roll out pastry to 1/4-inch thickness and about 8-inch diameter. Prick dough. Place over filling, folding edge under and fluting with thumb and forefinger. Bake in 450°F. oven 10 minutes; reduce oven setting to 350°F., and continue baking 35–40 minutes.

Note: Peel and slice apples or peaches; wash and hull berries, or halve and stone plums. The amount of sugar will depend on tartness of fruit being used; if using blueberries or winter-stored apples, include 1 tablespoon lemon juice in filling for better flavor; if fruit is dry, sprinkle with 2 tablespoons water. For such juicy fruit as fresh berries, prevent boiling over by inserting small foil funnel or cone at center. Remove before serving pie.

Apple-crumble Pie

Pastry for single-crust pie
4 cups peeled, cored, sliced apples
1/2 cup brown sugar, firmly packed
1/3 cup sifted all-purpose flour
1/4 cup butter or margarine
1/4 teaspoon mixed nutmeg and cinnamon

Line 9-inch pie plate. Arrange apples on crust. Make crumble topping by blending sugar, flour, butter or margarine and spices together until fat is well distributed and grains are the size of peas. Sprinkle over apples. Bake in 425°F. oven 30–35 minutes or until apples are tender.

VARIATIONS:

Mincemeat–Apple-crumble Pie: Combine 2 cups canned or homemade mincemeat with 2 cups sliced apples.

Peach-crumble Pie: Sprinkle 1 tablespoon quick-cooking tapioca over pastry-lined pie plate. Use 4–5 cups peeled sliced peaches.

Custard Pie

3 eggs
1/3 cup sugar
1/4 teaspoon salt
2 cups hot milk, scalded
Pastry for single-crust pie
1 teaspoon vanilla extract
Freshly grated nutmeg

Beat eggs just enough to mix. Add sugar and salt, and slowly stir in hot milk. Strain mixture, and allow to cool while preparing pastry and lining 9-inch pie plate. When milk mixture is completely cool, add vanilla, and pour into pastry shell. Sprinkle top with freshly grated nutmeg. Place pie in oven preheated to 450°F.; after 5 minutes reduce heat setting to 325°F. After 35 minutes test filling with silver knife; if it comes out without custard adhering, pie is done. If not, leave another 5–10 minutes to complete baking.

Note: With this method, pastry will start to cook immediately at high heat, thus preventing soggy crust; liquid mixture, slower to heat up, will bake at reduced temperature and form smooth firm custard.

Pumpkin Pie

    2 eggs
    1/2 cup milk
1 1/2 cups mashed cooked pumpkin or 1 (15-ounce) can
        pumpkin
    2/3 cup evaporated milk or light cream
    2/3 cups brown sugar, lightly packed
    3/4 teaspoon cinnamon
    1/2 teaspoon ground ginger
    1/2 teaspoon salt
    1/4 teaspoon nutmeg
Pastry for single-crust pie

Beat eggs well, and stir in milk. Combine all remaining ingredients, except pastry, and stir in

milk mixture. Line 9-inch pie plate with pastry, and pour in filling. Place in 450°F. oven; after 5 minutes reduce temperature setting to 350°F. Bake 40–50 minutes or until silver knife inserted in center comes out clean.

Lemon Meringue Pie

    1 cup sugar
    3 tablespoons cornstarch
    3 tablespoons all-purpose flour
    1/4 teaspoon salt
1 1/2 cups boiling water
    3 egg yolks, beaten
    1 tablespoon butter or margarine
    1/4 cup lemon juice
    2 teaspoons grated lemon rind
    1 baked 9-inch pie shell, cooled
    3 egg whites

Combine first 4 ingredients in top of double boiler. Slowly add boiling water, stirring to avoid lumping. Place directly over moderate heat, and cook, stirring constantly, until thick and no taste of raw starch remains. Gradually stir hot mixture into beaten eggs; return all to double boiler, and cook over simmering water 2–3 minutes until egg is smoothly incorporated. Remove from heat immediately. Stir in butter or margarine, lemon juice and rind. Let cool almost completely before turning into pastry shell. Top with MERINGUE FOR PIES.

Note: Use 3 leftover egg whites in meringue, and substitute one tablespoon lemon juice for vanilla. Or whipped cream may be used instead of meringue.

Lemon Chiffon Pie

    1 envelope powdered gelatin
    1/4 cup cold water
    3/4 cup sugar
    2 teaspoons grated lemon rind
    1/2 teaspoon salt
    2/3 cup boiling water
    3 egg yolks, beaten
    1/2 cup lemon juice
    3 egg whites
    1 baked 9-inch pie shell, cooled

Soften gelatin in cold water. In top of double boiler combine 1/2 cup sugar, lemon rind and salt; stir in boiling water, then softened gelatin, stirring to dissolve. Add a little of this mixture to beaten egg yolks; then return all to double boiler, and cook over simmering water, stirring constantly 9–10 minutes or until mixture is custardy and coats spoon. Remove mixture from heat, and stir in lemon juice. Pour into bowl, and place in refrigerator or in pan of ice water; let stand, stirring occasionally, until partially set. Beat egg whites to glossy peaks, and gradually add remaining sugar. Fold meringue into gelatin mixture. Pile into pastry shell, and chill in refrigerator for several hours until firm.

Strawberry Chiffon Pie

    1 envelope powdered gelatin
    1/4 cup cold water
    2 cups strawberries, washed and hulled
    2/3 cup sugar
    2 teaspoons lemon juice
    1/2 teaspoon salt
    2 egg whites
    1/2 cup heavy cream
    1 baked 9-inch pie shell, cooled

Soften gelatin in cold water. Reserve about 1/2 cup of choicest strawberries for garnish. Mash remainder, adding sugar, and let stand until latter is absorbed. Dissolve gelatin over boiling water; add lemon juice, salt and mashed berries. Place mixture in refrigerator or pan of ice water until partially set, stirring occasionally. Beat egg whites to glossy peaks; then beat into mixture. Whip cream, and fold in. Pile into pastry shell, and chill in refrigerator until filling is firm. Garnish with whole berries before serving.

Cream Pie

        2 cups milk
    1/2 cup sugar
        2 tablespoons all-purpose flour
        2 tablespoons cornstarch
    1/2 teaspoon salt
        3 egg yolks, beaten
        2 tablespoons butter or margarine
        1 teaspoon vanilla extract
        1 baked 9-inch pie shell, cooled

Scald 1 1/2 cups milk. Combine dry ingredients in top of double boiler, and gradually add 1/2 cup cold milk, blending until smooth. Stir in scalded milk. Set directly over moderate heat, and let come to boil, stirring constantly. Remove from heat. Stir thick sauce very gradually into beaten egg yolks; then return all to double boiler, and cook over hot water about 2 minutes, stirring constantly. Remove from heat, and add butter or margarine and vanilla. Cool almost completely before pouring into pastry shell. Top with meringue, whipped cream, toasted shredded coconut or whole strawberries.

VARIATIONS:

Butterscotch Cream Pie: Replace sugar with 2/3 cup brown sugar, and add 1 extra tablespoon butter or margarine.

Chocolate Cream Pie: Melt 2 1-ounce squares unsweetened chocolate in scalded milk; increase sugar to 2/3 cup.

Pecan–Syrup Pie

    1/2 cup butter or margarine
    1/3 cup sugar
    3/4 cup corn syrup
    1/4 cup maple syrup
        3 eggs
        2 cups pecan halves
        1 teaspoon vanilla extract
        1 unbaked 9-inch pie shell
    Whipped cream

Cream butter or margarine thoroughly; add sugar gradually, continuing to cream. Stir in syrups, a little at a time. Beat eggs slightly, and add to mixture. Stir in nuts and vanilla. Combine well. Turn into pastry shell. Bake at 325°F. 1 hour. Cool. Before serving swirl whipped cream on top.

Meringue for Pies

FOR 8-INCH PIE

        Few grains salt
        2 egg whites
    1/4 cup (4 tablespoons) sugar

FOR 9-INCH PIE

    1/4 teaspoon salt
        3 egg whites
    1/3 cup (6 tablespoons) sugar

Add salt to egg whites, and beat until rounded peaks are formed. Add sugar very gradually, about 1 tablespoon at a time, continuing to beat after each addition. After all sugar has been beaten in, continue beating until mixture is stiff but still glossy. Beat in vanilla. Pile meringue on top of pie filling that has been allowed to cool completely. It is best to start at rim of pie and work toward center. Do not leave any space between meringue and rim; otherwise topping may shrink or "weep." Swirl into crests or peaks for attractive effect. Put pie into preheated 375°F. oven, and bake for 10–12 minutes until meringue is delicately browned. Let pie cool at room temperature away from drafts. To cut meringue topping easily, dip sharp thin knife in water, shaking off excess before inserting. Or butter knife before using.

Note: Do not bake meringue on instant pudding- or pie-mix fillings. Vary your meringue flavoring according to filling being used; for lemon pie substitute lemon juice for vanilla.

Maple Cream Pie

        2 tablespoons soft butter or margarine
        2 egg yolks
        1 cup maple syrup
    1/2 cup commercial sour cream
    1/4 cup flour
        1 teaspoon vinegar
        1 teaspoon vanilla
        1 unbaked 8-inch pie shell
        2 egg whites
    1/4 teaspoon salt
        4 tablespoons sugar

Beat butter or margarine and egg yolks until thick. Gently fold in next 5 ingredients. Pour into pie shell, and bake at 425°F. 20 minutes. Lower heat to 325°F., and cook 30 minutes more or until set (metal skewer should come out clean). Beat egg whites, salt and sugar until very stiff, and swirl over pie. Bake at 350°F. 15 minutes or until lightly browned. Serve at room temperature.

Eggnog Pie

    1 envelope powdered gelatin
    1/2 cup milk
    1 1/2 cups commercial eggnog
    Vanilla, brandy or rum extract to taste
    1 cup heavy cream, stiffly beaten
    1 9-inch SIMPLE CRUMB CRUST or baked pastry shell
    1/2 cup chopped nuts
    2 tablespoons chopped candied pineapple

Soften gelatin in milk, and heat over hot water until melted. Remove from heat; don't worry if it curdles. Whisk in eggnog and vanilla slowly. Chill until mixture thickens. Fold in 3/4 cup whipped cream. Pour into pie shell, and chill until set. Sprinkle center with nuts, and garnish edge with remaining whipped cream and bits of pineapple.

Sherry Chiffon Pie

        Dash salt
        3 eggs, separated
        2/3 cup sherry
        1/3 cup sugar
        1 envelope powdered gelatin
        1/4 cup cold water
        1/4 cup sugar
        1 9-inch SIMPLE CRUMB CRUST
        3/4 cup heavy cream, stiffly beaten

Add salt to egg yolks, and beat until thick. Add sherry and 1/3 cup sugar, and beat well. Cook in double boiler until mixture coats spoon; remove from heat. Soften gelatin in cold water; add to hot mixture. Chill until partially set. Stiffly beat egg whites, and slowly beat in 1/4 cup sugar. Fold into custard, and pour into crust. Chill until set. Spread with whipped cream.

Fancy Pastries. Fancy pastries range from choux and sweet pastry to crumb and nut crusts.

Crumb and Nut Crusts

These pie shells are quickly made and very satisfactory for cooked and cooled cream fillings, whipped cream and the like. The crumbs must be finely pulverized with a rolling pin and the nuts must be finely ground.

Simple Crumb Crust

        1 1/2 cups crumbs (1 cup graham cracker crumbs,
                1/2 cup crushed cornflakes)
            1/3 cup sugar
            1/2 cup butter or margarine, melted

Mix crumbs, sugar and butter or margarine together. Press firmly into 9-inch pie plate. Chill about 1 hour before filling.

Graham Cracker Crust

        1 1/3 cups graham cracker crumbs
        1/4 cup sugar
        1 teaspoon cinnamon
        1/3 cup butter or margarine, melted

Combine fine crumbs, sugar and cinnamon, and stir in butter or margarine. Reserve 3 tablespoons mixture for topping. Press crumbs into 9-inch pie pan, covering bottom and sides evenly but making no edge on rim. Bake in 350°F. oven 10 minutes. Cool completely. Fill with cream or chiffon filling, and sprinkle with reserved crumbs. Chill in refrigerator several hours before serving.

VARIATIONS:

Use gingersnaps or chocolate or vanilla wafers in place of graham crackers, and omit sugar. A tangy lemon filling is particularly good in gingersnap-crumb crust.

Cereal Crumb Crust

        4 cups cornflakes
        1/4 cup sugar
        1 tablespoon all-purpose flour
        1/4 cup butter or margarine, melted

Crush cornflakes very fine; then measure 1 cup. Combine with sugar and flour, and blend in melted butter or margarine. Spread over 9-inch pie pan, allowing greater thickness over bottom than against sides. Bake in 350°F. oven 8–10 minutes. Cool completely before filling; keep chilled until serving.

Crisp Coconut Crust

        2 tablespoons soft (not melted) butter or margarine
    1 1/2 cups flaked or shredded coconut

Spread or brush butter evenly over bottom and sides of 9-inch pie plate. Pat coconut into butter or margarine. Bake in 350°F. oven 8–10 minutes or until shell is crisp brown. After filling with cream or chiffon mixture, refrigerate several hours before serving. Or fill with vanilla ice cream just at serving time; drizzle butterscotch sauce on top, and sprinkle with toasted coconut.

Brazil Nut Crust

    1 1/2 cups (about 3/4 pound) finely ground Brazil nuts
        3 tablespoons sugar

Combine nuts and sugar in 9-inch pie pan. Press mixture with back of spoon over bottom and sides to cover evenly. Bake in 400°F. oven 6–7 minutes or until lightly browned. Cool completely before filling; keep chilled until serving.

Meringue Pie Shell

1/2 cup (about 4) egg whites
1 cup superfine sugar
1/4 teaspoon cream of tartar
Pinch salt

Beat egg whites until stiff but not dry. Combine sugar, cream of tartar and salt. Add mixture 1 tablespoon at a time to egg whites, beating after each addition. After all mixture has been added, continue beating until very stiff but still glossy. Grease 9-inch pie plate, and sprinkle lightly with flour, shaking off excess. Turn in meringue, and spread just to rim. Mound meringue slightly at center. Bake in 275°F. oven for 1 hour or until delicately browned and crisp to the touch. Set pie plate on cooling rack in place away from drafts but at room temperature. Meringue will crack and fall in center, but that is the way it should be, in order to make shell suitable for filling. If cooled pie is not to be used immediately, store in covered container in cool, dry place. If shell becomes sticky from moisture, reheat in 250°F. oven 15 minutes. Cool before filling, and fill just before serving.

Note: Drained, diced fruits, fresh or canned, make good fillings, with or without whipped-cream topping, as does well-thickened, cooled filling for LEMON CHIFFON PIE, to which 1 cup whipped cream has been added, or sliced fresh strawberries lightly folded into sweetened whipped cream.

To Make Puff Paste

Puff paste consists of hundreds of layers of paper-thin dough, which remain separate because of the many thin layers of fat interspersed. During baking, moisture trapped in the layers becomes steam, forcing dough to rise. After baking, steam evaporates, leaving pastry high, crisp and flaky.

Older recipes for puff pastry involve washing butter to rid it of salt and to obtain plastic, waxy consistency. With unsalted (sweet) butter, however, washing isn't necessary. But the consistency of the butter is extremely important; if too cold and hard, it will break up dough when rolled; if too soft, it will ooze out. Butter should be of about the same consistency as the dough.

Do not try to make puff paste during hot weather unless your kitchen is air-conditioned.

Puff Paste

3 cups all-purpose flour
1 1/2 teaspoons salt
1 pound unsalted (sweet) butter
1 1/4–1 1/3 cups icewater

Sift together flour and salt. Cut in 2 tablespoons butter with pastry blender. Sprinkle with a little ice water, adding it gradually and mixing in lightly with fork. Continue adding and mixing ice water until 1 1/4 cups have been incorporated. If dough is firm and slightly sticky as it should be, don't add any more water. Turn dough onto lightly floured board, and knead 5–8 minutes or until very elastic and smooth. Cover with cloth; invert large bowl over it, and let stand 10 minutes. While dough is resting, flatten block of butter into oblong about 3″ x 5″ x 1 1/2″.

Roll dough to 1/8-inch thickness, in shape about 3 times as long as wide. Place flattened butter at center of 1/2 dough. Fold other 1/2 over butter. Seal edges of dough to enclose as much air as possible. Pat down until enclosed butter spreads to within 1/2 inch of all edges. Fold one end under and other end over, to form 3 layers of pastry. Wrap, and chill about 20 minutes.

Now roll out pastry evenly to 1/8-inch thickness, keeping it longer than it is wide. Lift pastry from board frequently to prevent sticking; dredge board with flour if necessary. Fold each end of dough rectangle to meet in center. Give dough 1/4 turn, and repeat rolling and folding in thirds as before. Chill. Repeat rolling, folding and chilling 3 more times. Then roll and fold ends to center, and double parcel again, making 4 layers. Chill until dough is stiff before using.

Patty Shells

1 recipe PUFF PASTE

Roll well-chilled dough to 1/4-inch thickness. Cut 3-inch rounds with cookie cutter. Remove

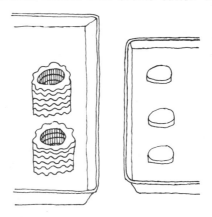

2-inch centers from 1/2 the rounds. Moisten edges of full rounds, and lightly press 1 ring shape on top of each. Place well apart on ungreased cookie sheet. Bake in 500°F. oven 5 minutes; then lower

heat by 50°F. at 5-minute intervals until temperature is down to 350°F. Bake about 10 minutes at 350°F. Makes 12–16 large patty shells or 24–30 small shells.

Note: The cut-out centers from the rings may be baked and used as lids for filled patty shells.

Napoleons or Cream Slices

1 recipe PUFF PASTE
1/2 cup confectioners' sugar or icing
1/2 cup chopped nuts
2 cups heavy cream, stiffly beaten and sweetened,
  or flavored or 1 recipe FRENCH CREAM FILLING

Roll out puff paste to 1/8-inch thickness to fit 10″ x 14″ ungreased cookie sheet. Let stand on sheet in refrigerator 15 minutes. Prick paste all over with fork. Bake in 400°F. oven about 15 minutes; lower heat to 300°F., and continue baking 40 mintues. Pastry should be well puffed and light brown. Allow it to cool thoroughly. Trim off all edges with serrated knife, and split pastry horizontally, making 2 layers. Lay bottom 1/2 on flat surface, spread with stiffly beaten cream (or filling) cover with remaining 1/2. Sprinkle with confectioners' sugar, and chopped nuts. Chill 1 hour before cutting into strips 3 inches wide and then into 1 1/2-inch slices. Yield: 18–24 Napoleons.

French Cream Filling

1 cup milk
1/3 cup sugar
2 tablespoons flour
Pinch salt
3 egg yolks, beaten
1 teaspoon vanilla extract

Heat 3/4 cup milk in saucepan over medium heat. Combine sugar, flour and salt; add remaining 1/4 cup milk, and blend to a smooth paste. Stir paste into hot milk, and cook, stirring constantly, until mixture thickens. Remove from heat. Add hot mixture, a little at a time, to egg yolks; then return all to saucepan. Place over low heat, cook a few minutes longer, stirring well, but do not boil. Add vanilla, and cool as quickly as possible. Refrigerate. Stir well before using. Mixture may be thinned if desired by beating in a few spoonfuls of rich milk.

VARIATIONS:

Chocolate Cream Filling: Melt 1 1/2 squares unsweetened chocolate, and beat thoroughly into mixture after removing from stove.

Deluxe Cream Filling: Soften 1 envelope powdered gelatin in 1/4 cup cold water; set container in hot water to dissolve; stir into cooled filling, and fold in 1 cup heavy cream, stiffly beaten; flavor as desired. Chill before using.

Cream Puffs, Eclairs, Bouchées

These pastries are easier to make than you think. They're made from basic CHOUX PASTE. They keep well if stored in a closed container. During hot humid weather they may soften somewhat but will be completely restored if reheated at 400°F. about 10 minutes.

A pastry bag equipped with a plain round tube about 3/4 inch in diameter is the ideal utensil to prepare pastry for baking. But a tablespoon or teaspoon, depending on the size wanted, can be used with complete success. Follow specific baking instructions in recipe. Puffs will collapse if they are not baked long enough; or they may be soft instead of crisp. In that case, just return them to oven, and let them puff again until they become crisp.

Filling should not be added until just before serving. Split puffs, and fill with sweetened whipped cream, FRENCH CREAM FILLING, or ice cream. Top with sifted confectioners' sugar, sweetened fresh fruit or sundae sauce. Tiny bouchées are generally filled with savory mixtures: chicken salad, hot creamed lobster and the like.

Choux Paste

    1/2 cup butter or margarine
    1 cup boiling water
    1 cup all-purpose flour
    1/4 teaspoon salt
    4 whole eggs, unbeaten

Bring butter or margarine and water to boil in saucepan. Add flour and salt all at once. Beat vigorously over low heat until mixture leaves side of pan and forms a ball. Remove from heat, and beat about 3 minutes as mixture cools to luke-warm. Drop in 1 whole egg at a time, and after each addition beat until smooth. When all eggs have been added, continue beating until mixture is glossy.

VARIATIONS:

Cream Puffs: Drop paste by spoonfuls onto greased cookie sheet, using tablespoon for large puffs, teaspoon for small ones, or press through

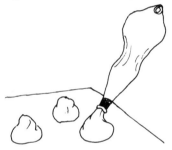

pastry bag, fitted with plain round tube. Space puffs about 2 inches apart. Mound paste, and swirl tops. Bake at 375°F. 40–45 minutes or until

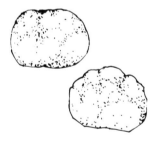

light and crusty. Remove from oven, and cut two slits on sides of each puff. Turn off oven heat

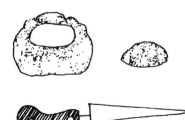

and return puffs to oven about 10 minutes to dry out centers. Cool. Fill with whipped cream

or other filling. Spread with APRICOT GLAZE or other appropriate glaze. Makes about 18 medium puffs. Recipe can easily be halved for smaller quantities.

Eclairs: Shape paste into rectangles, about 1″ x 4″, using pastry bag or spoon. Round sides and top. Bake as for CREAM PUFFS.

Bouchées: For each tiny bouchée, use 1 scant teaspoon of paste. Drop onto greased cookie sheet, and shape into high mound with spoon. Bake at 375°F. 25–30 minutes. Cut slits, and return to oven 10 minutes after heat has been turned off. Cool.

Apricot Glaze

    1 cup sieved apricot jam
    1 tablespoon orange curaçao or apricot brandy

Heat jam in saucepan; when it reaches simmering point, add curaçao. Spread while still warm over filled cases. Makes 1 cup.

VARIATIONS:

Currant Glaze: Use 1 cup red currant jelly, and flavor with a little wine or brandy.

Chocolate Glaze: Instead of jam melt semisweet chocolate, and add 1 tablespoon hot water or rich milk.

To Make a Fruit Flan

Fruit flan is a European dessert that is almost unknown in North America. Its special sweet pastry has a tender, crumbly consistency, because of its egg ingredient. The flan is a prebaked shell, and traditionally it is made in a flan ring, which is simply a straight-sided 2-inch-wide hoop of metal into which rolled circle of dough is fitted; the whole structure rests on a cookie sheet while baking. After cooling, shell is removed from supporting ring and filled, generally first with thick custard or cooked cream mixture and then with lightly stewed or glazed fruit or fresh berries, sliced peaches, and the like, arranged in decorative pattern. For topping, melted red currant jelly is frequently poured over fruit, or meringue is swirled on and baked until delicately colored and set.

Instead of the flan ring, a 9-inch layer-cake pan can be used satisfactorily. In order to get the necessary depth for the special filling, the sides should be built up slightly higher by means of a band of heavy aluminum foil fitted around the inside of the pan before putting in the pastry.

Sweet Pastry

    2 cups sifted all-purpose flour
    2 tablespoons sugar
    1 teaspoon salt
    3/4 cup butter or margarine or mixture of 1/2 butter and
        1/2 shortening
    2 egg yolks, slightly beaten
    1 tablespoon water
    1 tablespoon lemon juice

Sift flour, sugar and salt into mixing bowl. Cut in butter or margarine (which should not be ice-cold) with pastry blender, or work it in with fingers until mixture resembles cornmeal. Combine egg yolks, water and lemon juice thoroughly; sprinkle over flour mixture, and toss lightly to make soft dough. Work quickly so that butter does not become too oily. Turn out on floured board, and knead gently 5 or 6 times; wrap tightly in waxed paper, and chill 1 hour in freezing compartment of refrigerator. Watch timing, for if dough becomes too cold it is difficult to roll out; it should be firm yet "give" when pressed with the fingers. Roll out on lightly floured surface to scant 1/4-inch thickness. Then cut and shape according to your requirements for flan or regular pie shell or tart shells. Makes 1 9-inch shell (with leftover trimmings) or 10–12 medium tart shells.

Note: Sweet pastry may also be baked along with filling, as in MINCE PIE, CUSTARD PIE and fresh-fruit pies.

Cream Cheese Pastry

        1 cup sifted all-purpose flour
        1/4 teaspoon salt
        1/2 cup butter or margarine
        1 1/2 (3-ounce) packages plain cream cheese

Sift together flour and salt. With pastry blender or 2 knives cut in butter or margarine and cheese. When well blended, wrap in waxed paper, and chill 2 hours. Roll to 1/8-inch thickness, and cut according to desired use. Bake at 450°F. 12 minutes.

Note: This pastry can be used as the base for APPLE–CRUMBLE PIE, as small tart shells, for turnovers filled with jelly or plain in dainty rounds, diamonds and strips served warm with soup or salad course.

Tarts

Tarts take to a variety of fillings. Use chiffon mixtures; such cream-pie fillings as butterscotch, vanilla and chocolate, or cooled RAISIN PIE filling. Prepare filling several hours before serving time; cool; then fill shells. Top with meringue, and bake until delicately colored. Or just before serving top tarts with whipped cream or sprinkled coconut, chopped nuts, orange rind or shaved chocolate, according to filling. Fruit fillings for pies are great in tarts. Custard mixtures, PECAN-SYRUP PIE filling, and the like.

The fluted tart tins, muffin pans and custard cups used in preparing tarts, vary greatly in size and shape. Therefore, it's best to cut pastry rounds 1/4 inch larger than perimeter of inverted container.

PLAIN PASTRY, FLAKY PASTRY, SWEET PASTRY or CREAM CHEESE PASTRY may be used for tart shells.

Roll pastry to 1/8-inch thickness, and cut in desired size with pastry cutter. Or mark dough first with round can or lid, and cut out with pastry wheel. Fit pastry into tart pan; if necessary place on cookie sheet, and fill 2/3 full with prepared filling. Bake as directed in specific recipe.

Often you will wish to prepare baked tart shells, to be filled later with cream or custard mixtures, jam or jelly. To keep small shells nicely shaped and prevent shrinkage, fit pastry circles over outside of fluted tart pans or custard cups, and place upside down on cookie sheet for baking. Prick with form to prevent puffing. Bake at 450°F. 10–12 minutes. Cool thoroughly before removing from pans.

Lemon Filling

    3 eggs
    3/4 cup sugar
    1/3 cup butter or margarine
    3 tablespoons grated lemon rind
    1/3 cup lemon juice

Beat eggs in top of double boiler; then beat in sugar, butter or margarine and lemon rind. Place over boiling water and cook 5 minutes. Add lemon juice, and continue cooking 5 minutes, stirring until thickened. Remove from hot water. Chill mixture thoroughly. Fill medium tart shells, and refrigerate until shortly before serving time. Fills 10–12 medium shells.

Glazed Fruit Filling

    1 (3-ounce) package plain cream cheese
    1 teaspoon orange or pineapple juice
    Prepared peaches, sweet cherries, raspberries and so forth
    1/2 cup red currant jelly
    1 tablespoon hot water

Blend cream cheese and orange juice together. Spread thin layer of mixture in bottom of cooled, baked tart shells. Fill with well-drained fresh or frozen fruit. Prepart glaze by melting jelly and mixing with hot water. Spoon over fruit in tarts. *Note*: Do not use uncooked pineapple.

Strawberry–Cream Filling

    1/2 cup milk
    1/2 cup sugar
    1 tablespoon all-purpose flour
    1 egg, well beaten
    1/8 teaspoon salt
    1/2 teaspoon vanilla extract
    1/4 cup heavy cream, stiffly beaten
  1 1/2 cups strawberries, washed, hulled and drained
    1/4 cup (or more) red currant jelly

Scald milk in top of double boiler. Combine sugar, flour, beaten egg and salt. Pour hot milk slowly over egg mixture, stirring; return all to double boiler, and cook over boiling water until thick, stirring constantly. Add vanilla, and cool. Just before using, fold in whipped cream. Fill tart shells half full of mixture. Arrange layer of strawberries on top of each. Heat currant jelly until it melts, and pour a spoonful on top of each tart. Fills 6 large tarts.

Zabaglione Tarts

    6 egg yolks, beaten
    1/3 cup sugar
    1/8 teaspoon salt
    1/2 cup Marsala or medium-dry sherry
    1 cup firm whole berries or peeled sliced peaches
    8 baked tart shells, cooled

Beat egg yolks, sugar and salt in top of double boiler. Cook, beating over hot water until thick and smooth. Gradually beat in wine, keeping mixture thick and smooth. Cool. Spoon over fresh berries in tart shells. Makes 8 tarts.

Main Dish Pastries. For savory pies with the sort of fillings that might be absorbed by the pastry—BEEFSTEAK AND KIDNEY PIE for example— a plain pastry is best or the special type called ROUGH PUFF PASTRY. The latter is flaky and many-layered like PUFF PASTE, so that it builds up a high crust, but it is not so rich or delicate as is the latter. This kind of pastry may be used to make VOL-AU-VENT SHELLS, which are useful, filled with creamed chicken, sweetbreads and mushrooms and so forth, as luncheon dishes.

Rough Puff Pastry

    2 cups sifted all-purpose flour
    1/2 teaspoon salt
    1/3 cup lard
    1/3 cup unsalted butter or margarine
    1/2 teaspoon lemon juice
    6 tablespoons ice water

Sift flour with salt. Cut lard and butter or margarine into 1-inch cubes. Cut lightly into flour mixture. Add lemon juice to ice water, and mix in lightly. Continue to blend in water gradually until all has been added. Dough should be fairly stiff. Roll dough into oblong shape. Fold in 3. Turn so that folded edges are at right and left. Roll out away from you, fold and turn again. Repeat this process 4 times. Then allow dough to rest at least 1/2 hour and preferably 1 hour in refrigerator. Then roll it out, and shape to make single top crust for 9-inch pie or in any other suitable shape or size.

Vol-au-Vent Shells

These shells may be made of PUFF PASTE or ROUGH PUFF PASTRY, depending on type of filling you wish to use. Make pastry as directed; roll out, and cut dough into circles. Size will vary according to your needs. For bouchées and cocktail-hour specialties, make very small; for a luncheon dish you will want larger shapes. For the latter, cut circles about 3 inches in diameter. Set enough aside for number of servings planned. With remaining dough circles, cut a round out of each center, leaving rings like doughnuts. These rings will be used to make "walls" on complete circles and will hold filling in place. Set whole circles on baking sheet; on each stack 2 rings. Bake at 450°F. 8–14 minutes or until done; baking time will depend on size. On separate sheet bake small rounds cut from rings. As they are small, they will bake in less time. When all are baked and out of the oven, fill shells, and place 1 small round on top.

Beefsteak-and-Kidney Pie

1 1/2 pounds round or chuck steak
1/2 pound lamb kidneys
1/4 cup all-purpose flour
1 1/2 teaspoons salt
1/2 teaspoon thyme
1/2 teaspoon ground ginger
3 tablespoons shortening or cooking oil
1 tablespoon Worcestershire sauce
1 tablespoon chopped parsley
5–6 small onions, peeled
2 1/2 cups boiling water
FLAKY PASTRY or ROUGH PUFF PASTRY for single-crust pie, chilled

Cut beef into 1-inch cubes, trimming away all fat. Wash kidneys, trim away outer skin and any fat or tubes and slice. Mix flour, salt and spices; combine with meat, coating all sides. Heat shortening in skillet, and put in meat and seasoned flour. Cover and brown thoroughly; turn meat several times so that all sides are brown. Reduce heat, and add remaining ingredients except pastry, stirring to blend water with flour and fat mixture. Cover, and simmer about 1 hour. Turn into casserole. Roll out pastry to fit top generously; slash for steam vents; arrange over top, pressing to seal edge against moistened rim of dish. Bake in 425°F. over 35–40 minutes. Serves 5–6.

Tourtière

1/2-inch slice salt pork, diced, or 3 slices bacon, diced
1 small onion, chopped, (1/4 cup)
1/2 clove garlic, crushed (optional)
2 pounds lean shoulder pork, ground
3/4 cup meat stock or bouillon or consommé or 2/3 cup water and 2 tablespoons meat glaze
2 tablespoons chopped celery leaves
2 tablespoons chopped parsley
1 1/2 teaspoons salt
1/2 bay leaf
1/8 teaspoon mace
1/8 teaspoon chervil
Pinch ground cloves
Pinch cayenne
1 slice day-old French bread
2 recipes PLAIN PASTRY or ROUGH PUFF PASTRY for double-crust 8-inch pie

In large skillet sauté salt pork over low heat until crisply browned. Add onion and fry, stirring until it is transparent; add remaining ingredients, except bread and pastry. Simmer, stirring occasionally, about 45 minutes. Crumble French bread into mixture to absorb some of juice and keep meat mixture from spreading out of hot pastry when you cut it later. (If pie is

to be served cold, omit bread.) Let mixture cool before turning into pastry. Roll out 1/2 the pastry, and line 2 8-inch pie pans. Trim edges, and add filling. Dampen rims, and roll out remaining pastry for top crusts; put in place, and seal edges. Bake at 425°F. 15 minutes; reduce heat to 350°F., and continue baking 25–30 minutes. Serves 6–8.

Onion–Custard Pie

PLAIN PASTRY for single-crust 9-inch pie shell
5 medium onions, approximately 4 cups
3 tablespoons butter or margarine, melted
1 cup commercial sour cream
3 eggs, slightly beaten
2 tablespoons dry sherry
1 teaspoon salt
1/4 teaspoon black pepper
1/2 teaspoon celery seed
1/4 teaspoon chopped parsley
1/4 teaspoon sage
2–3 bacon strips, lightly fried
1 tomato, sliced

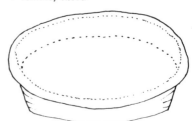

Line 9-inch pie plate with pastry, and chill. Slice onions thin, and sauté gently in butter

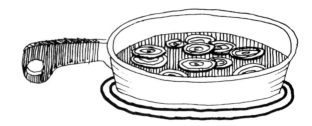

or margarine until transparent but not browned Heat sour cream and stir gradually into eggs.

Add sherry and seasonings, mixing well. Turn cooked onion into lined pie plate, and pour egg

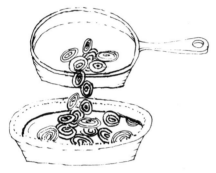

mixture over. Bake at 450°F. 10 minutes. Reduce heat to 350°F., and continue to bake another 1/2 hour or until filling is set. About 15 minutes before end of cooking time, arrange bacon strips

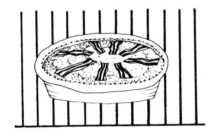

in diagonal effect on top, with slice of tomato between strips. Serves 4–5.

Oyster Pie

    1 1/2 cups combined oyster liquor and rich milk
    2 tablespoons butter or margarine
    2 tablespoons chopped celery
    1 tablespoon chopped parsley
    2 egg yolks beaten
    2 tablespoons fine bread crumbs
    1/2 teaspoon salt
Dash paprika
Dash Worcestershire sauce
    2 cups oysters, fresh or canned
PLAIN PASTRY for single-crust 8-inch pie
    1 tablespoon milk

Put oyster-liquor and milk mixture in saucepan, and add butter or margarine, celery and parsley. When hot pour gradually into egg yolks. Add crumbs, seasonings and Worcestershire sauce; stir thoroughly. Arrange oysters in greased shallow baking dish, and pour hot sauce over. Roll out pastry, prick and cover dish. Seal edge, and brush top with 1 tablespoon milk. Bake at 375°F. 30 minutes or until pastry is golden. Serves 4.

Savory Turnovers

1 recipe PLAIN PASTRY or ROUGH PUFF PASTRY
    for single-crust 8-inch pie
1 egg white, slightly beaten (optional)

Roll out pastry to about 1/8-inch thickness, and cut into 4-inch squares. Place 2 or more tablespoons suitable savory filling just off center of each square. Brush edge of each square with water, and fold pastry over to make a triangle; press edges together with fork tines. Place on cookie sheet, brush with egg white, and bake in 450°F. oven about 20 minutes. Makes 4.

Note: Fill with about 3/4 cup finely ground cooked meat, moistened with gravy, slightly diluted canned mushroom soup or chili sauce and seasoned to taste; or with 3/4 cup finely flaked and cooked fish (all bones removed) moistened with cream and sprinkled with chopped stuffed olives.

Chicken Pie

    4-pound stewing chicken
    3 cups boiling water
    1 large onion, sliced (1/2 cup)
    2 stalks celery, diced (1/2 cup)
1/4 teaspoon paprika
Salt to taste
    5 or 6 carrots, sliced (1 cup)
    2 tablespoons all-purpose flour
    2 tablespoons soft butter or margarine
PLAIN PASTRY or ROUGH PUFF PASTRY for single-crust 9-inch pie

Cut chicken in serving pieces, and cover with boiling water. Add onion, celery, paprika and

salt. Bring to boil. Reduce heat, and simmer about 2 hours until chicken is tender, adding carrots for last 1/2 hour of cooking time. Strain off stock, and chill quickly, uncovered. Cut chicken meat from bones; dice large. Heat 3 cups chicken stock (water or milk may be added if necessary to make up quantity). Blend flour and butter or margarine and use to thicken hot broth, continuing to stir until sauce is thick and smooth. Add diced meat and additional seasoning to taste. Cool again. Fill large or individual casseroles with chicken mixture. Cover with sheet of pastry, cut slits to release steam. Flute edge, and bake, allowing 12–15 minutes at 475°F. for small pies and 20–25 minutes at same heat for 2 large ones, or bake until pastry is golden brown. Serves 4.

Note: Suitable vegetables, pre-cooked, may be added: green peas, mushrooms, tiny new potatoes and the like. The chicken filling can be served as stew without pastry. Creamed leftover cooked chicken may be substituted for pie fillings.

Chicken à la King in Pastry Shells

        2 tablespoons butter or margarine
        3 tablespoons all-purpose flour
        1 cup chicken stock or consommé
        1 cup rich milk
        1/2 teaspoon salt
    Dash pepper
    Dash paprika
        2 egg yolks
        1/4 pound mushrooms
        1 tablespoon butter or margarine
        3 cups diced cooked chicken
        1/2 cup chopped sweet red or green pepper
        1 teaspoon lemon juice
    4–6 PATTY SHELLS

In top of double boiler over direct medium heat melt 2 tablespoons butter or margarine; blend in flour, and gradually add stock and milk, stirring constantly until thick and smooth. Add salt, pepper and paprika to taste. Beat egg yolks until thick and lemon colored. Stir hot mixture very slowly into eggs; return all to double boiler, this time over hot water. Sauté mushrooms lightly in 1 tablespoon butter or margarine; add, along with chicken and sweet pepper, to hot mixture. Just before serving stir in lemon juice. Spoon into patty shells. Serves 4–6.

FREEZING

Do not freeze custard pies, cream fillings and puddings, unwhipped gelatin desserts, unwhipped heavy cream and such cooked egg-white mixtures as meringues, macaroons and boiled icings. Most baked goods, however, freeze very well. A major factor is proper packaging—poorly wrapped cakes and breads will take on an undesirable "freezer flavor." Detailed instructions on wrapping and storing will be found in your freezer manufacturer's booklet.

How To Freeze Breads. All yeast breads and quick breads can be frozen very successfully (uncooked bread dough should not be frozen). Prepare and bake as usual, and let cool to room temperature. If desired, frost buns or fancy breads before freezing; or leave frosting until after thawing.

To Package

Wrap in freezer wrappings (foil, plastic film, freezer paper), or insert in plastic bags, excluding as much air as possible. Seal. Items that you like to reheat before serving—rolls, French bread or coffee cakes—should, for later convenience, be wrapped in foil, so that they are ready to warm in the oven. Such reheating must never be done in waxed or plastic wrappings, which will melt. The inexpensive aluminum-foil baking pans are useful in their various sizes for wrapping complete with contents for freezer storage.

To Thaw

Allow frozen baked goods to thaw in their wrappings at room temperature. If they are foil-wrapped and you wish to serve warm, place parcels in preheated 300°F. oven 15–30 minutes, depending on size. Unwrap as soon as heated through; otherwise they may develop a steamed texture. Allow 2 hours thawing time at room temperature for yeast breads, tea breads and square quick breads like CORNBREAD. Allow 1 hour or less for thawing rolls, muffins, scones and sweetened mitxures. Waffles, pancakes and presliced bread will thaw when toasted or heated under broiler.

How To Freeze Cakes. All kinds of cakes can be frozen—fruit, sponge, angel food, chiffon and butter cakes. Prepare and bake as usual; cool to room temperature.

Cakes may be frosted before freezing. The uncooked butter frostings are best for this purpose, as boiled or 7-minute frosting tends to become gummy when frozen, and the fudge type will crumble.

Large iced layer cakes sometimes pose a storage problem. When freezing, do not use cream fillings; instead, use butter icing between the layers, or resort to jam or cooked fruit fillings like date, raisin and the like.

Fill and frost cooled cake. Place it unwrapped in freezer 2 hours to set icing; then wrap.

To Package

Place cake, frosted or unfrosted, on piece of foil-covered cardboard; wrap with freezer wrappings (oil, plastic wrap), or insert in plastic bag, excluding as much air as possible; seal. Freeze; then place cake in cardboard bakery carton or any firm container to protect cake from other packages during storage period.

For luncheon use, halve, quarter or slice cake; wrap securely in individual portions, according to your requirements, and freeze.

To Thaw

Always leave cake in freezer wrappings during thawing period. Allow 2–3 hours for square or loaf cakes; 1–1 1/2 hours for layers, and as much as 4–5 hours for large iced layer cake. Fruit cakes, being quite solid, require about 1 hour per pound. To speed thawing of any cake, place package in stream of air blown from electric fan.

How To Freeze Cookies. Cookies of standard types may be frozen baked or unbaked. It will save space in your freezer to store dough and bake as needed. Bars and squares, however, must always be baked before freezing.

To Prepare Dough

Refrigerator-cookie dough can be shaped into roll and wrapped as usual, then placed in plastic bags and sealed before storing in freezer. Drop or molded cookie doughs may be handily packed in bulk in airtight freezer containers. Another way is to drop batter by spoonfuls or in balls onto a baking sheet and freeze 1 hour. Transfer frozen shapes to rigid container, placing a couple of sheets of waxed paper between layers.

To Thaw Cookie Doughs

Refrigerator-type dough should be sliced as soon as knife will cut roll. Other bulk cookie dough should stand at room temperature and be used when soft enough to handle. Preshaped cookies should be placed in their unthawed state on greased baking sheet and put into oven immediately, allowing longer baking time.

To Package Baked Cookies

If you wish to freeze baked cookies, let them cool thoroughly; pack in firm containers with lightly crushed waxed paper between layers; overwrap tightly with freezer wrapping. For such special occasions as Christmas, decorated fancy cookies can be arranged on trays with freezer paper between layers and the whole overwrapped before storing.

To Thaw Baked Cookies

Leave in freezer wrapping at room temperature; time will depend upon size of container and type of cookies. Date and oatmeal cookies and brownies require longer thawing time than do rolled sugar cookies.

How To Freeze Pies. Double-crust fresh fruit pies and mince pies are better frozen *unbaked*, with special preparation. On the other hand, pies and tarts with pecan-syrup or chiffon fillings should be baked and cooled before freezing. *Do not freeze custard or cream-filled pies*, baked or unbaked.

To Prepare Fruit and Mince Pies

Use regular or foil pie pans. When preparing filling allow 1/3 more thickener (flour, cornstarch, tapioca or the like) to control extra juices of frozen fruit. For example, if berry-pie recipe specifies 3 tablespoons flour, increase amount to 4. Do not make slits in top crust. Put unwrapped pie into freezer; package after it has frozen firm. Use cardboard bakery cartons, or cover top with inverted foil pie pan; overwrap with freezer wrappings.

Note: On a real baking day, you will probably have a fair amount of pastry trimmings after cutting out pie shapes. Why not cut out these scraps in fancy shapes with a cookie cutter and freeze for elegant decorations on casserole or pudding a month from now?

To Bake Frozen Fruit Pies

Remove unthawed fruit or mince pie from wrappings. Place immediately in preheated 450°F. oven. After first 10 minutes of cooking cut 2 or 3 slits in top crust. Bake, without reducing temperature, 60–70 minutes more.

To Freeze Baked Pies

Prepare chiffon pies or other types according to your recipe; cool. Freeze 1 hour; remove from freezer, and press circular foil or plastic wrap over filling. Package as for unbaked fruit pies.

To Thaw Baked Pies

Leave in freezer wrappings at room temperature 30–60 minutes.

How To Freeze Pastry. As bulk pastry dough takes a long time to thaw, it is advisable to roll it out before freezing. After rolling, cut into circles of size required to fit your pie pans. Have ready a heavy cardboard circle about 3/4 inch larger than pastry round; cover cardboard with aluminum foil; on top of it stack pastry circles, separating each layer with 2 thicknesses of waxed paper. Wrap and stack in freezer wrapping, and store in freezer.

To Thaw Pastry Dough

Leave wrapped stacks of pastry circles at room temperature until dough is soft enough to fit into pie pans.

Freezer Storage Life for Baked Goods. The following suggested periods for freezer storage of various home-baked products are conservative and must be considered only approximate (they are maximums for well-packaged foods held continuously at 0°F. or below). It is always desirable, however, to use items from freezer regularly and replace them as soon as convenient.

Yeast breads and quick breads, 3 months
Angel food and chiffon cakes, 2 months
Chocolate layer cakes, 4 months
Yellow pound cakes, 6 months
Fruitcakes, 12 months
Unbaked cookies, 6–8 months
Baked cookies, 12 months
Unbaked fruit and mince pies, 8 months
Chiffon and other baked pies, 2 months
Unbaked pastry, 6 months

APPROXIMATE BAKING TIMES AND TEMPERATURES

1 loaf bread takes 45–60 minutes at 375°–400°F.
Sweet rolls take 15–30 minutes at 350°–400°F.
Baking-powder biscuits take 10–15 minutes at 450°F.
Tea breads take about 60 minutes at 350°F.
Coffee cakes with baking powder take about 25 minutes at 375°F.
Coffee cakes with yeast take about 25 minutes at 400°F.
Layer cakes take about 30 minutes at 375°F.
Rectangular cakes take 30–45 minutes at 375°F.
Cupcakes take about 20 minutes at 400°F.
Sponge cakes take 50–60 minutes at 300°–325°F.
Pie shells take about 15 minutes at 450°F.
Double-crust pies take 15 minutes 425°F., then 30–45 minutes at reduced heat according to filling.

APPROXIMATE SIZES OF CAKE PANS *

Round layer pans 8″ or 9″ x 1 1/2″ deep
Square cake pan 8″ x 8″ x 2″
Square cake pan 9″ x 9″ x 2″
Oblong cake pan 13″ x 9″ x 2″
Sheet pan (for jelly rolls) 15″ x 10″ x 1/2″
Loaf pan 9″ x 5″ x 3″
Loaf pan 8″ x 4″ x 3″
Tube pan 8″ x 3 1/2″ deep
Tube pan 10″ x 4 1/2″ deep
Spring-form pan 9″ x 3 3/4″ deep
Spring-form pan 10″ x 4 1/2″ deep

*Sizes for most frequently used pans.

5
~
An Introduction to Gourmet Cookery

A gourmet evaluates cooking critically and is an epicure, or lover of good eating. The person who is a gastronomer practices the art of preparing fine foods. Although the controversy over whether gastronomy is an art or a science has not been resolved we fortunately remain free to explore all possibilities for fine cooking. The recipes in this chapter range from simple to complex. In all of them always assemble materials and utensils before starting preparation, and follow procedures, times and temperatures given. Omit or replace certain seasonings or flavors to suit your taste.

It is wise to try these recipes privately before serving to guests. Gourmet cooking more than any other kind improves with practice.

Equipment. A selection of good sharp knives is essential for slicing, dicing, chopping, boning and skinning. If you happen to find the type known as a "French chef's knife," buy it. It has a carbon-steel blade, which can be sharpened more quickly and easily than can a hard stainless-steel edge.

A heavy chopping board of good size—at least twice as large as an ordinary bread board—is another essential. There should be surface enough to let you undertake several cutting jobs at one time without overlapping, and the board should rest firmly, flat and even, on your kitchen counter or table.

Whisks, or wire whips for beating eggs and sauces, are not easy to find, but when you acquire one you will find it as indispensable as the European cook does. They are made in various sizes, with short or long handles, so try them out for "feel" and choose 2 or 3—perhaps 1 in the true whisk shape and the others with continuously coiled wire around an oval stirrer. Without these simple devices, intended for brisk whipping and beating by the right hand while the left is adding ingredients, the encyclopedia of French sauces could never have been achieved.

A rubber scraper is a great tool for folding, creaming, stirring and scraping. And a food mill, of the kind used to strain mixtures for a baby's diet, is frequently in use in gourmet kitchens for pureeing soups, and the like; an electric blender is generally a quicker, easier, neater substitute. The original blender, used in the days of Escoffier and for centuries before him, was the mortar and pestle; it is still used throughout Europe for the crushing of herbs, spices and nuts. The wire salad basket for efficient washing and drip-drying of greens was a familiar everyday tool in French kitchens long before it appeared on this side of the Atlantic.

Heavy-bottomed pans that conduct heat evenly and hug stove burner or element are desirable. Copper pots have been traditional in French kitchens, frequently handed down through generations of *bonnes femmes*, but they are both costly and heavy, and their interiors have to be retinned frequently. Today's stainless steel, with exterior bases of copper or with heavy cast aluminum bottoms, is an efficient compromise. Enameled cast-iron equipment for both top of the stove and oven is austerely handsome in design and color (the color does not tinge or otherwise affect food); but even empty, the weight, especially of the large covered casseroles, is formidable. On the other hand, very lightweight pots and pans are not recommended. Their instability makes them even dangerous to use, and foods tend to burn and scorch on thin bottoms.

To stock your kitchen satisfactorily, consider the various cooking jobs to be done, rather than the visual appeal of matched equipment. Several heavy frying pans of various sizes are a must. Reserve one with a rounded base and medium size for your omelet pan. Never wash it in the dishpan, and never let water come in contact with its cooking surface; otherwise your omelets may stick. Use clean dry cheesecloth or paper towels to wipe out pan after each omelet session.

Earthenware, oven-glass, or very hardy ceramic cooking equipment offers many styles and sizes of dishes suitable for both cooking and serving. The ceramic containers are impervious to direct heat and can even be transferred directly from cold refrigerator to gas flame or preheated oven. Earthenware cannot be used this way, yet for centuries the good cooks of continental Europe have prepared their traditional soups and ragouts in this fragile baked clay, which must never be exposed to extremes of temperature. There is a secret, of course. For cooking on top of the stove a protective asbestos mat is always used between heat source and clay pot; the pot is also allowed to cool slowly before being washed in hot water. When certain foreign recipes direct you to "brown the meat cubes and onion in melted fat, using an earthenware marmite over medium heat," the unstated assumption is that you know all about the essential asbestos mat that will keep the container from cracking.

The Dutch oven is a deep heavy metal pan, which may have a removable rack, and a tight-fitting cover. It is indispensable for slow-cooked meat dishes either on top of the stove or in the oven. The bain-marie is the French double-boiler, which is quite like ours, though sometimes with a porcelain lining in two metal sections. Another familiar sight in French kitchens is the series of graduated "melters," little metal containers with handles or thumb-pieces

Hair sieves, sometimes cone-shaped; wooden spatulas and spoons; the metal flan rings that are often used in place of pieplates for baking pastry shells; tiny brushes for glazing with fat or sugar syrup: larding needles for threading slivers of fat into solid meat before roasting; jelly molds in elaborate designs; cake pans; baking sheets for rows of small confections, and straight-sided soufflé dishes are all part of the ideal gourmet kitchen.

Types of cookery other than French sometimes call for such special equipment as the Japanese hibachi or charcoal grill for indoor or outdoor use and the cast-iron cornstick baking pan from the southern United States, which cooks cornbread in the shape of miniature corncobs. The list could go on endlessly and still be incomplete.

Notes on Basic Ingredients.

Butter

When heated, butter foams, and when the foam subsides the butter starts to brown and will eventually burn. Cook your omelet in butter just after foaming subsides. Oil is often used with butter to allow it to be heated to a higher temperature, especially in browning meats.

Clarified butter

Clarified butter is the clear yellow liquid obtained when butter is heated and the milky sediment settles on the bottom. Called "ghee" in India, clarified butter is popular in the Far East and other areas for sautéeing foods that require very delicate browning and also for certain sauces.

Oils

Oils vary greatly in kind and flavor around the world. Salad oil from vegetable sources is satisfactory for most cooking, especially for delicate French dishes.

Olive oil, so popular in Spain, Italy and other Mediterranean areas, is too definite in character for many kinds of cooking. In this section, unless otherwise specified, "oil" refers to cooking oils.

Flour

When flour is called for in recipes on following pages, it is the type known as "all-purpose," unless otherwise specified. This hard-wheat flour produces smoother sauces than do the varieties used for pastry and cakes.

Bouillon, Broth and Stock

These liquids are called for in many recipes. As homemade stocks are time-consuming to prepare, it is suggested that canned or dry-base types be substituted, according to flavor specified. Use consommé only if called for in recipe, as it tends to be slightly sweet.

Seasonings

Seasonings for bouquet garni and other purposes are discussed under herbs and spices.

A Guide to Seasoning with Herbs, Spices and Seeds. Get acquainted with the ancient "sweet herbs," treasured by good cooks for centuries. Use them fresh and green from the market or your garden. Dry or freeze them for a ready supply months later. (But remember that dried herbs are 6 times stronger than fresh-picked ones; the traditional "pinch" should be not more than 1/16 teaspoonful.) Store dried or crushed herbs well removed from cooking steam, and renew your supply of seasonings at least once a year. Study tropical spices, and learn their wide-ranging characteristics; investigate savory seeds, and experiment with today's newly available seasoning combinations.

Herbs, since the beginning of civilization, have been an important factor in everyday living, whether for medical or for culinary uses. Nowadays "sweet herbs" (the old term for the edible kinds) are becoming almost a necessity in our kitchens.

Many people grow their own herbs, and the space allotted may vary from 1 or 2 windowsill pots to a formal herb garden. Climate, space and taste dictate the kinds grown.

To Dry Leaf Herbs

Choose plants just beginning to blossom, and pick on sunny morning after dew is off leaves. Cut about 2/3 the length of the stalk, with side branches and stems. Rinse off earth clinging to lower leaves, and remove yellow or decayed leaves. Spread herbs (each variety separately) on trays or papers in warm dry room or airy attic. Turn every day until dried; it takes about 3–4 days. Strip off leaves, using glove to protect your fingers, place each variety in screw-top jar and store in dark room for 1 week. If moisture appears in jar, remove contents to cheesecloth-covered screen, and leave a few days longer. Store in opaque container, and make sure it is tightly covered.

To dry in bunches, tie stems together and hang from line in warm room until leaves are crackly. Spread papers underneath to catch leaves or seeds.

To Dry Herb Seeds

Dill and other herbs should be left to develop flower heads and cut while still in flower. Allow to dry as for leafy herbs, turning on trays or papers in dark dry room. Harvest seeds by rubbing heads between palms of hands. Store as for leaves, and be sure to check for moisture before finally putting seeds in containers.

To Freeze Herbs

Herbs most suitable for quick freezing are basil, chives, fennel, marjoram, spearmint, sage, tarragon and thyme. Frozen herbs cannot be used for garnishes, but are handy for chopping or crushing in cooked dishes, salads, sandwich fillings and iced drinks. Herbs may be blended for specific dishes like soups, salad dressings and poultry stuffings.

Have ready small plastic freezer bags and pint cartons in which to pack them. Cut herbs with tender tops, allowing sufficient stem to tie in bunches. Wash under cold running water and dry on paper toweling.

Arrange sprigs together (either one kind or a blend), and tie with thread, making loop sufficiently large to hold them when they are dipped in boiling water. Have large saucepan of boiling water ready, and keep it at boiling point. Nearby have pan of ice water. Immerse herbs in boiling water, and hold 1 minute; then transfer to ice water, and hold 2 minutes.

Rinse under cold running water, and drain. Place in freezer bags, and seal. Pack as many bags as possible in freezer carton, but do not crush. Label, and freeze. Before using, allow to thaw at room temperature, and use immediately.

Do not refreeze leftovers, but add thawed leaf herbs to wine vinegar for interesting flavor.

Herb Blends

Some herbs cancel out one another's flavors, whereas others tend to dominate. The bland or "blender" herbs are parsley and chervil. Pungent herbs requiring generous accompaniments of blending herbs are rosemary, tarragon and sage. Herbs with dominant but not too powerful flavors are dill, fennel, mint, marjoram, oregano and savory. Pair with each other or with a "blender." Chives and green or dry garlic go well with any combination.

Any desired blend can be assembled and frozen, following directions given previously. Dried herbs also can be blended and stored, but leave uncrushed until just before using.

How to Use Herbs

Herbs and spices should provide interesting accents to food, rather than overwhelm it. Remember, dried herbs are almost 6 times stronger than freshly picked ones. To substitute in recipe calling for 1 tablespoon chopped fresh herbs, use 1/2 teaspoon dried herbs or flakes or 1/4 teaspoon powdered herbs.

Use dried herb leaves or flakes when long cooking is required and broth can be strained. For dishes cooked in short time make infusion of dried herbs in any liquid to be added—tomato juice, milk and stock—and let stand 1 hour; then strain. To test taste of an unfamiliar herb, steep 1/2 teaspoon in 1/2 cup water for 1 hour; then sip brew, and make your decision, remembering that flavor will not be *that* strong when mingled with other ingredients.

Fines Herbes are combinations of several fresh leaf herbs, chopped and added near end of cooking period. They are used in soups, sauces, stews and omelets and in melted butter over steaks.

Bouquet Garni is a combination of fresh or dried herbs tied in small bunches and added to soup stocks, stews and casseroles for part or all of cooking period, then removed before serving. Basic herbs used are bay leaf, thyme, and parsley, often accompanied by celery leaves. Other suitable herbs are basil, marjoram, savory or chervil. Tie sprigs of fresh herbs together with long string and attach to handle of cooking pot. Place dried herbs in scrap of clean cheesecloth, as for pickling, and tie with string. Either way bundle can be easily removed.

Types of Herbs and Their Uses. *Here are the "sweet herbs," used in small amounts for seasoning. "Pot herbs" are vegetable greens like spinach* *that are cooked in quantity. "Salad herbs" are lettuce, chicory and the like.*

Angelica   The dried, usually candied green stalks of an herb native to Europe. Used in fine baking, often as decoration in elaborate frosting; roots are used in cordials.

Basil   Often called "sweet basil." Aromatic minty flavor; much used in Italian cookery; wonderful with tomatoes in any form; also a good choice for bouquet garni.

Bay Leaf   Not an herb but the leaf from the laurel tree. A very powerful flavor, and 1/2 dried leaf is usually enough for seasoning soups, sauces or aspics.

Chervil   A relative of parsley, which it resembles, with fine lacy foliage and sweeter, stronger flavor. Used in salads, omelets, fish dishes, cooked vegetables and soups.

Chives   A member of the onion family, very delicate in appearance, with a mild onion flavor. Used in fresh form only; has wide application; snip with scissors.

Dill   Chop fresh green foliage over salads, especially cucumber, hot vegetable or fish. Use dill seeds in cooked dishes only as pungent touch for eggs or lamb.

Fennel   Looks like celery but has distinctive licorice flavor. Use leaves in salads, soups, fish dishes; whole seeds in eggs, cheese dishes, cakes, apple pie.

Garlic From a hardy plant cultivated for its strongly flavored bulb. Esteemed by ancient Greeks and almost as popular now fresh, dried, powdered or in salt.

Horseradish Comes from long root of a coarse plant. Sharp piquant flavor and odor. It is sold grated and vinegared to go with meats (especially beef) or in sauces; it is also available in powdered form.

Oregano An aromatic herb, with a taste midway between sage and marjoram. Much used in Italian cookery; good with beef, meat loaves; powerful—use with discretion.

Marjoram One of the most popular herbs; aromatic, with flavor like delicate oregano. Good in soup, stews, cheese dishes; excellent with beef in any form and also with mushrooms.

Mint The finest fresh flavor. Use green leaves as garnish; in vinegars, jellies and cold drinks; with fruits or hot vegetables, and fresh or dried in sauce for lamb.

Parsley The mainstay of the bouquet garni; familiar last touch to salads and cooked dishes. Snip with scissors for easy chopping. Dried parsley flakes are handy.

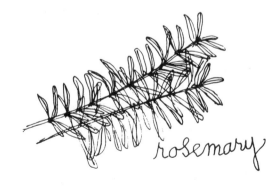

Mustard Young leaves are cooked or served raw. Tiny seeds add tang to pickles and various vegetables; they are dried and ground for packaged mustard.

Rosemary Poets used to sing of it. The leaves resemble pine needles and have tea-like fragrance. Use fresh or dried, but sparingly. Good with lamb, fish and poultry.

sage

thyme

Sage The well-known pungent herb, traditional in poultry stuffings, good with pork, spareribs, cheeses, soups, sauces. Use fresh or dried but always with caution.

savory

Savory Belongs to the mint family, possesses a highly aromatic leaf with strong flavor. Valuable either dried or fresh for stuffings, pork cuts, hot vegetables. Do not overdo.

Scallions Belongs along with chives, shallots and garlic, to family group of onions and leeks. Like young green onions, with slim, long top.

Shallots Small, rather pear-shaped member of the onion clan; has cloved structure like garlic. Much favored in European cuisines for salads, sauces, meats and so forth.

tarragon

Tarragon Delicately pungent herb, long prized by epicures for flavoring salad vinegars and dressings. Excellent with fish, chicken and vegetables, but do not use too much.

Thyme Another pungent herb, admired as a garden plant and for its flavorful leaves. A subtle touch for soups, meats, seafoods. Use dried thyme sparingly.

Types of Spices and Their Uses. *Familiar spices like pepper and nutmeg, plus costlier rarities: filé powder for Creole cookery or saffron, 1 pound of which requires 70,000 hand-picked autumn-crocus blossoms.*

Allspice A dried berry from the West Indies: tastes like mixture of clove, cinnamon, nutmeg. Whole or ground; use in pickles, cookies, cakes, meat seasoning.

cinnamon

Cinnamon Adds warm sweet flavor to many foods. Two imported types: dried bark (in sticks or ground) and cassia buds (whole or ground). Countless uses in all kinds of cookery.

Cayenne Prepared by grinding dried pods and seeds of red peppers or chilis. Fiery in taste; can burn mouth; use in minute amounts to liven sauces, salad dressings, pickles.

Chili Powder A blend of dried ground Mexican chili peppers, both "hot" and sweet types; may also contain oregano and ground cumin. Adds zest to meats, sauces, rice, beans, soups.

cloves

Cloves | The dried unopened flower buds of the Zanzibar clove tree. Pungent aroma, biting taste. Use whole or ground, but carefully. Has a great many uses.

curry

Curry Powder | A ground mixture of many herbs and spices; turmeric supplies the yellow-brown color. Packaged brands vary greatly in strength. Use with meats, fish, rice, soups and sauces.

Filé Powder | Made chiefly of dried sassafras; comes from Louisiana. Used in Creole gumbos; stirred into hot liquid after removal from heat, flavors and thickens.

ginger

Ginger | Root of Asian plant, grown in many tropical areas. Powdered, crystallized, preserved or dried. Delightfully fragrant, pungently flavored. Many uses.

Juniper | The aromatic fruit of a bush that grows wild. The unusual flavor (as in gin) is sometimes enjoyed in stuffing for game or in sauce for fish.

mace

Mace | Obtained from casing of nutmeg. Flattened, it is called a "blade." Otherwise in powder form. Smooth, gentle; used alone or in spice blends.

Nutmeg | Dried seed or nut from fruit of nutmeg tree. Available whole or ground. Adds delicate warm taste to eggnogs, desserts, baked products, certain soups and vegetables.

Paprika | From ground dried pods of sweet red or chili peppers; rich dark red; flavor mild to pungent. Use for both color and seasoning in batters, sauces and the like.

pepper

Pepper | Black and white from same dried berry; milder white is ground after hulls removed. Peppercorns are whole berries. Gourmet kitchens stock both.

Saffron | Powder made from stigmas of autumn-crocus blossoms. Gives golden color, pleasant flavor to rice, meats, breads, pastry. Steep saffron in recipe's liquid.

saffron

Turmeric	Belongs to ginger family; a dried root, ground, added to curry blends and condiments. Sweet tangy flavor; adds interesting color to pickles, sauces and so forth.

The Savory Seeds. *Nutlike sesame scattered over a cake; tiny celery seeds for piquancy in potato salad; old fashioned caraway blended with creamy cheese.*

celery seed

anise seed

Anise	The aromatic seed of a small fruit. Has distinctive licorice flavor (as in anisette, the French liqueur). Use whole or ground in baking, candies, and cheese.

Caraway

CARAWAY

Caraway	Highly distinctive flavor, which wins ardent devotion or strong opposition. Baked in "seed cake"; served with mutton or sauerkraut; often blended into mild cheese.

Cardamon

cardamon

Cardamon	An exotic flavor, like anise or licorice plus strong coffee. Used in mixed pickling spices. Featured in Spanish cookery and Scandinavian baking.

Celery	Celery seed has a very pronounced celery flavor. Useful in soup stocks, pot roasts, vegetable salads (especially potato), French dressings and pickles.
Coriander	The ancients prized this seasoning for its unusual sweetish taste. Uses range from pea soup and pickles to gingerbreads.
Cumin	Like coriander, this is a tiny fruit treated as a seed; with a long history too. Added to curry blends; used alone to flavor meats, hot vegetables, cheese.
Nasturtium	This homely garden plant is almost entirely edible. Young seed pods can be pickled in vinegar, like capers. Tender leaves, flowers are spicy salad touches.
Poppy	From an annual plant of the poppy tribe. White seed available but blue seed more popular. A favorite topping for breads; browned in butter for rice, and stews.

sesame seed

Sesame	Aromatic seed of a flowering plant. Has rich nutty flavor, which makes it useful in cakes, candies. Toasted and browned a worthy addition to salads, casseroles.

| Vanilla | An aromatic tropical bean, which, steeped in alcohol, gives the well-known flavoring extract for sweet dishes. Dried bean is used in *haute cuisine*. |

Combination Seasonings. *These are legion on today's market: packaged condiment sauces thick or thin, tomato pastes, blends of spices, seasoning salts.*

Angostura Bitters	An aromatic liquid spice made from gentian and other plant flavors in alcoholic solution. Add by drops to beverages. Extremely powerful, use with caution.
Monosodium Glutamate	White powder chemically produced from glutamic acids in sugar beets, wheat or corn. Add before or during cooking to enhance food flavors. Various brands. Referred to as M.S.G.
Poultry Seasoning	Term applied to packaged ready-mixed dried herbs suitable for use in stuffings. For 4-pound chicken, 1/2 teaspoon is basic recommendation; increase to suit taste.
Soy Sauce	The essential touch for Chinese savory dishes, replacing salt. An almost-black liquid made from fermented soy beans. Flavor is pronounced.
Hot Pepper Sauce	A red sauce, aged before bottling. Use only 1 or 2 drops at a time.

The Great Wines: Types and Origins. Wines are generally classified according to color: red or white (the latter actually a tone of yellow or gold), with the addition of the pinks, or vin rosé. There are further classifications as well. Wines may be dry or sweet, "dry" ("sec"), meaning lack of sweetness rather than total sourness, and in-between types like "demi-sec." Certain vintages are further grouped as full-bodied or light-bodied. Good "body" means a well-rounded combination of strength and flavor, resulting in what

the French esteem as "solidité." Fortified wines are those that have brandy added after the desired characteristics have developed in the wine. Aromatic wines, like vermouth, are fortified and infused with selected herbs and spices.

Selecting and Serving

The choice of wines to be served at a single meal depends upon personal preference, and budget. One dry wine—champagne, a red or white table wine or vin rosé—may be served throughout the meal.

At informal or formal luncheons or dinners champagne is often served throughout. Wine may be withheld during the salad course if the latter is accompanied by a pronounced vinegar dressing, as the flavors wouldn't be compatible.

Wines with Menu Courses

With hors d'oeuvres serve champagne, vin rosé or white wine.

With soup, dry sherry or Madeira is the traditional choice.

With fish, shellfish, ham, pork, omelets, cold fowl and light entrées, serve light dry wine or vin rosé.

With roast chicken, turkey, veal, lamb and ragouts, serve light-bodied red wine or full-bodied dry white wine.

With roast beef, steak, venison and game birds serve full-bodied red wine. With desserts, serve sweet white wine, champagne, Madeira, dessert sherry or port.

With cheese, fruits and nuts, port is traditional, but any full-bodied red wine may be offered.

Choice of Glasses

Wineglasses are best colorless so that the tone and life of the wine are well displayed. Stemmed glasses are nice but not essential. The glass should be of 6–8 ounce capacity, preferably tulip-shaped to collect the smell or bouquet of the wine at the top of the glass. The average serving of wine is 3–4 ounces, regardless of the size of the glass.

There is an all-purpose wineglass, which will serve any kind of wine and is satisfactory, both in appearance and use, also reduces the cupboard storage problem.

Temperatures for Serving Wines

Serve all white wines, sparkling wines and rosé wines well chilled at 40°–45°F. Several hours in refrigerator will bring wine to this temperature.

If you have a wine cooler for use in the dining room, by all means use it. Pack chilled bottle in crushed ice 1/2 hour before dinner, and rotate from time to time.

Serve still red wines at room temperatures, 65°–70°F. If brought from cellar with temperature of 50°F., allow wine to stand several hours in dining room. Some light-bodied red wines are more palatable served at 60°F., or slightly under room temperature.

Open still red wines an hour or so before serving, to permit them to "breathe." Sparkling wines should be opened just before serving.

Sherries, Madeiras and appetizer and dessert wines are pleasanter when served slightly chilled.

Care and Handling of Wines

Wine should be handled very gently. Shaking, twirling bottle or serving wine too soon after its arrival at your home is apt to damage it.

To open, use lever-type corkscrew, and work precisely and gently to insert as far as it will go. Then turn lever with steady motion to remove cork; do not try to pull. Removing cork from

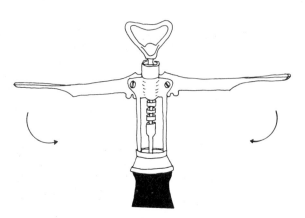

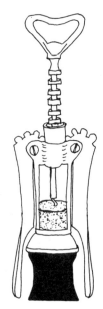

champagne is often quite tricky, requiring patience, dexterity and strength. After removing foil, take off wire very carefully, grasp cork, give it a turn to the right and then push out. Hold bottle at an angle after opening, so that pressure does not force a great deal of wine out of bottle.

Store all unfortified wines in cool, dark, dry place, laying bottles *on their sides* in order to

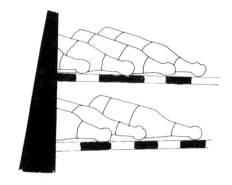

keep corks moistened and tight. These "living" wines continue to develop and mature within the unopened bottles; thus they deserve this slight extra care. Burgundies stored under proper conditions will last from 10 to upwards of 30 years, depending on the vintage. Bordeaux takes much longer to mature, and many vintages in the past were practically indestructible. The wines from the Rhone Valley are the most robust of all red wines produced in France. They are fine with game, cheese or other heavy dishes. The white and rosé wines of the Rhone Valley are also heavier-bodied than similar wines from other sections. On the other hand, the fortified wines

—sherry, Madeira and port—have more stable natures and can be stored upright. Of all the different classes of wines, sherry is the least subject to deterioration. Even after months of exposure to air, a 1/2 filled bottle of sherry offers the same quality as originally; indeed some experts maintain that it will show improvement.

The Fortified Wines

In this grouping are the sherries, dry or sweet; Madeira and Marsala, which, like sherry, can be chosen for either appetizer or after-dinner use, and port and Malaga, both of which are dessert wines. In all cases brandy is the fortifying agent, with the result that the alcoholic content of the wine may range up to 21 percent of volume.

Sherry comes from Spain; its name is an anglicizing of Jerez, the area where this renowned wine is produced. There are 4 recognized classes of sherry:

Manzanilla—very dry, sometimes called the world's driest wine, but not too well known outside Europe. Served as a chilled aperitif.

Fino—also very dry; universally prized as an appetizer. Serve chilled or "on the rocks" as a cocktail; often used as accompaniment to soups.

Amontillado—medium dry and darker; popular as appetizer.

Oloroso—deep gold in color; medium dry; usually served with desserts or sauced dishes. When blended with aged sweetening wines for export, Olorosos become the famous dessert sherries and usually have the word "Cream," "Brown" or "East India" in their brand titles.

Madeira hails from the Portuguese island of Madeira off northwest Africa. There are 4 tra-

ditional types: Rainwater, very light and dry appetizer wine; Sercial, darker but quite dry; Malmsey, rich and heavy and Boal, richest of all, an after-dinner wine.

Marsala from Sicily is somewhat sweeter than Spanish sherry; it is generally dark and rich.

Malaga from Spain is a deep red, richly sweet wine for after-dinner use.

Port is the famous red wine of Portugal, named after its shipping center of Oporto. A fortified and usually blended wine, it is famous for dessert or after-dinner use.

The Red Wines

Red Burgundies: Burgundy or the Côte d'Or is made up of 2 districts: Côte de Nuits and Côte de Beaune. Well-known vineyards in the Côte de Nuits district include Romanée-Conti, La Tâche, Les Richebourg, Le Chambertin, Clos Vougeot and many others. In the Côte de Beaune district, Pommard is the most famous name, and Aloxe-Corton and Volnay are almost as well known. They are pleasant, soft wines, good choices for those who sometimes complain that red wines taste "sour."

Red Bordeaux: Wines produced in the area around Bordeaux are dry and a little tart. They go well with meat and poultry of all kinds and especially with foods that are not too spicy or pungent.

Famous wines exported from Bordeaux are from the Médoc district: Château Margaux, Château Mouton-Rothschild and Château Latour. Château Haut-Brion comes from the Graves district. From Saint-Emilion comes Château Cheval-Blanc; from Pomerol Château Pétrus.

Beaujolais: These wines are brighter in color and lighter in flavor than the Burgundies and come from the area south of the Côte d'Or. Beaujolais wines are well known the world over and are sold under district and township names (see section on labels). Township names to remember are: Saint-Amour, Fleurie, Moulin-à-Vent, Juliénas. The neighboring Chalonnais district produces a similar wine.

Rhone Valley Wines: These wines come from the district south of Burgundy, are robust or full-bodied and consequently good with game and rich meat dishes. Best known are Hermitage, Côte Rôti and Châteauneuf-du-Pape.

Italian Red Wines: The great red wine is of course, Chianti: Brolio, Villa Antinori, Ruffino. Soave is a delicious white wine, as is Falerno. But this is the merest guide, as the Italians believe in drinking what you like. Ask your wine merchant for his recommendation.

The White Wines

White wines are easier to become familiar with than red, perhaps because there are fewer of them but mostly because in this country we enjoy chilled drinks. Flavors available range from green, acid wines to fruity, ripe ones, with most good wines somewhere between these extremes.

White Burgundies: Three of the most famous dry white wines in the world are Montrachet, Chablis and Pouilly-Fuissé. (The last-mentioned is hard to pronounce, which may make it easier to remember.) These great wines come from France's Burgundy district and are the classic selections to serve with oysters, fish, ham and pork in any form, cold buffets and picnics. Montrachet is described as a "deep" wine. Chablis has established its fame with just a few hundred acres of vineyards planted to one type of grape.

White Bordeaux: The best known are medium dry, soft wines from the Graves district and are particularly good served with seafood, fish and ham. Famous names to look for are Château Bouscaut, Château Carbonnieux and Château Haut-Brion.

Vouvray: This wine is exceptional; it's produced in the Loire district from a sweet grape that loses its sweetness as the wine develops, resulting in wine ranging from fairly dry to quite sweet.

Alsatian Wine: Alsace is the only important French region that does not have vineyard control laws; in addition, it markets its wine under German grape names: Riesling, Sylvaner, Traminer (a spicy wine), to name a few. These wines range from sharp and dry to pleasantly flowery in taste.

German Wines: All good German wines are white, light in body and excellent with fish, ham and pork. The labels are confusing if you are

unaccustomed to the language. However, the names of the town, district and vineyard are clearly noted on the center of the label. The Rheingau district produces Germany's finest wines: Schloss Johannisberger and Schloss Vollrads Steinberger.

Moselle: This wine, considered the most delicate of all white wines and sometimes almost in the "sparkling" class, comes from vineyards around the Moselle River and carries the names of the producing towns or villages. Names to look for: Zeltingers, Josephshofer, Bernkastelers and Piesporter. Saar wines are similar to Moselle but lighter and are usually consumed as festive or holiday drinks.

Italian White Wines: These wines are widely produced for home consumption. They range from dry to sweet, and there is even a white Chianti, which is winning friends among travelers there. Two of the oddest and best-known names outside Italy are Est! Est! Est! and Lachrima Christi.

Champagne: One of the great wines of the world, champagne is versatile and can be served any time anywhere, with many combinations of foods. The champagne vineyards are north of Burgundy and east of Paris, and in the strict

French sense champagne can be produced only there. The making of the wine is a long delicate process involving 2 fermentations; at the second fermentation, a sugar syrup is added to the bottle to sweeten it. The label describes the degree of sweetness; Brut has less than 1 percent sugar; Extra Sec has less than 2 percent; Sec has 3–5 percent; Demi-Sec and Doux have 8 percent and 10 percent respectively. Champagne is a blend of wines; therefore it is known by makers' brand names.

Dessert or Sweet Wines

Asti Spumanti is a sweet sparkling wine from Italy. Tokay is an unusual dessert wine from Hungary; it is very famous and quite sweet.

Among white Bordeaux, Château d'Yquem is the most famous of the sauternes and Barsac district wines. Others are Château la Tour-Blanche and Château Climens. These wines are sweet or medium-sweet and make their appearance with rich pastries and elegant desserts of *haute cuisine*.

American Wines

From California we have varietal wines, named after the principal grape from which they are produced:

Zinfandel: claret and port
Berbera: hearty reds
Pinot Noir: Burgundy reds
Semillon: sauternes
Muscat: muscadet
Cabernet: red
Palomina: sherry
Johannisberg Riesling: Rhines

From New York's Finger Lakes, we have these varietal wines:

Catawba: sweet white
Niagara: dry white
Delaware: red and white

and vin rosés, sherries, champagnes and dessert wines of all types.

Cooking with Wines. *Discover what a touch of wine can do for soups, ragouts, meat sauces, fish dishes, the dessert course. But remember: Introduce it only once in a menu, and add cautiously.*

A wine of any dependable quality may be used, as long as the flavor is compatible with dish and menu. A good general rule is to use the wine that you intend to serve with the meal.

When a specific wine is called for in recipe, it is wise to use that type. Otherwise there may be a clash of flavors. Generally speaking, white wines are used in preparing white meats, fish and poultry, for the practical reason that red wines tend to discolor the food. There are exceptions, however, notably in the case of coq au vin, in which the goal is both to darken and flavor with red wine.

In Cooked or Uncooked Dishes

Even such simple dishes as creamed chicken or a quickly heated canned soup take well to wine. The nutritional values remain undisturbed —indeed, the alcoholic content of wine or spirits is dissipated by heat, and only the flavor remains. When such ingredients are added to uncooked dishes, as in cut-up raw fruits for dessert, they retain their full strength, of course,

and should not overpower the foods. Add a small measure at a time, and check by tasting before going further.

Dregs from long-opened bottles should be tasted before being incorporated with any foodstuff. If there is noticeable deterioration or souring, avoid using; let the "turning" process continue until you have vinegar, which may add a flavorsome note to FRENCH DRESSING. Always strain off sediment before adding wine to any dish for the table.

The following suggestions for flavoring familiar dishes are grouped according to the type of wine or spirit that you may have handy for such touches.

Sherry: Add to taste to beef broths or soups; any dark, thick soup or sauce; beef and kidney stew; ragouts of beef and mushrooms. For desserts, add to CUSTARD SAUCE, whipped cream and hot sweet sauces. Sherry may be substituted for brandy to moisten and mellow fruitcake.

Dry White Wines: Add sparingly to canned consommé; use to flavor fish dishes during cooking; baste over lamb, mutton or veal during cooking, or add to gravies or sauces (caper sauce especially) for these meats; substitute for vinegar in salad dressings or for cold vegetable hors d'oeuvres.

Dry Red Wines: These wines are highly compatible with beef stews and variety meats like liver and kidney. Use to marinate and baste pork or duck; add to savory fruit sauces (raisin, for example) to accompany meats; substitute for vinegar in FRENCH DRESSING for tossed green salad.

Sweet Wines: Beat small jar of red currant jelly into a little port wine; serve with cold fowl. Before adding to desserts, test wine's sweetness; rich dessert wines often eliminate the need for sugar in desserts. Many fruits, raw or cooked, are enhanced with a little wine. Add sauterne to cut-up fresh fruits; chill before serving. Leftover chilled champagne is a delicious touch on fresh fruit cup or melon balls, seedless grapes and peaches. For a quick but elegant dessert, put drained cooked prunes into a serving dish; cover with drained, quartered canned pears; top with hulled strawberries: pour over just enough port wine to impregnate fruit with sweetness and flavor, and serve cold.

Spirits and liqueurs: Rum, brandy and the various cordials are those chiefly used in fine cookery. The first 2 are much prized for their "flaming" qualities in sweet specialties; all these types can bring gourmet flavoring touches to fine desserts—ice creams, rich cakes, frosting, fillings, hot or cold sauces, cooked or raw fruits, fritters and many more. Use sparingly and, especially with liqueurs, adjust sugar content carefully.

Liver in Red Wine Sauce

            3 tablespoons butter or margarine
        1/4 pound mushrooms, sliced (about 1 1/4 cups)
            1 pound baby beef liver, sliced thin
        1/4 cup dry red wine
            1 teaspoon chopped parsley
            1 teaspoon lemon juice
    Salt and pepper to taste
    Onion salt to taste (optional)

Melt butter or margarine in frying pan over low heat; add mushrooms and cook lightly. Remove mushrooms and keep hot. Turn heat higher, and add liver slices to pan; brown thoroughly on both sides. Reduce heat to simmer. Add mushrooms, wine, parsley and lemon juice. Cover pan, and cook slowly for 10–12 minutes. More wine may be needed during cooking. Season with salt, pepper and onion salt just before serving, preferably over hot rice, with unthickened pan sauce poured over. Serves 4.

Wine Barbecue Sauce

        1/2 cup red wine
        1/2 cup salad oil
            2 tablespoons white-wine vinegar
            1 clove garlic
            1 medium onion, finely chopped
                (approximately 1/2 cup)
            2 teaspoons salt
        1/2 teaspoon pepper
        1/4 teaspoon thyme
        1/4 teaspoon marjoram
    Few grains cayenne

Mix all ingredients in bowl, stirring until salt is dissolved. If wine is very dry, add a little sugar. Use uncooked sauce as marinade over chops, spareribs, cut-up chicken, and the like, and baste meat while it cooks. Makes 1 cup.

Note: This sauce will be at its best if made the day before using, in which case remove and discard garlic clove after preparing.

Chafing-dish Beef (Fondue Bourguignonne)

    4 pounds sirloin or tenderloin steak, 1–1 1/2 inches thick
    1 cup dry red wine
    16 large lettuce leaves
    Butter or margarine
    Salad oil
    6 hot and savory sauces

Trim fat, and cut steak into 1–1 1/2 inch cubes. Pour wine over cubes, and let stand at least 1 hour. Drain. Arrange in lettuce leaves on each individual plate required number of cubes for 1 serving, and set 2 forks at each plate. About 15 minutes before summoning your guests to the table, heat 2 inches butter or margarine and salad oil in bottom of chafing dish or electric skillet; let come to 360°F. or hot enough to brown 1-inch cube of stale bread in 1 minute. Each guest spears meat cube with fork and fries it in hot fat to desired degree—rare, medium or well done. He then dips it in 1 of sauces. First fork is set aside for second turn at chafing dish; second fork at each plate is used for eating.

Note: The selection of hot and savory sauces generally includes the following types:

Horseradish Cream: Combine 1/2 cup drained prepared horseradish and 1/2 cup sour cream, adding dry mustard, salt, pepper and sugar to taste.

Chutney–Curry Sauce: Combine 1/2 cup chutney, 1 tablespoon soy sauce, 1 tablespoon chopped onion and 1 teaspoon curry powder.

Hot Tomato Sauce: Simmer together 5 minutes 1 8-ounce can tomato sauce, 1/2 cup marinade from beef, 2 crushed garlic cloves, 3 broken chili peppers and 1 teaspoon dark steak sauce.

Savory Tartar Sauce: Combine 3/4 cup TARTAR SAUCE, 1/4 cup each finely chopped green pepper and onion and 2 tablespoons lemon juice.

Pickle Sauce: Blend 3/4 cup mustard-pickle relish with 1/4 cup chopped olives, 1 tablespoon chili sauce and 1 teaspoon dry mustard.

Desserts Flambés. One of the most memorable specialties of *haute cuisine* is the flaming dessert, like the world-famous *crêpes suzette*. The purpose of setting fire to a prepared dish is to add flavor, plus glamour and excitement, just before serving to guests who have watched the whole

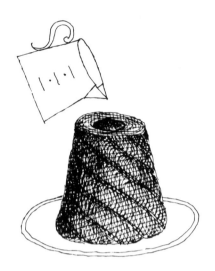

procedure. There are, of course, certain classic recipes for meats, calling for blazing during specific stages of the cooking process. This blazing is usually done in the kitchen, although brochettes and kebabs are sometimes brought to table on flaming swords or skewers. In this case, a ball of absorbent cotton, placed on end of skewer, is saturated with warm spirits and ignited.

The word "flambé" in culinary parlance describes any food enveloped in flame from spirits of high alcoholic content. Cognac, rum, vodka and even whiskey are used, although the first 2 are most frequently employed with desserts.

It is advisable to rehearse privately before attempting flambé display for guests. It is also desirable to have all necessary equipment and food assembled on serving table or cart, well removed from draughts, curtains and other possible hazards. A chafing dish, heat-proof platter or individual dishes may be chosen for the job; avoid delicate china, as it will almost certainly crack from heat of flame.

Allow 2–4 ounces spirits for recipe designed to serve 6 or follow specific directions in recipe. Warm measured spirits in glass placed in hot water. When ready to ignite, pour warm spirits around edges of food, and set aflame. For dramatic effect lower room's lights just before igniting.

Pudding Flambé: Any steamed or baked pudding of reasonably firm texture may be set aflame. Turn pudding onto heat-proof platter. Cut hole about 1 inch deep and 1 inch across in top, fill with warm brandy and pour additional 1/4 cup brandy over surface of pudding. Ignite small reservoir of spirits, and flame will spread rapidly.

Café Brûlot: The simplest version of flaming coffee is made as follows: Add 1 tablespoon warmed brandy to 1 cup very hot black coffee; do not stir. Place 1 sugar cube on teaspoon, and fill spoon with more warmed brandy. Hold spoon over filled cup, set match to brandy and sugar, lower into coffee and stir until flame burns out.

Coffee Soufflé

       18 ladyfingers or strips of sponge cake
        2 envelopes powdered gelatin
      1/2 cup cold water
        8 squares semisweet chocolate
   2 1/4 cups light cream
        6 eggs, separated
      1/4 cup sugar
        2 teaspoons vanilla extract
      1/2 teaspoon salt
      1/4 cup coffee liqueur
        1 teaspoon instant coffee
   2 1/2 cups heavy cream, stiffly beaten
      1/4 cup sugar
        1 recipe TOASTED ALMOND SAUCE
   Whipped-cream rosettes
   Slivered almonds

Butter inside of 7- or 8-inch soufflé dish. Line loosely with ladyfingers, standing upright. Tie collar of greased parchment or double thickness waxed paper around outside of soufflé dish, allowing it to stand 3 inches above rim of dish. Soften gelatin in cold water. Melt chocolate in top of double boiler, and add light cream. Stir occasionally until hot and smoothly blended. Combine egg yolks and 1/4 cup sugar, and stir into chocolate mixture. Turn heat low, and stir until chocolate custard is thick and smooth. Remove from heat, and add vanilla and salt. Combine liqueur with instant coffee, and add to chocolate custard, add softened gelatin. Stir until gelatin dissolves. Chill in refrigerator until mixture begins to thicken to consistency of thick white sauce. Fold in whipped cream. Beat egg whites until stiff but glossy, and beat in 1/4 cup sugar. Fold chocolate cream into egg whites, and pour into soufflé dish. Chill 2–3 hours. Garnish with whipped cream rosettes and slivered almonds. Remove collar from soufflé dish, and serve with toasted almond sauce. Serves 10–12.

Note: This dessert is just as good if made the day before serving.

Toasted Almond Sauce

      1/2 cup slivered blanched almonds
      1/2 cup butter or margarine
      3/4 cup dark brown sugar
        1 cup light cream
   Pinch salt
        2 egg yolks, slightly beaten
      1/4 cup brandy

Sauté almonds in butter or margarine in top of double boiler, taking care not to burn butter. Stir in sugar, and place pan over hot water. Add cream and salt; heat, stirring until sugar melts. Combine egg yolks with 2 tablespoons brandy, and add to pan and stir till thickened. Turn heat very low, and keep sauce hot until time to serve. At serving time, pour sauce into serving dish, and flame by warming 2 tablespoons brandy, setting it alight and pouring it over surface. Or sauce may be served icy cold, diluted with 1–2 tablespoons cream.

Cherries Jubilee

        3 cups canned Bing cherries and juice
        1 teaspoon arrowroot or cornstarch
        1 tablespoon cold water
      1/3 cup brandy or kirsch
        1 quart vanilla ice cream

Drain cherry juice into blazer pan of chafing dish (or use upper part of double boiler). Bring to boil over direct heat, and simmer until volume is reduced to about 2/3. Dissolve arrowroot in cold water, and quickly stir into hot juice. Cook a few minutes longer. Add cherries, and set pan over hot water to let cherries warm. Pour brandy into center; warm without stirring. Have ice cream ready in individual heat-proof serving dishes. Set sauce ablaze, and spoon immediately over ice cream. Serves 6–8.

Kirsch is generally used; brandy is equally applicable.

Note: This dessert is just as good if made the day before serving.

Flaming Apricot Omelets

        6 eggs
        2 tablespoons cream
        2 teaspoons sugar
      1/2 teaspoon salt
        3 tablespoons butter or margarine

1/2 cup apricot jam
1/2 cup cream, stiffly beaten
2–3 tablespoons orange juice
1 tablespoon grated orange rind
3 tablespoons sugar
2 tablespoons rum
2 tablespoons kirsch

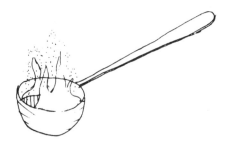

Beat eggs with 2 tablespoons cream, 2 teaspoons sugar and salt until fully blended. Heat individual omelet pan or small frying pan, and melt 1/2 teaspoon butter or margarine until it foams. Spoon in 3 tablespoons egg mixture. Brown on one side, turn and cook lightly on other. Remove to baking sheet to cool. Repeat until mixture is used up. When ready to serve, combine jam and whipped cream, and spread on omelets. Roll up, and arrange in chafing dish or other heat-proof server. Sprinkle with orange juice and rind, and dust generously with 3 tablespoons sugar. Warm rum and kirsch, pour over omelets, and set aflame. Serves 6.

Note: If apricot jam is lumpy with fruit pieces, sieve; then measure required amount. For this delicate dessert, the omelets are usually made in the kitchen, allowed to cool, and set alight at table.

Bananas in Rum

3 tablespoons butter or margarine
4 firm bananas peeled and halved crosswise, then lengthwise
2 tablespoons brown sugar
1 teaspoon lemon juice
1/4 cup rum, warmed

Melt butter or margarine in blazer pan of chafing dish over direct heat; or use heavy skillet on stove. Put in bananas. Turn heat to medium high. As bananas soften, sprinkle slices with a little brown sugar and a drop or two of lemon juice. Turn once, sprinkle other side with sugar and juice and cook until soft but not mushy. When ready to serve, turn down heat, pour in warmed rum and set alight. Serves 4.

To Flame Crêpes Suzette

5 lumps sugar
1 peeled orange with peel
1 peeled lemon with peel
1 1/2 cups orange juice
3 tablespoons unsalted butter
1 recipe CREPES SUZETTE
3–4 tablespoons brandy, warmed

Rub each sugar lump over outside of orange and lemon peels to extract flavor and color. Put sugar into blazer pan of chafing dish over direct heat, and set low. Crush lumps, add orange juice and simmer gently 1 minute. Add butter, and

blend. Fold each pancake twice to make triangular shape and put in to heat; turn frequently to absorb sauce. When ready to serve, pour in warmed brandy. Set alight. When high flames die down, serve crêpes, spooning sauce over. Serves 4 generously. Rum, Grand Marnier or orange curaçao may be used in place of brandy.

Note: Bring ingredients, chafing dish, and warm dessert plates to table, and prepare sauce and flame before your guests.

A World of Cheeses. *Crumbly or smooth, dark-veined or white as snow, stone-hard like Parmesan or soft and velvety like Brie, rare and costly or plain everyday fare.*

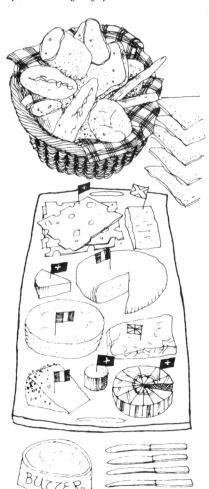

Basically cheese is made from the milk of cows, sheep, goats, buffalo, yaks, even reindeer and camels. The milk is coagulated or curdled, either naturally by souring or by the addition of rennet or lactic acid; this process results in separation of curds from whey. The curds, or solids, are then ripened by the action of molds or bacteria to develop characteristic flavors of cheeses. This description, of course, oversimplifies the whole science of cheesemaking.

The world offers some 500 varieties of cheese from 18 basic cheese "families," and volumes could be written on the subject.

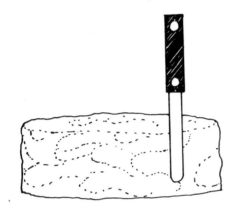

The Aristocrats

Roquefort, Gorgonzola, Stilton and blue (bleu) are world-famous and can be considered the champagnes of cheeses. They are characterized by their sharp, piquant flavor and the blue-green veins marbling their creamy, crumbly interiors. They are primarily dessert cheeses and have their maximum appeal served with crisp slices of fresh pears or apples. They also enhance salads and salad dressings and have a place of honor on cheese trays.

Roquefort is probably France's most famous cheese. By French government ruling, only the product of the Roquefort town area in the Department of Aveyron can use the name. Sheep's milk is used exclusively, and an added feature is the incorporation of bread-crumb powder that has been allowed to develop a greenish mold. Originally the cheese was made by shepherds and aged in local caves; it is now produced in cheese factories under carefully controlled conditions but still goes to the same caves for ripening.

Gorgonzola is produced in the Lombardy region of Italy from cow's milk. When exported it usually has a thin clay-like coating on the surface and is sometimes packed in wicker containers.

Stilton is England's contribution to the blue-blooded cheeses. Made from cow's milk, with cream added for extra richness, it is frequently exported in earthenware jars.

Blue (bleu) cheese, made from cow's milk by a process similar to that for Roquefort, probably originated in France but has been produced in all parts of Europe for hundreds of years.

Danish blue is very well known in America.

Also rated high among the aristocratic cheeses is *Camembert* from France. It has a comparatively strong flavor and aroma. A soft cow's milk cheese, ripened with a yellow, almost fluid, interior, it is one of the more complicated types to produce. Camembert is usually shipped before ripening has been completed, but if it is held too long in warehouse or store, it may develop a thickened crust around a runny center and a strong scent of ammonia, which signify definite over-ripeness; the cheese should be discarded. Good Camembert requires several hours at room temperature before serving, in order to attain the desired mellowness and softness of texture. By all means refrigerate after purchase, but keep in least cold part of box. Serve Camembert as the leading member of a dessert grouping of crackers and fruit, with coffee or wine.

Brie has a history several centuries longer than that of Camembert; both are of the same cheese family. There are many French regional names for Brie, but the cheese remains the same: smooth in texture, finer than Camembert, more delicately flavored and always with a reddish crust.

Limburger, originally developed in Belgium, has an almost overpowering aroma and generally dominant personality. This cheese goes with strong fare; dark bread, spicy meat and beer. The texture is soft, and, although the flavor is definite, it is less pungent than the smell would suggest.

Liederkranz is a United States creation to meet the need for a mild version of Limburger.

Famous Types the World Over

Among the pedigreed cheeses beloved of the gourmet are the smooth, semisoft varieties known generally as Trappist, referring to the order of monks who produce fine cheese in various parts of the world. *Oka* from Quebec belongs to this group and enjoys great popularity. *Port salut* hails from the Trappist abbey in France and is undoubtedly the most famous, with its richly mild, soft-textured, pale yellow body. Served as a dessert cheese, it has an affinity with fine port.

Muenster (Münster) is a mild, semisoft cheese generally used for sandwiches. In its native Germany it is sharp, highly flavored cheese, as the ripening or curing period is much longer.

Brick, similar to Muenster, but a native American cheese, is so named because of its shape and the fact that bricks were originally used to hold down the presses. It is creamy in color, with tiny irregular holes and flavor ranging from mild to nippy yet with a sweet pungent taste. It is used mostly for sandwiches and buffet service.

Cheddar is the most versatile of all cheeses, possessing flavors and textures to suit all tastes; it is splendid both in cooked dishes and plain. Cheddar is also known as "store" cheese.

From the same family come *Monterey Jack* cheese of California and *sage green*, a green mottled cheese, native to Vermont, which is produced by the addition of green sage leaves to the curd.

Dutch and Swiss Specialties

Two exclusively Dutch cheeses, *Edam* and *Gouda*, are distinguished by their spherical and cannonball shapes and sometimes by bright red wax coating. Edam is a firm, mild-flavored cheese, whereas Gouda is softer in texture with more tang; sometimes they are smoked or spiced. Baby Goudas weighing less than 1 pound each are popular and make an attractive and colorful addition to the cheese tray.

Leyden, another Netherlander, is sometimes known as "Delft" or "Hobbe." It is a firm cheese with dark brown surface, spiced with caraway, cumin and cloves.

Emmanthaler (Swiss) cheese from Switzerland has a delicate, nutty, sweet flavor, firm texture, and distinctive eyes or holes. This cheese is very versatile—garnish for salads, thickly sliced for hot or cold sandwiches, in cooked dishes and on dessert trays.

A slightly sharper version is *Gruyère* cheese, with smaller "eyes" and firmer texture. At the beginning of the twentieth century, Switzerland developed a method of processing Gruyère. Triangular-shaped pieces weighing about 1 ounce each are wrapped in foil and packed in round boxes of a dozen wedges. It is an excellent dessert cheese with a mild, sweetish flavor.

Sapsago is historically one of the oldest cheeses, tracing its origin back to the thirteenth century in the Canton of Glarus, Switzerland. It is very hard, dry, green cheese, with pleasant aroma and nippy flavor. The green color comes from dried aromatic clover grown especially for this use. Sapsago is available in grated form chiefly and is used in cooked dishes.

Italian Cheeses

Italy provides us with two wonderful cooking cheeses—Parmesan and Romano. Many a main dish would be dull without either or both of these lively cheeses.

Parmesan is an extremely hard or "grana" cheese, which cannot be cut but is broken and then grated. It is in this form that it is so widely used in cooked dishes, hot breads, appetizers, soups and sauces. Parmesan, with its sharp distinctive flavor and good keeping qualities, is the gourmet cook's ally.

Romano is very similar to Parmesan but a little softer in texture. In Italy it can be purchased freshly made and used much as we use Cheddar; on this side of the Atlantic we can also buy it grated. The flavor ranges from mild to sharp, which may be attributable to the different milk used—from cows, sheep or goats—and are designated respectively as Vacchino, Romano, Pecorino Romano and Caprino Romano.

Provolone, another Italian cheese used principally in cooking, has recently become very popular. It is the cheese of so many shapes that you see hanging by cords or ropes in Italian grocery stores or specialty food shops. Flavors vary from mild to nippy, and the cheese is usually smoked and well salted. It is hard cheese, sometimes with rather stringy texture.

Caciocavallo (literally "horse-cheese") is a member of the same family. It is unsmoked, white and beet-shaped and is generally grated. Two others are *Scarmorze* and *Mozzarella*, both pizza cheeses used fresh or just slightly ripened.

Bel Paese is the brand name of a Brie-type cheese made in Italy and esteemed by discriminating palates in every country. A soft, sweet, light-textured cheese with delicate flavor, it is a superb dessert choice.

Scandinavian cheeses

Noekkelost, a popular Norwegian cheese similar to Leyden, differing only in the proportions of spices used.

Mysöst, one of the most famous and ancient cheeses, is made from whey obtained in production of other cheese. It is light brown in color, with buttery texture and mild sweet flavor. It is a good cheese for sandwiches and buffet service.

Gammelost, from Norway, is made from skimmed sour milk. A semihard cheese, well aged with a sharp flavor. It is ideal for the informal buffet.

Gjetost (or primost), also from Norway, is a dark chocolate-brown cheese with a sweet flavor.

Cream and Cottage Cheeses

Cottage Cheese is the simplest cheese of all and has been a familiar item in the United States since early pioneer days. This uncured cheese from cow's milk is produced in many countries and under various names, such as pot cheese, Dutch cheese and smearcase. In America, cottage cheese is made commercially in large quantities from pasteurized skim milk, sometimes with cream added. It is a very nutritious cheese and versatile, with many uses in cooked dishes, salads, sandwiches and appetizers.

Cream Cheese is a soft uncured cheese made from pasteurized milk with cream added: it's coagulated with lactic acid rather than with rennet. It has very smooth texture and rich mild flavor, both in plain form and when packaged with such other flavors as pineapple and pimento.

Neufchâtel is a soft rennet cheese made from cow's milk in much the same manner as cream cheese but with higher moisture and lower fat content. Other names for this type of cheese are petit carré, petit suisse, Malakoff and bondon. It's used mostly as a dessert and sandwich cheese and is available plain or with added flavor ingredients.

Ricotta Cheese, like Scandinavian Mysöst, is made from whey obtained in production of other cheeses. This Italian cheese usually has whole or skim milk added and is soft in texture, with a mild flavor. It is frequently used in lasagna and ravioli dishes and in its native land is served also in sweet mixtures.

Care of Cheese

To care for a wheel of Cheddar or a block of Swiss cheese, cut off a wedge or slice sufficient to fill your needs for 1 week, and rewrap cheese. If cheese has come wrapped in cheesecloth bandage, replace loose part carefully over cut surface, and seal with melted paraffin wax. If cheese is rindless (today many Cheddars and Swiss cheeses are ripened within their own transparent paper and do not develop rinds), seal cut surface with melted paraffin wax, and replace original wrappings as much as possible. In both cases, overwrap cheese with heavy foil. Refrigerate or store in cool, dry place.

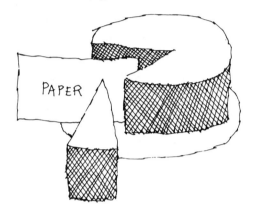

Cheese Service at Table

Contemporary cheese trays come in all shapes and sizes with beautiful wood finishes. They are ideal for buffet service, as well as for appetizer and dessert cheese assortments. Arrangement of

cheese, crackers and fruit can be highly individual and very colorful. For small dinner parties or family groups, it's fun to use the old-

fashioned slope-topped cheese dish, either heirloom or modern; 1 or 2 generous wedges can be accommodated under the cover. An antique cheese bell is difficult to find, but if you can acquire one, it will be a lifetime conversation piece. (Wedgwood made some beautiful cheese bells in the traditional blue or green jasper ware.)

For cheese-tray service a variety of shapes and portions makes for both eye appeal and convenience. Leave Gouda or Edam cheese whole, with thin slice of top removed and a cheese scoop (like a melon-ball cutter) nearby for guests to help themselves. Crumbly, well-ripened or wined Cheddar is best left in the piece; younger, springier types may be neatly sliced and grouped. If Swiss cheese is sliced, let portions be at least 1/4 inch thick. Individually wrapped wedges of Gruyère, Roquefort and the like are served in their packaging, but larger wedges can be unwrapped. Semisoft cheeses like Liederkranz, Bel Paese and Limburger seem to develop their best textures when cut in individual portions just after removing from refrigerator and then allowed to mellow at room temperature. For some cheeses a wire cutter with a sturdy handle is more useful than a knife.

When serving cheese, crackers and fruit for dessert, provide individual plates and fruit knives; pass serving dish with butter curls or pats. Occasionally, instead of whole fresh fruits, offer unpeeled apple or pear wedges dipped in lemon juice to prevent discoloration.

Here are some good dessert combinations:

Roquefort and blue, accompanied by chilled pineapple slices, fresh or canned, garnished with whole strawberries; pass the sugar caster.
Swiss cheese with tangerine or fresh mandarin orange sections and muscat raisins on stems.
Gorgonzola and Camembert, with lemon-dipped apple and pear wedges.
Liederkranz and Bel Paese, with Tokay grapes and fresh apricots.

Nice additions for any of the above: nuts in shells or salted; French bread and melba toast, and sweet or salted butter.

FRENCH GOURMET COOKING

The French make use of everything edible and extract the maximum flavor and palatability. The choicest fresh fruits and vegetables, eggs, butter and cream, wines and seasonings are treasured. The farm style (paysan), as with poached eggs in broth; "Regional," representing local variations in such famous dishes as CASSOULET; careful family cookery (*de la famille*), and finally, "haute cuisine," the chef's professional artistry.

The French have their own mealtime habits. Breakfast is simple; rich tender CROISSANTS or BRIOCHES, sweet butter, perhaps a confiture like cherry jam and CAFE AU LAIT or hot chocolate. Déjeuner, the leisurely noon meal, may consist of 4–5 courses: hors d'oeuvres, main course, vegetable or salad, cheese and raw or cooked fruit. Dinner follows the same ample pattern but with seafood or fruit appetizer in place of hors d'oeuvres, clear soup added and, instead of fruit, a rich dessert. Very few of the foodstuffs used in French cookery are not available here—the absentees include fresh truffles, certain mushrooms and some types of fish. Cooking techniques here differ only when we omit or rush certain steps in preparing a dish. Time itself may be considered the basic ingredient that the French cook willingly adds to all her projects. In order that texture and flavor may be at their best, she chops, sifts, beats, simmers, skims. Some of these essential processes can be accomplished with greater ease and speed in the American kitchen, with its electric grinders, blenders and mixers. But French recipes are not designed for saving labor.

Hors-d'oeuvres Variés

In France, hors d'oeuvres are strictly knife-and-fork fare, eaten at table, and bear no resemblance to the canapés and finger foods that are sometimes called "hors d'oeuvres" in America. A French hostess will serve 2 or more varieties, depending upon the occasion, choosing from cooked and raw vegetables, smoked and cooked fish and delicacies sold in *charcuteries* or pork shops.

Hors d'oeuvres may be hot or cold, but often they are leftovers, chilled and cooked. They **are** served in small amounts or as the main course at a summer luncheon, in which case as many as 6 or 7 hors d'oeuvre specialties may be set out, each in its separate dish, on a buffet table. Accompany them with a pleasant wine, and follow them with a light dessert, perhaps fruit.

Here are some items that frequently appear in French hors d'oeuvres:

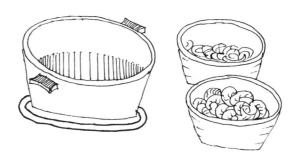

Anchovy fillets	Asparagus vinaigrette
Smoked salmon	Jellied eggs
Smoked oysters	Salade de boeuf
Stuffed eggs	Smoked turkey
Pâtés	Green and black olives
Shrimp in HERBED MAYONNAISE	Sliced tomatoes
	Pickled beets
MUSHROOMS A LA GRECQUE	Sliced sausage, all kinds

In selecting hors d'oeuvres, always balance foods and flavors against rest of the meal. If hot dish is to follow, omit fish; if pork is the main course, avoid sausage and rich pâtés at the start. If menu is lengthy and grand, open meal with just 1 appropriate appetizer, possibly caviar on toast rounds with lemon garnish.

Vegetables à la Grecque

Briefly, vegetables are cooked in consommé or bouillon until just tender; broth is boiled down and poured over solids, which are then put to chill and glaze. Suitable vegetables are tiny white onions, celery, zucchini, eggplant, cauliflower, frozen artichokes, baby carrots and so on. Cut larger vegetables into generous bite-size pieces; parboil less tender items like cauliflower 3–5 minutes before cooking à la grecque.

Mushrooms à la Grecque

     2 1/2 cups water or stock
       1/4 cup salad oil or olive oil
       1/4 cup lemon juice
         2 tablespoons chopped green onion
       1/2 teaspoon salt
     Bouquet garni (tied in cheesecloth)
         6 sprigs parsley
         6 peppercorns
         2 sprigs celery leaves
         1 pound mushrooms

Place all ingredients except mushrooms in 2-quart saucepan, cover and simmer 10 minutes. Prepare mushrooms; quarter large ones, and leave small ones whole. Add to liquid and simmer,

covered, until just tender, about 10 minutes. Remove mushrooms with slotted spoon. Reduce liquid by boiling rapidly until 1/2 the quantity remains. Strain over mushrooms; then cool, cover and refrigerate. Mushrooms will keep 3–4 days. Sprinkle with chopped fresh herbs before serving.

Vegetables Vinaigrette

Marinate raw or cooked vegetables in basic FRENCH DRESSING or VINAIGRETTE SAUCE 1 hour before serving. To cook vegetables, simmer until just tender in well-seasoned water or broth. Cool before marinating; drain off excess liquid before serving. Cooked vegetables suitable for serving with vinaigrette sauce are asparagus, cauliflower, celery, sliced or tiny beets, leeks, and green beans. Raw vegetables include tomatoes, cucumbers and thinly sliced mushrooms.

Vinaigrette Sauce

1 cup salad or olive oil
1/4 cup wine vinegar or lemon juice
1 teaspoon finely chopped green onions or 2 tablespoons
        chopped chives, tarragon or basil
Salt and pepper to taste

Combine all ingredients in jar or bottle, cover tightly and shake well. Use as needed for hors d'oeuvres.

Salade de Boeuf Vinaigrette (Beef Salad Vinaigrette)

Cold boiled or roast beef, thinly sliced
Thinly sliced mild onion rings
VINAIGRETTE SAUCE
Lettuce, tomatoes

Marinate beef and onion rings in separate bowls in sauce about 1 hour before serving. Drain off sauce, and arrange beef slices alternately with onion rings on lettuce-covered platter. Garnish with tomato wedges.

Quiche Lorraine

6 slices bacon
2 cups cream or rich milk
PLAIN PASTRY or FLAKY PASTRY for single-crust pie
6 ounces Swiss cheese, sliced thin
4 eggs
1/2 teaspoon salt
Dash freshly ground black pepper
Dash cayenne

Broil bacon, but do not crisp it. Heat cream slowly. Line a 9″ pie plate with pastry, and make firm double rim. Arrange bacon on pastry;

into 450°F. oven about 15 minutes; reduce heat as quickly as possible to 300°F., and continue baking until custard is firm, about 1/2 hour, or until silver knife inserted in center comes out clean.

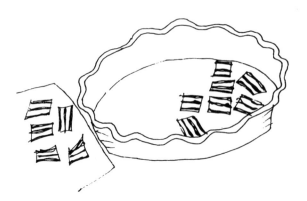

cover with cheese slices. Make custard mixture by beating eggs with fork and adding hot cream and seasonings. Pour into pastry-lined pan. Put

Note: Quiche Lorraine is a savory cheese custard pie served warm, in small segments for the hors d'oeuvre course or in larger wedges as the luncheon entree.

It's quite uncomplicated to make, as this recipe shows. Some cooks prefer to cut bacon into small pieces. The Swiss cheese may be grated and added to the custard filling. For extra flavor, scatter a little chopped raw onion over pastry bottom before filling.

Potato Croquettes in Bacon

3–4 cups seasoned mashed potatoes
1/4 cup finely chopped pimento
1 tablespoon grated Parmesan cheese
Dash cayenne
1 egg, beaten
1 cup bread crumbs or crushed cornflakes
10 bacon slices, halved lengthwise
Toothpicks

Combine first 5 ingredients, and form into small log-shaped croquettes, about 20 in all. Roll in crumbs; then rap in bacon slices. Secure with toothpicks. Place in shallow pan on rack; refrigerate until needed. Bake at 400°F. about 20–30 minutes. Serve with steak. Serves 6.

VARIATION:

Omit pimento. Roll croquettes in mixture of slivered almonds and Parmesan cheese, rather than bread crumbs.

Potatoes Anna

    6 cups peeled potatoes, sliced as thin as possible
    1/2 teaspoon salt
    Pepper to taste
    1/2 cup soft butter or margarine

Soak potatoes in ice-cold water, drain and dry well on towel. Season with salt and pepper. Butter round baking dish (6-cup size), and line bottom and sides with potato slices. Arrange layer of potatoes, and spread liberally with butter or margarine; repeat until all potatoes are used up, saving some butter or margarine for top. Bake at 425°F. 45–50 minutes or until potatoes are tender when tested with toothpick. To serve, invert baking dish on hot platter so that potatoes slip out in molded form, brown and crusty. Garnish with parsley. Serves 6.

Vegetables French Style

The French prepare certain vegetables with a blanching technique similar to that used in our home-freezing procedures; they cook them quickly in plenty of boiling water until just tender, drain and add butter or sauce. If vegetable is to be served hours later it is immediately cooled under running water, dried and refrigerated until needed. The following recipe is excellent when advance preparation is desirable.

Haricots Verts à la Mornay (Green Beans with Mornay Sauce)

    2 pounds fresh young green beans
    4–5 quarts boiling water, plus 1 tablespoon salt
    3 tablespoons butter or margarine
    3 tablespoons flour
    1 cup warm milk
    1 cup warm chicken stock
    1/3 cup grated Parmesan cheese
    3 tablespoons Swiss cheese, cut in small pieces
    1 tablespoon butter or margarine

Wash, string and cut beans diagonally into slices about 1 1/2 inches long. Drop into rapidly boiling salted water, and return water quickly to boil. Cook uncovered at slow boil 10–15 minutes or until just tender (depends on maturity of vegetable). Drain in colander, and cool immediately under running water to stop further cooking. Spread beans on towel to dry, place in bowl and refrigerate until needed. When ready to serve, melt butter or margarine, blend in flour over low heat, remove from heat and briskly stir in milk and stock. Cook over medium heat, stirring constantly, until mixture comes to boil. Remove, and blend in 1/2 the Parmesan cheese plus Swiss cheese until melted. Season to taste. Cover bottom of serving casserole with 1/3 the sauce, top with green beans and pour remaining sauce over all. Sprinkle with remaining Parmesan cheese, and dot with butter or margarine. Bake at 350°F. 30 minutes or until thoroughly heated and the top lightly browned. Serves 6–8.

Moules Marinière (Steamed Mussels)

    48 fresh mussels in shells
    1 1/2 cups dry white wine
    4 finely chopped shallots or 2 tablespoons finely
        chopped onion
    1/4 teaspoon pepper
    1/4 teaspoon powdered thyme
    3 tablespoons chopped parsley
    3 tablespoons butter or margarine
    1 tablespoon flour

Brush and scrape mussel shells thoroughly, and wash in several waters. Place in deep kettle; add wine, shallots, pepper and thyme. Cover, bring to boil and simmer 6–8 minutes until shells open. Remove mussels in shells to large deep casserole or serving platter, and cover with hot, damp towel to keep warm. Carefully strain broth through cheesecloth into another saucepan to remove sand. Bring to boil, and reduce to 1/2 the quantity. Add parsley. Blend butter or margarine and flour, and add to broth, stirring constantly until thickened. Taste for seasoning, and pour sauce over mussels. Serve immediately in soup dishes, and use cocktail forks to eat mussels directly from shells.

Coquilles St. Jacques (Scallops St. Jacques)

    1 cup dry white wine
    2 tablespoons chopped green onion or shallots
        (approximately 2 1/2 cups)
    1/2 teaspoon salt
    1/2 bay leaf
    1 pound scallops, washed
    1/2 pound sliced fresh mushrooms
    Water
    3 tablespoons butter or margarine
    3 tablespoons flour
    1 cup milk
    2 egg yolks
    1/4 cup cream
    1/2 cup grated Swiss or Parmesan cheese
    Salt and pepper to taste

Simmer together wine, onion, salt and bay leaf 5 minutes. Add scallops and mushrooms, and sufficient water just to cover ingredients. Cover and simmer 5 minutes. Remove scallops and mushrooms, return liquid to boiling and rapidly reduce to 1 cup. Melt butter or margarine in saucepan, blend in flour, remove from heat and stir in hot cooking liquid and milk. Bring to boil, stirring rapidly; boil 1 minute. Blend egg yolks and cream in mixing bowl; add hot sauce gradually, stirring constantly. Return sauce to pan, and bring mixture to boil. Add 1/4 cup grated cheese, and season to taste; thin, if necessary, with cream. Slice or quarter cooked scallops, and add to 2/3 the sauce along with mushrooms. Divide mixture among 6 buttered scallop shells or ramekins, cover with remaining sauce and sprinkle with 1/4 cup cheese. Refrigerate if serving later. To heat, place shells in 350°F. oven, and bake 15 minutes. Place directly under broiler to brown lightly. Serves 6.

Note: Almost every visitor to Paris has sampled this elegant scallop-and-mushroom concoction. Ideally you should use scallop shells, which are generally available; otherwise, earthenware or oven-glass ramekins of up to 1/2-cup capacity will do nicely. This dish can be made ahead and reheated just before serving. Serve as a main course for luncheon or as a starter at an important dinner. Accompany with chilled dry white wine.

Bouillabaisse

    8 pounds firm fish fillets (cod, haddock, etc.)
    1 pound tomatoes, peeled and sliced
    2 onions, sliced
    1 green pepper, chopped
    1 tablespoon salt
    1 bouquet garni
    1 teaspoon saffron
1/2 cup olive oil
1/2 cup dry white wine
Water or fish stock
    1 dozen raw oysters and liquid
    1 dozen clams and liquid
    1 cup cooked lobster meat or 1 dozen cooked shrimp

Start bouillabaisse about 1/2 hour before serving; cooking time will depend on size and thickness of fish pieces. Use large kettle. In it put fish fillets, tomatoes, onions, green pepper and seasonings. Pour in olive oil, wine and sufficient water to cover. Bring rapidly to boil, uncovered, and boil over high heat about 10 minutes. Reduce heat, add remaining ingredients and simmer another 10 minutes. Serve in large soup plates with generous portions of solids surrounded by bouillon, or lift fish onto separate dish, garnish with lemon and serve after soup itself is served from big tureen. Croutons or toasted FRENCH BREAD may be floated on top of soup. Serves 8–10.

Note: In Marseilles, its city of origin, this famous dish, which is both soup and fish course (and was originally created to use up miscellaneous leftovers from the daily catch), is a standby in modest homes and expensive restaurants alike. And even in the United States it's often a subject of argument concerning choice of ingredients and seasonings. Although the Mediterranean fish are not available to the cook, she will discover that bouillabaisse is one of the most flexible French dishes for adaption, as long as a few general principles are observed.

The basis is firm-fleshed fish; in Marseilles they use 5 or 6 kinds in a single kettle or bouillabaisse, but 1 or 2 can do nicely. Shellfish in variety are added, and it is good to follow suit if you want to achieve the true gourmet touch. Olive oil and saffron are "musts" in any version; on the other hand, tomatoes are a matter of personal taste. In Marseilles it is customary to allow 1 pound fish fillets per serving. You may reduce the quantity if desired.

If your fish has been filleted to your order at fish counter bring home trimmings too. Cover them with water, boil 1 hour, strain and use this stock with, or in place of, water.

Poulet Marengo (Chicken Marengo)

    2 2 1/2–3 pound broiling chickens
    3 tablespoons butter or margarine
    3 tablespoons salad oil or olive oil
    2 tablespoons flour
    2 cups peeled chopped fresh tomatoes
    1 cup chicken broth or bouillon
1/2 cup dry white wine
    2 tablespoons tomato paste, mixed with 1/4 cup water
    1 clove garlic, crushed
1/2 teaspoon thyme
1/2 teaspoon salt
Pepper to taste
    14 peeled small silverskin white onions
1/2 pound fresh mushrooms, sliced
        (approximately 2 1/2 cups)
    3 tablespoons butter or margarine, melted
    2 tablespoons chopped parsley

Wash and dry chickens and cut into serving pieces. Heat 3 tablespoons butter or margarine and oil in large heavy frying pan. Fry a few pieces of chicken at a time until golden brown all over. Keep cooked pieces warm until all are browned. Add flour to pan juice (if latter is too brown, clean pan, and start fresh with 2 tablespoons butter or margarine). Blend, and cook 2 minutes. Add tomatoes, broth, wine, tomato paste and garlic. Blend thoroughly, and bring to boil, stirring constantly. Let simmer 5 minutes;

add thyme, salt and pepper. Return chicken pieces to sauce, add onions and spoon sauce over all ingredients. Cover tightly and cook over low heat 35–40 minutes or until chicken is tender (or place in 350°F. oven about 50 minutes). In the meantime, cook mushrooms in melted butter or margarine over low heat about 10 minutes. Add mushroom mixture to chicken sauce, and bring to boil. If too thin, let simmer gently to evaporate; if too thick, add a little chicken broth or wine. Taste for final seasoning. Pour sauce over chicken, and sprinkle with parsley. Serves 6–8.

Note: This classic dish is named after one of Napoleon's famous victories. There are many versions of this recipe—some with olives, some without; some with red wine, some with white wine; some banning butter entirely. Usually they're all very good. The traditional finishing touch is to ring the platter alternately with small fried eggs on fried bread squares (remove crusts from bread before frying in butter) and cooked large shrimp or lobster tails. Use pullet eggs if available.

Coq au Vin (Chicken in Wine)

      1 3-pound roasting chicken, cut up, or ready-cut
          chicken pieces
      2 tablespoons brandy
    1/2 cup flour
Salt and pepper to taste
    1/4 cup butter or margarine
     10 mushroom caps
  1 1/2 cups red wine
     10 silverskin onions, peeled
Bouquet garni (bay leaf, thyme, parsley, bouquet of
          celery)
    4–5 slices bacon
      1 tablespoon chopped parsley

Wipe chicken pieces with damp cloth, and pat dry. Heat brandy, pour over chicken pieces and flame. Combine flour with salt and pepper. When flame dies down, roll chicken pieces in flour. Melt

butter or margarine in skillet, add chicken and cook over medium heat, turning frequently, until all surfaces are thoroughly browned. Add mushrooms, and brown them 1–2 minutes. Add wine, onions and bouquet garni. Reduce heat, and simmer gently, covered. Cook until chicken is perfectly tender, about 40 minutes. Fry bacon until crisp; drain and keep hot. When chicken is ready, turn out on hot platter, and garnish with bacon and chopped parsley. Serves 4.

Note: This fine chicken dish is dark and fragrant with red wine, hearty with some of the ancient paysan influence but elegant enough to be included in *haute cuisine* the world around. There are many versions: Some specify salt pork, others bacon; occasionally onions and mushrooms are cooked with the pork. A flame-resistant casserole may be used for browning and cooking chicken. A little flour may be incorporated at end for extra thickening, but in France coq-au-vin sauce is preferred on the thin side.

Cassoulet

  2 1/2 pounds pork loin
    1/2 teaspoon salt
    1/4 teaspoon sage
Pepper to taste
      5 cups dry white beans
      4 quarts boiling water
    1/2 pound lean salt pork
      2 quarts cold water
      1 cup sliced onion
      1 large bouquet garni in cheesecloth (6 sprigs
          parsley, 3 short stalks celery, 3 whole cloves,
          1/2 teaspoon thyme, 2 bay leaves)
    1/2 pound fresh pork rind, tied in a bundle
1–1 1/4 pounds whole Polish or garlic sausages, in casings
      2 pounds boned shoulder of lamb
    2–3 tablespoons hot pork drippings
      2 cups chopped onions
      4 cups beef stock or bouillon
  1 1/2 cups dry white wine
      1 (8-ounce) can tomato sauce
      2 bay leaves
    1/2 teaspoon thyme
      2 cups coarse bread crumbs
    1/2 cup chopped parsley
    1/4 cup pork drippings, butter or margarine

Trim excess fat off pork loin and rub salt, sage and pepper over surface. Place in 325°F. oven and roast until meat thermometer registers 185°F., slightly under 2 hours. Set aside to cool. Reserve juices. Add beans to boiling water, and cook 2 minutes after water returns to boil. Remove from heat, and let stand 1 hour. Freshen salt pork by adding to cold water and bringing to boil. Drain. Add salt pork, sliced onions, bouquet garni, and pork rind to soaked beans. Bring to simmer, skim and simmer uncovered 1 1/2 hours. Add boiling water from time to time to keep beans immersed. Add sausages for last 1/2 hour of cooking. Remove sausages, pork rind and salt pork, and set aside. Discard bouquet garni. Cut lamb in 2-inch cubes. Brown meat on all sides in 2–3 tablespoons drippings. Remove meat, lower heat and brown chopped onions lightly. Return meat to pan with stock, wine, tomato sauce and herbs. Cover, and simmer 1 1/2 hours or until meat is tender. Remove meat, and skim off fat. To lamb liquid add cooking juices saved from roast pork.

Cut pork rind into strips, and slice salt pork. Skin sausages, thickly sliced. Drain beans, reserving liquid. Cut roast pork into 1 1/2-inch chunks. Arrange pork rind on bottom of 8-quart casserole, cover with layers of beans, lamb, roast pork, salt pork and sausage slices respectively. Repeat layers, ending with beans. Pour meat juices over all, and add enough bean liquid to come to top of last layer. Spread top with bread crumbs and parsley, and dot with 1/4 cup drippings. Cover. Refrigerate if you wish to serve another day. When ready to serve, leave cover on. If casserole has been refrigerated, place in 375°F. oven 25 minutes; reduce heat to 325°F. and continue baking 1 hour. Remove cover, and bake 30 minutes longer. Add more bean liquid if mixture seems dry. If it hasn't been refrigerated, bake covered 1 1/2 hours at 325°F. Serve from casserole. Serves 10–12.

Note: Cassoulet is a renowned French regional dish. The ingredients vary greatly from section to section, causing many lively disputes. It is rich country fare, a combination of beans and meats, and requires long cooking and a fair amount of patience. It is easier to spread the making of this dish over 2 or even 3 days, well in advance of when needed for a weekend crowd.

Beef Tenderloin in Pastry

> 4-pound piece beef tenderloin
> 1/4 cup Burgundy wine
> 1/4 cup garlic-flavored FRENCH DRESSING
> 2 (10-ounce) packages frozen puff pastry shells, thawed
> 1 pimento, diced

Trim excess fat from meat. Set meat on platter. Combine wine and dressing, and pour over meat. Marinate in refrigerator 4 hours, turning meat several times. Thaw cream puff dough according to package directions, about 1 hour before serving time, drain meat, saving marinade. Brush off excess marinade from meat with pastry brush, or pat with paper towel, and place meat in a shallow pan. If there is a thin end, pin it under with toothpicks to make tenderloin uni-

formly thick. Press thawed pastry shells together. Roll out into oblong. Wrap around meat completely, clamping edges and sealing firmly. Bake at 450°F. 30 minutes or until meat thermometer barely registers 140°F. Decorate top with diced pimento. Serve on heated platter with POTATO CROQUETTES and garnishes. Serves 6–8.

Note: One of the elegant diversions of *haute cuisine* is the introduction in the early courses of a meal of such tender, flaky pastry as tartlets holding richly sauced mushrooms or seafood for hot hors d'oeuvres or a handsomely decorated wrap for a whole baked ham, or a length of the tenderest of all beef, the fillet of tenderloin. This recipe offers a simplified version utilizing the frozen puff pastry shells to cover top and sides of meat. If you prefer, use traditional puff pastry recipe.

The Great French Sauces. There are several basic sauces, notably béchamel, velouté and brown. The first 2 are French forms of our familiar white or cream sauce. Béchamel sauce uses equal parts sweet butter and flour blended together; hot milk is added and mixture cooked slowly over boiling water. Sometimes 1 beaten egg yolk is stirred in after pan is removed from heat. Velouté sauce begins in same way, but hot chicken or veal stock replaces milk. Various seasonings are used in either case, but always with discretion. Brown sauce is basically gravy but with these differences: Chopped onion and carrot are first browned in fat; liquid—boiling water or stock—always includes tomato puree, and sometimes browned meat bones are added for color. Brown sauce takes readily to many seasoning touches, and a dash of dry sherry is often added before serving.

Other famous sauces, perhaps more temptingly unfamiliar to American tables, include the following:

Sauce Béarnaise

> 4 egg yolks
> 1/4 cup light cream
> 2 tablespoons tarragon vinegar
> 1 tablespoon finely chopped onion
> 1/2 cup butter or margarine
> 1 tablespoon finely chopped parsley
> 1/2 teaspoon salt
> Few grains cayenne

Put egg yolks, cream, vinegar and onion in top of double boiler over gently simmering water. Stir constantly, or use wire whisk in French manner. When mixture starts to thicken, add butter or margarine gradually (not more than 1 teaspoonful at a time). Continue stirring and adding until all butter or margarine is smoothly blended in, about 15 minutes. Remove from heat; add parsley and seasonings. Serve immediately over steaks, chops or fish.

Sauce Américaine

    3 cups cooked fresh or canned tomatoes
    2 teaspoons sugar
    2 tablespoons butter or margarine
    1 tablespoon olive oil
    2 tablespoons chopped onion
    1 tablespoon chopped parsley
    1 clove garlic
    Pinch chervil
    2 tablespoons brandy

Simmer tomatoes with sugar, uncovered, over low heat until most juice has cooked down. Meantime heat butter or margarine and oil in saucepan; add onion, parsley, garlic and chervil. Cook gently until onion is clear. Press tomatoes through sieve; then add to onion mixture, increase heat, and simmer 15 minutes. Remove garlic, and stir in brandy. Heat thoroughly, but do not boil.

Note: This sauce is a good accompaniment for meats, fish, eggs and green or dried beans.

Sauce Mornay

    1 cup hot BECHAMEL SAUCE or white sauce
    2 egg yolks, slightly beaten
    1 tablespoon butter or margarine
    1 tablespoon grated Parmesan cheese

Stir a little béchamel sauce into egg yolks, return all to saucepan, add butter or margarine and cheese, and heat less than 1 minute over hot water. Serve with fish or vegetables like broccoli or asparagus. Serves 4.

Salade Française (Tossed Green Salad). Salad flavor depends upon quality of young fresh greens, well washed, well dried and thoroughly chilled. Select greens in season, and wash with cold water as soon as possible after purchasing. Dry by twirling in salad basket, or pat with towel. Store, loosely packed, in covered container or plastic bags in refrigerator. Romaine, escarole, chicory, watercress, spinach and head and leaf lettuce are excellent for salads.

To make salad, tear greens into bite-sized pieces, allowing 1–1 1/4 cups greens per serving. You can rub wooden salad bowl with cut clove of garlic. Add greens: then place such other suitable ingredients as diced tomatoes, snipped chives, sliced radishes and anchovy fillets on top. Refrigerate until ready to serve; add dressing and toss lightly.

Herb Dressing

    1/3 cup salad or olive oil
    2 tablespoons wine vinegar or lemon juice
    1 teaspoon herbs (any variety)
    1 teaspoon salt
    1/4 teaspoon dry mustard
    1/8 teaspoon freshly ground pepper

Mix all ingredients together well, pour over salad and toss.

Note: This recipe makes enough dressing for 6 cups greens, and it is much nicer when freshly made.

French Desserts

Croquembouche

The Croquembouche pyramid must be assembled quickly, or the syrup used to assemble it will harden and have to be reheated. Therefore be sure to read the recipe through thoroughly before starting to work. And have all ingredients near the stove, so you dip the puffs and set them in place quickly.

    1 cup dark corn syrup
    5 dozen (60) small cream puffs, custard-filled (from the
        bakery, or homemade)
    1/4 cup confectioners' sugar

Cut a 9-inch circle from cardboard and cover with foil. Set the circle on a board near the stove. Have the filled cream puffs close at hand.

Cook corn syrup over high heat until candy thermometer reaches "hard ball" stage (240°F.), or until a small drop of the syrup forms a soft ball in cold water. Turn heat off.

To build the pyramid, lightly dip the bottom of a cream puff in syrup and set on the edge of the circle, syrup-side down. Repeat with 9 more puffs, forming a ring. For the second row, arrange a slightly smaller ring of puffs over the spaces between the puffs of the first row, inclining the second row slightly inward. Fill in the center with more puffs, for support.

Continue building the pyramid in decreasing rings (see color illustration), filling in center for support as needed, until you have completed 8 rows.

Top with one puff. Sprinkle the Croquembouche lightly with 1/4 cup sifted confectioners' suger. To eat, just pull one or two puffs at a time off the pyramid, starting from the top. Serves 8–10.

Note: If syrup begins to thicken before pyramid is completed, add a teaspoon of water and stir over low heat. Do not let syrup burn.

Paris–Brest Dessert

1 recipe BASIC CREAM PUFF PASTRY
2 cups heavy cream plus 2 tablespoons sugar, or 2 (2-ounce) packages whipped topping mix
2 tablespoons sherry or lemon juice
1/4 cup light corn syrup
2 tablespoons green pistachio nuts, coarsely chopped pecans or walnuts, or slivered almonds

Preheat oven to 400°F. Cut a 9-inch circle out of heavy brown paper, place it in center of cookie sheet and oil it lightly. Make CREAM PUFF PASTRY. Place pastry around edge of paper circle in heaping tablespoons, leaving a 4-inch circle bare in center. Smooth pastry with a spatula, making an even ring. Bake 50 minutes at 400°F.

Remove ring from oven. Cut off top with sharp knife. Scoop out any soft dough. Turn oven off, place ring back in, and let it stand in oven with door slightly open for 15 minutes. Remove from oven and cool on wire rack away from drafts.

Whip heavy cream with sugar until stiff (or prepare two packages whipped-topping mix, following package directions). Fold in sherry or lemon juice. Fill bottom of pastry ring with whipped cream or topping. Replace top of ring and brush lightly with corn syrup. Sprinkle with green pistachio nuts, coarsely chopped pecans or walnuts, or slivered almonds. Serves 6–8.

Pots de Crème au chocolat (Individual Chocolate Cream)

1/2 pound unsweetened chocolate
4 eggs
2/3 cup sugar
1/2 cup soft butter or margarine
1/2 teaspoon vanilla extract
1 tablespoon brandy
1 cup heavy cream, beaten

Melt chocolate in top of double boiler. Separate eggs, and beat yolks until light, gradually

beating in sugar. Add melted chocolate, and continue beating. Add butter or margarine very gradually, beating well after each addition. Beat

egg whites very stiff; fold into mixture with brandy and vanilla. Spoon into individual soufflé cups or little pots. Chill thoroughly before serving.

Note: Butter that has been allowed to stand at room temperature for several hours will need creaming only a few moments before adding; otherwise soften it over warm water, but do not let it liquefy.

Crème Caramel (Caramel Custard)

    1/2 cup sugar
    2 tablespoons water
2 1/2 cups light cream
    3 eggs
    3 egg yolks
    1/2 cup sugar
Pinch salt
    1 teaspoon vanilla extract

In 4-cup ring mold, about 3 inches high and 5 inches in diameter at base, place 1/2 cup sugar and water; set over medium heat until syrup caramelizes. Tilt mold carefully to cover sides as well as bottom with syrup. Plunge mold, almost to its edge, in basin of cold water several seconds to cool and set glaze (do not let any cold water splash into mold). Set aside while you make custard. Scald cream. Beat eggs and egg yolks until well blended, beat in 1/2 cup sugar until mixture is light and foamy. Add salt and, gradually, scalded cream. Add vanilla, and strain into caramel-lined mold. Set in shallow pan of hot water, and bake at 325°F. about 60 minutes or until silver knife inserted in center comes out clean. Let custard cool, then refrigerate. At serving time, run a knife around custard, separating it from mold. Invert round platter on top, hold in place firmly and with one quick motion reverse plate and mold to remove custard in neat mound. Add spoonful of warm water to caramel adhering to mold, and pour around custard before serving. Serves 4–6.

Note: This delicate custard, made with extra egg yolks, is always served unmolded to display its rich caramel glaze.

Soufflé au Grand Marnier

    4 or 5 ladyfingers
Grand Marnier liqueur
    2 tablespoons butter or margarine
    1 tablespoon flour
1/2 cup milk
Few drops almond extract
    6 egg yolks
    5 tablespoons sugar
    6 egg whites
    1 teaspoon sugar
    1 teaspoon Grand Marnier

Crush ladyfingers and sprinkle with sufficient Grand Marnier to moisten; set aside. Melt butter or margarine in saucepan, stir in flour, remove from heat and add milk gradually, stirring to keep smooth. Cook, stirring constantly, over low heat until mixture thickens. Add almond extract sparingly. Beat egg yolks with 4 tablespoons sugar. Add almond mixture, a little at a time, to egg yolks. Return to low heat barely 1 minute,

stirring continuously. Let mixture cool slightly while egg whites are beaten stiff; add remaining 1 tablespoon sugar to beaten egg whites to keep them glossy and prevent drying. Fold whites gradually into warm yolk mixture, using up-and-down folding motion to incorporate thoroughly without destroying frothiness. Have ready a buttered straight-sided soufflé dish (1 1/2-quart size). Sprinkle 1 teaspoon sugar and 1 teaspoon Grand Marnier over bottom. Turn in 1/2 the mixture, cover with soaked ladyfinger crumbs and add remaining mixture. Run rubber spatula around outer edge of soufflé, separating it slightly from side of dish; smooth top. If mixture more than half fills your dish, prevent spilling and encourage rising by tying doubled strip of buttered waxed paper as a "collar" around top edge. Bake in medium hot oven, 375°–400°F. about 20 minutes or until soufflé has risen and is delicately browned. Remove collar before serving. Serve immediately. Serves 4–5.

Note: There is only one problem with a soufflé: it will not wait. When full-blown and beautifully, crisply golden on top it must be sped from oven to table for immediate serving; otherwise it will crumple into ruin. A dessert soufflé is admittedly one of the most challenging to achieve, because it goes in over at the time the main course is being served and should be puffed and perfect in about 20 minutes. This soufflé is often served without sauce; sometimes it is accompanied by sauce dish containing chilled boiled custard folded into an equal amount of whipped cream and lightly flavored with liqueur.

Riz à l'Impératrice (Empress Rice)

    1 cup finely diced mixed candied fruits (cherries, citrus, peel, pineapple)
    3 tablespoons brandy or kirsch
1/2 cup rice
1/2 cup cold water
1 1/4 cups cold milk
    1 envelope powdered gelatin
    1/4 cup cold water
    4 egg yolks
    1/2 cup sugar
Pinch salt
    3/4 cup hot milk
    1/2 teaspoon vanilla extract
    1 cup heavy cream, whipped to soft peaks

Marinate 3/4 cup fruits in brandy. Cover rice with 1/2 cup cold water, bring to boil and simmer 2 minutes. Drain, and rinse with cold water. Return rice to saucepan, add cold milk, bring to simmer, cover and cook until rice is very tender (about 30 minutes) and milk absorbed. Do not stir. Soften gelatin in 1/4 cup cold water. Combine egg yolks with sugar and salt in top of double boiler, add hot milk gradually and place over hot water, stirring constantly until custard is thick and smooth. Remove from heat, and stir in gelatin and vanilla until gelatin is dissolved. Strain into cooked rice, blend thoroughly and chill until mixture begins to set. Carefully fold in marinated candied fruits and whipped cream. Put into lightly oiled 6-cup ring mold or cylindrical fancy shape. Chill at least 4 hours, preferably overnight. To unmold, run knife around upper edge of mold; invert serving plate on top and reverse plate and mold together. Wring out tea towel in boiling water, and apply to mold, pressing over all surfaces. Repeat several times, and contents will drop free from mold. Decorate with remaining candied fruits cut in strips, circles, petals and diamond shapes. Pour STRAWBERRY SAUCE around shape, or serve separately. Serves 8–10.

Strawberry Sauce

    1 cup strawberry jam
    1 cup red currant jelly
    3 tablespoons brandy or kirsch

Melt jam and jelly over medium heat. Add brandy, blend thoroughly and simmer 1 minute. Put through sieve, allow to cool, beat until smooth and serve.

EXOTIC DISHES FROM SPAIN

Characterized by spices, nuts, fruits, fish, rice, olive oil and the renowned sherries.

The cuisine of Spain has its vivid, exciting moments, like the landscape and the life of the country itself. It is less complex and far-ranging than the *haute cuisine* of France; indeed in Spain almost any traditional dish can be undertaken with confidence. Spanish cuisine has a heritage from the long Moorish occupation of the country centuries ago. Spices, especially saffron, cinnamon, nutmeg and mace, are popular. Rice appears on almost every menu, whether in soups, chilled salads, hot accompaniments to entrees or final sweet courses. Nuts, particularly almonds, add interest to many dishes. Chocolate (introduced after the conquest of Mexico) is of great importance and is even used in grated unsweetened form over certain baked fish or meats. Many varieties of fish and shellfish from the Atlantic and Mediterranean coasts, plus freshwater trout and other inland fish, are used abundantly; but the popular dried salt cod continues to be imported from Canada's Atlantic shores.

Olives, olive oil and the country's inimitable sherries play a leading role in fine cookery. Fruits of all kinds, notably melons, grapes, and members of the citrus family, make the grand finale of the Spanish gourmet's 10 P.M. dinner a highly colorful affair.

Sopa de Almendras (Almond Soup)

    2 tablespoons butter or margarine
    1 tablespoon grated onion
    2 tablespoons flour
    6 cups chicken broth
    2 cups blanched almonds
    1/4 teaspoon nutmeg
    1/8 teaspoon mace
    Salt and pepper to taste
    2/3 cup heavy cream
    2 egg yolks, lightly beaten
    1 teaspoon grated lemon rind
    Watercress leaves

Melt butter or margarine, add onion and cook gently 1 minute only. Blend in flour, stir in chicken broth and cook until smooth and boiling. Grind almonds to paste in electric blender or fine nut chopper. Combine with seasonings and stir into soup. Cover, and simmer 15 minutes. Combine cream, egg yolks and lemon rind; gradually blend in 1 cup hot soup. Pour slowly back into saucepan, stirring constantly. Heat, but do not boil. Serve garnished with leaves of watercress. Serves 6–8.

Cacerola de Conejo (Rabbit Casserole)

    2–3 tablespoons flour
    Salt and pepper to taste
    1 tender young rabbit, cut up
    4–5 tablespoons salad oil
    1 medium onion, chopped (approximately 1/2 cup)
    1 clove garlic, crushed
    1/2 cup dry white wine
    1/2 cup (approximately) consommé or pale meat or
        vegetable stock or water
    3 sweet red peppers, cut in strips
    1 eggplant, peeled, thinly sliced and quartered
    3 cups hot boiled rice or 4–5 slices fried or toasted
        bread
    Ripe olives
    Parsley

Combine flour with ample salt and pepper. Dredge rabbit pieces in mixture. Heat 3–4 tablespoons salad oil in skillet; add meat, onion and garlic. Turn meat to color all sides light golden. Set oven at 350°F. and scrape contents of pan into heated casserole. Add wine and just enough consommé to keep meat moist. Cover casserole, and bake about 1 1/2 hours or until rabbit is perfectly tender. About 15 minutes before serving, heat remaining 1–2 tablespoons salad oil (or butter or margarine) in skillet; add pepper, eggplant. Fry gently about 10 minutes or until tender. Arrange cooked rabbit pieces on shallow bed of well-drained rice; strain casserole sauce, and pour over; garnish platter with hot vegetables, ripe olives and sprigs of parsley. Serves 4–5.

Note: Rabbit, either wild or commercially produced, is frequently featured as the main course. This recipe is an adaptation of the Spanish version; the sweet peppers, and eggplant are typical accompaniments. The casserole sauce may be thickened if desired, with 1 tablespoon flour blended with same amount cold water; stir into casserole 10 minutes before taking from oven.

Truchas al Jerez al Horno (Baked Trout with Sherry)

        6 brook trout
    1/2 lemon
    Salt and pepper to taste
        3 tablespoons salad oil or olive oil
        1 cup day-old bread crumbs
        3 tablespoons chopped parsley
        1 clove garlic, crushed
    Juice of 1/2 lemon
    1/3 cup dry sherry

Rub fish with lemon, and season with salt and pepper. Heat oil, and add bread crumbs, parsley and garlic. Spread 1/2 the mixture on bottom of shallow baking pan. Arrange fish on top, cover with remaining crumbs and sprinkle with lemon juice. Bake in preheated 350°F. oven 10 minutes. Add sherry, and bake 10 minutes longer, basting occasionally. Serves 6.

Pastel de Pescado (Fish Pie)

        3 tablespoons olive oil
    1/2 cup almonds, blanched and halved or coarsely
            chopped
        2 medium onions, chopped (approximately one cup)
        1 clove garlic, crushed
        2 cups raw tomatoes, peeled and chopped, or 1 (1-
            pound, 4-ounce) can tomatoes, drained
        2 teaspoons salt
    1/2 teaspoon black pepper
        1 bay leaf
        4 fillets white-fleshed fish, cut in pieces
        3 cups seasoned mashed potatoes

Heat oil in saucepan, add almonds and let color on all sides. Lift out with slotted spoon, leaving oil. In same pan gently sauté onions and garlic until transparent but not brown. Add tomatoes and seasonings, and simmer about 10 minutes, stirring occasionally. Heat oven to 400°F. Butter casserole and lay fish fillets over bottom. Place in oven, and bake 5 minutes, or until fish loses raw look. Add 1 1/2 cups hot to-mato mixture, then almonds, and cover with mashed potatoes. Bake 20–25 minutes; if necessary brown topping briefly under broiler. Simmer remaining hot tomato mixture to reduce slightly, and serve over casserole. Serves 4–5.

Note: Any tender white-meat fish, either fresh or frozen (partially thawed), may be used. Additional browned almonds may be scattered over potato topping.

Paella (Rice, Chicken and Seafood Casserole)

        3 tablespoons olive oil
        8 small pieces frying chicken
    1/2 pound sliced fresh mushrooms
            (approximately 2 1/2 cups)
    1/4 cup sliced green onions
    1/4 cup diced green or sweet red pepper
        2 cloves garlic, sliced
        1 teaspoon salt
        1 cup long-grain rice
    3 1/2 cups water
        2 chicken bouillon cubes, crumbled
        1 broken bay leaf
    1/2 teaspoon saffron
    1/4 teaspoon chili pepper seeds
        1 (10-ounce) package frozen peas
        1 (16-ounce) package frozen shrimp or about 2
            pounds fresh shrimp, cooked and peeled
        1 (12-ounce) can clams, drained
        2 tablespoons butter or margarine
    Sautéed mushrooms
    Sliced stuffed olives
    Hard-cooked eggs

Heat oil in large heavy pan, and lightly brown chicken. Add mushrooms, onions, pepper, garlic and salt. Cover, and turn heat low. Cook slowly 15 minutes. Sprinkle rice around chicken pieces, and add next 5 ingredients. Cover, and bring to boil. Reduce heat, and cook 20 minutes or until rice is tender. Add peas, cover and cook 5 minutes. In another pan sauté shrimp and clams in butter or margarine for 2 minutes; then pile on top rice mixture, or stir through. Reheat thoroughly. Garnish with sautéed mushrooms, sliced stuffed olives and hard-cooked eggs. Serves 8.

Note: Paella is the specialty dish of Valencia, the name of both a city and a province on the Mediterranean, which is a constant source of the seafood featured in this and many other recipes. The name "paella" actually refers to the large, shallow pan, round or oval but always with side handles, in which this dish is prepared and served. Paella is a colorful production with many ingredients and is too much effort for only 2 or 3 people, but it is ideal party fare. This recipe can be extended in the Spanish way by adding other suitable ingredients rather than increasing the base. Spicy smoked sausage is sometimes sautéed separately in 3 or 4 slices and then mixed in. 1 (9-ounce) package partially thawed frozen artichokes may be added at same time as peas. Cutup boiled fresh lobster meat is another extender heartily approved by the Spanish gourmet.

Churos (Spanish Fritters)

      1 cup water
  1/4 cup butter or margarine
  1/4 teaspoon salt
1 1/4 cups flour
      3 eggs
      1 tablespoon grated orange rind
Shortening for frying

Put water, butter or margarine and salt into saucepan over medium heat. As soon as it boils up and butter is melted, remove from heat and add flour all at once, stirring hard with wooden spoon to make very smooth choux paste. Return to stove over low heat, and continue stirring. When paste comes away from sides of pan, it is ready for eggs. Break them, 1 at a time, into a saucer; beat each slightly, and incorporate into paste thoroughly before next addition. Add orange rind. Have ready a good-size saucepan, filled with simmering shortening to a depth of 4 inches. When shortening has reached 375°F. on your deep-frying thermometer (or hot enough to brown a cube of day-old bread in 40 seconds), it is ready for cooking fritters. The traditional method is to put choux paste into pastry bag equipped with metal nozzle 1 1/2 inches wide. Press mixture through tube in 10-inch strips. Fry few at a time, as fritters swell and corkscrew as they cook. Lift out when golden brown, drain on paper towel and keep hot until batch is finished. Serve hot, sprinkled with confectioners' sugar. Serves 5–6.

Note: This highly distinctive Spanish delicacy is often served as the only accompaniment for breakfast hot chocolate. These long, twisting fried puffs could be an evening snack novelty or a tempting hot dessert after a salad luncheon.

Sherry–Cream Sauce

    2 egg yolks, beaten light
1/2 cup sugar
1/4 cup canned pineapple juice
1/4 cup orange juice
1/4 cup lemon juice
    3 tablespoons medium-dry sherry
3/4 cup heavy cream, whipped to soft peaks

Combine egg yolks and sugar in top of double boiler. Blend in fruit juices, and set over hot water. Cook, stirring constantly, until sauce coats spoon. Cover, and chill. Add sherry, and fold in

whipped cream. Serve over any colorful combination of sweetened fresh, canned or frozen fruits arranged in individual dishes.

LIVELY ITALIAN CUISINE

The nation that invented pasta and pizza has a robust tradition of colorful fare, and the variation in types and flavors, region by region, only adds to the excitement. Except for stock soups and slow-cooked sauces, most dishes are quickly prepared for immediate serving.

The colors of Italian foods are lively—the red sauces of the South, the Adriatic's pink scampi

(distant relatives of prawns or large shrimp), the fish soups, the green dishes of the North, the vivid shades of fresh fruits and vegetables, the frothy egg whips (sometimes added to savory liquids, sometimes beaten with wine for dessert) and the pronounced tones of the wine accompany all major meals.

To Italians the good cooking of the peninsula is known by its regional type: there are Florentine, Neapolitan, Venetian, Genoese, Roman and many other styles. The same dish may be presented to the visitor under 4 different names in many regions.

Pasta South, Rice North. Although pasta is always associated with Italian cuisine, it too is regional, belonging to the South; the rice of Piedmont is the pre-eminent grain staple of the North.

Pasta in its many shapes and sizes is produced in factories for mass distribution and by household and restaurant cooks for immediate use. The wheat-flour base is the same in all cases, but the factory product differs in that it is specially dried before packaging, which accounts for the longer boiling required, in contrast to the "5 minutes" directed for homemade pasta. Depending on thickness and shape, pasta should cook to the point of tender firmness, *al dente* ("to the tooth" or chewy), in 8–25 minutes. A large pot is a must, in order to hold sufficient water and allow a rolling boil; in Italy the rule is 6 quarts water for each pound raw pasta. Gluey overcooked pasta would horrify the Italian gourmet.

The rice or "risotto" of Italy is entirely different from that of the Chinese, Arabs, and other rice-eating peoples—different in crop variety and more similar to the long-grain rice of the southern United States. It's different in cooked results as well. Only a comparatively small amount of liquid is used in its preparation; this proportion and slower cooking provide a creamy texture.

Meats and fish, accompanied by cooked or salad vegetables, are considered the ideal main courses for dinner in Italy, as elsewhere. When they are replaced by pasta or rice, served with cheese sauce, it's generally in the interests of thrift.

Cheese, Fruits, Custards. Cheese occurs at some point in almost every menu, often with fruit for dessert.

There are sweet dishes in the various regional cuisines—fritters, sweet chestnut mixtures, custards, ices—but their range is limited compared with the great variety available in France, the British Isles and North America.

The best Italian cooking is based on generous use of fresh raw materials. The long hours or even days of preparation that French chefs put into *haute cuisine* are not the rule in Italy.

Antipasto (Italian Hors d'oeuvres)

Most mid-day meals in Italy start with a plate of appetizers regardless of whether the menu includes pasta. Plates and platters attractively arranged present many kinds of small fish, sausages, chilled raw and cooked vegetables, hot fritters, and miniature pizzas. Vegetable antipasto, like French vegetable hors d'oeuvres, can be served as a main-course salad for luncheon. Here are 3 suggested platters:

ANTIPASTO 1

Shredded red cabbage
Tuna fish pieces
Anchovies
Large green olives
Capers
Diced celery
Chopped parsley
Salt and pepper
Olive oil

Arrange cabbage on large platter, and scatter remaining ingredients on top. Season with salt, pepper and olive oil.

ANTIPASTO 2

Thinly sliced salami or thinly sliced prosciutto, if available
Mortadella sausage
Stuffed egg halves
Strips of red and green peppers marinated in oil

Arrange salami, ham, sausage and eggs in rows on large platter, and garnish with pepper strips.

ANTIPASTO 3

Green onions
Cherry tomatoes or tomato wedges
Radishes
White asparagus spears
Small melon wedges
Celery
Shredded lettuce

Arrange first 6 ingredients in groups on bed of shredded lettuce. Serve with crusty Italian bread.

Soups. The soups of Italy, with such various ingredients as vegetables, spaghetti and poached ground-meat balls in well-flavored stock can be served as luncheon main dishes.

Pasta in Brodo con Fegatine e Piselli (Pasta in Broth with Chicken Livers and Peas)

3 ounces vermicelli
1 pound fresh young green peas, shelled, or 10-ounce package frozen green peas
6 cups hot chicken broth
1 tablespoon butter or margarine
10 (approximately) chicken livers, coarsely chopped

Break vermicelli into 2-inch lengths. Cook with peas in boiling salted water. Drain. Add to hot broth, and bring to boil. Reduce heat, and simmer. Melt butter or margarine, add livers and cook over low heat. Add livers and butter to broth.

Note: Pass a dish of grated Parmesan cheese with the soup. Serves 4–6.

Brodo alle Mandorle e Funghi (Broth with Mushrooms and Almonds)

6 cups beef broth or consommé
Salt and pepper to taste
2 tablespoons butter or margarine
1/2 cup almonds, blanched and slivered
1 cup sliced fresh mushrooms
1 teaspoon chopped parsley
1/8 teaspoon powdered oregano

Heat broth to boiling, and season with salt and pepper. Keep hot. Melt butter or margarine, add almonds and cook slowly until light yellow in color. Add mushrooms, stirring 5 minutes. Add parsley and oregano, and blend well. Combine with hot broth; serve immediately. Serves 4–6.

Ways with Pasta. The sauces for pasta are as distinctive and various as the Italian regions. Naples is renowned for its spicy tomato sauce. In Calabria anchovies are scattered over the pasta platter. An interesting clam-and-tomato sauce is occasionally encountered.

Neapolitan Sauce for Pasta

1/4 cup olive oil
1 small onion, chopped (approximately 1/4 cup)
1 clove garlic, crushed
1 (6-ounce) can tomato paste
2 cups boiling water
3 cups canned tomatoes (1 pound, 13 ounce can)
1 cup red wine
2 teaspoon salt
1 teaspoon sugar
3/4 teaspoon dried oregano
3/4 teaspoon basil
1/4 teaspoon pepper
Few grains cayenne

Heal oil in heavy saucepan; cook onion and garlic until soft and lightly colored. Thin tomato paste with boiling water. Add tomatoes, tomato paste, wine, salt, sugar and seasonings. Bring just to boil; then reduce heat, and simmer, uncovered, at least 1 hour or until sauce has thickened. Stir frequently. If desired, put through sieve. Serve over well-drained, cooked spaghetti, macaroni shells or other pasta, and accompany with bowl of grated Parmesan cheese. Makes enough sauce for 6–8 servings.

Note: Some Italian gourmets maintain that sauce improves after standing, then reheating.

VARIATION:

For tomato–meat sauce, brown 1 pound ground lean beef in 2 tablespoons fat in frying pan; turn and stir vigorously to brown thoroughly over medium heat. With slotted spoon, remove meat from fat and add to sauce 1/2 hour after putting it to cook. Check seasonings before serving.

Fettucine all'Alfredo (Noodles Alfredo)

1/2 pound broad noodles
Boiling salted water
1/2 cup soft unsalted butter
1/2 cup grated Parmesan cheese

Cook noodles in plenty of boiling salted water until just tender. Drain, and place in large heated bowl. Add butter and cheese, and using long-handled spoon and fork, toss together quickly until noodles are thoroughly coated. Serve immediately on hot plates. Serves 6.

This recipe offers probably the simplest and most excellent method for preparing pasta. The trick is to plan a suitable menu (perhaps with big salad bowl of crisp vegetables and finely diced cooked ham or bacon bits), to have everything ready at table and everyone waiting to sit down, and to serve without a moment's delay so that all can enjoy this fresh main dish piping-hot.

Cannelloni alla Genovese (Genoese Stuffed Pasta)

2 eggs
2 tablespoons skim milk
1 1/2 cups sifted flour
1 teaspoon salt
Boiling salted water
3 tablespoons butter or margarine
1/2 cup chopped onion
1/2 cup chopped celery
1 carrot, scraped and chopped (approximately 1/4 cup)
1/4 cup mushrooms, chopped
1 (1-pound) can Italian plum tomatoes
1/2 cup dry white wine or chicken broth
1 teaspoon salt
1/4 teaspoon pepper
1/2 pound hot Italian sausages
1 (10-ounce) package frozen chopped spinach

1/4 cup chopped canned roasted peppers
6 slices mozzarella or pizza cheese

Beat eggs until frothy. Add milk, flour and 1 teaspoon salt; mix with fork until dough comes together. Knead on heavily floured board until dough loses stickiness and becomes smooth. Cover, and let stand 30 minutes. Divide dough in 1/2. Roll each piece as thin (1/16 inch thick) as possible on lightly floured board to approximately 12″ x 16″. Cut into 12 4-inch squares. Drop into boiling salted water; cook just until tender. Lift out, and drain on paper towels.

Melt butter or margarine in large skillet. Add onion, celery, carrot and mushrooms; sauté until onion is golden. Stir in tomatoes, wine, 1 teaspoon salt and pepper. Cover, and simmer 1 hour.

Remove sausage meat from casings, and sauté in skillet until cooked and golden. Drain off excess fat. Add frozen spinach and peppers; cook until spinach has thawed and separated. Cool. Divide spinach mixture evenly among noodle squares. Roll up. Place seam side down, 1 layer deep, in 3-quart baking dish. Spoon tomato sauce over rolls, and top with cheese. Bake in moderate oven, 375°F. 30 minutes or until golden on top and bubbly. Serves 6.

Spaghetti Siciliani

3 tablespoons olive or cooking oil
1/2 cup chopped onion
1/4 cup chopped celery
1 tablespoon chopped parsley
1 clove garlic, crushed
1 (2-pound, 3-ounce) can Italian plum tomatoes
1 (6-ounce) can tomato paste
1 teaspoon salt
1 bay leaf
1/2 teaspoon basil
1/2 teaspoon oregano
1/4 teaspoon pepper
1/2 pound spaghetti or linguine
1/2 cup (approximately) olive oil or cooking oil
1 large eggplant, peeled and sliced 1/2 inch thick
1 cup grated Parmesan cheese
1 cup grated Romano cheese

Heat 3 tablespoons oil in skillet. Add onion, celery, garlic and parsley; sauté until onion is golden. Stir in next 7 ingredients. Cover, and simmer 1 hour. Remove bay leaf.

Cook spaghetti by package directions; drain. Heat 3 tablespoons oil in large skillet, and sauté eggplant slices, a few at a time, until golden on both sides. Add more oil to skillet as needed. Layer tomato sauce, spaghetti, eggplant and cheeses in an 8″ x 8″ x 2″ baking dish, ending with spaghetti, sauce and generous sprinkling of cheese. Bake in moderate oven, 350°F. 20–30 minutes or until brown and bubbly. Serves 6.

Gnocchi alla Romano (Gnocchi in the Roman Style)

1/2 pound ricotta or cottage cheese
1/2 cup sifted flour
1/3 cup grated Parmesan cheese
1/4 cup of butter or margarine, melted
3 egg yolks
1/2 teaspoon salt
Pinch nutmeg
Salted water
1/4–1/2 cup butter or margarine, melted
1/2 cup grated Parmesan cheese

Press ricotta through sieve into small bowl. Add next 6 ingredients. Mix well. Spoon mixture into pastry tube or bag, fitted with large plain tip (no. 6–8). Bring large kettle of salted water to very gentle boil. Hold bag over kettle, and force contents through tube, snipping into 1-inch pieces with scissors. Work quickly. Cook gnocchi 5–7 minutes; remove with slotted spoon, and drain on paper towels. Divide gnocchi among 8 small oven-proof shells, or place in 1-quart shallow casserole. Pour 1/4–1/2 cup butter or margarine over all. Sprinkle with 1/2 cup grated Parmesan cheese, and bake in moderate oven, 350°F. 10 minutes; then brown a few minutes under broiler. Serves 4 as main dish, 8 as side dish.

Other Italian Dishes

Scallopine Mozzarella (Veal Cutlets Mozzarella)

1/3 cup flour
1 teaspoon salt
1/4 teaspoon oregano
1/4 teaspoon thyme
1/4 teaspoon garlic powder
2 pounds veal cutlets
1 egg, slightly beaten
1/4 cup milk
1 cup fine dry bread crumbs
1/4 cup butter or margarine
2 tablespoons olive oil or salad oil
1 (8-ounce) can tomato sauce
6 thin slices mozzarella cheese

Combine flour with seasonings. Cut meat into 6 serving pieces, and lightly coat with flour mixture. Dip meat in egg-milk mixture, then in bread crumbs. Brown on both sides in hot butter or margarine and oil. Cover bottom of large shallow greased casserole or heat-proof platter with tomato sauce. Place cutlets in single layer, and cover with cheese. Bake, covered, at 350°F. 15–20 minutes or until fork-tender. Brown lightly under broiler. Serves 6.

Pollo alla Cacciatore (Chicken Hunter Style)

1 (4-pound) frying chicken, cut in serving pieces
1/2 cup flour
1 teaspoon salt
3 tablespoons butter or margarine
3 tablespoons oil
1 cup chicken broth
1 cup coarsely chopped peeled tomatoes, or 1 (1 pound, 1 ounce) can tomatoes
6 small whole onions, peeled
1 pimento, finely chopped
1 clove garlic, cut in fine lengthwise strips
Salt and pepper to taste
1 cup sliced fresh mushrooms
1 tablespoon chopped parsley

Combine and roll chicken pieces in flour and salt mixture. Brown on all sides in hot butter or margarine and oil in large skillet. Add remaining ingredients, except mushrooms and parsley. Cover, and simmer slowly 1 hour. Add mushrooms and, if more moisture is needed, extra chicken broth or a little dry white wine. Cover, and cook 15 minutes longer or until chicken is very tender. Garnish with parsley. Serves 4–6.

Chicken Tetrazzini

1 (4 1/2–5 pound) roasting chicken
2 teaspoons salt
Few stalks celery
1 onion, peeled
1 1/2 pounds mushrooms, wiped and sliced
1/4 cup butter or margarine
1 pound spaghetti
1/3 cup butter or margarine
1/3 cup flour
1 cup heavy cream
3 tablespoons sherry
2 teaspoons monosodium glutamate
1 1/2 teaspoons salt
1 cup grated Parmesan cheese

Put chicken in large pot with water just to cover. Add 2 teaspoons salt, celery and onion. Bring to boil; simmer, covered, until tender. Cool chicken in broth. Remove skin from chicken, and cut meat into bite-size pieces. Reserve broth to use in sauce. Sauté mushrooms in 1/4 cup butter or margarine until tender. Set aside. Cook spaghetti by package directions. Drain.

Melt 1/3 cup butter or margarine in a saucepan. Stir in flour. Gradually add 3 1/2 cups reserved chicken broth and cream, stirring and cooking until smooth and thickened. Add sherry, monosodium glutamate, salt and 1/2 cup cheese. Simmer 10 minutes longer. Place 1/3 spaghetti in bottom of greased 4-quart casserole. Spoon 1/3 the mushrooms and 1/2 the chicken over spaghetti, topped by 1/3 the sauce. Add another 1/3 the spaghetti, the remaining mushrooms and

chicken and 1/3 sauce. Top with remaining spaghetti and sauce. Sprinkle casserole with remaining 1/2 cup cheese. Bake in very hot oven, 450°F. until brown on top, 30–40 minutes. Serves 8–10.

Piselli al Prosciutto (Green Peas and Ham)

2 tablespoons chopped onions
2 tablespoons butter or margarine
1 tablespoon oil
1/2 cup prosciutto, cooked bacon or ham, cut in strips
1 pound fresh green peas, shelled or 2 (10-ounce) packages frozen peas
1/4 cup bouillon or water
Salt and pepper to taste
1 tablespoon chopped parsley

Sauté onion slowly in butter or margarine and oil until transparent but not brown. Add ham and cook 3–4 minutes. Add peas, bouillon, salt and pepper; cover, and cook 10–15 minutes, stirring constantly. Sprinkle parsley on top. Serves 4.

Panettone (Italian Christmas Bread)

2 (1/4-ounce) packages active dry yeast
1/2 cup lukewarm water
1 1/2 cups lukewarm milk
3 eggs, beaten
1/3 cup sugar
1/4 cup softened butter or margarine
1 1/2 teaspoons salt
1/4 teaspoon allspice
2 drops yellow food coloring (optional)
6 cups sifted flour
1/2 cup raisins
1/2 cup chopped, mixed candied fruit
1/3 cup chopped almonds
1/3 cup chopped candied lemon peel

Soften yeast in 1/2 cup lukewarm water. Add milk, eggs, sugar, butter or margarine, salt, allspice and food coloring (optional). Mix well. Gradually mix in flour. Cover with a damp cloth and let rise 30 minutes in a warm oven.

Stir dough down. Add raisins, chopped fruit, almonds, lemon peel. Stir until well mixed.

Spoon dough into 3 well-greased 1-pound coffee tins. Bake for 45 minutes at 375°F. Let stand 5 minutes before removing from tins. Makes 3 cakes. Serves about 15.

4 FAMOUS DISHES FROM CENTRAL EUROPE

Hungarian goulash, steeped in paprika gravy; sauerbraten, Germany's hearty pot roast with sharp sweet sauce; Vienna's Esterházy steak in casserole, and a layered dessert torte.

Gulyas (Hungarian Goulash)

1/4 cup shortening or fat
4 cups chopped onions
2 tablespoons fat
2 tablespoons paprika
1 tablespoon flour
1 teaspoon salt
3 pounds beef chuck, cut in 1 1/2-inch squares
2 cups meat stock
1 cup coarsely chopped peeled tomatoes or 1 (1 pound, 4 ounce) can
Salt and pepper to taste
2/3 cup sour cream

Melt 1/4 cup shortening in Dutch oven or other heavy pot. Add onions, and cook until soft and transparent; remove from pan. Add 2 tablespoons fat. While fat is heating, combine paprika, flour and 1 teaspoon salt and roll beef in flour mixture. Brown in hot fat. When meat is well browned, return onions and any remaining paprika mixture, to pan. Add stock and tomatoes. Season with salt and pepper to taste. Cover tightly, and simmer gently 1 1/2–2 hours or until meat is very tender. Season to taste. Immediately before serving remove from heat, and stir in sour cream. Serves 6–8.

Note: Goulash is the national dish of Hungary, and the term is applied to all meats or combination of meat cooked or stewed this way. The liberal use of paprika, without creating a "burning" taste, is one of its features, and depending upon the region, these foods may be included: sour cream, sauerkraut, spices, tomato paste or raw sliced potatoes. The flavor of GULYAS is improved if it is allowed to stand overnight. In this case, omit sour cream. Cool stew rapidly, uncovered, and refrigerate. Remove hardened fat before reheating; stir in sour cream just before serving.

Sauerbraten (German Pot Roast)

2 cups water
1 cup vinegar
2 carrots, sliced (approximately 1/4 cup)
1/4 cup chopped onion
1 stalk celery, chopped (approximately 1/4 cup)
4 peppercorns
4 cloves
2 bay leaves
3–4 pounds top round of beef
1/4 cup flour
1/4 cup shortening
1/4 cup chopped onion
1/4 cup chopped carrots
1/4 cup chopped parsnips
1/4 cup chopped celery
1 teaspoon salt
Pepper to taste
8–10 gingersnaps, crushed

Combine first 8 ingredients in saucepan; bring to boil, and remove from heat. Pour over beef in earthenware (never metal) bowl, and cover tightly. Refrigerate from 24 hours to as long as 4 days. Turn meat occasionally. To cook, remove meat from marinade (reserving marinade), wipe dry and flour lightly. Melt shortening in heavy enamel kettle or Dutch oven. Brown meat on all sides, remove and add fresh vegetables. Cook, stirring, 5 minutes. Return meat to pan; add strained marinade, salt and pepper. Cover, and simmer 3 hours or until meat is tender. Remove meat to platter, and keep warm. Stir crushed gingersnaps into sauce, and cook until thickened. Pour a little over meat, and serve remainder in sauce boat. Serves 6–8.

Note: Marinating is an essential part of preparing SAUERBRATEN.

Esterházy Rostbraten (Viennese Steak)

1/4 cup shortening
4 medium carrots, coarsely chopped (approximately 1 cup)
2 medium onions, coarsely chopped (approximately 1 cup)
2 parsnips, coarsely chopped (approximately 3/4 cup)
2 celery stalks, diced (approximately 1/2 cup)
2 tablespoons flour
1 1/4 cups beef broth
2 tablespoons thick meat sauce
2 teaspoons capers
1 teaspoon paprika
Salt and pepper to taste
3 pounds round steak cut 1 1/2 inch thick
2 tablespoons melted butter or margarine
1 cup sour cream

Melt shortening, add prepared vegetables and sauté lightly until soft. Sprinkle with flour, and blend well; stir in broth, meat sauce, capers and paprika. Bring to boil, season with salt and pepper and remove from heat. Brush steak with melted butter or margarine, and broil in preheated broiler for 2–3 minutes on each side. Season with salt and pepper. Place in large casserole, and pour vegetable sauce over. Cover tightly, and bake in preheated 325°F. oven 40–45 minutes or until meat is tender. Five minutes before serving, add sour cream, and return to oven. Serve in casserole. Serves 6–8.

Note: This Viennese dish, named to honor the famous Esterházy family, is only second in popularity to Wiener Schnitzel, the egged, crumbed and pan-fried veal cutlet beloved of Austrians.

Viennese Almond Tortes. Central Europe, especially Vienna, is famous for tortes—those luscious cake-confections, rich with butter-cream frosting, nuts, almond paste, whipped cream and liqueur. They vary in structure from 1–12 layers made from meringue mixtures, rich butter cakes and sponge cakes mortared together with jams, cream fillings and nut fillings. A torte is not an item to run up in a hurry; component parts can, however, be made and baked ahead of time, stored or frozen and carefully assembled.

Crisp Almond Torte

    2 thin ALMOND-MERINGUE LAYERS
    1 cup raspberry jam
    1 ALMOND-SPONGE LAYER
    1/2 cup apricot jam
    1 recipe CHOCOLATE BUTTER CREAM
1 1/2 cups toasted, thinly sliced almonds
    1/4 cup confectioners' sugar

A pedestal cake dish is an effective choice. Place one meringue layer on server. Spread 1/2 cup raspberry jam over it. Split almond-sponge cake in half horizontally; place 1 layer on top of raspberry jam, and spread with apricot jam. Place other layer of sponge cake on top, and spread with remaining 1/2 cup raspberry jam. Top with meringue layer. Spread sides of torte with chocolate butter cream, and cover with toasted almonds. Use decorating tube to make border of butter-cream rosettes around top of torte. Sift confectioners' sugar over center of torte before serving.

Almond–Meringue Layers

    3 egg whites
    1/8 teaspoon cream of tartar
    1/8 teaspoon salt
    3/4 cup sugar
    1/3 cup sifted cornstarch
    1/4 cup blanched almonds, finely ground
    1 teaspoon vanilla extract

Preheat oven to 325°F. Combine egg whites, cream of tartar, and salt in large mixer bowl, and beat at medium speed until egg whites hold soft peaks. Add 1/2 cup sugar, 1 tablespoon at a time, beating constantly until meringue is stiff but not glossy. Combine cornstarch, almonds, vanilla and remaining 1/4 cup sugar, and fold into meringue. Grease and flour large baking sheet, and make 2 circles by pressing rim of 9-inch round pan into flour. Spread meringue mixture evenly within circles. Bake in 325° oven 35–40 minutes. Cool, and store; or set aside until needed. Makes 2 thin layers.

Note: Finely ground almonds are suitable for both meringue and sponge layers but must be prepared in an electric blender. Prepared sliced almonds are also handy for decorating torte.

Almond–Sponge Layer

    3 egg yolks
    2/3 cup sugar
    3/4 cup blanched almonds, finely ground
    2 teaspoons lemon juice
    1 teaspoon grated lemon rind
    3 egg whites
    3/4 cup sifted all-purpose flour

Preheat oven to 375°F. Beat egg yolks and sugar until light and foamy. Add almonds, juice and lemon rind and combine thoroughly. Beat egg whites until very stiff, and fold into egg yolks, carefully alternating with flour, until mixture is well blended. Pour into greased 9-inch spring-form pan, and bake 375°F. 25–30 minutes or until cake springs back when touched in center. Cool, and remove from pan. Store or freeze until ready to assemble torte.

Chocolate Butter Cream

    1/2 cup soft butter or margarine
    1 package (6 ounces) semisweet chocolate, melted and cooled
    1 egg yolk
    2 teaspoons brandy
    1 teaspoon vanilla extract

Cream butter or margarine until fluffy, and beat in chocolate, egg yolk and flavorings. If desired, add 1 teaspoon instant-coffee powder for mocha flavor. Store in refrigerator if not using immediately. Bring to room temperature before spreading.

TRANSLATIONS FROM THE SCANDINAVIAN

The Nordic cuisine introduced smorgasbord into the gourmet's lexicon; pioneered with fish puddings of rich, airy elegance; developed the open sandwich.

Nordic cuisine offers much of interest to the gastronome: different ways of cooking fish, distinctive seasonings, the subtle use of sour cream in many dishes, the combination of dried fruits with meat and poultry and breads of all shapes, sizes and grains, along with coffee cakes.

Scandinavian countries serve a type of hors d'oeuvre known as "smörgsbörd" in Sweden, "koldt bord" in Norway and "smørrebrød" in Denmark. The Swedish smorgasbord is well known on this side of the Atlantic, where it has been adapted by some restaurants, offering choices ranging even up to 50 dishes. In the home, 4–5 selections are usually offered, and they probably include tiny sausages or meat balls, liver pâté, smoked fish or shellfish, cheese and an egg or macaroni dish, along with crisp breads.

Danish open sandwiches or smørrebrød are wonders of creative talent and patience and are not served too often outside Denmark. There are literally hundreds of variations of these attractive sandwiches, some piled high, some flat, some covered with a single filling, others arranged in sections with 3 or more fillings. Among the last, the "Hans Andersen Favorite" is an example: rows of crisp bacon on light rye bread, sliced liver pâté on 1/2 the bacon, tomato slices on the other half sprinkled with grated horseradish, the whole topped with strips of firm aspic jelly. Any firm-textured bread may be used; it is always thinly sliced (never more than 1/2 the thickness of our machine-sliced type) and lightly buttered with unsalted or whipped butter. These open sandwiches are served for luncheons or late suppers, generally accompanied by beer or spirits.

Norwegian mayonnaise, frequently served with koldt bord fish and shellfish, is made with these additions to regular mayonnaise: 1 cup mayonnaise plus 1/2 cup thick sour cream with a restrained touch of horseradish and chopped dill over all.

Fish Pudding

    2 pounds fresh cod or haddock fillets or 1 pound each
    1 cup butter or margarine
1/4 cup flour
    2 teaspoons salt
1/2 teaspoon white pepper
1/8 teaspoon nutmeg
    1 cup light cream
    4 egg yolks, lightly beaten
    4 egg whites, stiffly beaten
    1 cup heavy cream, stiffly beaten
Fine cracker crumbs

Remove any skin or bones from fillets. Put fish through meat grinder 3 times, using finest blade. Add butter or margarine, and put through grinder again. Sift flour with salt, pepper and nutmeg; combine light cream and egg yolks. Add flour and egg mixtures alternately to fish mixture, a little at a time. Fold in egg whites and cream carefully, a little at a time. Have 8-cup mold, loaf pan or round casserole ready. Butter inside, and dust with crumbs. Carefully pour in fish mixture; mold should be 3/4 full. Set dish in pan of hot water, and bake in preheated 325°F. oven 1¼ hours or until firm. Let stand 5 minutes. Loosen edges with spatula, and strike bottom of dish gently on table. Place serving platter on top of mold, and invert together to turn out neatly. Serves 6–8.

Note: All the Scandinavian countries cook fish superbly, and their rich, fine-textured fish puddings and soufflés—almost always present at family parties and special occasions—are renowned. It is important not to skimp grinding procedures or careful combining of ingredients. These dishes are quite easy to make. Fish puddings could be the fish course at a formal dinner or 1 of 2 hot entrees on a small buffet. Garnish with small sautéed shrimp, and surround with tiny patty shells containing creamed spinach and creamed mushrooms. Serve LOBSTER SAUCE separately.

Lobster Sauce

    3 cups medium white sauce
    1 cup cooked lobster, cut up small
Salt and pepper to taste
    2 tablespoons sherry

To white sauce add lobster. Season, and stir in sherry just before serving.

Rum Cream

    2 cups milk
    5 egg yolks
2/3 cup sugar
    1 envelope powdered gelatin
1/4 cup cold water
1/4 cup rum
    1 cup heavy cream, stiffly beaten

Scald milk in double boiler. Remove from heat. Beat egg yolks and sugar until thick and lemon-colored. Add hot milk gradually, stirring constantly. Return to double boiler, and cook over hot water, continuing to stir until mixture coats spoon. Soften gelatin in cold water; add to custard, and stir until dissolved. Let mixture cool. Blend in rum: then fold in stiffly beaten cream. Turn into 4–5 cup mold or individual sherbet glasses. Chill several hours or overnight. Serve with fresh strawberries, fruit sauce or whipped cream. Serves 6.

Note: Chilled desserts, similar to Bavarian creams, are very popular in Scandinavian countries, and rum is widely used as a flavoring.

FROM THE LAND OF PILAFF AND KEBAB

The Eastern Mediterranean peoples are specialists with main-dish kasha, barley, rice.

Races, religions, economic conditions, climate and terrain have all influenced the eating habits of the various countries clustered in the eastern

Mediterranean area. In Israel and the Moslem communities, pork is not eaten. In districts where conditions are poor for cattle grazing, the popular meats are lamb, mutton, goat and kid. Freshly-caught fish and colorful vegetables and fruits—some unfamiliar to Westerners—are typical and usually abundant commodities in the markets. Local cheeses and honey, plus herbs and spices of ancient lineage, provide interesting touches. But the mainstay of the diet is to be found in the range of inexpensive cereal products like lentils, rice, wheat, kasha and pastas.

Pilaff is actually a method of cooking rice. The name varies with the region–"pilaf," "pilau," "pelo"—but, call it what you will, it's a first-class culinary trick to have at your fingertips. The Balkan peoples, Greeks, Turks and Persians have for centuries achieved notable success with this way of serving their staple cereal. Many extensions and combinations can be made with basic pilaff. Long-grain or converted rice is preferable in the following recipes, as the grains stay quite separate. For palatable flavor, butter or margarine is specified in place of the traditional olive oil.

Kasha (buckwheat groats) is one of the cereal staples of Russia and the Ukraine, as well as of the Mediterranean countries. It is served in much the same way as the Italians serve pasta—in soups, as a side dish with meats or by itself. It develops a nutty flavor during cooking and makes an interesting occasional replacement for potatoes; it is also unusual stuffing for poultry.

Pilaff

    1/4 cup butter or margarine
      2 cups rice
      4 cups boiling consommé or broth
    Salt and pepper to taste

Melt butter or margarine in heavy saucepan; add rice and stir constantly over medium heat about 5 minutes or until rice is golden. Add boiling consommé, cover and allow to cook over low heat 20 minutes or until liquid has been completely absorbed, leaving rice tender and just moist. Season with salt and pepper. Serves 4–6.

Barley Pilaff

    1/2 cup butter or margarine
    1/2 pound mushrooms, thinly sliced
          (approximately 2 1/2 cups)
    1/2 cup coarsely chopped onion
  1 1/3 cups pearl barley
      5 cups hot chicken broth

Preheat oven to 350°F. In 2 tablespoons butter or margarine, sauté mushrooms until tender, 4–5 minutes. Lift out mushrooms with slotted spoon, and set aside. In same skillet heat remaining butter or margarine; sauté onion until golden, about 5 minutes. Add barley, and cook over low heat, stirring frequently, until barley is golden brown, another 5 minutes. Remove from heat; stir in mushrooms and 2 cups hot broth. Turn mixture into 2-quart casserole, and bake, covered, about 30 minutes. Stir in 2 more cups hot broth, cover and bake another 30 minutes or until barley is tender. Finally, stir in remaining broth, and bake 20 minutes longer. Serve with veal, chicken or ham. Serves 8.

Note: You can prepare broth with 6 chicken bouillon cubes dissolved in 5 cups boiling water.

Kasha with Mushrooms

    1/3 cup butter or margarine or salad oil
    1/4 cup chopped onion
    1/4 cup chopped green pepper
      2 cups kasha
      4 cups hot chicken broth or water
    Salt and pepper to taste
      1 cup sliced mushrooms, sautéed in butter or
          margarine or 1 cup slivered almonds, sautéed
          in butter or margarine

Melt butter or margarine, add onion and green pepper and sauté lightly 5 minutes. Add kasha and mix thoroughly. Transfer to casserole. Add hot broth. Season. Cover, and bake in preheated 325°F. oven 1 hour. Check every 15 minutes to see if more liquid is needed, but be cautious as the kasha grains should be tender and dry when done. Add sautéed mushrooms, bake 10 minutes longer. Serves 6.

Note: A well-beaten egg may be stirred in along with mushrooms to bind mixture.

CURRIES OUT OF INDIA

Sometimes fiery to the tongue, but just as often mild and delicate, based on cautious mingling of spices.

India's cuisine has many points of appeal for American cooks. It is not difficult to master, and lends itself ideally to buffet service for company occasions. Curries improve by being made ahead and reheated for serving. Serve curried dishes buffet style, surrounded by a variety of accompaniments selected for flavor contrast, like fruits, nuts, hard-cooked eggs, chutneys, ham slivers, bacon bits and vegetables.

Mild Curry Powder

> 3/4 cup coriander seeds
> 2 1/2 tablespoons dried chili peppers
> 1 tablespoon poppy seeds
> 1 tablespoon cumin seeds
> 1 tablespoon mustard seeds
> 1/4 cup saffron
> 2 tablespoons salt
> 1 teaspoon garlic powder

Pound and rub seeds and chili peppers to fine powder. Add saffron, salt and garlic powder. Mix thoroughly. Bottle, and cork tightly.

Coconut Milk

> 1 coconut (white meat), grated, or 2 cups shredded dry coconut
> 4 cups milk, scalded

Add coconut to scalded milk, and let stand 1 hour. Strain through double layer of cheesecloth, and squeeze coconut meat until dry.

Note: Some curried dishes call for coconut milk.

Curried Shrimp

> 1 1/2 pounds fresh jumbo shrimp or 1 pound frozen shrimp
> Water
> 1 teaspoon salt
> 4 medium onions (approximately 2 cups)
> 1/4 cup raisins
> 2 tablespoons cold water
> 1/4 teaspoon lemon juice
> 1/4 pound butter or margarine
> 3–4 tablespoons curry powder
> 1 teaspoon salt
> 3 tart apples, peeled, cored and chopped (approximately 2 cups)
> Sugar to taste

Cook raw shrimp in water to cover with 1 teaspoon salt. Remove black veins; reserve cooking liquid. Or cook frozen shrimp according to label directions. Peel and chop onions. Soak raisins in cold water with lemon juice. Melt butter or margarine in skillet; sauté onions until transparent. Add curry powder and 1 teaspoon salt; sauté 3 minutes, scraping pan to prevent sticking. Remove from heat, and add apples, drained raisins, shrimp liquid and shrimp. Put back on low heat, and simmer very gently at least 1/2 hour; if necessary add a little extra liquid. Add sugar and seasoning after carefully tasting. When it is just right, remove from heat, and keep in refrigerator overnight. Reheat over low heat or boiling water. Serve with hot fluffy rice, and accompany with chutney, chopped hard-cooked eggs, salted nuts, fresh coconut chips, drained pineapple chunks, and so forth.

Note: Good curry is a nice balance between sweet, sour and hot flavors. To achieve it, you have lemon juice, sugar and curry powder.

Amount of curry powder depends on its strength and your taste.

Lamb Curry

> 2 1/2 pounds shoulder or leg lamb
> 1/4 cup flour
> 1/2 cup butter or margarine
> 2 cups thinly sliced onion
> 2 cloves garlic, crushed
> 1 cup chopped peeled apples
> 2 tablespoons curry powder
> 2 1/2 cups hot water or chicken broth
> 1/4 cup raisins
> 1/4 cup grated coconut
> 1 tablespoon barbecue sauce
> 2 teaspoons salt
> Salt and pepper to taste

Cut meat into 1 1/2-inch cubes, and roll in flour. Melt butter or margarine in large skillet, and sauté onions and garlic until lightly browned, about 5 minutes. Lift out vegetables, and set aside. Sauté meat cubes in pan, adding more butter or margarine if necessary; cook meat about 10 minutes, stirring constantly. Return garlic and onions to pan; add apples and curry powder, and cook 5 minutes. Add next 5 ingredients, bring just to boil, cover and reduce heat. Simmer 1–1 1/2 hours or until meat is tender. Season with salt and pepper to taste. Serve with SAFFRON RICE. Serves 6.

Note: Curry sauce may be thickened, although proper Indian curry is generally served without extra thickening. Blend 2 tablespoons flour with 4–5 tablespoons cold chicken broth or rich milk; stir into hot mixture, and simmer another 10 minutes, stirring constantly.

Saffron Rice

> 1 cup raw rice or 1 1/3 cups quick-cooking rice
> 1/4 teaspoon powdered Spanish saffron or 1/2 teaspoon dried saffron, steeped 1/2 hour in 1/2 cup warm water

Note: Genuine saffron is expensive and sometimes hard to find in groceries, though generally available in pharmacies.

Add rice and saffron to correct amount of water just before it reaches boiling point. If using dry saffron, strain into rice while it cooks. Serves 6.

Chicken Korma

> 2 small frying chickens, cut in serving pieces
> 1 cup buttermilk or yogurt
> 4 cloves garlic, crushed
> 1/3 cup butter or margarine
> 2 onions, finely chopped
> 1 1/2 teaspoons salt
> 1/2 teaspoon ground pepper
> 1 2-inch stick cinnamon
> 1/2 teaspoon ginger
> 2 whole cloves
> 1 tablespoon curry powder
> 2 teaspoons ground or finely chopped almonds
> 1 recipe RICE PILAU FOR KORMA

Wash and dry chicken pieces. Mix buttermilk with 2 cloves garlic; marinate chicken in buttermilk 2 hours at room temperature, turning occasionally. Melt butter or margarine in casserole or heavy saucepan, and cook onions and remaining garlic with salt, pepper, cinnamon, ginger and cloves 5 minutes, stirring frequently. Add curry powder and almonds and cook another 5 minutes. Add chicken and marinade; cover and simmer 1 1/2–2 hours or until chicken is tender. Discard whole spices. Add chicken mixture to rice, being careful not to break chicken pieces. Cover and let stand over low heat or in slow oven until flavors blend. Serves 6–8.

Note: Chicken Korma, one of the great dishes of the subcontinent, is served on national festival days by the Moslems and usually presented buffet-style in both India and Pakistan. A large serving dish or platter is set on brass or silver tray and surrounded with accompaniments; eggplant or okra fritters and bowls of such condiments as tart sauces, chutney and chopped fresh relishes.

Rice Pilau for Korma

> 1/2 cup butter or margarine
> 1 medium onion, finely chopped
>   (approximately 1/2 cup)
> 1 clove garlic, crushed
> 5 whole cloves
> 5 cardamom seeds
> 1 3-inch stick cinnamon, broken in half
> 1/2 teaspoon allspice
> 1 pound long-grain rice
> 1 teaspoon salt
> 1/3 teaspoon saffron, steeped in 1/3 cup warm water
> Boiling water
> 1/2 cup light raisins
> 1/2 cup dates, cut in strips
> 1/3 cup blanched almonds, sautéed in butter
>   or margarine
> 1/2 cup pistachio nuts, sautéed in butter or margarine

Melt butter or margarine, and sauté onion, garlic, whole spices and allspice 5 minutes; remove whole spices. Add rice, and stir over low heat 5 minutes or until golden. Add salt, saffron and sufficient water to cover rice by 2 inches. Cover tightly, and steam over heat about 25 minutes or until rice is tender and water is absorbed. Stir in raisins, dates and nuts. Serves 6–8.

FROM THE FAR PACIFIC

The "rijstafel" or rice table of Indonesia can be perfectly adapted to a special-occasion party, and the carefree "luau" from Hawaii has great possibilities too.

Indonesia. In the islands that comprise Indonesia the rijstafel is considered the most luxurious experience in leisurely feasting. Far back in history this "rice table" simply consisted of several side dishes added to the Javanese daily bowl of rice. But the tradition was expanded by the Dutch population into an elaborate repast involving as many as 30 special accompaniments, necessitating a troop of serving boys and a kitchen as well staffed as it was well stocked. The rice table thus emerged as the *chef-d'oeuvre* in exclusive clubs and hotel restaurants, and inevitably its secrets and subtleties were carried back to the Netherlands to become the featured daily event in the high-priced restaurants of Amsterdam.

Wherever you encounter rijstafel, you will find it surrounded with certain ceremony. A major-domo enters bearing the great bowl of steaming rice, followed by a queue of waiters, each with 1 or 2 accompaniments. Everyone at the table is served a generous mound of rice in an old-fashioned rimmed soup plate, and then the waiters, 1 by 1 proffer the side dishes. Each food is placed, with its sauces, on the bed of rice; according to the guest's preference, the individual pieces may be eaten separately or the whole pyramiding mass may be approached as one concoction. Rice table experts generally find that the second method is better, as the extremely hot seasonings have a chance to mingle with blander items and reduce the shock to the taste buds. Ice-cold beer provides some relief too.

Although it would hardly be possible to duplicate all the ingredients of the authentic rice table, the basic plan of the feast is workable in any part of the world.

Here is a simple menu of reasonable proportions. The Dutch spirit, schnapps, or a gimlet cocktail with light canapés might precede. Boiled rice, with each grain dry and separate, should be prepared in quantity and served very hot.

Rijstafel Chicken Dishes

These dishes include any or all of the following: curried chicken breasts with pineapple chunks; cubed chicken in coconut milk slightly thickened with arrowroot and powdered ginger; cubed chicken with green-pepper strips in gravy flavored with soy sauce; chicken livers braised with chopped skinned peanuts and flavored with orange rind.

Fish and Seafood Specialties

Fish and seafood dishes include shrimp sautéed with a little onion and garlic in peanut oil and served with fresh lime wedges; baked white fish seasoned with lemon juice and hot red chili peppers, and basted with melted butter or margarine and soy sauce; flaked boiled white fish in a rich sauce of coconut milk and heavy cream, flavored and colored with saffron.

Meat Selections

These dishes may run the full gamut. Raw lamb cubes, first marinated in vinegar and enlivened with ginger, garlic, cumin and ground chili pepper, are speared on skewers, brushed with peanut oil (or salad oil) and broiled until well browned. Ground cooked chicken and ham, moistened with thick sauce, are formed into tiny croquettes, dropped into raw egg and crumbs and fried. Strips of beefsteak are braised with spices and both sweet and hot peppers, then served as filling in thin rolled-up pancakes.

Indonesian Sambals

The sambal is basically a fiery pepper sauce made of butter, onion, peanut butter and milk (or coconut milk or both), the whole brought almost to "the point of danger" by the native "demon of sauce" known as "sambal oelik." In place of the last-mentioned, seldom obtainable here, use fresh or dried hot red peppers—but handle with discretion! Serve with 1 or more of the cooked dishes featured on the rice table; meats; hot hard-cooked eggs or freshly cooked vegetable mixtures like green beans with sliced celery, marrow with mushrooms, bean sprouts with water chestnuts.

Condiments

The range here too is limited only by the cook's imagination. Bananas sautéed in cinnamon butter and lightly dusted with sugar are frequently encountered. Fried onions, alone or with celery, are a good choice. A raw salad of shredded cabbage, chopped cucumber and sweet pepper offers welcome relief from hot spices. Chutneys, sliced ginger and hot roasted peanuts are almost always present as accompaniments.

Hawaii. Hawaii and the Polynesian Islands present a cuisine derived from such various sources as China, Japan, Portugal and the Philippines. The many fine restaurants catering to the tourist trade have expanded their basic French techniques to include these influences and add local tropical overtones.

Staple foodstuffs of the islands are taro (the starchy root of a large-leaved field plant), breadfruit, yams, bananas, pineapples, rice, fish and shellfish. Pork and chicken are the most popular meats. They are often served "Hawaiian style," which anywhere on the globe today implies the presence of pineapple. The great pineapple industry had its beginnings early in the nineteenth century with seeds left by Spanish sailors.

The best-known Hawaiian dining ritual is the luau, an institution not unlike the American clambake but featuring suckling pig, the festival choice in most of the South Pacific islands.

Luau Menu 1

Fruit punch
Assorted nuts: macadamia, and pili
Lomi-lomi   Poi
Kalua pig   Laulaus   Sweet potatoes
Baked bananas   Steamed shellfish
Chicken luau
Haupia   Pineapple   Watermelon

The punch can be mild, using tropical fruit juices, or it is sometimes the "scorpion" type made with rum and other spirits plus lemon and orange juices and served in bamboo cups or coconut shells with gardenias floating on top.

Lomi-lomi is an appetizer of thinly sliced raw fish soaked in fresh lime juice—a Japanese method of preparation. Poi is an authentic native item, but unsuited to many outsiders' tastes. *Kalua pig* is young pig cooked underground in an imu (bed of hot volcanic rocks, ashes and wet ti leaves). *Laulaus*, sweet potatoes, bananas in their skins, raw unpeeled shrimp and live lobster or crabs are arranged around pig, covered with more leaves and earth and left to steam for 4–5 hours. When done, the foods from the imu are unpacked, carved and cut in finger-sized portions and served on ti leaves or in large shallow wooden bowls. *Chicken luau* is a combination of fried chicken and taro leaves (similar to spinach) cooked in coconut milk. *Haupia* is a stiff blanc mange made with coconut milk, molded in a flat pan and cut in diamond shapes. The watermelon is served in strips or wedges.

The setting is out of doors. Broad green leaves are spread on the ground for the tablecloth or on long low tables, with nuts, fruits and flowers down the center. Individual wooden bowls or firm ti leaves are used for service, never china and glass. Cutlery is not used, as food is strictly to be eaten with fingers. Sometimes steaming perfumed towels are supplied at end of feast, more welcome than finger bowls. Entertainment and dancing carry on long after the feast is over.

For gourmets wishing to translate this tropical fun and feasting to American terms, it is possible to adapt the luau menu for either outdoor or indoor entertaining. Plenty of real or artificial greenery and all the flowers possible, including some to float on punch, will help create a tropical atmosphere.

Here is a suggested menu based on a typical luau but a little less demanding on the cook.

Luau Menu 2

Punch   Toasted coconut chips   Crisp relishes
TERIYAKI   Fried shrimp
Barbecued spareribs or chicken
LAULAUS MAINLAND STYLE
Baked sweet potatoes   CORN ON THE COB
Baked or fried bananas
PINEAPPLE LUAU   Watermelon fingers

Teriyaki

1 1/4 pounds beef sirloin cut 3/4 inch thick
1 (1 pound, 4 1/2 ounce) can pineapple chunks, drained
3/4 cup pineapple syrup from drained fruit
1/4 cup soy sauce
1 small clove garlic, crushed
3/4 teaspoon powdered ginger
20 stuffed olives

You will need 20 metal or wooden skewers 4 inches long. Cut beef in cubes about same size as pineapple chunks. Combine pineapple syrup, soy sauce, garlic and ginger. Pour over meat, and marinate 1 hour at room temperature. Alternate beef and pineapple on skewers, ending with 1 stuffed olive. Broil 3 inches from heat, turning once; allow about 10 minutes' cooking time altogether. Serve hot. Serves 6–8.

Note: This version of a Japanese-Hawaiian dish can be served as hot appetizers or as a main course.

For a main course, use regular kebab skewers. Heat marinade and thicken with 2 teaspoons of cornstarch blended with 2 teaspoons cold water. Serve in sauce dish as accompaniment for teriyaki on bed of hot FLUFFY RICE. Serves 4.

Laulaus Hawaiian Style

24–36 large spinach leaves
1 1/2 pounds fresh salmon
1 teaspoon salt
2 pounds lean pork
1 medium onion, finely chopped (approximately 1/2 cup)

Wash spinach leaves thoroughly in several changes of water, and dry. Place 2 or 3 in slightly overlapping arrangement on 12 6-inch aluminum foil squares. Cut salmon into 1 1/2-inch cubes; sprinkle with salt. Cut lean pork into 2-inch cubes. Place 2 or 3 pieces of fish and same amount of meat on each spinach serving. Sprinkle with chopped onion. Roll up spinach, wrap securely in foil package and tie with thread. Place in larger steamer or on trivet in Dutch oven. Keep plenty of water boiling in bottom of pot. Cover, and steam 2 1/2 hours. Remove thread from packages and place on serving tray. Serves 6.

Note: These steamed, leaf-wrapped packages can be made with a variety of savory fillings—meat, fish, vegetables, with seasonings. In place of Hawaii's giant taro greens, select largest leaves you can find in 2-pound bag of very fresh, green spinach.

For a shorter steaming period, make laulaus with precooked meats. Cubed cooked chicken and lightly fried diced salt pork are a good combination, requiring only 1 1/2 hours steaming in their spinach packages.

Laulaus Mainland Style

3 2-inch cubes lean raw pork
Salt and pepper to taste
Ground ginger to taste
6 pineapple chunks, drained
3 green pepper strips
1 green onion, sliced
1 small tomato

Sprinkle pork cubes with salt, pepper and ginger. Place meat, pineapple and vegetables on 12-inch aluminum foil square. Fold into package. Arrange packages as in single layer in baking pan. Bake at 350°F. 2 hours. Serves 1.

Note: If there is sufficient oven space, bake sweet potatoes and foil-wrapped ears of corn (completely husked and buttered) for last hour. Serve with tiny individual bowls of melted butter.

Pineapple Luau

1 fresh pineapple
Toothpicks

Cut thick slice from top and bottom of 1 fresh pineapple; set slices aside. With long thin-bladed knife cut out fruit in 1 solid cylinder and remove. Cut fruit in half lengthwise, and remove core; then cut in lengthwise spears. Fasten bottom slice to pineapple shell with toothpicks, and fill with prepared spears. Replace top to resemble whole pineapple.

ORIENTAL MEALS

For the crispest cooked vegetables, the most elegant tidbits of meats, fish, poultry, the salty tang of soy sauce, the blend of sweet and sour, follow the example of the Chinese and Japanese.

Chinese Cookery. Chinese cookery is basically thrifty, probably as much because of famine and other national disasters as of individual families' economic status. No doubt it was during times of stress that such unlikely items as bamboo shoots were first put to culinary use. Whatever the cause, Chinese cooks have learned to create literally countless dishes from all available edibles, each introduced in cautious quantities and brought to perfection with well-chosen seasonings. Monosodium glutamate, now widely sold in packaged form, has long been used in China.

Crisp tender vegetables, bright fresh colors and smooth clear sauces are characteristic. The vegetables require patient chopping, dicing, slicing or shredding, and the sauces require accurate timing. Chinese cooking has been described as "active"—dishes left to slumber undisturbed in oven or pots are extremely rare in this cusine. The stir-and-cook or "stir-fry" method, handed down over the centuries, is recognized everywhere today as one of the best ways to preserve valuable nutrients, plus distinctive food texture and color.

In an authentic Chinese dinner, the number of dishes often reaches a dozen or more—as many as 30 at a banquet. Appetizers like barbecued spareribs, egg rolls and fried shrimp are followed by various main dishes served at once along with the indispensable rice. Desserts are not important, and if served at all usually consist of fresh, candied or preserved fruits, possibly with special cookies. Bread with butter never appears on the table. Fragrant China tea is almost always present, to be sipped in its pale clear state toward end of meal.

Stir-Fry

This dish is a crisp mixture of many ingredients, each used in quite small quantity. The Chinese method of preparation is to group certain foods together beforehand and to cook each group separately before combining for serving. In this recipe 3 skillets are required. The numbered groupings are arranged in order of cooking.

GROUP 1

1 tablespoon salad oil
1/2 cup fresh green peas or 1/2 (10-ounce) package frozen peas, thawed
1 (5-ounce) can water chestnuts, drained and sliced
6 fresh mushrooms, sliced
2 stalks celery, sliced
1/4 teaspoon salt

Heat 1 tablespoon oil in skillet. Add peas, chestnuts, mushrooms and celery. Sprinkle with salt. Stir-fry 1 minute; then cover, and braise 3–4 minutes until peas are tender.

GROUP 2

1 tablespoon salad oil
1 clove garlic
2 slices raw ginger root or 1/2 teaspoon powdered ginger
1/2 pound lean ground ham
2 tablespoons soy sauce
2 tablespoons water
1 tablespoon dry sherry
1 teaspoon cornstarch
1/4 teaspoon pepper
1/2 teaspoon sugar

Heat oil in second skillet, and sauté garlic and ginger. Add meat, and stir-fry for 1–2 minutes. Blend soy sauce, water, sherry and cornstarch, and add to skillet with remaining ingredients. Bring to simmer, reduce heat, cover and braise several minutes.

GROUP 3

1 tablespoon salad oil
1/2 cup blanched almonds
1/2 head Chinese lettuce, coarsely chopped
1/4 teaspoon salt

Heat oil in third skillet, add almonds and sauté until lightly colored. Lift out nuts with slotted spoon. Add coarsely chopped lettuce, sprinkle with salt and braise in hot oil until just tender.

Serve Group 1 on bed of hot rice; cover with Group 2; surround with lettuce from Group 3, and sprinkle almonds from Group 3 over all. Serves 4.

Sweet-and-Sour Pork

    1/2 cup pineapple juice
    1/3 cup brown sugar
      3 tablespoons vinegar
  1 1/2 tablespoons cornstarch
      1 tablespoon water
      1 teaspoon salt
    1/2 cup flour
      2 eggs
    1/4 cup milk
    1/2 teaspoon milk
    1/2 teaspoon salt
      1 pound pork tenderloin, cut in 1-inch cubes
  Hot oil
    1/4 cup peanut or salad oil
      1 large green pepper, cut in 1-inch squares
      1 cup pineapple chunks
      1 clove garlic, finely chopped
      1 recipe SWEET-AND-SOUR SAUCE
      1 cup firm red tomatoes, cut in 1-inch pieces

Combine pineapple juice, sugar and vinegar in saucepan, and bring to boil. Cool a few minutes. Combine cornstarch with water and 1 teaspoon salt, and stir into warm mixture. Set aside until needed.

Beat flour, eggs, milk and 1/2 teaspoon salt together, to make batter. Dip meat cubes in batter, and fry in oil 1 inch deep preheated to 350°F. 5–8 minutes until golden brown. Heat 1/4 cup oil in large skillet. Add pork, green pepper, pineapple and garlic; cook together, stirring gently, 5 minutes. Add SWEET-AND-SOUR SAUCE, and blend. Cover pan, and cook over low heat until thickened, about 5 minutes. Fold in tomatoes, being careful not to crush; cook 3 minutes. Serves 3 generously.

Lobster–Almond Din

    1/2 cup green celery, cut in 1/2-inch slices
    1–2 teaspoons water
    1/4 cup peanut or salad oil
    1/2 pound fresh lobster meat, cooked
    1/2 cup sliced water chestnuts (1 5-ounce can)
    1/2 cup green pepper, cut in 1-inch squares
    1/2 cup (1 4-ounce can) button mushrooms, halved
      3 tablespoons canned pimento, cut in 1-inch squares
  1 1/2 teaspoons salt
    1/4 teaspoon pepper
    1/4 teaspoon garlic salt
    1/4 teaspoon monosodium glutamate
    1/2 cup chicken broth
      1 tablespoon cornstarch
     20 whole toasted almonds

Cook celery in water in covered pan 5 minutes. Heat oil in skillet; add lobster, chestnuts, green pepper, mushrooms, pimento and celery, and cook over medium heat 5 minutes, stirring constantly. Add seasonings and cook 2 minutes more. Blend chicken broth and cornstarch, and add to skillet. Cover, and cook 2 minutes more. Blend chicken broth and cornstarch, and add to skillet. Cover, and cook 5–6 minutes longer, stirring once or twice. If too thick, add more broth. Place in serving dish, and scatter almonds over top. Serves 3–4.

Note: If dish is to be only entree, recipe should be doubled.

Beef Strips with Green Pepper

      1 pound round steak
      2 tablespoons soy sauce
      1 tablespoon dry sherry
      1 clove garlic
    1/2 teaspoon sugar
  Small piece ginger root
      3 medium tomatoes
      2 green peppers
      3 tablespoons salad oil
      2 teaspoons cornstarch
      2 tablespoons water or stock

Cut meat into 2-inch cubes, then slice very thin for quick cooking. Place in bowl, add next 5 ingredients and let stand 1/2 hour. Quarter tomatoes. Remove stems, seeds and white membranes from peppers, cut into 1 1/2-inch squares. Start cooking about 10 minutes before serving. Heat oil in skillet over strong heat. After discarding garlic, turn in contents of marinating bowl, and be prepared for mixture to sputter. Stir-fry vigorously as meat strips brown. After about 5 minutes add tomatoes and peppers. Continue to stir-fry over strong heat only 2 minutes, to keep color and texture of vegetables. Blend cornstarch smoothly with water, and add to skillet, stir as it thickens. Turn contents of skillet over hot rice on serving dish. Serves 4.

Chinese Fried Rice

    1/2 cup butter or margarine
      3 eggs, slightly beaten
      3 cups cooked rice
  1 1/2 cups cooked diced chicken, pork, ham or shrimp
      1 can (1 pound) bean sprouts, drained
    1/2 cup (1 4-ounce can) sliced mushrooms, drained
    1/4 cup green onions, cut fine
      2 tablespoons soy sauce
  Salt and pepper to taste

Melt butter or margarine in large skillet. Add eggs, and cook until firm but not hard, stirring with fork. Add rice, and cook 5 minutes, stirring constantly. Add remaining ingredients, and cook 10 minutes; if mixture seems dry add 2 tablespoons butter or margarine. Serve in bowl, or pack in warm buttered mold, and turn out on platter. Serves 6–8.

Fry cooked rice in butter or oil first, stirring to smooth out lumps; then add vegetables and meat. When thoroughly heated, push contents of pan back to leave hollow in center; scramble eggs in hollow, as soon as they begin to set, stir all ingredients together to incorporate. Add seasonings, and serve.

Hong Kong Meatballs

    1 pound boneless fresh pork (leg slices, or shoulder
        chops), including a little fat
    4 or 5 water chestnuts
    4 medium mushrooms
    1/2 cup cooked crabmeat
    1/2 teaspoon sugar
    Salt and pepper to taste
    Few drops lemon juice
    1/4 cup fine cornmeal
    2 eggs, lightly beaten
    Peanut oil or salad oil

Cube pork. Drain water chestnuts. Wash mushrooms. If canned crabmeat is used, drain thoroughly, and pick over for any bits of shell. Put pork, chestnuts, mushrooms and crabmeat through grinder twice, using medium blade. Sprinkle with sugar, salt, pepper and lemon juice. Shape with teaspoon and fingers into firm balls about 1 1/2 inches in diameter. Roll balls in cornmeal, then in eggs and again in cornmeal. Have ready saucepan containing simmering oil to depth of 2 inches. Cook balls 15 minutes. Lift out with slotted spoon; keep in warm oven until all are cooked. Serve on platter with hot fluffy rice, hot bean sprouts and garnish of parsley and small tomatoes, halved. Accompany with soy sauce. Serves 4.

From the Japanese. Japanese cuisine is very similar to Chinese but more restricted in variety of foodstuffs. Fish, rice, plenty of vegetables, nuts and fruits are basic fare, along with such popular Oriental seasonings as Shoyu (soy) sauce, ajinomoto (monosodium glutamate), shiitake (dried mushrooms) and sesame-seed oil, which imparts both distinctive flavor and richness to many cooked dishes. It has been said that Japanese food is prepared as much for eye appeal as for taste.

Sukiyaki

    1 (10-ounce) can beef bouillon
    1/3 cup soy sauce
    1/4 cup dry sherry
    1/4 cup brown sugar
    Pinch of powdered ginger
    1 1/2 pounds top round or beef sirloin sliced 1/8 inch thick
    3 onions, thinly sliced
    1 cup thinly sliced large mushrooms
    1 cup shredded spinach
    1 cup celery, sliced thin diagonally
    1 cup sliced canned bamboo shoots, drained
    1 green pepper, cut in thin strips
        (approximately 1/2 cup)
    4 green onions, sliced (approximately 1/4 cup)
    1/3 cup oil

Combine beef bouillon, soy sauce, sherry, sugar and ginger; marinate beef in this mixture for about 2 hours. Arrange prepared vegetables artistically in separate dishes on tray. Drain meat, and reserve marinade. Take everything to table to be cooked. Put 2 tablespoons oil in skillet, add 1/3 the meat slices and brown on both sides. Add 1/3 the vegetables, and cook briefly 3 minutes. Add 1/3 the marinade, and simmer, covered, 5 minutes. Serve immediately, accompanied by hot boiled rice, to 2 of your hungry guests. Repeat procedure twice. Serves 6.

Note: Sukiyaki is considered a "foreigners' dish," and restaurants specialize in cooking it at table on brazier or in chafing dish. An electric frying pan or skillet on good-sized hibachi would be ideal for home use in our country. For more than 6 servings, prepare enough extra ingredients, use second electric frying pan and get help.

Shrimp Tempura

    2 pounds large uncooked shrimp with tails
    1 cup all-purpose flour
    1/2 teaspoon salt
    2 eggs
    1 cup water
    Oil

Wash and peel shrimp without removing tails, slit down each back, remove black vein but do not separate halves. If shrimp are quite large, flatten halves butterfly fashion. Pat dry. Sift together flour and salt; beat in eggs and water to make smooth batter. Add more water if mixture seems thick. Dip shrimp by tails into batter, coating thoroughly. Fry in deep hot oil (360°F.) until golden brown, 3–5 minutes. Drain on absorbent paper and serve hot with TEMPURA SAUCE and boiled rice. Serves 4.

Tempura Sauce

    1 cup beef bouillon
    1/4 cup soy sauce
    2 tablespoons sherry
    1 tablespoon sugar
    1/4 teaspoon powdered ginger
    1/4 teaspoon monosodium glutamate

Mix all ingredients in saucepan, bring to boil and keep hot until needed. Pour into 4 individual sauce dishes as dip for each person's shrimp.

Japanese Broiled Chicken

            2 small tender broiling chickens
        1/4 cup soy sauce
        1/4 cup sherry
            2 tablespoons horseradish
            2 tablespoons chopped onion
            1 tablespoon sugar
            1 tablespoon powdered ginger

Split broilers. Combine soy sauce, sherry, horseradish, onion, sugar and ginger. Marinate chicken in mixture 1 hour. Broil chicken, basting with marinade. Serves 4.

MEXICO'S SPICY THEME

Until the conquest of Mexico by Cortes and his Spaniards, Europeans had had no knowledge of tomatoes, pineapples, avocados, peanuts, turkeys, cacao beans, sweet potatoes and various other subtropical foodstuffs. The seed, slips and turkey chicks that the conquistadores brought back to Spain were to contribute to an important expansion in diet, first at the royal court, then among a wider public. At the same time, the native tribes of Mexico were receiving education in Spanish cookery through the missionaries and learning to grow and use such transplanted material as livestock, rice, figs, oranges, dates and olives. Today, a typical Mexican menu draws its colorful features from both native and Spanish traditions.

The "corn cuisine" of the country is in itself an almost never-ending study for outsiders.

Tortillas, the native bread for centuries, are extremely thin, round pancakes made of cornmeal and water. They are next to impossible to learn to make, unless, as the smiling Mexicans declare, you start at the age of 5. But they can be bought in quantity from Mexican restaurants and in cans. The basic *tortilla*, rolled or folded and frequently deep-fried, becomes an enchilada when served with hearty, spicy filling; a taco, somewhat similar to an enchilada, but less substantial; a tostado or toasted tortilla or any of a dozen other variants according to region.

Tamales are made with a dough of fine cornmeal and shortening, which is spread on washed and softened cornhusks, then topped with thick, spicy tomato sauce. Husks are folded to enclose contents, tied, steamed, then stripped back for serving. The baked tamale pie is constructed of 2 thicknesses of cornmeal mush with meat-sauce filling.

Frijoles are beans—white, brown, red, purple, black—which accompany virtually every hot meal, either cooked to delicious thick consistency or "refried."

Guacamole (Mexican Avocado Dip)

            1 large ripe tomato, peeled
            2 large avocados, peeled and seeded
            1 tablespoon lemon or lime juice
            1 teaspoon grated onion
        3/4 teaspoon salt
        3/4 teaspoon chili powder

Chop tomato very fine in wooden bowl; add pulp from avocado, and mash with silver fork or wooden spoon. Blend in remaining ingredients; mix thoroughly.

As a dip, serve in bowl surrounded with crisp crackers or raw vegetables. For salad dressing, increase lemon juice to 3 tablespoons, and omit chili powder. If made some time before using, spread thin layer of mayonnaise over top of mixture to prevent discoloration (a tendency of peeled avocado).

Mole de Guajalote (Turkey Mole)

            8-pound turkey, cut into serving pieces
            2 quarts (approximately) water
            1 tablespoon salt
        1/2 cup olive oil
        1/3 cup toasted almonds
        1/3 cup raisins
            1 slice toasted dry bread
            2 tablespoons sesame seeds
            1 (1-ounce) square unsweetened chocolate
            2 green peppers, chopped (approximately 1 cup)
            1 small onion, finely chopped
                (approximately 1/4 cup)
            1 clove garlic, chopped
        2–4 tablespoons chili powder
            1 teaspoon cinnamon
            3 cups turkey broth
            2 cups tomato sauce
        Salt and pepper to taste

Simmer turkey pieces in water to cover until almost tender, adding 1 tablespoon salt at midway point. Remove pieces from broth. Reduce broth to 3 cups. Set aside. Dry turkey pieces, brown on all sides in 1/4 cup hot oil in skillet, and place in large casserole or Dutch oven. Grind together almonds, raisins, bread, sesame seeds and chocolate. Heat remaining 1/4 cup oil; add peppers, onion and garlic; cook stirring constantly, about 5 minutes. Add ground mixture, plus chili powder and cinnamon. Stir, and cook until smooth. Stir in turkey broth and tomato sauce; cook over low heat 5 minutes. Add extra salt and pepper to taste. Pour sauce over browned turkey pieces in casserole; cover tightly, and cook at low temperature until meat is perfectly tender in 350°F. oven 1–1 1/2 hours. Stir sauce occasionally. Remove turkey to hot platter. If sauce seems thin, cook down until of desired consistency. Serve in sauceboat; accompany turkey platter with hot rice. Serves 5–6.

Buñuelos (Dessert Pancakes)

        3 cups all-purpose flour
        1 tablespoon sugar
        1 teaspoon baking powder
        1 teaspoon salt
        4 eggs
        1 cup milk
        1/4 cup butter or margarine, melted
        1/4 cup cold water
        Mild salad oil or shortening for deep frying
        Sugar and cinnamon or honey

Sift dry ingredients together in bowl. Break eggs into mixture, and add milk and butter or margarine. Beat with rotary beater, adding few drops water at a time—just enough to make dough that can be easily kneaded. Turn onto floured board, and knead 8 times. Cut dough, and shape into uniform small balls the size of walnuts. Cover with cloth, and let stand 20 minutes. Roll out each ball into very thin round pancake; let stand another 5 minutes while heating oil to good cooking depth in saucepan or skillet. When fat reaches point at which stale bread cube will fry golden brown in 60 seconds, it is right for buñuelos. Cook a few at a time; when golden, drain on absorbent paper, and keep warm. Serve sprinkled with mixture of sugar and cinnamon or with honey. Serves 6.

Note: For a late evening snack, accompany buñuelos with hot chocolate.

Basic Chili Sauce

        1/2 cup salad oil
        1 large onion, chopped
            (approximately 3/4 cup)
        2 cloves garlic, crushed
        1/2 cup all-purpose flour
        5 cups hot beef stock
        2 cups (1 pound, 4 ounce can) sieved
            tomatoes
        1/4 – 1/2 cup chili powder
        1/4 cup cold water
        Salt and pepper to taste
        Few grains cayenne

Heat salad oil in heavy pan, and gently sauté onion and garlic until soft and slightly colored. Blend in flour, and stir until mixture is smooth and bubbling. Combine hot stock with tomatoes;

add to first mixture, and stir constantly until thick. Blend chili powder to smooth paste with cold water. Add to simmering sauce, stirring thoroughly to combine. Continue simmering 1/2 hour; put through sieve. Add salt, pepper and cayenne. Makes 1 quart.

Note: Sauce should be cooled completely before covering and storing in refrigerator. Reheat with diced cooked chicken or other meats, using amount of sauce to taste.

Beef Chili

        1 cup or more BASIC CHILI SAUCE
        1/2 pound ground beef
        1 tablespoon fat

Sauté beef in fat. Add sauce to beef in skillet, simmer 10 minutes. Serve over hot unsweetened cornbread, tortillas or other pancakes. Serves 4.

Note: Extend beef and sauce with 1 cup fine stale bread crumbs; fill 4 large green pepper shells, and bake in oiled pan in medium hot oven.

CANADIAN TRADITIONS

Canada is today a mosaic of many ethnic ways. Some of the country's liveliest culinary traditions have been handed down virtually unchanged by generations of French Canadians. Food patterns have also been influenced by the immigration from the British Isles, Europe and the United States.

Pâté de Nöel

        1 7–8 pound turkey
        1 3-pound roasting chicken
    1 1/2–2 pounds veal knuckle
        3 quarts (12 cups) cold water
        4 teaspoons salt
        1 sliced onion
        1 stalk celery, sliced
        1 bay leaf
        1 sliced carrot
    Few peppercorns
        2 cloves
        1/8 teaspoon thyme
        1 1/2 pounds ground pork
        1/2 cup cognac
    PLAIN PASTRY for 2 double-crust pies
        1 tablespoon salt
        1/2 teaspoon pepper
        1/4 pound mushrooms, sliced
            (approximately 1 1/4 cups)
        1 recipe FLAKY PASTRY FOR PATE
        1 egg white, unbeaten
        1 egg yolk, slightly beaten, plus 2 teaspoons water

Skin turkey and chicken, reserve skin. Cut meat from bones in large pieces, 1/2 inch thick. Remove fat, gristle and tendons, reserving. Slice meat from veal knuckle into similar-sized pieces. Refrigerate sliced meats. Pile bones, skin and trimmings in preserving kettle; add cold water and next 8 ingredients. Bring gently to boiling point, and skim off foamy scum that will appear. Cover, turn heat low and simmer 3–4 hours. Drain broth into bowl; then return broth to pan alone, and continue simmering, uncovered, until reduced to 4 cups. Meanwhile pick over bones, and save any cooked meat bits. Strain reduced broth through cheesecloth, and cool to room temperature. Blend ground pork with cognac and 1/2 cup broth.

Roll plain pastry about 3/16 inch thick. Line 3-quart oblong, round or oval pan, preferably about 4 inches deep, loose-bottomed pan is ideal if you wish to remove finished pie to platter for serving. Sprinkle raw sliced meats with one tablespoon salt and pepper. Fill pastry-lined pan to top with alternate layers of dark meat, light meat, ground pork mixture and mushrooms. Roll flaky pastry 3/16 inch thick, and cover pie. Trim and seal pastry edges with egg white. Cut 2- or 3 1/2-inch openings in center of pastry lid. Cut out pastry leaves or triangles and arrange over vents; you can also braid strips of flaky pastry to decorate edge. Brush whole top with egg yolk. Bake pie in preheated 400°F. oven 1 1/2 hours; reduce heat to 350°F., and bake 3 1/2 hours. Cool pâté to room temperature, and lift off pastry leaves. Using funnel, pour reduced broth through pastry slits until pie is well filled. Tip pan several times as you pour, so that all spaces between meats are filled. Refrigerate overnight, and serve cold. Serves 30.

Note: French Canada's famous Christmas pie, made with turkey, chicken, and various seasonings, can be served all through Christmas week. It's always served cold, its thick slices encased in firm natural jelly of the meat broth. The pie is completely in pastry—plain for bottom and sides, especially flaky for top. It may be served on platter or left in oven-glass casserole or other suitable bake-and-serve dish.

Flaky Pastry for Pâté

        3 cups sifted all-purpose flour
    1 1/2 teaspoons salt
    1/3 cup soft shortening
    3/4 cup hard shortening (lard, cold butter or margarine)
        1 egg yolk, beaten
    1/2 cup ice-cold water
        2 teaspoons lemon juice

Sift flour and salt into bowl; rub in soft shortening until texture is very fine. Cut hard shortening into 1-inch cubes, and cut into flour with pastry blender to distribute evenly throughout. Combine egg yolk, water and lemon juice, and sprinkle over mixture. Stir with fork until crumbs cling together. Form ball, and chill 30 minutes. Roll out 1/2 inch thick on floured board in rectangle twice as long as wide. Fold in 3; give dough 1/2 turn, and roll out again 1/2 inch thick. Repeat once more, and wrap in waxed paper. Refrigerate 20 minutes. Roll and chill 3 more times; then refrigerate until needed for PATE DE NOEL.

Casserole of Atlantic Shellfish

        2 cups fresh or frozen scallops, thawed
    1 1/2 cups boiling salted water
        2 chicken bouillon cubes
        2 cups fresh or (thawed) frozen oysters, with liquor
    1 1/2 cups shrimp, shelled and deveined
    1 1/2 cups lobster meat, cut in bite-size pieces, or 1 1/2 cups crabmeat
    1/2 cup butter or margarine
    1 1/2 cups sliced fresh mushrooms
    1/4 cup finely chopped onion
    1/4 cup diced pimento
    1/4 cup diced green pepper
    1/2 cup flour
    2 1/2 cups fish broth and milk combined
        1 cup light cream
        1 teaspoon barbecue sauce
    1/2 teaspoon mustard
Salt and pepper to taste

Quarter scallops, and simmer in boiling salted water 5 minutes. Remove scallops. Add bouillon cubes to scallop stock, and dissolve. Heat oysters in their own liquor just until edges curl. Strain oyster liquor into stock. In a large bowl toss together scallops, oysters, shrimp and lobster meat. Set aside. Melt butter or margarine and sauté mushrooms 5 minutes. Add onion, pimento and green pepper to mushrooms and cook 5 minutes longer, stirring constantly. Sprinkle flour over vegetables, and blend. Add fish broth-milk mixture and cream and flour in pan, stirring until mixture is smooth and bubbling. Add barbecue sauce and mustard. Season with salt and pepper to taste. Ladle 1/4 the sauce into buttered 2 1/2-quart casserole, and arrange seafood and sauce in layers, ending with sauce. Bake in preheated 300°F. oven 45 minutes or until bubbling. Serves 8–10.

Note: The casserole can be made in advance, refrigerated, and heated in buttered individual ramekins or scallop shells, allowing 15–20 minutes in a 375°F. oven. Buttered soft bread crumbs and grated Parmesan cheese make a nice topping.

Roast Brome Lake Ducklings

        2 4–5 pound ducklings
        2 teaspoons salt

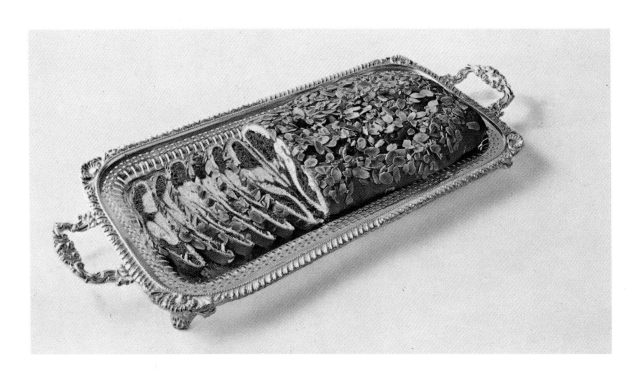

Stollen. *Credit: Henry Sandbank.*

Panettone. *Credit: Henry Sandbank.*

A French Table.
Credit: Henry Sandbank.

Cheese and Fruit Platter.
Credit: Henry Sandbank.

Onion Soup topped with
bread slices and cheese.
Credit: Henry Sandbank.

An Oriental Table. *Credit: Henry Sandbank.*

An Indian Table. *Credit: Henry Sandbank.*

Sweet and Pungent Pork.
Credit: Henry Sandbank.

Curried Shrimp.
Credit: Henry Sandbank.

Onion Bread, Dill Bread, Garlic Puffs, Saint's Loaf. *Credit: Faulconer/Fenn.*

Crown Roast of Lamb. *Credit: Elbert Budin.*

Roast Tenderloin of Beef. *Credit: Bernard Gray.*

A table for an outdoor party, featuring a main course of Lamb Kebab. *Credit: Bernard Gray.*

Daisies and balloons are everywhere at this children's birthday party setting. *Credit: Henry Sandbank.*

Cruller and Candy Apple. *Credit: Bernard Gray.*

An elegant buffet table arrangement. *Credit: Henry Sandbank.*

Croquembouche. *Credit: Bernard Gray.*

Paris-Brest Dessert. *Credit: Bernard Gray.*

Tea Sandwiches (in a long loaf of scooped-out French bread), Frosted Grapes, Fruit Tartlets, Petits Fours. *Credit: Arthur Beck.*

Crème Caramel. *Credit: Richard Litwin.*

A fruit and cheese tray. *Credit: Bernard Gray.*

Six-Layer Mocha Cake. *Credit: Bernard Gray.*

Seafood Cocktail. *Credit: Bernard Gray.*

Crescent Rolls. *Credit: Bernard Gray.*

A Buffet, including Seafood Cocktail and Boeuf en Gelée. *Credit: Bernard Gray.*

1/4 teaspoon pepper
2 large onions, chopped
    (approximately 1 1/2 cups)
2 apples, cored and chopped
    (approximately 1 cup)
2 stalks celery, thinly sliced
    (approximately 1/2 cup)
1/4 cup chopped parsley
1 cup apple cider or apple juice
1/4 cup butter or margarine
1/4 cup brandy
2 tablespoons flour

Scrub birds thoroughly, inside and out. Pat as dry as possible. Mix salt and pepper, and use 1/2 to rub cavities. Combine onions, apples, celery and parsley; divide mixture evenly, and stuff birds. Skewer, truss and rub skins with remaining salt and pepper. Place on rack in open roasting pan, and prick breasts. Bake in 325°F. oven, allowing 20 minutes per pound. At end of first 30 minutes, remove accumulated fat from pan. Repeat in another 30 minutes. In the meantime, heat apple cider and butter or margarine; add brandy. Baste birds with this mixture, and continue to baste at 10-minute intervals until end of roasting period. Remove ducks, and keep warm. Skim off all fat, reserving 2 tablespoons, measure pan juices and add water or cider to make 1 1/2 cups. Combine 2 tablespoons duck fat with flour, and blend into hot pan juices, stirring briskly. Cook until boiling and thickened. Adjust seasonings, and serve very hot. Serve with roast ducks, surrounded with glazed or FRIED APPLE RINGS and parsley. Serves 6–8.

Note: Fine-flavored ducklings are raised in Brome County, Quebec. The recipe could be used for any tender young duck.

Wild Rice and Chicken Livers

1 cup wild rice
3 cups boiling water
1/2 teaspoon salt
1/4 teaspoon pepper
1/4 teaspoon thyme
1/4 cup butter or margarine
1/2 cup chopped onion
1 pound chicken livers, chopped
2 tablespoons chopped parsley
2 tablespoons butter or margarine

Wash rice thoroughly and soak in cold water 30 minutes. Drain; add boiling water and seasonings. Cover, and simmer 40–45 minutes until rice is tender. Stir frequently, and add extra water if necessary. Melt 1/4 cup butter or margarine, sauté onion until golden, add chicken livers and cook, stirring gently, 5 minutes. Place cooked rice in buttered 1 1/2-quart casserole. Add onions, livers and any pan juices. Add parsley,

and combine thoroughly. Season to taste. Dot with 2 tablespoons butter or margarine, and bake in preheated oven (350°F.) 20 minutes. Serve from casserole as main dish or as side dish with poultry or game. Serves 4–6.

Note: Wild rice is very expensive. An excellent substitute is a packaged mixture of long grain and wild rice.

VARIATION:

Wild Rice and Mushrooms

Omit chicken livers, and substitute 3/4 pound sliced fresh mushrooms and 2 tablespoons chopped green pepper.

Maple Meringue Tarts

2 tablespoons butter or margarine
1/4 cup flour
1/4 cup sugar
2 egg yolks
1 cup maple syrup
1/2 cup cold water
1/2 cup seedless raisins
12 medium tart shells, baked in 3″ muffin pans
2 egg whites
1/4 cup sugar
1/4 cup chopped pecans

In saucepan cream butter or margarine; add flour and 1/4 cup sugar, and blend thoroughly. Beat in egg yolks, combine maple syrup and water, and gradually stir into pan. Cook over medium heat, stirring constantly until mixture comes to boil and is thickened. Remove from heat, and stir in raisins. Cool to lukewarm, stirring once or twice. Divide filling evenly among tart shells, leaving plenty of space at top for meringue. Preheat oven to 375°F. Beat egg whites to soft peaks, gradually add sugar and beat until stiff. Pile on top of maple filling, and spread to edge of crust; or swirl on, using pastry bag and tube. Sprinkle with chopped pecans. Brown in 375°F. oven, 10 minutes or until meringue is lightly browned. Serves 12.

Note: The ritual of "sugaring off" goes back to pioneer days, when maple syrup and honey were the only sweeteners generally available and annual syrup making was an important project and social event. Even today, with modern equipment, the process of producing 1 gallon of maple syrup from 30–40 gallons of sap involves a great deal of work and expense. Ontario, Quebec and New Brunswick produce excellent syrup, with Quebec producing the greatest volume. A dish of maple syrup served with fresh hot tea biscuits is the traditional way to enjoy its unique flavor. With PANCAKES, WAFFLES, FRENCH TOAST or CORN BREAD, maple syrup is the perfect sauce. There are also many fine recipes featuring maple syrup. For best results use the proportions of syrup specified; do not expect full results with substitute flavorings, plain brown sugar and the like.

Fresh Blueberry Roll

Note: Here is a luscious, rich dessert. Serve it freshly baked and warm, with a brown sugar or lemon sauce.

        1/2 cup soft butter or margarine
      1 1/2 cups brown sugar
          2 cups all-purpose flour
          4 teaspoons baking powder
        1/2 teaspoon salt
        1/3 cup shortening
        3/4 cup milk
          2 cups fresh blueberries

Cream butter or margarine and sugar until fluffy. Set aside. Sift flour, baking powder and salt together. Cut in shortening finely. Add milk, and stir with fork to make soft dough. Turn on to floured board, and knead gently 8–10 times. Roll out in rectangle, 9″ x 12″ and about 1/4 inch thick. Spread surface with creamed butter or margarine and sugar. Place berries on top to within 1/2 inch of edge. Roll up as with jelly roll, starting from longer side. Dampen edges, and seal. Cut roll into uniform slices, and place, cut side down, in well-greased baking dish. Bake at 375°F. 15–20 minutes. Serves 8.

REGIONAL COOKING IN THE UNITED STATES

There's ample gourmet potential in the distinctive cookery of New Orleans and the Atlantic seaboard states, as well as in the later creations of the Southwest and California.

American foods in the beginning were whatever the early settlers could find to keep themselves alive: fish, game, corn, wild fruits and roots. All were prepared as far as possible in the established ways known "at home," which could, according to the individual family or community, mean England, Holland, France or Spain. Eventually the precious seeds and cuttings brought from fields and gardens of Europe bore their harvests, and dining took on a more expansive atmosphere compounded of both Old and New World influences. With each wave of immigration and each new frontier opened, this pattern continued, region by region, and it was not until the mid-nineteenth century's great surge forward with farm production, manufacturing and transportation that these diverse food customs began to intermingle and develop along lines that were recognizably "American."

New Orleans. The creole cookery of New Orleans is quite unlike any other cuisine in the United States or elsewhere. French, Spanish and other European culinary arts have intermingled and come to perfection through the cooking genius of the Negro. The first French settlers learned from the Indians the use of filé (powdered sassafras) as a thickener for sauces. Boatloads of African slaves brought with them the plant known as "kingombo" or "okra," which was added to Louisiana stews, turning them into gumbos. Later filé was used to thicken gumbos, and some versions now specify only filé.

When this extravagant, fun-loving colony was ceded to Spain in a cousinly gesture by the French king, the Spanish influence emerged through the addition of olive oil, rice, paprika, garlic and hot chili peppers to the already colorful menus. By the time Louisiana became part of the United States, the distinctive character of the area, with its almost legendary plantation life, tracts of sugar cane, riverboats and the closely laid-out city behind the levees, had been set.

New Orleans' famous restaurants of today have retained the elegant and traditional dishes of creole cookery, much to the delight of gourmets. Here are several typical recipes.

Creole Gumbo

          3 tablespoons bacon fat or oil
          4-pound frying chicken, cut in serving pieces
        1/2 pound lean ham, diced
          2 cups sliced fresh okra or 2 (10-ounce) packages
            okra, thawed
          1 large onion, chopped (approximately 3/4 cup)
          2 cups peeled chopped tomatoes or 2 cups drained
            canned tomatoes (1 pound, 13 ounce can)
        1/4 teaspoon thyme
          3 drops hot pepper sauce
          8 cups water
    Liquor from 1 pint oysters
        1/3 cup chopped parsley
    Salt and pepper
      1 1/2 tablespoons filé powder
          1 pint oysters

Heat bacon in soup kettle; sauté chicken and ham until lightly browned. Remove meat from kettle. Add okra and onion to pan, with additional fat if necessary, and sauté until okra has ceased to "string." Add tomatoes, thyme, and pepper sauce and return chicken and ham to kettle. Add water and oyster liquor, bring just to boil, cover and reduce heat. Simmer 30 minutes. Add parsley, salt and pepper, cook over low heat 10 minutes or until chicken is tender. Remove from heat, and stir in filé powder and oysters. *Do not reheat.* Accompany with hot rice. Serves 4.

Note: Okra contains a gummy substance that "strings" when cooking, but it eventually disappears and need not cause concern. If filé powder is not available, thicken gumbo with 2 tablespoons flour added to fat in pan after onions and okra have been sautéed.

New Orleans Oyster Loaf

    1 large French or 3 small French loaves or 6 individual
        crusty rolls
    1 clove garlic
    1/4 cup butter or margarine, melted
    3 dozen oysters and liquor
    Salt and pepper to taste
    Dash hot pepper sauce

Split loaf lengthwise but not quite through. Scoop out soft center, leaving crusty shell 1 inch thick. Tear soft bread into coarse crumbs with fork, and set aside. Rub insides of shells with garlic, and brush inside and out with 2 tablespoons melted butter or margarine. Drain oysters, reserving liquor; sauté oysters in remaining butter or margarine just until edges curl, about 5 minutes. Fill loaf with oysters. Combine 1/2 crumbs with 1/2 cup oyster liquor, and use to complete filling. Sprinkle with salt, pepper, hot pepper sauce. Wrap loaf in moistened cheesecloth (use milk if desired), twisting ends tightly and folding under bread. Bake on sheet in preheated 350°F. oven 30 minutes. Unwrap to serve. Slice large loaf, halve small loaves. Serves 6.

Note: Popular for 2 centuries in the night-life city, this specialty was known as "la médiatrice" (The Peacemaker). A husband returning home in the early hours of the morning would buy one at the cafe and proffer it, piping hot, to pacify his angry wife.

Jambalaya

    2 tablespoons butter or margarine
    1/2 pound garlic sausage, thinly sliced
    1/2 pound cooked ham, diced
    2/3 cup chopped onion
    2/3 cup chopped green pepper
1 1/2 cups long-grain or converted rice
    1 cup diced peeled tomatoes or 1 cup drained canned
        tomatoes (1 pound, 4 ounce can)
    1 teaspoon salt
    1/4 teaspoon thyme
    1 bay leaf, crushed
    2 cups chicken or fish stock
    2 cups cooked shrimp, deveined
    1/4 cup chopped parsley (optional)
    Salt and pepper to taste

Melt butter or margarine in a good-sized saucepan. Add sausage, and cook until lightly browned; remove from pan. Add ham, and cook about 5 minutes, stirring constantly; push to one side. Add onion, and green pepper, and cook until soft. Add rice, and stir until well coated with fat. Add tomatoes, 1 teaspoon salt, herbs, and stock. Bring just to boil, lower heat and simmer gently 20–30 minutes or until all liquid is absorbed and rice is tender. Add cooked shrimp and parsley. Combine gently with rice or scatter over top. Add extra salt and pepper to taste. Cover, and reheat over hot water or in slow oven 10–15 minutes. Serves 4–6.

Note: Jambalaya is a rice dish that reflects the Spanish influence on New Orleans cooking. It is much like PAELLA of Spain, and there are many versions, using a variety of meats, poultry and fish. The original jambalaya used ham ("jambon") from which it gets its name.

The Southern States. *Abundant seafood from the coastal waters has inspired many wonderful dishes, especially those using the hard and soft-shelled crabs.*

Deviled Crabs

    1 pound cooked crabmeat
    3 tablespoons butter or margarine
    2 tablespoons chopped onion
    2 tablespoons flour
    1 teaspoon dry mustard
    1/2 teaspoon salt
    1/2 teaspoon sage
    1/8 teaspoon cayenne
    1 cup milk
    1 tablespoon lemon juice
    1 tablespoon barbecue sauce
    1 egg, beaten
    1 tablespoon chopped parsley
    1/2 cup soft bread crumbs
    2 tablespoons melted butter or margarine

Remove cartilage from crabmeat, Melt butter or margarine, and sauté onion until tender. Blend in flour and seasonings. Add milk gradually, and cook until thick, stirring constantly. Add lemon juice and barbecue sauce. Blend a little hot sauce into beaten egg; return all to saucepan, mix well and add crabmeat and parsley. Fill 6 cleaned crab shells or buttered ramekins. Mix bread crumbs with melted butter or margarine and sprinkle tops. Bake in 375°F. oven 15 minutes or until lightly browned. Serves 6.

Country Captain

```
1/4 cup flour
Salt and pepper to taste
  3–4 pound roasting or frying chicken, cut in serving
        pieces
  1/2 cup (approximately) shortening
    2 onions, finely chopped (approximately 1 cup)
    2 medium green peppers, chopped
        (approximately 1 cup)
    1 small clove garlic, crushed
    3 cups canned tomatoes
    1 tablespoon chopped parsley
  2–3 teaspoons curry powder
1 1/2 teaspoons salt
  1/2 teaspoon pepper
  1/2 teaspoon powdered thyme
Medium-dry white wine or water or combination of both
    2 cups hot cooked rice
  1/4 cup dry currants, soaked
    1 cup whole blanched almonds, toasted
Parsley sprigs
```

Combine flour and salt and pepper to taste. Roll chicken pieces in mixture. Melt shortening in frying pan; brown chicken on all sides, and remove to casserole or roasting pan equipped with tight lid. Add onions, green peppers and garlic to hot fat (if too brown, discard and melt fresh shortening); cook slowly for 5 minutes, stirring constantly. Add tomatoes, parsley, spices and seasonings. When hot, pour over chicken; add wine to bring liquid not quite to top of chicken pieces. Cover casserole, and bake at 350°F. 45 minutes or until chicken is tender. Place chicken in center of hot platter, and arrange circle of hot rice around it. Add currants to sauce in casserole, and heat to boiling; pour sauce over rice. Scatter almonds on top, and garnish with parsley sprigs. Serves 4.

Syllabub

```
4 cups heavy cream
2 cups milk
2/3 cup bourbon or rye whiskey
1/2 cup sugar
```

Use big deep bowl; otherwise foam will spill out. Combine ingredients. Beat with rotary beater until mixture is well covered with foam. Skim off top, and place in individual parfait glasses or goblets. Continue beating-and-skimming process until bowl is empty and glasses filled. Chill thoroughly before serving. Syllabub will keep 4–5 days in refrigerator. Serves 8–10.

Note: In some cookbooks, syllabubs are listed under beverages, in others among desserts or pudding sauces; but most books haven't included them at all. Actually syllabub is first cousin to eggnog and a traditional Southern dessert for holidays and gala occasions, generally served in tall parfait glasses or goblets, accompanied by rich cake. Syllabub came from England by way of early Colonial settlers and has remained a specialty in Virginia, the Carolinas and Georgia.

The Eastern Seaboard. The New England clambake became part of American tradition when the settlers first copied the Indians' custom of cooking shellfish. Layers of lobsters, clams and green corn were buried in pits heated with stones; seaweed was stuffed between the layers and on top, and the whole mass was covered with earth and allowed to steam for hours. Even when family groups moved on west, south or north, this tradition of the communal cookout went with them. Instead of clams, they made do very nicely with potatoes and corn baked in hot ashes and generally served with fried chicken; and perhaps they contributed some Down East skills to the "burgoos" or the barbecues of the nineteenth century Southwest, where often a whole steer would be spit-roasted during a week of festivities.

New England recipe names are delightful in themselves.

Anadama Bread. Made with cornmeal, white flour and molasses, said to be the invention of a fisherman with a very lazy wife named Anna.

Cherry Bounce. Sweet black cherries soaked and served in rum.

Hasty Pudding. Sometimes called "stir-about pudding," served with meat and gravy or with maple syrup for dessert.

Flummery. A cornstarch-thickened pudding of cooked fruit, sugar and water, served with cream.

Sizzlers. Blueberry or apple turnovers or small pies fried in deep fat.

The old controversy between supporters of New England clam chowder, made with milk and potatoes, and Manhattan clam chowder, with tomatoes instead of milk, goes on. It's a matter of taste.

Lobster Stew

```
    2 2-pound fresh lobsters, cooked
    1 quart cold water
    1 medium onion, sliced
    2 stalks celery, sliced
    1 bay leaf
  1/3 cup butter or margarine
    4 cups hot milk
    2 egg yolks
    1 cup cream
Salt and pepper to taste
Paprika to taste
```

Cut meat from cooked fresh lobsters into small pieces, leaving claw meat whole. Put water, onion, celery and bay leaf with cracked lobster shells in saucepan. Cover, and simmer 30 minutes; then uncover, and reduce broth to about 2 cups. Strain and reserve broth. Melt butter, and sauté lobster meat gently; add milk and reserved broth; heat to boiling. Beat egg yolks with cream; stir in 1 cup hot stew very gradually and then return all to kettle. Stir constantly until hot; do not let mixture boil. Season to taste. Serve with piece of claw meat in each bowl, and dust top with paprika. Serves 4–6.

Fresh Cranberry Betty

```
    1 cup sugar
  1/2 cup orange juice
  1/2 teaspoon cinnamon
    2 cups cranberries
  1/2 cup butter or margarine, melted
    3 cups soft bread crumbs
```

Bring sugar, orange juice and cinnamon to boil. Add cranberries, and cook 2 minutes. Pour butter or margarine over crumbs, tossing with fork to distribute evenly. Arrange alternate layers of crumbs and cranberries in buttered baking dish, ending with crumbs. Cover with lid of aluminum foil, and bake in preheated 375°F. oven 20 minutes. Uncover, and bake 15 minutes longer until top is brown and crisp. Serve warm with sweetened whipped cream to which 1 teaspoon grated orange rind has been added. Serves 6.

Note: The tart, crisp, juicy cranberry has altered little (except in abundance) since the Indians used it for food and medicine and the first Cape Cod housewife boiled down a "mess" with some of her carefully hoarded sugar.

Vichyssoise

```
    4 large leeks, sliced in 1-inch lengths
    1 small onion, chopped
      (approximately 1/4 cup)
  1/4 cup butter or margarine, melted
    4 cups chicken broth (3 10 1/2-ounce cans)
    4 medium potatoes, peeled and sliced
      (approximately 4 cups)
Salt and pepper to taste
    2 cups light cream
Chopped chives
  1/4 teaspoon nutmeg (optional)
```

Sauté leeks and onion gently in butter or margarine until transparent but not brown. Add 2 cups broth, cover and simmer 15 minutes. Cook potatoes until tender, drain well and crush with fork. Add to leeks with remaining broth. Simmer 5 minutes. Put through sieve or food mill (twice if necessary to obtain smooth mixture) or use an electric blender as manufacturer directs. Season with salt and pepper. Cool, and chill overnight. Before serving, add cream, blending well. Serve very cold in chilled dishes, and sprinkle with chives and a little nutmeg. Serves 6.

Note: New York's own soup, one of the great soups of the world, invented in the early part of this century by the great French Chef, Louis Diat, for 40 years ruler of the kitchens in New York's Ritz-Carlton Hotel. Shortly before his death he declared that, in casting about for a special chilled soup to tempt the appetites of Ritz patrons during a Manhattan heat wave, he remembered his mother's leek-and-potato soup and how she used to cool it with chilled milk for summer breakfasts. He named it after his native Vichy district.

The Southwestern States. *A blend of influences. Spanish and Mexican.*

Caesar Salad

```
    1 clove garlic
  3/4 cup salad oil
1 1/2 cups 1/4-inch bread cubes
    8 cups romaine lettuce
  1/4 cup lemon juice
    1 egg, boiled 1 minute
  1/4 teaspoon dry mustard
  1/2 teaspoon black pepper
  1/2 teaspoon salt
  1/2 cup grated Parmesan cheese
    6 anchovy filets, diced (optional)
```

Quarter garlic, and add to 1/4 cup oil; set aside several hours. Toast bread cubes until golden in 300°F. oven about 20 minutes. Tear lettuce in bite-sized pieces, and place in serving bowl. Cover, and refrigerate all ingredients until needed. At serving time, combine in small bowl remaining 1/2 cup oil, lemon juice, very soft egg removed from shell and seasonings; beat well. Discard garlic from oil prepared earlier; toss oil with toasted bread cubes. Add egg mixture, bread cubes, cheese and anchovies to chilled greens. Toss gently but thoroughly, and serve immediately. Serves 6.

Note: It is an ideal first course salad to serve while the "chef's" specialties from the charcoal broiler are cooking.

California Strawberry–Cheese Pie

```
PLAIN PASTRY or FLAKY PASTRY for 10-inch single-crust pie
    4 (3-ounce) packages cream cheese
  1/2 cup sugar
    3 egg yolks, beaten thick
    1 teaspoon vanilla extract
  1/2 teaspoon almond extract
```

3 egg whites, beaten stiff
1 cup commercial sour cream
1 tablespoon sugar
1 teaspoon vanilla extract
1 pint (or more) strawberries, washed, dried and hulled
1/4 cup sugar

Line a 10-inch pie plate with pastry. Blend cream cheese and 1/2 cup sugar. Add beaten egg yolks, 1 teaspoon vanilla and almond extract. Combine thoroughly. Fold in egg whites. Spoon filling into shell, and bake at 325°F. 40 minutes. For topping, combine sour cream, 1 tablespoon sugar and 1 teaspoon vanilla. Spread on hot pie, increase oven temperature to 400°F. and bake pie 10 minutes longer. Cool; then chill. Just before serving, roll strawberries in 1/4 cup sugar, and arrange on top in ring, starting at edge of pastry. Continue, making 3 circles of berries, but leaving center uncovered. Serves 6–8.

INTERNATIONAL GOURMET MENUS

Mediterranean Sunday Lunch

Bourride
Rouille
Tray of raw vegetables
(carrots, cauliflower, radishes, cucumbers)
Fresh peaches, poached in white wine

Bourride

2 tablespoons olive oil
1 cup finely chopped onion or diced frozen onion
2 cloves garlic, crushed
2 pounds red snapper or frozen fish fillets
1/2 pound prepared smelts
1/2 pound shrimp, shelled and deveined
2 (6-ounce) packages frozen crabmeat
1 (8-ounce) bottle clam juice
2 tablespoons chopped parsley
2 teaspoons salt
1/4 teaspoon black pepper
1/4 teaspoon thyme
1 twist orange peel
8 slices French bread
1/2 cup olive oil
1 teaspoon garlic powder

Heat 2 tablespoons olive oil in large saucepan. Stir in onion and crushed garlic. Sauté 5 minutes, stirring occasionally. Cut red snapper into 1-inch pieces, discarding skin and bones. Add to onion mixture together with smelts, shrimp and crabmeat. Pour in clam juice. Stir in chopped parsley, salt, pepper, thyme and orange peel. Cover and simmer 15 minutes. Meanwhile, sauté

French bread in hot olive oil to which garlic powder has been added.

To serve, place sautéed bread in soup bowl and spoon bourride over it. Serve with ROUILLE. Serves 6–8.

Note: Almost as famous in Marseilles as its cousin the bouillabaisse is this fish stew-soup. Unlike bouillabaisse, bourride has no saffron and generally no tomatoes. But like bouillabaisse, it's ladled into soup dishes over slices of toasted French bread. Stir a spoonful of garlic-scented ROUILLE or mayonnaise into broth to give it flavor and a slight hint of thickening.

Rouille

1/4 cup fresh white bread crumbs
2 cloves garlic, crushed
1/4 cup fish liquid (from BOURRIDE)
1/3–1/2 cup oil
Dash of hot pepper sauce

In blender, combine bread crumbs, garlic and fish liquid. Blend on low speed 30 seconds. Add oil in slow, steady stream to achieve consistency of mayonnaise.

Note: Make quickly by adding 2 cloves crushed garlic and 2 or 3 drops hot pepper sauce to 1/2 cup mayonnaise.

Special Dinner for 4

Double consommé
ROAST PHEASANT STUFFED WITH GRAPES AND NUTS
GREEN BEANS AND ONIONS AU BEURRE
Steamed rice
Pots de crème au café
Demitasse

Roast Pheasant Stuffed with Grapes and Nuts

2 (3-pound) pheasants, dressed and larded
3/4 cup butter or margarine
18 dried juniper berries, crushed, or 1/4 cup gin
1 tablespoon salt
1/2 teaspoon thyme
1/8 teaspoon fresh ground pepper
2 pounds seedless grapes, washed
1 cup mixed broken nut meats (walnuts, hazel nuts, hickory nuts or pine nuts)

Remove any pinfeathers from birds, and singe off hairs. Melt butter or margarine, and mix in juniper berries, salt, thyme and pepper. Rub birds well inside and out with seasoned butter. Mash 1/2 the grapes; mix with remaining grapes, nuts and remaining seasoned butter or margarine. Stuff each bird very well, skewer openings shut and truss. Wrap remaining stuffing in aluminum foil. Place birds on rack in open roasting pan, and roast in very hot oven, 425°F. for 15 minutes. The foil-wrapped stuffing can be placed in roasting pan beside birds. Baste with drippings, reduce heat to moderate (350°F.) and continue to roast 30 minutes more or until birds are tender, basting every 10 minutes with drippings. Serves 4–5.

Green Beans and Onions au Beurre

1 (9-ounce package) frozen green beans
1/4 cup butter or margarine
4 small onions (approximately 1/2 cup)
2 tablespoons wine vinegar
Salt and pepper to taste

Cook beans according to directions on package. Meanwhile, melt butter or margarine in skillet. Peel onions, slice thin and add to skillet. Cook until transparent. Drain cooked beans, and add to skillet. Cook until beans and onions begin to brown. Add vinegar, salt and pepper to taste, stir and serve hot. Serves 4.

Note: Cut, Italian, and Frenched green beans are all equally delicious prepared this way; this dish may be prepared in advance and reheated at serving time.

Luncheon or Dinner for 2

Olives, carrot curls and gherkin fans
CHESTNUT-STUFFED CORNISH GAME HENS
CREAMED ONIONS WITH WALNUTS
FLAMING PEACHES

Chestnut-stuffed Cornish Game Hens

1 cup chopped canned cooked chestnuts
1/4 cup golden raisins
1/4 cup sautéed onion
1 small winesap apple, chopped
(approximately 1/4 cup)
2 tablespoons diced celery
2 small Cornish game hens
1/4 cup butter or margarine, melted

Combine chestnuts with raisins, onion, apple and celery. Use to stuff hens. Roast at 375°F. 1 hour or until done, basting several times with melted butter or margarine. Serves 2.

Creamed Onions with Walnuts

1/2 (1 1/2-ounce) package white-sauce mix
1 cup light cream
1 (15 1/2-ounce) can small white onions, drained
1/2 teaspoon salt
1/4 teaspoon nutmeg
Dash black pepper
1/2 cup broken walnuts

Make up white-sauce mix, using cream. Cook over medium heat until thickened. Stir in onions. Add salt, nutmeg and pepper, heat through. At serving time, stir in walnuts. Serves 2.

Flaming Peaches

3/4 cup boiling water
3/4 cup sugar
2 large canned peach halves
1/2 teaspoon lemon juice
1/2 cup macaroon crumbs
1/4 cup cognac or rum

Place 3/4 cup boiling water and sugar in saucepan over high flame. Add peach halves and lemon juice. Boil 2 minutes. Meanwhile, make 2 mounds (1/4 cup each) macaroon crumbs on each serving plate. Turn off flame under peaches.

Place peaches and syrup in blazer pan of chafing dish. Arrange serving plates with macaroon crumbs on tray. When ready to serve, carry chafing dish and serving plates to table. Heat peaches and syrup over medium flame. Pour cognac gently over peaches in syrup. Do not stir.

Light cognac with match, which will be easy after cognac has heated slightly in hot syrup. Place peach half on each mound of crumbs. Spoon 6 tablespoons cognac mixture over each peach half. Serve warm. Serves 2.

Note: Peaches, poached in syrup, set like a golden crown on a mound of macaroon crumbs and, finally, flamed with cognac, make a perfect dessert.

International Luncheon for 8

WATERCRESS SOUP
COCONUT CURRIED SHRIMP
Hot muffins
Lemon sherbet
TUILES

Watercress Soup

> 3 (12-ounce) cans chicken consommé
> 1 cup water
> 5 scallions, washed and sliced thin (include some tops), approximately 1/2 cup
> 2 1/2 cups watercress leaves and tender shoots, washed
> Freshly ground pepper to taste
> Lemon or lime slices (optional)

Place consommé and water in saucepan; bring to boil. Add scallions, reduce heat to low and simmer 3–4 minutes. Add watercress leaves, turn off heat and let soup steep about 1 minute. Serve at once, seasoning each helping with pepper and garnishing with lemon slices. Or chill soup, skim off fat and serve cold. Serves 8.

Coconut Curried Shrimp

> 2 pounds fresh or frozen shrimp, peeled or unpeeled
> 1/2 teaspoon salt
> 2 1/2 cups boiling water
> 2 chicken-bouillon cubes
> 1 cup cream
> 1/3 cup fresh grated or flake coconut
> 2 tablespoons butter or margarine
> 2 tablespoons salad oil
> 1/2 cup diced celery
> 1/3 cup chopped onion
> 1 clove garlic, crushed
> 1/4 cup flour
> 1 tablespoon curry powder
> 2 tablespoons lemon juice
> 1 teaspoon Worcestershire sauce
> 1/8 teaspoon chili-pepper seeds
> 1/4 teaspoon grated lemon rind
> 2 tablespoons chopped parsley

Add shrimp and salt to boiling water. Cover, and bring to boil. Turn heat low, and simmer 2–5 minutes (small shrimp will take 2 minutes, large shrimp 5 minutes). Drain, reserving liquid. Crumble chicken-bouillon cubes into liquid, and set aside. Peel and devein shrimp if necessary.

Heat cream and coconut together until bubbly; set aside. Heat butter or margarine and oil, and add celery, onion and garlic. Sauté slowly until vegetables are transparent, about 5 minutes. Stir in flour and curry powder; then slowly add shrimp liquid, and cook until smoothly thickened. Add next 4 ingredients and coconut mixture. When blended, add parsley and shrimp, and reheat thoroughly. Salt to taste. If thick, dilute with cream or dry sherry. Serve over hot FLUFFY RICE. Pass chutney, raisins and sliced bananas.

Coconut Shell Servers

> 1 coconut
> Boiling water

With corkscrew drill holes through 2 eyes of coconut. Drain milk, and add cream to make 1 1/4 cups and use in place of 1/2 pint cream in COCONUT CURRIED SHRIMP. Leave meat in shell. Cut about 1 1/2 inches from top of coconut with meat or fret saw. Rinse well to remove bits of shell. Fill with boiling water, and let stand until heated; drain, and fill with coconut curried shrimp. Or rinse, fill, and set upright in pan of sand or coffee can in 300°F. oven to keep hot until serving time. Fill second coconut with fluffy hot rice.

Tuiles

> 1 cup butter or margarine
> 1 3/4 cups sugar
> 5 eggs
> 2 2/3 cups cake flour
> 1 cup finely chopped blanched almonds
> 2 teaspoons almond extract

Preheat oven to 350°F. Cream butter or margarine with sugar until fluffy. Add eggs, 1 at a time, beating after each addition. Sift flour all at once and mix well. Stir in almonds and almond extract. Drop by teaspoons onto greased baking sheet 3 inches apart. Bake 8–10 minutes or until light brown around edges. Remove from sheet immediately, and roll around handle of wooden spoon (if cookies should firm up before being removed from baking sheet, set back in oven a minute to soften them). Makes about 15 dozen cookies.

American Sunday Luncheon

BRAISED CHICKEN IN MUSHROOM SAUCE
Buttered Noodles
Glazed Carrots
AMBROSIA CREAM CAKE

Braised Chicken in Mushroom Sauce

1/4 cup fat (1/2 oil, 1/2 butter or margarine)
2 pounds frozen or fresh raw chicken breasts or legs
1 tablespoon lemon juice
Salt to taste
1 tablespoon flour
3/4 cup hot water
1 (10-ounce) can mushroom soup
1/4 teaspoon thyme
1/4 cup dried parsley

Heat fat in electric frying pan or large skillet, and add separated pieces of chicken. Sprinkle with lemon juice and salt. Sauté about 10 minutes until brown on both sides. Pour off all but 2 tablespoons fat, and stir in flour. Mix hot water with soup and thyme, and add to chicken. Cover and simmer about 30 minutes or until chicken is tender. Lift chicken to hot platter, and stir sauce in pan to smooth slightly. Pour over chicken, and serve sprinkled with parsley. Serves 4.

Ambrosia Cream Cake

3/4 cup crushed vanilla wafers
1/2 cup toasted coconut
3 tablespoons butter or margarine, melted
1 3/4 cups unsweetened orange juice
1/2 cup flour
3/4 cup sugar
1/4 cup lemon juice
2 eggs, separated
2 teaspoons grated orange rind
1 (8-ounce) package cream cheese, softened
10–12 mandarin orange sections, drained (optional)

Combine first 3 ingredients, and spread 1/2 in greased 8-inch square pan. Heat 1 1/2 cups orange juice in top of double boiler. Beat flour, 1/2 cup sugar, remaining orange juice, lemon juice and egg yolks together, and pour into hot juice. Cook, beating until thick and smooth, about 7 minutes. Add orange rind. Beat cheese in small bowl, then beat in hot orange mixture. Stiffly beat whites with remaining sugar, and fold in. Spread over crumb layer, and sprinkle with remaining crumb mixture. Chill. Garnish with orange sections. Serves 10–12.

6

~

Parties
Large and Small

Being a good party hostess is really quite simple. All you need to do is create a festive atmosphere and make your guests feel at home. It's best to attend to your food and decorations in advance, and, if you have no help, don't plan a formal dinner for 20 people; have several smaller, informal parties instead.

Select your guests imaginatively—some who are talkers and some who are not and an extra man or a guest from abroad, if possible. Include some people whom you know and can count on.

Plan your menu around your guests and upon the mood of the party (formal or informal, buffet, sit-down, and the like). Do take full advantage of dishes that can be prepared in advance, and try to remember any medical, religious or other restrictions on your guests' diets.

Suggested Procedure

Guest List

If it's to be a large party, you can safely invite people of varying tastes and backgrounds. For a small group, it's wiser to be sure your guests will like one another and share similar interests.

Date and Time

Try to pick a time convenient to all. For example, many working people dislike late party nights during the week, but drinks before dinner are usually okay; a luncheon for ladies is usually best on a weekday.

Invitations

A word-of-mouth invitation is in itself indication of an informal occasion. More formality is

implied when you mail little printed cards or write personal notes; and full formality is suggested by engraved cards, as for a coming-out dance or a wedding. The last should be sent 3 weeks or a month in advance; for other types of parties allow 10 days to 2 weeks. Be sure every invitation of whatever type explicitly mentions guest's name (or names), type of party, time, place and date. A suggestion for the kind of clothes to be worn is appreciated, for example, "black tie" to signify dinner jackets. If you wish to know the exact number of guests for the occasion, specify RSVP. There are always some who neglect to answer invitations promptly. If you can possibly manage without knowing how many are coming, let it go. If you must know, telephone, and ask them if they plan to come.

Set the Keynote

Is the party a special event like an anniversary or homecoming? Is it to be formal dinner, intimate supper, buffet luncheon, cocktail party? Work out your plan according to the over-all theme and the number of guests.

Choose the Menu

Decide what foods to serve and how. Note which items you can prepare ahead of time and which ones need attention the day of the party. Get as much as posssible done beforehand, and keep kitchen duty to a minimum.

Check Your Equipment

Look over your platters, serving dishes, flatware, table linen and other supplies. Make sure you have what you need for the menu planned and the number of guests invited. Have enough plates and glasses so that dishwashing isn't a problem.

Organize Your Shopping

A pre-party shopping plan should cover candles, favors, place cards and other decorations. Flowers should be ordered for delivery the day of the party, but in plenty of time for you to arrange them. Buy any extra table equipment you may need. If serving special beverages, order them and accompaniments in advance. Plan to have plenty of ice cubes ready in refrigerator. Make sure you have enough cigarettes, coasters, ashtrays and matches.

Break down your menu into a complete grocery list, and assemble all nonperishable foods you will need. Place orders well in advance for any specialties you may need from baker and grocer.

Make a list of all items to be bought at the last minute—salad materials, cream, breads and so on.

If you look at your lists from time to time you'll be able to catch missing details.

How Much Formality?

The degree of formality is usually a personal decision, but here are some rules for formal entertaining.

The Tablecloth

A white damask or lace cloth is called for. If the former is used, you need a table pad underneath. If you decide on lace or cutwork cloth, you should use individual pads where needed for placement of hot plates, platters and serving dishes.

Places and Spaces

In arranging places, allow about 2 feet of space for each guest. If you measure space from dinner knife at one place setting to that at the next, you can be sure you have allowed enough space so that each diner is uncrowded.

Arranging Flatware

Place all flatware uniform distance from edge of table—not less than 1/2 inch and not more than 1 inch—and well clear of rim of the dinner plate, so that it won't be disturbed when plates are served or removed. All flatware should be placed in order in which it will be used, working from outside in toward plate. Forks go at left, with tines pointing up. Knives are placed at right, with cutting edges turned toward the plate. There are some exceptions, though. A fish-cocktail fork, for instance, should not be placed on left with other forks, but on extreme right. The butter spreader should not be ranged with the other knives, but should be placed across butter plate at left of dinner plate, handle pointing to the right, so that it can easily be picked up in the right hand.

Spoons go to right of knives. Again placement is in order of use: Soup spoon at far right and dessert spoon next. It will simplify your service if dessert spoon and small fork are arranged above plate area. Special serving pieces like relish spoons, butter knives or pickle forks are placed on table, each parallel to dish for which it is intended.

Napkin Folding and Placement

Napkins are usually placed to left of each place setting. A small luncheon napkin may be folded in triangular shape. In that case folded

edge is placed parallel to forks. A larger napkin should be folded square and then oblong and should be placed so that open corner is toward guest.

Preliminary Preparation. Several days beforehand get out china, and if necessary wash it. Check linen and silver. Table may be set the day before and covered with a sheet.

On the day of the party, arrange flowers, set out ashtrays and coasters, guest towels for the bathroom, and so on.

The menu should match the party. If the latter is formal, the food should be too. If you have no help, you might make a soufflé for a small party of 4, but not for a much larger number.

Only a very experienced cook or a hostess with plenty of help should attempt an elaborate menu for guests. It's better to plan something you know you can prepare well and easily.

Unless you plan to make CREPES SUZETTE or unless cooking is part of the party (barbecue, fondue, SUKIYAKI or the like) try to avoid last-minute cooking.

Make the most of serving aids: tea carts, serving carts and folding tables; a cart with thermostatically controlled top that keeps food hot; chafing dishes, electric frying pans, deep fryers and griddles, and, of course, aluminum foil and plastic film, disposable broiling pans, cake tins and so on.

And use your imagination. An ancient soup tureen can become a conversation piece, and even baked beans can be festive served on colorful earthenware plates.

Setting The Dinner Table

Your aim is to serve your guests conveniently and easily, and common sense usually is the best guide.

For a formal dinner, a large china service plate is set at each place before guests are led to dining room. If the menu opens with a cold appe-

tizer, it too is in position, in its own container on a small plate placed on the service plate. When the opening course is finished, the small plate and container are removed, but service plate remains, ready to receive the next course—perhaps fish in a ramekin or soup in a bouillon cup or plate—which also is served on its own smaller plate. Not until main course is reached is the service plate removed and replaced by a warmed dinner plate for hot meat and vegetables. At the formal dinner table of today, bread-and-butter plates are frequently used; they're placed at left of each place setting and about 1 inch above forks.

If 1 kind of wine is served, glass is placed below water glass, slightly to the right. If you are serving several wines, place glasses in diagonal line to right of water glass, in order in which they are to be used. Don't however, use more than 3 wine glasses at a place setting. The glass nearest the water goblet is filled first, though always after guests have been seated.

Condiments and relish dishes and other small accessories should be placed convenient to each place setting. For formal dinners, individual salt and pepper servers are placed directly above each place setting. For informal meals, have salt and pepper servers within easy reach of your guests.

If you are setting a formal or semiformal table, you will probably want to use a centerpiece. Flowers, fruits, dried arrangements and china figurines are all acceptable. But make sure that they are low enough to provide a view of the guest opposite.

Candlelight is always correct after dusk, but be sure that candle flames are above eye level or placed very low for a less formal occasion.

Seating Guests. If no place cards are being used, the hostess can direct each guest to his or her place at the table. A guest of honor, if it is a

woman, should be seated at the host's right; a man should be placed at the right of the hostess. Place cards are customary at formal dinners but can be used even at less formal parties.

Serving Procedures. The guest of honor is served first, the hostess last. If a maid is serving, the used plates are usually taken from the right and the food served from the left of each guest. Some people find it less confusing to have all food service from the left. In any case, all beverages are served from the right.

Informal Entertaining. For easy-going cooking and serving, casserole recipes are great. Food can be prepared well in advance, and meat and vegetables may be cooked together. Serving can be postponed if a guest is late or if no one is in a great hurry to come to the table. Food stays hot in a warm oven and can come to table in a colorful casserole dish.

BLANQUETTE DE VEAU, BOEUF BOURGUIGNON, CHICKEN PAPRIKA and COQ AU VIN are some foods to prepare in advance. Serve with rice or potatoes, and add salad or vegetables. Make dessert at leisure the day before, or serve an assortment of French pastries from the bakery. Or make a cheese board with several kinds of cheese, and have a bowl of fresh fruits, which guests may peel at the table.

Appetizers or crisp relishes can be made early in the day, arranged for serving, covered with plastic wrap and kept in refrigerator until your guests arrive. Your salad, too, can be made in advance and kept covered in refrigerator; plan to add dressing at table, and toss lightly.

Step-by-Step Procedure. Before dinner serve canapés with drinks in living room, and relax with your guests. Other appetizers or relishes may also be passed in living room; when you are ready to serve, you can concentrate on the main course.

Set casserole on a candle warmer or electric plate warmer at 1 end of table, with rice or potatoes and dinner plates nearby. With your hus-

band seated at head of table and you opposite, you can divide work of serving.

Autumn Menu for 6–8 People

SALADE NIÇOISE
BOEUF BOURGUIGNON   Parsleyed Potatoes
GARLIC BREAD
NESSELRODE PIE (or poached pears and strawberries)

Salade Niçoise

```
      1 head lettuce or other greens
      1 (7-ounce) can tuna in oil, drained
      1 cup cooked green beans, chilled
      1 green pepper, diced
          (approximately 1/2 cup)
      1 red onion, sliced thinly
          (approximately 1/2 cup)
  1/2 cup diced celery
  1/2 cup cooked diced potatoes
      2 quartered hard-cooked eggs
      1 tomato, cut in eighths
      6 anchovy fillets
    10 Greek black olives
      3 parts olive oil
      1 part wine vinegar
Salt and pepper to taste
```

Make bed of lettuce. Place drained tuna in center. Arrange beans, green pepper, onion, celery and potatoes in mounds around it. Garnish with ring of egg quarters alternating with tomato sections. Place anchovy fillets, crisscrossed, in center. Scatter olives on top. Make vinaigrette sauce with oil, vinegar and salt and pepper. Toss salad with vinaigrette sauce at table. Serves 6–8.

Boeuf Bourguignon

```
      4 pounds lean stewing beef, cut in 1 1/2-inch cubes
  1/4 cup hot butter or margarine
      3 tablespoons flour
Salt and pepper to taste
1 1/2 cups red wine
      2 onions, coarsely chopped (approximately 1 cup)
      2 shallots, finely chopped
      1 carrot, cut up
      1 clove garlic, finely chopped
Bouquet garni
      1 veal knuckle, cracked
Water
      1 pound mushroom caps
  1/4 cup Madeira (optional)
      2 tablespoons brandy
```

In heavy casserole brown beef in 2 tablespoons butter or margarine. Sprinkle meat with flour, blend in thoroughly and add salt and pepper and red wine. In small frying pan, brown onions in 1 tablespoon butter or margarine. Add onions to meat, together with shallots, carrot, garlic, bouquet garni and veal knuckle. Add just enough water to cover meat, cover and simmer over low flame 3 hours or until meat is very tender and sauce is rich, dark brown. Half an hour before serving time, add mushroom caps, Madeira and brandy. Remove bouquet garni, and serve *boeuf bourguignon* with parsleyed potatoes. Serves 6–8.

Garlic Bread

                1 (14-inch) loaf Italian bread
            1/2 cup soft butter or margarine
                3 cloves garlic, crushed
                1 teaspoon parsley, chopped
            Grated Parmesan cheese

Cut bread diagonally in 1-inch slices. Blend butter or margarine, parsley and garlic. Put bread together again with butter mixture between. Sprinkle top liberally with cheese. Wrap in foil. Heat in hot oven (400°F.) 10 minutes. Serves 6–8.

Nesselrode Pie

                1 (9-inch) baked pie shell
                1 envelope powdered gelatin
          1 1/4 cups milk
            1/4 cup sugar
                1 tablespoon cornstarch
            1/4 teaspoon salt
                3 egg yolks
                1 teaspoon vanilla extract
                3 egg whites
            1/4 cup sugar
            1/2 cup heavy cream
            1/2 cup quartered maraschino cherries

Chill pie shell. Soften gelatin in 1/4 cup milk. Mix 1/4 cup sugar, cornstarch, salt, and remaining milk. Cook over boiling water, stirring constantly, until thickened. Cover, and cook 10 minutes more. Add softened gelatin, and stir until dissolved. Beat egg yolks, and slowly add to milk mixture. Cook over hot water 3 minutes more; chill until slightly thickened. Add vanilla. Beat egg whites in deep bowl until stiff, gradually beating in 1/4 cup sugar. Fold cold gelatin mixture gently into egg whites. Whip cream until stiff. Fold whipped cream and cherries into mixture. Turn into pie shell, and chill. Serves 6–8.

Shopping List

            1/2 pound green beans
                1 green pepper
            1/2 bunch celery
                1 (7-ounce) can tuna fish in oil
            1/2 dozen eggs
                1 tomato

            Small jar or can Greek black olives
                1 (3 1/2-ounce) tin anchovy fillets
                1 head lettuce
            Olive oil
            Wine vinegar
                3 pounds new potatoes
                1 loaf Italian Bread
            Parmesan cheese
                4 pounds beef (chuck or rump)
            Red wine
            Red onions
            Carrots
            Garlic
            Shallots or green onions
            Parsley
                1 veal knuckle
            Brandy
                1 pound mushroom caps
                1 package pastry mix
                1 package gelatin
                1 pint milk
            Cornstarch
            Salt
            Vanilla extract
            Sugar
            Flour
            Butter
            1/2 pint heavy cream
            Small jar maraschino cherries
            Coffee
            Coffee cream

Preparation Plan

The day before:

Make and bake pie shell.
Prepare beef, cool and refrigerate, covered.
Chop parsley, and refrigerate in foil.
Crush garlic and cream with butter; refrigerate in covered container.
Make salad dressing.
Dice celery and green peppers for salad; refrigerate in covered container.

The day of the Party:

Make filling for pie, fill shell and refrigerate.
Scrub potatoes, and put in pan with water and salt.
Slice bread, butter and wrap in foil.
Cook beans.
Assemble salad, except for dressing.

At Serving Time:

Boil potatoes, and dress with butter and parsley.
Heat BOEUF BOURGUIGNON.
Heat bread in oven.
Toss salad with dressing.

Winter Menu for 6–8 People

CLAM–TOMATO BOUILLON
CHICKEN PAPRIKA with steamed rice
Green bean–celery salad
ORANGES ARABIAN

Clam–Tomato Bouillon

2 1/2 cups bottled clam juice
2 1/2 cups tomato juice
1 teaspoon celery salt
6 pats butter (1 teaspoon each)

Combine juices. Season with celery salt, and serve hot in mugs or cups with lump of butter in each. Serves 6.

Chicken Paprika

1 5-pound fowl, disjointed, with giblets
3 cups water
1 small onion, sliced
3 or 4 sprigs parsley
2 teaspoons salt
4 whole peppercorns
1 bay leaf
1/2 cup finely chopped onion
4 tablespoons butter or margarine
1 cup flour
1/3 cup paprika
1/3 cup cream
1 1/2 cups thick sour cream

Place giblets in saucepan with water, sliced onion, parsley, 1 teaspoon salt, peppercorns and bay leaf. Simmer, covered, 1 hour. Sauté chopped onion in skillet in 2 tablespoons butter or margarine until soft but not brown. Remove onion, leaving butter or margarine in skillet. Combine flour, reserving 2 tablespoons for later use, remaining salt and 2 teaspoons paprika in paper bag. Shake chicken pieces in bag until coated with flour mixture. Brown meat well in butter or margarine remaining in skillet. Add 1/2 cup giblet broth, and cook, covered, over low heat until chicken is tender, 1–1 1/2 hours, adding more chicken broth to prevent pan drying out. In saucepan, heat remaining 2 tablespoons butter or margarine and blend in reserved

2 tablespoons flour. Add remaining giblet broth, sweet cream and remaining paprika. Stir over low heat until smooth and thickened. Add sour cream gradually, stirring vigorously. Pour sauce over chicken, and cook over low heat 3 minutes, turning chicken and stirring sauce. Do not boil, or sour cream will curdle. Serves 6.

Oranges Arabian

6 large oranges
2/3 cup chopped dates
1/2 cup shredded almonds
2/3 cup orange juice
1/2 cup brandy
1 cup heavy cream, stiffly beaten

Peel oranges, and slice very thin. Mix dates and almonds and scatter over oranges. Pour orange juice and brandy over, and chill thoroughly before serving. Pass lightly sweetened beaten cream. Serves 6–8.

Spring Menu for 6–8 People

AVOCADO PASADENA
BEEF STROGANOFF, noodles
Fresh asparagus with lemon butter
STRAWBERRY TART   Coffee

Avocado Pasadena

2 1/2 cups frozen king crabmeat, drained
2 tomatoes, peeled, seeded and chopped
1 1/2 cups BLENDER MAYONNAISE
2 tablespoons chili sauce
1 tablespoon vinegar
1 tablespoon parsley, tarragon or chervil
1 teaspoon chopped chives
1 teaspoon Worcestershire sauce
Salt to taste
3 avocados
3 tablespoons lemon juice
3 ripe olives, halved and pitted

To crabmeat, add tomatoes, mayonnaise, chili sauce, vinegar, parsley, chives and Worcestershire sauce. Mix all together, and season. Peel avocados, halve them and remove pits. Brush with lemon juice. Fill avocado halves with crabmeat mixture, and garnish each with 1/2 ripe olive. Serves 6–8.

Blender Mayonnaise

2 egg yolks or 1 whole egg
1 teaspoon salt
1 teaspoon dry mustard
1 1/2 cups oil
3 tablespoons tarragon vinegar or lemon juice
Dash hot pepper sauce

Put eggs in container of blender; add salt, mustard and 1/2 cup oil. Turn motor on and off a few times. With motor on low, *very slowly* add rest of oil. When mixture is thick and stiff, flavor it with vinegar and hot pepper sauce. Makes 1 1/2 cups.

Beef Stroganoff

    2 pounds (trimmed weight) fillet of beef (tail end) or
        sirloin or porterhouse steak
    2 tablespoons butter or margarine
    3 tablespoons brandy
1/2 pound fresh mushrooms, sliced
    1 teaspoon crushed garlic
    2 tablespoons flour
    1 tablespoon meat glaze
    1 tablespoon tomato paste
    2 cups beef stock or canned bouillon
Salt and pepper to taste
    1 cup sour cream
    2 tablespoons fresh dill, chopped

Trim all fat from beef, and cut into fingers about 1/2 inch thick. Heat butter or margarine in deep, heavy pan. Sear meat in butter or margarine a few pieces at a time, very quickly. Meat should be very rare. Remove, and set aside. Heat brandy, pour into pan and stir with wooden spoon to scrape up all glaze. Add mushrooms to pan with garlic. Cook over low heat 2–3 minutes; then stir in flour, meat glaze, and tomato paste. When smooth, add stock. Season with salt and pepper. Stir over fire until thickened; cool. Beat in 1 cup sour cream and fresh dill. Just before serving, heat sauce over hot water, and return meat to sauce to heat through. Keep meat rare. Serve with noodles or wild rice. Serves 6–8.

Strawberry Tart

    1 teaspoon cornstarch
    1 package frozen strawberries, defrosted (reserve
        1/4 cup juice)
    1 recipe RICH TART PASTRY baked and cooled
1 1/2 pints large perfect strawberries, hulled

Dissolve cornstarch in reserved strawberry juice, set thawed strawberries aside. Fill tart shell with hulled strawberries, standing pointed ends upright. Puree packaged strawberries (in blender or strainer). Stir in dissolved cornstarch. Heat over moderate heat to boiling point, stirring with whisk until clear and thickened. Pour over strawberries in shell, and cool before serving. Serves 8–10.

Rich Tart Pastry

    2 cups all-purpose flour, sifted
1/2 cup butter or margarine
1/4 cup margarine or other shortening
    3 tablespoons sugar
    2 teaspoons grated lemon rind
1/2 teaspoon salt
    3 hard-cooked egg yolks, mashed
    2 raw egg yolks

Place flour in bowl, and make well in center. Add butter, margarine, sugar, lemon rind, salt and all egg yolks to well. With fingertips, make paste of center ingredients, gradually incorporating flour to form smooth, firm ball of dough. Work quickly so butter does not become oily. Wrap dough in waxed paper, and chill until firm enough to roll. Roll pastry between sheets of waxed paper. Fit into 10-inch pie plate, and chill in refrigerator until ready to bake. Prick bottom all over with fork before baking. Bake at 375°F. for 15–18 minutes. Prick 3–4 times during first 10 minutes of baking to prevent bottom of pastry from puffing up. Cool. Serves 8–10.

Summer Menu for 6–8 People

CLEAR CELERY SOUP
VITELLO TONNATO
GREEN RICE SALAD WITH TOMATOES
Bread sticks   Hot sesame rolls
COLD ZABAGLIONE
Iced coffee

Clear Celery Soup

    1 cup sliced celery
    1 quart clear beef broth
Lemon juice to taste
Stiffly beaten cream, salted (optional)

Simmer celery in broth 1/2 hour. Strain, and add lemon juice. Serve hot in cups garnished with beaten cream. Serves 6–8.

Vitello Tonnato (Veal with Tuna Sauce)

    3 1/2 pounds rolled, boneless leg of veal
        2 (7-ounce) cans tuna in olive oil
    10 anchovy fillets
        4 stalks celery
        4 stalks parsley
        2 cloves garlic, peeled
        1 carrot, sliced
    1/2 sour pickle, sliced
    1/2 teaspoon thyme
Salt and pepper to taste
        2 cups white wine
        1 cup olive oil

In heavy saucepan place veal, tuna and oil from cans, anchovy fillets, celery, parsley, garlic, carrot, sour pickle, thyme, salt and pepper. Add wine and olive oil and bring to boil. Cover pan, lower heat and simmer gently until veal is tender. Let veal cool in juices; then remove to platter, and slice very thin. Strain juices from pan through very fine sieve, and taste for seasonings. Serve sliced meat with cold sauce and tiny gherkins. A cold rice salad mixed with finely cut vegetables and VINAIGRETTE SAUCE goes well with this dish. Serves 6–8.

Green Rice Salad with Tomatoes

    1 1/2 cups uncooked rice
        6 tablespoons olive oil
        3 tablespoons wine vinegar
    1/2 teaspoon black pepper
        1 teaspoon salt
    1/2 teaspoon tarragon
    1/2 cup cucumber, cut into small cubes
    1/4 cup chopped green pepper
    1/4 cup chopped parsley
    1/4 cup chopped chives
    1/4 cup chopped green onion
    VINAIGRETTE SAUCE
    Salad greens
        2 hard-cooked eggs, sliced
        2 sliced ripe tomatoes

Boil rice according to directions on package. Drain, and mix at once with olive oil, vinegar, black pepper, salt and tarragon. Let stand to cool. Then mix with cucumber, green pepper, parsley, chives and onion. Mix in VINAIGRETTE SAUCE to taste, heap on greens and garnish with eggs and tomatoes. Serves 6–8.

Cold Zabaglione

        6 egg yolks
    1/2 cup sugar
    1/2 cup Marsala
        1 cup heavy cream

In top part of 2-quart double boiler, beat together egg yolks and sugar until thick and pale in color. Gradually beat Marsala into mixture. Place over boiling water, and continue beating until mixture foams up and begins to thicken. Scrape sides and bottom of pan often. Place pan in bowl of cracked ice, and continue beating until cold. Whip heavy cream until stiff, and fold into cooled zabaglione. Pour into cups, and chill in icebox. Serves 6–8.

St. Valentine's Day Dinner

QUICK BORSCH
OSSO BUCCO   RISOTTO MILANESE
Romaine salad
VALENTINE BAVARIAN   Coffee

Quick Borsch

        2 (1-pound) cans julienne beets
        3 cups chicken broth
    Juice of 2 lemons
    1/4–1/3 cup sugar
        Salt and pepper to taste
    1/4 cup sour cream
        1 tablespoon chopped fresh dill or parsley

Drain beets, reserving juice. Combine beet juice with chicken broth, lemon juice, sugar, salt and pepper. Heat mixture to boiling, pour over reserved beets and chill. Serve in cups, garnishing each with a dollop of sour cream and sprinkling with dill or parsley. Serves 8.

Note: Make sure chicken broth is free of fat.

Osso Bucco

        8 veal shanks 2 inches thick
    1/4 cup flour
        Salt and pepper to taste
    1/2 cup olive oil
        2 cloves garlic, finely chopped
        1 cup white wine
        1 cup tomato puree
    1/3 cup chopped parsley
        2 anchovy fillets, finely chopped
    Grated rind of 2 lemons

Dredge veal shanks in flour, salt and pepper, and brown in olive oil. Add garlic, wine and tomato puree, and cover pan. Simmer 1 hour. Add the parsley, anchovy fillets and lemon rind. Blend thoroughly, and heat through. Serve with RISOTTO MILANESE. Serves 6–8.

Note: When you buy veal shanks, tell butcher what you want them for, so he will give you shanks with plenty of meat on them.

Risotto Milanese

        1 large onion, sliced
            (approximately 3/4 cup)
    1/4 cup butter or margarine
        1 cup uncooked rice
    2 1/4 cups stock, broth or bouillon
        1 bay leaf
    Salt to taste
    1/4 cup grated Parmesan cheese

Brown onion in butter or margarine, and add the rice. Cook over low heat 4–5 minutes, stirring. Mixture should be lightly colored. Heat liquid to boiling point, and pour over rice. Place bay leaf on top. Cover pot tightly, and bake in 350°F. oven 25–30 minutes or until all liquid is absorbed. Salt to taste. Serve sprinkled with cheese. Serves 6–8.

Valentine Bavarian

    1 (1 pound, 2 1/2 ounce) package white-cake mix
    2 packages powdered gelatin
    1 (3-ounce) package cherry gelatin
2 1/2 cups hot water
    1/2 teaspoon almond extract
Few drops red vegetable coloring
    1 pint (2 cups) cherry ice cream
    1 (2 1/8-ounce) package dessert topping, prepared
        according to package directions
    1 cup flake coconut
    1/2 cup heavy cream, stiffly beaten

Prepare cake mix according to package directions. Pour 2 cups batter into each of 2 heart-shaped cake pans. Use remaining batter for cupcakes. Bake at 350°F. 15–20 minutes or until cake springs back when lightly touched in center. Cool, and remove from pans. Dissolve plain and cherry gelatin in hot water, adding almond extract and coloring. Stir in ice cream to dissolve; chill until thick and creamy. Whip dessert topping, and fold gently into jellied mixture. Divide in 2 and spread in lightly oiled heart-shaped pans. Chill to set. Place 1 cake layer on plate, unmold jelly heart on top, add second cake layer and top with second jelly layer. Decorate with coconut and whipped-cream rosettes. Serves 8–10.

Party for George Washington's Birthday

CHERRY SOUP
Ham baked in vermouth
Sautéed sweet potatoes   Pureed spinach
CHOCOLATE LOG   Coffee

Cherry Soup

    2 (1-pound) cans dark, sweet cherries, pitted
Water
    3 cups chicken broth
    2 tablespoons lemon juice
    1/2 pint heavy cream, stiffly beaten and lightly salted

Quarter and reserve 4 cherries per person for garnish. Simmer remaining cherries and juice (and enough water to make 2 cups) 5 minutes. Puree in blender (or push through fine strainer), stir in chicken broth and heat again to boiling. Add lemon juice. Put 4 quartered cherries in bottom of each bouillon cup. Pour hot soup over, and garnish with whipped cream. Serves 6–8.

Chocolate Log

    6 eggs, separated, at room temperature
    3/4 cup sugar
    1/4 cup unsweetened cocoa
    2 tablespoons sifted flour
1 1/2 teaspoons vanilla extract
    1/2 cup confectioners' sugar
    2 cups heavy cream, chilled
    1/3 cup sifted confectioners' sugar
    1/4 cup cognac
    2 tablespoons slivered toasted almonds

Preheat oven to 350°F. Grease bottom of 15 1/2" x 10 1/2" x 1" jelly-roll pan. Line with waxed paper. In large bowl, beat egg yolks with 3/4 cup sugar at high speed until thick and pale-lemon colored. With beater at low speed, mix in cocoa, flour and vanilla. Place egg whites in second large bowl. Beat at high speed until stiff but not dry. With wire whisk or rubber scraper, gently fold whites into egg-yolk mixture. Pour into prepared jelly-roll pan. Bake 12–14 minutes or until surface springs back when touched lightly. Sift 1/2 cup confectioners' sugar onto clean tea towel, covering it completely. Turn cake onto towel. Cool slightly. Peel off waxed paper. Trim edges with sharp knife or scissors. Beginning at long edge, roll cake up, jelly-roll fashion, and place on wire rack with seam side down. Cool completely.

Whip heavy cream until stiff. With rubber spatula gently fold in 1/3 cup confectioners' sugar and cognac. Unroll cake, and carefully remove towel. Spread with 1/2 the filling. Re-roll. Place, seam side down, on serving platter. Frost with remaining filling. Sprinkle with slivered almonds. Chill until serving time. Serves 6.

May Day Dinner

ARTICHOKE HEARTS VINAIGRETTE
New potatoes with chives
Roast saddle of lamb   Coffee
Petits pois
RASPBERRY TART

Artichoke Hearts Vinaigrette

2 (1-pound) cans or 3 (9-ounce) packages frozen artichoke
    hearts
1 recipe vinaigrette sauce
2 cloves garlic, crushed
Salt and pepper to taste
8 large lettuce leaves
8 lemon wedges

Drain canned artichoke hearts, or cook frozen ones according to package directions. Pour vinaigrette sauce, garlic and salt and pepper over hearts, and refrigerate overnight. Drain, and serve on lettuce leaves with lemon wedges. Serves 8.

Raspberry Tart

    1 recipe RICH TART PASTRY, baked and cooled
    1 quart fresh raspberries, hulled
    1 (6-ounce) jar currant jelly
    2 tablespoons cognac

Fill pastry shell with raspberries. Heat jelly to melting point, stir in cognac and spoon over raspberries in tart shell. Serve cold, or heat slightly before serving. Serves 8.

Note: Frozen raspberries *will not* do.

The Buffet Party. Setting up a buffet party gives you plenty of scope for dramatic linen, china, decorations and food. Best of all, you can forget about serving each guest individually. In addition to helping the hostess, self-service adds to the fun of a party because it encourages guests to mingle. And you can cope with many more guests when you're not limited to the number you can seat around your dining room table.

Almost any type of meal can be served this way—Sunday supper, breakfast, luncheon, dinner or refreshments for an evening party. It can be set out in recreation room, living-dining area or patio, and of course the dining table can become the focal point. It's important, too, to leave plenty of room around the table so that guests can help themselves without crowding one another. For entertaining more than 12 people at a buffet, you might set out platters of foods, and bread at each end of table. If possible, group plates, silver and napkins, at each end also. This grouping will relieve congestion in serving and prevent a slow-moving line around table. If you have no table long enough, it's a good idea to set up a trestle table. Use boards, a slab of plywood or even a smooth, level door laid across trestles. Cover with large cloth and let cloth hang down to hide supports.

When setting the table for either small or large buffet party, place dishes, flatware, napkins and food in order in which they will be picked up. A nice idea is to place small tables of the nested or stacked type around the room or in adjoining living room, so that guests may put their plates down if they wish.

Someone, host, hostess or other help, should be at buffet table to slice meat or help with other foods that require special service.

To prevent clutter on the main table, have a separate small table nearby to take used plates and flatware. Someone should keep an eye on this table, removing items before there is a large, untidy accumulation.

Coffee is usually served from a separate table. Cups, saucers, cream, sugar and spoons can be ready for use. But, of course, if you prefer, the coffee can be served from the buffet table after the table has been cleared of platters and the rest.

Buffet Menu

Cold baked ham   POTATOES AU GRATIN
Pineapple slices topped with spiced crab apples
MUSTARD PICKLES   Carrot curls   Celery hearts
Tossed salad with Swiss and bleu cheese
Hot buttered rolls   FRENCH BREAD
Assorted French pastries   Coffee

Procedure

A precooked ready-to-serve ham will save you hours of preparation time. If you wish to stud it with cloves and glaze it in a slow oven, by all means do so. Make it a morning operation, and allow about 5 minutes' cooking time per pound. Chill. For a large crowd, it is best to slice ham beforehand.

To make casserole, boil potatoes in the morning or the day before. For each guest, allow 1 medium potato. Cover, and refrigerate. On morning of party make 4 cups medium white sauce; season, add grated cheese and cover. About 1 hour before serving, combine sauce and cubed potatoes; turn into 2 casseroles, sprinkle with grated cheese and bake at 350°F. for 30–40 minutes or until bubbly.

Make salad in early afternoon. Use assorted crisp greens—lettuce, romaine, endive, watercress. Wash, and drain. Arrange in 2 salad bowls, and top with peeled tomato sections. Sprinkle 1 salad with crumbled bleu cheese, the other with slivers of Swiss cheese. Cover bowls with damp towels, then with plastic wrap to keep crisp. Refrigerate. Set on buffet with several types of dressing nearby.

Buffet Menu

CURRIED SHRIMP   ANISEED BEEF
Rice
Chopped peanuts   Chopped green onion
Mango chutney   Chopped hard-cooked eggs
Grated coconut   Crumbled bacon
TROPICAL DELIGHT
Coffee   Tea   Beer

Curried Shrimp

2 pounds medium shrimp, cooked, and cooking liquid
1/2 cup chopped green apple
1/2 cup chopped onion
2 tablespoons butter or margarine
3 tablespoons fresh curry powder
2 teaspoons lemon juice
1/2 teaspoon salt
1/4 teaspoon ground cloves
1/4 teaspoon dry mustard
2 cans (10 1/2 ounces) frozen cream of shrimp soup

Peel and devein cooked shrimp. Finely chop green apple and onion. Sauté in butter or margarine until soft. Mash to paste, and add curry powder, lemon juice, salt, cloves and mustard. Cook slowly about 10 minutes. Heat soup. Add 1/2 can shrimp liquid and 2 tablespoons (or more) curry paste. Simmer 20 minutes. Add cleaned shrimp, and heat through. Serve over plain boiled rice. Serves 8.

Note: Curry paste will keep about 2 months if kept in covered jar in refrigerator.

Aniseed Beef

2 pounds shin beef
4 cups water
1/3 cup soy sauce
2 tablespoons sugar
4 slices ginger root
2 tablespoons sherry
4 aniseed stars or 1 1/2 teaspoons anise seeds
1 teaspoon sesame-seed oil

Trim beef, and cover with water. Bring to boil, and skim. Add soy sauce, sugar, ginger, sherry and anise and cook over medium heat about 2 hours. Add sesame-seed oil, and cook about 20 minutes longer. Slice meat, and serve hot or cold. Serves 8.

Tropical Delight

2 large ripe bananas
3 canned peach halves and 1 cup juice
1 (6-ounce) can frozen orange juice
2 cups sweetened pineapple juice
Juice of 1 lemon
2 eggs

Put bananas, drained peaches and orange juice in blender container. Blend until smooth (or press bananas and peaches through a fine strainer). Combine puree with juices and eggs in large bowl or mixer, and beat at medium speed until fluffy and light. Pour mixture into refrigerator trays. Freeze until a border of crystals forms (about 1 inch thick) around edges; beat again until mushy, and return to freezer. Serves 6–8.

Procedure

Cook and clean shrimp the day before. Make sauce, and add shrimp. Store in covered container in refrigerator. Cook beef, and cool in liquid before chilling. Make dessert, and freeze. Set serving table, and cover.

The day of party, fix side dishes, and cover them. Chill beer, and prepare coffee pot. Slice meat thin, and place on platter. Cover with plastic wrap. About 3/4 hour before serving, reheat curry gently. Cook rice. Remove dessert from freezer to refrigerator to soften slightly. Plug in coffee pot. Heat water for chafing dish.

At serving time, put curry in chafing dish. Place everything except dessert on table.

Buffet Menu

Guacamole   Corn chips
CHILI CON CARNE   Tamales
Radish salad
MEXICAN FLAN or melon balls and liqueur   Coffee

Chile Con Carne

1/3 cup bacon drippings
3 onions, chopped (approximately 1 1/2 cups)
3 1/2 pounds ground round or chuck steak
2 teaspoons chili powder
1 teaspoon salt
1/2 teaspoon pepper
1/2 teaspoon garlic powder
Pinch cayenne
4 (1 pound) cans red kidney beans and liquid
1 large (1 pound, 13 ounce) can tomatoes
3 tablespoons tomato paste

Melt drippings in large heavy skillet. Sauté onion until golden brown; then add meat. Stir continuously until beef is brown all through and moist from its own juice. Add chili powder, salt, pepper, garlic powder and cayenne. Mix well. Then add kidney beans with their liquid, tomatoes and tomato paste. Combine thoroughly, and simmer, covered, stirring occasionally about 30 minutes. Serves 12–14.

Note: For hot chili, increase amount of chili powder.

Mexican Flan

8 eggs
2/3 cup granulated sugar
2 (14 1/2-ounce) cans evaporated milk
2 teaspoons vanilla extract or 1 teaspoon brandy
1/2 cup packed light-brown sugar

Preheat oven to 350°F. Beat eggs until well blended. Add granulated sugar, and mix in well. Beat in undiluted milk, and add vanilla. Sift brown sugar into bottom of 9″x5″x3″ loaf pan, and pour custard gently over it. Place in shallow baking dish containing hot but not boiling water. Bake in 350°F. oven for 1 hour or until knife inserted in center comes out clean. Do not cover. Refrigerate overnight. Before serving, run knife around edge of pan, and turn out onto a small platter. Serves 12.

Summer Buffet

Cold BORSCH
POACHED SALMON WITH HERBED MAYONNAISE
Potato–cucumber salad
Pumpernickel sandwiches
Lemon mousse   Coffee

Poached Salmon with Herbed Mayonnaise

    2 cups water
    2 cups white wine
    4 peppercorns
    4 parsley stems
    2 stalks celery
    1 carrot
    1 onion, sliced
  4–5 pound piece of salmon
    1 recipe HERBED MAYONNAISE

Combine all ingredients except salmon and mayonnaise. Simmer 15 minutes, wrap fish in cheesecloth and lower gently into simmering liquid. Cook 7–8 minutes per pound; test for doneness with toothpick. If not cooked, return to broth a short time. Let cool in liquid, and remove with aid of cheesecloth. Serve with HERBED MAYONNAISE. Serves 8–10.

Herbed Mayonnaise

    1 cup homemade or commercial mayonnaise
    3 tablespoons chopped parsley
    2 shallots or green onions, finely chopped
    1 tablespoon chopped chives or fresh dill

To mayonnaise add all other ingredients. Makes one cup.

Buffet Menu

HAM RING and SOUR CREAM–HORSERADISH SAUCE
Deviled eggs
SPINACH–RAW MUSHROOM SALAD
Hot buttered rolls
EASY CHEESECAKE   Coffee

Ham Ring

    2 pounds ground ham
  3/4 pound ground veal
    1 cup finely diced pineapple
    4 slices bread, trimmed
    1 cup milk or water
    2 teaspoons prepared mustard
  Pinch pepper
    1 egg
  Whites of 3 eggs

Combine meats and pineapple. Cover bread with enough milk to soak; add to meat mixture. Add mustard and pepper. Mix well. Add whole egg, then whites, 1 at a time, mixing well after each addition. When mixture is finished, put into ring mold, and bake, covered, in pan with a little water at 350°F. 35–40 minutes. Cool slightly before unmolding. Serve cold garnished with crab apples, pineapple slices and SOUR CREAM–HORSERADISH SAUCE. Serves 8.

Sour Cream–Horseradish Sauce

    1 cup thick sour cream
  1/3 cup horseradish
    1 tablespoon grated lemon rind
  Salt and white pepper to taste

Combine all ingredients and mix well. Makes 1 1/3 cups.

Spinach–Raw Mushroom Salad

  1 1/2 pounds young spinach, well washed and drained
  1/2 pound fresh mushrooms, wiped clean and thinly
      sliced
  Salt and pepper to taste
  1/2 cup FRENCH DRESSING

Cut off tough stems of spinach, and break leaves into eating-sized pieces. Combine with mushrooms. At serving time, add salt and pepper, and toss well with dressing. Serves 8.

Easy Cheesecake

    3 (8-ounce) packages cream cheese
    5 eggs
    1 cup sugar
  1/2 teaspoon vanilla extract
  1/4 teaspoon almond extract
  1/4 teaspoon salt
    1 cup SOUR CREAM TOPPING
  Shaved chocolate

Combine all ingredients except topping and chocolate in large bowl. Mix with electric mixer at medium speed 10 minutes. Scrape bottom of bowl occasionally. Pour into greased spring-form pan, and place in 350°F. oven 50 minutes. Allow to cool 20 minutes. Spread with topping, and return to oven 350°F. 10 more minutes. Cool, chill and sprinkle with shaved chocolate. Serves 8–10.

Sour Cream Topping

    1/2 pint sour cream
    2 tablespoons sugar
    1/2 teaspoon vanilla extract

Mix all ingredients. Makes 1 cup.

St. Patrick's Day Buffet

Corned beef
Boiled potatoes in jackets   Quick-cooked cabbage
Boiled yellow turnips   Beets   White onions
Carrots   Assorted mustards
RYE BREAD with butter
Beer   IRISH COFFEE

Irish Coffee

Make very hot, strong, sweet coffee. Flavor it with Irish whiskey, and serve in demitasse cups or small glasses topped with unsweetened whipped cream.

Italian Buffet

Antipasto platter
CANNELLONI WITH SAUSAGE
Tossed green salad with oil and vinegar
Bread sticks
FROZEN LEMON PIE   Coffee

Cannelloni with Sausage

      2 cups sifted all-purpose flour
    1/4 teaspoon salt
      2 eggs, slightly beaten
    1–2 tablespoons water
      3 quarts boiling salted water
      1 pound ground beef
      1 Italian sausage, sliced
      1 onion, chopped (approximately 1/2 cup)
      1 clove garlic, crushed
      2 tablespoons butter or margarine
      1 teaspoon salt
      2 tablespoons flour
    1/4 teaspoon thyme
      1 (10 3/4-ounce) can minestrone or beef soup
    4–5 cups tomato sauce
    Sliced mozzarella cheese
    1/4 cup Parmesan cheese

Sift 2 cups flour and 1/4 teaspoon salt into bowl, and stir in eggs and water with fork. Press mixture together with hands to form stiff dough. Knead lightly, and roll out to very thin sheet, about 16" x 16". Cut into 16 4-inch squares. Drop squares in boiling salted water, and cook until just tender. Drain on clean dry towel. Stir-fry meats, onion and garlic in butter or margarine until pinkness disappears. Then stir in 2 tablespoons flour, 1 teaspoon salt, thyme and soup. Simmer until very thick; then season, and cook to lukewarm. Heap some meat mixture along edge of each cooked pasta square, and roll up. Place in buttered baking dish. Cover with 2 cups tomato sauce and mozzarella slices. Cover dish, and bake at 350°F. about 40 minutes. Uncover, and sprinkle with Parmesan cheese. Broil quickly until lightly browned. Pour remaining sauce over rolls at serving time. Serves 8.

Frozen Lemon Pie

      3 eggs, separated
    1/2 cup sugar
    1/4 cup lemon juice
    1/2 cup flaked coconut
    1/2 teaspoon grated lemon rind
      1 cup ice-cold evaporated milk
     24 chocolate wafers, crumbled (1 cup)

Beat egg yolks slightly in top of double boiler. Add 1/4 cup sugar and lemon juice. Cook over hot water until mixture thickens, stirring constantly. Add coconut and rind. Beat egg whites stiffly with remaining sugar, and fold into egg-yolk mixture. Cool. Whip evaporated milk until very stiff. Fold in lemon mixture. Line 2 refrigerator ice-cube trays with 1/2 the wafer crumbs, pour in custard and top with remaining crumbs. Freeze. Serve in wedges. Serves 4–5.

CATERING FOR A CROWD

When faced with large numbers to feed, a basic plan is essential. Get all the help you can, and make sure it is coordinated.

If you belong to any large organization, someday you may find yourself in charge of organizing the entertainment and the feeding of 100 people. There could even be 200–300 (especially if it's a fund-raising event), but let's make a modest beginning, and consider catering for 100 first.

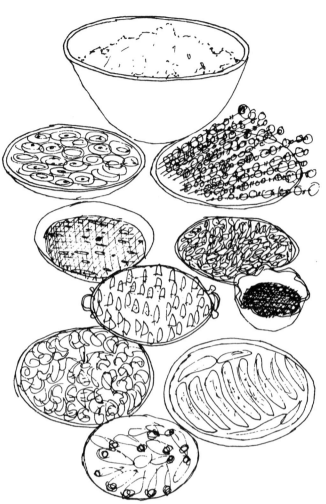

Smorgasbord Approach. One way to feed such a group can be called the "smorgasbord approach." It's worked around a wide variety of dishes, with contributions cooked separately by a number of women in their homes and brought in all ready to serve.

One member might make a crock of home-baked beans, for example; another might contribute steamed browned bread to go with the beans. Someone could bring in some huge bowls of potato salad, someone else a large batch of

deviled eggs. And using the organization premises, several people might prepare hams studded with cloves and baked with sugar crust.

International Accents

If your group includes members who come from other countries, you might plan an International food sampling. Ask the members to prepare some of their countries' famous dishes, but be sure that each participant knows what the others are doing.

The invitations or notices for this sort of party should specify, of course, that the guests are invited to sample foods of other lands cooked by members of the group. It would be a very good idea to have some such standard fare as a large baked ham and a jellied veal mold planned as well, to be sure there's something all the guests like.

Committee Approach. This approach requires more work from fewer people and a more familiar menu. The committee will need a long table to work on and plenty of sharp knives, bowls of various sizes, stacks of plates, and a supply of foil and plastic wrap for wrappings. And if you're making sandwiches and cakes for an evening party with tea or coffee you'll have to calculate quantities closely.

Assembly-line Sandwiches

For sandwiches, set up an assembly line. Have first person slice bread; use whole unsliced bread, and slice lengthwise rather than across. The next in line spreads slices with softened butter or margarine. Next someone spreads fillings and tops with second buttered slices, or rolls up slices for pinwheel sandwiches. The last in line slices sandwiches into small, easily managed pieces and arranges them on platters, covers them with foil or plastic wrap and refrigerates them until serving time.

A helpful tip: Have several varieties of filling made up ahead of time, but you will find it easier and quicker to spread 1 at a time; then go on to the next kind.

Cakes by the Yard

While gathered together for the sandwich job, the committee might also like to make petits fours, those attractive little bites of cake, decoratively iced. To make them you need large sheet cakes baked ahead of time. Cut them into small squares and diamonds, and have several bowls of icing—the simple kind made with confectioners' sugar and milk, one, white; one, chocolate; one, pink perhaps. Then you need an assortment of silver candies, chocolate sprinkles and so on. If one of your members has artistic tendencies, you are set.

Estimating Quantities

How much food can 100 people eat or 200–300, for that matter, and how much coffee will they want with it?

A general guide would be to calculate two 2-slice sandwiches for each person (thus 2 sandwich loaves per 10 people, and 1 pound butter or margarine for 3 loaves). But your sandwiches usually are cut into fancy shapes and small sizes, and a guest may eat 8–10 of them very easily. It's up to you to decide hcw ample your servings are to be. It could very well depend on the hour at which refreshments are served, what has gone before, and so forth.

Coffee for a Crowd

To make coffee for 100 people, buy 2 1/2 pounds regular-grind coffee, and put it in cheesecloth bag large enough to hold *double* that amount—size is important because coffee swells. Put bag in large boiler with 20 quarts boiling water, cover tightly, and reduce heat so that water is no longer boiling. Let it stand, keeping hot but not boiling, about 20 minutes. Then, using kitchen tongs, grasp bag and move it up and down in coffee several times to extract maximum flavor. Remove bag, and continue to keep coffee hot for serving. For each 100 cups of coffee, allow about 2 quarts light cream, and 2 pounds sugar.

To make instant coffee for a crowd, use 16 quarts (4 gallons) boiling water, remove from heat, add 8 ounces (4 1/2 cups) instant coffee and stir until dissolved.

Buffet Menus

Cold Buffet

Lobster and chicken salads, 4 gallons each
Thin slices rare roast beef
(18 pounds, uncooked weight, rolled sirloin)
Horseradish and mustards

Hot Buffet

Lasagne with tomato sauce,
6 (13″ x 18″) pans
Italian bread sticks
Orange and grapefruit sections with rum, 4 gallons
Assorted cookies, 13 pounds
Coffee   Cream   Sugar

COFFEE AND TEA PARTIES MORNING OR AFTERNOON

These parties are an easy, inexpensive way to entertain small or large groups. You can accompany the morning coffee with cream cheese and smoked salmon on toasted bagels, with some IRISH SODA BREAD with sweet butter or UPSIDE-DOWN TOAST.

Note: Other suggestions include Danish pastry, warm brioches with strawberry jam, blueberry–cream muffins, rich biscuits, quick coffee cakes.

Irish Soda Bread

```
  4 cups flour
1/2 cup white raisins
1/2 cup black raisins
  2 tablespoons caraway seeds
  1 tablespoon sugar
  2 teaspoons baking powder
  1 teaspoon salt
  2 eggs
  2 cups (approximately) buttermilk
  1 tablespoon butter or margarine, melted
  1 teaspoon cream of tartar
  1 teaspoon baking soda dissolved in 1 tablespoon water
```

In large bowl combine flour, raisins, caraway seeds, sugar, baking powder and salt. In another bowl beat together eggs, 1 1/2 cups buttermilk, butter or margarine, cream of tartar, and baking soda. Add wet ingredients to dry ingredients, stir with spoon and add more buttermilk if mixture is too dry. Put into buttered, floured 9-inch round pan. Make cross on top of bread, spreading open. Bake at 350°F. 40–60 minutes or until lightly browned on top. Makes 1 round loaf.

Upside-down Toast

```
  2 tablespoons butter or margarine
1/4 cup brown sugar
1/4 cup crushed pineapple, drained
  1 egg
3/4 cup milk
1/8 teaspoon salt
  4 slices bread
```

Preheat oven to 400°F. Melt butter or margarine in 9-inch square baking pan. Into butter or margarine stir brown sugar and pineapple. Spread mixture evenly over bottom of pan. In bowl beat together egg, milk and salt. Soak bread in milk mixture until soft, then lay over pineapple mixture in pan. Bake 25 minutes or until lightly browned, and cool 1 minute before inverting on heated serving platter. Serves 4.

For the casual afternoon coffee or tea, you can use a silver tray and service, or any type of tray covered with a fresh cloth. Arrange the tray in the kitchen and add a plate with a few small sandwiches made with very thin bread and/or some cookies on their own plate. Don't forget milk, cream, sugar and lemon slices.

The Large Occasion. For a more formal coffee or tea, the dining room is the best setting and your best cloth, china and silver are appropriate. Flowers can help dress up the room. For large bridal showers, receptions for out-of-town guests, club meetings, church groups, and so on, it's often an ideal way to entertain. Use at least 2 services if more than 20 guests are expected, and place 1 complete service at each end of the table.

Some help in the kitchen for washing cups and saucers—or catering service—is a good idea. And if you can have someone (maybe a friend can help you) look after filling tea and coffee pots and see that sandwich and cookie plates are replenished from time to time, you'll be free to mingle with your guests. In general, for a guest list of 20, 2 or 3 in help would be perfect. For a party of 75 guests, about 8 would be necessary.

Choosing the Menu. The menu pattern is usually uncomplicated and light, with food as dainty and as decorative as possible, harmonizing with flowers and setting.

Menu

Small sandwiches
(avocado–watercress triangles,
anchovy–egg pinwheels)
Party rolls with pâté
Tiny puffs filled with shrimp salad
SWEDISH SHORTBREADS   PINEAPPLE CAKE
ALMOND MERINGUES
Coffee   Tea   Punch

Make pâté and pinwheel rolls the day before, wrap in plastic wrap and refrigerate or freeze. Avocado–watercress sandwiches should be made the day of party and wrapped in damp towel until serving time. Puffs may be made in advance and filled the day of the tea. Assorted cookies can be made days in advance, freezer-wrapped and frozen until needed.

Swedish Shortbreads

```
  1 cup butter or margarine
1/2 cup confectioners' sugar
  2 cups sifted flour
  1 teaspoon vanilla extract
```

Cream butter or margarine and sugar together. Add flour; then add vanilla. Refrigerate until dough is chilled. Roll teaspoonfuls in balls. Flatten with fork. Bake at 350°F. 10 minutes. Makes 3 dozen.

Pineapple Cake

    2 1/2 cups sifted flour
        1 tablespoon baking powder
    1/4 teaspoon salt
    3/4 cup butter or margarine
    1 1/2 cups sugar
        1 teaspoon vanilla extract
        4 egg yolks, well beaten
        1 (8-ounce) can crushed pineapple,
            undrained
        4 egg whites

Sift flour with baking powder and salt. Cream butter or margarine and sugar until fluffy. Stir in vanilla and egg yolks. Blend well. Add crushed pineapple. Fold in sifted dry ingredients. Beat egg whites until stiff but not dry, and fold into batter. Pour into 10-inch, well-greased tube pan, and bake in moderate oven, 375°F. 25 minutes and then at 350°F. 25 minutes. Makes one 10-inch cake.

Almond Meringues

        1 cup soft butter or margarine
    1/2 cup almond paste
    1/2 cup light brown sugar
        1 egg
        2 cups sifted flour
    3/4 cup raspberry jam
        3 egg whites
    3/4 cup granulated sugar
    1/2 cup slivered almonds

Cream butter or margarine with almond paste; gradually beat in brown sugar and egg. Blend in flour. Pat in lightly buttered 13″ x 9″ x 2″ pan. Bake in moderate oven, 325°F. 20 minutes. Spread with jam. Beat egg whites until frothy; gradually beat in sugar, and beat until stiff meringue is formed. Fold in nuts; spread over jam. Return to oven about 20 minutes. Cool in pan. Cut into 1 1/2-inch squares. Store in airtight containers. Makes about 54 cookies.

Sandwiches

Use sandwich loaves; bread should be 1 day old for easy slicing, except for rolled sandwiches, which require fresh bread. Cream butter or margarine for easy spreading. Prepare batch of assorted fillings in advance.

To make triangles, tiny square, or circles; trim crusts from whole unsliced sandwich loaf, and slice lengthwise, spread butter or margarine, then filling, over 1 whole long slice, cover with second buttered slice; cut into shapes, wrap and chill before serving.

To make rolled sandwiches, remove crusts from fresh unsliced sandwich loaf, slice across loaf and spread slices with butter or margarine

and filling. Roll each slice, and secure with wooden pick. Wrap, and chill before serving.

To make pinwheel sandwiches, remove all crusts from fresh unsliced sandwich loaf, and slice lengthwise. Spread with butter or margarine and filling, roll each slice using long side, wrap in foil and chill. Before serving, slice into pinwheels.

Suggested Sandwich Fillings

Eggs, finely chopped green onion, and mayonnaise
Mashed sardines, onion, lemon juice and chopped parsley
Liver sausage, cream cheese and cognac
Crabmeat, tarragon and MAYONNAISE
Shrimp with CURRY MAYONNAISE
Chicken, almonds and MAYONNAISE
Thin-sliced cucumber
Raw mushrooms

Other Suggested Accompaniments

Sunshine Cake

    1 1/2 cups sifted cake flour
        1 teaspoon cream of tartar
    1/2 teaspoon salt
    1 1/2 cups sugar
    1/2 cup water
        5 egg whites
        5 egg yolks
        1 teaspoon vanilla extract

Sift first 3 ingredients together several times. Boil sugar and water together 10–15 minutes until syrup forms thread when dropped from spoon about 6 inches over saucepan. Beat egg whites till stiff, and pour syrup slowly over them, beating all the time. Continue to beat until mixture is cool. Beat egg yolks together with vanilla, and add to egg-white mixture. Fold in sifted flour mixture quickly, and pour batter into large *ungreased* tube pan. Bake at 325°F. 1 hour. Turn pan upside down to cool, and remove cake from pan when completely cool. Serves 12.

Chocolate Butter Icing

    1/3 cup butter or margarine
    1 1/2 ounces (1 1/2 squares) unsweetened
            chocolate, melted
        1 egg yolk, well beaten
    1–1 1/2 cups confectioners' sugar
    1/2 teaspoon vanilla extract

Cream butter or margarine very thoroughly; to it add chocolate and egg yolk, and beat hard to incorporate. Gradually beat in sugar until mixture is of spreading consistency. Add vanilla, and frost cake. Makes about 1 1/2 cups.

Butterscotch–Nut Bread

2 cups sifted all-purpose flour
3/4 teaspoon baking powder
1/2 teaspoon baking soda
1/4 teaspoon salt
1 egg
1 cup brown sugar, firmly packed
1 1/2 tablespoons melted butter or margarine
1 cup sour milk
1/2 cup chopped walnuts

Sift flower, baking powder, soda and salt together. In large mixing bowl beat egg, and add sugar gradually, beating until light. Add butter or margarine, and blend thoroughly. Add flour mixture, a little at a time, alternating with sour milk. Stir to keep mixture smooth. Add nuts. Turn into greased loaf pan, 9″ x 5″ x 3″, and bake at 350°F. 1 hour or until done. Cool loaf completely. Serve in slices, buttered. Serves 8.

Rich Orange Drops

3 1/4 cups sifted pastry flour
1/2 cup superfine sugar
2 tablespoons baking powder
3/4 teaspoon salt
1/2 cup butter or margarine, chilled
1 egg, well beaten
1/2 cup strained orange juice
2 tablespoons grated orange rind

To flour add sugar, baking powder, and salt and sift twice. Cut in butter or margarine to make fine particles. Mix together egg, juice and orange rind. Make well in flour mixture, and add liquid; mix all together lightly with fork. Drop dough from tip of teaspoon, well apart, onto greased baking sheet. Bake at 350°F. about 18 minutes. Makes 60–70 drops, depending on size.

SUNDAY BRUNCH PARTY

Sunday-morning brunch is great for family entertaining so do include children. It should be a casual, relaxed affair in atmosphere as well as in dress. If you start meal with fruit, or juice, or bloody marys, everyone will have a chance to relax and chat a few minutes. If your specialty is omelets, you might plan your meal around them, or, with aid of an electric griddle, make buttermilk or buckwheat pancakes right at table. Ham steaks grilled in the broiler and fried eggs cooked on griddle or electric skillet are also nice. Brown-and-serve rolls, biscuits, butterflake rolls or cinnamon rolls, the kind you buy at the supermarket and keep refrigerated, need only be popped in the oven. In fact, keep in mind all the ready-to-bake products available. Try muffin mixes with your own variations, like a spoon of marmalade hidden at the center of each muffin.

Another idea is French toast; you can vary it by serving with bacon or sausage and maple syrup, by sprinkling with cinnamon or by using orange juice instead of milk as liquid.

Brunch Menu 1

Grapefruit and pineapple juice
Creamed codfish on toasted English muffins
Broiled tomatoes
Coffee

Brunch Menu 2

Broiled fresh pineapple, brushed with honey
Sautéed chicken livers with sherry in toast cups
Danish pastry
Coffee

Easter Brunch

STRAWBERRIES IN RASPBERRY SAUCE
STUFFED EGGS MORNAY
Asparagus wrapped with ham
Hot rolls or brioches
Coffee

Strawberries in Raspberry Sauce

1 quart fresh strawberries
1 (12-ounce) package frozen raspberries, defrosted
1/4 cup kirsch

Hull and wash strawberries. Place in crystal bowl. Purée defrosted raspberries in blender (or push through fine strainer), and strain over strawberries. Stir in kirsch. Chill until serving time. Serves 6.

Stuffed Eggs Mornay

6 hard-cooked eggs
1/2 cup cooked mushrooms, finely chopped
2 tablespoons soft butter or margarine
Salt to taste
1 3/4 cups MORNAY SAUCE
3 tablespoons Parmesan cheese

Halve eggs lengthwise; press yolks through strainer, mix with mushrooms and butter or margarine and season with salt. Pile mixture back into whites; spread 1 cup MORNAY SAUCE in flat baking dish. Lay eggs on top of sauce, and spoon remaining sauce over. Sprinkle with cheese, and heat in 350°F. oven until sauce bubbles. Serve at once. Serves 6.

Hunt Breakfast

Grapefruit juice   Champagne or sherry
Smoked kippers
Veal, kidney and mushrooms sautéed
Scrambled eggs
Toast   English muffins   Rolls
Marmalade   Jellies
Coffee

This meal doesn't require a "call to the hounds." You can serve in the traditional manner, from a sideboard (or server) with silver or copper chafing dishes, keeping foods hot as guests serve themselves. Wine is the customary opener.

LUNCHEON PARTIES

Offer an aperitif, a simple 2–3 course luncheon and time to linger over coffee.

If your guests are all women, a seasonal theme is particularly pleasant—there are appropriate decorations for Valentine's Day, Easter, and the fall. Use linen place mats with plain or patterned napkins, luncheon plates and appropriate glasses and silver.

If you are playing bridge, for example, you might save dessert and coffee until after you've finished your game.

Some Luncheon Menus

Luncheon for 6–8 People

Clear chicken broth
CHICKEN AND ALMONDS IN SESAME SHELLS
Fresh fruit salad   Melba toast
PETITS FOURS   Tea with lemon

Chicken and Almonds in Sesame Shells

        1/4 cup slivered, blanched almonds
        3 tablespoons butter or margarine
        2 (6-ounce) cans mushrooms and juice
        1/4 cup chopped green pepper
        2 tablespoons chopped onion
        3 tablespoons flour
        1 (10 1/2-ounce) can cream of chicken soup
        2 tablespoons pimento juice
        1/2 cup evaporated milk
        2 egg yolks, slightly beaten
    2 1/2–3 cups diced cooked chicken
        1/4 cup diced pimento
        8 large baked sesame tart shells
    Chopped parsley

Sauté almonds in butter or margarine until golden. Add drained mushrooms, green pepper and onion. Cook until tender. Blend in flour; add mushroom juice, soup and pimento juice. Cook, stirring until thick and smooth. Combine milk and egg yolks, and add to pan. Cook 2 minutes longer. Add chicken and pimento. Reheat in double boiler. Fill tarts. Sprinkle with chopped parsley. Serves 8.

Note: Make sesame shells by adding 1/4 cup toasted sesame seeds to your favorite flaky pastry —mix before adding water.

Bridge Luncheon for 8

Tomato consommé
DEEP-DISH SALMON TART
MUSHROOM BÉCHAMEL SAUCE
Asparagus with LEMON BUTTER
LADYFINGERS   Coffee   Platter of fresh fruit

Deep-dish Salmon Tart

    Rich pastry for 2-crust pie
    1 1/2 pounds canned salmon and juice
    1 1/2 cups bread crumbs
        2 eggs, beaten
        1 cup milk
    1/2 cup grated, peeled cucumber
        2 teaspoons onion juice
        1 teaspoon grated lemon rind
    1/2 teaspoon salt
        1 teaspoon lemon juice
    Salt and black pepper to taste
    Dash celery seed
        6 hard-cooked eggs, sliced
    Melted butter or margarine or beaten egg

Roll out sufficient pastry, and line a deep oblong baking dish, 9″ x 6 1/2″ x 2″. Turn salmon and its juice into bowl. Discard dark skin; mash bones and salmon with juice. Add next 7 ingredients. Taste, and season with lemon juice, salt and pepper to taste and celery seed. Place alternate layers of egg slices and salmon mixture in pastry-lined dish. Dampen edge, and roll out remaining pastry for top crust. Seal edges, and trim. Prick with fork, and brush with melted butter or margarine or beaten egg. Bake at 400°F. 30 minutes, reduce heat to 350°F., and bake another 30 minutes. Serves 8.

Note: Serve with MUSHROOM BÉCHAMEL SAUCE, or pass sauce separately so that guests may serve themselves.

Mushroom Béchamel Sauce

    1/3 cup butter or margarine
        2 tablespoons chopped onion
    1/3 cup flour
        2 cups milk
        1 (4-ounce) can mushroom pieces with juice
    Pinch cayenne

Dash nutmeg
Salt and pepper to taste
2 or 3 egg yolks
2 tablespoons cream

Melt butter or margarine, do not brown it. onion. Heat until onion is transparent; blend in flour. Add milk slowly, and cook, stirring until smoothly thickened. Add mushroom pieces and juice, with cayenne, nutmeg, and salt and pepper. Transfer to double boiler over hot—not boiling—water. Combine egg yolks with cream, and add to sauce. Stir 2–3 minutes to heat through, and serve hot over SALMON TART. Makes about 3 cups.

Lemon Butter

1/2 cup butter or margarine
1/3 cup lemon juice
1 teaspoon sweet paprika

Melt butter or margarine, do not brown it. Stir in lemon juice and paprika. Serve over fresh asparagus spears. Makes about 3/4 cup.

Ladyfingers

3 eggs, separated
2/3 cup superfine sugar
1/4 teaspoon salt
1/2 teaspoon vanilla extract
1/3 cup sifted all-purpose flour
1/4 cup superfine sugar

Beat egg whites until fluffy. Add 1/3 cup sugar gradually, and continue beating until stiff. Beat egg yolks until thick, and beat in 1/3 cup sugar, vanilla and salt. Fold egg-yolk mixture and flour into egg whites. Spoon mixture into pastry tube or bag, with a plain 1/2-inch opening. Press tube to form fingers 3 inches long on ungreased heavy brown paper placed on cookie sheet. Sprinkle with 1/4 cup sugar, and bake at 360°F. 10–15 minutes. Cool, and lift from paper with metal spatula. Put fingers together in pairs with LEMON FILLING or jam, or serve singly. Makes 6 dozen single fingers.

Informal Cold-day Luncheon for 4

ANOTHER MANHATTAN CLAM CHOWDER
Sea toast or pilot crackers
Tossed green salad with roquefort dressing
Warm apple pie   Coffee

Another Manhattan Clam Chowder

1/4 pound salt pork
3 medium potatoes, cubed (approximately 2 cups)

1 large onion, chopped (approximately 3/4 cup)
2 leeks, halved lengthwise and thinly sliced
(approximately 1/2 cup)
2 stalks celery, thinly sliced
(approximately 1/2 cup)
1/2 small green pepper, chopped (approximately 1/4 cup)
1/2 bay leaf
1/2 teaspoon thyme
3 tomatoes or 3 cups canned tomatoes
Boiling water
4 cups cold water
1 quart shucked clams and liquor
Salt and pepper to taste
1/2 tablespoon chopped chives
1/2 tablespoon chopped parsley

Dice salt pork. Fry lightly in deep kettle. Reduce heat, and add potatoes, onion, leeks, celery, green pepper, bay leaf and thyme. Dip 3 tomatoes in boiling water, then quickly in cold water; peel, seed and chop, then add to kettle with 4 cups water. Drain liquor from clams, add it to pot and season lightly with salt and pepper. Cover kettle, bring to boil over high heat; reduce heat and simmer 30 minutes. Meanwhile in wooden bowl, finely chop clams. Add to kettle, and poach over medium heat 4 minutes. Stir in chives and parsley. Serve at once with toasted and buttered sea toast crackers or New England pilot crackers.

Dieter's Luncheon for 4

BUTTERMILK—TOMATO SOUP
OLD-FASHIONED PRESSED CHICKEN
Vegetable bouquet
FRUIT CREME

Buttermilk–Tomato Soup

        2 cups skimmed buttermilk
        1 (10-ounce) can condensed tomato soup
        1 teaspoon chopped onion
        1/2 teaspoon salt
        1/4 teaspoon Worcestershire sauce
        1/8 teaspoon hot pepper sauce
        4 lemon slices

Mix first 6 ingredients well together. Chill, and serve garnished with lemon slices. Serves 4. Calories per serving: 94.

Note: This pink and tangy soup is also a good introduction to summer lunch or supper.

Old-fashioned Pressed Chicken

        1 (2 1/2–3 pound) broiler-fryer chicken
        Water
        1 onion
        1 stalk celery
        4–5 peppercorns
        1 teaspoon salt
        1/2 cup white wine
        Salt and pepper to taste
        1 envelope powdered gelatin
        1/4 cup cold water or stock
        1 (7-ounce) jar pimentos, sliced
        4 pitted ripe olives, sliced, or bits of truffle
        1 hard-cooked egg, sliced
        Watercress

Simmer chicken until tender in water to cover with onion, celery, peppercorns and 1 teaspoon salt. Cool in stock; then remove. Reduce stock by boiling 10 minutes; strain, and chill, so that fat can be removed. Remove skin and bones from chicken. Slice breast meat; chop remainder. Measure 1 cup chicken stock; add wine, and season well with salt and pepper. Soften gelatin in cold water. Dissolve over hot water, and add to stock-wine mixture. Cover bottom of 1-quart mold or loaf pan with thin layer of gelatin mixture, and chill until set. Arrange some of the pimentos, olives and egg slices in attractive design; then add sliced white meat of chicken in even layer. Cover with thin layer of gelatin mixture, and chill until firm. Chop remaining egg slices. Chill remaining stock until syrupy; fold in remaining chicken, pimentos and chopped eggs to fill mold. Chill until firm. Unmold on platter, and garnish with watercress. Slice, or cut in squares. Serves 4–5. Calories per serving—approximately 185.

Fruit Crème

        1/2 (6-ounce) can frozen orange-pineapple juice
                concentrate
        1 envelope powdered gelatin
        1/4 cup cold water
        1 tablespoon orange curaçao or Cointreau
        2 teaspoons liquid sugar substitute
        1/4 cup nonfat dry milk
        1/4 cup ice water
        Whole strawberries

Reconstitute juice concentrate as directed; bring juice to boil, and cook 2 minutes. In large mixer bowl, soften gelatin in cold water. Add hot juice, liqueur and sugar substitute, stirring to dissolve gelatin. Chill until mixture becomes thick and syrupy. Combine dry milk and ice water; beat at high speed in mixer until mixture holds its shape. Fold into gelatin; spoon into 3-cup mold. Chill until set. Garnish with strawberries. Serves 4. Calories per serving: 83—add 4 calories for each strawberry used as garnish.

You may also substitute raspberries or sliced fresh peaches as garnish.

Note: If you don't cook juice at the beginning, enzymes in pineapple juice will prevent mixture from becoming firm.

Summer Luncheon for 8

Melon with lime wedges
Cold lobster with CAVIAR MAYONNAISE
Watercress   Cherry tomatoes
PINEAPPLE ROYALE   Iced coffee

Caviar Mayonnaise

        1 cup mayonnaise
        1 ounce (2 tablespoons) caviar
        Few drops lemon juice

To mayonnaise add caviar and lemon juice. Makes 1 cup.

Pineapple Royale

        2 large firm ripe pineapples
        1/4 cup superfine sugar
        1/4 cup rum or brandy (optional)
        1 quart orange sherbet
        6 egg whites
        1/8 teaspoon salt
        3/4 cup sugar
        1/4 cup flake coconut

Set pineapples on their sides, and, starting at base of each, quarter lengthwise right through green leaves. Discard core, and cut out flesh with small sharp knife or spoon, being careful to keep shell intact. Dice pineapple meat and sprinkle with 1/4 cup sugar and rum. Cover, and chill. Wrap green leaves in foil, and place shells on cookie sheet in refrigerator. Scoop 8 large balls of sherbet into waxed paper-lined pan, and set in freezer. At serving time make stiff meringue of egg whites, salt and 3/4 cup of sugar. Spread partially drained pineapple in shells. Add scoops of sherbet, and cover fruit and sherbet completely with meringue. Sprinkle with remaining fruit, sugar and coconut. Bake at 450°F. 4 minutes or until lightly browned. Remove foil from greenery, and serve immediately. Serves 8.

Note: Omit sherbet if you wish, and instead pile extra diced or sectioned fresh fruit in shells; cover with meringue, or swirl whipped dessert topping over sherbet, and serve without baking.

COCKTAIL PARTY

Here's a party at which the hostess can be almost as carefree as her guests. As guests will be going on to dinner when they leave, appetizers and snacks are the rule, and they can be made ahead of time. It isn't really necessary to offer a great variety of drinks, as long as there's enough of whatever you do serve. And ginger ale and juices should be available along with alcoholic beverages.

Make sure you have enough glasses to go around and more. It's possible to rent an ample supply of glasses from a caterer, if necessary.

Make sure, too, that you have enough ice. If you make plenty of cubes in advance, you can keep them in plastic bags in your freezer compartment until time for the party.

Set out necessities for making drinks separately from food. You can arrange bar in any corner where supplies will be safe from being knocked over. Set out bottles, ice bucket filled with cubes, pitcher of water, mixers, jigger measures and tray of glasses. Mixers—ginger ale, soda, tonic and so on—should be kept cool in refrigerator and put out a few bottles at a time, as they are needed.

You may prefer to fill glasses in the kitchen and take them around on a tray. In this case, drinks are mixed in larger quantities and kept well chilled until serving time.

Your Guests. People are apt to do a lot of wandering about at cocktail parties. If you can manage it, arrange a few corners in other rooms, so that groups can gather for talk away from main crowd.

Seating is always difficult at a cocktail party, but no one seems to mind very much. You can put a stack of cushions at foot of stairs, so that people can sit on stairs if they wish.

Accessories. You'll need plenty of ashtrays scattered liberally about room so that people can dispose of toothpicks or cigarettes as they talk. Coasters should be in good supply also, on every flat surface where you might reasonably expect someone to stand a glass. Small cocktail napkins are useful too.

Food. The food you serve should be finger-size if possible, as some of your guests will be standing, holding a glass in one hand and eating a bite here and there as they move about talking to other guests. Juggling doesn't come easily to most people. Circulate fresh supplies as long as party lasts—regular or open-faced sandwiches, plates of relishes, potato chips, salted nuts, and a hot specialty like tiny sausage rolls. Each is best handled separately. Occasionally cocktail-party food is set out as for small buffet, with a stack of small plates for those who wish them. Provide plenty of toothpicks or forks for spearing moist snacks.

Cocktail food generally is most appealing when sharply flavored—salted nuts, olives, flavorful crackers, crisp "munchies," herring tidbits smoked oysters, smoked salmon, pâtés, cheese spreads, dips, spreads, cocktail toast, seasoned toasts, nuts wafers, cheese wafers, and stuffed eggs.

Strips of toasted bread make good appetizer foundations. Trim crusts from thinly sliced bread, cut in 1-inch strips and toast on both sides under broiler before spreading with savory mixture. To cut bread into assorted shapes, slice before spreading with savory mixture. To cut bread into assorted shapes, slice unsliced sandwich loaf lengthwise, and trim crusts. Then cut out shapes. Or buy small dinner rolls, and slice thin, to make small toast circles with less waste than cutting rounds from square slices of ordinary bread.

For the finishing touch on canapés, here are a few suggestions:

Anchovy paste, asparagus tips and Parmesan cheese on toast strips
Onion sandwiches

Smoked salmon and capers on pumpernickel
Caviar with mimosa garnish (sieved egg yolk) on
toast
Sardines, onions and MAYONNAISE on toast
Shrimp butter and shrimp on toast
Ground ham and Swiss cheese on rolls, heated
Toast, BLUE-CHEESE SPREAD and onion garnish
CLAM COCKTAIL SPREAD on toast triangles decorated
with anchovy curls, grilled

Clam Cocktail Spread

    1 (7-ounce) can minced clams, drained
    1 (8-ounce) package cream cheese
    2 tablespoons sour cream
    1 tablespoon chopped chives or 2 tablespoons grated
        onion
    Dash hot pepper sauce or cayenne

Mix all ingredients except hot pepper sauce
together, and combine well. Add hot pepper
sauce very carefully, tasting to make sure you do
not overdo it; too little seasoning can be cor-
rected, whereas too much cannot. Makes approximately 1 cup.

Note: Spread on crackers or toast shapes, or
double amount of sour cream to make a dip.

Blue Cheese Spread

    1/2 cup cottage cheese
    2 ounces blue cheese
    Dash Worcestershire sauce

Blend cottage cheese and blue cheese in bowl
previously rubbed with garlic. Season with
Worcestershire sauce. Makes 3/4 cup.

Cocktail Puffs

These puffs are made of CHOUX PASTE and can
be bought ready for filling or made at home.
They usually take sweet fillings—custard or
whipped cream—but can be adapted to appetizing cocktail bites.

Make 1 recipe CHOUX PASTE. To fill, cut slit in
side of each puff; or cut top of each shell, spoon
in filling and replace top. Use creamed salmon,
creamed shrimp, creamed chicken or ham.

Hors d'oeuvres Suggestions

STEAK TARTARE
STUFFED MUSHROOMS
Turnovers (ham and anchovy, sausage, mushroom or
EMPANADAS)
SHRIMP TOAST
CHICKEN IN PAPER
BUTTERFLY SHRIMP
BAKED SESAME CLAMS
KEFTETHES

TIROTRIGONA
Cherry tomatoes stuffed with GUACAMOLE
Black olives in olive oil with crushed garlic and sliced
lemon

Steak Tartare

    1 pound finely ground lean beef
    1/2 cup finely chopped parsley
    1/3 cup grated onion
    2–3 teaspoons dry mustard
    1 1/2 teaspoons salt
    1 clove garlic, grated
    1–2 dashes Worcestershire sauce

Mix beef with parsley, grated onion, mustard,
salt, garlic and Worcestershire sauce. Heap in
bowl, and pat smooth. Surround with thin slices
rye or pumpernickel bread, cut into fingers, or
thin slices toasted rye or pumpernickel. Let
guests spread their own, and have pepper
grinder near by for those who like to top with
freshly ground black pepper. Serves 6–8 for
appetizer.

Note: Have butcher grind beef twice.

Stuffed Mushrooms

    1 pound medium mushrooms
    1/4 cup butter or margarine
    2 shallots, finely chopped
    1 clove garlic, finely chopped
    1/2 cup dry white wine
    2 tablespoons chopped parsley
    2 tablespoons anchovy butter
    1/3 cup fine bread crumbs
    1/4 cup buttered crumbs

Wash and dry mushrooms; remove caps and
finely chop stems. Sauté caps very briefly in 1/4
cup butter or margarine; remove caps and set
aside. In same pan sauté shallots and garlic until
soft. Add mushroom stems, wine, parsley, and
anchovy butter. Cook, stirring, over low heat 3
minutes. Stir in 1/3 cup bread crumbs. Fill caps
with mixture, sprinkle with buttered crumbs and
brown lightly under broiler. Makes approximately 14–15.

Empanadas

    1/2 cup lard
    1 tablespoon oil
    1 3/8 cups flour
    3 eggs
    1/2 cup (approximately) water
    1/3 cup lard
    1 large red pepper, diced
        (approximately 1 cup)
    1 large green pepper, diced
        (approximately 1 cup)
    1 medium onion, chopped
        (approximately 1/2 cup)

1/2 clove garlic, crushed
1 pound chopped beef
1/4 cup raisins
3/4 cup beef stock
Canned green chilies, peeled and chopped
2 tablespoons cornstarch
2 tablespoons water
Salt and pepper to taste
1 egg
Hot oil for deep-frying

Cream 1/2 cup lard until fluffy. Add oil, flour and 3 eggs, and mix well. Add 1/2 cup water, a little at a time, until dough has smooth consistency. Mix dough well until it does not stick to fingers. Let rest 1 hour before using. Meanwhile, melt 1/3 cup lard in pan. Add red and green peppers, onion and garlic. Sauté a few minutes. Add beef, and cook until it turns color; add raisins and stock. Simmer until meat and vegetables are cooked. Add as many chilies as desired. Dissolve cornstarch in 2 tablespoons water, thicken filling, season and let cool.

Roll dough out on floured board, thinner than a dime. Use empty 1-pound coffee can to cut out empanadas. Remove all dough cut away from circles. Beat 1 egg, and brush on each circle. Place 2 tablespoons filling on each circle. Fold over to form 1/2-moon shape. Twist ends closed by overlapping dough, as on pie shell. Fry in deep fat 375°F. until brown. Makes 12–14.

Shrimp Toast

1/2 pound shrimp
6 water chestnuts
2 1/2 tablespoons cornstarch
2 tablespoons pork fat, chopped fine
1 egg
1 teaspoon sherry
1 teaspoon salt
6 pieces bread, cut in triangles
Hot oil for deep-frying

Finely chop shrimp and water chestnuts. Add egg, cornstarch, pork fat, sherry and salt. Mix well. Spread mixture on triangles of bread, mounding in center. Fry, shrimp side down, in hot (375°F.) oil until bread is golden brown and crisp, turning once. Drain on paper towels. Serve at once. Makes 24.

Chicken in Paper

1 large whole uncooked chicken breast
1 tablespoon dry sherry
1 tablespoon soy sauce
1/2 teaspoon salt
1/2 teaspoon sugar
4 scallions, each cut into 5 pieces
2 slices fresh ginger root
Hot oil for deep-frying

Skin and bone chicken breast (or have butcher do it). Cut each 1/2 into 10 slices. Marinate in sherry, soy sauce, salt, sugar, scallions and ginger 20 minutes. Grease 20 6" x 6" squares waxed paper with few drops of oil. Place chicken slice and scallion piece in center of each and wrap as an envelope. Heat oil to 375°F. Fry 3 or 4 packages at a time about 3 minutes, turning once. Drain and serve at once. Makes 20.

Butterfly Shrimp

1 pound (15–18) uncooked shrimp
Juice of 1 lemon
1/2 cup flour
1 teaspoon baking powder
1/2 teaspoon salt
1 cup cold water
1 tablespoon oil
Hot oil for deep-frying

Shell and devein shrimp, but leave tails on. Squeeze lemon juice over shrimp, and let stand 20 minutes. Dry on paper towels so that batter will adhere properly. Mix remaining ingredients except oil, and let stand 10 minutes. Heat oil to 375°F. Coat each shrimp with batter, leaving tails uncoated, and fry, a few at a time, until crisp and golden, 3–4 minutes. Drain. Serve hot with English mustard or Chinese "duck" sauce. Serves 6–8 as an appetizer.

Baked Sesame Clams

4 stalks celery
2 leeks
1 medium onion
3 cloves garlic
1/2 can bean sprouts
1/2 cup butter or margarine
3 dozen clams and juice
Salt and pepper to taste
1/2 teaspoon grated fresh ginger
1 1/2 teaspoons cornstarch dissolved in 1 1/2 teaspoons water
1 1/4 cups MORNAY SAUCE
1 1/4 cups sesame seeds

Finely chop celery, leeks, onion, garlic and bean sprouts. Sauté in butter or margarine, but do not brown. Chop clams, and add to sautéed vegetables. Cook few minutes longer, add clam juice and season with salt, pepper and ginger. Thicken with cornstarch. Place filling in clam shells, cover with MORNAY SAUCE and sesame seeds. Glaze under broiler 5 minutes. Serve hot. Makes 36.

Keftethes (Parsley Meat Balls)

1/3 cup fine dry bread crumbs
1/2 cup milk
4 green onions, finely chopped
(approximately 1/2 cup)
1/2 cup finely chopped parsley
3 tablespoons olive oil
2 pounds ground chuck
2 egg yolks
2 cloves garlic, crushed
2 teaspoons salt
Ground pepper to taste
2 tablespoons butter or margarine
3 tablespoons lemon juice
1/2 teaspoon dried oregano

Soak bread crumbs in milk until soft. Sauté onions and parsley in 2 tablespoons oil until limp, and mix thoroughly with ground meat, egg yolks, garlic, salt and pepper. Add soaked bread crumbs. Shape into balls 1 inch in diameter. Sauté balls in remaining 1 tablespoon oil and butter or margarine in large frying pan, turning to brown all sides. Pour lemon juice into pan, and sprinkle meat balls with oregano. Heat a few minutes, scraping up browned drippings. Makes about 3 dozen appetizer meat balls; serves 6 as entree.

Tirotrigona (Cheese-filled Triangles)

1/2 pound blue cheese
1/2 pound feta cheese
1 pint large-curd cottage cheese
1 (8-ounce) package cream cheese
3 eggs
2 tablespoons finely chopped parsley
Dash of pepper
3/4 pound prepared strudel leaves
1 cup butter or margarine, melted

Cream all cheeses together until smooth. Add eggs, 1 at a time, beating until smooth. Mix in parsley and pepper. Lay out strudel leaves, 1 at a time, and brush each leaf all over with melted butter or margarine. Then, cutting across width of dough, cut each leaf into strips 2 inches wide. Place heaping teaspoon cheese filling on 1 end of each pastry strip, and fold over 1 corner to make triangle. Continue folding from side to side in shape of triangle until entire pastry strip covers filling. Proceed in this manner with leaves and filling until all are used. Place triangles on buttered baking sheet, and bake in preheated 350°F. oven 15 minutes or until golden brown. Serve hot. Makes about 6 dozen.

A Menu Suggestion

SHERRY–CHEESE LOAF
Fresh figs with walnuts and prosciutto
Raw mushrooms
Celery and cucumber sticks
TANGERINE FRAPPÉ

Sherry–Cheese Loaf

1 (6-ounce) can pecans
1/2 cup soft butter or margarine
3 tablespoons sherry or brandy
2/3 cup crumbled blue cheese
1 (4-ounce) package cream cheese
2 tablespoons Parmesan cheese
Dash hot pepper sauce
Parsley sprigs
Melba toast circles

Put nuts in blender, and blend 3–4 seconds or until finely chopped. Scrape nuts onto square of waxed paper. Measure butter or margarine and sherry into blender, and blend until smooth. Gradually add remaining ingredients, except parsley and toast, blending after each addition. Stop blender occasionally, and scrape down sides. When smooth, turn onto nuts, and shape into log. Coat well with nuts. Roll up in paper to smooth and shape, and chill. To serve, unwrap, and decorate with parsley and melba toast circles. Makes about 2 cups.

Note: 1/2 cup toasted sesame seeds may be used in place of pecans.

Tangerine Frappé

1 (6-ounce) can frozen tangerine juice
2–3 tablespoons lemon or lime juice
2 tablespoons grenadine
3/4 cup water
2 egg whites, unbeaten
1 cup soda water

Open top and bottom of juice can, and press frozen juice into blender. Add next 4 ingredients, and cover. Blend about 1 minute or until mixture is smooth and foamy. Add soda water, and pour over crushed ice. Serve in 5-ounce cocktail glasses, and pass savory appetizers. Makes about 26 ounces.

ENTERTAINING WITH CHEESE AND WINE

A cheese and wine party is a different and casual way to entertain a large group. You can make it an after-ski party, an evening event or a porch party. Invitations can be given by telephone, and preparation is simple. All you need is bread, crackers, wines and several kinds of cheese, arranged attractively. Set things out on dining table or server. A colored linen cloth or polished surface without mat echoes the note of informality. A checked cloth and candles in empty wine bottles can give the party a "cellar" atmosphere. Arrange wine and glasses at 1 end, and place food where it is easiest to reach and looks best. Wine glasses can be on large tray to avoid stains on tablecloth.

Identify Each Cheese. Group cheeses on 1, or at most 2, trays or boards. The effect of great variety is lost if you put each kind of cheese on a different plate. It's a good idea to set up a small flag (speared with a toothpick) identifying each kind of cheese with its name and country, so that guests can note and remember their favorites.

Have several napkin-lined baskets of various kinds of sliced bread and crackers, a bowl of sweet butter and plenty of table napkins.

Selecting Wines. Two kinds of wine, 1 red and 1 white, are enough; but you can serve as many as you like. Red wines should be opened some time before they are to be used. As a general rule, serve white wines chilled and red wines at room temperature. Don't be afraid to ask expert's advice. Any wine shop or wine importer will be happy to answer your questions.

Wines

Bordeaux reds	California reds
Burgundy reds	Champagne
Rhone Valley reds	Port

Breads and Biscuits

French or Italian bread	Water wafers
Dark and light rye bread	Melba toast
Biscuits, salted and unsalted	Sesame wafers

Cheeses

Brie	Gruyère
Bleu	Gouda
Camembert	Edam
Cheddar	Muenster
Caerphilly	Oka
Crème Chantilly	

DESSERT AND COFFEE PARTY

Most desserts can be prepared the day before, except for sauces or fillings. Everything can be laid out on dining table or on small tables in living room.

Some dining tables look best without cloth, with candles, silver and china on the polished surface, but a linen cloth can also be used. A low flower arrangement in center looks best, with candles on either side, but if table is against the wall a higher centerpiece is striking.

Put coffee tray at one end, with cups arranged around it. Put out both demitasse and larger cups; don't be afraid to mix your china, and provide dessert plates, spoons, forks and table napkins.

It's a good idea to have an alternate dessert for calorie counters—fruit compote or lemon sponge, for example. Be sure to have enough of each, though, for all your guests to take the same thing.

Somewhere on the table have a large pitcher of ice water and glasses. Little dishes with salted nuts and colored candies round out table display nicely. If you wish, liqueur may be served in tiny glasses with coffee.

There are many ways to prepare coffee. Just what flavor and strength depends on personal taste. Generally, after-dinner coffees are stronger than those served at mid-morning coffee breaks, for instance. Similarly, for these dressed-up versions, it's wise to start with good strong coffee. You're adding other flavors, so you need coffee that doesn't get lost in the mixture.

Coffees

Vienna Coffee

Serve 2/3 cup coffee diluted with 1/3 cup hot milk. Top with whipped cream.

Café Brûlot

Put sugar lump into teaspoon, pour over it a little brandy and set alight. Pour hot strong coffee into cup, and stir in flaming sugar.

Café Royale

To each cup of strong black coffee, sweetened to taste, add jigger of brandy. Or serve brandy separately for each guest to add as desired. Pass thick cream separately.

Liqueur Coffee

Fill demitasse cups about 3/4 full. To each, add 1 tablespoon of any liqueur. Try curaçao, Cointreau, crème de cacao, Tia Maria.

Coffee Chantilly

Serve strong black coffee, and top with whipped cream, sliding it gently onto surface of coffee, so that cool cream blends with hot coffee in each sip. If you want to make a production of it, you might try *unwhipped* whipping cream, but it takes a little practice. Pour thick cream over back of spoon held so that its tip is just at surface of coffee. And for a refinement in either of these methods, blend a little of any liqueur into the coffee (if you use Irish whiskey, it becomes Irish coffee).

Mocha Coffee

Make hot coffee, add equal amount of hot cocoa, pour into large cups or mugs and top with whipped cream and a little grated chocolate.

Desserts

Strawberry Torte

          4 egg whites
      1/4 teaspoon salt
          1 cup superfine sugar
      1/2 teaspoon almond extract
          4 egg yolks
      1/3 cup sugar
      1/8 teaspoon salt
      1/2 cup flour
    1 3/4 cups hot milk
          1 teaspoon vanilla extract
          1 quart fresh strawberries, 12 halved and remainder sliced
          1 cup heavy cream, stiffly beaten
      1/2 cup strawberry jelly
          1 tablespoon hot water

Mark 3 (8- or 9-inch) circles on sheets of heavy brown paper, and grease circles. Beat egg whites and 1/4 teaspoon salt until stiff and glossy; then beat in 1 cup sugar gradually, 2 tablespoons at a time. Add almond flavoring. Spread mixture evenly within circles. Set on cookie sheets, and bake at 300°F. 30–40 minutes or until very lightly tinted. Cool, and remove from paper with metal spatula, taking care to keep circles intact. Let meringue circles dry overnight, uncovered. Beat egg yolks, 1/3 cup sugar and 1/8 teaspoon salt together till thick, and beat in flour. Add milk, and cook in double boiler till thick and smooth. Stir in vanilla, and cool. To put torte together, spread 1/2 the custard on 1 meringue circle, and cover with layer of sliced strawberries; then spread with 3/4 cup cream, whipped, and cover with second meringue circle. Repeat sliced strawberries and whipped cream, and top with remaining meringue circle. Press layers together very gently, taking care not to crumble meringue. Make border of strawberry halves, cut side down. Heat jelly with hot water, and spoon over strawberries.

Chill; then garnish center and sides of torte with remaining whipped cream, swirling it with spoon or piping it in circles with icing bag. Allow torte to stand in refrigerator a few hours before serving. Cut in wedges. Serves 8–10.

Note: This torte can be made with any other fruit in season or with canned fruit, well drained and cut in pieces.

Glazed Cherry Torte

          2 (1-pound) cans sour pitted red cherries in syrup
      1/3 cup butter or margarine
    1 1/2 cups sugar
          2 eggs
    1 1/2 cups plus 2 tablespoons sifted all-purpose flour
      3/4 teaspoon baking soda
      1/2 teaspoon double-acting baking powder
      1/8 teaspoon salt
          1 cup coarsely chopped walnuts
      1/2 envelope (1 1/2 teaspoons) powdered gelatin
          2 tablespoons cold water
          1 cup heavy cream
      1/2 cup sugar
          2 tablespoons plus 1/2 teaspoon cornstarch
      1/2 teaspoon red vegetable coloring
    Chopped green pistachio nuts

Preheat oven to 375°F. Grease round cake pan 10 inches in diameter and 2 inches deep with butter or margarine, line bottom with waxed paper cut to fit and grease paper with butter or margarine. Drain cherries in sieve over pan, to reserve syrup. Measure out 2 1/4 cups cherries, and return to sieve to drain again. Chop cherries coarsely, and return to sieve to continue draining. Cream butter or margarine, and add 1 1/2 cups sugar, creaming well. Beat eggs until frothy, and add to creamed mixture. Sift flour, baking soda, baking powder and salt. Add to creamed mixture alternately with chopped cherries. Fold in chopped walnuts. Turn into pan, and bake at 375°F. 30–35 minutes, or until top is resilient when touched and toothpick inserted in center comes out clean. Cool in pan on rack 5 minutes; turn out on rack after loosening sides with knife, and immediately remove waxed paper. Cool.

In small measuring cup soften gelatin in the cold water; then place cup in small pan of hot water, stirring till gelatin is dissolved, about 3 minutes. Cool slightly. Whip cream stiff, and beat in dissolved gelatin gradually. Turn cooled cake onto plate; if you plan to use cake stand, make sure it will fit in your refrigerator. Spread cream mixture over top of cake only, as smoothly as possible, without swirling. If you don't have a flat round serving dish and are using a dinner plate, cake will sink in middle; it's all right, but put more topping in middle to even up. Put cake in refrigerator while making glaze. Combine 1 cup reserved cherry juice, 1/2 cup sugar, cornstarch and coloring in saucepan, and cook, stirring constantly, until thick and transparent. Cool, stirring frequently, till almost cold, about 30 minutes. Then refrigerate about 5 minutes. When almost cold, spread on cake, being sure to cover most of whipped cream. Sides of the cake are left plain, but you may let some glaze drip down decoratively. Arrange pistachio nuts around edge of cake. Refrigerate cake; as it's a 10-inch cake, your cake cover may be too small, in which case insert toothpicks through glaze around edges of cake, with 1 in center, and cover all with plastic wrap, tucking under plate. Holes made by toothpicks will not show later. Serves 14–16.

Rum Mousse

        2 eggs, separated
    1/4 cup superfine sugar
    1/2 cup milk
      1 envelope powdered gelatin
      3 tablespoons cold water
      1 cup heavy cream
      1 cup chopped glacé cherries
    1/4 cup light or dark rum
    1/2 cup whipped cream
     12 whole glacé cherries

Beat together egg yolks and sugar. Warm milk, and pour over egg mixture. Pour into top of double boiler, and cook over boiling water until thickened, stirring constantly. Remove to basin, and allow to cool about 5 minutes. Soften gelatin in cold water, dissolve in top of double boiler and add to cool custard. Whip cream until thickened, and add to custard with 1/2 cup chopped cherries and rum. Beat egg whites until stiff, and fold into mixture. Pour into mold (preferably a tube mold) rinsed in cold water, and chill until set. Unmold, and fill the center with remaining chopped cherries topped with whipped cream. Arrange whole cherries around mousse. Serves 6.

SUNDAY-NIGHT SUPPER

Everyone, including guests, can pitch in for a supper of soup, HAMBURGER SOUFFLE with BEARNAISE SAUCE, rolls, BUTTERED BROCCOLI, COLORFUL CABBAGE SALAD and CHOCOLATE RIBBON DESSERT.

Sunday-night Supper Soup

        2 slices bacon
    1/2 cup chopped onion
      2 (10 1/2-ounce) cans condensed green-pea soup
      2 (10 1/2-ounce) cans beef bouillon
    1/8 teaspoon thyme
    1/8 teaspoon pepper
      1 cup coarsely grated raw carrot

Fry bacon until crisp; drain on paper toweling. Sauté onion in 2 tablespoons bacon drippings. Combine pea soup, bouillon, thyme and pepper. Simmer 1 minute. Just before serving, add carrot. Crumble bacon over top. Serve with popcorn. Serves 4.

Hamburger Soufflé

    3 1/2 tablespoons butter or margarine
    4 1/2 tablespoons flour
    1 1/2 cups evaporated milk
      1 cup ground lean beef
    1 1/2 tablespoons instant minced onion
      2 teaspoons Worcestershire sauce
      1 teaspoon dried or fresh chopped chives
      1 teaspoon chopped parsley
      1 teaspoon salt
    1/4 teaspoon pepper
      6 eggs
    3/4 cup SAUCE BEARNAISE

Preheat oven to 400°F. Melt butter or margarine in medium saucepan over low heat. Stir in flour. Slowly add milk, stirring until mixture thickens. Remove from heat; add beef, onion, Worcestershire sauce, chives, parsley, salt and pepper. Separate eggs, and beat yolks well. Stir into meat mixture. Stiffly beat egg whites. When mixture cools, gently fold in stiffly beaten whites (for higher soufflé, add 2 extra whites). Pour into well-greased straight-sided 2-quart casserole. Bake 45 minutes; serve immediately. Serves 4–6.

Buttered Broccoli

      1 bunch or 2 (10-ounce) packages frozen broccoli
      2 tablespoons melted butter or margarine
      1 teaspoon lemon juice

Wash and trim hard stems from broccoli. Place in vegetable steamer over hot water. Cover, and steam 20 minutes or until tender. Dress with butter or margarine and lemon juice.

Colorful Cabbage Salad

      1 small head white cabbage
      1 small head red cabbage
    3/4 cup blue-cheese salad dressing
    1/2 cup red Italian onion rings

Halve cabbages; remove outer leaves and hard stalks. Chill in ice water several hours; drain. Finely shred on slaw board or with sharp knife until lacy thin. Line salad bowl with white cabbage leaves. Toss together equal parts white and red cabbage with salad dressing. Garnish with onion rings. Serves 4–6.

Caraway Sticks

    1 (8-ounce) package refrigerated crescent rolls
    1 egg yolk, beaten
    1/4 cup caraway seeds
    2 tablespoons coarse salt

Preheat oven to 375°F. Prepare crescent rolls, following package directions. Brush tops with egg yolk; sprinkle with caraway seeds and salt. Bake 10–13 minutes. Makes 8 rolls.

Chocolate Ribbon Dessert

    2 (3 3/4-ounce) packages vanilla whipped-dessert mix
    2 teaspoons sugar
    1/2 teaspoon mint extract
    1/2 teaspoon green vegetable coloring
    1 (3 3/4-ounce) package chocolate whipped-dessert mix
    2 teaspoons sugar
    1 (1-ounce) envelope unsweetened no-melt chocolate
    1/4 teaspoon vanilla extract
    1 recipe MARBLED WHIPPED CREAM

Prepare 1 package vanilla dessert mix, following package directions, adding 2 teaspoons sugar to mix and mint extract and food coloring to water. Pour 1/2 mixture into 7 1/2″ x 3 1/2″ x 2 1/2″ loaf pan; chill. Meanwhile prepare chocolate dessert mix, following package directions, adding 2 teaspoons sugar to mix and chocolate, and vanilla to water. Pour over mint layer, and chill, Pour remaining vanilla mixture over chocolate layer. Chill 1 1/2 hours, or set in freezer 1/2 hour. Garnish with whipped cream. Serves 6.

Marbled Whipped Cream

        1 cup heavy cream
        2 tablespoons chocolate syrup

Whip cream until stiff; gently fold in syrup to give marbled effect. Makes 1 cup.

Sunday-night Supper Menu

SPRINGTIME CASSEROLE
SPICED PEACHES
Green salad   Corn sticks
Coffee layer cake with chocolate frosting
Coffee

Some leftover baked ham, combined with peas and new potatoes, can become a SPRINGTIME CASSEROLE. You can make it on Saturday.

Springtime Casserole

    1/2 cup butter or margarine
    1/2 cup flour
      5 cups milk
      1 cup cream
    1/3 cup grated Cheddar cheese
      1 teaspoon salt
    1/2 teaspoon white pepper
      2 pounds cooked fresh peas or 2 (10-ounce) packages frozen peas
      2 pounds cooked new potatoes, peeled
      8 slices (1 1/2 pounds) cooked ham

Preheat oven to 350°F. In saucepan melt butter or margarine, blend in flour. Add milk and cream, stirring until mixture is smooth and thickened. Add cheese, salt and pepper. Continue cooking and stirring until cheese is melted. Add peas, potatoes and ham; spoon mixture into 3-quart casserole. Bake 30 minutes until golden and bubbly. Serves 8.

BON VOYAGE OR FONDUE PARTY

If you're having friends in to say goodbye to the Joneses, you might ask each guest to bring some small travel aid as a parting gift to decorate a traveler's tree. This tree actually grows in the West Indies, but you can make your own by decorating a room divider or screen with attractive branches of oak, maple, pine or shrubbery from which to hang gifts. Feel free to set a maximum price.

Types of Menu. You can serve food to make your departing friends think back on America or ahead to their destination. If they're going to Switzerland, do have a Swiss fondue party.

You'll need an earthenware casserole and spirit lamp or chafing dish. Rub casserole with garlic first. Fondue is made by stirring 1/2 pound shredded Swiss cheese, dusted with flour, into 1 cup dry white wine and heating it very slowly in casserole over flame until cheese melts and combines with wine in creamy-white mixture. Just before serving time, stir in 2 tablespoons kirsch.

For the ceremony of eating, set your table with a plate of bread cubes for each person. Cubes should be about 1 inch in size. A glass of white wine, too, should be at each plate, and you'll need long-handled forks; there's a special kind of fork with a heat-resistant handle, for a fondue. Each person takes a cube of bread on fork, dips it into fondue and swirls it around the bottom of casserole in figure-8 movement, to keep mixture from hardening on casserole bottom.

Fondue is sometimes made with white-sauce base. You can start cooking in kitchen; make your white sauce with 2 tablespoons each butter or margarine and flour for each cup milk. Stir in cheese, and pour mixture into casserole ready for serving over flame at table which keeps it hot during eating.

Swiss cheese is used for this dish because it melts more smoothly than any other. But if mixture does begin to get a little stringy while guests are twirling their bread cubes in the mixture, as it will, simply add more kirsch.

Menu for a Fondue Party

STEAK TARTARE
Swiss-cheese fondue with French bread cubes
Tossed green salad   PEARS BURGUNDY
Coffee

Pears Burgundy

    3 (1-pound) cans pear halves
    1 (4/5 quart) bottle red Burgundy
    1/2 cup light corn syrup
    1 tablespoon grated lemon rind
    1 1/2 teaspoons cinnamon
    3/4 teaspoon allspice
    1 teaspoon cloves

Drain pear halves, saving 2 cups liquid. In medium saucepan mix liquid with Burgundy, corn syrup, lemon rind, cinnamon, allspice and cloves. Simmer 10 minutes. Add pear halves. Cool. Refrigerate at least 4 hours. Serve with DATE SQUARES. Serves 6–8.

A HOME-MOVIE PARTY

You can rent 35 mm. movies by mail! Why not try a Keystone Cops comedy as the feature, and invite guests to bring their own home-movie efforts as short subjects. Set the living room up to look like a theater, and darken it when guests arrive. Usher guests to their seats with a flashlight; hand them a bag of popcorn and some old-fashioned licorice sticks. Have soft drinks on hand for intermissions.

After the show, serve an ice cream-parlor treat of waffles with strawberry topping.

Waffles with Strawberry Sauce

    1 (12-ounce) package frozen strawberries, thawed
1 1/2 tablespoons cornstarch
    1/3 cup orange juice
    2 teaspoons lemon juice
    3 (5-ounce) packages frozen waffles, cooked according to package directions

Drain strawberries, and save juice. Blend juice with cornstarch, orange juice and lemon juice in medium saucepan. Stir until smooth. Bring to boil; stir until thick and translucent. Add strawberries. Serve warm over waffles. Serves 8.

Friday-to-Sunday Menus

Friday-night Supper

CIOPPINO
Green salad
Toasted FRENCH BREAD
ROSÉ FRUITS   Cookies   Coffee

Cioppino

    1 1/2 cups chopped onion
    1 cup chopped green pepper
    1/4 cup olive oil
    3 cloves garlic, mashed with 1 teaspoon salt
    1 (1 pound, 13 ounce) can tomatoes
    2 cups red table wine
    2 cups tomato juice
    2 cups fish stock made from lobster body and fish trimmings
Herb bouquet (bay leaf, parsley, basil)
    3 pounds sea bass
    1 live lobster
    1 pound (or more) jumbo shrimp
    1 pint clams or mussels or oysters or all three
    1/2 cup chopped parsley

Sauté onion and green pepper in olive oil until just soft. Add next 6 ingredients, and cook 10 minutes. Remove herb bouquet, and taste for seasoning. In large kettle with cover, arrange all fish and seafood in layers. Pour sauce over, and cover pan. Simmer over low heat 20–30 minutes or until fish is just done. Serve in deep bowls, shells and all, and sprinkle liberally with chopped parsley. Have plenty of big paper napkins on hand. Serves 6–8.

Rosé Fruits

1/2 cup honey
1/2 cup rosé wine
Small bunch mint leaves, broken
    1 cup sliced strawberries
    1 cup sliced bananas
    1 cup melon balls
    1 cup fresh diced pineapple or any fresh fruits in season
    1 quart vanilla ice cream

Heat honey; remove from heat, and add wine and mint leaves. Chill 1 hour. Strain, and pour over fruits. Chill until serving time. Spoon over scoops of vanilla ice cream. Serves 8.

Saturday Breakfast

Orange juice
Blueberry pancakes with maple syrup   Bacon
Coffee

Saturday Lunch at the Lake

Thermos ice cold martinis
Cold broiled tarragon chicken
FRENCH POTATO SALAD   CAVIAR EGGS
French loaf
Miniature French pastries (from bakery)

French Potato Salad

    3 pounds (6–8 medium) new potatoes
Boiling water
Pinch salt
1/2 cup olive oil
    3 tablespoons wine vinegar
    1 teaspoon salt
    1 teaspoon freshly ground black pepper
    1 cup chopped green onions
1/2 cup chopped parsley
    2 hard-cooked eggs, sliced

Wash potatoes, and place unpeeled in boiling water to cover. Add pinch salt, and cook in boiling water until just done. Test by piercing with point of sharp knife. Do not overcook. Drain at once, and run a little cold water over. Peel quickly, and slice. Place in deep bowl, and add olive oil, vinegar, 1 teaspoon salt and pepper. Mix well. Set aside to cool; then chill in refrigerator. About 2 hours before serving, add onions, parsley and additional oil if necessary. Taste for seasoning, and add more salt and pepper if needed. Serve in salad bowl, and garnish with egg slices. Serves 6–8.

Note: Potatoes should still be warm when seasonings are added.

Caviar Eggs

    6 hard-cooked eggs, halved
    2 tablespoons MAYONNAISE
    1 small (2-ounce) jar black caviar
    1 tablespoon chopped parsley
    1 teaspoon onion juice
Salt to taste

Scoop out egg yolks, and mash. Add mayonnaise, caviar (reserving a little for garnish), parsley and onion juice. Taste for seasoning, and add salt if necessary. Heap mixture into egg whites, and garnish with caviar. Chill. Serves 6.

Saturday Dinner on the Porch

Raw vegetables with ANCHOVY MAYONNAISE
Grilled thick sirloin steaks   MUSTARD SAUCE
Baked potatoes with garlic butter
Green beans and corn
Strawberries and cream   Coffee

Anchovy Mayonnaise

    6 anchovy fillets, mashed to paste
3/4 cup mayonnaise
Lemon juice to taste

Add anchovy fillets to mayonnaise, and season with lemon juice. Makes 3/4 cup.

Mustard Sauce

    1 cup sour cream
1/2 cup sharp mustard
    1 teaspoon vinegar
    1 teaspoon chopped parsley

Mix all ingredients together. Let stand in refrigerator 2 hours before using. Makes 1 1/2 cups.

Sunday Brunch

Peaches and raspberries in orange juice
CHICKEN HASH IN CREAM
Broccoli with butter   Toasted English muffins
Coffee

Chicken Hash in Cream

    3 cups diced poached chicken, white meat
1 1/2 cups light cream
    2 tablespoons butter or margarine
    2 tablespoons flour
1 1/2 cups milk
Salt and white pepper to taste
    1 egg, slightly beaten

Place chicken and 1 cup cream in saucepan, and simmer until cream has reduced to about 1/2 cup. Melt butter or margarine in separate saucepan; add flour, and cook 2 minutes. Add milk, and cook over medium heat, stirring constantly, until thick and smooth. Stir in remaining cream; add salt and pepper. Add 1 cup of this sauce to chicken-and-cream mixture. Place hash in flat oven-proof dish; combine egg with remaining cream sauce, and spread over hash. Bake in 350°F. oven until heated through and glazed on top. Serves 6–7.

HOLIDAY ENTERTAINING

Traditional Thanksgiving Dinner

MUSHROOM CONSOMMÉ
ROAST TURKEY   CHESTNUT STUFFING
Brown giblet gravy
Mashed white potatoes   Candied yams
Creamed white onions
Puréed yellow turnips   Buttered green beans
Cranberry jelly
Celery hearts   Green and black olives
Pumpkin pie with whipped cream
Fruit   Nuts   Coffee

Mushroom Consommé

3 tablespoons butter or margarine
1/2 pound mushrooms, chopped
   (approximately 2 cups)
4 (13-ounce) cans consommé Madrilene
2 tablespoons chopped parsley
2 tablespoons sherry (optional)

Melt butter or margarine in saucepan. Add mushrooms, and cook lightly a few minutes, stirring often. Add consommé, heat. Sprinkle with parsley, and add sherry. Serves 10.

Chestnut Stuffing

1 pound chestnuts
Boiling water
6 cups stale coarse bread crumbs
1/2 cup butter or margarine
1/4 cup boiling water
1 cup sliced celery
3 or 4 sprigs parsley
1 onion, quartered
2 teaspoons salt
1 teaspoon thyme
1 teaspoon savory
1 teaspoon sage
1/2 teaspoon pepper

Gash chestnut ends, and simmer in boiling water 20 minutes. Remove shells and membranes. Chop in blender 1 cup at a time. Mix ground nuts with crumbs. Measure all remaining ingredients into blender, and whizz at high speed to paste-like consistency. Pour over crumb-nut mixture, and toss lightly. Makes enough dressing for 10–12-pound turkey.

Trim-the-Christmas-Tree Supper

HOT SEAFOOD MEDLEY
COLD ROAST FRESH HAM
RELISH CHRISTMAS TREE   CHEESE BALL
Assorted breads
Dark or LIGHT FRUITCAKE
Coffee or yuletide eggnog

Hot Seafood Medley

4 (10 1/2-ounce) cans frozen shrimp soup
1 1/2 cups milk
6 cups cooked fish and seafood (flounder, cod, shrimp, crabmeat, lobster)
2 tablespoons sherry (optional)

Combine soup and milk. Heat. Add fish and seafood. Heat, and add sherry. Serve in ready-baked PATTY SHELLS, or buy frozen ones and bake according to package directions, allowing 1 per serving. Serves 8–10.

Cold Roast Fresh Ham

1 (10–14 pound) fresh ham
Salt and pepper to taste

Rub ham with salt and pepper. Place, face side up, on rack in open roasting pan. Insert meat thermometer through fat side into center of roast. Roast in slow oven (325°F.) until thermometer registers 185°F. (well done)—6–7 hours. Score and garnish if desired. Cool well before slicing thin. Serves 15–18.

Relish Christmas Tree

Buy a piece of styrofoam shaped like a Christmas tree. Cover with heavy green wrapping paper. Stick with toothpicks and then with assorted vegetables and pickles—tiny tomatoes, cauliflower pieces, radishes, pickled onions and tiny cucumber pickles.

Cheese Ball

4 pounds soft Cheddar cheese
1 (8-ounce) package cream cheese
1 cup chopped parsley
Strips sweet red pepper
1 small tomato or twisted pepper strip

For large cheese ball, shape Cheddar cheese into ball (keep out of refrigerator until right temperature to shape easily). Chill. Cream cream cheese to spreading consistency. Spread over ball. Cover ball with chopped parsley, and press in lightly. Arrange strips of sweet red pepper down sides of ball, and press in lightly. Top with tomato or twisted pepper piece. Makes 32 servings.

Light Fruitcake

    1 pound almonds, blanched and slivered
    1/2 pound candied red cherries, halved
    1/4 pound candied green cherries, halved
    1/2 pound golden raisins
    1/2 pound candied citron, chopped
    1/4 pound candied pineapple, chopped
    4 cups unsifted all-purpose flour
1 1/2 cups butter or margarine
    2 cups sugar
    6 eggs, separated
    3/4 cup milk
    1/4 cup brandy
    1 teaspoon almond extract
    1 teaspoon cream of tartar
Candied strawberries
Angelica strips

Grease 10-inch tube pan, line with brown paper and grease paper. Combine almonds, cherries, raisins, citron and pineapple; sprinkle with 1/2 cup flour. Cream butter or margarine, gradually add sugar and beat until creamy. Beat egg yolks well, and add to butter mixture; beat thoroughly. Combine milk, brandy and almond extract; add alternately with remaining flour to butter mixture. Pour over fruit and nuts, and mix well. Beat egg whites until foamy; add cream of tartar, and beat until stiff. Fold into first mixture. Pour into prepared pan. Bake in slow oven (275°F.) about 3 hours. Let stand 30 minutes. Remove cake from pan, and carefully tear off paper. Cool to room temperature. Decorate with candied strawberries and strips of angelica. Wrap in moisture-proof paper, and store in cool place.

Christmas Dinner

Oysters on half-shell
Roast goose   Wild rice
Chestnut purée   Brussels sprouts
Plum pudding   VELVET SAUCE
Christmas pound cake   Coffee   Brandy

Velvet Sauce

    2 eggs
    1 cup confectioners' sugar
    3 tablespoons lemon juice
    1 tablespoon grated lemon rind
1 1/4 cups stiffly beaten cream

Beat eggs well until thick and lemon-colored. Add sugar slowly; beat well, and add lemon juice and rind. Fold in stiffly beaten cream. Makes about 2 cups.

New Year's Eve Buffet Supper

CRUSTY BUFFET HAM   BRAISED TURKEY WITH HERBS
Lump crabmeat with Russian dressing
Hot corn sticks   Parker House rolls
LAZY-SUSAN SALAD
Mincemeat tart   CAFÉ BRÛLOT

Crusty Buffet Ham

    1 (4–6 pound) ready-to-eat boneless ham
    1 egg, slightly beaten
Pastry mix for 2-crust pie
Water
    2 teaspoons dry mustard
    2 teaspoons ground cloves
    2 teaspoons sugar
    1 egg yolk
    2 tablespoons water
Endive
Pimento stars

Remove casing from ham. Stir egg into pastry mix; add just enough water to make stiff dough. Roll out on well-floured board in rectangle, about 9″ x 14″ and 3/8–1/4-inch thick. Combine mustard, cloves and sugar, and sift over pastry. Set ham, fat side down, in center of pastry, and dampen edges. Bring edges up to overlap and completely enclose ham. Seal edges and ends by folding and pinching pastry. Roll back and forth to smooth edges, and place in baking pan, fat side up. Score diagonally without cutting through. Prick every other diamond with fork; combine egg yolk and water, and brush on pastry. Bake at 350°F. for 1–1 1/2 hours, depending on thickness of pastry. Cool at room temperature; then chill. To serve, slice crust from face of ham and discard. Set ham on platter garnished with endive, and dress crusty top with star-shaped pimento cutouts, if you wish. Serves 8–10.

Braised Turkey with Herbs

Turkey giblets, back and neck
    4 cups water
    1 teaspoon salt
    1 handful celery leaves
    1 piece bay leaf
    1/3 cup flour
1 1/2 teaspoons salt
    6–7 pound turkey, cut into serving pieces
    1/4 cup butter or margarine
    3 tablespoons salad oil
    1 cup white wine or French vermouth or consommé
    1/4 cup sliced green onion
    1/2 clove garlic, crushed
    1/2 teaspoon tarragon
    1/2 teaspoon chervil
    1/2 teaspoon thyme
    3 tablespoons soft butter or margarine
    3 tablespoons flour
    2 teaspoons tomato paste
Salt and black pepper to taste
Chopped parsley or pepper cress

Cover back, neck and giblets with 4 cups water; add 1 teaspoon salt, celery leaves and bay leaf. Cover, and simmer 2 hours or until liquid is reduced by 1/2. Strain. Remove bones from meat, finely dice giblets and bits of turkey, add to stock and set aside. Combine 1/3 cup flour and 1 1/2 teaspoons salt. Dredge serving pieces of turkey in flour mixture; heat butter or margarine and oil together in large shallow roast pan. Turn turkey pieces to coat well, and slip pan in hot oven (400°F.). Roast until 1 side is browned, about 20 minutes; then turn pieces over, and brown another 20 minutes. Combine wine, onion, garlic and herbs, and pour over turkey. Cover tightly, and reduce heat to 325°F. Bake 1–1 1/2 hours or until tender, turning turkey pieces once during cooking. Add more wine if necessary. Remove turkey to hot platter, and cover. Keep warm in oven while making sauce. Scrape pan juices into saucepan, and skim off excess fat. Add giblet stock; make smooth roux of 3 tablespoons butter or margarine, 3 tablespoons flour and tomato paste, and stir in. Whisk until smoothly thickened. Add salt and pepper. Pour sauce over turkey, and sprinkle with parsley. Serves 8.

Note: Have butcher cut turkey into pieces, so that you have legs, thighs, wings, 4 pieces of breast and back and neck separate.

Lazy-Susan Salad

Arrange assortment of vegetables, each in its own dish, on lazy Susan. Dress with VINAIGRETTE SAUCE, and dust with chopped parsley. Some vegetables you might choose: whole crisp green beans, raw cauliflowerettes, whole cherry tomatoes, tiny carrots cooked until crisp, cooked whole white onions, sliced zucchini.

New Year's Day Open House

Toasted hazelnuts   Spiced ripe olives
Smoked mussels   Cheese wafers
Sliced smoked turkey
Bread-and-butter sandwiches
OYSTER STEW
Beaten biscuits   Oyster crackers
Caraway cakes
Fruitcake   Christmas cookies
White-wine punch   Eggnog

Oyster Stew

    3 pints oysters and their liquor
    1 pint milk
    1 quart cream
    1/2 cup butter or margarine
    Salt, pepper and cayenne to taste

Drain liquor from oysters, and heat with milk and cream. While it is cooking, heat 8 bowls, and add 1 tablespoon butter to each bowl to melt. Season hot liquid with salt, pepper and cayenne, and add oysters. Let mixture come just to boiling, but do not boil. When steaming hot, pour into bowls, and serve with toasted FRENCH BREAD. Serves 8.

POKER PARTY

When all the guests are men, the accent should be on hearty food—a casserole and salad, some filled sandwiches, a platter of corned-beef hash, and so on. Set out plates, cups, saucers and napkins. Have casserole ready to heat through in the oven or sandwiches covered with damp towel in refrigerator. Fix coffee pot, and have sugar and creamer handy.

Menu

DANISH MODERN SANDWICHES   Cold beer
Fresh fruit   Toasted pound cake
Coffee

Danish Modern Sandwiches

    2 (8-ounce) packages cream cheese
    1/2 cup commercial sour cream
    1/4 teaspoon salt
    6 slices dark rye bread
    1 tablespoon butter or margarine
    1 1/2 pounds smoked salmon, sliced
    6 hard-cooked eggs, sliced
    1 large Italian or Spanish red onion, sliced
Fresh dill
Salad greens

Cream together cream cheese, sour cream and salt. Spread bread lightly with butter or margarine. Spread cream-cheese mixture on salmon slices; fold salmon over, place on bread. Arrange egg and onion slices between salmon-cheese rolls. Garnish with dill; serve on salad greens. Serves 6.

CHILDREN'S PARTIES

Parties for the very young (1–3) should be limited to a small group of youngsters whose mothers will accompany them. Provide simple toys for the guests to play with; they're not ready for games yet.

The children will enjoy seeing the birthday cake and candles but probably will not be too interested in eating it. Cookies or cupcakes are more easily handled by this age group, as are plastic bowls or cups of ice cream, jello or custard. Milk and fruit juices are suitable beverages.

Don't insist that children remain at table too long; their attention span is short. Coloring books and crayons may occupy the time while you serve cake and coffee to adult guests.

As soon as you notice signs of restlessness among the children, try to indicate gracefully that the party is over. Get out some gifts for the children to take home with them, which will please them, and let them know that it's time to leave.

The most satisfactory children for a party are 4–7 year-olds. They are old enough to enjoy it and young enough to be unself-conscious about it. Hats, streamers, noisemakers—all the conventional party accessories—are appropriate. Use a pretty paper tablecloth, matching napkins and plates and cups. A charming place card can be made from a balloon: Write each child's name with a felt-tipped marker on a balloon (before inflating), tie with string and attach 1 to each chair.

If you have invited them for lunch, keep food simple—sandwiches of cream cheese or peanut butter and jelly, tuna fish, egg salad and perhaps a plate of cocktail frankfurters. Heated shoestring potatoes; carrot and celery sticks, the birthday cake, ice cream and chocolate milk or fruit juices will complete the menu.

If you are going to play games, have all the equipment gathered in advance. Children like such old favorites as pin-the-tail-on-the-donkey and musical chairs. Have some prizes for the winners; in fact have a small prize for everyone.

When you call to give the invitations, tell the mothers that you will arrange for the children to get home. This way you can decide when the party is over.

After the age of 8 you may have to alter the style of the party. Boys, particularly, are not very enthusiastic about dressing up for an afternoon of ice cream and cake. A backyard cook-out would be more to their liking. Thick, juicy hamburgers; grilled frankfurters; a platter of hard-cooked eggs; small whole tomatoes; and black, crusty potatoes baked in coals and eaten by hand with butter and salt would be a feast for them. Lots of milk and soft drinks, ice cream and cake or cupcakes are nice for dessert.

If weather permits, some games can be organized to occupy them before mealtime. Sack races, potato races, three-legged races, volleyball and touch football are all fun, as are certain indoor games like Nok Hockey, Ping-Pong and other action games. Again, prizes are nice.

Girls older than 8 seem content with the traditional ice-cream and cake routine, varied with some records and space for dancing. Girls love to make things too. You could provide paper plates and some odd feathers, flowers, ribbons and the like and stage a hat-designing contest.

Halloween Party

Everybody loves to dress up, especially children, and Halloween offers unlimited opportunities. Issue invitations far enough ahead for mothers to plan children's costumes.

Games Need Space

The number you invite, of course, depends on the space you have. And games—especially children's games—require a great deal of space. Have as much Halloween in the decor as possible—orange paper pumpkins pinned on doors, and big clusters of orange and black balloons tied to the hall light, and the stair posts—give a carnival look to the house.

When the children arrive start a game—maybe charades for an opener. Do keep the pace brisk, and go on to the next game before they tire of the first. Be sure to include bobbing for apples —it's messy but fun. And older children might enjoy some dancing.

Food and Beverages

Right from the start, with so much action, children will be thirsty. Have big pitchers of cold apple cider or fruit juice on hand all evening.

When suppertime comes, produce a good choice of easy-to-manage food arranged on a table—sandwiches, filled rolls, deviled eggs, squares of cheese, celery and carrot sticks, olives, gherkins. For something sweet, try pumpkin or mince tarts, crullers, candied apples, hermits or other spicy cookies. Hot chocolate served with whipped cream or hot chocolate milk is a good beverage choice.

Menu

Peanut butter-and-jelly sandwiches
Franks in hot rolls
Deviled eggs   Cheddar cheese squares
Celery   Carrot sticks
Olives   Gherkins   Dill pickles
Popcorn   Potato chips
Rye bread and butter
Pumpkin tarts   Crullers   Hermits
Candied apples
Hot chocolate milk
Hot chocolate and whipped cream
Salted nuts   Turkish taffy

Making Candy. From a child's point of view, candy makes a party "a party." Homemade candy making with tasting privileges is the most delightful activity they can ever imagine.

Halloween is the ideal time for children and candies to come together, and for "trick or treat" homemade candies can't be beat.

If you think you're going to enjoy candy making, a candy thermometer is a good investment. But you can manage without one, though the results aren't quite so predictable, and it takes a little practice. The test of "doneness" consists of putting a drop of the cooked sugar mixture into glass of cold water. If you are making soft candy like fudge, the mixture is done when drop of syrup forms a soft ball in cold water but does not hold its shape (236°–238°F.). In making caramels, cook longer, until the syrup forms a firmer ball (244°–250°F.). For taffy, drop should form a hard ball in cold water and hold its hardness when taken out (258°–266°F.). Butterscotch mixture should form threads when dropped into cold water, which soften when taken out (290°–300°F.). Brittle candy like PEANUT BRITTLE needs a slightly higher temperature; syrup forms brittle threads, which snap off when taken from water (300°–310°F.), sometimes known as "hard crack."

Use heavy saucepan to prevent mixture from burning on bottom, and have it large enough to allow mixture to boil vigorously without boiling over. A wooden spoon is best for stirring or beating candy mixtures.

Note: Do not attempt to make candy on a humid day!

Peanut Clusters

8 ounces semisweet chocolate
8 ounces roasted shelled peanuts

Melt chocolate in bowl over hot water. Remove from heat, cool slightly and stir in peanuts. Spread sheet of waxed paper on cookie sheet, and drop teaspoonfuls of chocolate-peanut mixture onto sheet. Place cookie sheet in refrigerator overnight to chill thoroughly. Makes 1 pound.

Candied Apples

6 medium-size red apples
6 wooden skewers
2 1/2 cups light corn syrup
2 1/2 cups sugar
1 cup water
1 teaspoon red vegetable coloring

Wash and dry 6 medium-size red apples. Dry well. Insert wooden skewers firmly at stem ends. In medium saucepan, mix sugar, corn syrup and water. Stir over medium heat until sugar dissolves. Add 1 teaspoon red food coloring. Bring to boil; cook until candy thermometer reads 300°F. (hard-crack stage). Remove syrup from heat. Quickly dip each apple in syrup, coating completely. Place on well-greased baking sheet while coating hardens. When cool, wrap individually in clear plastic wrap. Serves 6.

Raisin–Peanut Clusters

8 ounces semisweet chocolate
2 1/2 cups seedless raisins
1 cup shelled roasted peanuts
1/4 teaspoon salt

Melt chocolate in bowl over hot water. Remove from heat, and cool slightly. Stir in raisins and peanuts, add salt and mix well. Drop teaspoonfuls on waxed paper on cookie sheet, and chill overnight in refrigerator. Makes about 2 pounds.

Pralines

1 cup granulated sugar
1 cup firmly packed brown sugar
1 cup buttermilk
1/2 teaspoon baking soda
1/8 teaspoon salt
1 1/4 cups pecan halves
2 tablespoons butter or margarine
1 teaspoon vanilla extract

Mix sugars, buttermilk, baking soda and salt in heavy 4-quart pan, and stir over low heat until sugar is dissolved. Boil over moderate heat till thermometer registers 230°F. or till mixture forms soft balls in cold water. Remove from heat, and stir in nuts, butter or margarine and vanilla; beat until mixture is thick and slightly sugary. Set saucepan over low heat or hot water, to prevent mixture from hardening any further, and drop tablespoonfuls onto waxed paper on cookie sheet. Make each patty about 2 1/2 inches across. Cover with waxed paper, and chill before using. If pralines are to be used for gifts, wrap each separately in cellophane, or set in fluted paper cups. Makes about 1 1/2 pounds.

Lollipops

         2 cups granulated sugar
         1 cup water
       2/3 cup light corn syrup
       1/2 teaspoon oil of lemon
       Few drops yellow vegetable coloring
        24 sticks

Wrap wet cloth around long-handled fork, and use during cooking to wipe off crystals that accumulate around sides of pan. Grease lollipop molds or any flat surface (cookie sheet or shallow baking pan, turned upside down, will do). Put sugar, water, and syrup into heavy saucepan, and cook over low heat, stirring, until sugar dissolves. Continue to cook without stirring until hard-crack stage is reached (310°F.). Quickly stir in oil of lemon and food coloring. Pour mixture into greased lollipop molds or drop from end of spoon onto flat greased surface, spreading to make round shapes. Press 1 end of lollipop stick into each pop as soon as mixture is poured from spoon, working quickly before candy cools and hardens. Loosen lollipops from surface as soon as they are firm but before they are quite cold, and wrap each in cellophane. Makes 24.

Note: To form faces, use 1/2 gumdrop for mouth and raisins for eyes, and scatter coconut around top for hair. Set out all ingredients for decorations in advance, ready to add while pops are hot and before they harden.

Uncooked Fondant

         1 egg white
       1 1/2 teaspoons water
         3/4 teaspoon vanilla extract
       2 3/4 cups confectioners' sugar

Beat egg white, water and vanilla in bowl until well blended; add sugar gradually, beating until mixture is very stiff. Knead with hands until smooth. Wrap in waxed paper, and store in refrigerator.

VARIATIONS:

Chocolate Fondant: Add 2 squares melted unsweetened chocolate to fondant. Blend thoroughly.

Fondant Chocolate Peppermints: Add few drops essence of peppermint to fondant. Mix it thoroughly. Melt 2 squares unsweetened chocolate in top of double boiler. Make small balls of fondant, and flatten into patties. Dip in melted chocolate. Place on waxed paper to dry.

Coconut or Chocolate Fondant Balls: Make fondant balls; roll in shredded coconut or melted chocolate.

Peanut Butter–Fruit Confections

         1 cup pitted dates
       1/2 cup seedless raisins
       1/2 cup currants
         1 cup peanut butter
       1/4 cup sweetened condensed milk
         2 tablespoons confectioners' sugar (optional)

Chop fruit or put through mincer, and mix well with peanut butter and milk. Press mixture firmly into bottom of 8″ x 8″ x 2″ pan, which has been buttered and sprinkled with confectioners' sugar. Sprinkle top with confectioners' sugar. Chill until firm; cut into squares. Makes about 1 1/8 pounds.

Magic Rum Balls

         3 cups finely crushed vanilla wafers
         1 cup finely chopped walnuts
   1 1/3 cups (15-ounce can) sweetened condensed milk
         1 teaspoon rum extract
       1/4 cup confectioners' sugar or chocolate or colored
             sprinkles

Combine wafer crumbs and nuts. Add milk and rum extract, and blend well. Chill about 1 hour. Dip palms of hands into confectioners' sugar. Shape by teaspoonfuls into small balls. Roll in confectioners' sugar or sprinkles. Store in covered container in refrigerator. Balls will keep moist and fresh for several weeks. Makes about 48.

Nougat

         2 cups sugar
       1/2 cup honey
       1/4 cup water
         2 egg whites
       1/8 teaspoon salt
       1/2 cup chopped filberts
       1/4 cup chopped candied cherries

Combine sugar, honey and water. Cook to hard-ball stage (285°F.). Meanwhile beat egg whites with salt until stiff. Add syrup gradually, beating constantly, until mixture stands up in peaks. Spread in greased shallow square pan, and scatter nuts and cherries over top. Cool, and cut into 24 rectangular pieces.

Turkish Delight

      3 tablespoons (3 packages) unflavored gelatin
    1/2 cup cold water
      1 pound (2 1/4 cups) sugar
    1/2 cup hot water
    1/4 teaspoon salt
      3 tablespoons lemon juice
    Few drops vegetable coloring
    Flavoring as desired
      1 cup finely chopped nuts
    1/4 cup confectioners' sugar

Soften gelatin in cold water 5 minutes. Bring sugar and hot water to boiling point. Add salt and gelatin, and stir until gelatin has dissolved. Simmer covered 20 minutes; remove from heat, and cool. Add lemon juice, coloring, flavoring and finally nuts, and allow mixture to stand until it begins to thicken. Stir again; then pour about 1 inch deep into pan that has been rinsed with cold water. Let stand overnight in cool place. Moisten sharp knife in boiling water. Cut in squares. Roll each piece in confectioners' sugar.

Note: The mixture may be divided into several parts and each colored and flavored differently.

Chocolate Fudge

      2 squares (1 ounce each) unsweetened
          chocolate
    2/3 cup milk
      2 cups sugar
    1/8 teaspoon salt
      2 tablespoons butter or margarine
      1 teaspoon vanilla extract

Break chocolate into small pieces. Add to milk in saucepan. Cook over low heat, stirring constantly until mixture is smooth. Add sugar and salt, and stir until sugar is dissolved and mixture boils. Cook slowly, without stirring, until small quantity dropped into cold water forms soft ball (236°F.). Remove from heat, and add butter or margarine and vanilla, without stirring. Cool to lukewarm (110°F.). Beat until fairly thick; pour at once into greased pan. Cool, and cut into squares. Makes about 1 1/4 pounds.

VARIATION:

Brown-sugar Fudge: Substitute 1 cup firmly packed brown sugar for 1 cup granulated sugar.

English Toffee

      1 cup sugar
      1 cup butter or margarine
      3 tablespoons water
      1 tablespoon corn syrup
    3/4 cup finely chopped almonds or peanuts
      1 small chocolate bar, finely chopped

Cook sugar, butter or margarine, water and corn syrup until few drops tested in cold water crack (290°F. on candy thermometer). While syrup cooks, sprinkle almost all the nuts over bottom of pieplate. Pour hot syrup over nuts, and sprinkle with chocolate bar and remaining almonds. When cool, break into pieces. Makes about 1 1/4 pounds.

Butterscotch

      2 cups brown sugar
      1 cup water
    1/4 cup light corn syrup
    1/4 teaspoon salt
    1/3 cup butter or margarine
    1/4 teaspoon vanilla extract

Place sugar, water, corn syrup and salt in saucepan, and cook over low heat, stirring, until sugar dissolves. Continue cooking without stirring until mixture reaches temperature of 290°F. Add butter or margarine, remove from heat and add vanilla. Pour into buttered shallow pan. Cool slightly, and mark into squares. When cold, break into pieces. Makes about 1 1/8 pounds.

VARIATIONS:

Lemon Butterscotch: Substitute few drops oil of lemon for vanilla.

Butterscotch Lollipops: Cook sugar mixture to 290°F., then stir in butter and vanilla quickly, and pour into greased lollipop molds; or drop from end of teaspoon onto greased flat pan. Place stick in each pop.

Peanut Brittle

    1 1/2 cups shelled peanuts
      1/4 teaspoon salt
        1 cup sugar
      1/2 cup light corn syrup
      1/2 cup water
    1 1/2 tablespoons butter or margarine
      1/2 teaspoon lemon extract

Sprinkle nuts with salt, and warm them in oven. Put sugar, corn syrup and water in pan, and stir until mixture boils. Wash down sides with wet pastry brush, and cook to 300°F. or until mixture is very brittle when tested in cold water. Add butter or margarine, lemon extract and nuts; pour into shallow greased pan. As soon as it's cool enough to be handled, turn mass over, pull and stretch as thin as possible and break into irregular pieces. Makes 1 1/4 pounds.

Popcorn Balls

```
        1 tablespoon butter or margarine
   1 1/2 cups corn syrup
        1 cup sugar
        1 teaspoon salt
        1 teaspoon vanilla extract
Few drops vegetable coloring (optional)
        4 quarts popped corn
```

Melt butter or margarine. Add syrup, sugar and salt. Boil over medium heat to very hard-ball stage (260°F.). Add vanilla and coloring. Pour syrup over popcorn, stirring thoroughly while pouring. Butter hands lightly, and shape mixture into balls. Makes 12–14 balls.

VARIATIONS:

Cereal–Popcorn Balls: Substitute 3 cups puffed cereal for 3 cups popcorn, and mix before adding syrup.

Molasses–Popcorn Balls: Omit corn syrup, and use 1 cup molasses.

Nut–Caramel Corn: Add 1/2 cup nut kernels to popcorn before adding syrup.

Teen-Age Parties. Teen-age standards are extremely casual—but their own. The condition of the house doesn't interest them much, as long as they can move around, eat what they like, and listen to their own kind of music. At parties, teen-agers seem to have fun eating from paper plates and drinking from plastic mugs, so let them. You can use a strip of bright plastic or canvas for a table cover, and toss some cushions on the floor; and, of course, have dishes of nuts, potato chips, candies, and bowls of popcorn to sustain them until the "real food" is ready.

Buying the Food

Just see that there is plenty—which usually means twice as much as adults would eat. Buy loaves of French, rye or for that matter any bread; sliced chicken, ham, bologna, salami, even peanut butter; pickles, relishes, tomatoes and lettuce. Or you might prepare a big basket of crisp fried-chicken pieces, to be eaten cold. A sandwich grill makes a marvelous adjunct to a teen-age party—a blender is helpful for making shakes and malteds. It's good to provide low-calorie sodas, as well as other soft drinks and milk.

They Like to Cook

If you have a sizeable kitchen, you might even turn it over to them when they arrive, and suggest something like pancakes and sausages, or spear-your-own shish kebabs. The shish-kebab makings can be prepared ahead and left to marinate until it's time to cook them. They can be broiled under the grill or barbecued if it's summer time. You're in luck if your own teen-ager takes the responsibility for supervising the cooking and cleaning up.

A simple casserole—chicken and rice or ham and potatoes—or pizza from a mix or made on English muffins would be a change from the usual. Your child would probably appreciate a little help from you before the party. Here's a casserole idea most teen-agers can manage easily:

Turn canned chili con carne into casserole—how many cans depends on number of guests and size of their appetites, but it should be enough to fill casserole about 3/4 full. Over it, spoon strips of corn-bread batter, made from a mix. Between rows, place ripe olives. Bake in moderate oven (375°F.) about 20 minutes until corn bread is lightly browned and chili con carne is bubbling hot and tempting.

If you have individual casseroles, so much the better; bake in small portions, 1 for each guest.

Menus

Breakfast After the Senior Prom

Scrambled eggs   Sausage patties
Buckwheat pancakes   Maple syrup
Creamed chipped beef on toasted English muffins
CAPPUCCINO

Cappuccino

```
3 tablespoons instant espresso coffee
3 cups boiling water
3 cups hot milk
Ground cinnamon
```

Pour boiling water over instant coffee. Stir well. Pour hot coffee and hot milk into cup at same time. Sprinkle with cinnamon. Serves 8.

Note: Top with sweetened whipped cream if desired.

After-the-game Buffet

BOSTON BAKED BEANS   Cold baked ham
COLESLAW WITH A BOILED DRESSING
QUICK CORN RELISH
Steamed brown bread (from can)
SPICED CHERRY COMPOTE and cream   Soft drinks
Hot chocolate

Boston Baked Beans

    3 cups (1 1/2 pounds) pea or navy beans
1/2—pound piece salt pork
    1 large onion, whole
    1 small onion, finely chopped
        (approximately 1/4 cup)
    2 cups boiling water
1/2 cup dark molasses
    2 teaspoons salt
    1 teaspoon dry mustard
1/3 cup brown sugar

Soak beans in water to cover. Next day, drain beans, cover with cold water and bring to boil. Skim; then simmer till tender. Halve salt pork; then slash each piece to rind at 1-inch intervals. In bean pot (or deep earthenware casserole with tight-fitting cover), put whole onion; combine chopped onion, boiling water, molasses, salt and mustard separately. Put into pot 1/2 the beans, then 1/2 the salt pork, then remaining beans. Pour molasses mixture over, and top with the brown sugar. Put remaining pork on top. Cover, and bake in very slow oven (250°F.) 5–6 hours or until beans are very tender. Every 1/2 hour, replace boiling water that has been absorbed; the last time, leave pot uncovered. Serve with sliced cold baked ham. Serves 10.

Note: A time-honored test for beans is to spoon up a few beans and blow on them; if the skins pop off, they are done.

Coleslaw with a Boiled Dressing

    3 egg yolks, well beaten
    1 tablespoon sugar
1 1/2 teaspoons salt
3/4 teaspoon dry mustard
    1 cup milk, scalded
1/3 cup cider vinegar
    1 large head cabbage, shredded

In top of double boiler combine egg yolks with sugar, salt and mustard. Gradually stir in scalded milk. Cook over hot water, stirring constantly, until thick and smooth. Remove from heat, and stir in vinegar. Pour hot dressing over shredded cabbage. Cool; then refrigerate. Serves 8–10.

Note: This dish is pretty garnished with radish "roses."

Quick Corn Relish

    1 cup cider vinegar
1/4 cup light corn syrup
1/4 cup firmly packed brown sugar
    1 tablespoon dry mustard
    1 tablespoon celery seed
    2 teaspoons salt
    1 cup chopped onion
    2 (10-ounce) packages frozen corn
1/2 cup chopped green pepper
1/4 cup chopped sweet red pepper

Combine vinegar, corn syrup, brown sugar, mustard, celery seed and salt. Bring to boil, add onion and simmer 10 minutes. Add corn and green and red peppers, and bring to boil. Simmer about 5 minutes. Chill. Makes about 4 1/2 cups.

Spiced Cherry Compote

    3 (1-pound) cans sour pitted cherries
Water
    4 whole cloves
    3 lemons, thinly sliced
1 1/2 cups sugar
    2 sticks cinnamon
    1 tablespoon cornstarch, dissolved in 2 tablespoons
        water
Few drops red vegetable coloring (optional)

Drain cherries, reserving liquid. Add enough water to cherry juice to make 2 cups. Stick cloves in lemon slices. Combine juice with sugar, cinnamon, cloves and lemon slices; simmer, uncovered, until syrup is reduced to 1 cup. Thicken with cornstarch. If color is poor, add coloring. Serve hot with heavy cream. Serves 8–10.

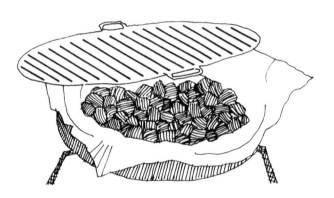

SUMMERTIME ENTERTAINING

The Barbecue. As far as the hostess is concerned, the barbecue offers great flexibility in entertaining. It's usually informal but can be elegantly served. You may invite your guests at any hour from late morning to the dinner hour, and numbers can range from 1/2 dozen to as many as the premises can hold.

Elaborate equipment isn't necessary, but if you plan to cook outdoors more than once or twice a year, you might invest in a grill with a

large fire basket that can be raised and lowered with ease. An electric spit and hood are marvelous additions if you are interested in spit cooking.

Making the Fire

Although successful grilling can be accomplished with nothing more than a supply of seasoned wood, most people use charcoal briquets to make their fire. It will help if you use a starter of some type—liquid, paste, electric or a simple homemade one from a clean discarded 1-gallon oil can. Cut both ends out, pierce a few holes in sides for ventilation, cut 3 squares from around the bottom and place can upright in firebox. Squeeze 3 sheets of newspaper into tight balls, and drop in can. Cover with 10–15 briquets, and light paper from below. Let fire burn briskly until all briquets are glowing. Slip can from around coals with tongs, and let briquets fall freely into firebox; arrange them to the size of the meat you are cooking, adding more if necessary. When coals are all encrusted with white ash, cooking may begin.

Cooking

If you have a large wicker basket, you might keep it permanently ready with your outdoor equipment. Bring it outdoors with you, and you'll have all the things you need right at your fingertips. Restock after the party, and you're set for the next time.

As most grills cannot accommodate all the food for your meal, plan to prepare some parts of it indoors, or use an electric skillet or cooker at the table. Warming trays can be used most advantageously to keep food warm outdoors.

Have your fire good and hot, use a sprinkler of some sort to keep flare-ups at a minimum, turn meat frequently and check by making small cut with sharp knife toward end of prescribed cooking time to see that it has reached desired degree of doneness. Care is just as important outdoors as in.

Sturdy tables and chairs or benches are necessary, as are candles in protective holders after dark. Torches on poles stuck into the ground nearby can augment candles.

Earthenware, pottery, painted tin, plastic or coated-paper plates are in order. Sturdy glasses, stainless-steel tableware and large paper napkins or terry fingertip towels to use as napkins are a good idea too.

Barbecue Checklist

Grill: Brazier, roll-about or portable type

Accessories: Starter (fluid, electric or can)
Fuel (wood, charcoal, briquets or paper)
Tongs, long spatula, aprons, sturdy salt and pepper shakers and hinged or basket grill

Basket Equipment: Terry fingertip towels (or paper napkins)
Metal or plastic dishes
Plastic cutlery tray and cutlery
Salt and pepper, sugar, cream containers
Paper bags (for garbage)
Clothes damper (to put out flare-ups)

(Line large basket with tablecloth; keep all equipment in it; after use, wash and return utensils to it.)

Other Equipment: Plastic containers in various sizes and shapes with tight-fitting covers, paper frank holders, straw holders for paper plates, plastic holders for paper cups, large candles and hurricane globes (or oil lamps, lanterns and the like), insect repellent, umbrellas (large and small) and snack tables.

Barbecue Menus

Menu #1

SPINACH-STUFFED TOMATOES
Shashlik   PILAF
SYRIAN COLESLAW
Apricots in honey   KOURAMBIEDES   Coffee

Spinach-Stuffed Tomatoes

1 (10-ounce) package frozen chopped spinach, thawed
1/2 cup pine nuts (pignolia)
2/3 cup olive oil
2 onions, finely chopped
(approximately 1 cup)

2 cloves garlic, chopped
1 cup cooked rice
Salt and pepper to taste
6 medium tomatoes, hollowed out
Salt and pepper to taste
Generous pinch dried basil

Drain spinach, and press out all moisture. Sauté nuts in 1/3 cup oil until golden. Add onions and garlic, and sauté slightly in oil. Remove from heat. Add spinach, rice, and salt and pepper. Sprinkle insides of tomatoes with salt, pepper and basil, and stuff with spinach mixture. Arrange in baking pan, pour 1/3 cup oil over and bake until tomatoes wrinkle, about 15 minutes. Chill. Serve cold. Serves 6.

Syrian Coleslaw

2 small cloves garlic, mashed to paste with 1 tablespoon salt
1/4 cup olive oil
Dash wine vinegar
Juice of 2 lemons
1 small head cabbage, shredded
1 cup fresh mint leaves, chopped fine

Make dressing of garlic, oil, vinegar and lemon juice. Toss cabbage in dressing, add mint leaves and toss well again. Refrigerate overnight for flavors to blend. Serves 6–8.

Kourambiedes (Greek Cookies)

2 cups soft sweet butter or margarine
3/4 cup sifted confectioners' sugar
1 egg yolk
1 1/2 tablespoons brandy
4 1/2 cups cake flour, sifted twice
48 whole cloves

Cream butter or margarine well; gradually add 3/4 cup sugar, then egg yolk, creaming well. Add brandy. Gradually work in flour to make soft dough. Refrigerate 1 hour. Shape dough into balls about 1 1/2 inches in diameter. Stud each with clove. Bake on ungreased baking sheet, in preheated 350°F. oven, until they turn pale gold. Cool well on racks, and sift confectioners' sugar generously over them. Makes about 48.

Menu #2

GRILLED RANCH STEAKS
BLACK BEANS AND SOUR CREAM   SANGRÍA
Melon sherbet   Coffee

Grilled Ranch Steaks

1/4 cup lime juice
1/4 cup lemon juice
1/4 cup water
1/2 teaspoon hot pepper sauce
Salt and pepper to taste
8 rump steaks cut 3/4-inch thick

Combine juices, water, hot pepper sauce, salt and pepper. Pour over steaks in pan. Let steaks stand 4–6 hours (out of refrigerator), turning occasionally. Grill over *hot* fire 3–4 minutes on each side for rare. Increase cooking time for medium or well-done steaks. Serves 8.

Black Beans and Sour Cream

1 pound black beans
Water
2 stalks celery
2 stalks parsley
1 small onion, sliced
1 bay leaf
Ham bone
Salt to taste
Dash of hot pepper sauce
1 tablespoon cornstarch dissolved in 1/4 cup water
1/4 cup cognac
1/2 pint cold sour cream

Soak beans overnight. Next day, add more water to cover, celery, parsley, onion, bay leaf and ham bone. Cook until beans are tender; add salt and pepper sauce. Drain beans, discarding vegetables and seasonings. Thicken liquid with cornstarch. Transfer beans and liquid to casserole; add cognac, and bake in 350°F. oven until well heated. Serve with sour cream. 6–8 servings.

Sangría

1 cup water
1/2 cup sugar
3/4 cup light corn syrup
1 orange, sliced
1 lemon, sliced
1 lime, sliced
1 bottle inexpensive Chilean, Spanish or Italian red wine
1/4 bottle (or more) club soda

Boil water and sugar together 10 minutes. Cool. In 2-quart pitcher, place 3/4 cup syrup and fruit slices. Pour in wine, add ice cubes and about 1/4 bottle club soda (more if you wish). Stir with wooden spoon or paddle.

Menu #3

GRILLED CRABMEAT WITH BACON
GARLIC-BROILED SHRIMP   BARBECUED SPARERIBS
Spitted chicken rubbed with tarragon
BARLEY WITH MUSHROOMS   Romaine lettuce
FRENCH DRESSING
Platter of fresh fruits   Coffee

Grilled Crabmeat with Bacon

1 (6-ounce) package frozen king crabmeat, thawed
6 bacon strips, cut in halves

Wrap lumps crabmeat in bacon strips. Secure with toothpicks, and place in basket grill. Grill over coals until bacon is crisp. Serve with hot English mustard. Makes 12 pieces.

Garlic-Broiled Shrimp

1 pound (12) jumbo shrimp
1 cup olive oil
Juice of 1 lemon
3 cloves of garlic, crushed
2 tablespoons chopped parsley
1/4 teaspoon ground cloves

Split shrimp shells down back with scissors, and remove the veins; wash shrimp, leaving shells on. Make marinade of olive oil, lemon juice, garlic, parsley and cloves. Marinate shrimp 2–3 hours; drain, and place in basket grill. Grill 3 minutes on each side. Let each guest remove his own shrimp from shells. Serve a little marinade if desired. Serves 6.

Note: Shells are left on to keep in shrimp juice while cooking.

Barbecued Spareribs

1/4 cup soy sauce
1 1/2 tablespoons vinegar
1 tablespoon catsup
1 tablespoon chili sauce
1 tablespoon dry sherry
1/2 tablespoon sugar
1 clove garlic, crushed
1 tablespoon honey
2 pounds or 1 small rack young spareribs

Combine soy sauce, vinegar, catsup, chili sauce, sherry, sugar and garlic. Pour over spareribs, laid out flat in roasting pan. Marinate at least 4 hours, turning often. Drain, reserving marinade. Broil slowly over charcoal 20 minutes, turning often. Mix honey into reserved marinade, and brush on ribs on both sides while cooking another 20 minutes. Cut into individual ribs to serve. Serves 6 for appetizers.

Barley with Mushrooms

1 large onion, chopped (approximately 3/4 cup)
3/4 pound mushrooms, sliced (approximately 1 cup)
1/3–1/2 cup butter or margarine
2 cups pearl barley
4 cups chicken broth
Salt to taste

Sauté onion and mushrooms in butter or margarine until soft in oven-proof casserole. Add barley, and brown lightly. Pour 2 cups broth over barley, and cover casserole. Bake at 350°F. 1/2 hour. Uncover, add 2 cups broth and continue cooking until liquid is absorbed and barley tender. Add salt before serving. 6–8 servings.

Menu #4

RED CABBAGE SALAD
GRILLED ITALIAN SWEET SAUSAGES WITH
GREEN PEPPERS
LENTIL CASSEROLE
FIGS WITH ALMONDS AND RICOTTA
Iced espresso coffee

Grilled Italian Sweet Sausages with Green Peppers

4 onions, peeled and quartered
4 green peppers, seeded and quartered
Olive oil
Salt and pepper to taste
2 pounds sweet Italian sausages

Cover onions and peppers with olive oil. Add salt and pepper. Marinate at least 1 hour. Halve sausages, and thread on skewers alternately with onions and peppers. Grill slowly over coals 30–40 minutes, turning frequently. Serves 6.

Lentil Casserole

2 cups "quick-cooking" lentils
Water
1 bay leaf
1 onion stuck with 2 cloves
Pinch salt
2 large onions, sliced (approximately 1 cup)
2 tablespoons butter or margarine or bacon fat
4 or 5 bacon strips
1/3 cup Parmesan or Romano cheese

Put lentils in kettle with water to cover, add bay leaf, onion stuck with cloves and salt. Bring to boil, lower flame and simmer gently until lentils are tender, 25–30 minutes. Do not let them get mushy. Drain, and save liquid. Discard cooked onion and bay leaf. Sauté sliced onions in butter or margarine. In large casserole put layer of lentils, layer of onions, more lentils and remaining onion. Top with remaining lentils. Pour lentil liquid over casserole, and bake in a 350°F. oven 40 minutes. Cover top of casserole with bacon strips, and continue baking until bacon is crisp and brown. Sprinkle with cheese. Serves 6–8.

Figs with Almonds and Ricotta

1/2 pound ricotta cheese, sweetened with 2 tablespoons confectioners' sugar
1 box calimyrna figs, split
1/2 cup shelled almonds, blanched

Place cheese in small bowl; surround with figs and almonds. Let each guest help himself by sandwiching cheese and almonds between fig halves. Serves 6–8.

Menu for a Clambake

Clam broth STEAMED CLAMS Drawn butter
CHARCOAL-BROILED LOBSTERS Steamed corn
Sliced tomatoes and cucumbers
Watermelon Beer Coffee

Steamed Clams

> Washed wet seaweed
> 12 small potatoes, wrapped in foil
> 12 small ears corn, husked and wrapped in foil
> 4 dozen steamer clams, well scrubbed

Fill bottom of enamel clam boiler with seaweed. Add water just to cover, and place over high heat. When water boils, add potatoes and another layer of seaweed. Cover pot. Steam 35 minutes. Add corn, and cover again. After 10 minutes, add more seaweed and clams. Cover, and steam until clams open. Drain liquid, and strain through linen napkin into cups for drinking and dipping. Have plenty of butter or margarine on hand for corn and potatoes. Serves 12.

Charcoal-broiled Lobsters

> 6 (1 1/2-pound) lobsters, split and cleaned
> 1 cup butter or margarine, melted
> Paprika to taste
> Lemon wedges
> Salt and pepper to taste

Brush lobsters with a little butter or margarine, and sprinkle with paprika. Grill over charcoal fire 6–7 minutes on each side. Serve with melted butter or margarine, lemon wedges and salt and pepper. Serves 12.

Garden Parties. If the weather's with you, this is a perfect way to entertain. A garden party can be anything from a simple cup of coffee to an elaborate reception. Cocktail parties, women's luncheons, large buffets are all suitable. Whatever it is, you'll need some garden chairs, a table and some lawn cushions. Try to arrange for groupings as you would indoors: cluster 3 or 4 chairs and a table in 1 corner of the garden, 2 or 3 cushions under a tree or giant umbrella. But most people do expect to stand or wander about at this sort of gathering.

Service

Unless you can hire caterers and waitresses, the kind of service you choose requires careful thought. The simplest way might be to serve most of the food from a large table indoors and let guests themselves take their plates outside. Even at self-service parties, a few helpers make a difference, even if they're your children and their friends passing plates and taking second helpings to people.

A beautiful luncheon can be arranged with a serving table near the house and small tables seating 4 arranged at intervals around the garden. As guests come into garden, they pick up their food in passing and settle down at small tables. No matter how you serve, though, it's important to plan ahead. You'd be surprised how much can be done several days before the party.

A Basket Luncheon

For small groups, an informal basket luncheon can be fun. In the middle of a small basket lined with a colored paper napkin, put a glass of fruit juice or other cool drink. Around it in basket arrange assortment of sandwiches, and let each guest take her own basket into the garden. All that is needed to complete the menu is coffee, organized in the kitchen ahead of time.

Remember, tablecloths and napkins are quick to blow away. Whether they are linen or paper, anchor them with a few heavy things like ashtrays or cutlery. Don't use tall vases of flowers—they will inevitably fall over.

Foods

Garden parties seem to make people unpunctual and relaxed, so it's wise not to serve food that should be eaten the moment it's ready. It's a losing game to cut meat with one hand and balance plate with the other while standing up, so serve easy-to-manage foods, unless you can arrange for people to sit down at a table or at least with firm trays on their knees.

Garden-reception Menu

JELLY PINWHEELS MINT SANDWICHES
White meat of chicken on buttered bread
MOCK MADELEINES SCOTCH SHORTBREAD
6-LAYER MOCHA CAKE
Sparkling punch Coffee

Jelly Pinwheels

> 1 (8-ounce) package cream cheese
> 4 ounces currant jelly
> 1 drop vegetable coloring (optional)
> 1 loaf white bread, unsliced

Blend cream cheese and currant jelly together in small bowl of electric mixer. If necessary, add coloring to turn mixture pale rose. Cut all crust from bread, to make perfect oblong. Spread longest side generously with cream cheese mixture; then, with serrated knife, cut off spread side in thin even slice. Roll as for jelly roll, press together and repeat to end of loaf. Wrap in damp cloth, and chill 2 hours; then slice each roll into thin sandwiches. Count 2 to 3 sandwiches per guest. Makes about 50 sandwiches.

Mint Sandwiches

    1/2 pound (1 cup) sweet butter
      2 cups sifted confectioners' sugar
    1/4 cup chopped spearmint leaves
      1 loaf white bread, sliced
      1 loaf protein bread, sliced

In small bowl of electric beater or by hand, cream butter, and add sugar gradually. Beat at high speed 4 minutes or 20 minutes by hand. Stir in spearmint leaves. Butter white bread heavily with mint butter, cover with protein-bread slices, trim crusts and cut each sandwich into 3 finger strips. Chill in refrigerator, covered with damp cloth.

Mock Madeleines

      1 package pound-cake mix
    1/4 cups sifted confectioners' sugar

Prepare pound-cake mix according to package directions. Put 1 level tablespoon batter into each well-greased fluted 2 1/2-inch tart pan. Bake at 325°F. 20 minutes. Remove from oven. Sprinkle tops lightly with sugar.

6-Layer Mocha Cake

    1 (1-pound 2 1/2-ounce) package devil's food cake mix
    2 cups heavy cream
    2 tablespoons sweetened instant cocoa mix
    2 teaspoons dry instant coffee

Prepare cake batter, following package directions. Bake in two 8-inch layers, dividing batter evenly between pans, according to package directions. Cool in pan 5 minutes. Loosen sides with spatula. Remove to wire rack. Cool completely. Combine cream, cocoa mix and instant coffee. Chill 30 minutes. Beat at high speed until thick and spreadable. Carefully divide each cake layer horizontally into 3, making 6 layers total. Sandwich layers together, using 1/3 cup frosting between each pair. Frost top and sides with remaining frosting. Chill 1 hour or until serving time. Serves 6–8.

Country Weekends. Ask people well ahead, as a trip out of town usually involves extra planning. If your house is hard to find, send a map and include time it takes to get there, as well as the approximate time you expect people to arrive and leave.

Once your guests have arrived, show them their beds and bathroom facilities, and point out any local rules (swimming arrangements, car or boat parking and so forth). Let them know about mealtimes, if you run on schedule, and let them know of any plans you've made (visits to other friends, fishing or sight-seeing expeditions and the like).

Plan your menus carefully, and do as much as you can before guests arrive. Even the vegetables can be washed and cut up ahead of time. Just wrap in plastic bags, and keep cool. One-dish wonders are ideal—stews, meat or fish pies and of course salads. As an appetizer, prepare a platter of sliced tomatoes just off the vine, sprinkled with chopped chives or green-onion tops.

Breakfast

Breakfast can cause concern to both sides: the guest who looks forward to a long morning in bed and the hostess who wonders how she'll ever get on with her day; or the opposite. So make plans, and let your guests know what they are.

You can serve breakfast at a fixed time, or you can set out a do-it-yourself arrangement. Leave coffee hot and ready in percolator; put out fruit, individually packaged cereals, jug of milk, bread, butter, toaster and marmalade. If late-comers want eggs and bacon, makings and equipment are ready in the kitchen. As a hint you might also indicate some preorganizing for dish-washing, with pan, detergent, mop and towels in readiness. But if sleepers-in take over breakfast cleaning up—and generally they don't mind—change the shift for other meals.

Help-yourself Luncheons

Do-it-yourself luncheons are good for you and your guests. They'd probably prefer to eat when they want to, so set out platters of cold meats, tomatoes, lettuce, bread and butter, pickles, cheeses, assorted crackers and if it's a cold day, a big pitcher or tureen of hot soup can be added, and fresh fruit for dessert. Don't hesitate to use paper plates.

Meals to Suit Programs

If your guests are fishing enthusiasts, picnic lunches will be needed. Hearty sandwiches with meat or cheese filling, a vacuum or 2 of hot and/or cold drinks (coffee, tea, soup, fruit juice and so on) and some fruit.

A beach or country weekend offers opportunities for picnics, berry-picking expeditions, swim-suit snacks on the dock, corn roasts, songs around the bonfire and other events that can't be duplicated in the city. Take advantage of them.

7
~

The Bridal Corner

JUST MARRIED

After the honeymoon, when your husband and, most likely, you are back at work, you probably won't have too much difficulty in managing simple meals for the 2 of you. But sooner or later, depending on your disposition, you'll wind up entertaining. Whether your guests are friends for coffee, your in-laws for dinner or a crowd for cocktails, you can make the occasion successful.

The road to success is called "preparation." For a planned party, everything should be ready before guests arrive—matches handy to light candles, guest towels in bathroom and you at the door ready to greet guests on time. Being prepared encompasses impromptu occasions—emergency supplies in cupboard or freezer, place mats ready in the linen cupboard, lots of peanuts and potato chips to serve guests while you start dinner and set table.

Any entertaining, elaborate or spur-of-the-moment, goes more smoothly if your work area is well organized. Your kitchen shouldn't be overcrowded. If shelves are scarce, you can store large trays, seldom-used vases, a giant roast pan and so on somewhere else—even in a locker. You can save drawer space by keeping place mats and extra tea towels in linen cupboard or dresser drawer.

You can expand your cupboard space with cuphooks, rubber turntables and shelves. Plastic bins stacked under sink will hold cleaning supplies. And when you shop, select sizes that will fit your cupboard shelves—the small saving on giant boxes of detergent, potato chips, flour or cereal is not worth the frustration of finding a place to store them.

You can hang your new pots, serving imple-ments, spice shelf or waxed paper dispenser on a wall. Let the refrigerator aid your space pro-gram—use it to store catsup, Worcestershire sauce, canned juices and fruit, canned consommé, mustard, canned meat and fish, jams and jellies, even though these items do not need refrigeration until after they have been opened.

If work space is inadequate, clear toaster, mixer, frying pan, canisters (at least the big flour one) off the counters.

Silver, China, Linen. Keep all your china and silver clean and ready for use. If you have ster-ling and use it often, it's enough to treat it with a tarnish preventative and store it in chest or felts. (Incidentally, silver acquires a lovely soft glow if used constantly.) If you use your silver only occasionally, plastic wrap will keep it from blackening. Platters, entree dishes and tea sets can be protected with tissue or felts and stored airtight in plastic garbage bags. Stainless steel doesn't require any special care.

China should also be ready for instant use. If you keep your good dishes in your cooking area, protect them from scratches, and place large paper napkins or paper towels between plates, slide piles of 3 or 4 into plastic bags. Crystal stored in kitchen for any length of time will almost certainly have to be washed, unless wrapped with tissue or plastic.

Table linen can be stored in linen closets, chests or even dress boxes, but store carefully—avoid finding napkins that are all wrinkled be-cause they were put away slightly damp or table-cloth fresh from cleaners that is badly creased from overcrowding. Hang tablecloths on special hangers if it eases the space problem.

There are several little extras you can have on hand to make a meal a party—candles for the table, artificial flowers and fruit, dried flowers and leaves, stored in plastic bags for instant cen-terpieces. Extra ashtrays, coasters and dishes (or individual salad bowls) for pre-dinner appetizers should be on hand.

Planning a Dinner Party. First, decide how many guests to invite—bearing in mind the size of your apartment, what your kitchen can ac-commodate, seating arrangements and number of place settings. Until you're more experienced, you might want to hold your guest list to a minimum.

Invite your friends enough in advance for them to hire baby sitters, and be sure, especially if you have a job, to leave yourself enough time to get ready before your guests come. On a weekday, cocktails at 7:00 and dinner at 8:00 usually satisfy all.

What to Serve. The next step is to decide on a menu. Three courses—appetizer; meat, vegetables and salad; dessert and coffee—are enough.

In deciding on specific dishes consider your silver and china—if you don't have bouillon spoons, serve seafood instead of soup. And an easy way to bring elegance to a table is through wine. One word of warning to apartment dwellers: Choose mild-flavored vegetables like carrots, peas, beets, asparagus, spinach and so forth. There's nothing less appetizing to arriving guests than strong aroma of cabbage cooking.

Two Dinner Menus for Beginners

Menu 1

Seafood cocktail and sauce
FRENCH-FRIED CHICKEN BREASTS   New potatoes
Asparagus with cheese sauce
Salad and Dressing   Rolls   Wine
Fresh fruit   Coffee

French-Fried Chicken Breasts

   8 pieces chicken breasts
   2 cups hot chicken broth or diluted consommé
   1 cup unsifted all-purpose flour
1 1/2 teaspoons baking powder
  1/2 teaspoon salt
  1/4 teaspoon thyme
  1/4 teaspoon onion salt
   1 egg, well beaten
  3/4 cup milk
Deep hot oil

Place chicken pieces in large saucepan with broth. Cover tightly, and simmer gently until almost tender, about 15 minutes. Drain and cool, reserving liquid. Carefully remove bones and heavy fat from chicken. Sift dry ingredients into bowl; mix egg and milk, and stir in. Beat until smooth. Heat about 3 inches of oil in deep pan or deep-fat fryer to 370°–375°F. Dip each chicken piece in batter, and drop into hot fat. Fry until golden brown, 4–5 minutes. Drain, and serve hot with MUSHROOM GRAVY. Serves 8.

Note: Chicken may be cooked the day before and chicken and broth refrigerated until needed.

Mushroom Gravy

  2 cups skimmed chicken broth (add water if necessary)
1/4 cup flour
1/4 cup chicken fat or butter or margarine
1/4 pound fresh mushrooms, sliced
     (approximately 1 1/4 cups)
  2 tablespoons butter or margarine
3–4 tablespoons heavy cream
Pinch cayenne

Bring broth to boil; combine flour and fat in smooth mixture, and stir into broth. Whisk until smoothly thickened. Keep hot. Sauté mushrooms in butter or margarine, and stir into gravy. Dilute with cream; add cayenne and taste for seasoning.

Menu 2

TONGUE–LIVER PÂTÉ
CHICKEN AU GRATIN
Tossed green salad with dressing
Bread and butter   Wine
APPLE SAVARIN   CRÈME PÂTISSERIE   Coffee

Tongue-Liver Pâté

   1 pound raw chicken livers
1/2 pound sausage meat
   1 egg, beaten
   1 cup soft day-old crumbled French bread, crusts removed
1/4 cup milk or dry white wine
   2 tablespoons chopped parsley
1/2 clove garlic, crushed
3/4–1 teaspoon salt
1/4 teaspoon freshly ground black pepper
1/8 teaspoon thyme
1/2 pound bacon
   6 slices tongue, cut in strips

Mince chicken livers, and mix liver and liver juice with sausage meat and egg. Soak crumbs in milk a few minutes, and mash well. Stir into meat mixture with next 5 ingredients. Line 9″ x 5″ x 3″ loaf pan with strips of bacon set side by side lengthwise. Spread about 1/4 the liver mixture evenly over bacon. Cover tongue strips, and repeat layers, ending with liver mixture. Press down lightly, and lay bacon strips across top. Cover with foil, and set pan in second pan or dish of hot water. Bake at 350°F. 2 hours. Lift out of water, and drain off some of liquids. Cool slightly. Place weight on top, and refrigerate 24 hours. Serve sliced as appetizer or main-course meat dish with marinated cold asparagus and FRENCH POTATO SALAD. Serves 6.

Chicken au Gratin

1/2 pound sliced mushrooms
     (approximately 1 1/4 cups)
   6 tablespoons butter or margarine or chicken fat
   6 tablespoons flour
1 1/2 cups chicken broth
  3/4 cup light cream
   3 cups cooked egg noodles
   2 cups cut-up cooked chicken
2–3 tablespoons sherry
Salt and pepper to taste
   3 slices processed cheese, cut in triangles
Tomato wedges
Chopped parsley

Sauté mushrooms in butter 3 minutes. Stir in flour, then chicken broth, gradually. Cook until thick, and stir in cream. Reheat 1 minute. Add next 3 ingredients. Season, and spread in buttered 1 1/2-quart casserole; bake at 400°F. 20 minutes or until bubbly. Top with cheese triangles, and bake 3–5 minutes until cheese melts. Garnish with tomato wedges and chopped parsley. Serves 6.

Apple Savarin

```
    1 envelope (1/4 ounce) active dry yeast
1/4 cup lukewarm water
1/2 teaspoon sugar
1/2 cup milk
1/4 cup butter or margarine
1/4 cup sugar
    1 teaspoon salt
    2 eggs, beaten
    1 teaspoon lemon rind
    1 teaspoon vanilla
2 1/4 cups sifted all-purpose flour
    APPLE TOPPING
    APRICOT GLAZE
    CREME PATISSERIE
```

Dissolve yeast in lukewarm water with 1/2 teaspoon sugar. Scald milk, add butter or margarine, sugar, salt and stir until dissolved. Cool until lukewarm, then add yeast, eggs, flavorings. Beat in the flour, a little at a time. Set bowl in a warm place and let mixture rise until doubled. Butter an 8 1/2-inch tube pan. Add batter. Again let rise until double. Bake at 400°F. 20 minutes, or until tester comes out clean. Cool slightly, then unmold.

Apple Topping: Cover cake with a ring of cored, peeled apple slices which have been stewed for 5 minutes in 1 cup water, 1/4 cup sugar and 1/2 teaspoon lemon rind. Drizzle topping and warm cake with APRICOT GLAZE and decorate with a few maraschino cherries. Accompany dessert with CRÈME PÂTISSERIE or rum-flavored whipped cream.

Apricot Glaze: Heat 1-pound jar apricot preserves and strain. Add a tablespoon rum or orange juice.

Crème Pâtisserie: Scald 1 cup light cream in the top of a double boiler. Beat 2 egg yolks, 1/4 cup sugar and 2 tablespoons flour together. Stir in a little of the hot cream until smooth, then scrape mixture into remaining cream in double boiler. Cook and stir until thickened and smooth. Add a dash of salt and vanilla or almond flavoring to taste. Cool before serving. If mixture is too thick add 2 or 3 tablespoons additional cream.

Neither of these meals is difficult, especially if you use prepared foods like seafood sauce, cheese sauce, ready-mixed salad dressing and heat-and-serve rolls.

Shopping and Final Preparation. Convert your menu into quantities for a shopping list, by thinking the whole party through from cocktails to coffee. This way you won't forget olives for martinis or cream for coffee. Next make a checklist that includes everything you must do—order flowers; shop; polish glassware; wash plates if necessary; chill wine and soft drinks; prepare seafood and seafood sauce; prepare salad material, vegetables and fruit (store in plastic bag in refrigerator); make dip; set table; arrange coffee tray, coasters and ashtrays; set out food containers, utensils and plates in kitchen; place guest towels in bathroom, and so on.

The Night Before. When food is prepared and refrigerated, start arranging things on counters —dishes for nuts and candy, cocktail glasses, jigger, ice bucket, shaker, underplates for shrimp dishes, dessert plates, bread basket and napkin, cooking utensils, dinner plates, entree dishes, meat platter.

Next set table. Start by putting underpad on the table and then smooth on tablecloth, making sure it hangs evenly with crease in center. Then fix your flowers, keeping arrangement low. If you're using candles have them above or below eye level and strategically placed.

Allow at least 2 feet for each place setting, and line up silver as precisely as you can. Set out bread-and-butter plates, folded napkins, wine glasses, water goblets, ashtrays. Arrange serving implements conveniently so you will have enough room for meat platter and entree dishes. Refer to your checklist to make sure you haven't forgotten seafood forks, salad servers or gravy ladle.

Organize your clothes for the party, place ashtrays, matches and coasters around living room.

Party Day. In the morning you can serve breakfast on trays at the coffee table if kitchen is too crowded. If you work, make bed, do breakfast dishes, put guest towels in bathroom and, if you have an automatically timed oven, put food in and set timer before you leave.

If you're rushed when you get home, clean up and dress first. Then fill bowls with nuts and candy, put out dip and take olives out of refrigerator for martinis. (If anyone comes early, you will at least look ready.)

Still following your checklist, do your final preparations: Line dishes with lettuce, arrange seafood, add seafood sauce, store in refrigerator; put vegetables in cooking pots; have butter or margarine and chopped parsley beside stove; prepare and add dressing, cover with plastic wrap and return to refrigerator.

After you welcome your guests, show them where to leave their coats, and offer drinks and food to nibble on.

Shortly before meal, drain vegetables, dress them and keep warm in covered entree dishes; put meat on the platter and fill gravy boat. Place salad, butter and rolls or bread on table. Wrap napkin around wine bottle if you wish, and put appetizer on table. Light candles, and dinner is ready.

Buffet. If your dining table seats only a small number, you can plan a buffet. For suggestions on what to serve see Chapter 6.

Arrange flowers and candles behind food if table is against wall. If your table is small, however, you will need all 4 sides to accommodate food. In this case, have your flowers and candles in center. Your centerpiece needn't be low, as for a sit-down dinner; just be sure it doesn't overshadow the food.

Set your table so items are in order they will be picked up; for example, consommé, spoons, plates, noodles with serving spoon, stroganoff with ladle, salad with servers, salt and pepper, basket of garlic bread wrapped in napkin, forks and napkins. If you wish, wine may be served to guests after they have carried their plates to their seats. Most men hate to eat from their laps, so try to seat them by end tables or near the coffee table.

The Cocktail Party. Decide on what drinks to serve and what refreshments to serve with them —deviled eggs, stuffed mushrooms, shrimps on toothpicks to be dipped in savory sauce, miniature cheese balls and so forth. Be sure you have enough of everything.

Set up bar: more glasses than you think you'll need, ice bucket, jigger, lemon slices, maraschino cherries, liquor bottles and chilled mixes. Arrange food on plates or tray, set bowls of salted nuts and potato chips around the room. Put out lots of ashtrays and coasters, and you're ready.

Another version of the cocktail party is the simple affair to which you invite a few friends to come about eight and at which you serve drinks and light refreshments. At around 10:30 you can pass around sandwiches, celery and olives, cookies and coffee. Or you can dress up your table buffet style and serve lasagne and salad, buttered dark rye bread, dessert and coffee.

The Impromptu Dinner. It's really not that difficult to serve dinner to an unexpected guest —or guests. What do you think a casserole would involve? You can make one by combining canned chicken à la king, tuna fish and mushrooms and adding sherry. Top with buttered bread crumbs. You can serve rice or potatoes, a frozen or canned vegetable and a tossed green salad as accompaniments. Canned fruit cocktail will do nicely as an appetizer, pie from the bakery for dessert and wine are easy enough to serve, and coffee completes the meal.

The impromptu affair in fact is often more fun than the well planned party. There's less preparation involved, and if your emergency shelf is sensibly stocked food won't be a problem.

Here are some foods you can keep on hand:

For appetizers, canned and packaged soups, fruit and vegetable juices, fruit cocktail.
For main courses, macaroni and cheese, ravioli, lasagne, spaghetti, eggs, chicken à la king, baked beans, canned fish and meat, mushrooms and vegetables, pastas, rice, potato flakes, biscuit and muffin mixes, instant sauces and gravies, creamed soups for quick casseroles, dried parsley, paprika, poppy seeds, Cheddar and Parmesan cheeses, soy sauce, sherry, bread crumbs, olives and pickles.
For desserts, canned fruit, applesauce, ice cream, sauce, instant puddings, whipped topping.
For extras, crackers, cheese, potato chips, nuts, wine (red wine is better than white for instant entertaining, as it usually doesn't have to be chilled).

Meals from the emergency shelf needn't be dull. Serve croutons with the soup, wine with the fruit cocktail. Grate Cheddar cheese over canned spaghetti, and top with bacon strips and thick tomato slices before baking. Dress up baked beans with catsup and onion rings. Combine tuna chunks and canned macaroni and cheese, and top with buttered bread crumbs. Pour cream soup over canned salmon and peas, heat until bubbly and top with biscuits made from mix. Follow package instructions for baking time and oven temperature.

Dress up vegetables with instant sauces or undiluted cream soups. Sprinkle parsley, paprika or poppy seeds on pale vegetables; crisp bacon bits, mushrooms, water chestnuts, Parmesan cheese, slivered almonds or grated hard-cooked egg white on green ones.

Splash wine into canned fruits or top with shredded coconut or whipped topping. Serve maple syrup and slivered almonds on ice cream.

Puree frozen raspberries in your blender, and fill parfait glasses with layers of vanilla ice cream and berries. Garnish scoop of orange sherbet with mint sprig, and pour on some crème de menthe.

Impromptu Menus

Menu 1

Consommé with lemon or sherry
Corned beef hash   HARVARD BEETS
Frozen green beans   Bread sticks
APPLE CRISP   Coffee

Menu 2

EGGS À LA RUSSE
SEAFOOD BROILER CASSEROLE
Asparagus with lemon   Potato chips
Fruit compote with sour cream   Coffee

Eggs à la Russe

6 hard-cooked eggs
2/3 cup mayonnaise
1/3 cup of chili sauce
2 tablespoons India relish
1 tablespoon wine vinegar
6 large lettuce leaves
Pimento strips or capers

Halve eggs. Make Russian dressing by combining mayonnaise, chili sauce, India relish and vinegar. Place large lettuce leaf on each plate; lay 2 egg halves, cut side down, on each lettuce leaf. Spoon dressing over egg halves, and garnish with crisscrossed strips of pimento. Serves 6.

Seafood Broiler Casserole

1/2 cup frozen chopped onion
1/4 cup diced green pepper or 1 small can pimento, cut in strips
2 tablespoons butter or margarine
1 (6 1/2-ounce) can crabmeat, drained
1 (6 1/2-ounce) can lobster, drained
1 (5-ounce) can shrimp, drained
2 teaspoons Worcestershire sauce
1 (10 3/4-ounce) can cream of celery or cream of mushroom soup
2 teaspoons Worcestershire sauce
2 teaspoons curry powder (optional)
Salt to taste
Pinch of cayenne
1/2 cup bread crumbs
1/4 cup grated Parmesan cheese

Sauté onions and green pepper lightly in butter or margarine. Break seafood into bite-size pieces, and add; stir in soup. Add Worcestershire sauce and seasonings, heat thoroughly and pour into shallow baking dish. Top with crumbs and cheese, and place under broiler 10–15 minutes or until top is bubbling and golden brown. Serve with rice. Serves 6.

VARIATION:

Substitute 1/2 pound fresh scallops for 1 can seafood, but scallops will have to be cooked first. Cut each scallop into 4 pieces, and sauté gently with onions and green pepper 5–10 minutes before adding seafood and soup.

The most important part of any entertaining is to enjoy yourself, for if you don't no one else is likely to.

PARTIES FOR THE BRIDE

A wedding in the family brings with it a great deal of entertaining. Someday, *you* may have to give 1 or more of the following kinds of parties.

The Announcement Party. Of course, such a party is not necessary for making an engagement official, but it is fun. The bride's parents can give this party for friends and relatives of both families. The invitations should be handwritten on informals or notepaper and should simply state details of time and place.

If space permits, this party is likely to be large. A luncheon may be the occasion for the announcement, but a cocktail party or supper is usually preferred. The cocktail buffet would be an almost perfect answer because it is neither too formal nor too difficult to execute.

A bar (or 2 if the house is large) and bartender (especially if the party is large) are the first requisites. Set up the bar with the makings for the kinds of drinks you'll serve, and include fruit juice or punch and low-calorie drinks. Champagne is a great drink to serve and you can, if you want, then dispense with the bar. This move simplifies service and is no more expensive in the long run. It's also sensible to rent glasses. They come clean and can be returned dirty, and you needn't be too concerned about breakage.

The house can be decorated with flowers— perhaps sweetheart roses. For the table, a pale pink or white cloth is appropriate. Soft lighting from candles lends atmosphere.

Use chafing dishes, warming trays, electric frying pans, and so on to keep hot foods at proper temperatures. Small plates of cold foods, replenished often, are more attractive than large platters left to dry out on the table.

Sliced smoked turkey   Thin sliced roast beef
Sliced tongue
Small rolls, split   Assortment of breads
Mustard   Horseradish
Mushroom turnovers
Cold shrimp with green mayonnaise
Baked sesame clams
Large bowls of SALADE NIÇOISE
Champagne   Coffee (for late stayers)

The Bridal Shower. If you're entertaining for a bride-to-be, you should consider her schedule and needs (find out if anyone else is having a shower for her) to avoid conflict. Usually the guest list includes the mothers of both bride and groom and the attendants too. You can set a theme for the shower—kitchen, bathroom, linen, lingerie, china, paper, and so on, or have a miscellaneous one.

The Paper Shower

The only things your guest of honor can see at first are a pair of huge red firecrackers. They contain gifts, all made of paper, wrapped individually, signed and packed into a pair of bedroom wastebaskets. The baskets are then wrapped in red paper and tied at each end. The red paper covering the baskets is pin-punched around the middle so that the cracker will "pop" with a sharp tug. Paper-gift suggestions include playing cards, notepaper, stationery, cookbooks, telephone pads, monogrammed paper napkins, shelfpaper rolls, and similar things.

Or, instead of firecrackers, you might like to present gifts in a large carton decorated with headlines appropriate to the bride's activities, her future home, her life ahead and so on. Just make a patchwork of words and phrases clipped from newspapers. Instead of the usual gift wrapping, you can decorate box tops only. This cuts down on work for the gift giver and saves time and clutter at the shower party.

Lingerie Shower

Nightgowns, petticoats, slips, stockings and breakfast coats would all be appropriate gifts (to ensure proper fit include bride's sizes on invitations).

A pretty, feminine table is in order, maybe with pink cloth and pink flowered napkins. Remove fabric from an old umbrella, and cover it with pink fabric or paper, and attach nosegays to ends of spokes and at center junctions. Choose your gayest china and silver. Serve food in keeping with the occasion.

Suggested Menu

Sliced avocado and grapefruit sections with
FRENCH DRESSING
COQUILLES ST. JACQUES
Broccoli with lemon
Butterflake rolls
COEUR À LA CRÈME WITH WHOLE STRAWBERRIES
Coffee

Coeur à La Crème with Whole Strawberries

1 pound cottage cheese
1 pint sour cream
3 tablespoons sugar
1 teaspoon vanilla extract
1–1 1/2 pints whole strawberries

Line strainer with double thickness of cheesecloth. Force cottage cheese through it. Beat cottage cheese, sour cream and sugar together at low speed 8–10 minutes. Stir in vanilla extract. Line strainer (or heart-shaped basket) with double thickness of cheesecloth, and pour mixture into it; place over bowl. Refrigerate 24 hours (with bowl underneath) to catch any liquid. Unmold and surround with strawberries. Serves 8.

China Shower Brunch

Ideal for career girls' group is the Saturday shower brunch. Friends might band together to start the bride-to-be on her favorite pottery or china. From there everything follows in reverse order from the usual program. The refreshments are served on the china, and the guest of honor discovers it's all hers as the set is packed away, complete with gift card. This idea could be adapted for presentation of flatware or crystal pieces.

Recipe Shower

The hostess tells each guest what others are contributing so that there won't be any overlapping. Cards for a recipe file are sent out, and each guest is asked to type or clearly write her favorite recipe. A gift accompanies each card, and a natural choice is a pan or utensil associated with that particular recipe.

When gifts are unwrapped, recipe cards are collected and presented in recipe filing box. For refreshments, some of the recipes on the cards received can be put to good use.

Suggested recipes and gifts: muffin recipe and muffin pans; cookie recipe, baking sheet and cookie press; cake recipe and cake pans; soufflé recipe and soufflé dish; fruit-bread recipe and loaf pan; angel food cake recipe and tube pan;

jellied salad-ring recipe and ring mold; custard recipe and glass custard cups; omelet recipe and omelet pan; ragout recipe and casserole.

Here are some main-dish menus that are easily prepared ahead of time and can be adapted to any number. Start with grapefruit or tomato juice, serve main dish with green tossed salad and chunks of crusty FRENCH BREAD and with fruit salad.

Baked Lasagna

    1/2 pound ground beef
    1/2 pound ground pork
    1 medium onion, chopped
            (approximately 1/2 cup)
    2 teaspoons chopped parsley
    1 clove garlic, crushed
    2 tablespoons olive oil
    2 cups water
    1 (6-ounce) can tomato paste
    1 teaspoon salt
    1/2 teaspoon pepper
    1 pound lasagne noodles
    5 quarts salted water
    1 pound mozzarella cheese
    1/2 pound ricotta or cottage cheese
    2 tablespoons grated Parmesan cheese

Brown ground meats together with onion, parsley and garlic in olive oil. When meat has browned, add 2 cups water, tomato paste, salt and pepper. Simmer slowly 1 1/2 hours. Break noodles into shorter pieces, and boil in salted water till tender but not limp, about 20 minutes. You will have to stir frequently to prevent noodles from sticking together or brush noodles with oil before boiling. Drain, and arrange layers of noodles, meat sauce, mozzarella and ricotta in shallow casserole, with ricotta on top. Sprinkle with grated Parmesan, and bake at 375°F. about 20 minutes or until cheese is melted and top is browned. Serves 8.

Note: If doubling recipe, make 2 separate casseroles, as it is difficult to cook larger amount of noodles at 1 time.

Chicken Marguerite

    2 (3 1/2-pound) chickens
    2 cloves garlic, halved
    Salt and pepper to taste
    1/3 cup butter or margarine
    1/3 cup olive oil
    1 onion, sliced (approximately 1/2 cup)
    2 cups cold water
    1 cup dry sherry

Halve or quarter chickens (or buy chicken pieces, allowing 1 piece for each serving). Rub generously with garlic, and sprinkle with salt and pepper. Brown pieces in butter and olive oil (or use all olive oil). Remove chicken pieces to small roasting pan or to 2 or 3 casseroles just large enough to hold chicken. Brown onion slightly in frying pan, add water and sherry, and simmer a few minutes before pouring over chicken pieces. Bake chicken uncovered at 400°F. 30 minutes; then turn chicken pieces, and cook 30 minutes more. A little more water may be added if chicken seems dry. Serve with un-thickened sauce poured over pieces with steamed rice or creamed potatoes. Serves 10–12.

Kitchen Shower

To furnish the heart of the home, you might suggest a shower of gifts for the kitchen. You can make this party an informal party, lunch or supper perhaps, and serve refreshments from trays. Set them up before with red-and-white checked paper mats, white plates and a red nosegay pinned to each napkin. Place trays on dining table; at serving time, food will be arranged on them, and guests can carry them to comfortable spots for eating.

Menu for Tray Luncheon

Cup of lobster bisque
Asparagus–ham–cheese sandwiches
Ice-cream snowballs
Coffee or Tea

Asparagus–Ham–Cheese Sandwiches

    1 (10-ounce) package frozen asparagus
    1 tablespoon butter or margarine
    3 (4" x 4") slices Cheddar cheese
    6 slices white bread
    2 tablespoons butter or margarine
    6 slices (approximately 1/2 pound) cooked ham

Cook frozen asparagus according to package directions. Drain well and toss with butter or margarine. Cut cheese slices diagonally, making 6 triangles. Spread bread thinly with 2 tablespoons butter or margarine. Roll 3 or 4 stalks asparagus in each ham slice. Place rolled ham and asparagus diagonally on buttered bread. Top with cheese triangles. Broil 5 minutes or until cheese is slightly melted and edges of toast golden brown. Serves 6.

Surprise Party for the Bride and Groom. This party would be particularly suitable for a group of married couples whose last single member is being married. It could be given on a cooperative basis with each wife contributing 1 dish for a smorgasbord. The hostess would be responsible for beverages and for preparing table.

The table can be covered with a bright blue cloth with napkins of mixed red, blue, purple, yellow and green, and a tray of fat candles of varying heights would be a striking centerpiece.

Here are some gifts you can consider: monogrammed towel sets, pair of beach towels, cocktail apron for her and bar apron for him, monogrammed stationery.

Menu

HERRING SALAD   Shrimp in dill
Smoked salmon
Pickled beets   Cucumber salad
FISHBALLS WITH SHRIMP SAUCE
Meatballs in cream gravy
Danish liver pâté (canned)
CAVIAR EGGS   MIXED-VEGETABLE SALAD
Cheese Board:
Caraway, Swiss, goat's milk, Crema Danica
Basket of breads:
sour rye, Swedish flatbread, limpa, Ry-Krisp
Imported and domestic beer
Swedish short breads   Coffee

Herring Salad

1 (2-ounce) jar herring in wine sauce, drained
4 potatoes, boiled and peeled
2 apples, peeled
2 onions, peeled
1 (8-ounce) can diced beets, drained
Sour cream
Salt and pepper to taste
Chopped dill or parsley

Dice herring, potatoes, apples and onions to approximately same size as beets. Mix together with beets, and add just enough sour cream to bind mixture; add salt and pepper. Garnish with dill. Serves 8.

Fishballs with Shrimp Sauce

2 (10-ounce) cans frozen cream of shrimp soup
2 (1-pound) jars or cans Swedish fishballs and liquid
1 soup can heavy cream
1 small (5 1/2-ounce) can or jar shrimp, drained
2 tablespoons dry sherry
Salt to taste

Dilute frozen soup with 1 soup can liquid from fishballs and cream. Heat to boiling, and simmer 5 minutes. Gently stir in drained fishballs, shrimp, sherry and salt. Cook until heated through. Keep hot over boiling water until ready to use. Serves 8.
Note: If you can't get imported fishballs, you can improvise with hors d'oeuvre-size gefilte fish.

Mixed-Vegetable Salad

2 (10-ounce) packages frozen mixed vegetables
3/4 cup mayonnaise
1/4 cup sour cream
1 tablespoon grated onion
Salt and pepper to taste

Cook vegetables until just done. Drain, and rinse with cold water to cool quickly; drain again. Mix mayonnaise, sour cream, onion, salt and pepper with vegetables. Chill before serving. Serves 8–10.

The Bride Entertains Her Attendants. This luncheon should be an intimate party for bridesmaids and maid of honor. It would be appropriate to present them with gifts and to let them peep at trousseau and wedding gifts.

Because it is a sentimental occasion, the decorations can be sentimental too. An old-fashioned bouquet for the centerpiece and a miniature replica for each guest are effective. An organdy tablecloth or mats and flower-sprigged china would be lovely, but by all means improvise with what you have. As the group will be small, you can fix individual warmed plates in the kitchen. Set them in front of each guest to keep table uncluttered.

Menu

HAM ROLLS WITH MELON
FILLET OF SOLE WITH GRAPES AND MUSHROOMS
Mixed green salad
Pineapple or lemon sherbet with crème de menthe
Coffee or Tea

Ham Rolls with Melon

1 large melon
32 (1-inch) strips thinly sliced prosciutto or ham
Black pepper to taste

Cut melon into 8 wedges, and scoop out seeds. Make ham rolls of prosciutto slices, and arrange 4 rolls along center of each melon wedge. Chill thoroughly. Pass black pepper at serving time. Serves 8.

Fillet of Sole with Grapes and Mushrooms

Celery tops, parsley and thyme to taste
1 bay leaf
Juice of 1/2 lemon
1/2 teaspoon salt
Boiling water
2 pounds fillet of sole
1/2 pound sliced mushrooms
(approximately 2 1/2 cups)
3/4 cup chopped onion

1/4 cup butter or margarine
1/4 cup seedless green grapes
1/4 cup flour
3/4 cup chicken broth
3/4 cup heavy cream
1/2 teaspoon salt
1/4 teaspoon tarragon
Dash pepper
Pinch thyme
Pinch marjoram
3/4 cup fresh white bread crumbs

Add celery tops, parsley, thyme, bay leaf, lemon juice and 1/2 teaspoon salt to 1/2 inch boiling water and poach sole about 5 minutes. Use large covered skillet, and sauté mushrooms and onion in butter or margarine until golden brown. Drain fillets, and place 1/2 in greased baking dish. Cover with onions, mushrooms and grapes. Place remaining sole over filling. Make cream sauce of remaining ingredients except crumbs, and pour over fish; sprinkle with crumbs. Bake at 325°–350°F. 20–30 minutes. Serves 6.

The Rehearsal Dinner. This party includes just the inner circle—the bridal couple's family and closest friends, members of the wedding party and their husbands or wives (or dates). It is customary to have it following the wedding rehearsal itself and is usually given by the bride's parents at home or in a club, although a close friend can be host too. As it's a fairly large party, buffet service is a wise choice.

In selecting a menu, plan food that will not suffer from delay. Choose foods that can be prepared in advance and need little or no attention at the last minute. It's not necessary to have 5 or 6 courses. A main dish, salad, buttered rolls and dessert are ample, as long as there's enough of each.

Menu

HORS-D'OEUVRES VARIES
VEAL BIRDS on rice
Buttered rolls or FRENCH BREAD
PETITS FOURS   GLACE FRUIT TARTLETS
FROSTED GRAPES

Veal Birds

1/4 pound prosciutto
2 tablespoons chopped parsley
1 clove garlic, chopped
Salt and pepper
Oregano to taste
1 large onion, cut into 4–5 slices
1 1/4 pounds rump of veal, thinly sliced and cut in 4-inch squares (approximately 4–5 pieces)
1/4 cup olive oil
2 cups canned tomatoes

Chop prosciutto, and mix with parsley, garlic and seasonings. Place 1 tablespoon mixture and 1 slice onion on each veal square, and fasten with toothpick. Heat oil in skillet, and brown rolls quickly. Add tomatoes, cover and cook slowly 30 minutes. Serves 4–5.

Glacé Fruit Tartlets

These were inspired by the ones served at New York City's Four Seasons restaurant.

1/2 cup soft butter or margarine
1/4 cup sugar
1 egg white
1 cup sifted flour
3/4 cup blanched almonds, ground up
1/2 teaspoon almond extract
1/4 cup sugar
1 tablespoon cornstarch
1 cup milk
2 egg yolks
3/4 teaspoon vanilla extract
1 box medium-size strawberries
1 cup fresh raspberries (or whole frozen raspberries)
1 cup fresh blueberries
1 cup fresh or canned Royal Ann cherries
1 (3-ounce) package lemon gelatin
1 1/2 cups water
Lemon leaves

A Day Ahead

Shells: Preheat oven to 375°F. In a medium bowl, combine soft butter or margarine and 1/4 cup sugar. Beat in egg white. Add flour, almonds and almond extract. Use hands to mix. It will be very stiff. Use 1 teaspoon dough to line each 1 1/2 x 1/2-inch tartlet pan. Place tartlet pans on cookie sheet. Bake 10 minutes or until golden brown. Cool in pans for 10 minutes. Remove to rack. When cool, store in airtight tin.

Pastry Cream: In small saucepan combine 1/4 cup sugar, cornstarch, and milk. Bring to boiling point over medium heat. Remove from heat. Beat egg yolks in quickly. Mix in vanilla extract. Cool. Refrigerate covered overnight.

Next Day

To assemble: In each shell, place 1 teaspoon chilled pastry cream. Top with 1 big whole strawberry or 3 or 4 small berries, or whole cherry. Chill.

Prepare glaze by dissolving gelatin in 1 cup boiling water. Stir in 1/2 cup ice water. Chill until semi-set. Spoon a little glaze over each tartlet. Chill until set. Serve on platter decorated with lemon leaves. Makes 5 1/2 dozen.

Arranging a Wedding. The type of invitation depends on what type of wedding is planned. For the most informal wedding, a handwritten note from the bride's parents serves nicely. There are many versions of printed or engraved invitations. The wording can be varied slightly to suit your preference. The printer from whom you order them will be helpful in suggesting models for you to follow.

Invitations should be mailed to out-of-town guests about 4 weeks before the date; to those in town, 3–4 weeks ahead. The officiating clergyman and his wife are invited personally by the bride's mother.

Formal or Informal

Usually a formal wedding is held in the evening; the bride wears a long dress and veil and the groom, best man, ushers and fathers of the bride and groom wear formal clothing or military uniforms (formal clothing can be rented, by the way).

The bride's dress for the formal wedding is usually white, but sometimes a pastel color. For an informal wedding, the bride wears white or any color except black. A widow or divorcée usually doesn't wear white or a veil, but the groom's marital status doesn't affect the type of ceremony.

Dressing for a Formal Wedding

A long wedding gown with or without train, a headdress and veil are worn. If the dress has a train, the veil is 18 inches longer than the train; otherwise it's fingertip length. Unless the dress has long sleeves, plain white kid gloves would be nice. A single strand of pearls, white satin pumps, a white prayer book or bridal bouquet can also be part of the bride's attire.

The Informal Wedding

Here you can have more of a choice in clothes —a short or ankle-length wedding gown, headdress with shoulder-length veil, gloves, bouquet; simple floor-length white gown and shoulder veil; even an afternoon dress or going-away outfit in any color but black will serve.

Flowers

Bring to the florist swatches of the fabric of the bride's and other attendants' dresses, along with sketches of designs, if available. They'll help him plan colors and arrangements and to harmonize bouquets with dresses.

Flowers should complement, not dominate, colors of bridal gowns. Flowers alone look much richer against the lovely materials of the wedding gown and the bridesmaids' dresses. Consistency is important in that bridesmaids' bouquets should bear some relation to the bride's but should not overpower it. The boutonniere for the groom usually differs slightly from those of the other male members of the wedding party, but all are white.

The Receiving Line

After the ceremony, the bridal party leaves for the reception as soon as possible. The receiving line should be placed for least congestion, and guests should preferably approach from the left to make handshaking easier. The order of the line is bride's mother, groom's father, groom's mother, bride's father, bride, groom, maid of honor and bridesmaids (sometimes the bride's father or both fathers stand apart from the receiving line, greeting friends who may come up to them). The bride's mother, as hostess, greets each guest first, then introduces them to the groom's father and mother. The line proceeds along to greet the rest of the bridal party. The best man and ushers assist elsewhere to see that everything runs smoothly. When all guests have been greeted, members of the receiving line proceed to refreshment area.

Seating Arrangements

At a large formal sit-down reception, guests are served as soon as they have passed the receiving line. They sit at small tables for 6–8 people. The bride and groom join them when the line of guests has dwindled, usually between first course and dessert. The groom seats the bride at his right and the maid of honor at his left. The best man will sit at the right of the bride, and the bridesmaids and ushers take their seats alternately along 1 side of the table.

The bride's parents at a large wedding have a table of their own, sometimes with place cards. The groom's parents are seated there, bride's mother to the left of groom's father and the groom's mother to the right of bride's father. Others at this table may include close relatives or friends, as well as the clergyman who performed the ceremony.

At a smaller wedding with only a few attendants, the parents and clergyman often sit at the same table with the bride and groom. At a very small wedding reception, everyone may sit at the same table.

At many large receptions, the guests stand, as at any informal party, with trays of food passed around.

Small Reception at Home

There's no formal receiving line. The bride's and groom's parents greet guests as they enter, and the bride and groom together greet them in reception room. In a small room 2 or 3 small flower arrangements are all that are needed for decoration. Cover buffet table with cloth that blends with colors worn by bridal party and set wedding cake in center, with sandwiches, small cakes and small dishes of nuts and pastel mints surrounding it. Have small plates, napkins and forks available. Place coffee service and punch bowl at opposite ends. Guests proceed to buffet as they arrive, and when all have come the bride and groom cut the cake and the toasts begin.

Toasts

Whoever you wish may make the first toast—always to the bride. The groom responds and may then propose a toast to the bridesmaids, which is responded to by the best man or head usher. These toasts may be followed by a toast to the bride's mother, proposed by a family friend and responded to by the bride's father, and then a toast to the groom's mother, proposed by a family friend and responded to by the groom's father. All except the first toast are optional.

The Wedding Feast

Almost all weddings include a wedding cake and drinks. For a very small reception at home, no other food need be served. In general the type and amount of food and how it is served depends on the time of day, number of guests and size of the reception room, rather than on the formality of the wedding.

Sit-down Wedding Breakfast

A sit-down wedding breakfast (or lunch or dinner, for that matter) should be arranged only when the guest list is small enough or the reception room is large enough to seat everyone comfortably. If it is, such a reception is a natural choice after a morning wedding. If you are doing the catering yourself, have each course served in the kitchen or serving area and then brought inside. If guests and bridal party sit at 1 table, cake should be set on a small decorated table or tea wagon nearby, to be cut by the bride after main-course plates have been removed. A large

cake is too high for a centerpiece when there are place settings all around the table.

When To Have a Buffet

When the guest list is large and the room average size, a wedding buffet is best. After a morning or late-afternoon wedding, serve a fairly substantial hot or cold one. Have luncheon-size plates and forks, and make sure knives are not required for the food.

For an early-afternoon or late-evening wedding, buffet foods may be simple finger foods because the reception takes place before or after the dinner hour. Small plates and napkins, dainty sandwiches, hot appetizers and fancy tea cakes are placed on the buffet or passed around. They may be followed by dessert and coffee. Before wedding cake and punch are served, other dishes should be removed.

There's also a semi-buffet. Guests serve themselves from the buffet; then they sit at small tables and chairs grouped informally around the room. One large table is reserved for the bridal party.

Buffet Menus

Finger-Food Buffet

Dainty Sandwiches
Hot Appetizers
(Sausage rolls, savory seafood or
chicken tartlets, toasted asparagus
rolls, fish or cheese puffs)
Small cakes
(Shortbread, macaroons,
bars, drop cookies,
petits fours)
Ice cream molds   Salted nuts   Mints
Wedding cake   Punch
Coffee or Tea

Breakfast or Luncheon

Chilled melon garnished with fresh strawberries
Turkey and mushrooms in PATTY SHELLS
Asparagus tips
Hot corn sticks and crescent rolls
Raspberry sherbet or ice cream   Wedding cake
Punch   Coffee

Luncheon or Supper Buffet

Chicken or turkey salad, sliced cold ham, tongue
Molded mixed vegetables in tomato aspic
Lobster or shrimps in cream puff shells
Mixed green salad or relishes
Small sandwiches or small buttered hot rolls
Ice cream   Small cakes
Wedding cake   Punch
Coffee or Tea

The Wedding Cake

No matter what kind of wedding you plan the *pièce de résistance* is the wedding cake. Many bakers specialize in making them to order and will decorate them exactly as you like. Or you may prefer to buy just the cake and decorate it yourself. If you want to do the whole thing yourself from start to finish, try the CHRISTMAS OR WEDDING CAKE. With the most limited equipment, you'll be able to decorate it beautifully.

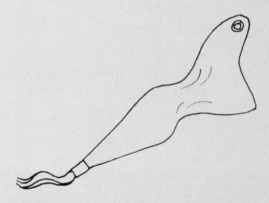

The first step is to buy a pastry tube. It can be made of nylon or plastic and comes with a set of nozzles in assorted sizes and designs, each of which will turn out a different type of decoration. Before you begin work on wedding cake itself, practice. Make up a batch of icing, get out pastry tubes and experiment with squeezing

icing out in a regular, smoothly flowing line. Then try making rosettes. After a little while, you'll probably be ready for the cake.

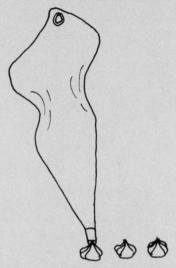

For the cake we illustrate here, all you need is one simple type of "swag." You can buy the more elaborate decorations; candied flowers are available at party shops or pastry shops. But you can also make delicate and beautiful flowers yourself very easily by using real flowers. Roses are best because of their petals. Pull petals from 3 or 4 white roses, and brush each petal with egg white that has been very slightly beaten. Over each side of each petal, sprinkle very fine sugar. Set petals on cookie sheet that has been covered well with the same kind of sugar, and sift more sugar over them. Then set in warm dry place until egg white has thoroughly dried. Do not cover; they will keep for several days if you leave them in dry place. Buds may be sugared whole. When you decorate cake, after all icing has set, make up a few "roses" using sugared petals; place a few silver dragees in center of each bunch of petals.

Decorating Icing

      1/2 cup butter or margarine
      1/2 teaspoon salt
        3 pounds confectioners' sugar, sifted
        5 egg whites, unbeaten
      1/4 cup cream
        2 teaspoons vanilla extract

Cream butter or margarine, and add salt. Work in part of sugar gradually, blending well; add a little egg white and more sugar, continuing to alternate until egg whites are used up. Then continue to add sugar, alternately with cream, until mixture reaches spreading consistency (a little more or less cream may be necessary to adjust texture). Beat well after each addition to make smooth mixture. Add vanilla last, and blend well. Makes about 5 cups, enough to cover 1 10″ x 10″ x 2″ layer or 2 8″ x 8″ x 2″ layers, plus enough to decorate with garlands or similar ornaments.

Note: While you are decorating cake, keep frosting covered with damp cloth, so that it stays moist for spreading.

WEDDING ANNIVERSARIES

Whether it's a first or thirty-first, an anniversary is a good time for a party. It can be arranged by either relatives or friends or by the people celebrating the occasion. When you give your own party, though, don't tell the guests it's an anniversary party until they arrive, or they'll feel obliged to bring gifts.

Gifts

In arranging an anniversary party for someone else, do tell guests how many years the couple has been married. Many guests like to buy gifts accordingly:

1. Paper	13. Lace
2. Cotton	14. Ivory
3. Leather	15. Glass or crystal
4. Silk or pewter	20. China
5. Wood	25. Silver
6. Iron or copper	30. Pearl
7. Wool	35. Coral or jade
8. Bronze or pottery	40. Ruby
9. Willow	45. Sapphire
10. Tin	50. Gold
11. Steel	55. Emerald
12. Linen	60. Diamond

Gauge Age and Interests

As a rule, early anniversary parties are informal, but as the years roll on they tend to become more formal. A fifth anniversary party could be an informal dance, supper, cocktail party or even a noisy evening of games in the recreation room. By the time a golden anniversary comes along, a more dignified reception would be appropriate. But the party should suit the people for whom it's given—a middle-aged couple celebrating their twenty-fifth anniversary would probably like a lively affair, whereas an elderly couple married for 25 years would probably prefer a quieter one.

Golden or Diamond Wedding Anniversaries. A golden or diamond wedding anniversary is usually given in the home of the guests of honor, but their children or friends do the arranging.

Unless the house can accommodate all the guests at one time, the party starts about 4:00 and goes on until 10:00 or 11:00, with friends dropping in at any time during these hours. It usually works out that 1 group appears between 4:00 and 6:00 in the afternoon and the rest after 8:00 in the evening. That means a lull around dinnertime, a break appreciated by the guests of honor. If you're finding it difficult to cut down your list, you can always have 2 parties, both the same, a week apart, which makes double work for the party arranger but may make it more comfortable for all concerned.

Carrying Out a Theme

Decorations should fit the anniversary—for a golden one, yellow roses, sprays of artificial gold flowers and leaves in vases and so forth. A low bowl of golden Christmas-tree balls or an arrangement of gold leaves and fruits makes a pretty centerpiece.

Food and Drink

On sideboard have a tray and on it a big bowl of iced punch, with pieces of fresh fruit floating in it.

Remember that most people will have to stand if it's a large party, so make the food easy to handle. Sandwiches, hot tartlets, canapés, tiny cookies, petits fours, little cakes or ice-cream strawberries can be managed with 1 hand while the guest holds a cup of tea or a glass of punch in the other.

A small side table in the dining room, covered by a damask or lace tablecloth, can hold the wedding cake for guests to admire as they arrive. Or it can be used as centerpiece for dining table. At about 5:00 or whenever crowd seems at a maximum, ask everyone to gather in the dining room for the ceremony of cutting the cake. This is done by the couple together, and the cake is then cut into small pieces for serving to guests. After cake has been passed, there will surely be some toasts, so be sure everyone's glass is full.

Menu for Golden Wedding Reception

Assorted sandwiches (egg salad, chicken salad, chopped ham—relish, lobster)
Hot crabmeat tartlets   Mushroom tartlets
Cocktail sausages
Caviar toast rounds   Smoked oysters on toast
Olives
Small chocolate brownies   Coconut macaroons
SUGAR COOKIES   Small iced cakes
Ice-cream strawberries
Nuts   Mints   Chocolates
GOLDEN WEDDING CAKE
PUNCH

Golden Wedding Cake

            4 cups sifted all-purpose flour
            2 teaspoons baking powder
            2 teaspoons salt
        1 1/2 cups canned pineapple chunks
            1 cup chopped candied citron
            1 cup candied cherry halves
            1 cup candied orange peel
            1 cup candied lemon peel
            1 cup light sultana raisins
            1 cup slivered blanched almonds
          1/2 cup shortening
          1/2 cup butter or margarine
            2 cups sugar
          3/4 cup milk
            8 egg whites

Sift flour, salt and baking powder together. Combine fruits and almonds, and stir into flour mixture. Cream shortening and butter or margarine together, add sugar and beat until mixture is light and fluffy. Stir in fruit mixture alternately with milk, and mix well together. Beat egg whites until they hold stiff peaks, and fold into batter. Pour into greased and brown-paper lined angel cake pan with tube center, and bake at 300°F. about 2 1/2 hours or until top springs back when pressed lightly with finger. Or bake in 4 1-pound coffee cans, putting 1/4 the batter in each tin, for 2 hours at same temperature. A sheet of heavy brown paper placed over top during last 45 minutes of baking will prevent it from darkening too much.

Punch

            2 cups water
            2 cups sugar
            Juice of 12 oranges
            Juice of 12 lemons
            2 quarts chilled ginger ale
            Orange and lemon slices
            Sprigs of mint

Boil water and sugar about 10 minutes. Cool syrup, and add to it orange and lemon juice. Chill well; immediately before serving add ginger ale, and garnish with orange and lemon slices and a few sprigs of mint. Serves 35–40.

VARIATIONS:

Be sure to add alcoholic beverage at the same time as the ginger ale, just before serving the drinks.

Champagne Punch: Substitute champagne for ginger ale, or use 1 quart champagne and 1 quart ginger ale.

Sherry Punch: Substitute quart medium-dry sherry for 1 quart ginger ale.

Quantities for Golden Wedding Reception Menu (35–40 guests)

(1 sandwich makes 4 pieces when cut into small triangles)

1 dozen egg-salad sandwiches
1 dozen chopped ham—relish sandwiches
1 dozen chicken-salad sandwiches
1 dozen lobster sandwiches
3 dozen cocktail sausages
3 dozen hot crabmeat tartlets
3 dozen hot mushroom tartlets
4 dozen melba toast rounds with red caviar, sprinkled with
        grated lemon rind or spread with anchovy paste
4 dozen smoked oysters on toast
2 dozen small chocolate brownies
2 dozen coconut macaroons
4 dozen small frosted cakes
2 dozen plain sugar cookies
6 dozen ice-cream strawberries

Appendix

GUIDE TO A PERFECT KITCHEN

Major Appliances. The basic equipment in any kitchen includes range, refrigerator and sink. But more and more often, appliances that once were considered luxuries are becoming essentials—dishwashers, disposals, freezers and so on.

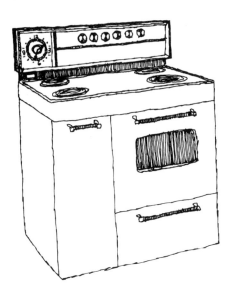

Ranges and Cooking Devices

Ranges, both gas and electric, have been improved in recent years so that the choice of the right one frequently narrows down to which range has the particular features you want and which fuel is the most economically and reliably supplied in your area.

Today's ranges (both gas and electric) include 3 general types; free-standing, built-in and slide-in models. Free-standing ranges, designed as separate units, are usually a good choice when replacing a range in an old kitchen without extensive remodeling. There are models available from compact 24-inch widths (with 3 or 4 surface burners or units and a single oven-broiler) up to ranges twice that width with 2 ovens, 2 broilers and 6 burners or surface units.

Built-in ranges have separate ovens (singly or in pairs) that are set into cabinets and surface cooking sections installed directly into counters. These units blend neatly into kitchen decor without dirt-catching crevices and cracks, and separate baking and broiling activities from surface cooking, so that there is less congestion. In almost every case, built-in ovens are elevated to avoid bending and stooping. Built-in ranges require more kitchen space for convenient use than do other types.

Recently, designers have worked out a third type that slides snugly between counters, looks built-in but has the advantage of separate models when service or replacement is necessary. Some of the newest ranges with this built-in look feature 1 or 2 ovens elevated above the cooking top at eye level; another oven may be under the cooking top to provide a very compact cooking center as small as 30–36 inches wide.

Both built-in and slide-in ranges fit nicely into plans for new or remodeled kitchens.

Electronic Cooking

Electronic ovens are special electric units that heat food incredibly fast: bacon and eggs in fractions of seconds, roasts in minutes instead of hours. The electronic rays heat food but not utensils, which must be glass, ceramic or other special materials. They can't be metal, which shields food from heat. Electronic cooking does not brown or char food and thus enhances flavor and appearance. It can be used with other cooking methods for speedy heating of frozen foods. Electronic ranges are in limited production and are expensive.

Controls for Easier Cooking

For almost every cooking assignment, time and temperature controls are available. They not only monitor heat during cooking but also keep foods hot until serving time without overcooking, even when you are delayed. The most important single control is still the one that controls oven heat because the food you bake and roast is often the most expensive as well as the most sensitive to heat. Some new oven controls are combined with timers and can be set to lower heat automatically when roast or casserole nears doneness, so that food keeps hot for several hours without overcooking. A new trend is very low-temperature roasting of meat, which means less spattering in the oven and less shrinkage of meat. A few ranges have special controls for this type of roasting.

Temperature-controlled surface cooking is one of the newer features of both gas and electric ranges. There is a sensor-operated heat regulator (a little disc mounted on springs so that it presses against the bottom of pans), which measures heat and keeps it at level you've set. You can leave stew to simmer for hours untended. These automatic units give best results with pans that are flat, so that they make good contact with the sensors. The controls are set for use with medium-weight aluminum pans because they heat evenly. With other kinds of utensils, it is usually desirable to set the control 25° lower than on the chart for a given type of cooking. With temperature-controlled gas burners, flame adjustments are set to lower levels for small pans and those of materials other than aluminum. Some ranges have built-in griddles with temperature controls that make it easy to bake pancakes, grill meat or scramble eggs successfully with little watching.

There are other features you will find on some ranges that save time and contribute to successful cooking. Rotisseries in ovens rotate meat and poultry under broiler heat to give juicy indoor-barbecued foods. Meat probes inserted in roasts and poultry signal when desired doneness is reached. Oven cleaning, long one of the most disagreeable kitchen chores, is made easier by removable Teflon panels that can be cleaned in the sink; in other ranges, ovens clean themselves by incinerating spatters so that a wisp of ash is all that's left. Ventilating systems designed into ranges or separate ovens are of 2 types; one is connected to a duct so that heat and odors are exhausted outdoors; the other refreshes the air and recirculates it.

Plug-in Cookers

Electric utensils handle some specialized cooking assignments very well, and they fill in when a range is unreliable or inadequate. Outstanding are automatic frying pans, griddles, deep-fat fryers and saucepans with temperature controls. Some models can be put directly into water for convenient cleaning, and many new ones have nonstick Teflon linings that are easy to clean. Broilers and rotisseries in various sizes often make it easy to broil or barbecue while oven is used for baking other foods. Other plug-in cooking devices include tea kettles, corn poppers, roasters and, of course, coffee pots.

Success with any of these electric appliances depends on having ample electric service, convenient outlets and circuits large enough to carry the load. The heat-producing appliances require most electricity, and adequate circuits are therefore most important; otherwise heating will be slow and, in severe cases of overloading, unsafe.

Refrigerators and Freezers

Refrigerators and freezers, with their specialized storage arrangements, have become modern home pantries. When these appliances are large enough, you can plan meals ahead and save time by shopping just once or twice a week. Aside from being inconvenient, a too-small refrigerator is less reliable in keeping food at its best. Without increasing outside dimensions, many modern refrigerators have more space inside because new, efficient insulation is more compact. An important recent development in refrigerators and freezers is the perfection of those that never need defrosting. They cost a little more to buy and a very little more to operate than do older types, but they save a great deal of time, and refrigeration is very uniform.

A handy refrigerator holds foods so that they are convenient to reach and provides temperature and humidity conditions for keeping them at their best. Important are moist-cold bins or drawers for tender fruits and vegetables; extra-cold lightly covered storage for meats; convenient shallow shelves on doors for small containers; shelves with head room for tall bottles and some large space for bulky foods like large melons or turkeys. Some models have shelves that can be adjusted easily, and some have ice makers as optional equipment. They are connected to the water supply and automatically maintain a bin full of ice.

Freezer storage can be part of a refrigerator or a separate appliance. In either case it's important that the temperature be maintained around 0°F. without exaggerated fluctuation. At high or fluctuating temperatures, food loses quality very rapidly. A steak that is good for 1 year at 0°F. loses flavor after 5 months if temperature rises to 5°F. At 10°F. quality begins to slip after 2 months, and in a 15°F. ice-cube compartment, steaks start to lose flavor after only 1 month.

There are freezer compartments in many refrigerator models, sometimes below the fresh-food section, sometimes above it or, in the newest ones, beside it. The choice is largely a matter of preference, but you do use the fresh-food section more frequently than the freezer part.

A glorified ice-cube section is not to be confused with a freezer; the latter has its own insulating wall and door to the section and often a separate control. If you are in doubt when you shop, do ask about performance.

Separate freezers can be shaped either like refrigerators or chests. Either can be relied on for excellent results. Generally, the upright freezer is more convenient to use because more foods are easily accessible.

A freezer makes it possible not only to stock up for the future, but also to prepare foods when you have time and to enjoy them later.

Sinks Are Pivot Points in Kitchens

The most convenient sinks are those with fairly large single bowls or with 2 small ones so that when 1 bowl is in use, the water supply is available in the other. With a single bowl, separate plastic dishpans and drainboard racks help a great deal. In any sink it's important to have a mixer faucet that blends hot and cold water to the temperature desired. A spray, either on the faucet or on a separate hose is helpful when washing foods or rinsing dishes.

Dishwashers

An automatic dishwasher can save as much as 1 hour a day. Models have changed tremendously in recent years. Today they clean everything inside the tub with improved spray systems of scalding-hot water. Water jets from 2 or more levels reach into bowls, cups and glasses to clean them thoroughly. There is more freedom in arranging dishes in dishwasher racks, and dishes do not need to be so carefully prepared before loading in the new machines as in the old.

New models have increased capacity—many accommodate service for 9–16 people but take up no more room. Capacity is rated in place settings—1 each dinner and salad plates, sauce dish, glass, cup and saucer plus silverware and serving pieces. For flexibility, new machines have cycles programmed to suit special loads, as well as the usual one for typical combinations of dishes and utensils. There are shorter cycles for glassware, a vigorous one for utensils, a dry "warm" one for heating plates and, newest, a "hold" cycle that pre-rinses dishes so that they can be held from one meal to another or until a sizable load has accumulated. Built-in portable dishwashers are available. The newest built-in models are a compact 24 inches wide, have firm, clean lines and come in colors to blend with other kitchen equipment. Some have kits for attaching panels to match kitchen cabinets, so that dishwasher can blend with the rest of the kitchen. Portable models are often just as automatic as permanently installed ones; they are rolled to the sink on casters and hooked up to faucets at dishwashing time. Some portable dishwashers can be plumbed in, and a few space-saver models fit under sinks or cooking tops in the smallest kitchens. For best results, dishwashers require 140°–150°F. water (some models have their own booster heaters). Dishwashers are used with special detergents that clean without foaming, as suds tend to buffer the cleaning action of the water. Different formulas or detergents have been developed for use in different kinds of water; sample several to find which works best with your machine and water.

Disposals

Disposals installed in sink drains grind up most kitchen food waste so that it can be washed away with the drain water. They handle peelings, parings, vegetable and fruit trimmings, egg shells, small bones, scraping from the table and even many soft unglazed papers like towels and napkins. Disposals, however, are not made to grind hard substances like tin and glass containers, harsh papers or very fibrous materials like bulky corn husks or artichoke leaves.

A disposal is a container with a grinding mechanism at the bottom, it is installed under the sink drain. Some are designed so that a batch of waste is loaded into the container; then a top is put in place and turned. When cold water is turned on, the grinding starts. With this arrangement, there is less chance of utensils or sponges sliding into the unit as it operates. Another mechanism, known as a "continuous-feed" unit, operates when a switch is turned and continues as long as necessary—food material can be added during the operation; a soft rubber-like baffle provides some protection at the drain. With any disposal, cold water is used to wash away the ground-up material; hot water would soften fat and grease in the disposal, but if they hardened later they might block the drain. The newest disposals are more efficient than were earlier models; they are faster and quieter too. Some models have reversing action, a very helpful feature that saves service calls when material is jammed in the mechanism.

Use And Care Of Kitchen Appliances. Modern appliances have more aids built into them than ever before, but they all do better when used and cared for as planned. Do read and follow the manufacturers' instructions for your particular models.

Success in Using Ranges

For surface cooking, choose pans suited to quantities of food and heating units or burners. Utensils should have flat bottoms for even heating, especially for successful automatic surface cooking.

Use high heat to bring utensil and food to cooking temperatures; then turn heat lower to maintain cooking speed desired (with automatic cooking, type controls lower heat). Cooking at proper temperature prevents scorching food.

For oven cooking, choose utensils suited to type of food being cooked—see section on cooking utensils. Generally, place foods in approximately the center of the oven, and arrange pans so there is air circulation around them.

For baked foods it is usually to your advantage to preheat oven to desired temperature as food is prepared. For most meats and casserole-type foods, preheating is not necessary.

There are timers available to turn ovens on and off while you are away. Do not let fresh meat stand more than 4 hours before cooking starts.

Easy Care of Ranges

The top of the range and the cabinet are easier to keep spotless if spills are wiped up after each meal. On enamel tops it is best to wait until sur-face is cooled; then wipe with sudsy sponge, and dry with paper towel. Never scrape, gouge or use caustic cleaners on enamel, anodized aluminum or chrome.

Broiler pans are easier to clean if detergent is sprinkled over grid after food is removed. Cover with dampened paper towels until dishwashing time. Drip pans and reflector pans under surface heaters can be removed and cleaned in dishpan. These areas can be lined with heavy foil, shaped to fit and (for those under electric units) cut out to allow the same space for ventilation as the section it protects. There are also liners available for these areas. In any case, they can be replaced when soiled.

Some ranges have ovens that clean themselves; others have easy-clean Teflon panels and throwaway foil linings. Still others have doors that fold down or remove to make it easier to reach the interior. For the ovens that still need cleaning in the old ways, however, and they are in the majority, here are some suggestions:

Wear rubber gloves to protect hands, and spread papers over floors and nearby areas, for some cleaning compounds are caustic.

If oven light comes on when the door is opened, tape switch "off" so that bulb will not get so hot it breaks if touched with cool spray or sponge. It's a good idea too to tape or shield sockets and controls in oven.

New special oven cleaners make cleaning easier. The spray-type cleaners with foaming action that keeps cleaner in contact with surface longer than liquids are effective. Do read labels, as some cleaners are more effective when used in warm oven, some sprays should be shaken well and some should not be agitated.

Another method is to place a small custard cup, with 1/2 cup ammonia diluted with 1/2 cup water, on oven rack while oven is still warm. The fumes help to loosen spatters and make oven cleaning easier.

After oven has been cleaned, heat it empty 5 minutes before adding foods, to prevent contamination of flavors.

Success in Using Refrigerators

For best operation, a refrigerator should be level, so that door will swing closed easily and seal completely.

Cold air in refrigerators holds less moisture than warm air, so fresh fruits and vegetables without natural coverings of their own should be stored in bins or containers provided, put in plastic containers or wrapped in foil or plastic. Carefully wrap foods with decided odors of their own (melons, cauliflower) so they will not spread to other foods. Also see that delicate foods like butter and other spreads are kept covered so that they do not pick up strange flavors.

Rinse ice trays with warm water as needed but avoid using hot water, for it tends to remove the special finish on ice trays that makes cubes easy to remove.

Meats should be kept in the very coldest part of the refrigerator and lightly covered. For storage life of meats see Chapter 2.

Easy Care of Refrigerators

All refrigerators require regular cleaning and care, even those that do not need defrosting.

To defrost nonautomatic models, choose a time when food supply is low. Defrosting should be done when icy frost is 1/4–1/2 inch thick or when special indicator is covered. Defrosting can sometimes be delayed by scraping off fluffy frost with frost scraper or pancake turner, using a scraping, not jabbing stroke. When scraping, collect frost on tray or newspapers. For complete defrosting of nonautomatic models, remove any contents from drip pan; turn control to "defrost" if there is such a position or to "off" if not. The melting of the frost can be speeded by using shallow pans of hot water in the evaporator or by using special electric defrosters (follow instructions for placing them to protect plastic sections).

How often a refrigerator needs cleaning depends on the use it gets, but at least once a month is a good average. Remove all contents, wash inside of cabinet, racks, shelves and door gasket with baking soda-and-water solution (1 tablespoon soda per 1 quart water). Refrigerators are easier to keep clean if spills are wiped up immediately.

A liquid or cream wax of the cleaning type, used on the outside, both cleans and leaves a pleasant sheen. Never use oily furniture polish or abrasive cleaners on any part of a refrigerator.

The coils at the rear of the cabinet of all older models and underneath food-storage section in some new models should be cleaned at least twice a year of dust and dirt that clings to them, as this accumulation reduces efficiency of the mechanism. A crevice tool of a vacuum cleaner is effective for this; a long-handled brush is also helpful. Some of the new refrigerators can be moved easily for cleaning. For others, it is important at least to move from the wall to reach the coils.

Success in Using Freezers

A freezer is more convenient to use if it is in or near the kitchen where the supplies can be selected easily and quickly. Like refrigerators, this appliance should be level.

Speedy freezing is a secret of quality. You can freeze any amount that will freeze solid within 24 hours. Usually, that's about 2 pounds for each cubic foot of freezer space when the temperature is maintained at 0°F. If you have more than that to freeze, keep some in refrigerator until first amount is solidly frozen. In fact, prechilling in refrigerator helps retain fresh flavor and good texture. Do remember, however, that freezing protects—rather than improves—foods. You will want to select good food to start with, the kinds known for successful freezing.

When loading a freezer, leave space between packages for air circulation, and try to keep new, warmer packages from touching those already frozen. For convenient use, you will want to follow a pattern for storing foods in freezer, so that you can quickly locate any needed food. You will find it helpful if meats are in one part, vegetables in another and desserts all together in still another. It will save time and guesswork in sorting out the makings of a meal later if you label each package with contents and number of servings. Also, date packages, and use older ones first. Freezer storage is drying, and it's important to wrap and seal packages to protect against dehydration and changes in flavor, texture and color. For packaging, choose materials, bags, containers made for freezers or some of the new utensils that take kindly to the temperature shock of going from freezer to oven. The lightweight household wraps and cartons for cottage cheese and ice cream, for instance, do not protect frozen food, at least for extended storage times.

When several layers of food like steak, chops, or ground-meat patties are to be frozen, put 2 layers of wrap between them to speed separation later. Separate foods like chops and hamburgers can be wrapped in clear plastic wrap or sandwich bags, then grouped in a large plastic bag.

When doing up chunky compact foods, mold foil or clear plastic wrap closely around them, and double-fold edges. Masking or freezer tape holds seams tight. These precautions seal out air that is harmful to flavors of frozen foods.

Easy Care of Freezers

The cabinets of freezers are cared for in the same way as those for refrigerators. Like refrigerators, the models that need no manual defrosting should be cleaned periodically; twice a year is usually enough.

STORAGE TIME FOR MEATS

COVERED LOOSELY IN REFRIGERATOR 36°–40°F.

Ground beef	1–2 days
Liver, heart, kidney	1–2 days
Sausages	2–3 days
Leftover casseroles, stews	2–3 days
Cooked meats	3–4 days
Wieners	3–4 days
Chops and steaks	3–5 days
Roasts	5–6 days
Bacon	6–7 days
Cured ham, whole	1–2 weeks

SEALED IN FREEZER WRAPPINGS IN FREEZER 0°F.
OR COLDER

Sausages	1–2 months
Ground beef	2–3 months
Casseroles, stews	2–3 months
Liver, heart, kidney	3–4 months
Wieners	3–4 months
Veal and pork chops	3–4 months
Lamb chops	3–4 months
Veal and pork roasts	4–8 months
Fish	6–9 months
Lamb roasts	8–12 months
Beef roasts and steaks	10–12 months

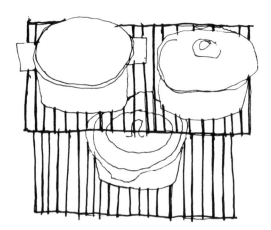

Choosing Cooking and Baking Utensils. Proper pans will increase your chances of successful cooking. The sizes and materials of utensils are both important. For baking, a utensil should suit the quantity of a recipe. If it's too small, food may run over edge; if it's too large, food will not brown properly. In addition, baking

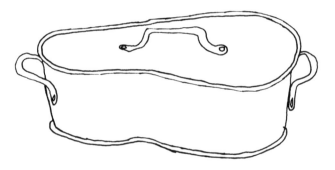

utensils or other pans should not be so large that they touch sides of oven, which blocks heat and results in uneven browning. Some new utensils have sizes stamped on bottoms for easy identification. To measure baking utensil (in case size is indicated in recipe), take inside dimension at top of pan. For depth, take inside perpendicular dimension. Casseroles, custard cups and many other oven dishes are measured by liquid capacity; and this measure is specified in many recipes. If you do not know size when buying, be certain to ask the clerk.

When baking, bright metals like aluminum usually give the most uniform heating and therefore the most even browning of baked foods like cookies, cakes and the like. Very dark pans, black by nature or from long-time use, tend to absorb more heat and give darker results. Oven glassware is efficient in absorbing heat and is excellent for pastry or casserole foods. When using it to bake cakes or more heat-sensitive foods, however, reduce oven heat about 25° to compensate for heat absorption. For casserole cooking, any oven-proof material may be used,

and it's desirable to consider materials that can go directly from refrigerator or freezer into oven —like durable ceramics and the new aluminum-lined casseroles.

For top-of-range cooking, pans should fit size of heating unit or burner and be adapted to quantity being cooked. The most useful utensils have flat bottoms, so that they receive heat evenly, and well-fitting covers to retain moisture. The medium-weight aluminum pans heat uniformly; stainless steel, ceramic, glass and porcelain are attractive and easily cleaned. They heat more slowly, however. They can be used successfully if the heat is adjusted lower than for aluminum, so that it is given a chance to spread evenly. Cast iron stays level and flat for long-time use. It heats slowly but evenly and holds heat well. It's heavy, thick and durable and may be heavy to handle. Iron improves with use if properly cared for, but it must be kept dry to prevent rusting. Some iron is coated with enamel to add color and improve appearance. Cast iron should not be confused with sheet-iron utensils, which are very lightweight and often warp and buckle with use. For this reason, they heat unevenly and give unreliable results.

Nonstick Surfaces

Almost every kind of utensil is easier to clean when lined with Teflon or similar materials. This coating, now found in aluminum, enamel, glass, iron and stainless utensils, gives an antistick finish that makes some foods easy to cook and cleaning much simpler. Many of these finishes are damaged by harsh treatment, however, so good care includes special tools (nylon- or Teflon-coated or wood) that are kind to the surface. Teflon-lined utensils should be washed in hot detergent water, for, although food particles are easily removed, lingering traces of fat tend to darken and discolor.

General Points

1. Choose saucepans and frying pans that are well balanced. An extra long or heavy handle makes a pan unsteady, and as a result it tips easily.

2. For any pan, choose designs that are free from hard-to-clean cracks and crevices.

3. Try lifting utensils to see if handles are comfortable to hold and balance utensil well. Heat-resistant handles mean pans can be used in ovens as well as on the surface.

4. Handles of utensils for surface cooking should not be so long that they extend over edge of stove. They will be easily knocked off and may cause serious burns.

5. Cooking utensils are so handsome these days that you will want to consider hanging some where they are convenient to use. For this purpose, look for handles with loops in the ends.

6. Very large pots, like kettles and soup pots, should have 2 handles, so that the heavy weight can be handled with assurance.

7. Utensils should be purchased with their own well-fitting lids. With cover in place, many foods can be steamed to save flavor, nutrients and cooking fuel.

Arranging a Convenient Kitchen. A kitchen that serves well is made up of labor-saving appliances arranged for easy, comfortable use.

Each major appliance—refrigerator, range and sink—should have an adjoining counter of at least 2 feet, which serves as a landing deck when serving and as a place to put utensils while working. If there is a separate oven, it should have its own counter of at least 15 inches to put roasts and baked foods on as they are removed. One counter in a kitchen should be at least 42 inches long if there is to be a comfortable mixing center for general food preparation.

The actual arrangement of working centers depends on room size and shape. But a good plan is to place sink between refrigerator and cooking surface, preferably in a triangular arrangement. A very good plan is an "L" shape on 2 adjacent walls. There are many convenient arrangements that can be worked out to fit available space, however. When counters are aligned on opposite walls, a 4-foot aisle should be planned between them.

At each main center there should be cabinets for storing utensils, tools and foods used there regularly. These include cabinets under counters for large utensils and packages, and wall cupboards for smaller ones. In planning storage, don't forget space for dishes, cleaning supplies, staples, small appliances, trays, timers, wastebasket, food wraps, towels. They will need cupboard room, not necessarily at main work centers.

Finally separate cooking and extracurricular kitchen activities. You will be glad if a place to eat or do the laundry, for instance, is near the kitchen but not located so that it interferes with food preparation.

COOKING TERMS USED IN THIS BOOK

À la grecque: In the Greek style. Food may be cooked in consommé or other liquid then chilled in the reduced consommé or liquid. This term may also describe food prepared with oil, garlic and/or other seasoning enjoyed by the Greeks.

À la king: Food served in rich cream sauce. Usually flavored with mushrooms and pimento.

À la mode: In the fashion. When referring to pie, with ice cream; referring to beef, marinated beef braised in marinade.

Angelica: The candied leaf stalk of an European herb used to decorate candies and desserts.

Antipasto: Italian hors d'oeuvres consisting of meat, fish, vegetables, etc.

Aspic: A savory jelly made from concentrated meat or vegetable stock and seasonings, with or without the addition of poultry, fish, vegetables, etc.

Au gratin: Food baked or broiled with a breadcrumb topping. Cheese may be included with the crumbs.

Baba: A French cake made with yeast batter. *Baba au rum*—a baba soaked in a rum-flavored liquid.

Bain-marie: A French double boiler or a large open vessel half filled with hot water in which saucepans are placed to keep contents nearly at boiling point.

Bake: To cook by dry heat as in an oven.

Barbecue: A unit or grill. To roast meat on a rack or spit, basting frequently with a highly seasoned sauce. A social entertainment with food cooked outdoors.

Baste: To pour liquid or melted fat over food during cooking to keep food moist and flavorful.

Batter: A mixture of liquid, flour and other ingredients that graduates in thickness from a pouring consistency to a spreading consistency.

Beat: To incorporate air into a mixture or to combine and mix ingredients into a smooth mixture with a spoon, beater or mixer.

Béchamel: French term for white or cream sauce.

Bisque: A thickened soup made from a puree of fish.

Blanch: To skin nuts or fruits by covering them with boiling water for two or three minutes, then immersing in cold water.

Blanching: To scald vegetables when preparing them for freezing.

Blend: To combine two or more ingredients until smooth. To mix ingredients in an electric blender if recipe specifies.

Boil: To cook in steaming liquid in which bubbles are breaking on the surface.

Bouchée: French: Literally "a mouthful." A tiny cream puff or puff pastry shell filled with a savory mixture.

Bouillabaisse: A French soup-stew made with fish and shellfish.

Bouillon: A clear broth made by simmering various combinations of meat and vegetables for a long time in water.

Bouquet: The particular fragrance of a wine.

Bouquet garni: A mixture of herbs and spices tied in a cheesecloth bag, cooked with other ingredients and discarded at the end of cooking time. Typical flavors used are celery, bay leaf, thyme, green onion.

Braise: To cook meat with a small amount of moisture in a covered saucepan or casserole.

Brazier: A large flat tray for holding burning charcoal.

Bread: To coat with fine bread or cracker crumbs prior to frying or baking cutlets, chops, croquettes, fish, etc.

Breathe: To open a bottle of wine an hour or so before serving to have the flavor at its peak.

Briquet: A brick-shaped block of artificial coal.

Broil: To cook food by searing the surface with direct heat on a broiler or over hot coals.

Brown: To briefly fry meat, poultry, etc., in a little hot fat until brown on the outside.

Brown Sauce: A French gravy seasoned with onions, carrots and tomato puree.

Brush: To spread thinly with a brush.

Canapé: A tiny piece of fried or toasted bread topped with savory mixtures of cheese, meat or seafood.

Caramelize: To melt granulated sugar over medium heat to a golden-brown syrup.

Cassoulet: A French dish made of beans and meat.

Chill: To refrigerate until thoroughly cold.

Chop: To cut in fine or coarse pieces with a knife, chopper or scissors.

Choux: A type of pastry made with eggs, used in making cream puffs, eclairs, etc.

Chowder: A hearty soup of fish, seafood or vegetables containing diced potatoes.

Citron: A fruit similar to a lemon, available candied for cookies, fruitcake, etc. "Citron" is the French for "lemon." Citron-melon—A species of watermelon with variegated coloring.

This small round fruit is preserved in syrup rather than eaten raw.

Coat: To cover thoroughly with a fine film of flour, crumbs, icing, sugar, crushed nuts, coconut, etc.

Compote: A mixture of fresh or stewed whole fruits.

Condensed milk: Canned whole milk, commercially concentrated by evaporation and sweetened with sugar.

Condiment: A pungent seasoning, such as pepper, mustard, vinegar or prepared sauce.

Consommé: Bouillon enriched with additional meat, poultry etc.

Cool: To let stand at room temperature until no longer warm.

Cream: To soften fat, or fat and sugar, with a wooden spoon or electric mixer until light and fluffy. The percentage of butterfat in: milk 3.5 to 4.3 percent; table and coffee cream 16 to 18 percent; cereal cream 8 to 15 percent; whipping cream 30 to 35 percent.

Creole: The cookery of New Orleans. It usually includes filé powder or okra.

Crêpes: French. Very thin pancakes.

Croquettes: A molded mixture of ground cooked foods with a crumb coating, fried in deep fat.

Croutons: Small bread cubes toasted, baked or fried until crisp and used to garnish soups, salads, etc.

Crumble: To crush a food such as crisp bacon or bread with fingertips until it resembles coarse crumbs.

Crush: To break up solids such as ice or cornflakes by force.

Curry: A mixture of meat, fish, vegetables or eggs seasoned with curry powder.

Cut in: To combine solid fat with dry ingredients using two knives, a fork or a pastry blender.

Dash: A quick shake from a small-necked bottle or 1/6 teaspoon.

Decant: To transfer wine from a bottle to a decanter by pouring gently to leave sediment behind.

Demitasse: A small cup for after-dinner coffee.

Dice: To cut into cubes with a sharp knife on a cutting board.

Dip: To immerse briefly in liquid.

Dissolve: To cause a dry substance to pass into solution in a liquid.

Dollop: A heaped-up mound of whipped cream, sour cream, creamed cheese, etc., spooned on a food to garnish it.

Dough: A mixture of flour, liquid and other ingredients, thick enough to roll, pat out or knead. Dough is thicker in consistency than batter.

Drain: To remove liquid from a food by placing it in a colander or sieve or by using a lid.

Dredge: To coat pieces of food with flour, sugar, etc. Dry ingredient and food pieces may be shaken together in a paper bag.

Drippings: The juice and fat extracted from meat or poultry during cooking.

Dust: To sprinkle lightly with flour, sugar, etc.

Dutch oven: A deep heavy metal pan with a close-fitting cover. It may or may not have a removable rack.

Eclair: Cream-puff base baked in oblong shape and filled with whipped cream or custard.

Entree: French: Usually refers to the main course of a meal.

Enzymes: Substances that cause chemical changes in foods.

Evaporated milk: Whole milk commercially concentrated by evaporation. It contains twice the minerals, protein, fat and sugar of ordinary whole milk. It can be whipped when chilled.

Fillet: A boneless piece of fish or meat; in beef, *beef tenderloin*.

Fines herbes: A blend of several fresh chopped or dried herbs. The blend usually includes parsley, tarragon, chervil or chives and is used to flavor omelets and sauces. Fresh herbs are preferable to dried.

Flake: To break into small pieces with a fork.

Flambé: Food enveloped in a flame from spirits of high alcoholic content such as cognac, rum or brandy.

Flan: An open tart containing fruit, traditionally baked in a metal flan ring.

Flute: To scallop the edges of a pie before baking.

Fold in: To combine ingredients with a gently up-and-over motion without releasing air bubbles that have been beaten into the ingredients. Cut down through mixture with a broad spatula, scraper or whisk. Lift some of the mixture from the bottom to the top with each fold. Give the bowl a quarter turn with each motion until all ingredients have been blended.

Fondant: Sugar syrup cooked to the soft-ball stage (234°F.), then kneaded until creamy.

Frappé: A partly frozen fruit ice, or liqueur or other liquid poured over crushed ice.

Fricassee: Food which has been browned, then simmered or baked in a sauce with vegetables.

Frost: To apply a topping or icing.

Fry: To pan-fry is to cook in a small amount of fat in a frying pan.

French-fry: Is to cook in fat deep enough to cover the food.

Garnish: To decorate with colorful and contrasting food.

Gash: To make cuts with a knife or scissors.

Gelatin: Use unflavored gelatin unless otherwise indicated.

Ghee: The clear yellow liquid obtained by melting unsalted butter and discarding the sediment settled on the bottom. A term used in Asian (not Oriental) cooking.

Glacé: Food coated with sugar syrup cooked to the "crack" stage, or frozen desserts.

Glaze: To add lustre to a food by coating with butter, egg, milk, syrup or jelly.

Goulash: A Hungarian meat stew usually flavored with paprika.

Grate: To shred food by rubbing it over a sharp-edged grater.

Grease: To rub and coat the inside of a baking pan with fat before pouring in batter, etc.

Grill: To broil.

Grind: To cut or crush finely in a food mill or a grinder.

Gumbo: A dish made with okra. Usually associated with Creole cooking.

Haute cuisine: Fancy French cookery.

Hibachi: Japanese barbecue unit.

Hors d'oeuvres: French for "outside the main work." Tidbits served to tease the palate, such as relishes, canapés, etc.

Jigger: A bar measure that contains 1 1/2 ounces of liquid.

Julienne: Matchlike strips of food such as carrots, potatoes.

Kebabs: See shish kebabs.

Knead: To work dough with a pressing motion accompanied by folding and stretching. Or to press dough with the heel of the hand, alternately folding, pushing and stretching the dough.

Larding: To thread slivers of fat with a larding needle through lean meat before roasting.

Leavening: An ingredient in baked products to make them light and porous by releasing or forming gas during baking.

Lukewarm: Eighty-five degrees or neither warm nor cool on the inside of your wrist.

Macédoine: A mixture of several vegetables or fruits, often diced.

Marinade: A savory mixture of acid liquid, seasonings, chopped or sliced vegetables and sometimes oil; may be cooked or uncooked depending on its use.

Marinate: To season and tenderize food by soaking it in a marinade.

Marmite: A clay cooking pot used in Europe. It is always placed on an asbestos mat as direct heat will crack it.

Mash: To reduce food to a smooth consistency by pressing it with a potato masher and then beating the food with a spoon or electric mixer.

Melt: To slowly heat a solid substance until it liquefies.

Meringue: A stiffly beaten mixture of egg whites and sugar. It is usually browned in the oven when used as a topping for pies and desserts. It can be folded into other ingredients or shaped and baked in layers for tortes or small cakes.

Mince: To grind, chop or cut into very small pieces.

Mix: To combine ingredients by stirring. Also a commercially prepared mixture of dry ingredients.

Moisten: To brush or spoon liquid over a food.

Mold: A container used for jelling mousses, jellied salads, etc. Oil mold lightly before pouring in a savory mixture; rinse mold in water before filling with a sweet mixture. To mold—form into shapes.

Monosodium glutamate: A chemical used on food to bring out the flavor. Often referred to as M.S.G.

Mornay: French. A white sauce blended with eggs and cheese.

Mousse: A mixture of sweetened whipped cream and other ingredients chilled without stirring. Or a light rich mixture of cream, fruit, meat, vegetables etc., poached, steamed or set with gelatin.

Oven-poach: To bake a dish of food by setting it in a larger dish containing water.

Pan-broil: To cook uncovered in a frying pan, pouring off the fat as it accumulates.

Parboil: To partly cook in liquid and complete cooking by some other method.

Pare: To peel off the outer skin.

Parfait: A frozen mixture of custard and whipped cream. It is usually served in tall glasses with alternating layers of frozen cream mixture or ice cream and sauces, then topped with whipped cream.

Paste: A smooth mixture of dry ingredients and liquid. Also pureed meat, fish, tomatoes, etc.

Pastry board: A board on which to knead or roll dough.

Pastry cutter: A utensil used to trim edges of pastry.

Pastry wheel: A utensil used for cutting decorative or straight edges on pastry.

Pat: To flatten with fingertips.

Pâté: A paste of meat or fish used for hors d'oeuvres and sandwiches.

Patty: Ground meat which has been shaped into a flat cake or patty. *Patty shells* are cases of puff pastry to be filled with creamed mixtures of chicken, fish, etc.

Peel: To cut away the outer covering.

Petits fours: Little fancy iced cakes made by cutting sheet cake into special shapes (squares, diamonds, etc.). Frosting is poured on and then decorations added.

Pilaff: Rice browned in fat until golden and then cooked in consommé.

Pinch: As much of an ingredient as can be held between thumb and index finger (1/16 tsp.).

Pipe: To ornament food with lines of icing, potato rosettes, etc., by forcing the mixture through a pasty bag with a metal tip.

Poach: To cook in or above liquid at simmering point.

Pot roast: A method of cooking cheaper, less tender cuts of meat by browning the surface of the meat in fat and then cooking it in a small amount of liquid in a covered dish in the oven or on top of the stove.

Pound: To break down and crush a food by hitting it repeatedly.

Preheat: To heat oven, fry pan, waffle iron, etc., to the correct cooking temperature before adding the food.

Press: To push down with the hands or the back of a spoon.

Prick: To pierce with a fork or skewer.

Puree: To press cooked food through a fine sieve or press or to mix in a blender. Also a soup thickened with sieved vegetables.

Rack: A grill or flat perforated utensil usually made of wire.

Ragout: French. A stewed or braised mixture.

Ramekin: An individual baking dish.

Reconstitute: To restore a food, such as frozen juice, to its natural strength.

Reduce: To simmer liquid uncovered until some of the water evaporates.

Render: To extract clear fat from the fat parts of meat or poultry.

Rest: To let yeast dough stand for ten minutes to make it easier to shape.

Roast: To cook uncovered in the oven.

Roll: To place on a board and spread thin with a rolling pin. A small shape made from dough and baked.

Rosé: A still or sparkling wine with a pinkish cast.

Roux: Flour blended with fat and used to thicken sauces, soups and main dishes.

Rub: To press against a surface with fingertips —to rub flour into meat, etc.

Sauté: To brown or cook pieces of food in a small amount of fat in a frying pan, turning pieces frequently.

Scald: To pour boiling water over vegetables, etc., draining at once or allowing to stand for a few minutes. To bring milk almost to the boiling point.

Scallop: To bake—usually in a casserole with sauce.

Score: To cut narrow grooves or slits partly through the outer surface of a food.

Sear: To brown the surface of food quickly over high heat in order to seal in juices when long slow cooking follows.

Sieve: To press food through a sieve.

Shortening: Fat suitable for baking or frying.

Shell: To remove shells from seafood or nuts.

Shish kebabs: In shish (sword) kebab (meat) cookery chunks of marinated meat and vegetables, fruit, etc. are threaded on skewers and broiled.

Shred: To cut into long pieces or to grate coarsely on a shredder.

Shuck: To remove shells from seafood such as clams and oysters. To remove corn husks.

Sift: To put one or more dry ingredients through a sieve or flour sifter.

Simmer: To cook in liquid just below boiling point on top of stove.

Skim: To spoon off fat or scum on the surface of stews, jams, etc. To remove cream from the top of milk.

Slice: To cut a thin flat piece off a large food mass such as a roast or a loaf of bread.

Sliver: To cut or shred into long thin pieces.

Smorgasbord: Scandinavian type of buffet with up to fifty selections of food.

Soak: To immerse in liquid for a time.

Soufflé: A hot soufflé is a delicate custard-like mixture containing cheese, fruit, chopped meat or vegetables, etc., made light with stiffly beaten egg whites. When cold, soufflés may contain whipped cream and gelatin.

Sparkling: A type of wine carbonated by natural fermentation.

Spice: Seasoning from bark, roots, stems, leaves, seeds, buds or fruit of certain tropical plants.

Spirits: Hard liquor such as rum, bourbon, whiskey, etc.

Spirit lamp: A lamp heated by methylated or other spirits and used for heating or boiling food.

Sponge: A high light cake, leavened with eggs and/or baking powder or soda or a batter made with yeast.

Spread: To smooth on a soft substance such as frosting, butter, etc. with a spatula or knife.

Sprinkle: To scatter a dry ingredient over top of food.

Steam: To cook food over steam rising from a pan of boiling water or other liquid.

Steam-bake: To cook in the oven in a pan or baking dish set in a pan of water for steaming.

Steep: To soak in a liquid just below boiling point to extract flavor, color or other qualities from food.

Sterilize: To destroy microorganisms by boiling in water, by dry heat, or by steam.

Stew: To cover and slowly cook food in liquid until tender.

Still: A wine which is neither sparkling nor effervescent.

Stir: To mix together with a spoon using a rotary motion.

Stir-fry: To stir a frying food constantly.

Stock: A liquid in which food (meat, fish or vegetables) has been cooked. Used as a base for soups and sauces.

Swirl: To spread with a circular motion.

Temperatures for baking: Slow oven—250°F. to 325°F.; moderate—325°F. to 400°F.; hot—400°F. to 450°F.; very hot—450°F. to 500°F.

Thaw: To defrost a frozen substance in the refrigerator, at room temperature, in the oven or on top of the stove.

Thicken: To add a thickening agent such as flour, cornstarch, egg yolks, etc.

Thin: To add liquid such as milk, water, stock, etc.

Timbale: An unsweetened custard or white sauce combined with vegetables, meat, poultry or fish and baked in individual molds.

Toast: To brown lightly by direct heat. Bread which has been toasted.

Top: To spread on top; to garnish.

Torte: A rich cake, usually made from crumbs, eggs and nuts. A meringue made in the form of a cake.

Toss: To mix ingredients lightly with an upward motion without mashing them.

Trim: To cut off the edges with a knife or scissors.

Truss: To tie a fowl or other meat so that it will hold its shape during cooking.

Tutti-frutti: Mixed preserved fruit.

Until set: Until a liquid has become firm—often refers to a gelatin or custard mixture.

Velouté: French. Sauce made with butter or margarine, flour and hot chicken or veal stock.

Vinaigrette: Sauce made of oil, acid and seasonings. May be used to marinate cooked food before serving.

Well: A hole made in the middle of dry ingredients into which liquid is poured before mixing.

Whip: To incorporate air into a mixture by beating rapidly with a beater, wire whip or electric mixer.

Whisk: To blend sauces, etc., with a wire whisk.

Zwieback: A kind of toasted bread or rusk.

Index